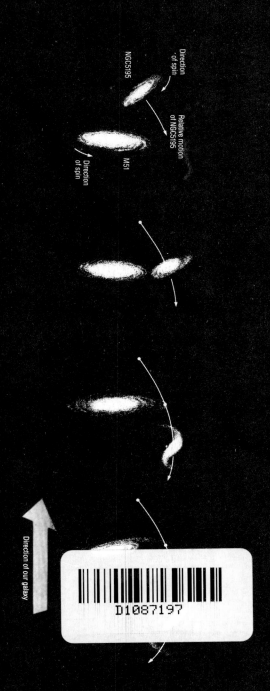

The conspicuous spiral galaxy M51 (= NGC5194) and its companion NGC5195 passed close to each other during the last several hundred million years; effects of the encounter may be seen in the elongated shape of the disk of M51 and the sprung pitch angle of its spiral arms.

M51-NGC5195 Interaction: Both M51 and its companion NGC5195 were badly distorted by a recent close encounter, as indicated in this "side view" that reconstructs their history over the past few hundred million years. NGC5195 is proceeding away from M51, but since it lies behind M51 as seen from the Milky Way the two galaxies look to us as if they were still entangled.

These two interacting galaxies raise the question: what is interacting? From our Earth bound vantage point, we see the ancient light of these clouds of suns, but if we were in the midst of that bent galactic arm, our view would be like our own night sky: the mostly black, mostly empty, void of space. What is bent is an arm of void! In time, space itself is bending!! The spacetime of one galactic arm is bending the spacetime of another galactic arm. Space is the ocean, stars are the foam.

D1087197

CREATION IN SPACE

a course in the
fundamentals of architecture

Volume 2:   DYNAMICS

Jonathan Block Friedman

KENDALL/HUNT PUBLISHING COMPANY
4050 Westmark Drive   Dubuque, Iowa 52002

FOR MARILYN

with love and gratitude

for Charlie and David

with pride and joy
with gratitude and love

This book was made possible in part by a generous grant from The Anna M Rockefeller Trust. Completion of this book was supported in part through the generosity of the MacDowell Colony.

Printed in the United States of America
10 9 8 7 6 5 4 3 2 1

Song, not poem

this lawn this edge from wood to sand
this kiss of color light radiant wine
soft as wind in spring white pine.
Trees make wind! Birch oak and
maple songs call forest kin
across the rolling waves of lawn.

Plant feet stretch ground earth up
to dancing head in mindful clouds
and fly to light, bird Bird and birdie
loft par chip putt drive an ace!

Silence is the space
for practicing your songs.

Practice is repetition and variety.
Profession is standard and invention.
Living is prediction and surprise.

Musician work is play
and play pays well in beauty.

(rest)

Volume 2: DYNAMICS

Contents

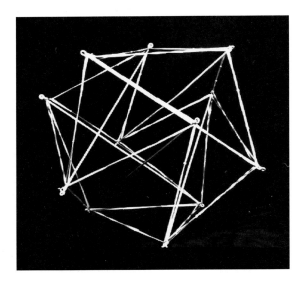

PREFACE TO VOLUME 2

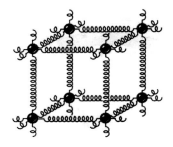

*Ingres is said to have created an artistic order out of rest.
I should like to create an order from feeling and, going stiill further, from motion.*
Paul Klee, September 1914

I didn't plan it this way, but the logic of the questions inevitably led this work along some of the most difficult paths in modern science.-- relativity, spacetime, gravitation, and quantum mechanics. The first volume of *Creation In Space* was relatively easy to write-- it was about what we all learned as beginning students in architecture. This second volume is about what we *should have* learned, and is thus much more difficult to write.

Volume Two comes out of a simple and straightforward question: "What happens to the models made in Architectonics when **time** enters the discussion?" This question arises out of another, which emerged relatively late in the inquiry: "What happens when the blocks of Architectonics get big-- big enough to live in-- and are therefore hollow?" The corollary to both these basic questions is "What happens when forces (like gravity and wind) are allowed to act on the perfect still lifes of Architectonics? These questions, innocent enough, and perhaps slanted towards the sense that a beginner in architecture should certainly have a *feel* for structures, materials, and construction, as well as form, light, and scale, have led to this new volume, *Dynamics*. Then all hell broke loose. What began as a 40 page simple handbook has now become two volumes, with a total of over 700 pages. Volume One was conceived in a weekend and completed and published within about three years; Volume Two was conceived in the same weekend, but has taken 12 more years to re-conceive and complete.

What follows is offered in the spirit it was created: an honest attempt to confront difficult and subtle phenomena from an architect's outlook; a maker of things who seeks the meaning of forms in space as they exist in time. I do not claim to be comprehensive, but I do not think the difficult questions raised by modern physics and philosophy can be avoided or ignored by any practicing, that is, thinking-*and*-doing artist in this day and age. More than one friend has suggested that I "get rid of the space-time stuff." I tried. I understand that in the everyday world of architecture as a business the primary question is how to resolve plan and program within the constraints of site and available budget. But I found myself returning to "the spacetime stuff" every time I tried to sense or express what space feels like and how architects unify their abilities to mold filled and empty solids into the comprehensive fabric of a building. I believe that if this books fails in its mission, it is not because the questions are wrong but because the answers are not yet clear.

I have tried to tell this story twice, in parallel, once in pictures and on the facing page again in words. Because my own background encouraged verbal before plastic expression, I have worked hard to strengthen my weakness first, like any beginner. Thus, I hope that this new volume will be found to make sense above all through the sequence of the images, the photos and drawings. If the words help to amplify the pictures, so much the better. I await the next generation, who may well be comfortable with virtual modeling, the evolution of plastic and elastic form, and travel in multiple frames of reference, to re-write this approach and re-tell the ever fresh and always enduring story of the comprehensive joy of making architecture with the clarity and passion it deserves.

Jonathan Friedman
11· 9 · 94   NHNH
11· 9 · 97   GCGC

ACKNOWLEDGMENTS

"It is time..." says the wise Rafiki in *The Lion King*. Maturity comes when gratitude greets opportunity. To make a book, to give shape to a fragment of the infinite, an author needs help from everywhere and everyone. An early portal to the limitless possibility of the mind is the grade-school blackboard: words and numbers and pictures come and go, changing, evolving. Even better than television, this dark window into intellect is like the night sky window to the cosmos. No wonder cleaning the erasers was an honor! Today the blackboard remains the plastic medium of the teacher, interpreter of signs. Pictured above is one day's blackboard a decade ago, linking architectural space with the evolution of structure. Questions in that class led me to the insight that the design of volumes follows the design of masses. So first I must thank all the students who gave me the chance to explore with them, to think out loud at the blackboard.

As the *tabula rasa* for architecture becomes more precise, with components of tracing paper, models, and monitors, the spirit of exploration and discovery infuses every medium. This new course, *Dynamics*, demands attention to structure, scale, materials, and space all at once. For many years, our modeling methods using a new Bag of Tricks were frustrating students. Joining pieces is time-consuming, and makes it difficult to experiment with other 3D program *parti* configurations. But then, a now anonymous student asked me if he could use the *Architectonics* Kit of Parts elements to model the program spaces in the *Dynamics* Concerto exercise. He (and everyone else!) was having problems visualizing volume relationships of the program spaces. Students needed to learn how to let the blocks of void, volume, space dance in the head and find their best positions on the site. As luck would have it, at 1/8" scale the 1" cubes made perfect 8' practice rooms and the 1/4" rods were close enough to model the circulation spaces. Cementing other cubes together could model the larger volumes. I suggested color-coding these elements by function to quickly see different *partis* of complex programs directly in 3D! Now a true and illuminating hierarchy of the stages of architectural design emerged: first program of volume locations, second surface relationships of continuity, opacity, transparency, third structural and material means. At last it became clear that first in *Architectonics* we learn to model mass in space then in *Dynamics* we learn to treat those filled masses as the empty volumes of architectural program: rooms, corridors, etc. The rest is easy! (Of course! "We coulda had a V8!") So, above all, I must thank the "guinea pigs"-- the students of the early years of this program -- for their patience, tolerance, immense talent, and support.

Special thanks to Dr. Julio San Jose, Guillermo Jullian de La Fuente and Anthony Eardley for their ongoing inspiration of joy and rigor in the pursuit of excellence. To Michele Bertomen for many conversations, including the crucial insight of a dynamics of spacial orders, rather than just of moving parts, which led me directly to the idea of program stresses on bowed and sheared space, as derived from the arch. To Dr. King Cheek and David McAlpin for their abiding encouragement and critical help. To the people of MacDowell colony for the essential gifts of time and space. To Dr. Sheldon Reaven, Dr. Woodrow T. Hundt, Dr. W. Stooder, and Dr. Iris Orens, for vital guidance and critical contributions. To my mother, Bernice Friedman, whose constant interest and direct questions led to the clearest formulation of many of these issues. To my brother Jeremy, for his love and care. To Dr. Matthew Schure and Dr. Edward Giuliano of NYIT for their support. To Russ Jordan for friendship and the ABS plastic "missing links". To my teaching colleagues and fellow Deans at NYIT, too numerous to name individually, for their continued interest and support. A few deserve special thanks: Judith Sheine, Paul Amatuzzo, David Diamond, Chris Chimera, Pascal Hofstein, Erin O'Keefe, Bill La Riche, Carl Karas, Michael Schwarting, Michael Kuenstle, Nick de Felice, Jim Weisenfeld, Harriet Kulka, Luis Navia. To wizards Mike Nolan, Debbie Huff, John Ringel, Steve Badanes, Kim Vlaun, Carloyn Chute, Anthony Brown, and Bob Stern. To Susan Niego for research and encouragement. To Maria di Natale, Maria Sola and Justin Faley for bringing order out of production chaos. To Traci Tager for patience and professionalism in producing myriad digital scans. To Ken Lin, who revealed wisdom in cold soup! To June Bukovinsky, for vast and vital help in preparing the manuscript. ***To Irma Roby for wisdom unlimited.***

To Bob Slutzky, pioneering plastic philosopher, whose articles are as beautiful and luminous as his paintings, the depth of my gratitude for his guidance, both skeptical and compassionate, cannot be measured. To Emilio Ambasz, inventor poet, my thanks for his time, razor mind, and gentle humor. To David Laur and Kirk Alexander at the Princeton Computer Lab. To Sally Fried, whose careful drawings revealed spacial issues in construction, and Bil Reyman, who made Harmony sing. To the many dedicated students who have kept excellence alive, including the Sowinski-Sullivans, Naomi Phillips, Ernie Di Maio, Clay Smook, Jon Reo, Kenny Jerome, Maria Parianos, Curt Taufman, Louis Trentadue, Rob Shoaff, Henry Hong, Tom Milano, and other twizzlers.

To Neil Ackerman, Ray Boz, Howard Stark, Peter Wayne, Todd Falb, and yes Terry Numanit, who demonstrated that the essence of play is the beauty achieved, when lofted arc settles close to the pin, and even in the less rare moments. To Jon Dyer for post-modern Merion. To neighbors Ann and Ed Fitzgibbon and to friends Diana and Sheldon Reaven, Janet and Jeff Kopito, Rick and Barbara Schwartz, Ellen and Lee Fawkes, Sue and Wayne Cohen, Greg Martin and Sue Aronson, Helen and Steve Chernicoff, David Lenson, Andrew Littauer. And to Lyco P. Sandbank, ace jazz sleuth.

To my family: Bernice Friedman, Aubrey Sverdlik, Jeremy, Lisa, Lindsay, and Caroline Friedman, Penny and Norman Schuster, Amy and Jeff Katz, Nancy Sverdlik, Linda and Sam Burton, Jenny and Irfan, Kate and Nate. To Elsie and Iris Turtz, Len and Judy Tager, Traci and Jay, Jennifer and Keith, Melissa Etlin. To the blessed memories of my father, Charles Friedman, my grandparents, Florence and Max Block, and Rose and Joseph Friedman. To those too soon lost still close to my heart, Minnie and Arthur and Howard Silber. And the best for last: to my sons Charlie and David, and my wife and friend Marilyn, my love and gratitude without end-- and my promise that it will never (and always) be like this again. At last, it is finished, now let the wild rumpus and PC games begin! "It is time...."

DEBBIE HUFF
(1954 - 1995)
IN MEMORIAM

*"Eenie meanie, chili beanie,
the spirits are about to speak"
Bullwinkle
"Not that lesson, this lesson..."
Rocky*

FOREWORD
by Emilio Ambasz

As the doctrine of Architectural Modernism is slowing receding -- standing remain only those glorious fragments that have survived the decay of their original cultural context -- so the teaching doctrines which Modernism engendered are brought into question. Like any colonizing catechism created to ensure self-perpetuation, it has also generated its own antibodies; as a matter of fact, the strongest battles against Modernism have been fought from within the doctrine itself. The main attack came about when some of the concepts it has much declaimed, but little explored, were examined thoroughly. Singular among these was "Space-time": the hymn generations of architects taught the next one to chant. However, beyond a cursory assimilation to journalistic notions of relativity, little attention had been paid as to what was actually meant by the idea of time. Once in a while, beachheads were established by a few authors who understood time as the essence of architecture conceived as process: the phenomena it undergoes in the stages of its coming into being. But even then, many wrong avenues had been taken; prominent among these was method-idolatry, later to be substituted by an intellectually undernourished confusion as to the architect's power to affect social behavior.

Perhaps, like in some notion of Paradise whereby it is understood not to be a place lost but a place around us to which we have been blinded, time as an analytical device for perceiving the reality of architecture was always there. We only needed to stretch our fingers to touch it. Essentially, it required supplementing the conceptual notion of architecture as a formal entity, and add to it another domain of concern: that of perceiving it as a phenomenological process. Not only the passage of time as measured by clocks, but more importantly, the process of architecture perceived sensorially, emotionally, and spatially, as well as observed as it impresses and modifies our perceptions through the very theories we created to explain it.

Friedman recognizes that time, conceived as an uninterrupted flowing line, is a very poor approximation to the phenomenon that concerns him. He perceives the process of time as an amalgam of conflicting phenomena, as an aggregate of often contradictory wills, as a juxtaposition of fragments which many times derive their meaning from the manner in which they're juxtaposed. By allowing such combinations, new meanings are deciphered, and sometimes, even ironies are generated.

His book is based on a sedimented conviction that theoretical constructs have usually deceived us, allowing in the meantime many horrors to be committed in the faithful pursuit of its tenets.

Friedman proposes a pathway, rather than a *methodos,* advancing an aggregate of insights and perceptions as a more trusting and durable device than so-called incontrovertible theory and ideology. Friedman's credo would highly please Merleau-Ponty, who would see in him the convert that arrived, not by the book, but through a true phenomenological way, that is to say, by experience.

To understand how Friedman arrived at his insights, and the refreshing optics he offers us, it is not out of place to imagine him as an aged-young-student. Now that he's more than fifty, he knows that education is wasted on the young, but he is also inclined to accepting the fact that there is no other choice, it must be poured on them. Paternalistically, the author seeks to encourage the student to see what is ahead. Perhaps he remembers himself and his student years at Princeton. Those were the years when a young generation of teachers pontificated the doctrine of Modernism, rewarding only the faithful acolytes. Notions of scale, composition, proportion, color, rhythm, and texture were denied a place in their own house. Similarly, transmitted experience about the effects of wind, climate, and sunlight on buildings were anathematized as the concern of the true infidel. In essence, Friedman's is a private pilgrimage for absolution. We are much obliged to him for taking us with him in this journey.

This book is an excellent collection of architectural insights. No formula is offered, for Friedman is too generous a soul to enslave. On the contrary, his hope is that by helping us gain an understanding of at least one essential point, he will have given us the key to understanding the quintessence of other essentialities. I acknowledge my great delight in reading it in an aleatory manner. Among the great assets of this book is the conviction that architectural theories are conceits of the mind. They do not exist in the nature of architecture. Perceptions, memories, sensations, images are the way nature affects us.

Conceived as a resplendent Breviary, this book should not be read in sequence -- any page can be opened at any time. The author has provided a taxonomy which, keeping reassuring company, gently allows us to cherish each insight that he provides within a delicate system of cross-references. Rather than a rosary, this book should be considered like a box of precious stones. While some are highly polished, others will become burnished only by cherishing them. We can take out one at a time, and adorn ourselves with them. By so doing, we may appreciate how they relate to each other and how they are to be juxtaposed, and by this procedure, we may realize we have learned the first of this book's many lessons.

This brick is hollow. The Vertical Assembly Building at Cape Kennedy Florida, where the Apollo moon rockets were assembled before launch, is a cube volume is so large that it makes its own weather. Clouds form inside it. The doors are large enough to wheel the United Nations Secretariat Building through them. It dwarfs the "moving brick" helicopter in the photo. However, while the VAB is more voluminous, great architecture like Frank Lloyd Wright's Falling Water or Le Corbusier's Algiers Tower are more spacial.

THIS ROOM IS MOVING.

THE ARGUMENT

"Architecture begins when two bricks are put carefully together." Mies

"If I were to define architecture in a word, I would say that architecture is the thoughtful making of spaces." Lou Kahn

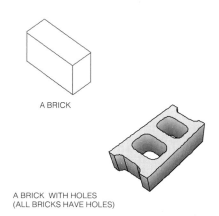

A BRICK

A BRICK WITH HOLES
(ALL BRICKS HAVE HOLES)

Architectonics satisfies the mind with order.
But what does architecture *feel* like?   Architecture feels dynamic.

The push and pull of organization is a dance in the mind. It is the food of thought as much as air is the food of breath. Forces within buildings shape and locate the volumes we inhabit. To a builder, a brick is a brick; to an architect, a brick is a room and a room is a brick. Both brick and room are rectangular solids. One is filled, one is empty. Masons pile up bricks to make rooms; architects pile up rooms to make space. The space of architecture is an ordered fabric of filled and empty solids.

Filled solids of brick, wood, glass or stone wrap empty rooms in walls, windows, floors, and ceilings. Forces like wind and gravity push and pull ceiling beams and panels, but what keeps these masses from crushing us is their structure-- the arrangement of filled solids to resist the motions constantly generated by the forces around and through them.

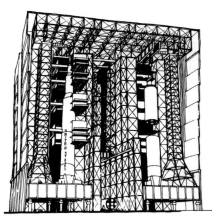

MEDIEVAL ROOM WITH HEAVY TIMBER BEAMS

Similarly, what keeps the empty rooms of a building from resisting confusion, decay, and neglect is the viability and endurance of their order-- that is, the arrangement of empty solids to produce desired light and satisfy program needs of the inhabitants. The masterful composition of volumes requires an understanding of how they push and pull against each other in seeking their correct location. This art is no less subtle than the skill of the structural engineer in ordering mass elements into bridge, arch, flying buttress, or space frame. It is the essential skill of the architect. The distinction between builders and architects is clear. For example, many freestanding suburban houses inexplicably locate the garage at the southeast corner, robbing the residents of the best morning light. They could have been transformed into wonderfully sunny homes at no extra cost-- if only the builder had turned the plans over before the concrete for the foundation was poured! The builder must know how easily the concrete flows; the architect must learn how **volumes** move in space. Architects make space out of volumes. This book is about how to do that. Composing in space and time is the melody of this book, an idea that evolves into theme and variations.

Architectonics teaches how mass elements can create order in three-dimensional space, but it cannot yet teach how to create an order **of** three-dimensional space. To do this we must first define volumes plastically and materially; then combine volumes by resolving forces developed between them; and finally organize volume fields of varying energies which balance internal and external forces. Force brings motion, altering place and *time*. In architectonics, the arrangement of masses seems as changeless as a still life. But in the real world, forces like wind and gravity never sleep. Beams deflect, floors sag, roofs leak. Materials and connections count. The constructor must use both ruler and clock to organize masses to resist any tendency to move in unwanted directions.

Dynamics is the study of how a geometry of solids changes in time. Dynamics equals architectonics plus time. Architecture orders both space and time. Architects master the fabric of all solids, both filled and empty, that compose rooms and the matter between them in every building. In truly plastic design, everything is in flux until unifying order is found and established. Time unifies the structure of volumes. To master the art of dynamic design, we must learn to feel time-- to sense the effects of time on space and space on time. Architecture feels dynamic. Architecture takes time to make space.

VERTICAL ASSEMBLY BUILDING:
INSIDE A BRICK

A book has time. This is before. The end is after.
Turning the pages makes space.
Study many times makes sense.
This page is for my father in spacetime.

INEFFABLE SPACE

by Le Corbusier
from *New World of Space*

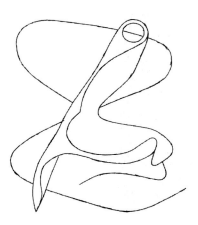

Taking possession of space is the first gesture of living things, of men and of animals, of plants and of clouds, a fundamental manifestion of equilibrium and of duration. The occupation of space is the first proof of existence.

The flower, the plant, the tree, the mountain stand forth, existing in a setting. If they one day command attention because of their satisfying and independent forms, it is because they are seen to be isolated from their context and extending influences all around them. We pause, struck by such interrelation in nature, and we gaze, moved by this harmonious orchestration of space, and we realize that we are looking at the reflection of light.

Architecture, sculpture and painting are specifically dependent on space, bound to the necessity of controlling space, each by it own appropriate means. The essential thing that will be said here is that the release of esthetic emotion is a special function of space.

Action of the work (architecture, statue or picture) on its surroundings: vibrations, cries or shouts (such as originate from the Parthenon on the Acropolis in Athens), arrows darting away like rays, as if springing from an explosion; the near or distant site is shaken by them, touched, wounded, dominated or caressed. Reaction of the setting: the walls of the room, its dimensions, the public square with the various weights of its facades, the expanses or the slopes of the landscape even to the bare horizons of the plain or the sharp outlines of the mountains - the whole environment brings its weight to bear on the place where there is a work of art, the sign of man's will, and imposes on it its deep spaces or projections, its hard or soft densities, its violences or its softnesses. A phenomenon of concordance takes place, as exact as mathematics, a true manifestation of plastic acoustics; thus one may speak of one of the most subtle of all orders of phenomena, sound, as a conveyor of joy (music) or of oppression (racket).

Without making undue claims, I may say something about the "magnification" of space that some of the artists of my generation attempted around 1910, during the wonderfully creative flights of cubism. They spoke of the *fourth dimension* with intuition and clairvoyance. A life devoted to art, and especially to a search after harmony, has enabled me, in my turn, to observe the same phenomenon through the practice of three arts: architecture, sculpture and painting.

The fourth dimension is the moment of limitless escape evoked by an exceptionally just consonance of the plastic means employed.

It is not the effect of the subject chosen; it is a victory of proportion in everything - the anatomy of the work as well as the carrying out of the artist's intentions whether consciously controlled or not. Achieved or unachieved, these intentions are always existent and are rooted in intuition, that miraculous catalyst of acquired, assimilated, even forgotten wisdom. In a complete and successful work there are hidden masses of implications, a veritable world which reveals itself to those whom it may concern, which means: to those who deserve it.

Then a boundless depth opens up, effaces the walls, drives away contingent presences, *accomplishes the miracle of ineffable space.*

I am not conscious of the miracle of faith, but I often live that of ineffable space, the consummation of plastic emotion.

Here I have been allowed to speak as a man of the laboratory, dealing with his personal experiments carried out in the major arts which have been so unfortunately dissociated or separated for a century. Architecture, sculpture, painting: the movement of time and of events now unquestionably leads them toward a synthesis.

He who deals with architecture (what we understand as architecture and not that of the academies) must be an impeccable master of plastic form and a live and active connoisseur of the arts. Now that the architect assigns to the engineer part of his work and his responsibility, admission to the profession should be granted only to persons who are properly endowed with the sense of space, a faculty which psycho-technical methods seek to reveal. Lacking that sense, the architect loses his justification and his function. To keep such candidates away from building, then, is a service to social health.

The illustrations in this book show an incessant desire to take possession of space by bringing into play architecture and city planning, sculpture and pictures, all capable of achieving that purpose through the never relaxed pressure of a continuing inventiveness.

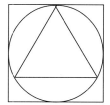

INTRODUCTION

SWING

LIFE on a SWING

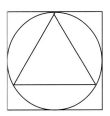

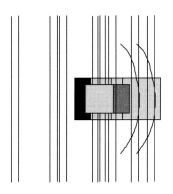

PENDULUM

tuning the universe

STUDENTS OF ACTION

"It don't mean a thing if it ain't got that swing."   Duke Ellington

Swing Time

We are all architects as children. Every day we grow and animate our world. Arranging blocks for elbow room, we become acrobats, builders, climbers, dancers, swimmers exploring space-- and we change. Five-year-old citizens of the playground test strength and balance in the give and take of living skin and bones. Children inhabit a fantasy of power when they make dream castles with wood blocks in their hands, but adults use true power, force in time, to extend a builder's reach beyond arm's length. As we mature, our blocks grow large and heavy but more temporary as the grip of time demands care to keep our bricks and beams in place. Yet a well-made home sets no limit to the soul. Making form organizes space and time.

Carpe diem! Seize the day! A swinging child pumps *now!* to catch the downward fall and add a burst of speed to amplify the arc even higher in resonant oscillation. The swing seat pendulum traces a sector of a cylinder of revolution about the crossbar above. This geometric solid exists in time as much as space. The moving child burns food energy and pumps knees to rhythmically shift weight and drive the dynamical system of volume force and motion that creates the swing-space. A nearby friend stands in a different local frame of reference than the swinger in the cylindrical swing-space. If the standing leg of one meets the flying foot of the other, both will hurt. The empty volume of the swinging child is a form as real and "solid" as any carved block of stone. Mass in motion defines space as much as any static set of walls and floors. Only a fool would stand in the middle of a highway because no 60 MPH car filled the space at that very moment.

To the swinging child, seat, rope, and hands look sharp against a blurred field of streaking trees and leaves. Clearly the moving space of the swing is not the same as the static space of the playground. In plan and section the swinging room also measure time. All things weave elaborate fabrics of mass and void through the loom of time. What complex geometric figure does our daily path trace along the world-line of a roving passenger aboard a spinning and orbiting planet whose central star makes its own vast 100,000 year circuit around the distant center of our Milky Way galaxy? And from whose point of view is the figure seen? How can an architect, master of architectonics as the science of arrangement of mass in light, come to grips with this kind of multiple experience and perception of space and time? If a picture is worth a thousand words, then a plan is worth a thousand pictures. If architecture is many plans and views at once, it is also one view or plan many times.

Death is eternal, changeless, and inert, but *anima*, the soul of life, is the motion that quickens the vital pulse of compassionate being. Motion is parent and again child of e-motion. Children are students of action as much as vision. While Architectonics may emerge from the five-year-old child in the midst of still and instantly ancient monuments, what emerges from the first childhood revolution of independence is *urgent vision*, the need to seek a new world with room enough to move and breathe, the need to live in the country that the ever-growing mind inhabits. Architects make realms for action, where gesture is a dance of body *with* mind. If ARCHITECTONICS is the study of relationships of mass and void poised motionless in space, then the study of the relationships between volumes and the forces that put mass and void *in motion* is herein called DYNAMICS.

ACTION IN SPACE

"Everything flows; nothing remains.... One cannot step twice into the same river." Herakleitos

The maturing child moves beyond playground swings and seesaws into ever shifting fields. Like an ocean-riding windsurfer, a player in the world arena must adjust to changing footings, horizons, and complex waves. Politics presents its own rhythmic undulations. Political terrain may move with geologic pace (at which even glacier flow seems frantic) or suddenly reform in avalanche catastrophe. It takes the skill of life's experience to learn to negotiate the dips and swells of social space and time. It takes further practice yet to master the art of flight-- that is to find balance in or on one's craft to ride the crest of opportunity into lofty heights. Rarer still are those who can then turn the world upside down and land smooth and upright in a shifting field with the poise to seek such daring launch again. Architects find in *plan* (both plastic vision and call to action) the courage and consolation to face relentless change. Thales (640?-546BCE), father of Greek mathematics and philosophy, argued that everything, even mist and earth, is ultimately water. He believed that heavenly bodies were water in an incandescent state; and that stars were not gods but were 'steam from a pot'. It is told that one day he fell into a ditch while gazing at the heavens. A woman scoffed, but he remained awed at the spectacle above him. Perhaps that sense of wonder arising from facing the rich glory of the cosmos is the true origin of *science,* as desire for knowing, and *art,* as expression of feeling. Thales today might well be windsurfing, body and soul immersed in heaving sea, ingenious as an engineer, sensitive as a weatherman ecologist, as close to a "free ride" as any economist. Awe is mind sport into unknown surf where physical reality demands the honest and noble humility of power in control.

Dynamics

All things tend to move. Architects arrange mass and void in fields of forces like wind or gravity in such a way that the configuration can resist change. Thus we walk on floors and under roofs that don't collapse. The volumes we inhabit are surrounded and supported not by inert lumps ignorant of the fields around them, but rather by "skin" and "bones" which ever shift to balance the forces that tug them. Dynamics is a call to action, to arrange mass and void into habitable volumes. *Dynamis* means "power" in Greek, and comes from *du* "to be able, to have the strength to do." The dictionary defines "dynamics" as both the branch of physics that treats the action of forces on bodies in motion or at rest (kinetics, kinematics, and statics, collectively) and the various forces, physical or moral, operating in any field. In music, dynamics determines the force (loudness or softness) of expression, distinguished from *tempo* (speed), *rhythm,* (pattern) etc. What architects do in the field of architecture is to organize action, specifically the inter-action of volume. As architect Lou Kahn said, "order is."

Spacetime: a Dynamic medium

No one picture of a windsurfer tells his or her story of acrobatic daring in such a restless realm. A sequence is needed at the very least, better yet a film, better yet a ride in the sea itself. Not only is the actor always in motion, always adjusting position, balance, muscular tension and grip, but so too is the field ever new. The surfer may leap off the wave at its crest, only to fall an extra 30 feet to find the surface at the wave's trough. The surfboard cuts the sea and shapes the wave even as the wave shapes the surfer's flight. To map the surfer's ocean playground, we need to know not only *where* every drop of water is in space, but also *when.* Modern physics tells us that every play between mass and void demands such spacetime measure too. Neither the sea nor space is static. The interstellar vacuum is filled with radiant waves of light and gravity. Space and time are stretched by matter just as matter is subject to the shapes of cosmic curvature. Space is in fact spacetime, a dynamic medium.

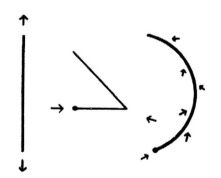

Wassily Kandinsky's illustration, in *Point and Line to Plane,* of "forces" applied to a point to produce straight, zigzag, and curved lines.

DYNAMIC MATTER: A WORLD OF MOTION

Glaciers are rivers of flowing ice. They may take thousands of years to move through the same course that a river of liquid ice, or water, would traverse in a few seconds. Why? Matter is dynamic at atomic scales as well as at the larger scale of our surrounding environment. A ship in Alaska can encounter one kind of matter in many states of motion. Ice flows down, clouds rise up, and water oscillates its surface at sea level. And beyond, whole galaxies wheel. Black holes more massive than a millions stars can apparently explode. Our universe is now best explained as having arisen from an infinitesimally small and infinitely hot Big Bang, not steady state but always in dynamic expansion. Temperature measures the action of the atoms and molecules that compose matter. The warmer a body is, the greater the motion of its constituent parts. Adding energy to any material in its solid state increases the vibration rate of molecules as they bounce like springs within the close-packed structure determined by their electromagnetic fields. Added energy increases motion, weakening the electro-chemical bonds. Eventually the material will flow as a liquid. Still more energy will dissociate the molecules completely. When each molecule is free to fly until it rebounds off another, the material is a gas.

Three Bags Full: ice, water, cloud

The same chemical compound, H_2O, can be water, ice, or steam, depending on how much its molecules will tend to move. The difference between them can be modelled with simple materials. Tightly wrap rubber bands around a plastic bag filled with stones or marbles. The bag and stones will move together as a rigid form. The same bag without rubber bands will deform to a new shape when pushed, and hold that shape until pushed again. The material in the bag has flowed under the effect of an outside force, and is thus roughly equivalent to a plastic liquid. A bag filled with springs will quiver when pushed, as the bag first deforms and then returns to its original shape "under its own power". This approximates the form of an elastic gas. (Curiously ice floats because crystal H_2O expands when it freezes, and is thus less dense than water. This is uncommon in phase changes.) The character of a material, whether rigid, plastic, or elastic, depends on the strength and orientation of the bonds between its constituent atoms. Even at molecular scales, creation is a balance between forces that tend to drive matter apart and gather it together. Perhaps this is the fundamental reason why architecture is sometimes called "frozen music".

States of Matter: the Properties of Materials

Building materials are distinguished by their strength in comparison to weight, which depends in part on how rigid, plastic, or elastic they may be. Bricks are quite rigid, while wet clay and mud are very plastic. A perfectly rigid material would fracture if you tried to twist or bend it. A completely plastic material could resist no load at all. (Imagine a house built of water!) The *modulus of elasticity* describes how a given material will "spring back" to its original shape when carrying a load, and is an important measure of its strength. Steel has a high modulus of elasticity, while cement has a very low modulus of elasticity. In a dynamic medium, it makes no sense to place one "pure" white cube on another. A cube of alabaster will crush a cube of cotton below it. Materials count, and the force of gravity stresses and deflects forms when loaded. Only after forces have acted on materials or structures long enough may their effects be visible. So time counts. *Before, during,* and *after* construction are all important, especially when the elements make spaces bigger than a human being. The grain in the stone of a Brancusi sculpture is a record of the stresses that pushed, pulled, and twisted it in its molten state. As it cooled, the molecules settled into the rigid but still vibrating crystal pattern it has maintained for perhaps billions of years. Even though this beautiful mass will outlast any human lifetime, it would vaporize in an instant of solar nova heat. The stone always swims through the river of time.

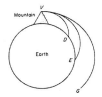

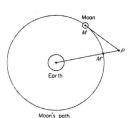

MOVING STONES

Galileo Galilei (1564-1642) saw mass moving in space. As a youth he watched a pendulum and saw that the time of its swing period remained constant whatever the width of the arc. Later, he discovered that falling objects travel 16 times the time in seconds squared, expressed as $s = 16t^2$, from which he determined the rate of acceleration due to earth's gravity. He noted that this expression did not include a value for the weight and therefore argued that stones released from the same height would reach the ground no matter how much they weighed. Legend tells that he demonstrated this to an astounded crowd at the Leaning Tower of Pisa by dropping stones of different weight which indeed arrived at the ground simultaneously. This event, which many historians claim marks the beginning of the modern science of structural engineering, seemed contrary to experience, but it led Galileo to predict the fact that, ignoring air resistance, a stone and a feather will fall to the earth at the same speed. This was confirmed by Astronaut David Scott on the airless Moon in 1971, when the hammer and falcon feather he released fell together in the vacuum of space and reached the moon's surface at the same time.

The precise shape of motion

Galileo established systematic principles for the investigation of the natural world. He sought to describe *how* things happened, rather than *why* they happened. Although at first this might seem like a retreat in understanding, a little reflection shows the power of Galileo's ideas. He did not need to justify any pet theory. Without prejudice he could describe how the world worked, and could predict how the world would work under certain conditions. Galileo said "religion tells you how to go to Heaven, not how heavens go." History records the controversy generated by Galileo's original idea to aim the newly invented telescope to the heavens, where his discovery of four moons orbiting Jupiter confirmed the Copernican heliocentric model of the solar system, and laid to rest forever the ancient illusion that the Earth was the still center of all movement in the universe. Threatened by the Church with charges of heresy, he officially renounced his scientific insights, but legend tells us he then muttered "yet it moves."

Isaac Newton (1642-1727) found a simple relationship between how an apple falls to earth and the Moon orbits our planet. In a basic thought experiment, he asked what would happen if a stone were thrown from a high mountain. He showed that the stone would follow the path of a parabola, and eventually fall to the ground. But what would happen if the stone were thrown so hard that it would travel completely around the earth, returning to the original mountain peak before it fell to the ground? He understood that the stone would then be in orbit around the earth, much as the moon itself is in orbit around our planet. Then one day, probably in the year 1665, while he was staying in the countryside to avoid the great Plague in London, he observed an apple from the tree above him fall to the ground. He realized that the apple and the Moon obeyed the same force of gravitation towards the center of the earth. With geometry and the calculus he invented, he was able to derive a universal law of gravitation that applied to all bodies in the heavens and on earth. A stone in a cathedral was subject to the same forces and motions that governed how the planets and the stars interacted. Along with a formula relating force, mass and acceleration ($F = ma$), and the principle that every action has an equal and opposite reaction, Newton's Law of Gravitation provides the basis for the mechanics, statics, and structural analysis that enables us to build domes, bridges, and towers of enormous dimension without fear of their collapse.

EMPTY STONES

Creating emptiness requires mastering the physical forces that determine how masses sustain and surround regions of void to establish structural stability. **Volume** is the result of mass poised carefully about a void. A volume is a perceptual and often habitable empty solid. At human scale, the dominant forces that determine the structure of volume are gravity and the electromagnetic bonds that provide an elastic material with the means to resist gravity. Even wind is ultimately gravitational in origin. Wind is the result of cold dense air being pulled closer to the center of the earth than the warmer lighter air which gets pushed up and sideways, out of the way, like bubbles in soda.

It is possible to read the history of civil engineering as the search for ever greater structural spans with ever less material. This becomes a twofold study: both the search for ever stronger and lighter materials and the search for ever more efficient structural geometries. The Pantheon, a hollow stone sphere, built almost 2000 years ago under the reign of the Roman Emperor Hadrian (c. CE 120-124), employs subtle refinements to overcome the inherent massiveness of its primary material, concrete, bonded with brick and internally clad with stone. The ceiling is lightened and strengthened by coffering, and as Brunelleschi discovered 1300 years after its construction, the span of the crown is constructed from a lighter volcanic rock than the perimeter spans. The external annular rings serve to direct the outward thrust of the span downward into the massive perimeter buttresses. Although the floor pattern reveals the inherent difficulty of unifying radial and orthogonal geometries in a single space, the Pantheon remains a marvel for its volumetric clarity, colossal size, and magical lighting from a single 27' diameter oculus skylight in the crown of the dome.

Volume and Space

The 142'-6" diameter sphere of the Pantheon is dwarfed by Goodyear's Air-Dock, which at its construction was the world's largest building without interior supports, spanning about 300 feet. The 1958 CNIT Building in Paris spans 780', the current record. Buckminster Fuller's (1895-1983) mid 20th Century proposal to cover all of central Manhattan with a vast dome is not impossible. A dirigible is an immense structure filled with helium that is lighter than air itself. Fuller suggested that it was possible to make city spheres several miles in diameter, utilizing the greenhouse effect, in which sunlight could heat the interior volume to a few degrees warmer than the surrounding air, which at large enough scale would make the weight of its geodesic skin structure and *the weight of all its inhabitants* negligible so that these cities would actually float! (See page 361 below for more on this idea.)

Exciting as these structural inventions are, to an architect they are still essentially "one-liner" stories. **Volume** is essential to architecture. Architectural **space** is the plastic interaction of volumes that result from the compositional forces of site and program. Architecture is the *play* of volumes-- large and small, round and square, light and dark; an order which appeals to sense as we experience the building and appeals to reason as we understand the logic of how volumes are organized to meet programmatic needs. As Le Corbusier says, "You have kept the rain off my head, and for that I thank you, but you have not yet touched my heart." A single massive volume, although a demanding problem of structure and construction, does not necessarily yield plastically rich architectural space. Pascal Quintard-Hofstein observes that while the stacked floors of a skyscraper may be a hundred times taller than a living room with a balcony, the room is more vertical. So too is Le Corbusier's Villa Shodan (see page 42) more spacial than the VAB at Cape Kennedy. There may be more volume in a hangar, but there is more space in a sponge.

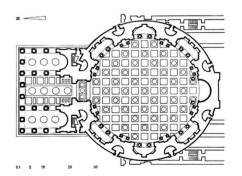

THE INTERIOR OF THE PANTHEON, SAMUEL H. KRESS COLLECTION, © 1997 NATIONAL GALLERY OF ART, WASHINGTON.

01 5 10   20   30

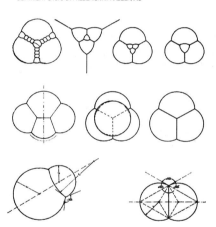

FROM *FREI OTTO: TENSION STRUCTURES* BY ROLAND.
COPYRIGHT © 1970 BY FREDERICK A. PRAEGER, INC

"The study of soap bubbles makes for a better understanding of pneumatic structural shapes... a soap bubble is always a "minimal surface'." Frei Otto

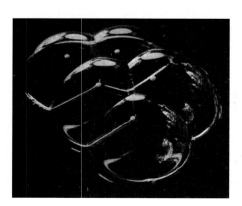

LIGHT AND HEAVY STONES

The nucleus of an atom is an island of mass surrounded by void. Molecules are like sponges of void punctuated with small and distant specks of matter. When molecules are cool, they can be arranged as crystals, closely packed, with little space between them. But as they are heated, they vibrate, and the average distance between molecules increases. When hot enough to be gaseous, they completely dissociate to fill a much larger volume than their actual aggregate dimensions, just as a moving swing fills a much larger space in the playground than a motionless wooden seat and metal chains. Hot air balloons are bags of gas, much less dense than an equivalent weight of stone, which can remain close-packed and crystalline. Adding heat to the air inside a balloon makes it so much less dense than the surrounding cooler air that it can lift itself and passengers off the earth's surface, floating into the upper reaches of our air-ocean like a bubble in the sea. On the other hand, it is easier to set a few stones in position and expect them to stay there than it is to hold hot-air balloons in position for very long at all. A castle is a collection of heavy stone cubic "bricks", while a balloon race is a collection of light spherical hot air bubble "bricks".

Close Packing

Different geometries can fill space with varying degrees of completeness. Space may be completely filled by an orthogonal geometry of rectangular solids, whereas a group of spheres will always leave wedges of excess void between the cells. Closely-packed rigid spheres exhibit strict geometries (which are very helpful for understanding physical chemistry). At least part of the reason why architects favor orthogonal cubic space may be the comprehensive spacial efficiency of this geometry. Orthogonal bricks surround orthogonal rooms, which contain orthogonal cabinets that carry orthogonal books or cereal boxes that are shipped in orthogonal cartons in orthogonal trucks, etc. Cubes may be arranged so that no joints show between them, unlike cylinders or pyramids. Perhaps because we are most used to it, cubes appear to us as the most "intuitive" version of close-packed space, accepted and elaborated by geometers from Euclid through Descartes. (Do Mongolians dwelling in circular yurts share this perception?) But other shapes besides cubes also fill 3D space. For example, tetrahedrons and their octahedron duals completely fill any extent of "triangular" space.

Dynamic Volume

While groups of massive or inflexible spheres like a jar of marbles will always leave gaps between them, elastic spherical volumes like balloons or soap bubbles can create a foam of mutually shared surfaces. Soap bubbles are empty balls whose skins are only a few atoms thick, which flow across the surface to equalize stress. The flowing material does not allow stress concentrations to occur anywhere in the film of either a single bubble or a group of them (except for minor differences in stress due to the weight of the soap film itself). Soap bubbles thus adopt the shapes that make the least surface area for the enclosed volume of air. A foam of soap bubbles is a dynamic volume as mass and void shift to resolve stresses into minimal surface geometry. The changing thickness of the soap film bubble skin refracts different frequencies of light, which is what gives them their multicolored iridescence. Architectural volume is not static but *dynamic*. Like bubbles, rooms need not be merely passive and mutually exclusive neighbors, but may interact with their own kind and each other. As bubbles near each other deform, so too can volumes interact, modifying each other's shape and position until the form of the whole bagful of bubbles (the building) comes to rest. A fleet of hot air balloons in flight can serve as an image of a "gas" of rooms not yet coalesced into decisive plan and section.

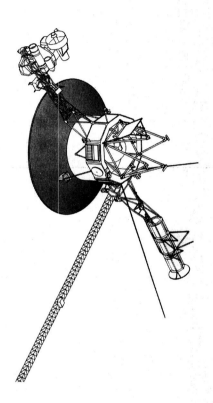

STONE'S THROW

Galileo's method of inquiry is still used as we throw sophisticated stones like the spaceship Voyager to worlds beyond his discoveries. Today, at the edge of technology, our "stone's throw" is becoming longer, and the controls needed to aim and position the 'stone' more delicate. The materials of our new 'stones' are more complex, and carving the volumes they inhabit requires utmost precision. Their targets move with great speed and are very far from us indeed. When mission scientists send signals to turn on a tape recorder on Voyager, the motion of the tape and the shift of its mass from one spool to the other alters the course of the ship. This change must be calculated and accounted for if the ship is to reach its destination. There are no brakes on board and there is no friction surface for the ship to grip. All changes must be accomplished by repositioning the ship's inertial mass and applying force in a chosen direction with small jets of gas. The ship reacts and changes direction while continuing to move at great speed. The engineering that accomplishes these wonders is a direct descendant of the principles pioneered in the investigation of forces and building structures from Galileo onward. Every rocket flight demonstrates Newton's Third Law of Motion, often stated as: "for every action there is an equal and opposite reaction." Unlike boats or airplanes, space ships do not push against any material to move. There is only void, the vacuum of space itself. The fuel goes out the back and the rocket moves forward. "Newton" works, and an exquisitely delicate dance of inertial guidance and celestial mechanics carries us to the stars. Human thought took flight, and the Eagle has landed.

When nuclear scientists investigate the smallest particles of matter like electrons they know that the light they shine will change the position of the electron. At the middle scale of everyday life, moving mass affects the design of forms. If an auto or airplane engineer were to discount the torque generated by the rotating shaft of an engine, the vehicle would not run true. The top of the Citicorp Building in New York carries a block of concrete on a railroad track, which is connected by computer to sensors which measure the force of the wind on the side of the building. When the wind blows, the block is automatically moved against that motion, to dampen the oscillations caused by the wind. For the arrangement of forms in space at all scales, motion matters. Not only do planets, spaceships, electrons and atoms move, but their associated electromagnetic, gravitational, etc. fields move as well. Today we find that mass determines the very shape of space, which in turn determines the motion of all things. Matter, movement, and space itself appear to be interrelated.

A Family Portrait

Michael Collins, pilot of the Apollo 11 Command Module on its historic mission to land Neil Armstrong as the first person on the moon, was orbiting the far side of the moon when the Eagle landed at Tranquility Base on July 20, 1969. Thus Collins was the first person out of radio contact with the earth and rest of humanity. When asked what that moment was like, he told this author, "You know how it is, if you are sitting in the middle of the Pacific Ocean in a rowboat on a clear moonless night, with stars everywhere above you?" (Of course, we've all had that experience!) "Well, it was just like that, except that there were stars everywhere below as well." Imagine, stars brilliantly vivid in coloir, too numerous to count, moving faster than any rocket... all around! Michael Collins took the photograph opposite as Armstrong and Buzz Aldrin returned from Tranquility Base. It shows three local stones in a single view, each an independent space-craft. In the foreground, the Lunar Module, humanity's most roving mobile home yet. In the middle ground looming dark and bright with promise, the Moon. In the distance, our mobile home planet, Earth....

THE GODZILLA: A UNIT OF DEPTH

HOW DEEP IS SPACETIME?

"You see, the mind is capacious." Benny Golson

A baby's fingers delicately brush your cheek. A slap in the face wakes you up. Lay a brick on your hand, or drop the brick onto the same hand from above your head. The bigger the mass, the faster the motion, the greater the impact. Try to stop an ocean liner! Dynamics describes events and motions not only in terms of positions in space and time but also in terms of causes-- the forces on objects and how objects respond. Dynamics studies what happens, how forces influence the motion of matter and shape of space. Physicist Robert Mills has said "The best focus for a discussion of dynamics is the pair of physical quantities *momentum* and *energy*. These are the basic conserved quantities of nature."

Momentum, force, energy, and power

Momentum, identified by Newton as the "quantity of motion" carried by a moving particle, is proportional to its velocity and mass. It takes *force* to change momentum and it takes *energy* to sustain that force over any opposition. The combined momentum and energy of a system is always conserved. (One billiard ball may hit another and stop, but the second will start to move.) Power, measured in the familiar unit of watts, is the rate of energy consumption. A 100 watt light bulb burns 100 standard units (Joules) of energy every second. In our universe, the speed of light is the only absolute. A second is now defined as how long it takes for light to go 299,792 kilometers (about 186,000 miles) and distance is measured in how far light can go in a given time span. Light takes 8 minutes to travel the 93 million miles from the Sun to Earth. In one year, a photon of light will cross 5,865,696,000,000 miles! A modest light bulb floods a room with light. But a whole planet full of electric light is no more visible to people from a nearby star than one candle flame in Los Angeles would be to a New Yorker. How many watts of energy are needed to send the light from M51 galaxy across 30 million light years to our eyes!? The answer is so vast that it is difficult to relate it to human scale.

A measure of depth

When we gaze at the ancient distant light of galaxies we see more than just the three dimensions of a brick. We *feel* something of the majesty of the awesome forces involved. For example, the cover of this volume (and the facing page) shows two galaxies interacting. The clearly bent arm of M51, the Spiral Galaxy, mostly boundless void, contains billions of stars of enormous momentum. Only the huge gravitational force generated by a passing galaxy could have altered their momentum and energy into the distorted pattern we see today. Every photograph captures the light not just of solid geometry, but also the forces involved in generating their configuration at that moment. To distinguish this sense from the usual three dimensions of left-right, up-down, and in-out, and to include some sense of the heft, or weightiness of such vision, let us identify the combination of momentum and energy as a measure of *depth*.

Golfers and galaxies. Above, © Disney Enterprises, Inc. Far left, photo by Harold Edgerton, inventor of the strobe light and strobe light photography. He could visually "stop time" in the thinnest slices. When one of Edgerton's graduate students asked "do you have time to talk to me about my project?" he answered " I can give you about 9 nanoseconds..."

An average golf swing (driving a golf ball mass some distance in a short time) measures momentum and energy at human scale, and is herein defined as one "godzilla". On page 20, a frieze of sequential frames from Walt Disney's *Sorcerer's Apprentice* shows Mickey Mouse's dance in time to Paul Dukas' music. The amount of momentum /energy for each frame transformation in Mickey Mouse's animated dance is clearly less than one godzilla. (Each bump from Mickey's slight frame would gently push you, whereas the golf swing would crack your jaw.) For finer gradation, and to celebrate the golden section, we shall arbitrarily define a scale of 1 godzilla = 1618 mickeys. About a gazillion godzillas = 1 light year's worth of light. A very large Golfer could accelerate one galaxy past another, and if the drive was accurate enough, not only bend the shaft of the Club, but also the arms of the galactic target. A sphere with a radius of one light-year fills $8.44942271943 \times 10^{38}$ cubic miles!! Plenty of room!! Plenty of depth!!

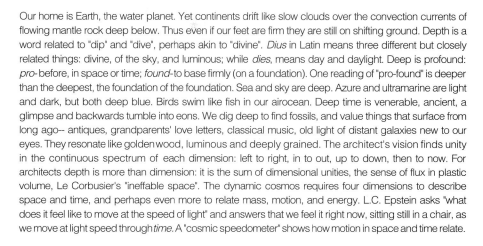

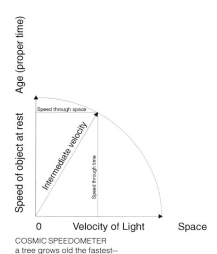

COSMIC SPEEDOMETER
a tree grows old the fastest--
it does not move, so it travels the least in space
and thus the most in time (if the earth stood "still")

LIGHT DOES NOT AGE

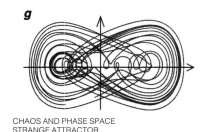

CHAOS AND PHASE SPACE
STRANGE ATTRACTOR

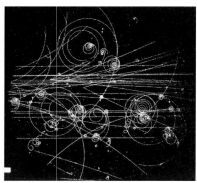

PARTICLE TRACES IN A BUBBLE CHAMBER, CERN

COMING TO LIFE

Depth

Our home is Earth, the water planet. Yet continents drift like slow clouds over the convection currents of flowing mantle rock deep below. Thus even if our feet are firm they are still on shifting ground. Depth is a word related to "dip" and "dive", perhaps akin to "divine". *Dius* in Latin means three different but closely related things: divine, of the sky, and luminous; while *dies*, means day and daylight. Deep is profound: *pro*-before, in space or time; *found*-to base firmly (on a foundation). One reading of "pro-found" is deeper than the deepest, the foundation of the foundation. Sea and sky are deep. Azure and ultramarine are light and dark, but both deep blue. Birds swim like fish in our airocean. Deep time is venerable, ancient, a glimpse and backwards tumble into eons. We dig deep to find fossils, and value things that surface from long ago-- antiques, grandparents' love letters, classical music, old light of distant galaxies new to our eyes. They resonate like goldenwood, luminous and deeply grained. The architect's vision finds unity in the continuous spectrum of each dimension: left to right, in to out, up to down, then to now. For architects depth is more than dimension: it is the sum of dimensional unities, the sense of flux in plastic volume, Le Corbusier's "ineffable space". The dynamic cosmos requires four dimensions to describe space and time, and perhaps even more to relate mass, motion, and energy. L.C. Epstein asks "what does it feel like to move at the speed of light" and answers that we feel it right now, sitting still in a chair, as we move at light speed through *time*. A "cosmic speedometer" shows how motion in space and time relate.

Strange Attractor

We can get a spoon to sit on the surface tension of a cup of coffee, balanced against the weight of its cantilevered handle hovering over the tabletop. It gently bobs up and down in time to drumming fingers or dancing feet. Those ripples measure an oscillation in the spoon-cup-earth system. If ripples get too high, they crest and break the surface tension. Then the spoon floods and drowns. The spoon/cup seesaw is a fragile construction, an *unstable* equilibrium: balanced, but unlikely to survive any external push or pull. The merest breath usually knocks it over. It is a simple system, yet unlikely to fall into perfect balance by accident. How much more unlikely is the balance between forces in every atom, yet protons are older than galaxies! How rarer still that we humans (with as many brain cells as there are stars in the Milky Way) survive and replicate our kind from one generation to the next. Yet life is as old as the seas! We swim through the chaos of chance events in time, yet somehow our kind endures.

Ocean surf is a chaotic system that can actually reveal structure in the way it describes a path in the **phase space** that plots position and speed together. The nodes around which the cycles cluster are called ***strange attractors.*** Repetition of randomness becomes a pattern, and chaos leads to form. Perhaps mass is a trough in the rippling fabric of spacetime, where energy dives toward a strange attractor of density and duration. Light feels age when it becomes mass. A soul is born into flesh. Gravity is the glue that keeps a pile of heavy stones in place on earth. But in the face of pounding ocean surf, stones break into sand, and whole mountain ranges return to the sea. Yet lighter structures survive when forces and materials resonate in equilibrium. A rigged ship sings in the wind. The sculptor Chillida created a series of steel coils set in rock against Atlantic surf in Northern Spain. Like a violin which vibrates but does not break apart when the strings are bowed, so too do Chillida's *Wind Combs* resist the thick and flowing fluids of ocean and air. The instrument holds its own, prevails, and even sings. Patterns persisting in time and space-- is not this life? Leafy branches of a tree each make shade to shape the paths of other growing branches, just as each tree seeking light shapes its neighbors. Chinese sages observed that the prince of a state is like a tree in the center of a forest, tall and straight and noble, protected from harsh winds and light by its retinue of neighbors. Interestingly, these sages often preferred the gnarled, stunted trees exposed at a cliff face-- these were the trees with "character".

THIS IS WHAT'S CALLED A "WOODEN" CHARACTER.

EACH EYE, EAR, ARM, HAND, FINGER, LEG, COLLAR, SHOE, etc. LOOKS THE SAME AS ITS COUNTER-PART. THE RESULT IS A VERY STIFF LOOKING POSE.

...THIS CHARACTER LOOKS MORE NATURAL SIMPLY BECAUSE EACH PART OF THE BODY VARIES IN SOME WAY FROM THE CORRESPONDING OPPOSITE PART.

EYES IN PERSPECTIVE

FINGERS THAT VARY GIVE THE HANDS A MORE DYNAMIC LOOK.

PAF!

ANIMATION: SEEING SPACE IN TIME

An infant learns to see by moving eyes and head to focus on objects and discover depth in vision. A mother's smile reveals *mother coming!* Later cause and effect join in the drama of perception: first *that* things move, then *how*, then *why*. Which projection can we use to show the spaces of both the swing and the playground, or the distinct perceptions of the standing child and the swinger? A plan, perspective, or axonometric alone is partial and incomplete. Position in space is not enough to tell these stories to the mind's eye. We need to set projection in time.

Just as Architectonics requires precise geometric **Projection**, so does Dynamics demand another way of seeing, extending planimetric, axonometric, and perspective projection into time. Fortunately, we are now all familiar with that new kind of projection-- it is called animation! **Animation** enables the geometric construction of volumetric relationships and the exploration of spaces from many different places and points of view. Animation differs from that other visual temporal medium, movies, as much as perspective differs from photography. Animation allows the designer to create new orders in space and time rather than simply record existing ones. Through animation we may design as well as describe the deflection of beams, flow of heat in a jet engine, or healing of earth's ozone layer. From the beasts at Altamira through Muybridge's study of a horse in motion to Picasso's dissection of a village ravaged by war in *Guernica* we can see the expressive potential of animated line, plane, and volume. To see images as still frames in an extended movie is to sense the play of forces on masses that produce motion. This means to *feel*. Consider these notes on the subject from the great masters of the medium, the artists of the Disney Animation studios:

"Too many of the men, old and new, were full of tricks and techniques that had looked great in cartooning school but did nothing for them at the Disney studio. The little shadows under the toes of the shoes, the slick line, the flashy verve of clothing reacting to violent exertion-- all these devices that had impressed us in high school were of little use anymore.

Signs were hung on many walls where the young trainees would be sure to see them, and the one we remember best was this: "Does your drawing have weight, depth, and balance?" -- a casual reminder of the basics of solid, three-dimensional drawing. Men had devoted their whole lives to the mastery of these elusive principles, and there was this sign about as pretentious as the one that said, "Buy Savings Bonds" or pointed to the nearest exit.

Another sign admonished us to watch out for "twins" in our drawings. This is the unfortunate situation where both arms or legs are not only parallel but doing exactly the same thing. No one draws this way on purpose, and usually the artist is not aware that he has even done it. This affliction was not limited to the thirties, for again in the seventies young animator Ron Clements was annoyed to find "twins" in his drawings no matter how hard he worked to keep them out. "It was one of the first drawing principles I heard at the studio. If you get into acting, you would never think of expressing an emotion with twins anywhere, but, somehow, in a drawing, if you're not thinking, it creeps in time and again."

Our main search was for an "animatable" shape, one that had volume but was still flexible, possessed strength without rigidity, and gave us opportunities for the movements that put over our ideas. We needed a shape that was a living form, ready to move-- in contrast with the static form. We used the term 'plastic,' and just the definition of the word seemed to convey the feeling of potential activity in the drawing: 'Capable of being shaped or formed, pliable.' "

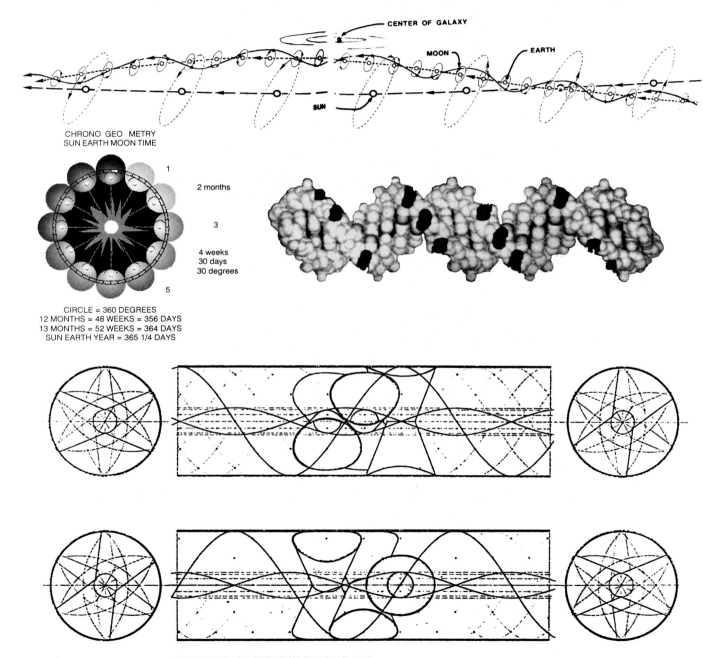

CENTER OF GALAXY

MOON   EARTH

SUN

CHRONO GEO METRY
SUN EARTH MOON TIME

1

2 months

3

4 weeks
30 days
30 degrees

5

CIRCLE = 360 DEGREES
12 MONTHS = 48 WEEKS = 356 DAYS
13 MONTHS = 52 WEEKS = 364 DAYS
SUN EARTH YEAR = 365 1/4 DAYS

STUDIES FOR A SPACE STATION, BY MICHAEL KALIL

CLOCK

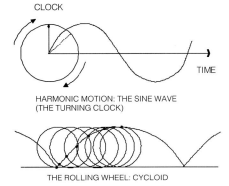

TIME

HARMONIC MOTION: THE SINE WAVE
(THE TURNING CLOCK)

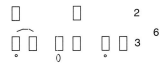

THE ROLLING WHEEL: CYCLOID

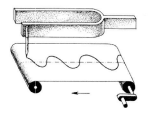

TUNING FORK SINE WAVE
the source of music, cycles per second

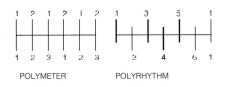

Music: rhythm: beat 2 against 3
B-dupp bump-a dup bump bup a dup

POLYMETER   POLYRHYTHM

CYCLES PER SECOND

A movie presents the illusion of motion by passing before the eye 24 sequential still frames every second. Early animators quickly learned that they could repeat sets of drawings in loops to convey periodic motion. A clock's second hand completes one revolution of the clock face each minute, and then repeats the cycle. The same path in space moves in another time. Plotting the height of the end of a clock hand as it goes around the clock face against a linear time track generates the unique curve of harmonic motion called the sine wave. The cycloid is another relationship of moving circle and line, a curve of the position of a point like a valve on a rolling bicycle wheel. Animation opens a whole new world of phenomena when we study how geometric figures move in time. Animation and mathematics permit us to be precise in constructing action.

Function

In living things, functions are characteristic, normal, natural actions, like digestion. In mathematics, a *function* is a variable dependent on the values of another variable. This is a powerful idea. For example, the magnitude of cycloid and sine curve values are functions of time and repeat each full cycle. Mathematical curves reveal the character of functions over a range of values. René Descartes (1596 -1650) showed how algebraic formulas expressing function relationships between variables could be graphed on paper. For example, $y = \sin t$ will plot the sine curve along two perpendicular axes called Cartesian coordinates, while the expressions $y = a(\theta - \sin \theta)$ and $x = a(1 - \cos \theta)$ can be used to plot the cycloid in another graphing system called polar coordinates. Sometimes curves are easier to mechanically construct than to plot from equations. The cycloid is a good example of such a curve. A pencil attached to one point on a coin rolled along a ruler will quickly generate a cycloid. Geometric construction preceded analytic algebraic geometry by two millennia: Euclid and Pythagoras used compass and straightedge, not equations, to discover mathematical relationships. A set of Function/Plot exercises is suggested for each study in Dynamics, so that even in this day of computer-generated mathematics and graphics, the hand and eye can teach the mind about precise relationships of functions. Modern architects use the term "function" to indicate that their forms derive from and depend on the logic of purpose, and perhaps also to signify the recognition that mathematics is essential to the foundation of beautiful form.

Music

Rhythm is tone in time, the flow or pattern of movement in time. As ethnomusicologist/percussionist Anthony Brown observes, accented beats in 2 against 3 polyrhythm and polymeter syncopations generate the tension and resolution that creates the driving dynamic of the music called be-bop and **swing.** Pitch is also a function of time. Higher tones vibrate our ear drums more frequently than lower ones. **Melody** is a rhythmic sequence of varying tones. **Harmony** also depends on frequency-- a pitch vibrates exactly half as fast as the tone one octave above it. **Music** is an order of the tempo and pitch of sound in time. *Chromatics* describes a spectrum of vibrations-- of tone in music and of light in color. There are remarkable affinities between musical scales and color intervals. *(See page 469.)* The spectrum of sound, like the spectrum of light is infinite and continuous. But standard intervals-- notes-- facilitate communication. Like keys on a piano, the limited notes of standard musical notation suggest the value of a limited palette. Limitation means that theme, variation, and improvisation are essential to music. If there can be a spectrum of plastic volumes of all possible frequencies, then architecture can be a music of space.

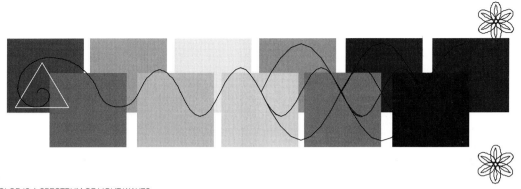

COLOR IS A SPECTRUM OF LIGHT WAVES
IS IT LINEAR OR CIRCULAR (CYCLICAL)?

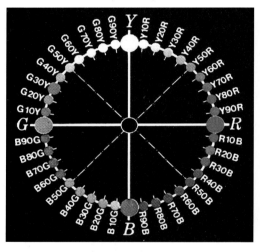

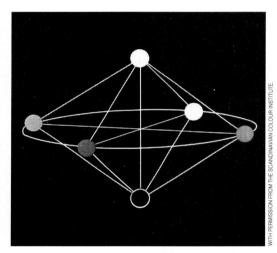

WITH PERMISSION FROM THE SCANDINAVIAN COLOUR INSTITUTE.

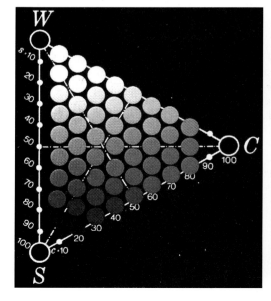

LIGHT AND COLOR

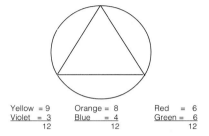

Yellow = 9   Orange = 8   Red   = 6
Violet = 3   Blue   = 4   Green = 6
    12   12   12

Goethe's scale: the sum of complementary pairs each
have the same numerical value, 12, but each is appor-
tioned according to its relative intensity.

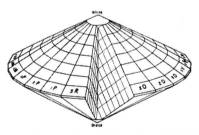

Ostwald Color System. Complete circle contains 24
hues, with the "psychological primaries" (red yellow sea
green and ultramarine blue) and their secondaries
(orange, leafgreen, ice blue, and purple) as a basis.

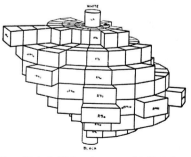

Munsell Color Solid. One of many possible illustrations.
Light colors appear at a level near white, and dark
colors at a level near black. Intense hues extend farther
from the gray scale than pale colors.

"The eye sees no form,
in as much as light, shade, and color
constitute that which to our vision distinguishes object from object...
from these three... we construct the visual world." Goethe

Color is visible light. Light is the vibration of the electromagnetic field propagating outward. Across a continuous range of frequencies, from about 1 vibration per second to over a trillion trillion per second, radiation carries energy everywhere in the universe, forever! Near the slow end, radio waves vibrate around 10^8 (100,000,000) cycles per second, while near the high end, gamma rays vibrate at 10^{22} cycles per second. Visible light is roughly in the middle of this logarithmic scale, vibrating at around 10^{14} cycles per second. Wavelength, the distance between crests in these vibrations, is inverse to frequency. Newton used a triangular prism to diffract (bend) "white" sunlight into separate angles for distinct frequencies, and thus discovered that the rainbow spectrum of visible light we call color is a range of wavelengths. Visible light occurs in wavelengths from red (7000 Å) to violet (4000Å), where Å is an Ångstrom unit, defined as one ten millionth of a centimeter. Beyond red lies infrared, which we sense as warmth. Beyond violet lies ultraviolet, whose high energy can cause sunburn on sensitive skin. Many animals see what remains invisible to us-- nocturnal owls see the infrared heat of their prey at night, and many insects respond to the ultraviolet patterns of flowers. Color phenomena vary according to how they are generated. For example, pigment is not the same as illumination: a mixture of primary-color illuminating lights will produce white (as in sunlight), while a mixture of primary color paints or pigments will produce brown or black. Color is independent of change in time or space. The *pattern* of shadow on a lawn is not concerned with color, nor does the flickering of a candle flame change the color of its light.

Color systems

Color seems to demand many dimensions to describe its order. Goethe's *Theory of Colours* related hues to each other through a proportional scale of relative intensities, so that the sum of complementary pairs remains the same total 12. Since then, numerous color systems have appeared to help organize the qualities of color phenomena like hue (red or blue), value (pink, or dark red), and chroma (bright or dim red). Ostwald created an early solid model. Munsell's important color model organized colors on a rotating sphere model. His three categories of color quality provide three different ways of navigating his color globe. Pure hues form a great color wheel along the equator. The sphere's axis of rotation measures value, from white to black, so that northern and southern hemispheres locate tints and shades respectively. Diameters measure chroma and their ends link complementary hues. Pure hues are the most saturated chromas, while the least saturated chromas lie along the polar axis. As the entire spectrum of color produces white light, the central gray represents not the absence of color, but rather, a balanced mix of compliments. Three coordinates (hue, value, and chroma) are necessary to position any color value in this matrix, allowing very precise descriptions of color. Other color ordering systems exist. Johannes Itten, in *The Art of Color*, describes seven color contrasts that account for most color interactions: hue, light/ dark (value), cold/warm, complementary, simultaneous [contrast], saturation (chroma), and exten- sion. The New Color-aid set of 314 colors, developed by Kim Vlaun, is based on the NCS, or Natural Color System, now the standard color notation system of Sweden. It claims to be a color language which will enable us to characterize and describe the 10 million colors the human eye can distin- guish. It exploits the theories of E. Herring and T. Johansson's "Natural Color System" and research led by Anders Hard since 1964 to produce yet another system of ordering color.

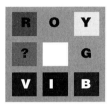

A square circle-- Cartesian color wheel. Cubechrome in two dimensions as a field

Re-T2	RO-T2		O-T2	YO-T2		Yw-T2	Y-T2		Y-T2		YGw-T2	YG-T2	YGw-HT2	Gw-T2		G-T2		Gw-T2	BG-T2		C-T2	Bo-T2	B-T2		Bw-T2	BV-T2	V-T2	RV-T2	M-T2	Ro-T2		R-T2
Re-HUE	RO-HUE	RO-EX	O-HUE	YO-HUE	YO-EX	Yw-HUE	Y-EX	YO-HUE	YG-EX	YGw-HUE	YG-HUE	YGw-HUE	Gw-HUE	Gw-EX	G-HUE	G-EX	Gw-HUE	BG-HUE	BG-EX	C-HUE	Bo-HUE	B-HUE	B-EX	Bw-HUE	BV-HUE	V-HUE	RV-HUE	M-HUE	Ro-HUE	Ro-EX	R-HUE	R-EX
	RO-S2		O-S2	YO-S2			Y-S2			YGw-S2	YG-S2				G-S2			BG-S2		C-HS2		B-S2				V-S2	RV-S2	M-S2			R-S2	

AMEDEE OZENFANT: *STILL LIFE WITH A GLASS OF RED WINE*, OIL, 1926

COLOR IN ARCHITECTURE

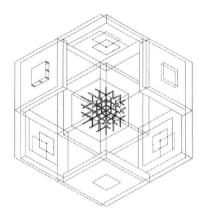

Teleology is the branch of philosophy that studies ends and existence, and its root, *teleos*, is related to *kyklos*, the wheel. Color offers us a teleological curiosity. Our eyes tell us that one order of colors has no end-- that the color wheel is a cycle which loops where red meets blue in violet. We also know that red and violet are the extreme ends of our visible spectrum. Is color a line or a circle? Marshall McLuhan said a light bulb is the basic unit of information-- it is either on or off. Black ink on white paper graphics is also basic information in a binary either/or mode. But as the maturing eye and soul discover, there are many shades of gray between black and white. And even more subtly, and quite mysteriously, there are infinite nuances to visible color relationships. Spectrum is a range of possibilities. With color, nothing is absolute. A red against a blue does not look the same as that very red against yellow. Dynamics introduces students to an *interaction of color*, following the insights and work of Joseph Albers. Color perception is perhaps as close as our brains [minds?] come to directly feeling. If eyes become fingers when we measure space, then minds become bodies of compassionate emotions when we enter into a world of color interaction.

Just as the Kit of Parts explores arrangement relationships with given spacial elements, so too we may study color with given chromatic intervals, using the commercially available digital spectrum "Kit of Color" papers called **Color-aid**™. A Color Rule is provided with this text as a "bookmark". It shows 34 hues, their tints and shades, and a range of grays taken from the Color-aid set. Its background is a neutral gray. Missing tints or shades are not provided with the current version of Color-aid. The reverse side of the rule gives the standard notation name for the colors. Pantone™ is another brand of color sample ranges useful to designers. Studying color in Dynamics is valuable not only for learning the science and techniques of color theory and color design, but more importantly for enabling the student to enter the whole realm of the powerful and intimate human experiences of feelings, emotions, and the subtle nuances of shades of meaning and responsive consciousness to evoke mood, climate, tone, even harmony and dissonance. In this sense, studying an *interaction* of color may rehabilitate our time, where too often the "real world" encourages us to abstract elements in isolation, too far removed from the unity of human awareness and divine creation.

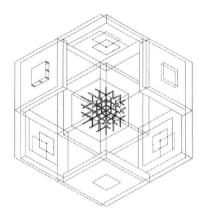
cHUbE cHrOME orthogonal color volume, by Slutzky

Beyond Graphics

Whereas Architectonics benefited from the heightened either/or distinction of black and white, which made vivid ambiguities of figure/ground and solid/void, Dynamics opens the window of vision to the full spectrum of electromagnetic radiation. Architect David Diamond notes that awareness of color phenomena is essential to all who are visually alert. He holds that interpretation of color effects is often automatic, unconscious, and spontaneous. Color provides vital data about the world around us, offering clues to relative distance, position in space, orientation and configuration. Without color, human movement in space would at best be full of surprises and at worst, fraught with peril. Understanding color theory and phenomena provides the plastician with a powerful and subtle tool for making and rendering compositions in space. Architects deal with color in at least three different ways: 1. local color (blue drapery is sometimes lighter or darker, but everywhere blue); 2. cartographic color (color as a code system: on a map, red is a highway, blue a local road); 3. metaphoric color (the structure of color relationships: pink to red is one contrast, blue to orange is another, pink to dark blue yet another). Color modulates space. Painter Robert Slutzky and his students at ETH in Zurich have begun a provocative exploration of polychromy in three dimensions which they call Cube Chrome. Many contemporary architects eagerly await its further development. The multiple cues color relationships can carry may yet enable us to see clearly phenomena in spacetime.

Study for *homage to the square*. 23 x 23". Josef Albers' last painting, at 88 years of age, in 1976.

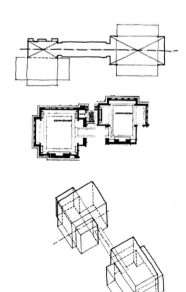

Frank Lloyd Wright: Unity Temple

Frank Lloyd Wright: Heller House

VOLUME IN ARCHITECTURE

The Birth of Volume

Solid is the generic term for any three-dimensional form, the next extension in the series point, line, plane. Solids may be filled or empty. A soap bubble is as much a spherical solid as a bowling ball; a glass is a cylinder whether or not it holds water. Void is revealed as volume when the masses that mark its boundaries define a perceptible solid (A sports stadium is a volume, even without a roof.) Since the surrounding masses might themselves be volumes, it is possible to define volume "without outlines" through its content of modulated energy, as much as a color may fill an area of a painting surface. Architects seek to compose volumes of light, color, temperature, sound, aroma, and feeling, with the same mastery and freedom that a musician develops to organize intervals of time and tone. In the best work, void itself becomes the primary presence. There is an ART to making volume visible and emptiness tangible which can be learned through study, guidance, practice and experience. This is how to make something from nothing!

Interaction of volume

If color is light at different frequenciesof electromagnetic radiation, then volume is void at different frequencies of duration, size, and depth. Like color, volume exists in a continuum-- a spectrum ranging from open to closed, from filled to empty, from light to dark, warm to cool. Like any color, no room stands alone in our perception. It is always experienced in the context of other volumes-- even if only the one (other) volume of the whole field of its site, of the "outside" of the room. Volume is never considered in isolation but always in relationship. Volume is never static, but always dynamic. There is an *interaction of volume* as well as an interaction of color.

Space as fluid

Volume is to architecture as color is to painting. Space is the medium of architecture as light is the medium of painting. Painters use pigment to modulate light. Architects use volume to modulate space. **Space,** in architecture, is a set of ordered volumes, identifiable solids both empty and filled. As Josef Albers'1976 study for *Homage to the Square* (opposite) suggests, the presence of space in a volume is like a swimming pool filled with blue. Volumes endure in so far as they are palpable to our senses, that is tangible and solid. Volume must be filled with **space**.

Whales can hear deep oceanic wavelengths. Astronomers speak of the music of the spheres. We may understand architectural space as plastic ***fluid***. Weight is the *feel* of mass in a gravity field- the interaction of the body (subject), force, sense, and another body (object). The density and weight of emotion, for example the loving recollection of beloved forebears. Architecture can be a spectrum of all vibrations of actions or loading conditions on plastic volumes. Perhaps this is the key to understanding Le Corbusier's notion of visual acoustics, an acoustic relationship of volumes. Consciousness is required to feel vibrations directly in the medium of space-and-time, reinforcing the whole body/mind in reverberating overtones. Just as there may be ambiguity in painting, as in Ozenfant's *Still Life with a Glass of Red Wine* on the preceding page, shared contours (edges) in two dimensions suggest shared surfaces (at least) in three dimensions. The overlapping reading of color planes in the two dimensional surface field of the painting suggest the possibility that in three dimensions volumes may overlap and intersect. Frank Lloyd Wright's 1905 *Unity Temple* and Heller House are compositions of intersecting volumes, a palette of solids both filled and empty that modulate the rhythm of architectural space.

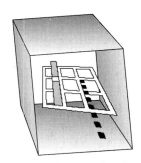

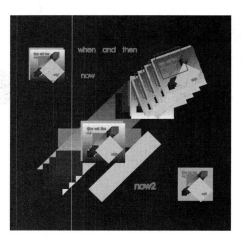

FRAMES OF REFERENCE

In 1908, Einstein recognized that local free-float reference frames are the spacetime equivalent of ideally rectangula postage stamps or ideally square townships; they are, in other words, "perfect pieces of spacetime." J. A. Wheeler

A room is a frame of reference

You set a chair in a room. Tomorrow, although the turning world has spun your chair through thousands of miles of space, you find your chair in the same spot-- *relative to the room*. The room is the frame of reference. Perhaps your chair and room are in a cabin in the woods, where you can sit and watch the seasons pass through your window-- snow in winter, green shoots through meltwater in spring, deep shade in summer, flaming forest glory in autumn. Such a cabin is a ship through time and a station in space-- it does not change its position relative to the landscape you survey. Consider another kind of ride: you drive a van on the highway while children play in the seat behind you. Accidentally, their ball pops into the front seat next to you. Angrily, you toss the ball back to them, reminding them how dangerous it is to throw things in a moving car. Does the ball hit anyone hard enough to break a bone? No, even though the ball, with the car, is moving at 60 miles per hour. Relative to the car, the ball hardly moves at all. You get in a car at home, out at your destination. While you are in the car, although the clock ticks, time seems unchanged. The car is a space-ship and a time station. If the car moved fast enough, that is at the speed of light, time would stop. You would not age. The volume you inhabit is your frame of reference, both in space and in time.

Still volume in motion

Three-dimensional tic-tac-toe requires three regular games stacked on trays above each other. A winning line can be vertical, horizontal, or even diagonal through three-dimensional space. It is possible to play a four-dimensional version of this, by imagining three cubes of the stacked trays to be placed sequentially in the same location. A winning line might be top left to bottom right through all three cubes, or the same square on all of them. These are "four-dimensional" straight lines, perpendicular to the three dimensions of everyday space. Our *action* of replacing one cube with another requires *time*. Einstein identified time as a fourth dimension in the physics of light.

Where and when is home to someone who lives in a helicopter? A harbor crane lifts a standard cargo shipping container and sets it on a barge. Will it sink the barge? That depends on what it holds, on how heavy it is, on its *density*. This is determined not only by what materials comprise its walls, but also what the box *contains*. A car uses less fuel to haul an empty mobile home over a mountain than to pull one that is fully loaded. What does it take to haul a room through time as well as space? A room that does not move (in relation to us) still evolves in time. Like a container on a barge, it may float or sink, depending on its density in spacetime. We might call its presence in space and time its ability to endure, its spacial temporal inertia-- its *spacetime density*. The fullness or richness of presence that we experience when we are there is a combination of just proportions, appropriate materials, use, and light, and some hint of the infinite eternal extent of this universe, our home. Perhaps this is what Le Corbusier identified as "ineffable space.' Like the chord of music that sends shivers down your spine-- this is a question of feeling that cannot be described but that is recognizable to those who have experienced it. While an engineer orders mass, an architect orders space. Volumes can vary in *architectural* density. Light, circulation, massing, and enclosure determine the relative "fullness" of an architectural space. Brunelleschi's Pazzi chapel is clearly such a place. Architecture is composed of a hierarchy of spacial densities. When architects order action, the result is room between things and things in their places. The architect can generate spacial density by ordering masses along lines and planes to create legible volumes that "read" as a unified three-dimensional zone. These zones endure in space and or time as a conceptual solids whose "name" is written in the characters of plan and section.

ROBERT COTTINGHAM. *ROLLING STOCK SERIES, NO. 9, FOR REID* 1988. ACRYLICS AND SAND ON CANVAS 6' SQUARE

Age (proper time)

Speed of object at rest

Speed through space

faster through space

Intermediate velocity

Speed through time

slower through time

0   Velocity of Light   Space

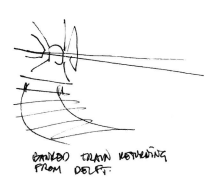

BANKED TRAIN RETURNING FROM DELFT.

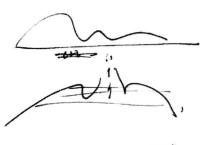

US 40 TO ALBUQ. GOING WEST

LOCAL AND NON-LOCAL

"Everything, including you, is always moving at the speed of light. How can you be moving if you are at rest in a chair? You are moving through time. "Lewis Carroll Epstein

Albert Einstein (1879 - 1955) said that he first thought about relativity at the age of sixteen, while riding a bicycle and wondering what the world would look like to a person whose bicycle moved at the speed of light. Bob Cottingham's 1989 painting *Rolling Stock Series, No. 9, for Reid* recalls the example often given in texts explaining the theory of relativity where light flashes from a moving train depict the independent perceptions of a passenger and someone at the station. The 1887 Michelson- Morley experiment demonstrated the constant speed of light in every direction, thereby destroying the contemporary explanation of light transmission in an invisible but very rigid medium called the luminiferous ether. This result forced Einstein to build a physics with light as measure of space and time, rather than the reverse. Now distance and time are both derived from the one constant, the speed of light. Thus a meter is a measure of time-- 1/299,792,000th of how far light travels in one second. In frames of reference moving relative to each other, light is constant but time and distance change as the frame moves. This is the essence of Einstein's Theory of Special Relativity, first published in 1905.

Frank Lloyd Wright built the Unity Temple in 1906 and the Robie House in 1908. It was these buildings that enabled Wright to claim he had "exploded the box", the traditional conception of an absolute distinction between outside and inside. The resulting flow of continuous space in his work demonstrates how architecture modulates volume within the frame of its container, whether room, building, or city, but always within the context of the full extent of its environment. Whether we call this "ineffable space" or spacetime, as architects we seek to suggest something more than simply extension in three dimensions. We seek to realize all the potential of space within a *parti* of limited volumes. A room is a box of energy in motion, flowing through spacetime. For physicists, the current understanding proposes that if we sat "still" in a chair like a tree rooted to our point in space, distant from any galaxy or planet, and therefore not moving relative to any other cosmic body, our world-line through space and time would run at a different rate along Epstein's cosmic speedometer than any other body accelerating through space relative to us. Our "stationary" frame of reference would move as fast as possible through time. Someone in another frame of reference, zipping through space at some fraction of light speed (greater than zero and less than 186,000 miles per second), would travel more through space and less through time, and would not age as fast as us. Light does not age. To light itself there is no flow of time, no past or future. For light, everywhere is now.

Einstein in the Desert

Some years ago, I rode a train at sunset from Delft to Amsterdam. Holland is so flat that as the train made its long banked turn, I could use the reflections of light in the windows on either side of the railroad car as a transit level to read the angle of its line against the horizon to determine the exact degree of the banked railroad track. More recently, I was driving east on US 40 toward Albuquerque New Mexico, some fifty miles away. On either side was the distant edge of mesas, mountains, buttes, and wide sagebrush country. Below were the rich subtle colors of the clay-red earth, above was the turquoise of the limitless sky. Ahead was the wall of the Sandia mountains, rising behind the grid of the distant city. An audio tape filled the car with CarlosNakai's clear Navajo flute music, seeming to echo off the hundred-mile boundaries of the bowl of space that surrounded me (Mr. Nakai thought the 'reverb machine' was invented for the Navajo!) For a brief moment, I felt I was in perfect stillness, in the center of all space, despite the fact that the car was speeding over 75 miles an hour. I watched the road roll beneath me, as if I were on an exercise treadmill, moving yet static in space and free in time.

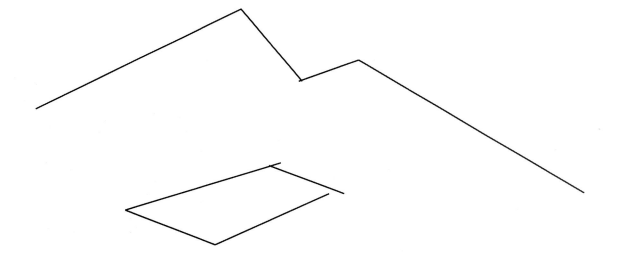

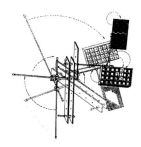

MULTIPLE REFERENCE FRAMES

Architecture imprints the local reference frame. In fact, architecture can imprint the density of all local frames of inhabitation, and there can be more than one for a given place. Architecture modulates volume within the frame of its container, whether room, building, or city, but always within the context of the full extent of its environment. Whether we call this "ineffable space" or spacetime, as architects we seek to suggest something more than simply extension in three dimensions. We seek to realize the all the potential of space within a *parti* of limited volumes. If this enables the student of design and commercial practitioner to understand that even in the design of a supermarket, the top and back and sides of the building are as vital as its front facade and floor plan, to understand that every home can be rescued from a life of darkness by simply deciding which way to flip over the off-the-shelf stock house plan according to solar orientation, then the sense of contingent but endless possibility of plastic order in space and time will have been revealed. Orthogonality is the most efficient three-dimensional packing scheme, but multiple orthogonalities may interact in the same physical location to produce multiple volume orders and multiple spacial reading, nearly simultaneously, somewhat akin to the polymeters and polyrhythms of jazz since the developments of be-bop and swing.

One stone in the Desert

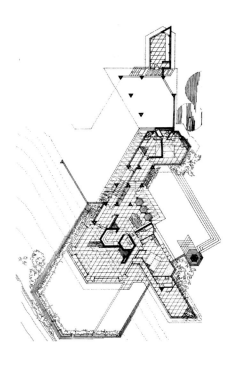

Frank Lloyd Wright was a master of space. The plan of the 1941 house for Mr. and Mrs. Carl Wall, in Plymouth Michigan shows his virtuoso capability for integrating multiple frames of reference within a single volumetric composition, the institution of a dwelling family. The *parti* sets two major hexagon lobes, one for the master bedroom suite, the other for the living room, apart from each other. They are connected by three parallel lines of circulation, with an internal staircase flanked by a colonnade of triangular piers on the garden side and a trellised entry from the carport on the public side. Along one face of the living-room hexagon two more bedrooms are extended, and beyond the master bedroom the garage and workroom are placed. The kitchen and dining area are at the hub, the intersection of all these zones, and the easy flow through and around them masks the complexity of geometry that occurs here. Wright exploits the property of the hexagon that the perpendicular to any of its diameters is parallel to the chord connecting two of the hexagon's sides. Thus the many local geometries are united by the underlying fabric of the diamond floor tile grid without any loss of the idiosyncratic collisions that surprise us everywhere in this house. Square, triangle, and hexagon happily coexist while maintaining their unique identities, like solo players in a jazz ensemble.

Taliesin West was Wright's winter home in the Arizona desert near Phoenix, a project he *began* when he was about 70 years old. To be in its space is a most remarkable experience. There are moments when volume seems solid, when the emptiness of a boundary or a beam of light seem to be as tangible as a beam of wood or steel. The right angle corner point of the low desert concrete retaining wall that builds the platform of tended lawn and pools amidst an arid wilderness, the "point" of Taliesin clearly marks an edge between human culture and suprahuman nature. Standing there, it is possible to discover how Wright found the geometry to resolve two frames of reference simultaneously: the orthogonal of the plan of the studio, library, and his own living quarters perpendicular to the studio are organized along an east-west axis, to provide full shade and shelter to the north, where vines and trellises have flourished. The apparently random rotation of the lawn suddenly locks into the landscape when the person at the point perceives that its grid is parallel to the grand structure of mountain ridges and long valley, marching to the horizon perhaps some 50 miles away!!

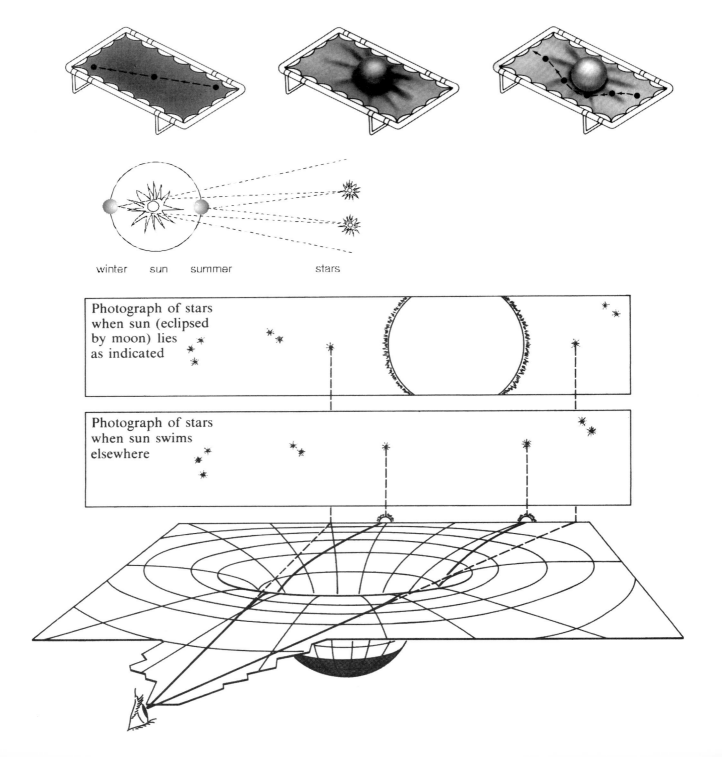

winter   sun   summer   stars

Photograph of stars
when sun (eclipsed
by moon) lies
as indicated

Photograph of stars
when sun swims
elsewhere

THE GEOMETRODYNAMIC

"Space tells matter how to move and matter tells space how to curve."
Misner, Thorne, and Wheeler, *Gravitation*

Movement, Matter, and the Shape of Space

Before 1915 there was a troubling problem about the orbit of Mercury. Albert Einstein suggested that the reason Mercury's orbit itself seemed to spin, or precess, had to do with the large mass and gravitational field of the nearby Sun. He proposed that the mass of the sun distorted the very geometry of space and time near it. He predicted the same distortion of spacetime would occur when we looked at the light of stars as they passed near the sun. Not until after World War I could Sir Arthur Eddington, astronomer and cosmologist, observe the stars seen at a solar eclipse and demonstrate that Einstein's radical explanation predicted the data to an accuracy of a few parts in a million. Newton's Universal Law of Gravitation quantitatively described how every bit of matter attracts every other body in the universe, directly proportional to their masses and inversely according to the square of their distances. But Newton could not explain how mass could act on mass across empty space without any apparent mechanical connection. It remained for Einstein, in his General Theory of Relativity, to describe a geometric interdependence between matter and space.

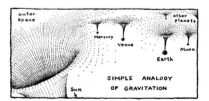

What Einstein's genius first saw clearly we can understand by means of a simple analogy. "Matter tells space how to curve, and space tells matter how to move", much in the way a bowling ball and a trampoline might interact. When a mass is large enough, modern physics tells us that it will actually "bend" the space around it. We can roughly visualize this dynamic geometry of spacetime by imagining small balls on a stretched but flexible trampoline. A marble rolled across the empty trampoline will travel in a straight path. Now imagine a bowling ball placed in the middle of the trampoline, increasing the curvature of its nearby surface. If the marble is rolled across the trampoline this time, its path will bend in the region of the ball--the nearer it passes, the stronger its deflection. The marble itself will cause some change in the shape of the trampoline and even, although perhaps in a very small way, a change in the position of the bowling ball. If we put a softball on the trampoline some distance from the bowling ball, it will make its own indentation in the surface of the trampoline. If the bowling ball and softball are moving as well as the marble, the surface of the trampoline will become a complex and ever-changing shape, and the path of the marble will respond accordingly. Now substitute the Sun for the bowling ball, the Earth for the softball, and light for the marble. The two-dimensional trampoline surface represents three-dimensional space and with time added is an analogy to the four dimensional spacetime continuum of our universe. Physicists now call this relationship between momentum, energy, space, and time-- the GEOMETRODYNAMIC.

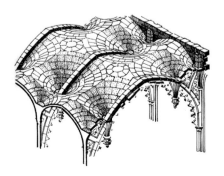

Geometrodynamic Architecture: Volume in Spacetime

If void defines the position and direction of moving matter as much as mass determines the shape of spacetime, the implication for architecture is startling. In a geometrodynamic universe, mass and void tug on each other. For architects, volume can be subject to force, as mass defines and shapes void into volume, just as volume reshapes space itself. We normally think of "solid" as matter, as in "solid rock" but we know that the geometric term "solid" describes a defined region of space, whether filled or empty. A room is a volume and a brick is a mass, and both are solids. Volumes can interact, and the force **OF**, as well as **ON**, one can change the shape and/or position of another. These forces can be programmatic as well as structural. The altered volume can in turn affect all other volumes in a site, a process which may continue until a fullly resonant architectural space is realized.

THE SENSE OF ARCHITECTURE

Medical observations in space indicate that long-term living in microgravity may reduce memory, coordination, balance, and general ability to interrelate a series of events. These abilities are related to functions of the inner ear, the vestibular organs of balance. Without gravity to push the calcium crystal otoliths against the cilia in the semicircular canals, our biological gyroscopes become disoriented. Astronauts begin to lose their congenital inertial guidance. Actual or imagined sequences of pleasing vestibular pressures may give rise to what Le Corbusier terms "plastic emotion".

We hear music through air vibrating against the ear's tympanum; we see painting through the light in our eyes; the touch of sculpture begins at the skin. Our deepest sensory nerves are the vestibular organs of equilibrium, archaic hollows within the bones of the skull itself. They may be reference for all other perceptions, navigation aids to determine direction, momentum, intention, providing a means to measure change in space. Our inner ear organic gyroscopes let us measure where we are in terms of where we have been and where we shall go. The sense of architecture is gyroscopic; we experience space through change in position and orientation. Visual perception remains pictorial, not truly volumetric, which is why for architects plans are not pictures but maps for mind wandering. The idea that we constantly measure change (and its lack!) reintroduces integrated human perceptions as a necessary ingredient in the plastic equation. As Guillermo Jullian has said, we must even know how a building smells. Carrying the weight of the body, seeing the play of light and shade, feeling the breath of the wind, sniffing the air, doing these things with attention we may begin to understand how architecture exists for and through the senses. The brain is the most complex junction of nerve endings in the body and may be regarded as the ultimate sense organ, particularly sensitive to integrated relationships. Thus to make architecture only for isolated decorative sensations is to deprive architecture of the connective transformations, the quickening pulse of life.

A sense of being

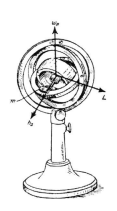

Grammatically, being is a gerund, a verbal noun ending in-*ing*. It has all the uses of the noun but retains such characteristics of the verb as the ability to take an object as an adverbial modifier, as in "playing the piano was one of his hobbies" The Latin-Sanskrit base of gerund (and gestate, gesture, jest, congest, digest, register, suggest) is *gerere*, meaning to bear or carry, to take on oneself, take charge of, to perform or accomplish. So Being is the gerund of existence, meaning to bear or carry *existence itself*. For Dynamics, Being is added to the four actions already modelled as the studio experience-- Thinking, Projecting, Doing, and Reflecting. The beginner need not consider Being-- it is enough to practice the ways of established mastery. But the journeyman and ultimate master must confront creation by becoming a participant in making the world, not merely a passive consumer. Buckminster Fuller said "I seem to be a verb." We create in space by inhabiting as well as arranging. We do this by recognizing that space, a *dynamic* medium of energy and action, is a plenitude, potentially filled or empty-- *equally*. The sense of architecture is available not to a disembodied intellect, but to anyone conscious of weight and work in the world and the contingent, participatory nature of being in space. A room, even a house, need be nothing more than a net mesh-- a humane, humanist architecture, of, by and for the body and mind. A hammock is an elegant example of a plane of woven linear elements warped into a complex curve by the interaction of gravity, fibre strength, and the resistance and shape of the body. It is comfortable, atavistically womb-like, deep in emotional and physical support. It is light, flexible, swinging, interactive, easy to clean, portable and beautiful-- structured space that literally models itself to body measure-- architecture at its best.

SOLID SPACE

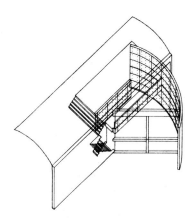

"…. How can we grasp the concept of spacetime curvature? Earlier we saw that the curvature of an automobile fender was revealed by the inability to lay down rectangular postage stamps in register on its surface. We can gauge the "imperfection"-- the curvature-- of a two-dimensional space by seeing how perfect pieces, postage stamps or ideal townships, fail to fit. Perhaps the same approach will work with spacetime. In 1908, Einstein recognized that local free-float reference frames are the spacetime equivalent of ideally rectangular postage stamps or ideally square townships; they are, in other words, "perfect pieces of spacetime." J. A. Wheeler

Usually one order of space resonates best to our long-term needs. You'd like to know where your things are located, at least all week. Dwelling is action in repose. The more resolved an architecture is, the more comfortably its spaces fit our bodies and our needs, even when these needs change. Volumes endure in so far as they are palpable to our senses, that is tangible and solid, whether filled or empty. **Space,** in architecture, is a set of ordered volumes. Architects work directly in the medium of space, composing volumes of light, color, temperature, sound, aroma, and feeling, with the same mastery and freedom that a musician develops to organize intervals of time and tone. In the best work, void itself becomes the primary presence. There is an ART to making volume visible and emptiness tangible which can be learned through study, guidance, practice and experience. This is how to make something from nothing!

The Kit of Parts for Architectonics is shown on page 143, Volume 1 through outlines of corners, edges, and surfaces. What is inside these solids? Wood, rock, concrete, air-- or nothing at all? Of course, we know that no real solid is completely filled with mass-- there are pores between the cells of wood, air bubbles in bricks, and virtually nothing at all between the electrons and nuclei of every atom, thousands of diameters apart from each other. At the atomic scale, mass occupies perhaps no more than a billionth part of the total void. Astronomic data reveals the same open weave to the fabric of the cosmos. Mass gathers in clumps at every scale, confounding our understanding of how a homogenous Origin at the unity of the Beginning could have evolved into the present clumpy distribution of matter in our vast Universe. Matter and void permeate and perforate each other. Architects often seek a continuity of space, a unity between inside and outside places. They learn to exploit the interplay between filled and empty intervals of three dimensions and seek to "tune out" objects to reveal space, much as we tune out static on a radio to hear the music. Let us be clear in an attempt to define architectural space in terms of these ideas. Although a room is "empty" of bricks or beams, we cannot see its dimension unless relatively opaque markers establish its extent and boundaries.

For a builder a brick is a brick. For an architect, a room is a brtick. For a builder, a wall is a fabric of bricks. For an architect, a building is a fabric of volumes. A volume is void defined by mass into a perceptible solid. Since we cannot inhabit mass, architectural space is primarily void transformed into an identifiable set of volumes. As design of the masses become more and more the result of volumetric intention, architecture becomes ever more a question of composing volumes. In the best work, void itself seems to become the primary presence. As the design ability of an architect grows in power and maturity, more and more the design of buildings becomes the design of spaces. Tadao Ando's volumetric composition is described in the drawing here. The photo opposite reveals a sense of space as a living presence of light, capacious and awaiting people. This may well be in part due to the degree to which mass is suppressed to make the intersection of "shoebox" and pie-slice volumes come forward in our perceptions. Transcending a limited materialist mentality, designers of equipment, furniture, rooms, buildings and cities (and perhaps whole planets) create compositions of related volumes which are only secondarily interrelated masses. Frank Lloyd Wright, quoting Lao Tse, said that "the reality of a room is not in the walls but in the space it contains." When architects organize action, the result is room between things and things in their places. This three-dimensional equivalent to Albers' sense of the interaction of color maybe called an interaction of volume.

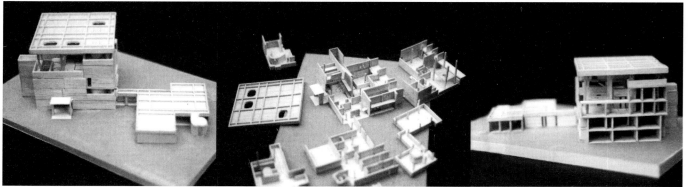

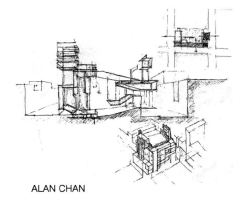

COMPOSING VOLUMES

Mass and void in space are like sound and silence in music. A musical scale is a set of tones or notes that may be composed together, selected to sound harmonious in combination. We suggest that proportioned volumes are the "notes" of architecture. A harmonic "scale" of volumes can be derived for a single project as Wright often did, or made more general as Palladio and Le Corbusier did (with Le Modulor). Just as structural engineers make use of a kind of animation of masses for their experimental thinking (if this block goes here, the bridge will stand, but if it goes over here, the bridge will be lighter yet still stand), so too is there an animation of volume for architects. "Move this here, then this can go here, and these can organize this, and if you just shove this over here, then there's room to get this in here..." describes the true action of architectural design in resolving *parti* by relocating program volumes (entry, bedroom, breadbox, city hall) until everything fits. "Fits" in architecture means the right size and tight place for all volumes, necessary and sufficient, no more, no less. Connection and location count. A kitchen may be next to the dining room, but whether it is placed at the top or bottom of a house significantly affects human order in space. To design by moving volumes through each other in the mind's eye is to make a DYNAMIC of volumetric composition.

Bubble Diagrams

Chemists who know the number of atoms in a molecule also need to study how its atoms connect. Changing the order of connection produces a different material. If there is any great value to the "bubble diagrams" architects claim to employ in design, it is as a tool for establishing essential connections between program volumes, independent of form. Bubble diagrams are useful for focusing on connections without worrying about the shape (cube, sphere, etc.) of any mass or void, but such conceptually elastic bubbles are often dangerously misleading because they may ignore real constraints like required light levels or exit corridor width. Bubble diagrams alone ignore the sense of architecture-- the play of opaque to transparent, of light to dark, or of long gradual ramp to rapid spiral stair. What has evolved for many designers is a kind of hybrid modelling technique, in which floor areas are accurately represented in proportion but not in shape. Scissors and tape make it easy to position areas in three-dimensional space and then trim excess width and re-tape it as additional length, etc. Thus shape may change, but the proportion of one program volume to others remains fairly constant. The ability to hold constants against variables in three or more dimensions is one of an architect's most valued skills. Making spaces which communicate such plastic speculation through permanent mass raises the service of building to the art of architecture.

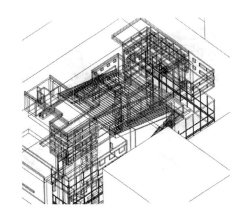

ALAN CHAN

The *Corpo Transparente*

For architects, seeing all rooms equally in a kind of mental x-ray, the body of a building is transparent. First volumes are treated as naked solids, wire-framed transparent boxes. Then surfaces can become opaque to modulate light or control privacy. From such an outlook, walls or floors can gain real presence; they are treated as filled solids and part of the ensemble, rather than as annoying obstacles that need holes punched in them to solve mundane concerns like illumination or fresh air. Le Corbusier's Villa Shodan, in India is a wonderful example of the plastic richness in both volumetric composition and material presence. One side is mostly opaque wall, seemingly a filled solid, while the opposite side exhibits mostly void. The roof, a floating plane that completes the cubic definition of the space also acts as a literal parasol to provide shade and natural convection air conditioning in this hot climate. To best see these volumes within volumes-- double height bedroom suites, roof terrace "room", master suite study opening to triple height entry-- we must study all the plans, sections, and models. We need mental x-rays to grasp the total harmony of this transparent body, this *corpo transparente*.

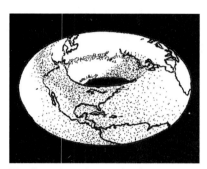

What if...   the earth were a donut?

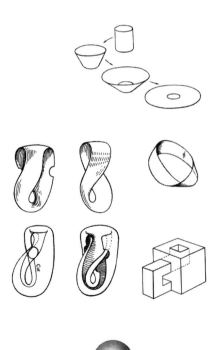

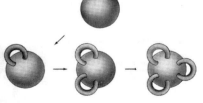

COMPLEX SPACE

Topology

Solid geometry carefully describes the differences between cube, sphere, and pyramid. But there is another branch of mathematics, called topology, in which these solids are essentially the same. Topology's founder, Henri Poincaré by 1900 had described topology as "geometry drawn by a bad draftsman." If we imagine solids to be composed of an infinitely stretchable material, we can discover some essential properties of their topology (not typology!) A teacup with its handle is topologically equivalent to a donut (a torus) and a drinking straw. In each case, no matter how much the shape of the mass is changed, there will always remain one loop of void. Topological curiosities include two dimensional single surface Mobius Strips (vs. double surfaces like a piece of paper) and three dimensional single surface Klein Bottles, which lack the distinct inside and outside surfaces of regular bottles. Architect Peter Carl once designed a Klein Bottle house. (Chateau Villandry is in some ways a Klein Bottle villa.) Topologies are distinguished by their degree of "hole-ness" and knottedness. A pretzel is a second degree topology, with three irreducible void loops and an irreducible intersecting knot. The degree and kind of perforations and intersections distinguish architectural spaces.

Perforation

Perforation means to bore or pierce through. Mass perforates void; void perforates mass. Together they generate volume. Volumes of multiple perforations are the essence of architectural space. "Solid" walls are in fact perforated volumes-- whether the mass of sheetrock and studs and the 16" voids between them (sometimes filled with insulation, itself composed of fiberglass mass suspended in dead air void), or the mass of cinder blocks around the voids of the holes in them. Even a brick wall can be seen as a kind of mesh of rigid clay block holes in a perforated but continuous plane of drying liquid mortar. Architecture is composed of multiply perforated volumes with windows, doors, chimneys, stairs, creating complex sets of spacial loops and knots. Aligned columns and balusters stacked on many floors can create a stair tower that is a hollow rod of many intersecting volumes. The central space at Wright's Larkin Building is a hollow solid that is consistently perforated in all three dimensions. Many readings of this rich spacial composition are possible, in which *volumetric* lines, planes, and solids intersect.

Modulated Volume: Plastic Rhythm

It is often to the engineer's advantage to define as large a volume with as little mass as possible. But this does not guarantee that the resulting space will be plastically rich beyond the fascination with its size. Architectural space, a mass/void continuum that defines an order of volumes, can be plastically rich independent of size. A small three story home like Le Corbusier's 1925 Maison Cook, with roof garden gallery opening to its double height living room, is more vertical than the 110 repetitive layers of the World Trade Center. Where you put the skin and bones qualifies the space of a given volume. The complexly perforated volume of Le Corbusier's 1957 Unite d'Habitation sets up rich spacial rhythms by the variation and placement of single and double height volumes, revealed through the balconies that create such deep relief in facade. Modulating volume is a new design tool for Dynamics. In Architectonics, we presumed that a cube was filled with mass. Now we understand that any cube may also be hollow. The design task becomes finding a *parti* by composing *volumes* rather than masses. Establishing the position and interval of such volumes creates plastic rhythm in both mass and void. It is in this sense that we mean that a room is the architect's brick. This is how architects modulate volume to make space.

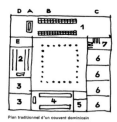

DESIGN DEVELOPMENT

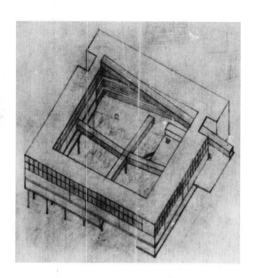

When children aspire to be "real" architects, they often attempt to make plans of houses by drawing the walls around the rooms. Many high school "architecture" courses teach only how to draft blueprints-- that is, plans and elevations of standard room layout. Compositional skills are perhaps engaged in locating furniture, circulation patterns, or window openings, but any connection between the actions of builder and architect remains unclear. Just as a carpenter locates cabinet boxes on wall planes in room volumes, so too does the architect organize and position bedroom room boxes around corridor rods, setting them above or below a planar volume of living room and kitchen. The true skill of an architect comes not in knowing how to locate these boxes at the first attempt, but in developing strategies for their rearrangement and repositioning until subtle and profound relationships are revealed. In the most accomplished instances, the locations of masses and volumes are inextricably interrelated.

Parti and plasticity

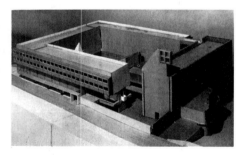

After determining what volumes are required by the program, an architect locates volumes within a three-dimensional order that answers relational needs to find a *parti* (keep children's bedrooms far from adult party areas and give them late-- not early!-- morning light), often in the crudest manner imaginable. Inspiration for the complex warped ramp of Le Corbusier's Strasbourg City Hall project (see page 297) may have been a chance juxtaposition of match box and adhesive tape dispenser on his desk. Usually what follows is a period of experimental rearrangement of volumes, circulation elements, etc. until a satisfactory *parti* is achieved. After the most important and inertially intransigent volumes are located and relational hierarchies are established, plastic modeling of mass and void commences. Only now do refinement of structural systems, materials, fenestration and the like move into the foreground of the designer's attention. Insights gained at these levels may force a reconsideration and reconfiguration of *parti*, which may imply new structural concerns, etc. For example, the increasingly plastic articulation of Le Corbusier's monastery La Tourette clarifies its *parti*. An axonometric projection establishes positions of major volumes and circulation on the hillside, and reveals that the archetypal Cistercian plan makes roof line rather than ground plane the horizontal datum. A later model eliminates the crude (and dumb!) exterior ramp to liberate the chapel box from the U-shaped residential wing while intensifying the void between them. Increasingly differentiated relief and proportioning of upper monk cells from lower communal levels render upper volumes more "massive" than the lower ones and thus levitate the whole residential ensemble, increasing upward pressure on the roof-level datum. The uninterrupted verticality of the mostly opaque chapel box contrasts with the horizontality of the other elements. Projecting cell balconies over lower public volumes creates deep shadows which reinforce the horizontal reading. Countless modifications like these finally create the fully realized three-dimensional plasticity of this built masterpiece.

Pro-position and Re-solution

It is one thing to offer a thought, but another to make it work. Proposition precedes solution. A conscientious designer reconsiders the solution as a new proposition and evaluates the success and failure of its configuration, especially in terms of internal consistency. Then the solution is solved again, to achieve re-solution (to become resolute!) and eventually arrive at what architect Chris Chimera calls "synthetic inevitability". Pro-position implies "something from nothing", while re-solution implies "something from something"-- or as James Joycemight have said, "newthing from samething". As architect Paul Amatuzzo suggests, "form follows form". For Dynamics, each major *etude* is presented in two chapters; the first establishes a proposal-- a Pro-position, while the second encourages reconsidering ideas and shapes toward a resolved form-- a Re-Solution.

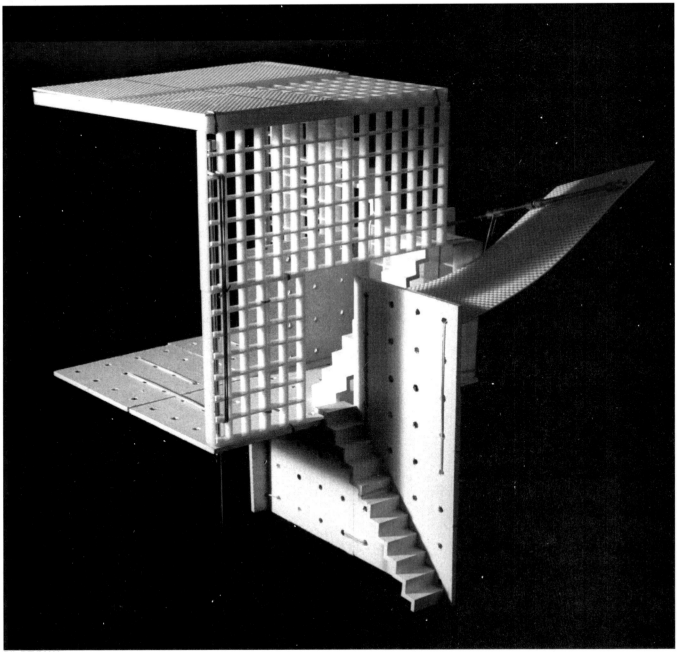

BIL REYMAN

ARCHITECTONICS

MASS

PRELUDE

DYNAMICS

PLANE
MELODY   LINE   POINT

INTERSECTION/UNION
HARMONY

TARTAN
CONCERTO

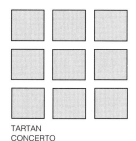

COLLAGE
SYMPHONY

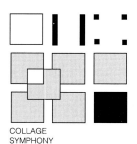

A NEW BAG

How Space Feels

We feel with our whole body and soul, we sympathize. We feel crushed by debts, tense with anxiety, and relaxed in comfort; we curl up in fear and jump for joy. Once we learn to look for the cues, we can sympathize with any physical structure. We can feel downward pull of gravity on the red octagon of a stop sign, the upright stiffness of its supporting stanchion, and the cutting shear on the connecting bolts pushed down by the octagon and up by the stanchion. Such stress and strain is the internal force and motion in a structure. From flying buttress to cantilever, structure can eloquently express how mass feels. In architecture, we may also consider how the structure of volume feels. Architectural space may be compressed, extended, twisted, etc. according to plastic factors akin to the physical forces on matter in spacetime.

Bag of Tricks

Every molecule in the ceiling above our heads is straining to float free, straining to accelerate towards the planet's center. But every molecule of wood or steel in those beams is also vibrating according to the structure of its material. It is the integrity of these intermolecular electrochemical forces that keep us from being crushed by the heavy weight overhead, so architectural space is made of volumes defined by mass elements chosen and positioned to *resist* their tendency to motion. When the internal workings of architectonic elements are brought to light, their play in fields of forces enters plastic design in architecture. The Kit of Parts, delineating geometric solids as ideal homogeneous masses and connecting them with an always-effective "magic" rubber cement that ignores load and joint conditions, is inadequate for modeling volumes subject to force and motion. We must replace rubber cement with rubber bands. For Dynamics, a new set of elements is introduced, called the **Bag of Tricks**. These perforated solids become a medium for modeling structure and light as well as volume at human scale. They permit non-orthogonal volumes (vaults from bent mesh, diagonals from eccentric cantilevers, etc.) to be established from load conditions rather than from any arbitrary drawing. Modeling volume directly through material structure is a powerful tool-- consider the difference between making a complex form by crumpling a piece of paper and describing that same crumpled form through constructive geometry, even with computer-aided design. (The Appendix, starting on page 437, gives more details about the Bag of Tricks.)

Perforated topologies

Every piece in the Bag of Tricks has at least one hole in it. A rubber band has a hole at the center of its continuous loop. Brass and ABS plastic tubes are topologically equivalent to rubber bands. Eggcrate, masonite, and mesh all have multiple perforations. Joints may be more "pretzel-like" in their topology. Now any void may be perforated with mass. Now a cube itself may be hollow-- perforated with void-- and may be externally defined or internally implied by surface planes, edge lines, and point corners. Perforated volumes can intersect each other in harmony (two cubes can overlap). Whole sets of volumetric order can permeate each other in tartan perforation. The student who masters Dynamics composes *partis* of volumes rather than masses, exploiting differences in topology, geometry, material, light, and function as the student of Architectonics exploits the differences between rod and cube, pyramid and cylinder, stair and ramp. Such a palette of spacial qualities and nested volumetric orders permits true architectural design at all scales, from construction detail to whole cities.

THE CROWN OF CREATION

*"The sun does not realize it is until after a room is made.
A man's creation, the making of a room, is nothing short of a miracle.
Just think, that a man can claim a slice of the sun."* Lou Kahn

Out of darkness into light

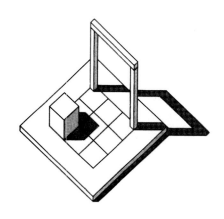

This cube is hollow. As we look up into the skylight over the entry well at Louis I. Kahn's British Art Museum at Yale in New Haven, Connecticut (shown opposite), we may well wonder--- how did this space get that way? What keeps those massive beams floating so lightly so far above our heads from crashing down upon us and crushing us? Similarly, why don't the ceiling joists above your room fall down at this very moment? We may also marvel at how light seems to fill the Yale entry, as if its volume were a balloon of concrete and stone inflated by pure energy, like a star radiant in all directions. Light glows! Light is the skin which radiance becomes on meeting gravity. This Kahn space becomes a vast light vessel, a chamber for holding light, sound, spirit. The architect has made a cube that is hollow-- a solid of volume rather than mass. How did this cube become so empty? How is it possible to design and arrange elements of empty space-- of nothing at all?! How is it possible to learn to think the way of composing volumes primarily-- the way of the architect? That is the primary subject of this second volume of *Creation in Space,* called *Dynamics.* In Kahn's space at Yale light comes down from the top, the sky, through the skylight, not from the clerestory sides as in a cathedral like Beauvais. All at once we find that there is a window to "up" as well as to "out". Now we know such frames of reference are only local, not universal. It is just as easy to lie on the earth and imagine the whole globe a giant backpack glued to our body by gravity as it is to think of it as a floor to hold "up" our feet. Now we can see that at least from the point of view of say the moon, trees grow out, not up.

Making Space, Taking Space

Making room is an action. To extend boundaries out beyond arms reach is to insure that habitation is not confining-- not a prison cell-- which is not a question of mere dimension (compare a prison cell with the stateroom of a luxury liner), but is rather more basically a question of the degree of freedom such space enables the individual to inhabit. Freedom may be described as the personally established order that meshes with the order of society. In spcial terms freedom is the extension of a dwelling to the horizon in unbroken continuum. In this sense, a wall can confine or **de**-fine. Definition is not imprisonment but rather enhancement of the localities on both sides of the wall, as Peter Carl has discussed regarding architecture and bifurcation. The masters of traditional Japanese garden design framed views of their gardens through doors and windows to "capture space" and extend a room. Later we will see that the free plan perforates habitable volume with the mass of a grid of columns.

But how to establish walls, floors, roofs, beyond the body? This becomes the skill of the constructor in the dance of the elements-- a juggling act in which the pieces never move from their appointed positions. That dance, when mastered, can become an insight into the vision of architecture-- a means to understand that space is not a static but a **dynamic** medium. First, the student must learn the ART of seeing space, to discover that space is more than three-dimensions by finding that surface is more than two dimensions. To do this one must learn to see not only things, but their context. Then the student needs to master the ART of making volume visible. Then the student may learn an algebra of solid geometric combinations and the ART of combining volumes. Following that, a student may learn the ART of combining sets of volumes in fields. Finally, the ART of pressurizing interacting volume sets into resonant and radiant instruments becomes apparent and ready to be tested. Beyond that, the Universe we inhabit beckons and everywhere offers the possibility of architecture.

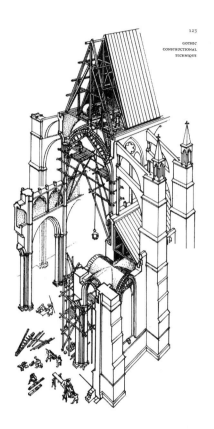

123

GOTHIC
CONSTRUCTIONAL
TECHNIQUE

BRIDGE: *REPRISE*

The nave of the Beauvais Cathedral, when first built c. 1282, fell and collapsed under its own weight, because the medieval builders tried a daring structural form to satisfy their desire to fill a lofty space with light and the energy of religious spirit. To throw a two-ton stone 200+ feet above your head and keep it there, and to make the supporting walls so thin and open that they seemed made more of light than of stone took daring, vision, and technical precision. The means were finally found to achieve what once seemed impossible. Since the Shuttle Challenger explosion, we must again find ways to keep stones of all kinds aloft as a testament to the human spirit.

We inhabit volumes larger than ourselves. Finding ways to put pieces beyond our reach so as to make *room* demands ingenuity in construction. Piling stones like the Great Pyramids in Egypt is a difficult way to create space. To create large volumes, to wrap material around a void and keep it there despite all the forces acting on it, is to make a span. Setting stones so as to counterbalance the forces between them can make an arch. The stones of an arch are kept in perpetual low orbit by the skill of the architect. The stones of Machu Picchu are in a higher orbit than the stones of Venice. Resolving the forces in elements that define volumes in space can produce magnificent plastic works. The Verrazano Narrows Bridge in NY Harbor, a great suspension bridge, levitates steel, concrete, highways and trucks like toys high above the sea, as much as half a mile from any support! Even more wonderful are human places like the Pantheon, Hagia Sophia, the cathedrals, the Eiffel Tower, where the economic, elegant and daring use of materials and structures have created wonderful spaces, producing architecture inhabited by both body and spirit!

Just as bamboo or trees bend in the wind, so does every part of a building respond to the forces around it. The ideal static geometry assumed for the study of ARCHITECTONICS must be augmented by an understanding of geometry in motion. DYNAMICS can reveal the forces that act to make spaces and forms. How to think about engineering of materials and structures as design investigations is the subject of the next course, called DYNAMICS. The medium for DYNAMICS includes both the space (solid and void) of ARCHITECTONICS, and *time* .

Where do we come from? Consider the chambered nautilus, a mollusc who seems to create its shell walls from an infinitesimally small origin. How did it begin to make its beautiful form, the logarithmic spiral? Life appears to make a leap, perhaps of faith, creating its reality by growing into the void. Evolution means literally "to turn or spin outward". "Volume" itself comes from the same Sanskrit root, "vol"— meaning "to roll".

We used to be completely anchored to the Earth. Now, however, humankind has succeeded in spanning space not just across the land, but also outward from our planet's center. Bruce McCandless, the astronaut who floated free above the Earth in the Manned Maneuvering Unit was not just "hovering out there in space". His forward thrust kept him falling around the earth as fast as gravity pulled him to the surface. McCandless maintained his position because he was spinning about the center of the earth at orbital velocity, which is 17,000+ MPH. So a picture of this astronaut is not only a still life, but also a movie.

And the ceiling of the nave of Beauvais Cathedral, a crown of creation, is not only up but also out.
Now it is time to explode the roof....

450 million light years

MAGNANIMOUS UNIVERSE

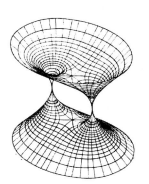

"An important distinction between Newtonian and Einsteinian cosmology is that in the former the galaxies are racing apart through a static, unchanging background of space, while in the latter space itself is expanding. The raisin bread analogy is closer to the Einsteinian model: Space, namely the bread between the raisins, is itself a dynamic entity." Anthony Zee

Anima, the root of animation (and animal) means soul, spirit, mind. The great etymologist Eric Partridge suggests it is the most onomatopoeic of words-- *a-* as breath in, *ni-* hiatus, *ma-* as simplest plosive, or breath out. *Anima*, like the Hindu mantra *om*, enacts as it names that most basic survival event and fundamental form of meditation, breathing. Inspiration, perspiration, and respiration all depend on *spire-*, also meaning breath. Insofar as the universe itself is a vast dialog of inward attraction and outward radiation creating alternating regions of density and sparsity, darkness and light, it is great spirited, great souled, great minded. In short, we live in a magnanimous universe.

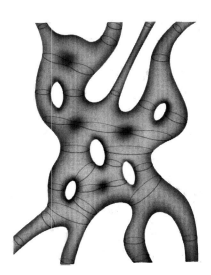

Background radiation coming from everywhere in the heavens at 3 degrees above absolute zero, identified by Arno and Penzias in 1965 as remnant glow from the primordial Big Bang, was thought to be evenly distributed throughout all the known universe. But COBE found that some regions of this radiation are slightly hotter than others. Margaret Geller and her associates have shown that galaxies are clumped together in some areas and virtually absent in vast cosmic deserts. Their computer model indicates surprising strings of galaxies, including one cluster they call the "Great Wall" that is almost 400 million light years long! we may see this figure as the head and extended arms of an enormous celestial person. We may also see voids, not matter, as primary structure. These bubbles of volume, perhaps as large as 100 million light years across, seem to reveal a sponge-like structure to the universe. The gathering of even a tiny mass locally distorts the fabric of spacetime into a gravity trough or well that attracts still more matter in ever increasing amounts, pulling it from the "thinner" and flatter regions of spacetime as a bowling ball on a trampoline would attract nearby marbles, in turn pulling the bowling ball deeper, attracting more distant marbles and bowling balls, and so on...

We now see, through astronomic instruments gathering all known radiation frequencies, from radio and visible light to X-rays and hard gamma rays that the universe is no stately clockwork, as Newton supposed, but rather a dynamic phenomenon of violent explosions. Theorists argue that spacetime is awash with gravitational waves as much as light and radio waves, although these remain undetected to date. Stars explode into novas and supernovas, whole galaxies collapse or devour other galaxies. The Big Bang model proposes that the entire cosmos was born in a single explosion some 10 to 20 billion years ago. The ubiquitous red shift of the most distant galaxies and quasars is evidence that the universe is still outwardly expanding everywhere. Every point in space, filled or empty, is receding from every other one like spots on the surface of an inflating balloon. Extrapolating backwards, scientists conclude that the universe was once infinitesimal, as tiny as possible, some 10^{30} times *smaller* than an atom! Perhaps it arose from vacuum as a fluctuation of quantum probability. Contemporary cosmologists seek to unify the quantum theory that describes the dynamics of matter at subatomic scales with Einstein's General Theory of Relativity, which describes the geometrodynamics of spacetime at the cosmic scale. What a ride to the center! What a burst of space out again! How wide is our swing! If animation is universal, if as some sense the universe itself is living *anima*, then Dynamics may provide insight to an architecture at all possible scales. Le Corbusier's definition of architecture as the "correct, masterful, and orderly play of volumes brought together in light" clarifies issues of Architectonics. But if light and mass are equivalent as energy, if matter moving at light speed becomes light, as Einstein's famous $E = mc^2$ proposes, perhaps we must extend the terms of architecture. The "correct, masterful, and orderly play" of movements is found in the phenomenon of music, whose chief characteristics are tone structure and rhythm. A working definition of an architecture of Dynamics might be:

Architecture is the structure and rhythm of energy.

DYNAMICS

"The springing flexibility of bamboo allows it to survive, even in the winds of change." I Ching
"Bamboo without mind, yet sends thoughts soaring among clouds." Wu Chen (1280-1354)

Prelude -- *ludere* to play *prae* before -- to play beforehand. **n.** 1. a thing serving as the introduction to a principal event, action, performance, etc; preliminary part; preface; opening. 2. in music, a) an introductory section or movement of a suite, fugue, etc. b) since the 19th century, any short romantic composition. **v.t.** 1. to serve as or be a prelude. 2. to introduce by or as by a prelude. **v.i.** 1. to serve as or be a prelude. 2. to play or provide a prelude.

Interlude -- to play *inter*, or between times or at intervals; a game between two periods of business, hence something light introduced to relieve heaviness, as in a medieval morality or mystery. [from Origins] (*ludus-* - a game; cf. O. Irish *loid*, a song. Old Celtic *leut-*, to be joyous.]

Syncopation comes from the Greek *sym* - together + *koptein* - cut. Webster: in music, a) to begin a tone on an unaccented beat and continue it through the next accented beat, or to begin a tone on the last half of a beat and continue it through the first half of the following beat. b) to use such shifted accents in a musical composition. *syncopation* - in which accented beats are played against the unaccented beats of an underlying rhythm.

Jazz -- a kind of music, originally improvised but now also arranged, characterized by syncopation, rubato, heavily accented 4/4 time, dissonances, melodic variations and unusual tonal effects on the saxophone, clarinet, trumpet, trombone, etc.

PRELUDE

PURIST PAINTING
plane volume plane

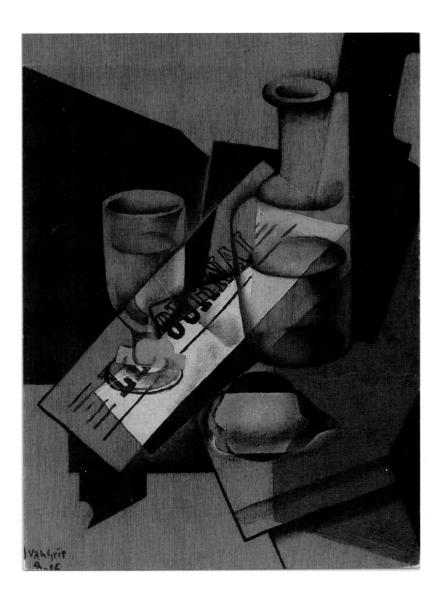

I work with the elements of the intellect, with the imagination. I try to make concrete that which is abstract. I proceed from the general to the particular, by which I mean that I start with am abstraction in order to arrive at a true fact. Mine is an art of synthesis, of deduction, as Raynal has said. I want to endow the elements I use with a new quality; starting from general types want to construct particular individuals.

I consider that the architectural element in painting is mathematics, the abstract side; I want to humanize it. Cézanne turns a bottle into a cylinder, but I begin with a cylinder and create an individual of a special type: I make a bottle-- a particular bottle- out of a cylinder. Cézanne tends toward architecture, I tend away from it. That is why I compose with abstractions (colours) and make my adjustments when these colours have assumed the form of objects. For example, I make a composition with a white and a black and make adjustments when the white has become a paper and the black a shadow: what I mean is that I adjust the white so that it becomes a paper and the black so that it becomes a shadow.

This painting is to the other what poetry is to prose.

Though in my system I may depart greatly from any idealistic or naturalistic art, in practice I cannot break away from the Louvre. Mine is the method of all times, the method used by the old masters: there are technical means and they remain constant.

Juan Gris Personal Statement 1921
in L'Esprit Nouveau No. 5

"Gravity and inertia are being overcome."
El Lissitzky (1926)

*"One needs three jaws in order to conduct oneself
and to 'eat' in space." Eduardo Chillida*

BOCCIONI, Umberto. *Developement of a bottle in space.* (1912) Silvered bronze
(cast 1931), 15 x 23 3/4 x 12 7/8" (38.1 x 60.3 x 32.7 cm). The Museum of Modern
Art, New York. Aristide Maillol Fund. Photograph (c) 1998 The Museum of Modern
Art, New York.

*The metaphorical model of Cubism is the***diagram***: the diagram being a visible, symbolic representation of invisible processes, forces, structures. A diagram will not eschew certain aspects of appearances: but these too will be treated symbolically as signs, not as imitations or recreations. The model of the diagram differs from that of the mirror [the metaphorical model of the Renaissance], in that it suggests a concern with what is not self-evident... The system of organization which the Cubists used leads us back to Cézanne, their other precursor. Cézanne raised and allowed the question of there being simultaneous viewpoints, and thereby destroyed forever the possibility of a static view of nature. (Constable's view, for all its bustling clouds, was nevertheless static.) The Cubists went further. They found means for making forms of all objects similar. They achieved this by reducing all forms to a combination of cubes, cylinders, and-- later-- facets and planes with sharply defined edges. The purpose of this simplification was to be able to construct the most complex view of reality ever attempted in the visual arts. The simplification was very far from being for simplification's sake. If everything was rendered in the same terms (whether a hand, a violin, or a window) it became possible to paint the interactions between them; their elements became interchangeable. Furthermore, the space in which they all existed could also be rendered in the same terms-- but in obverse. (Where the surface of an object was concave, the surface of the space was convex.)*

The Cubists created a system by which they could reveal visually the interlocking of phenomena. And thus they created the possibility of art revealing process instead of static states of being. Cubism is an art entirely concerned with interaction: the interaction between different aspects; the interactions between structure and movement; the interactions between solids and the space around them; the interactions between unambiguous signs made on the surface of the picture and the changing reality which they stand in for. It is an art of dynamic liberation from all static categories. All is possible [wrote André Salmon, a Cubist poet], everything is realizable everywhere and with everything....

The Renaissance artist imitated nature....
The Cubist realized that his awareness of nature was part of nature.

Cubism broke the illusionist three-dimensional space which had existed in painting since the Renaissance. It did not destroy it. Nor did it muffle it— as Gaugin and the Pont-Aven school had done. It broke its continuity. There is space in a Cubist painting in that one form can be inferred to be behind another. But the relation between any two forms does not, as it does in illusionist space, establish the rule for all the spacial relationships between all the forms portrayed in the picture. This is possible without a nightmarish deformation of space, because the two-dimensional surface of the picture is always there as arbiter and resolver of different claims. The picture surface acts in a Cubist painting as the constant which allows us to appreciate the variables. Before and after every sortie of our imagination into the problematic spaces and through the interconnections of a Cubist painting, we find our gaze resettled on the picture surface, aware once more of two-dimensional shapes on a two-dimensional board or canvas.... This makes it impossible to confront the objects or forms in a Cubist work. Not only because of the multiplicity of viewpoints— so that, say, a view of a table from below is combined with a view of the table from above and from the side— but also because the forms portrayed never present themselves as a totality. The totality is the surface of the picture, which is now the origin and sum of all that one sees. The viewing point of Renaissance perspective, fixed and outside the picture, but to which everything within the picture was drawn, has become a field of vision which is the picture itself.

John Berger— The Moment of Cubism

BEING

"O wad som pow'r the giftie gie us/to see ourselves as ithers see us..."
Robert Burns, *to a Louse*

Seeing and Knowing

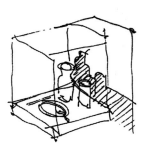

What is true? Look at the photograph on the left. What is strange about it is that we see what we know to be true, a rare visual experience indeed. The tablecloth looks to be made of right angle squares, the plate, bottle and glass are circles, and the shadows on the wall are exact profiles of the liquid containers. We usually see ovals and trapezoids instead of the circles and squares we *know* through the touch of our hands because the focussing plane of our eye or camera is rarely directly frontal and parallel to the shapes. We have learned to see lines which are actually parallel in space as visually converging towards an implied depth in a picture plane, and we call this perspective. This photograph of a breakfast table reveals the disparity between what our eye as still camera registers and what our brain as data processor and stereometric integrator learns. Seeing depends on an awareness of the conditions of looking, and involves noting relationships in space, in the visual field, and in the interaction between these. The Renaissance rediscovery of "true" perspective showed a "photographic reality" of the world, but at a cost. To "work", a perspective view demands observation from a single station point. Any change in position generates a different visual geometry. Thus we can only know what faces us in such an image. Is a cow etched on the back of the milk bottle? Is the tabletop horizontal, or is it vertical with only images of the crockery pasted to it, like a billboard? Such ambiguity, only partly overcome by the parallax of binocular vision, is inherent in the two-dimensional picture plane our eyes register and the three-dimensional world our bodies inhabit.

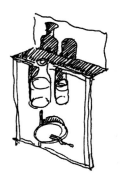

We experience phenomena in many dimensions. TV weather reports depict a complex spacetime reality. Animated satellite photos, national pressure/temperature maps, local radar scans, and 5-day forecasts all add up to a multi-format *model* of the weather environment around us. Does a fish see the sea? To truly see *our* spacial reality, to see *through* the world, we need vision, the simultaneous integration in the "mind's eye" of all relevant views, instructions, and diagrams. Before the event, we call it imagination. An architect imagines a house: will it be warm in winter and cool in summer, will the back be akin to the front, will the stair create a good hall upstairs and down? With such comprehensive "x-ray vision" it is not a difficult trick to design upside down-- a skill many architects develop from countless desk crits with students and clients.

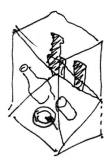

Before photography, the primary function of painting was *mimesis*, the imitation of nature. Since Impressionism, painters have sought a role for painting no longer needed just to copy scenes. Paul Cézanne realized that a perspective view creates an illusion, a hole-in-the-wall window onto a landscape not really there, requiring us to ignore the reality of the canvas, picture frame and wall on which the work is hanging. A painting is thus a kind of hole *on* the wall, and like a diagram it brackets its content, taking it out of context. A square in a square represents not just a two-dimensional visual field, but also the sense of the field itself in a context: on a wall, in a room, in other dimensions. The Cubist and Purist painters who followed Cézanne in the 20th century consciously tried to order this structure of perception. Just as our weight bends a floor, vision creates a kind of perceptual "load" on the picture plane before us. Although the surface of a painting is flat, through the illusion of depth it proposes space. Do we "read" a painting as a recess into or a projection out of its wall? Once we accept, along with Cézanne, that a painting is not only a simple window to an illusion of space beyond, but also the presence of a very real surface constructed of paint, we begin to feel the drama that can occur at the picture plane. Our eyes seek to resolve this tension between depth and flatness. Do we project the surface rotating about its central horizon or do we imagine a punch through the wall into depth, parallel to our confrontation? Such issues as the conflict as between frontality and rotation can order a "structural design" of perception.

"The most extreme combination of two- and three-dimensionality are illustrated in he right diagram. above Illustration A is a tracing from a wineglass in a painting by Picasso. Arrows at the top indicate the same kind of "thrust and return" as that analyzed in Cézanne's cup and saucer. But the top of the glass is seen from above while the bottom is drawn from a horizontal eye level. A combination of two- and three-dimensionality thus exists in the same object.

"Historically the same phenomenon can be traced back to Egyptian murals and Roman and Byzantine art. Illustration a is the general model for all three. I feel certain that Cézanne was not particularly interested in historical predecessors in this kind of drawing; but that he practiced it and very likely was responsible for suggesting it to Picasso and others is evident..."

Earl Loran, Cézanne's Composition

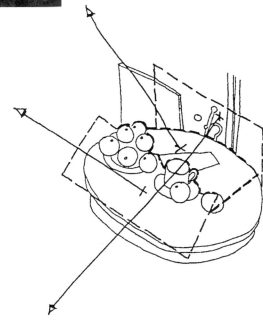

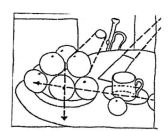

FALLING DOWN: GRAVITY
FALLING BACK: PERSPECTIVE
SLIDING ACROSS: BILLIARDS

MOVEMENT IN THE PICTURE PLANE

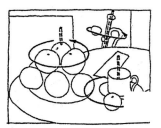

ROTATION INTO DEPTH

FREE BODIES IN SPACE

Forces Between Volumes

A painter or sculptor may see the play of solids and voids in the geometry of a bowl of fruit. An engineer may see the play of loads and forces in the same geometry. Newton revealed a physical relationship between force, motion and mass. This became the basis for the structural engineer's way of seeing forces: diagramming the magnitude, direction, and position of loads on masses and analyzing how they interact. The engineer's primary concern is to resolve these loads into stable structures, the branch of mechanics called statics, or into integrated moving systems, the branch of mechanics called dynamics. The architect's corollary is to be concerned with the transitions between states like the quality of light in a room over time, or the interaction between program and enclosure.

Gravity pulls each apple in a fruit bowl towards the center of the earth. The push of the topmost apple transfers to the bowl, table, and ultimately the earth itself. An apple in the middle of the pile might be supporting some fruit and sitting on others. The engineer's vision uses vectors and load diagrams to reveal these interactions of matter and forces. A wood or metal beam is a solid filled with matter. But a room is a solid that is essentially empty. The painter's apple has no weight on the canvas, yet Cézanne found a pictorial equivalent to the engineer's concern. Professor Diamond's and Erle Loran's diagrams of *Cup and Saucer with Plate of Apples* do not show literal structural loads on the fruit but rather the visual organization of pictorial elements in the composition. The relation between volumes in space and the relation between two-dimensional and three-dimensional space as recreated in the picture plane depend on the poised resolution of the kind of "forces" revealed in the Graphics studies of Architectonics while suggesting the movement of animation. Cézanne is the painter weighing apples, the painter weighing the space between apples, even the painter weighing light and space! Cézanne, the painter who is also an architect "in all but fact", found vision in the **interaction of volumes**.

Cézanne's Doubt

Paul Cézanne confronted the inadequacy of "scientific perspective" as a means of recording his experience of the physical world. Limited to a point fixed in space and time, perspective as a symbolic form was readily legible but limited. Cézanne's painting *Cup and Saucer with plate of Apples* breaks with the traditional use and display of perspective as the guarantor of fidelity to the world as we know it. Cézanne's canvas reveals fragments, seen by an eye in active motion, and reconstructed, more or less, as a continuous fabric. This fabric joins views from before, beside, and above, from various moments in time and space. Cézanne's process evolved into a way of structuring both the surface of the picture plane and the deep spaces it depicts. It enabled him to portray both the force of gravity pulling his apples to the ground and the force of perspectival recession pulling those same apples towards surrogate vanishing points through the surfaces of the rear wall. Diagrams of the painting shows how the axes of the apples lead the eye to the wall and trumpet behind them, how the tilt of the trumpet continues a circular motion in depth back to the foreground, and how a rotation of the cup and saucer continue this orbit. Cézanne painted in such a way that he revealed not only volumes, but also the forces acting on them. He found motion in still life. The viewer can participate in the spacial ambiguity between two-dimensional perception and three-dimensional movement by following the shifting viewpoints needed to see apples in space. Cézanne's paintings are the beginning of movies. The arrows in the analysis reveal Cézanne's recognition of a dynamic world of interacting volumes. Merleau-Ponty wrote of the wisdom of "Cézanne's ignorance"-- his refusal to subject looking to any single overall perspective as an artificial unifying fabric, in his quest to depict how we actually *see*.

LE CORBUSIER. *Still Life*. 1920. Oil on Canvas, 31 7/8 x 39 1/4" (80.9 x 99.7cm). The Museum of Modern Art, New York. Van Gogh Purchase Fund. Photograph (c) 1998 The Museum of Modern Art, New York.

"In this [*Still life with stacked plates, 1920*] the puzzling fragmented world of early Cubism was reintegrated, machined, polished, and endowed with static mathematical precision. Banal, everyday objects were reduced to the most generalized curves and rectangles, then disposed in flat planes parallel to the picture surface. The pictorial conception was not perspectival, but resembled an engineering drawing where the elevation and plan of the object might be included together on the same sheet. The Cubist principle of fusing different views here was regularized: the bottle top for example was treated as a pure circle. Objects and surfaces were contained in their outlines and were spliced together with purely abstract shapes in flat layers. Colour was also restricted by boundaries, and was painted in after the contour had been fixed by the drawing, whereas in analytical Cubism the method had been integral: take the colour away and nothing is left. The Purist range of colours included electric blues, light greys, pinks, ochres, earth reds, greens, black and white. Light was even, pearly, and opalescent." William Curtis

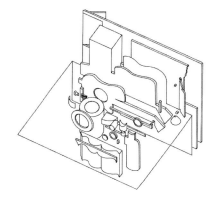

The notes above could almost be a program for building architecture...

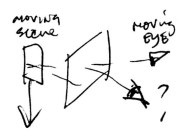

WORKING DRAWING

How can we draw what we know rather than what we see? Architects achieve something like this all the time, using the conventions of plan and axonometric projections to communicate not only what spaces they envision, but also the instructions for how to build them (in *working* drawings.) The painters Amedée Ozenfant and Charles-Edouard Jeanneret (who later as architect took the name Le Corbusier) developed **Purism**, a mode of painting which exploited the conventions of plans, sections, and elevations to render everyday objects like bottles and glasses without visual distortion, true in shape and proportion, in compositions depicting volume organizations in two and three dimensional spacial orders simultaneously.

René Magritte's *Ceci n'est pas une pipe"* *(this is not a pipe]* presents a dilemma. Clearly, a pipe is represented. But a representation of a pipe is only a drawing. In perception obvious truths may not always be valid or exclusive. The innocent question "what is this thing?" sparks inquiries into the nature of perception, truth, reality, and being. To understand "what is this thing?" we must understand "what does this thing represent?" as well as "what could this thing represent?" We must also determine the qualities of space in which this represented thing sits.

The Cubist painters sought to alter or eliminate traditional perspective, like the Post-Impressionists and Fauvists before them. Without a single vanishing point as arbiter of all resolutions within the depicted space, other cues to volume and depth were invented, like layering and transparency. Plan and section, by no means new inventions, were inserted along with other fragmentary evidence of the actual set-up and remain visible in the finished canvases. The new arbiter of spatial conflicts is the flat and vertical surface of the picture plane itself. Like a working drawing, a cubist painting displays traces of the time, movements, and methods of transformation.

We may think of a cubist canvas as a cross-section through the design studio. (Photographic evidence shows that Pablo Picasso and Georges Braque often worked directly from life, from the objects and spaces in their studios.) Plans, sections, elevations, perspectives, axonometrics, models, details and samples are all present as experimental tools for the laboratory of the canvas. Some refer to the evidence of the studio, others may be fragments from a previous structure, and still others to a yet unbuilt construction. The metaphor of the design studio also provides a sectional view through the creator's imagination to reveal two- and three-dimensional transformation constructions, processes which combine intuition and intellect, analytical and creative faculties. The painting is thus a meditation on the evolution of form, composition, association, and relationship. In this sense, solid form in space, like the physicist's concept of energy, always in flux and capable of transformation, is always conserved.

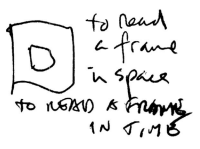

The traditional architect's education examines great monuments of the past, from Stonehenge through the Villa Savoye and beyond, in an attempt to discern that which is immutable. Scale, proportion, order, the use of logic, structure, and material, articulate relationships between architecture and man, the earth, and civilization. The enduring themes of truth, beauty and soul emerge through the eloquent spaces we call Gothic, Baroque, or Modern architecture. But we must also respect that which is temporal, changeable, in flux. The very essence of the act of design is mutation, metamorphosis, and transformation. Creating order, arrangement, and composition is how architects, artists, poets and musicians make meaning. We may explore countless manifestations of an idea before we accept a solution. At other times the variations themselves represent a solution.

MARVENE WORRELL

  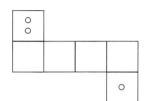

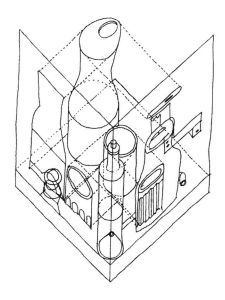

JOHN PAVLOU

A MARRIAGE OF CONTOURS

Purist painters achieved tension between surface and depth primarily through layering, color, transparency, implied folding, and shared boundaries, which they called "a marriage of contours".

> "A composition for Le Corbusier was like setting a table: the rectangle of the surface needed to be contrasted to the roundness of objects at differing scale. The convention of the table full of objects functioned for the Cubists like the theme of Madonna and Child for Renaissance painters. Instead of decomposing objects, however, the Purists insisted on respecting their geometric integrity and the truth of their form. Rather than fragmenting volumes, they pursued a method of densification, superimposing many elements on top of each other, which in 1924 they explained as a 'marriage of objects with the same contours in common.' According to Nivola, one of the things that fascinated Le Corbusier most was the opposition of empty and full and the filial dependency of vessels to containers: the empty glass was seeking its opposite in the full bottle."
>
> Richard Ingersoll

The real subject of a Purist painting is the relationship between object, void and perception-- between volumes and viewers. Like a blueprint, Le Corbusier's *Le Dé Violet* carries data that can be decoded to arrive at a possible working *process* of constructing plastic order. Its may be seen as a series of views from front, sides, and above which are taken from the picture planes around the objects and projected onto the canvas as a simultaneous composite. Note the double views from front and side of both glass tumbler and carafe. The vertical edge between yellow and gray sides of the canvas may then be a fold *line* projecting an outer corner of a cubic frame. On the left a shadow suggests that the bottle is a hole in the yellow surface. The bottom of the bottle reads as both inverted "punt" of the wine bottle and as egg in a cup also in front of the bottle. These cues contrast with the painting's right side, where a bottle, bright against its dark background and sitting on a convex base, projects its rounded shapes forward. While the tumbler's fluting and shared contours seem to embed it within the space of this right-hand bottle, the vertically stacked tilted circles (tumbler top, bottle neck, bottle top) tend to project the entire round construction forward from its picture plane. Thus the two halves of the painting present sets of layered planes sheared across the vertical center. Figure on the left becomes ground on the right, and vice-versa, compressing the space between these reference volumes. A third bottle along the central axis reinforces this reading with multiple depth cues. Its left shadows recess this bottle behind the painting's left foreground plane, and its right shadows push the bottle back into that foreground. Another reading of these central shadows has the left ones project the central bottle forward and the right ones pull the bottle to the deepest layer of the painting by merging with the dark background. The central cone both projects forward of the dark right side and joins with it, receding behind the light left side.

There is thus a simultaneous seesaw of spacial shears and torsions, a fulcrum at the center of the painting like the in-out doors of a cuckoo clock. The painting's English title The *Purple Die* (singular of dice) reveals an understanding of this drama. The bent rectangle with two dark dots in a light field becoming one light dot in a dark field could well be a construction manual for the entire spacial order. This figure describes an unfolded cube, marked to show two sides that cannot be parallel in any single perspective view, but which we know are equal faces in three dimensions. This a set of unfolding, refolding, layered, and twisted planes, this *origami*, becomes the "architectural plans" for reconstructing the play of figures the artist knows *and* sees. *Dé* also suggests dé *a coudre*, a thimble (literally "die for sewing"). This unfolded cube, midway between top and bottom, may well be both *parti* and plan of the whole painting. On the left dark it shows voids cut into the light reference plane while a bright figure projects from its dark surrounds. This in turn implies a projecting space on the left and a receding one on the right. In this sense the Die "sews" the two halves of the space together.

ROBERTO PETRUCELLI

AMBIGUITY AND SIMULTANEITY

To "read" an image, we must learn its conventions. Consider the trapezoid to the left. Alone, it reads as a flat two-dimensional geometric figure. When a square is added it is easy to read depth, as the trapezoid becomes a receding floor plane. Like any diagonal, the trapezoid is an inherently ambiguous figure rendering both flatness and depth. Ambiguity has been used to great advantage by Cubist painters and their followers. Transforming three dimensions into two-dimensional order generates multiple interpretations. A square in a square is an ambiguous figure, able to indicate many depth readings including a tilted plane, a bent surface, a cylinder, one plane behind another, and so on, as shown in the accompanying sketches. A figure that yields two or more visual readings yields them *at once,* even if we must process them in our brains sequentially-- ambiguity is simultaneous. A marriage of contours permits multiple depth readings for the same lines or color areas. A complex Cubist painting, like Juan Gris' *Fruit Dish and Newspaper* (1920) is no longer a simple still life. Depth cues of color, transparency, and overlap; tensions between shallow surface and deep relief; and simultaneous multiple views of plan and section, front and back, inside and outside, offer numerous spacial readings. Shifting interpretations make the painting cinematic, closer to a motion picture, a planar sieve catching forms and forces emerging from its depth.

An empty square on a page is already a figure in a field. The tension between a figure and the edge of its paper as frame creates a charged space between them, distinguishing the figure from its surroundings. Framing sets a figure apart from its embedded context. The frame can no longer be taken for granted. How thick is the frame!? Which is the hole? The sculptor Brancusi often devoted as much attention to the base as to the figure it supported. The Cubists had trouble with frames. Sometimes they put their paintings in ellipses, building up planar structures from the center outward, other times they twisted the space against the orientation of the frame-- as did Mondrian, and as does Juan Gris here. Must one frame architecture? Can we inhabit volumes whose plastic order is intrinsic?

With Cubism, the problem of painting became how to order the two-dimensional picture plane into a meaningful and revealing analog to three-dimensional reality. If contour and viewpoint may be manipulated, then a vertical picture plane can support the images of bottles etc. as much as a horizontal tabletop supports the physical bottles. The everyday surface of a table became an arena for changing pictorial/depth relationships, an endless source of the subject matter of perception, an orderable experimental microcosm. The world became simultaneously tabletop, sculpture garden, and picture plane. John Hejduk observed that the sky is a vertical picture plane as much as it is a horizontal dome. Is the checked tablecloth in the breakfast table photo on page 62 parallel to the ground (as tabletop) or to a gallery wall (as window)? The question shows how Cubist space maintains a flux of simultaneous spacial readings. Let us imagine the Cubist visual explorers sitting at a cafe in Paris before 1910, amidst the objects of everyday life. Drinking coffee, liquor, soda, reading newspapers, smoking pipes, they sketch the forms nearby, aligning utensils, studying light and shadow through transparent glass. Perhaps some street musicians come by. How does one draw the reality of a guitar in space? The wood box, with its mother-of-pearl inlay? But what of the music it makes? Its strings vibrate when plucked, turning the box and air inside into an acoustic resonator that shakes the air projecting out of the sound hole to fill even an auditorium with music. How does one draw that?! The room may be very big, yet the strings and wood of the guitar itself would make a tiny pile of mass. Even the volume of its interior is but a fraction of the volume that its music fills. Does that space resonate to the physical shape of the instrument? Can this be something perceptible in a drawing or model? Suddenly a connection is made between the space in a bottle and a clarinet, guitar and siphon! Plasticity!

Is this a flat trapezoid...

or floor in perspective?

THINKING

there are many ways to skin a cat.... anonymous

CUBISM AND ARCHITECTURE

Why should architects understand Cubism? We believe that such an investigation provides vital tools for the architect, even at the most fundamental level, helping to develop architectural skills and insights for the issues presented in Architectonics and especially Dynamics. The habit of seeing through space and time from all sides, in and out, top and bottom, front and back, then and now, forces an ongoing re-solving of continuity in space, and has led skilled plasticians to find opportunity where traditional forms have perhaps outlived their utility if not their presence as volumes in light, architectural spaces previously overlooked (gardens on the roof) or ignored (the back of the supermarket). Cubism, now almost a century old, is not just a "style" of painting. Fundamental understanding of its plastic principles and those of its cognates and derivatives, including Purism, Constructivism, Neo-Plasticism, Surrealism and Abstract Expressionism, is vital to architects in providing strategies for ordering solids, both filled and empty. The lessons of Cubism now underlay all the visual arts, music, literature and film.

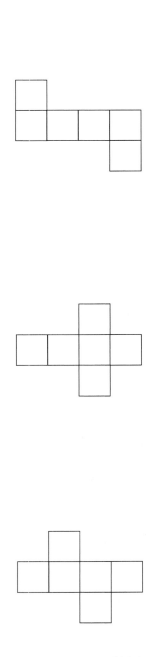

We can distinguish several levels of plastic spacial perception and design ability in students of architecture. This is not the same as the acquired skills of making pictures of workmanlike "professional" or currently stylish "artistic" or "intellectual" facades, showing on the one hand eaves, random shakes, or board and batten "traditional" siding, or on the other hand diagonal deconstructivist floors or rotated windows. Nor is it the same as the technical skills of a thorough knowledge of the application of codes, zoning, economics, etc. which are of course all necessary for the construction of a building-- but which alone are no guarantee that a building will in any real sense be architecture. As Le Corbusier wrote in Towards *a New Architecture:*

> "You employ stone, wood, and concrete, and with these materials you build houses and palaces. That is construction. Ingenuity is at work. But suddenly you touch my heart, you do me good, I am happy and I say: 'This is beautiful.' That is Architecture. Art enters in."

Let us be clear-- if architecture is a humanist discourse through the medium of space, then an understanding of the attributes of the medium is the prerequisite for its realization. These include three-dimensionality, plasticity, plan-section, frontality, light, structure, proportion and scale. Other concerns, like material and texture have an important effect on our experience of a space, but they are not the primary means for marking, developing, ordering, composing or molding space. The structure *of* **space** concerns not the columns that hold up floors, but rather the structure of the volumes--the array of columns within a space, their orientation to the site or other building elements, the rhythm of their spacing, the alteration of their intervals for events like entries, corners, and so on. A column grid may not only hold up floors in a building, but also contribute to its *spacial* structure. (See Brunelleschi's San Lorenzo Church (page 390) in Florence and Le Corbusier's Assembly Building (page 327) at Chandigarh.) Between two and three dimensions reside infinite possibilities. The diagrams to the left show not one but three ways to fold a (paper) plane of six contiguous identical squares into a cube. There are certainly others. Just as Cubist paintings generate numerous valid readings, so too does transforming two-dimensional order into 3 dimensions generate multiple valid interpretations. There is an art to making volume visible. Early Cubists confronted *seeing.* Borrowing techniques familiar to architects, they found means to make the multi-dimensional reality they inhabited come to the fore in plastic composition in sculpture, cinema, and most vividly, most clearly, in the two-dimensional medium of painting itself! This seems to be paradoxical until we recall the unique ability of the picture plane surface to carry multiple dimensional and color relationships simultaneously. You have already learned this in your Architectonics studies.

these are all cubes -- unfolded

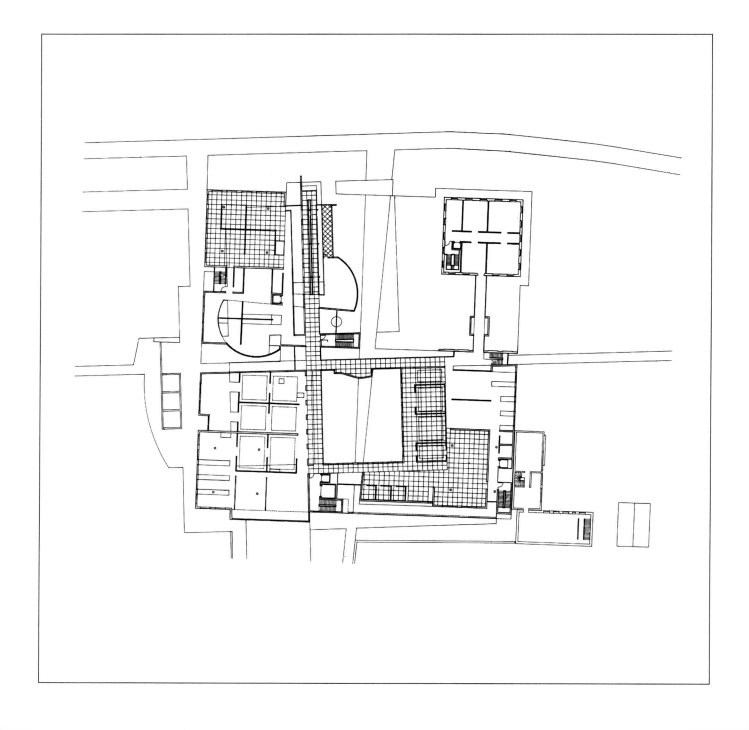

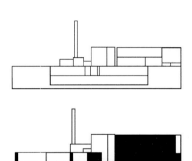

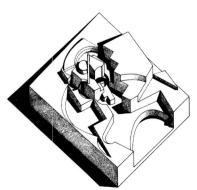

JOHN M. JOHN

Why do some plans look "klunky" and some don't? How does one attain a grace in resolving spacial conflicts? We can all recall those agonizing plans of octagon buildings, where each corner cranks so crudely that acute closets, elbowed walls, and overshaped (which is to say shapeless) rooms abound. Those designers have not yet learned the secrets: that void, not mass is the "lubrication"; that corners need not be turned by 45° plan bumpers or reflectors but rather by cuts in opposite walls (windows and doors aligning, inflection generated by an eccentric column against a wall); that an extra slot of space may always be invented to include a slipped entry; that paths can pinwheel about a gathering center rather than crossing. Since at least Michelangelo's plan of St. Peters, we have known how to impose more than one volumetric reading in the same space. But Renaissance plans still required carving of massive masonry piers and walls to establish such multiple readings, which made complex shapes of skin and bone, inconsistent in the round (that is to say front does not always result from or reveal back.) Yet in the free plan architecture inspired by Cubism and Purism each element may have a simple form integrity. Columns may be cylinders and walls simple slabs, but the space may yield a complex reading, just as in the paintings of Mondrian and Gris, where simple jigsaw cut out elements may create complex and ambiguous spaces in the overall composition.

"Spatial structure in both visual arts and built environment carries meaning. People can learn to read content and intention by understanding the clues as fragments of a larger whole. Design literacy contributes to the richness of urban experience. Developed, it facilitates appreciation of and demand for meaningful form. For students of design the analytic process provides an example that informs the synthetic process and is a clue to the ways in which we read and understand architectural space. For example, multiple space readings engender multiple plan solutions, i.e. layered/transparent orders of space (cues) at the same location. Architecture is perceived both two-dimensionally and three-dimensionally in the following ways: (1) We often experience architecture through drawings and photography where a system of codes like plan, axonometric or perspective projections provide clues to spatial resolutions. (2) As we inhabit space we encounter both two- and three-dimensional information, like a planar facade and a solid oblique corner. (3) Our understanding of architecture depends on an awareness of fluctuating visual clues, which are the simultaneous combination of flat and deep space perceptions that suggest a larger pattern of the plan, of which each visual clue is a fragment." David Diamond

Tantalizing speculations arise. Are the double height spaces Le Corbusier so loved a means to establish Purist layering -- the dotted line of the plan projection the equivalent to the tonal transparent overlays of a painting's picture plane? A corollary: was Le Corbusier's call for an "efficient height for the home" not only a way to get more stories into a building envelope, but also a device to extend Cézanne's compression of the picture plane's depth into the vertical dimension? Can the insights of Cubism lead to a way of not just marking space to make a box, but also to do things to and with the box? Suggestive examples include explosion of the box (Wright at Unity Temple), compression of the box (Le Corbusier at Villa Stein in Garches), bending the box (Alvar Aalto at MIT's Baker Dorm). Boxes can also be proportioned (Schindler and Meier) and intersected (Wright's Isobel Roberts House) in several dimensions simultaneously. Such "moves" mark of a certain sophistication in architectural skill, and are often in evidence in the classics of world architecture. Is this understanding then not a necessary development in the skill of an architectural student?

Painting, like architecture, is imbued with both two and three-dimensional structures. Comparative analysis through drawing and model may teach us a great deal about both arts. For example, models, transparent overlay drawings, diagrams and analytic drawings which map the three-dimensional structures described in a painting of Le Corbusier may reveal plastic analogs for structure, circulation, program, symmetry, pattern, etc. found in his architecture. This kind of study is revealing for architects and painters throughout the history of world culture.

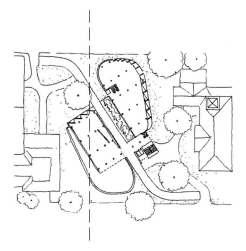

MARIA DI NATALE

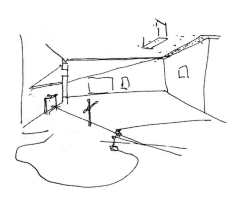

A ROOM IS A BRICK

The room is the architect's brick. A mason's brick is a filled solid we can easily see. A room is an empty solid that without its defining walls, floor, and ceiling would be "invisible". How can architects compose using empty solids? There is an art to making volume visible. We have observed that beginning students of architecture tend to evolve their perception of spacial order and skill in plan/ section and volumetric composition through the following major stages:

1. **Picturing sides:** the stage of flat space. The primary sense is that space is flat, that design is accomplished by drawing relationships within a plane. Hence an emphasis on design by drawing elevations or by making plans according to a linear sequence (I come in here, then go to vestibule here, then living room, then kitchen, *ad infinitum*].

2. **Relating Planes**: the stage of dawning consciousness of planar relationships in three dimensions. Plan and section or front and side elevations may be considered together for purposes of registration and "correctness"-- but not yet as informants to a spacial totality.

3. **Arranging Volumes**: the stage of an understanding of volumetric relationships, in an additive, and subtractive algebraic sense. For example, if 3 of room size **A** equals 1 room size **B**, then a double loaded corridor can accommodate both in the same length. This stage might also lead to a sense of depth relationships, so that if room **B** is double height, and the three **A** rooms are placed on the second level, the space under the three **A** spaces may establish an entry condition. Only rarely does this stage include a sense in which the spacial markings and events within one volume may influence the order of other volumes within the ensemble and throughout the site-- the beginning of plan and section "force" interactions. (This demands an understanding of phenomenal spacial transparency.)

4. **Composing Multivalent Volumes**: the stage of an understanding of how one space may read as part of several "moves" or orders of relationships. This can result in spacially ambivalent conditions of intersecting spaces, as in the Le Corbusier's Algiers Tower (opposite, far left). His design for the Carpenter Art Center at Harvard (plan, this page) gives multiple readings of the same volume in plan: the column grid in is parallel to the major orthogonal walls of the building, but the building itself is rotated to the diagonal of the local street grid. However, the diagonal of the column grid is actually orthogonal to the street. So in a sense to stand in the exhibition gallery is to be simultaneously part of two nonparallel but resolved orthogonal orders. Insights into figure-ground ambiguity, shared contours, and "hues of grids" become planning devices for eliminating "leftover" space in buildings, while helping to maintain the tension between flatness and depth.

5. **Composing light in space and time.** For the very best architects, there is a further possibility. What may be most important to architects about the Synthetic Cubist and Purist sensibility is that their strategies embrace spacial simultaneity and resolution of the total field, both extremely power-ful planning tools. This spacial understanding permits "both/and" situations to develop: both light and dark, both flat and deep; both plan and section, both opaque and transparent, both frontal and round, both orthogonal and diagonal oblique. The patient and attentive visitor can find a true sense of the presence of space in time, and the use of light to articulate spiritual and physical realities in the nave of the large chapel at La Tourette. As the sun sets in the west, it traces a beam of light up to and across the west wall through a narrow slot, converging on the altar, darkening to blood red. A skylight above reveals the deepest azure blue in contrast to the red as sun gives way to night.

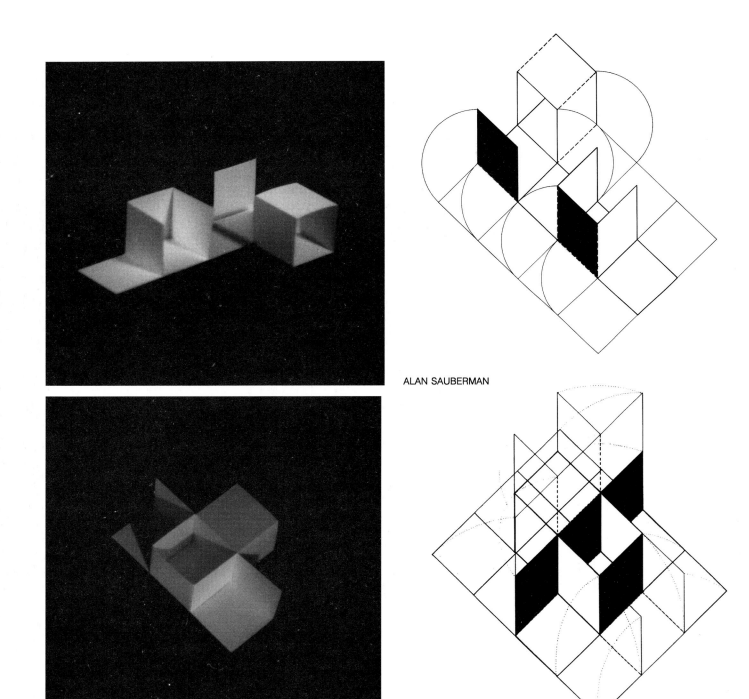

ALAN SAUBERMAN

PHIL SANTANTONIO

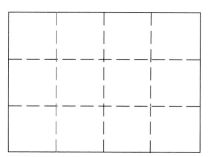

TIMESCALE: fold and cut one sheet = 12 minutes

impromptu

Cubism and Purism are particularly fascinated by the reciprocal relationship of the two dimensional world that lays across our eyes and the three dimensional world our bodies inhabit. This is perhaps one of the most crucial discoveries of 20th Century plastic arts, and is still uniquely suited to understanding our world vision today, where we must carefully time the meeting of a comet and a space mission so that their volumes will intersect, where we can see with sonograms babies before they are born and with CAT scans the inside of our skulls and the Earth, where lasers enable supermarket checkers to read the labels on canned goods from any angle and orientation, and where we understand that "live" television from Saturn takes hours to reach us. Cubism has presented us with a means to understand vision as a set of encoded views which can show complex volume and event relationships in both space and time. Our brains decode and recode these perceptions, so that a Cubist painting becomes a place to live in, an arena of and for animation. To further explore the relationship between dimensions, the following simple exercise explores a kind of *origami Purism* that reveals the plastic eloquence and power inherent in the transformation of surface into volume.

DYNAMICS

Origami Spaceframe

A. Fold one piece of standard 8 1/2 x 11" plain white bond or copier paper into a grid of three by four squares. Using folds and cuts (or careful tears) only, transform this paper into at least three cubes. The paper must stay intact as a single sheet, not broken into separate parts.
B. Repeat this exercise four more times, for a total of five *different* variations in all. Which is the strongest? Which is the weakest? Which configuration makes the richest space? Which the simplest? Which modulates light the most? etc...

Document each of these figures with the following:
1. A "plan" showing the unfolded plane, indicating torn edges with solid lines and folds with dotted lines.
2. A set of "final" views, either as projections (axonometric/perspective) or as photographs.

Just as sticks and stones can become rods and cubes (lines and points) in an architectonic order, so too can paper (plane) and perpendicular paper (fold line) generate volume. There is an implicit equivalence between mass and void. Plastic richness comes through a rhythm of filled and empty threads, a fabric of perforation. Thus does space, as the sum of filled and empty solids, become an arena of timeless change, of dramatic and creative tension.

It is interesting to note that the process of this exercise can be seen as a model of the phenomenon of the relationship between architect, builder, and client. The flat paper divided into twelve squares and notated to show cuts and folds is like the architect's plan. The act of folding the two-dimensional paper into three-dimensional volumes is like the contractor's construction of the house. And the final configuration of space defined by planes and volumes in light is like the dwelling the owner inhabits.

ANIMATION: In a series of as many frames of successive views as necessary, draw a set of instruction **diagrams** showing the operations required to transform the original plane into the final volume.

KEN JEROME

COLOR: 1. Value *2. Pre-collage* (See page 462 for more on these color exercises.)

THE DREAM, BOISGELOUP, JANUARY 24, 1932. OIL ON CANVAS, 51 1/4 X 38 1/8" (130 X 97 CM). ZERVOS VII, 364. COLLECTION MR. AND MRS. VICTOR W. GANZ, NEW YORK

ANIMATING

Time in Space: Sequence and simultaneity develop perception in depth

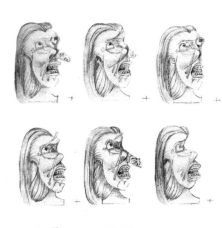

Picasso's famous painting *The Dream* is probably one of the clearest pictorial exploitations of the potential of simultaneous image-making. We see a woman whose head rests on her shoulder, eyes closed, obviously asleep. In profile, the lips are relaxed, the face is in repose. But then we note that the shadow that follows the forehead, nose, mouth, and chin also seems to separate the left side of her face from the right. The left side quietly levitates, animated with its own secret smile, brushing the first profile face on the lips with a kiss of-- of course!-- the dream! Once again we regard the full face in the whole painting, only now we cannot help but see the complexity of the image, frontal view and profile simultaneously, each with a shift of meaning, together a deeper pyschology than either alone.

When pictorial methods are combined for simultaneous spacial and psychological readings, the effect can be almost instantaneous, as in *The Dream* -- after all our eyes see all shapes in combination at once, even though our brains may unfold their meanings one after the other. When a single visual structure may be revealed as a set of images in sequence, each with its own plastic cues for simultaneous and ambiguous readings, every two-dimensional picture plane can become cinematic in its effect. Consider the following descriptive analysis of Picasso's study of a weeping woman:

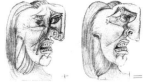

> In the old arts, horror was usually rendered through the distortion of the facial muscles, distortion of the open mouth, by enlarged and protruding eyeballs. Picasso intensified this approach by moving and distorting the usually immovable and undistortable elements of the body, such as the eyes, ears, and nose. In Guernica, he shifted the eyes away from their normal position; he turned the ears upside down. In the studies for the mural he transformed the eye into a cup and the lower eyelid into a saucer from which tears poured. He exposed the tongue of a screaming, horror stricken victim as a flame, at other times as a dagger to signify despair. In one of these studies he showed a dozen variations of a face, changing the profile of a young mother under the impact of unspeakable suffering-- into the distorted, crumbled features of an old woman. This was done through interweaving the features of a panicky, quickly aging, hideous creature, each expression growing out of the other without breaking the oneness. The same etching, if looked at upside down, solved the enigma by displaying the deteriorated, piggish face of Hitler, the cause of the bestial destruction. The old technique of the trashy "double image" postcards was used here with unusual subtlety to make the psychological spacetime as transparent as an x-ray photograph.
>
> from George Kepes, *Vision in Motion* Theobald, Chicago, 1969, p.250-51

The phenomenon of dimensional ambiguity becomes very clear (yet more mysterious) in color. If a violet area is placed where red and blue zones appear to overlap, layers of space become visible. This is a way to achieve depth without the devices of perspective such as diagonal, size hierarchy, or vanishing point. These devices are thus free as other means of expression. Implied overlapping can create ambiguities of transparency and shared contours. The careful choice of colors may create a visual field that seems filled with light, even though there is no clear or direct source of illumination. Multiple light sources can thus be introduced, which in turn can imply rotation, fracturing, spacial discontinuity with the visual field. Polychromy can translate these pictorial discoveries into the world of three dimensional (plus!) built form. Volume is implied in Cubist/Purist painting, not only through the "front" view of a traditional perspective but also through information about back, inside, and out-- the way architects see their building designs, in plan/section/elevation. Overlapping planes and cast shadows from many (perhaps conflicting) light sources, or from a general luminance of carefully selected color relationships without any shadow at all, create an essentially dynamical vision with roving and multiple viewpoints, as opposed to the fixed station point of classical perspective. These paintings record a perception of the forces that occur as volumes intersect and order each other.

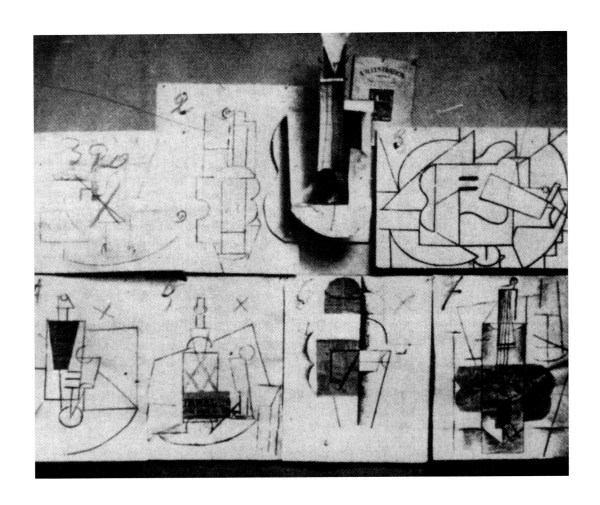

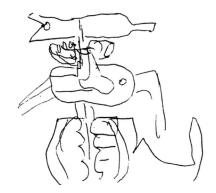

PABLO PICASSO. *GUITAR*. PARIS (1912-1913). SHEET METAL AND WIRE,
30½ X 13 1/8 X 7 5/8". COLLECTION, THE MUSEUM OF MODERN ART, NEW YORK.
GIFT OF THE ARTIST.

CUBISM: CONSTRUCTING SPACE FROM TWO TO THREE DIMENSIONS

"Only those who play can be serious." Marcel Duchamp, painter and chess player

There are many ways to skin a cat. Converting two-dimensional planes into three dimensional structures is both simple and complex. For example, take a piece of paper, crumple it in your hands. The result is easy to make, hard to draw, still harder to construct geometrically or plot in a CAD system. The resolution of the complex crushing forces is chaotic-- predictable to some general degree, but unpredictable in its local specifics. Even when the steps are simple and clear, there may be no unique connection between a three dimensional figure and its two dimensional origins. A cube can be made from many different configurations of folding six flat contiguous squares. To know that a solid is the source of many possible planar mappings is to enjoy the plastic and speculative nature of form in space. Cubism is the 20th Century's gift to vision-- it is a powerful way of both seeing and knowing the world through flux and change. Perhaps the most important work in 20th Century art is Picasso's and Braque's exploration of how inhabited space and pictorial vision meet in the picture plane, a way of seeing that has come to be called Cubism. From about 1905 to 1913, the very years Einstein developed his theories of relativity, Picasso and Braque extended the explorations they found in Cézanne's painting, and invented Cubism. Cubism enabled artists to concentrate on the plastic form of their world and the transition between feeling and looking as a viable subject matter in itself; the subject matter of the composition is the composition, not the pieces of the composition.

A beginner in the study of the interaction of volume sees stones and sticks as points and lines in empty space, arrangeable in piles, layers, or other mass configuration. An adept sees pregnant and solid volume marked by the position of linear and pointlike elements. Through cutting and bending, shifting and twisting, the expert also finds the means to transform planes into volume.

The visual structure of the 2D field implies many 3D interpretations. And the volumetric order of the 3D field implies many 2D renderings. Picasso exploited these insights in a witty and inventive manner. He found in the wooden mass and acoustic volume of a guitar a motif which suggested a re-presentation of spacial order through an arrangement of layers of cut, folded, and re-glued cardboard. The photo of Picasso's studio shows that the guitar construction was a three-dimensional "drawing" in a series of studies that included other guitar drawings (#2 and 3), but also contained studies of tabletops with the objects of a Parisian cafe-- newspaper, siphon, etc. (#4 and 5). Study # 5 shows virtually all the plastic elements in the guitar sculpture-- the long neck, the central box, the sound hole, the curved wall, and the diagonal pegboard at the end of the neck-- but now these elements are transformed into bottle stem, metal mesh over the glass bottle body, circular plan of the bottle, table edge, and newspaper, respectively. The essential form of the drawing and the picture space *remains the same,* even though the subject matter of the two works appear entirely different.

The real subject of these studies is the *arrangement* of elements, whether they make a guitar or cafe tabletop. The configuration of masses and volumes in space and the interplay between three-dimensional construction and two-dimensional vision is the primary concern. Picasso claimed that it didn't matter whether his paintings were upside down or right side up. He said he tested a painting's composition by rotating it through all four 90 degree orientations. Le Corbusier recounts a related incident. While flying over the Himalayas, between his home in Paris and his commission to design a new capital city for India at Chandigarh, he looked at a reproduction of one of his early still life paintings and discovered that by rotating the image 90 degrees he could find in it the visage of a bull. From this emerged his long and fruitful *Taureaux* (Bull) series of paintings.

EMILIO SUSA

DOING

DYNAMICS: SPACE PAINTING

Transform a Cubist or Purist painting into three-dimensional space.

Obtain a good color reproduction (museum post card or laser copy) of a Synthetic Cubist or Purist painting (Ozenfant, Gris, Le Corbusier, Picasso, Braque). Build its order of perceptions, ie the spaces it demands, simultaneous, transparent, overlapping, warped, diagonal, layered. Make small (4" to 6") study models using construction paper (or pasted together double-sided **Color-aid**), cutting directly with scissors. Discover how the folding, bending, and joinery become part of the volumetric structure as well as the order of construction. Folded paper can yield structural sections like I-beam and folded plates. An elegant solution may use no glue or tape at all, only tab-and-slot, folds, etc. to integrate construction. Note how perception of volumes as much as rendering of objects is the subject of Cubism. Relief may emphasize planar and frontal ambiguities, but at the expense of a fully realized spacial solution without "back" or "sides". Using material of a single color may highlight purely volumetric relationships, while color models can explore polarities within the painting-- such as black/white, complimentary contrast (red/green, blue/orange, yellow/violet), grouping (all the blues, etc.), or...

Another way to think about this study is that you are the architect/builder. You have just been issued the drawings. But it is only one page. Yet it is plan, section, perspective, elevation and axonometric simultaneously. Animate the transformations necessary to construct the volumes you mind will inhabit.

JOHN CONTE

In your model, explore the contrast between object and structure. Consider issues of representation and abstraction, which touch upon problems of composition, form, and meaning in painting collage and architecture. Subsequent models, based on the structure already discovered, will explore perceptions of depth. Locate/mediate foreground, middle ground, and background, using clues consistently interpreted from the cubist work. (overlapping, color/light contrast, oblique views, etc....) After exploring the ambiguities of structure and depth, determining a "correct" resolution becomes the next level of inquiry. Some suggestions on working methods for this project: Keep turning your model so as to be able to see it from all sides. If you only concentrate on the "front" view, the back will be undeveloped and unrelated to the whole. The same is true for top, bottom, sides. Remember, the model is a plastic 3D construction, **not** a picture. To go beyond a literal reconstruction of the color areas in the original painting, first imagine what views the painting would yield if its volumetric order were seen from the sides of the canvas, from the top, bottom, and back. Then, to avoid simply building a dollhouse shadow box, be sure to build perceptions of space as an accretion of views that reveal what you know to be true of the combined 2D-3D space of the painting-- a circle in plan becomes an ellipse in perspective but can be reconstructed as both circle and ellipse (or cylinder or sphere!) in model.

DOCUMENT the final model and other results of your studies through architectural means: plans, sections, elevations, axonometric, perspective, etc. in ink on paper. You may choose to draw the opacities, transparencies, and densities which the actual pieces of the model represent. Consider the "closure" within your model as partial, as more dense than outside the model while permitting continuous space to perforate the continuous mass of construction.

COLOR: 3. Hue. 4. Chroma. (See page 462 for more.)

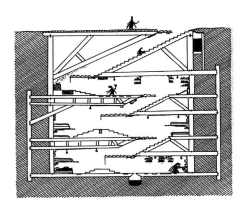

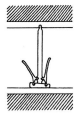

FROM *THE PLANIVERSE*,
BY A. K. DEWDNEY

THE HOUSE

The house was essentially a large, rectangular excavation subdivided by beams which were held together by double spikes and formed into a rigid, well-formed structure. Although it appeared to be very complicated, this structure consisted of only 13 horizontal, 16 diagonal, and 22 vertical beams, hardly enough pieces from which to construct a single, three-dimensional room! It is just as well that the Ardeans enjoy such an economy of means, for their construction methods are equally restricted. Nails are useless since they part any piece of material they may be driven through. Saws are impossible. A beam could only be cut with something like a hammer and chisel. Nevertheless, beams may be attached to each other by double-pointed spikes or by pegs driven into prepared holes. Glue supplements the holding power of spikes and pegs, sometimes even replacing them. In fact, glue comes close to being a universal fastener for the Ardeans, not just in houses but in every sort of construction.

The "swing stairs" are worthy of closer attention. For example, the swing stair at the entrance to the house had a hinge and a spring at one end.

A traveler from the west crosses the entrance to the house by stepping on the swing stair, which under the traveler's weight swings down, until it meets the stairway. The traveler descends three steps, ascends three steps, and continues on. Crossing the entrance from the east is only slightly more difficult: the traveler pushes down on the swing stair with his or her lower eastern arm, catching it with the eastern foot, and then ascending.

THE DOOR/WALL

This strange but useful device has just four moving parts: a hinged column, two levers, and a shoe. The shoe fits into the bottom of the column at an angle so that it acts like a wedge. It is pushed under the column in order to support the ceiling and it is pulled away to allow the column to hang freely.

Approaching the door/wall from the left, an Ardean pushes the lever, pulling the shoe from out from under the column. It is then possible to swing the column to the right as the Ardean walks under it. In order to return the door/wall once more to its supporting role, the Ardean now pushes the lever on the other side of the door/wall.

An Ardean passing under the door/wall in the opposite direction does precisely the same things, but pulls the lever instead of pushing it.

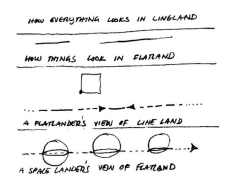

HOW EVERYTHING LOOKS IN LINELAND

HOW THINGS LOOK IN FLATLAND

A FLATLANDER'S VIEW OF LINE LAND

A SPACE LANDER'S VIEW OF FLATLAND

BEYOND THIS DIMENSION

It is hard enough to see empty volume. Can we ever see the four dimensions of spacetime-- or any other four-dimensional phenomenon? Whether or not we can record such images with our retina, we can understand them with our mind's eye. Mathematicians often lead the way into new visions of the reality the rest of us wake up a little bit later to discover they are perfectly evident to our eyes as well. As a way to introduce the abstract notions of geometry in more than three dimensions, Edwin Abbott wrote a wonderful little book called *Flatland*. The inhabitants of two-dimensional Flatland are lines and polygons, who occupy a planar realm. In a few revelatory dreams, one citizen, an open-minded square, encounters first Lineland and then Spaceland. Lineland is a one-dimensional domain inhabited by points and lines. Spaceland resembles our familiar surroundings. The square vainly attempts to enlighten the king of Lineland about the richness and superiority of Flatland. Linelanders, trapped in their one-dimensional line world, are unable to see beyond or to pass their adjacent neighbors. Flatlanders enjoy lateral as well as forward-and-backward movement, and thus are free to assemble and choose their neighbors at will. However, when the open-minded square meets a sphere from Spaceland, who grows in Flatland from point to circle and back to point before disappearing, the square has difficulty imagining a third dimension which doesn't conform to his everyday experience. Spacelanders are free to circulate "upward not northward", heresy in Flatland. "Upward, not northward," implies a privileged plan overview, unimaginable to Flatlanders.

The story helps us understand perception in many dimensions. Linelanders can see only points, whether they are points, lines seen on axis, planes, or geometric solids pierced by the trajectory of Lineland. Likewise, Flatlanders can see only points and lines, be they points, lines, polygon planes or cross-sections through geometric solids seen edgewise. They cannot see planes, even though they themselves are planar. We who seem to live in 3D Spaceland see only two-dimensional shapes on the planar surface of the retina. Our knowledge of solid space and depth depends on perception from another dimension. We must move out of space and into time to build the fully stereometric qualities of Spaceland from the picture plane images in our memory. A "fourth-dimensional" awareness of space and time demands the accumulated experience of all our senses. Video, film, newspapers, software, and blueprints all present many dimensions of experience together. If a picture equals a thousand words, then a plan may equal a thousand pictures.

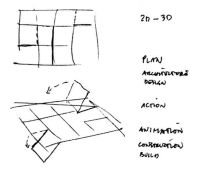

2D — 3D

PLAN
ARCHITECTURE
DESIGN

ACTION

ANIMATION
CONSTRUCTION
BUILD

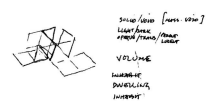

SOLID/VOID [MASS-VOID]
LIGHT/DARK
OPAQUE/TRANS/REFL

VOLUME

INHABIT
DWELLING
INHABIT

Another mathematician, A.K. Dewdney, wrote *Planiverse,* an extended meditation on how Flatland might really work. His marvelous book explores the biology, mechanics, art, and architecture (naval and aeronautical as well as domestic) of a Flatland civilization as complex as our own. By solving digestion, traffic, security, in two dimensions, he provides insight into thinking beyond assumed dimensional limits. For example, inside our own bodies the complex weave of blood vessels and nerves is akin to how plumbing and wiring in a building manage to avoid cutting each other. Yet how rarely is this topological sophistication applied to a problem like traffic-- only on some highways do cloverleafs and overpasses keeping crossing roads from intersecting. And only in such evolved plans as Olmstead's Central Park in New York City do such weavings keep cars from hitting people and people from slowing down cars.

Perhaps painters too are mathematicians-- mind learners of a mathematics of the infinite Present always before us in the here and now as light cascades into our brain in an electromagnetic and chemical continuum of boundless configuration. Wayne Thiebaud, with only a little help from the topography of San Francisco, shows us in *Holly Park Ridge* that the plan of a city may also be the picture plane of an apartment window. In what dimensions does this vision exist?

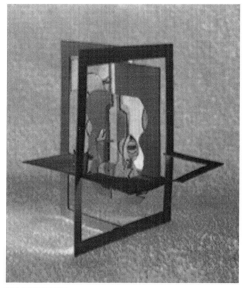

YU CHI YANG

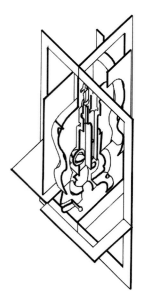

RICHARD PRESTON

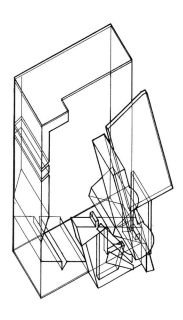

RAY GUITIERREZ

REFLECTING

What do Cubism and Purism suggest for architects? How are these masterful paintings guides for making architecture? How do you draw the plan of the space and time of a child's swing? Recent studies hint that the path between the brain's optic lobe and the eye's retina is reversible, suggesting that vision and imagination may inform each other (a good argument for an architect to travel with sketchbook in hand). Alissa Feldman, a student who pursued these studies entirely in the virtual space of computer modeling, said of her images, "This is a *sketch* model..." To the architect or plastician who composes volumes, hard line precision and shaded rendering remain means, not ends, and the quest is not just superficial pictorial pleasantry, but deeper spatial order, perhaps simultaneously in the multiple dimensions of surface, solids, and spacetime.

Robert Slutzky, a painter, has long been a wonderful teacher and critic of architecture. Reviewing student work he is like a surgeon, cutting right to a problem's essence, which invariably is one of an unclear or improperly formulated geometric conception. (He is known to ask a seemingly simple question like "Why is it symmetric?" that comes as a revelation to the designer. *Of course!! Shrinking the east and expanding the west gardens will solve parking entry and privacy problems, after all sunrise and sunset are similar but basically different phenomena --I coulda had a V8!!*) We are privileged to sample his writings on the pages immediately following. Cubism and Purism teach that each plastic element may be formally simple and clear without sacrificing complexity in the whole. Like the art of Gris and Picasso, Slutzky's paintings show how plastic elements may be interlocking shapes which create compositions of multiple space perceptions in both two and three dimensions.

The Space Painting study usually produces quite revealing results. At first almost everyone tries to make a dollhouse "model" of the "picture", seeking identifiable objects-- tables, bottles, flowers, doorways-- to build what that would "really be". When students realize that Cubism can communicate *perception* of objects, they begin to abandon their literal fantasies of the space of the painting. Realizing that a Cubist painting can be about how to construct the everyday vision we operate with simultaneously-- how to synthesize in a single image or model that experience of complex multivalent spacial ambiguity that is the swirl of our true everyday experience and how to confront the actuality of the picture plane (avoiding Caravaggio's illusion of a hole or Veronese's false window)-- almost everyone tries to make a simple relief. At this point a very effective critique is "what would such a space look like from the side, top, back, etc.?" Only then is plane transformed into volume, is depth implied through layer and rotation, and is the ambiguity of spacial overlap exploited. Further study may reveal, for example, how Gris deliberately played a fabric of planar symmetries against spacial asymmetries. This can lead to greater skill in clarifying form to articulate plastic possibility and in resolving plans by making one space read as several things simultaneously.

SUGGESTED READINGS:

Abbott, Edwin. *Flatland*
Dewdney, A.K. *Planiverse*
Huizinga, J. *Homo Ludens*
Ingersoll, Richard. *Le Corbusier, A Marriage of Contours*
Konig, H. G. *The Planar Architecture of Juan Gris*
Le Corbusier. *Creation is a patient search*
Loran, Erle. *Cézanne's Composition*
Matisse, Henri. *Jazz*
Rosenblum, Robert. *Picasso and the Typography of Cubism*
Rubin, William. *Picasso Braque*
Slutzky, Riobert. *Transparency 1 and 2, Cube Chrome, Aqueous Humor*

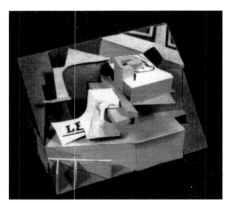

JAMES SCALA

APRES LE PURISME

by Robert Slutzky

You know these joys: to feel the generous tummy of a vase, to stroke the delicate neck, to explore the subtleties of its lines… letting oneself be gently seduced by the fascinating enamels, by the splendor of the yellows, and by the velvetlike blues; to witness the lively struggle of the brutal black masses and victorious white elements.
Le Corbusier, in a letter to Perrin, 11 June 1911

The painting PHYSICALLY is a masterly massage appliance.
Ozenfant and Jeanneret, Après le cubisme, 1918

Verre et Journal, a little known Juan Gris still life of 1917, now in the storage racks of the Kunstmuseum in Basel, offers the opportunity to open yet another discourse between Cubist and Purist aesthetics. The latter first took issue with the former in a manifesto entitled *Après le Cubisme*, coauthored by Amedée Ozenfant and Le Corbusier (then still Charles Edouard Jeanneret) in 1918. In this document, general praise of Cubist geometries is dimmed by sharp criticism: the Cubist distortion of objects, wrote the authors, had the effect of diminishing the "credibility" of still-life painting; presumably taking to task Picasso, Braque, and perhaps Gris, they cited the "fallacies" of triangular pipes and square guitars. The two collaborators proposed to rescue such objects-types from pictorial misrepresentation by accentuating their inherent architectonic qualities, depicting them through the more "honest" and universal definitions of plan, section, and elevation.

Within this idealized image, a happy *marriage des contours* was to take place, the interaction of concavities, convexities, and orthogonalities engendering a dynamic unfolding of space and surface. To guarantee the preservation of object identities, Ozenfant and Jeanneret prescribed a palette derived from academic painting.

What this systematic vision of the external world entailed was a rather Protestant notion of aesthetics. The mass-produced object of daily use was to be elevated to the highest order of representational importance: mundane utensils were to occupy a place formerly reserved, in still-life paintings of the sixteenth through nineteenth centuries, for the nobler elements of nature, and earlier, before the invention of the still-life genre, for gods and persons of highest standing. Whereas the Cubists had sought to invigorate inert bottles and guitars with the presences of daily life - fruits, bread, newspapers, household patterns and textures - the Purists undertook to ban such pictorial stuff from the canvas, celebrating instead the refinement and elegance of containers of machined shape.

Yet if one looks closely at Le Corbusier's own paintings of this period, one sees how transparency and contour acquire a figural presence not really consonant with the Purist program. It does not require much imagination to suggest that Apres le cubisme is more the polemic of Ozenfant than Jeanneret. A comparison between the still lives of both painters reveals that whereas the former hones his canvases closely to the prescribed rules of composition and palette, the latter tends immediately toward the subjective and arcane, suggesting, even if in ever so muted a way, the anthropomorphic characteristics latent in the products of a rational technology. Thus pitchers, glasses, bottles, carafes, siphons, pots, dishes, dice, boxes, lanterns, architectural moldings, books, violins, and guitars become actors on the stage of a still-life theater (notwithstanding the curious inclusion of musical instruments in the repertory of mass production). Reclining guitars become surrogate odalisques; bottles bad jugs double as orators and statesmen. The "noun" definitions proclaimed in the manifesto give way, in effect, to a syntax nuanced by "adverbial" modifications and "adjectival" qualifiers.

These early Purist efforts of Le Corbusier, often perfunctorily included in the pantheon of modernist art and only recently reexamined within the canon of the architect's work, frequently amount to energetic and complex

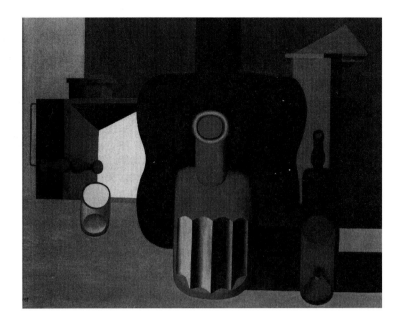

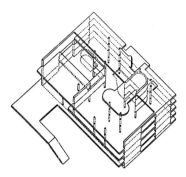

formal and chromatic cadenzas. They not only expose a painterly original-ity, but also recall, in strong metaphors, the history and culture of West-ern painting. But before looking at a few of these works, we must return to the small but monumental Gris still life in the Basel museum's reper-tory. In doing so, we should recall Le Corbusier's praise of Gris: "the strongest of the Cubists."

In the Gris painting we have a seemingly typical Synthetic Cubist still-life arrangement that upon first glance suggests a traditional foreground-middleground-background schema. The orange-browns are appropriately deployed to configurate a table leg in the lower left corner, a tableau in the center supports an unclear cluster of objects, while a piece of wall paneling in the upper right corner completes the flattened but essentially Renais-sance recessional reading of objects in space. The style of rendering is peculiarly Cubist, but it is imbued with a disturbing quality of predeter-mined diagonal symmetries. A pair of opposing and reversed dark shapes in he upper left and lower right corners folds the rest of the composition back into the painting's center, illuminating other sets of complementary shape oppositions that also draw attention to the first and last two letters of the newspaper banner, LE JOURNAL. This syntax of mirror symme-tries triggers a revelatory new reading: gender, hinted at by the concavity and convexity of various object-shapes, now surfaces linguistically. Thus in the black-on-white LE diagonally concluded by the gray-on-black AL, a seemingly innocent play of metonymic fragments opens up the possibil-ity of assigning gender to the painting's pictorialized nouns. LE remains a masculine article (French), but now stimulates the reversal of AL to LA, the feminine article (French). This sudden dialogue of gender reverber-ates back to LE, causing its reversal to read EL, masculine (Spanish). And so a subliminal game of gender interchange, one that Gris will employ much more consciously in his later paintings (for example, Le Canigou, where an over play of Freudian readings overlays a "conventional" still-life composition), becomes an added, witty investment into presumably "dumb" objects. At the same time the reversal of French to Spanish sug-

gests the painter's own relation to Paris, a rather significant layer of autobiographical reference.

I have undertaken this somewhat extended reading of a literary-visual pun in the Gris painting to dramatize the potency of Cubist abstraction to generate new meaning. In the canvases of painters like Picasso and Gris, all manner of anthropomorphic and sexual references disguise themselves within a highly organized pattern of innocent geometries. The Euclidean object definitions, nouns of traditional representationalism, are transmo-grified by their displacements and reconstructions into poetically allusive roles. Tellingly, a mass-produced object like the daily newspaper, a fa-vored point of departure for the Cubist literary-transformational game, is excluded from the Purist vocabulary. One can only speculate why this and other typographical material are so thoroughly banished: perhaps words and letter in themselves were seen as too culturally determined to be "primary" enough for the universal comprehension to which Ozenfant and Le Corbusier polemically aspired.

In Cubism, metaphor functions as the subversive and emancipatory instru-ment of a pictorial system in which precise geometries work to fragment objects into alchemical othernesses. The oscillation between surface and depth definitions, between two-dimensional infrastructures and illusion-istic representation, provides a friction of contradiction that radically extends the duration of aesthetic time. It is no accident that Cubism attracted the attention of the poets. It no doubt attracted a side of Le Corbusier as well, despite his and Ozenfant categorical demotion of Cubist idiosyncrasies. If it was the academically trained young architect from a Swiss watchmak-ing town who would naturally have gravitated toward the technical ratio-nalism and pictorial precisions of the Purist program, then it was the traveler to the East, exposed to the exoticisms and sensory seductions of an altogether other culture, then immersed in the intoxicating expansive-ness of a Parisian milieu with its attendant cast of luminaries, who would have been susceptible to the pull of a much more liberating aesthetic.

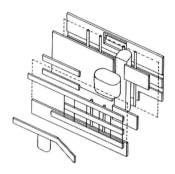

Three Purist-period paintings by Le Corbusier in the La Roche collection in Basel prompt an elaboration of this hypothesis. The *Nature morte a la cruche blanche sur fond bleu* (1920), we are struck by the refinement of interpenetrating and overlapping forms that, in sharing either contiguous contours or common color values, disintegrate the literal spatial emplacements of the objects being represented. Thus, for example, the circularity of the mouth of the goblet in the lower left foreground seems to be inextricably bound to the hemicircular motif of the red-topped architectural molding (open book?), which, in its shared relation to a darker red, flat-axonometric upper half of a guitar lying behind, completes a triadic relationship of expanding hemicircles. The same goblet's transparent adhesion to the dark bottle behind it to the left, and its sharing of the gray value in its right-hand portion with a second bottle above it to the right, dematerializes the prominent stage position of this frontal actor so that it gets subsumed by its taller "parents." What emerges is a metaphor of family - embodied by the goblet and both tall glass containers, the one to the right most anthropomorphic of all by virtue of the strange convexity of its neck/head, the threesome proudly posing in what finally reads as an architected interior space composed by a rescaled vision of ordinary subjects.

Meanwhile the pitcher on the right is attempting to escape its compressed imprisonment. It is checked, however, by the thin surrounding field at its right, but its alliterating bottom curvature completing the half-guitar to its left, and by its circular handle, which triangulates with the round mouth of the goblet at lower left. At the same time, the pitcher's spout nudging the painting's right-hand edge is almost symmetrically countered by a wedge-shaped fascia on the left, a form seeming to belong to the tuning-neck of the guitar and located a hair's breadth from puncturing the left-hand edge of the canvas. These two projective elements, the pitcher's spout and the trapezoidal wedge, create a state of extreme middleground tension by their counterpoint with the compressive vertical elements.

The title conveys further ambiguities. The blue field is almost totally obscured by the coulisse arrangement of objects in front of it, while the white pitcher is nearly mirrored diagonally by a shaped lantern(?) face, which through its echoing scale and color value effects a contradiction between a background element and one in a more prominent fore- or middleground position. The coloration of the whole speaks mysteriously of complementarity - not a typically Purist device - with a predominant red-green-gray interplay inflected by bleached yellows and shaded blues. One also notes the way the offset "navel" of the canvas is stated by a shift of the mouth of the fluted drinking glass diagonally upward to the left of the painting's actual center.

This latter pictorial device is also seen in *Composition a las lanterne et a la guitare* (1920), where the circular opening of the fluted bottle is shifted to the upper right, and in the later *Verres, pipes et bouteilles sur fond clair* (1922), where the eye-level rim of the central goblet splits the painting into equal top and bottom halves. This perfectly centered horizontal anticipates Le Corbusier's predilection to establish a reflective center line or oculus in his architectural and urban elevations, for example the middle-rise housing blocks of the Ville Contemporaine. In the Composition a la lanterne et a la guitare, a palette reminiscent of Gris - red-browns, orange-browns, pale ocher-grays, and blue-grays - organizes a decidedly asymmetrical composition in which a sparse area of light color and chunky elements on the left counterpoints a dense, dark-brown field on the right characterized by compressed verticals. This counterpoint between left and right enframes the two nearly symmetrically aligned main figures, which shift rightward and constitute an intermediary section of light-on-dark and dark-on-light articulations, thus weaving the left-hand side of the canvas through the right side. What is striking about the two central actors is the interchange of figural meanings: the guitar is cropped at the top so as to leave out its tuning board and thus reads as a fat, flat flask; the bottle in turn pirates the guitar's sounding hole, fretboard, and string parts, becoming less a container of liquid and more one of sound. Thus

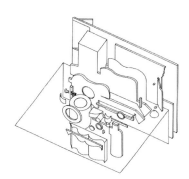

liquidities and acoustics reverse their respective vessels, completing a surrealistic exchange of subject and object. The highly articulated fluting on the front bottle also suggests the hand of the sculptor/musician/painter/architect - multiple roles that Le Corbusier would aspire to embody.

Nor is such a painting all that far from the metaphysical atmosphere of a De Chirico. And in light of Le Corbusier's own affirmation of the role of his painting in the formation of his architectural concepts, we can already see premonitions of the more arcane presences that will lurk within the distorted forms and poetic encadrements of some of his later architecture. The Purist surface manipulations of plan-section-elevation, intended to elucidate the concealed structures of presumably ordinary objects, now in fact have just the opposite effect: that of engendering ambiguously related animistic subjects, trapped within a garden of delights rather more mechanistically inspired than that of Bosch. In the case of the 1922 still life, there is an attempt to infuse translucency into earthy opacities; ocher-orange-green-grays tinted and shaded within a compressed range of values work to release the central black modeling of the fluted goblet, thereby minimally yet powerfully asserting its paradoxical presence. This curious overlapping distortion in what should have been a polemically clear representation recalls the figural excesses of the Gris pointing discussed earlier and definitively signifies Le Corbusier's transition from the Purist vocabulary of reasonable clear tectonic projections to a painterly repertory with distortive and enigmatic characteristics.

Taken together, these four paintings - three by Le Corbusier, one by Gris - offer more than a glimpse of the new poetics of modernist still-life painting. With Gris, the wedding of Euclidean and Orphic impulses will be consummated in his late works of the 1920s. With Le Corbusier, the constraints of Purist aesthetics, of compositional literalness, will be radically loosened, giving way to more ambiguous space and content and allowing the artist's psychic energies to overflow into his work - not only from the containers being represented, but also from the larger, more metaphorical ones that become the canvases and architectural projects

themselves. Just as the Dom-ino is succeeded by the subtler and darker intricacies of the Jeanneret-La Roche house and villas Savoye and Garches, so these, in turn, will be replaced by the more outward energies of the Pavillon Suisse, the Palace of the Soviets, and the Algiers Obus, and, still later, by the poetic imagination of Ronchamp and La Tourette, two structures that encapsulate the subliminal and the sublime.

What could you not find contained in a canvas if you could obtain the painter's confession? But the canvas goes out alone, making or mot making its way, bearing its message. There is a world in a painting or a building as there is also in a work of city planning. Seek, and you shall find. Look into the depths of the work and ask yourself questions. There are illuminations and scenes; there are hours of fullness, agonies, radiant or menacing skies, houses and mountains, seas and lagoons, suns and moons. And there are besides all the cries of the subconscious, sensual or chaste, and everything you can imagine.

Le Corbusier, *New World of Space*, 1948

"Tout calice est demeure." (Every vessel is a dwelling place.)
Jean Laroch, quoted in Gaston Bachelard, Poetics of Space

Notes

My thanks to Joan Ockman for her essential collaboration on this effort. This paper is published in German in *Le Corbusier und Raoul La Roche: Architekt und Maler*, Bauherr und Sammler (Basel: Architekturmuseum in Basel, 1987), p. 53-59. It is reprinted here with the kind permission of Ulrike Jehle-Schulte Strathous.

1. For an extended discussion of this theme, see Robert Slutzky, "Aqueous Humor," Oppositions 19-20 (Winter-Spring 1980): 27-51.

COLOR/STRUCTURE/PAINTING

The primary subject matter of my painting is color. For this reason I call it color/structure painting. Consciously turning its back on illusionism and allegory, this kind of art attempts to define its own universe of meanings, and thus, in the polemical act of purifying itself from extraneously derived languages and imageries, aspires to ineffability. How, then do I presume to talk about it? The very notion of talking about an ineffable object is paradoxical.

To be sure, the "unspeakable" painting aspired to by modernist abstraction has frequently had to bear the noisome burden of an irrelevant, often arcane, and sometimes brutish critical language claiming to interpret it. Relatively young (in the perspective of five hundred year of Western art) and therefore fragile, it has been far more vulnerable than representational painting to the violations of a prose language using methods of scientism to verify its seeming simplicity, its overt pictorialness.

The Russian linguistic critic Roman Jakobson distinguished two aspects of language, derived from two conventional tropes of classical rhetoric, the metonymic and the metaphoric. The metonymic mode tends, in the realm of literature, to describe the language of narrative prose. It proceeds by a chain of associations based upon relationships of contiguity and by the substitution of representative parts of wholes. Because contiguity implies a logic of cause-effect, and the associational chain leads to a piling up of "relevant" details, it is strongly realistic. The visual form to which it may be said to correspond most closely is representational painting, which, like realistic literature, may be fruitfully analyzed in terms of its fidelity to or distortion from its subject, and its use of "local color." In this form of painting, the primacy accorded to the mimetic and narrative image tends to assure the authority of the painting's content.

Metaphor, on the other hand, is the predilection of poetry, of rhyme over reason. It is a touchstone, a quantum leap out of the constraints of conventional causality into a transforming relationship based on some aspect of analogous structure. Metaphor connects "pig" to "fig" sheerly by virtue of sound, as well as to "glutton" by a conceptual jump; metonymy, moving from the whole to its parts, would connect it to "ham" and "oink." Funda-

mentally unstable and momentaneous, and in this sense opposite from the metonym, which becomes codified by time-honored "trains of thought," the metaphor lives and dies in an atemporal, self-combustible instant of interaction between its two (or more) juxtaposed ideas. But its effect is universal and revelatory: "the metaphor is not the enigma but the solution of the enigma" (Paul Ricoeur).

In the world of painting, color, when inseparably bound to structure, and immersed in a total relational matrix of pictorial cohesion, resonates with metaphoric energies. The effects of juxtaposition, transposition, and competition lead color/structure painting by way of metaphor from revelry in the pure vibrancy of analogous structure, to revelation, finally to reverie, the contemplative dream of an aesthetic world outside of chronological time.

It is in this sense that metaphor is the language of ineffability. The oxymoron suggests the precariousness of the condition. For the ineffable language has to be both daring and cautious so as not to shackle its pulsating subject in linguistic chains, using its technique of analogy as a deferential probe, coaxing to the surface whatever meanings might emerge from the hermetic envelop of color/structure. It speaks through the power of evocation rather than description, extracting essences and cultivating presences. It prefers the more subtle probes of the etymologist to the transfixing classificatory pins of the entomologist, reaching into the unconscious memory of culture, impregnating rather than impaling its mute subject, always seeking to render visible the essential mystery without reducing it.

The color/structure painter discovers his motive for metaphor in conjuring "the half-colors of quarter-things" (Wallace Stevens).

Let us attempt to use this metaphoric language of illumination in discussing some qualities of the painter's cosmos. What is a canvas but the substantiation of an ideal two dimensional plane? Quadrilateral or not, when frontally manifested to the eye, this plane possesses certain innate energies that distinguish it from all other planes. Its existence is further transformed by stretching it over a supportive frame. The raw canvas not only has its own coloration but its own texture, which possesses a specific reflective quality. Its tooth determines the way it grips the pigment and sucks in the medium, and these prehensile and oral activities together with its confrontational display of surface, suggest a physiognomic entity, a visage, a face. The frame behind this anthropomorphized canvas, like the skeleton and muscle behind the skin, invests the plane with a certain resiliency, a tone that is taut yet impressionable, a complexion that gives and takes. Unlike other planes that get pinned to hard surfaces or are those surfaces, the stretched canvas, in its elastic buoyancy, awaits the first thrusts and parries of the painter.

The painter usually prepares his raw canvas with a ground, applying layers of white gesso or lead-white to heighten the surface's luminosity and tame its tooth. The word ground is fertile with meaning. When coupled with the Gestalt term field, it assumes the significance of earth-ground, suggesting a horizontal plane/plain of landscape awaiting growth through man's cultivation. It is the beginning of culture - from the Latin *colere*, to cultivate, to live in, to bestir oneself, to be busy; related to agricola, farmer; also to the French *cueillir*, to gather, to cull; to such English derivatives as colonize; and even to the Anglo-Saxon word wheel, by way of the Indo-European root *kwel-*, to move around; all of these progeny of colere sounding so fortuitously akin to the root of color, *celare*, to conceal; and to the Latin *occultus* (from *occulere*), hidden, secret. Perhaps we can now appreciate the color-wheel as the vehicle to uncover, cultivate, and be busy within earth-fields - hence painting as a primal mode of habitation, dwelling, living... as culture.

The pictorial field is, of course, most decidedly vertical, suspended, as it were, by our voluntary suspension of disbelief, flipped up in defiance of gravity to a direct confrontation with our eye. Thus the surrogate, possibly even paradigmatic, relationship between the canvas and the human body is established. This amplified context is superimposed on what was formerly seen as a neutral and relatively meaningless picture plane of quadrilateral geometry. Figure and field become indissolubly fused, face and earth linked in a coexistent paradigm of the vertical and the horizontal; and the unpainted canvas assumes the character of an androgynous entity.

We here arrive at the astounding awareness that the most conceptually non-figurative aesthetic is describable in anthropomorphic language. And this canvas earth-face possesses still further analogical qualities. On the basis of its size, its proportions, and its reflectivity, our metaphoric vision is led to extract invisible yet intrinsically present structural characteristics. An emergent awareness of foreground/middleground/background dawns on us, created by an inevitably unequal weighting of space, from lighter top to heavier (gravity-bound) bottom, and by "feelings" of tension and compression generated across the surface by natural laws of proportional relations. The innate latitudinal and longitudinal tension/compression in turn recalls tableaux of landscape, interior, and still-life subjects, whose spatial types we know from their paintings. In such manner, the blank field, presumed by scientists and psychologists to be devoid of pictorial meaning, in fact provokes our fictive and fantasizing perceptions, attracting to itself an infil of extrinsic imageries, at this stage still vague, disordered, and even dreamlike, yet deeply rooted in our past experience and in our historical and cultural memory.

Once the actual marking of the canvas begins, vagaries give way to specificities, and a quantum jump is made into purposeful composition, that traditional process of making form and meaning "significant", which takes place even when the artist pretends to avoid it. The maternal earth-field is plowed by the fertile concept (a masculine word, as Gaston Bachelard points out, in virtually all languages that make gender distinctions), and figuration arises from the union. The introduction of the figure into the field is nothing less than the installation of Adam in Eden, his mythical arrival in a still pure world that is nonetheless destined to self-knowledge. The figure in the field becomes the surrogate of man's early existence. And the multiplicity of figures, or configuration, is the surrogate of his society. But only in ways that resist literalness of interpretation: if a metaphor of human existence may be said to be implicit in the evolutionary development of all pointing, it is in the profound realm of structural similarities, in the domain of the deepest possible analogical relationships between figure(s) and field, figure(s) and ground.

And what of the concomitant of structure, color, "the pain of light" in Goethe's

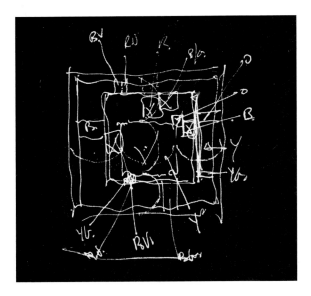

beautiful personification? Does it too have deep metaphorical and linguistic affinities with the anthropo- and geological? Pigments were originally vegetable dyes and essences of earth, refined in air of fire, then bound by a liquid medium. Black, a word by now cloaked in the opacity of its Anglo-Saxon evolution, has its root in the Latin for fire - as in conflagration - signifying burning, the dye-stain of smoke, the ultimate carbonization of life (bones, ivories). White, conversely, is etymologically akin to words for light, dawn, brightness; but also fascinatingly - closely related in Old English to the word for wheat, with its whitish grain and flour, suggesting fields of wheat, white-gleaming fields of wheat, reinforcing the canvas's early analogy, and recalling the image that Henry James used to describe the terrain of "poetry", whatever its artistic form: "the fields of lights." Black as fire, white as both light and fecundity - these associations suggest the impossibility of escaping elemental meaning even when we assume we are addressing the most neutral and austere manifestations of color.

We could pursue this etymological discourse through the rest of the spectrum, discovering relations between yellow and egg yolk, red and fish roe, purple and porphyra and porphyry (algae and mineral). The naming of chroma is literally rooted in earth, water, and sky with their animal, vegetable, and mineral offspring. But what does all this mean to the color/structure painter? Can color in its non-objective and structural role within relational painting be made to capture and exude in essences the variegated richness inherent in these etymological roots? Indeed the earth colors, the marine colors, the colors of fruit and minerals, when unsealed like genies from the painter's tubes and jars and put into the hermetic context of the earth-field, are revitalized by their metaphoric existence. Once in the painterly field, they participate in totally new and highly specific relationships. These relationships are not only a matter of optics: the metaphoric consciousness activates chromatic fantasy. It reveals to the artist that his act is a veritable alchemy, a transmutation of base elements into the combinatory luminosity of painting.

"The painter said: 'If one where to imagine a bluish orange, it would have to feel like a southwesterly north wind.' 'No, that would be a reddish green.'

said the other painter. 'It is all the same to me,' said Roy G. Biv. Blessed art thou who bringest forth fruit of the bronze: bells and pomegranates, thunder and lightning. Blessed art thou who brought forth nought of the lead, save Roy G. Biv." - John Hollander, "Orange", from Spectral Emanations; Roy G. Biv's name is an acronym for the colors of the spectrum.

It is no coincidence that the advent of abstract painting was heralded by a return to a basic palette of earth colors - black and white mixed with browns and sparing amounts of blue and green. By 1911, Mondrian, along with Picasso and Braque under their "muddy banner of Cubism" (Ortega y Gasset), had forged a revolutionary pictorial space in which minimal color began to be accorded a structural function. Having transported, so to speak, Cézanne's chromatically pellucid late landscape indoors into their urban studios, these painters subtracted chromas as they also compressed and heavied space. The surrogate slice of verdant landscape, flipped up into the frontalized picture plane, lost its verdancy and gained instead earthy opacity and compaction. Abstracted geometric abbreviations of extrinsic subject matter, metonymic tropes of still-life objects, took root in this leaden yet fertile earthen field, as a radically new pictorial syntax sprouted. The earth matrix became colloidal, a suspension of pictorial multiplicities we now know as Analytical Cubism. This agglutination of form and meaning, in dynamic juxtapositions, in turn generated new form-meanings. Color, for the most part, merely recorded the temperature of this yeast-pot of metonymic and metaphoric images, behaving in an unobtrusive manner, simply warming to the degree of intellectual expansiveness in grisaille shades as it essentially subordinated itself to formal animation. Cubist painting became the poetry of an enlightened vision born from an umber and slate-gray plain.

The next event in the evolving infancy of color/structure was the replacement of the earthen palette by primaries. It was de Stijl and Suprematism that shattered the pictorial symbiosis of Analytical Cubism by declaring persona non grata those forces of figuration extrinsic to the elemental clarity of a reborn two-dimensional world. They proclaimed rigorist aesthetic utopias, aesthetic politics of abstention from the forbidden fruits of the full spectrum.

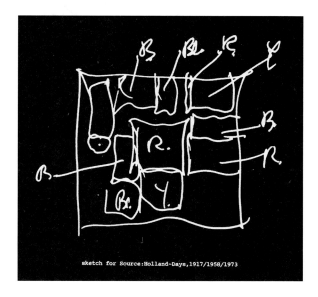

sketch for Source:Holland-Days,1917/1958/1973

In employing the unsullied and heraldic colors we call primaries and secondaries, they sought to purge Cubism and all other imagistic painting of its metonymic and mimetic proclivities, presuming the possibility of shutting out or neutralizing one world for the apparently infinite and self-motivated freedom of another. In the strange new world of non-objective space that they created, this self-imposed limitation of vocabulary perhaps represented a felt need to lean how to walk before learning how to run. But we now see (a half-century later) the traps and delusions of such self-denying hermeticism. Even though Mondrian heroically maintained to the end his exclusive formalism, we can already observe in such late paintings as the Victory Boogie-Woogie a latent illusionism that refers all the way back to his landscape House on the River Gein of 1900. Already, too, in his late New York City paintings, color becomes more complex, as "primaries" vie with other "primaries" for primacy (several blues of differing hues coexisting in the same canvas, for instance). We also know how Malevich, in delimiting his own primary field of action, succumbed to the signs, symbols, and spatial illusionism of geometric fragments traversing aerial fields much as the Sputniks would traverse deep space forty years later. The inadvertent image retained its uncanny ability to infiltrate the most polemically sanitized fields.

Some years later in this selective - and admittedly autobiographical - history, we find a parallel course being taken by another pioneer of color/structure, Josef Albers. (In citing Albers, Mondrian, Malevich, and the Analytical Cubists here as genealogical progenitors of the poetic development we are pursuing, we are clearly neglecting a number of others who cultivated the same or adjacent territory.) If Mondrian pared down the color palette to primaries in order to better explore the structural complexities of horizontal/vertical form, Albers reduced the formal dialogue to the primacy and simplicity of the square in order to explore the complex relational effects of color interaction. But Albers, too, in the abnegations of his rich asceticism, could only advance the discourse of color/structure so far. His paintings ultimately seem overly reductive, demonstration objects rather than provocatory instruments of that revelling, revelatory, reverie-inducing action of painted art that we spoke of earlier.

In the end, the square demanded - demands - a more poetic form of homage. Here we return to the canvas as surrogate I. Another fortuitous similarity of language enters our enriched pictorial cosmos: between occult (from occulere, to conceal; which in turn comes from celare, the root of color, as mentioned earlier) and oculus. The latter is the paradoxical counter-eye in the canvas, confronting artist and spectator alike, the two-dimensioned eye, the navel, the geographic center of the hermetic plane. The centered oculus transgresses the modernist canon of flatness to mark the void within the illusion, to remind us that what underlies the configurational shifts is the canvas itself, to turn space inside-out like a torus-glove and make figure and field ambiguously one, to still within the radius of its frame the turning wheel of the world.

At the same time this most positive and negative node unanchors our contemplative eyes for distant journeys and far-away places, loci of memories rebirthed. Images float by - a tempestuous painting by Giorgione, Adirondack woods, fog in rice fields, Venetian canals, anthracite tunnels, Saint Veronica's veil, the granite of Roman ruins; loom into view - Goethe's prism and Courbet's cavern, gray Gris, the brutish pink angulations of Avignon demoiselles; and disappear - the last gleam on a Pacific horizon, tidal shifts unsea-ing creatures of the depths and shallows; to yield still others, rescued from the edgeless boundary between invisible and visible - squares that are not, greens more red than not, flatnesses that warp, lines that stay and disappear, arid planes that seep and ooze, colors on the threshold of monochromy, the magnetic suction of black.

In short, the alluvial-allusive stuff within the ebb and flow of fictive and factitive perception. The crucible-crux of painterly metaphor.

Robert Slutzky
with Joan Ockman
August 1984
New York City

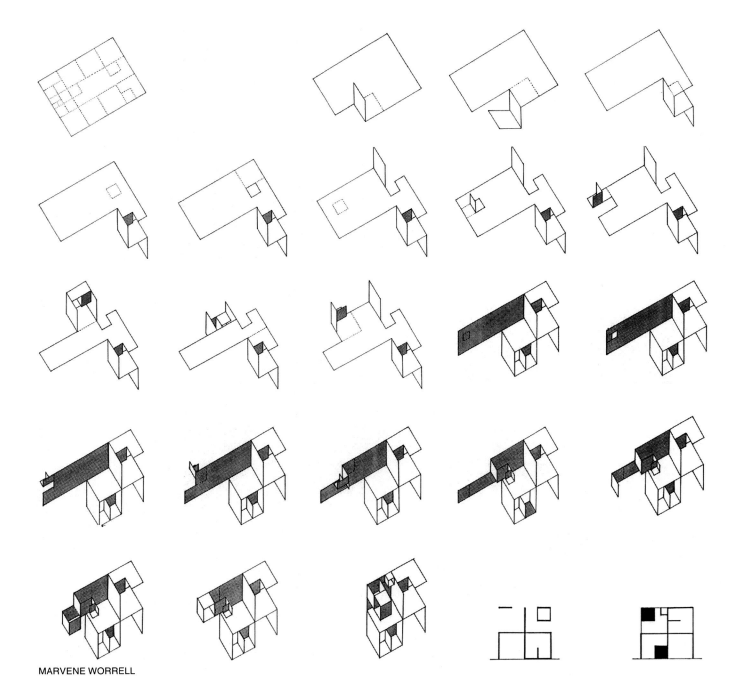

MARVENE WORRELL

A song is anything that can walk by itself.

Bob Dylan

Melody comes from the Greek for *song + to sing* and means the pleasing arrangement of sounds in sequence. In music it is a) a sequence of single tones, usually in the same key or mode, to produce a rhythmic whole. b) the element of form having to do with the arrangement of single tones in sequence: distinguished from harmony. c) the leading part, or voice, in a harmonic composition; the air.

Interval from Latin, literally *inter + vallum*, between two palisades or walls. 1. a space between two things; gap; distance. 2. a period of time between two points of time, events, etc.; intervening period. 3. the extent of difference between two qualities, conditions, etc. 4. in *music*, the difference in pitch between two tones.

Rhythm from Greek *rhuthmos*, a measured movement, akin to *rhein*, to flow. See also rhyme, stream, from Sanskrit *sravati*, it flows and (without the s) in Greek *rhusis* , flowing; in music, the pattern of movement in time.

Canon from Latin, measuring line, rule; Greek *kanon, kane*, a reed, rod. 1. a law or body of laws.... 2. any law or decree. 3. a standard used in judging something; criterion. ... 8. in *music*, a round; composition in which there are exact repetitions of a preceding part in the same or related keys. [also canon: reed, tube, cannon, canyon]

1. MELODY

SPACING

MELODY: *SPACING*

BEING

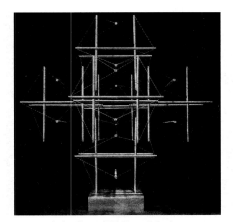

"Taking possession of space is the first gesture of living things, of men, and of animals, of plants and of clouds, a fundamental manifestation of equilibrium and duration. The occupation of space is the first proof of existence." Le Corbusier

Spacing

What is space? People often think of space as effortless absence, but carpenters and masons know that it takes *sweat* to keep things apart, to organize the emptiness of a room to sustain the heavy bricks and beams around it. Volume at human scale, amidst the crush of gravity, is a real achievement, not an accident. How remarkable then is the space created between the branches of a tree! When an oak was a mere acorn, the void it would come to occupy was just "airspace," a typical portion of atmosphere. But as the place between the branches of a leafy graceful giant, blessed in cool shade and dappled light, home to birds and other animals, the space of an oak is unique, present, and very real. Le Corbusier suggests that the first human act is to occupy space. We might say the first act of all is to establish the presence of something in nothing, not by stillness but by action. The empty interval between masses is as vital as the massive interval between voids. An array of holes makes room for bodies. Void permeates mass to create space.

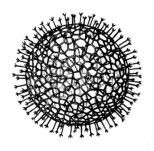

Spring Street, 1964. Kenneth Snelson

Spring

The sun's radiant energy agitates matter, driving atoms of organic aromatic hollow amino acid proteins into coiled DNA springs. An oak is a living community of vibrations that withstand wind and gravity for centuries, always growing and in motion. In each branch the cells grow larger on the bottom than the top to keep it from drooping as its cantilever reaches out from the trunk. Root-to-leaf nutrient channel fiber bundles stiffen the trunk's woody column and keep it vertical, even against storms. Like the tube of an auto spring formed by steel molecules forged into an airy coil, the emptiness of the tree is the geometric result of dynamic forces. Kenneth Snelson's poetic sculpture *Spring Street*, a vigorous but delicate balance of pushing and pulling, is also full of emptiness. It is almost intuitively clear that the thin wires of *Spring Street* are stretched in tension while the fatter rods resist collapsing in compression. What about the void parts of this sculpture? Do some volumes feel more squeezed, while other regions seem more stretched? Can empty solids be stressed as much as filled ones?

Silica skeleton of the radiolarian *Aulastrum triceros Hkl*

Making a Point

Without stars we could not measure the cosmos. An array of points reveals to consciousness the space between them. In reproduction, life concentrates mass. Oaks perpetuate the species through acorns, concentrated miniature carriers of essential information for being in space. The acorn is mostly space, largely empty between nuclei and electrons, between atoms and molecules, and between structures of cells that make tissue. Yet the acorn appears to us far more dense than the tree it becomes. How do earthly matter and solar energy get processed into root and branch, trunk and leaf? What does the tiny seed carry that reaches out to light, spiraling matter into the sky, weaving energy into such a benevolent spacious creature. DNA, the blueprint molecule inside each acorn cell, directs transformation of air, water, and soil into protein. The concentration of matter and intention into a single cell is a miracle of plastic organization. Like us the tree is a community of billions of such cells. Oaks and human beings are essentially identical in DNA genetic structure. Every seedpod is a birth of volume, which becomes a filigree of leaf and branch dense enough to catch light, a volume changing the world around it-- *making shade!!*

Acorn-- *quercus tomentalla*

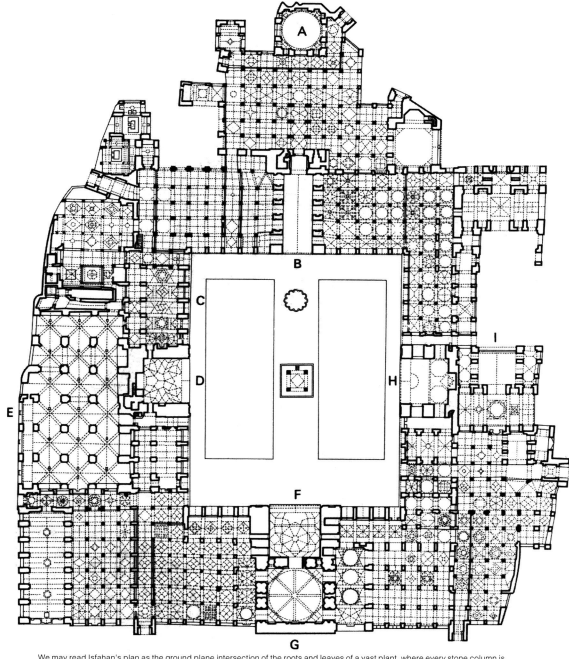

We may read Isfahan's plan as the ground plane intersection of the roots and leaves of a vast plant, where every stone column is a vessel between light and shade in a natural plumbing of wells of potential and fountains of kinetic energy. The plan is the generator!

THINKING

"I wish I was there when the column was invented"-- Lou Kahn

Foundation

The plan is the intersection of gravity and light. Tree branches mirror their roots. Buildings are honest, down to earth, built from the ground up. The plan is the measure of the foundation, the building's footprint and roots. The section measures loft and reveals light. Volume was rare and costly when human homes were caves in rock, more mass than void. Since we cannot inhabit mass, architects must bring the emptiness between masses into the foreground of design. The Great Pyramids of Egypt are huge masses, but they have only narrow burial chamber niches between heavy opaque stones. Their presence is massive and solid, but lacks volume.

Making Room

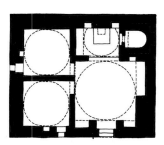

Trulli: many megarons

Room is related to "*ream*" which means to extend, enlarge, widen, or carve out. A megaron was a "great carving". The Italian trulli are additive cells amidst thick masonry bearing walls, whose voids are clearly organized as room volumes. While the mass of a structure can help insulate a room and keep its walls standing against strong winds, there is a distinct economical advantage to enclosing much space with little material. The ability to dwell more in void than mass was a difficult conceptual and technical struggle. Plan inventions, from cave to wall to column and span inventions, from corbel and beam to arch, vault and dome helped architecture evolve into mostly void solids. Using mass efficiently is a technical problem, but making volume visible and primary to experience is an architectural and plastic concern. How much mass must remain before a volume loses its identifying edges and shape? How much mass must remain before a set of volumes reverts to a reading as a single volume? Masses that mark boundaries need not fill every face and edge. A column can mark a corner as much as an intersection of two walls. Related spacial positions can reveal volume as much as literal enclosure. Walls and floors separate rooms, but volumes also become boundaries to other volumes. What happens at the boundary when volume abuts volume? In a sense, the answer is the whole history of architecture.

In Between

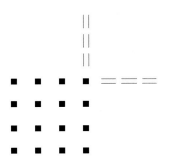

Column grid: a megaron without walls?

Matter and void permeate and perforate each other. What a true plastic invention is the idea of a column grid! It may be the first true architectural space, a *continuum* of mass and void. A grid is an equivalence of two kinds of "in between", the perforation of mass by void and the perforation of void by mass, permitting multiple readings of spacial relationships. The grid plan of the Greek Temple of Eleusis demonstrates an idea of space as something not only between but also *through* mass. The honeycomb of rooms between steel columns and beams in a high-rise is a three-dimensional grid of voids, just as those beams and columns are a three-dimensional grid of masses. Today we have the technology to build the rhythmically gridded spacial fabric of Isfahan in section as well as plan. Architects seek unity between inside and outside places to exploit the interplay between filled and empty intervals in three dimensions. Architectural space is a plastic intention. The hues of grids of the Friday Mosque in Isfahan Iran create architectural space as the fertile grounding of the sacred rituals of our everyday experience. The atrium heart of Isfahan is hollow: a grand courtyard within a complex of sacred and daily spaces, many of which have their own courtyards. These hollows within hollows provide breathing room and direct access to the sky, mixing shade and sun into dappled space for the city walker. The Persian saying "Isfahan is half the world" may refer to its beautiful spaces-- and their rhythm of darkness and light.

Carving is assembly in a negative mode, like embossing.

LIGHT SPACE: LIGHT IN ACTION

"A building begins with light and ends with shadows." Lou Kahn

When space as the medium of architecture becomes void as much as mass, it reveals another potential-- light. Light can be the qualifier of volume, rather than merely quantifier of perforated holes punched in a mostly massive skin. Melody is an *air,* a light-filled room. Hagia Sophia is a "bubble" filling emptiness with light. The southwest wall at Le Corbusier's Ronchamp chapel (see page 87 in *Architectonics* for its plan and axonometric projection) subtly transmits sunlight into the chapel, making the interior a radiant vessel of shafts of glowing color. The wall is a light/dark ambiguity as well as a figure/ground and solid/void ambiguity. The chapel wall is a vertical version of the plan of the Temple of Eleusis, in which rhythmic and syncopated shafts of light replace the regular grid of columns of mass. An array of masses makes space present to consciousness; an array of lights illuminates bodies. The medium for Dynamics is both space and time; and the carrier is light, which permits the ongoing evolution of mass into energy into mass. Architects design solids of light.

Voxel

The image of Ronchamp on the facing page is not a photograph, but a computer-generated image. A new technique for rendering computer graphics that has been developed to aid doctors, engineers, and others who like to look inside things is called *volume rendering* and promises significant improvement over older computer-aided drafting programs (CAD) rendering software that wraps contour lines around a three-dimensional structure and links them to create a surface shell composed of perhaps thousands of two-dimensional polygons. The computing power (and time!) it takes to transform these planes into proper visual perspective, and then to figure out which polygons must be subtracted from the ones appearing in front of them, as anyone waiting to mesh a building file can tell you, is enormous. But volume rendering stores a three-dimensional model as voxels (volume elements akin to the light points on a video monitor called pixels). An image of the model is rendered by casting imaginary rays from behind the model. As the rays move toward the picture plane, they accumulate data from each voxel they penetrate. At the picture plane, the data determines the color for the surface pixel. This software permits rapid change of view, removal of parts, or cutting a section for an inside look. Voxel-based imaging seems to be a necessity for the laser-scan confocal miscropes that permit biologists to observe the inner workings of living cells. This impressive technology will help reveal wonders in everything from anatomy to cosmology, but to an architect this is what sketching and building with light has always been about.

Distant solids

The Temple of Eleusis was sacred to Demeter, goddess of fertility. It was called the *Telesterium* which in Greek means literally *"distant solids",* as in (tele)vision and stereo (solid). The wide spacing of its column grid recalls a forest grove of trees making room between mass. Capacious like a pregnant womb, space is ever able to carry both bone and heart, both mass and volume. Is this not the essence of fertility? From the narrow caves inside the pyramids, to the light-filled bubbles of Hagia Sophia, to the nesting courts of Isfahan and the glowing space of Ronchamp, humankind has learned to make figures of emptiness, architectural vessels for human life and regeneration, extracting poetic meaning from every possible program need and plastic opportunity. Architects keep their feet on the ground and their heads in the clouds.

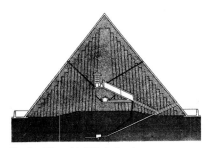

The Great Pyramid of Gizeh, Egypt section showing Royal burial chambers

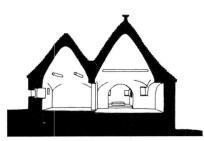

Trulli section, a good example of human-made "caves"

Temple of Eleusis, isometric reconstruciton.

HYPERCUBE
a 4D block of spacetime,
eight 3D cubes "unfolded",
a diagram of momenergy,
or mass/volume in motion.

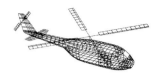

SKIN AND BONES

Skeleton

A dinosaur's fossil bones are the hard body parts that have resisted the ravages of geologic time. In addition, they reveal how the whole organism resisted the tug of gravity during its lifetime millions of years ago. The skeleton acts as a framework of stiffness working with muscles and ligaments to make the essential volumes for animal survival-- bellows of the lungs, chambers of the heart, cave of the stomach, pantheon of the brain. Structural engineers seek to build skeletons of hard parts (wood, concrete, steel) to make room, to keep the soft parts (people, air, light) alive. Galileo's investigations of the time things take to fall was perhaps the first study in modern structural engineering, applying reproducible experiment, observation, and numerical analysis to buildings. He attempted to predict and understand how structures would move before actually built. The collapsing cathedral as building experiment was eventually replaced by calculation on pencil and paper. Structural engineering grew under daring people like Brunelleschi, Soufflot, Eiffel, Roebling, and Fuller. Their lessons continue to guide and inspire architects in experiments with habitable volume to find out how to make a lot of room to live in using as little building mass and construction effort as possible.

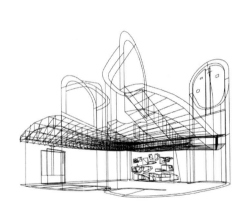

Wire Frame

Ideally, a structural solid would be defined by lines of mass only at its edges. Computer-aided drafting programs (CAD) now routinely delineate spacial designs through such *wire-frame models* of volume. The wire-frame model of Ronchamp here includes the deep window perforations in the south wall shown on the previous page. Finite-element analysis is a sophisticated dynamical modeling of wire-frame figures which has become essential in the design of complex structures like rockets and helicopters. The traditional study of materials, structure, and construction carry in them core issues about the movement of volumes in space. But whereas structural engineering courses usually emphasize using formulas to solve known problems in known ways, a design study of forces and volumes in motion may also approach materials and structures as open-ended explorations, informing the design process from the beginning. *Engineer* is related to the word *ingenuity*; another etymologically correct way to say "mechanical joint" is "harmony machine". Depth is more than a third dimension: it is the sum of dimensional unities, what Le Corbusier referred to as "ineffable space". The geometrodynamic cosmos requires a four-dimensional hypercube block of spacetime to make a wireframe model of momentum-energy, of filament as flame, of matter in motion.

Sky Light Weight

Architectural volume is most musical when its basic solids are cleanly revealed in the structure. New York's Penn Station, by McKim Mead and White, was a structure of perforated spans and skylights, a calligraphy of steel that created a feeling of fullness. It was an emptiness flooded with light. Today the stairs and tracks are used by the Long Island Railroad, but are covered over into darkness. The 1965 destruction of the space was a great loss. Before the building technology of steel and concrete, the order of stone masses was *the* Order (Doric, Ionic, Corinthian, Tuscan, etc.) New materials allowed these canons of dimensions to be stretched. What remained was the order of volumes. Penn Station was composed in the same volumetric order as the central hall of the Roman Baths of Caracalla, but with much less mass. (So much for "The Orders"!) We live in trees as much as caves. To build a void, one must place mass carefully, in space and in time. Depth is created and sustained by a well-timed structure of mass which remains in the background to reveal a well-timed structure of volume. The architect must keep bubbles empty- to make volumes of sky light, to make weight light.

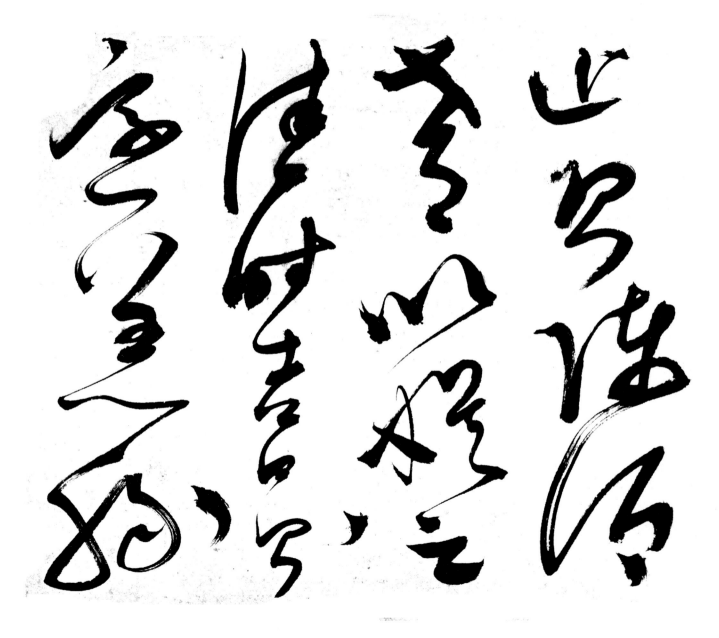

"When I put a stroke of ink on the paper, I realized that the black was where the light was not, and then I could really make a drawing, because I could be discerning as to where the light was not, which was where I put the black. Then the picture became luminous." Lou Kahn (*Between Silence and Light*)

AN AIR: IMPROVISING MELODY

How can you actually build a solid of light? How can you shape something you can't touch? How do you keep the placement of stones light enough so as not to crush the spirit of a volume? The answer is to *play*, to let things dance in space. At first you must juggle masses, testing their weight, balance, and extension while seeing the voids between them. In short, you improvise a structure around a theme. Volume is the theme, masses are its notes, and space is a melody. The origin of melody is intuitive-- a breath of fresh air, a gleaming light in the dark. But who tells the mason where to break his brick and mortar line to introduce a window hole when he's laying up a wall? Who helps him envision sun and breeze filling window and room? What if he's wrong? The architect experiments with positions of absence, of holes in walls becoming luminous planes, of voids becoming light-filled space. He learns to mark absence as a presence. To evolve such plans takes the courage to willingly follow intuition, to expect to be wrong and to use the error to build the next step in a line of successful "improvements". The Oriental calligrapher also improvises, eschewing hesitation and valuing spontaneity. An improvised line inhabits its plane, revealing time in action, even as it is preserved "frozen" out of time. Every line has character: a spring to the step, a liveliness in structure. The calligrapher paints white spaces with (and between) black brush strokes to build with light.

> "There is a Japanese visual art in which the artist is forced to be spontaneous. He must paint on a thin stretched parchment with a special brush and black water paint in such a way that an unnatural or interrupted stroke will destroy the line or break the parchment. Erasures or changes are impossible. These artist must practice a particular discipline, that of allowing the idea to express itself in communication with their hands in such a way that deliberation cannot interfere... The resulting pictures lack the complex composition and textures of ordinarypainting. But it is said that those who see well find something captured that escapes explanation... This conviction that direct deed is the most meaningful reflection, I believe has prompted the evolution of the extremely severe and unique discipline of the jazz or improvising musician."
>
> from IMPROVISATION IN JAZZ, Bill Evans' liner notes to *Kind of Blue*, by Miles Davis

First comes invention, later reflection and evaluation. The first step is intuitive. Improvisation is additive, aleatory, making do with what is at hand. Footsteps lead to giant steps to take us miles ahead, either on the road or off the beaten path. Spirit's horn of plenty brings one note, then another. Repetition brings figure and inversion as themes and variations (half new half old) blossom forth. Imagination molds form into eloquence, speaking in realms beyond the reach of words.

There is a kind of play at a restaurant table. Waiting for dinner, who has not begun playing with the forks and spoons, idly enjoying the pleasure of inventing (literally coming upon or discovering) space through structural experimentation? How often have we interlaced the tines of two forks to make an arch, or balanced the bowl of a spoon on the surface tension of a glass of water against the weight of cantilevered handle hovering over tabletop? We sharpen our sense of how things are poised in space, creating that pregnant emptiness in which the silverware balances, making empty volume ever more present. The daring spans of Gothic cathedrals evolved through invention, ingenuity, experiment-- through engineering *play*. The play of improvising order is as natural to the brain as breathing is to the lungs. For the musician, calligrapher, and builder, beauty only comes after perfecting one's "chops"-- the scales and changes, strokes and characters, or joints and intersections-- so well that performance becomes play. Practice not only makes perfect, it also gives freedom. As Marcel Duchamp has said "only those who play can be serious."

"Passion can create drama out of inert stone."
Le Corbusier

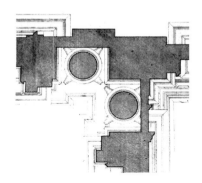

ANIMATING

Force Moves Mass

"Walking is a continually arrested falling." Erwin Straus

"Bag of bones" does not describe the dynamic system of a living human body. Muscles, ligaments and bones push and pull on each other to keep us upright as we walk or stand. The walls, floors, and ceilings around us form a similar dynamic system of structural muscles and bones arranged to resist wind and gravity's tendency to move them. Forces push and pull on every molecule of mass in beams and columns to load them in **compression** and **tension**, as well as to twist them in torsion and make them slide across each other in shear. Michelangelo's *Captive* seems to be working hard, arms and legs acting like the columns in the corners of the Ricetto at his Laurentian Library, some stretched in tension while others bulge in compression, The plan of the columns could be a cross-section through arms or legs and torso-- struggling in and with the heavy opaque mass of the stone around and above the columnar support.

At a tug of war, each side pulls on the rope with great **force**. They do not move, because although everyone is exerting great effort, the forces oppose each other and the resulting force is zero. To describe a force it is not enough to give its magnitude— direction must also be specified. A slanted beam exerts more force on its lower support than its upper one. We can understand the loads on any body in space by drawing the forces that act on them. ***Vectors*** are mathematical quantities that indicate both magnitude and direction. Using vectors, we can show all forces acting in a system. As "arrows" or lines of particular size and orientation, vectors can be added and subtracted graphically to find their resultant effect, which is particularly useful to architects and engineers working directly in plan and section. A diagram of forces acting on a body enables us to show how to *resist* motion. If the vector sum of all forces is zero, then the mass will not move (within its frame of reference). When all masses remain in stable position, the structural system is in **equilibrium**.

Free Bodies

An astronaut is a free body in space, in a state of "free fall" because the tug of gravity is countered by the million pound forward thrust of the orbital delivery rocket. Similarly, a keystone in an arch (or the lintel stones above the Ricetto columns) can be understood as a free body suspended above the surface of the earth, held in position by the upward thrust of the stones below it balancing the downward pull of gravity on its mass. To calculate and design building structures, we conceptually isolate each element in a structural system from its surroundings as a ***free body***. For purposes of analysis, we can consider every structural element in a system as a free body. Load vectors can be assumed to be acting on and from the center of the mass of a free body, which simplifies structural analysis. A ***free body diagram*** will show all force vectors acting on that body. (See page 488 for more on solving free body diagrams.) The angled walls of a keystone transfer its downward weight outward to the neighboring support stones. These supports carry both their own weight and outward thrust as well as that of the keystone. An unmoving free body is said to be in **static equilibrium**, since all the forces must be in balance. A keystone is in static equilibrium. Statics is the study of how to keep dynamical tendencies (forces) in balance to make a stable structure. An orbiting astronaut is in **dynamic equilibrium**, because her position relative to other elements in the system remains constant, even while she is in motion. If gravity and orbital thrust did not balance, she would either fall to earth or drift into deep space. The cover of *Creation in Space* is a movie as much as a still life.

THE PROFESSOR STEPS INTO AN OPEN ELEVATOR SHAFT AND WHEN HE LANDS AT THE BOTTOM HE FINDS A SIMPLE ORANGE SQUEEZING MACHINE. MILK MAN TAKES EMPTY MILK BOTTLE(A) PULLING STRING(B) WHICH CAUSES SWORD(C) TO SEVER CORD(D) AND ALLOW GUILLOTINE BLADE(E) TO DROP AND CUT ROPE(F) WHICH RELEASES BATTERING RAM(G). RAM BUMPS AGAINST OPEN DOOR(H) CAUSING IT TO CLOSE. GRASS SICKLE(I) CUTS A SLICE OFF END OF ORANGE(J) AT THE SAME TIME SPIKE(K) STABS PRUNE HAWK(L) HE OPENS HIS MOUTH TO YELL IN AGONY, THEREBY RELEASING PRUNE AND ALLOWING DIVER'S BOOT(M) TO DROP AND STEP ON SLEEPING OCTOPUS(N). OCTOPUS AWAKENS IN A RAGE AND SEEING DIVER'S FACE WHICH IS PAINTED ON ORANGE, ATTACKS IT AND CRUSHES IT WITH TENTACLES, THEREBY CAUSING ALL THE JUICE IN THE ORANGE TO RUN INTO GLASS(O).
LATER ON YOU CAN USE THE LOG TO BUILD A LOG CABIN WHERE YOU CAN RAISE YOUR SON TO BE PRESIDENT LIKE ABRAHAM LINCOLN.

T   A   0

MACHINES

"There are three departments of architecture: the art of building, the making of time-pieces, and the construction of machinery."
Vitruvius, 2000 years ago...

"A house is a machine to live in." Le Corbusier, 1922

Vladimir Tatlin's Monument to the Third Internationale

Machines are devices for changing the magnitude or direction of forces. We might think of them as "vector-benders" or "vector-stretchers" (or compressors). The three basic machines are the lever, pulley, and inclined plane. (TAO again!) All others are compounds of these. A wheel-and-axle is not a pulley with a hole, but actually a lever that is allowed to rotate through 360 degrees. A screw is an inclined plane twisted around a central axis. For a machine to work force must be applied against a resistance, and work is not done unless something moves. (A wheel is just a pizza until it rolls.) An inclined plane is just a triangular prism until a force is applied so that it will act as a wedge or a ramp. Machines enable force to put lines, planes, and volumes in motion, creating space.

The elements of a compound machine may move at different patterns and rates of vibration. Automobile engine pistons moving up and down connect through offset cams and gears to drive the crankshaft in rotary motion. The chassis sits on springs to isolate the oscillating engine from bumps in the road. The whole assembly is subject to uneven loads as the car makes a right turn, etc. Machines hold together by joining moving assemblies with devices which do not come apart under vibration. For example, threaded nuts and bolts bind the parts of the engine block together during the explosion of the ignited gasoline. The friction and enormous stress built up at the contact of nut to bolt assures that this connection will not shake loose when the rest of the car vibrates. Today we use simple machines to make increasingly complex ones for the most subtle and sophisticated applications imaginable. Such machines as lathes, dynamos, steamships, bicycles, cars, milling machines, tape recorders, airplanes, space shuttles, and satellites have revolutionized our world.

Moving Rooms

Elevators are rooms which move. (If one moved regularly between top and bottom floors of the building, it would trace a sine wave as the earth moved through space.) The trail of space made by a piston and cylinder in the engine of a moving car desribes a volumetric wave of simple harmonic motion. Buckminster Fuller saw the mobile home as an extrusion determined by the width of highways and the height of overpasses. Vladimir Tatlin's proposed *Monument to the 3rd Internationale*, a capitol building for the new Soviet Union designed in 1920 offered a daring exploration of the architectural possibilities of moving volumes. The cube, pyramid, and cylinder law chamber s suspended wityhin the inclined double helix spiral were to rotate once a year, once a month, and once a day, respectively. Kinetic architecture is still in its infancy. The MIR/NASA International space station moves around us at over 25,000 miles per hour. Is the space shuttle a machine or a house? Forms need not move to reveal the architectural potential of the lessons of machine motion. Felix Candela designed complex warps of concrete that were very strong and light. Utzon's Sydney Opera House is like clouds or sails floating on the skyline. Aalto's Baker dorms at MIT warps the space of the river edge into a wall as wave that activates and intensifies the experience of urban volume. Facades can reveal an intention to treat the stacked floors of a building as layers of a weaving, one level in, the next out. The free plan permits walls and volumes to weave around supporting columns. The flow of space in a building can sustain the melody of human movent through it, or it can act as counterpoint to enhance the volumetric experience of the inhabitants. Structure is timing of solids in space.

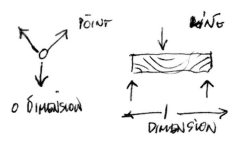
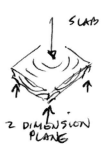

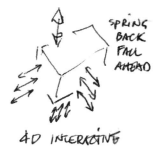

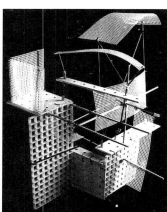

JOHN WILSON, JR.

STRUCTURE IS SPACING AND TIMING

Our restaurant service is slow. Drinks, but still no food. One hand rests on the bowl of a spoon, the other releases the stem end in frustration. The spoon clinks on the table. Gravity, like rust, never sleeps; it pulls on the ceiling above us as much as the spoon. Why don't the ceiling joists and lights and tiles also drop to the floor? What keeps the volume of the room itself from disappearing as the surrounding materials of its skin collapse into a heap on the floor? Why doesn't a strong wind blow the room's walls over, when even a light breath can tip the balance of the forks and spoons? The second hand on the clock barely turns. If time "stood still"--nothing could fall. That immutable permanence is the condition of Architectonics, where all designs seem to be made of magic pure solid stuff, without load or force to distort them. But what if we add a clock to the Kit of Parts?

> "Everyone thinks he knows the meaning of the word **structure**. We point to a stone wall or a bridge or a barn and say, 'That's a structure.' What is common to a steel bridge, a wooden barn, a jumbo jet, an iceberg, a starfish, a fern, a diamond jewel, an elephant, a cloud, a human baby? They are all structures. Some are more versatile than others, some last longer than others. Why? Why do wood or stone cohere at all? If we understood a little more about structure, it could lead to a better understanding of the political and economic dilemmas of our time. Political and economic systems are structures-- often so ill conceived so as to require constant local patching and mending.... We all have experiences of **pushing** and **pulling**, and we think of them as 180 degree experiences directly away from us or toward us. But pushing and pulling both produce 90 degree resultants, which we mistakenly call side effects, and vice versa.... Gravity and magnetism are embracingly contractive around-- and radially inward toward-- a center of gravity. With gases, pull is partial vacuum whereas push is an explosion: attraction vs. propulsion, tension vs. compression.... Contrary to common opinion (even that of engineers) structures are always dynamic and never static."
>
> R. Buckminster Fuller, *Tensegrity*

The whole world is in motion. Every atom vibrates to a temperature frequency above absolute zero. Although we may feel perfectly still, we rush through intergalactic space. A spoon handle actually bends, deflecting under its own weight. Structure is the careful arrangement of elements to accept wanted and resist unwanted motion; it is the means to sustain the positions of masses and to lend them duration, that is to keep mass in place in time. If we are careful, we may prolong unlikely states of balance, resolving push and pull in a structure to obtain a balance of masses and equilibrium of forces. Then everything is still-- or is it? *Making structure sets the tendency to* **resist** *motion.* Volume is the result of masses **not** moving, but trying to....

Structural Improvisation

Amazing! The spoon balances! It sits on the coffee's surface tension, balanced against gravity's pull on the cantilevered handle. The spoon gently bobs on ripples in the cup until they crest and break the surface tension. The spoon floods and drowns, and we try again. Structure *emerges* from mass-positioning improvisation, an activity of locating things in space that depends on the feedback of all masses in the local system. Structural improvisation is an evolution of weighing, moving, balancing, counterbalancing, etc. until an instant of rest arrives, where there is no motion relative to the local frame of reference. Masses find repose, and leave voids between them. Structural improvisation often proceeds outward from an elegant joining of several mass elements, first in one direction, then along another axis to provide stability. The improviser of spoons on a tabletop uses the feedback from fingers and eyes (and one's innate sense of balance!) to continuously re-establish equilibrium while adding pieces and spaces. We sharpen our sense of how things are poised in space, creating that pregnant emptiness in which silverware, stones, or steel balance, making empty volume ever more present. Structure is the art of reducing mass to increase volume. Structure is a question of **massing**-- putting piles of stuff near each other, **spacing**-- keeping the piles apart, and above all **timing**.

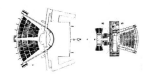

PALACE OF THE SOVIETS

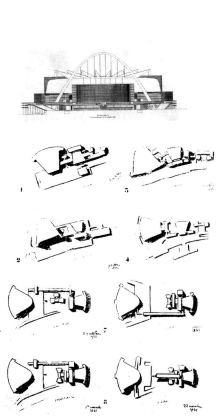

"These few photographs of the model of the Palace of the Soviets in Moscow reveal phenomena of harmony which have a tremendous intensity and which have not yet found a door open before them. The harmony is too pure. It is too strong, it is too new. Through these images it is possible to conceive part of the esthetic emotion which tomorrow holds in store for us... when men shall have once more become wise, aware, and courageous.... All the fixed forms are breaking up; academic teaching is failing. In imagination, try to harmonize the life of tomorrow with the promises that this vision suggests!"

Le Corbusier, *New World of Space, 1935?*

Plan improvisation

Le Corbusier's proposed Palace of the Soviets is about how to build a hollow balloon of "pure" volume in a field of real forces. The problem is how to make a really large span without interior supporting columns, because the issue was how to make a unified space for *people*, 14,000 of them at one time, both visually and acoustically right for everyone. His brilliant idea was to carry the structure on the exterior of the otherwise purely modeled acoustic shell. This was very much in the tradition of the cathedral, which as he wrote was a pure volume on the inside but "hirsute, [hairy] arrayed as an army" on the exterior, full of flying buttresses, crockets and finials, towers, etc. The resulting architecture, akin to its contemporary Russian Constructivism, celebrates structural solutions to program, reveals forces like gravity and exploits its site, all the time maintaining the integrity of each component of the ensemble. What is truly marvelous about this project is how the planning of the architecture reveals and amplifies the structural means. The studies to the left show exploration of massing and circulation relationships between large volumes, as well as access to the river and city. So many *parti* diagrams of independent elements arranged and rearranged to achieve balance though asymmetrical equilibrium! Eight versions (by a very talented architect) to arrive at "an obvious solution!" More subtle than Saarinen's Gateway Arch in St. Louis, the Palace of the Soviets plan is a set of bends in circulation and acoustic focus, the elevation is the bend of an arch, and the site is the bend of a river.

Evolving *Parti*

How wonderful is the architecture achieved by the sequence of structural decisions working to support possibilities of *parti*! First-- eliminate all columns in the great hall. This means a very large span. How to support it? Make the roof a thin and lightweight shell, shaped for best acoustic transmission, hung by cables from a series of giant joist-girder-beams above it, delicate yet robust. What holds up the beams? At the rear, a set of exterior pylons behind the lobby; at the front-- nothing at all!!-- except two massive feet, striding like the colossus of Rhodes, the base of a great parabolic arch, from which hang an octave of eight cords that support the girders which in turn suspend their own cables to the roof shell. The whole is an exercise in suspension and quite musical, formed like a violin with bridge, bow strings all tuned to a structural tension-compression equilibrium tensegrity.

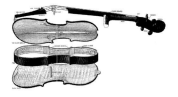

The evolution of the plan shows *parti* rearrangements that experimented with an aesthetic of separate elements composed as an interacting unity yet independent and valid as forms or program organs on their own. The work is a concerto of solo and ensemble volumetric compositions. Le Corbusier described his plan for the 1958 Phillips Pavilion "like a stomach". Here Frank Lloyd Wright and Le Corbusier converge: for both the *organic* suggested an organism of independent solids integrated into a system of organs, like human body. Program can stress volume in plan and section as we see in Le Corbusier's Palace of the Soviets.

THE GEOMETRY OF DYNAMICS

Woven Fingers

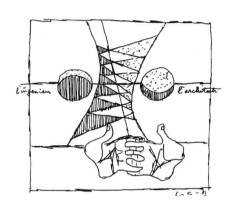

Geometry can solve structural problems. It can also express feeling. Beyond orthogonality there is a larger formal palette for architectural solutions. Le Corbusier sketched the related concerns of engineer and architect as a diagram of sun, moon, and the interlaced fingers of both hands. The vertical axis indicates material constraints (structure, etc.) while the horizontal axis indicates liberty of choice (composition, etc.). The engineer is mostly concerned with physical laws, while the architect is mostly concerned with laws of humanity and beauty. Le Corbusier's diagram recalls Wright's famous illustration of his principles of Organic Architecture, in which he first presented his two hands with palms facing and slipping apart, and then compared it with the fingers of his two hands interlaced. This demonstration of interrelated elements recalls both the rebar-concrete block fabric and the plans of his Usonian houses, where a public (living room, kitchen) wing often intersected with a private (bedroom, bath) wing at the entry.

Square Triangle Circle

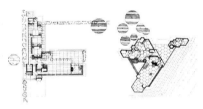

Le Corbusier diagrammed primary forms in his essay *On the Plastic* (see Volume 1.) Remarkably, the same diagram in the same order appears in Sengai's brush painting depicting Zen enlightenment. This figure also appears in three dimensions in Buckminster Fuller's design for an Octet Truss, as well as in the capital letter formulation of the English version of the Chinese philosophy of ecology wisdom called TAO. Square frames without diagonal bracing will rack. A triangle makes the strongest frame, since corners cannot flex or move because they are joined by lines of least distance. A circle has no corners. Each of these basic forms have extremely different properties, which appeal to three aspects of building human space. When filled with mass, a cube can be a strong block. But if the cube is hollow, it is intrinsically weak as a structure in a field of forces like gravity. However, four spheres may be closest packed into a tetrahedron; a successive layer of triangulated tangential spheres will form a cube-octahedron. If these sphere represent radial vector interaction between adjacent fields of energy, they maintain what Fuller calls the *vector equilibrium*. Note that square faces maintain right angle rigidity because every edge is also the edge of an equilateral triangle.

Cube Tetrahedron Sphere

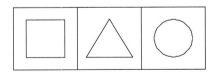

Four triangles can join to make a tetrahedron, the strongest three-dimensional frame. A civil engineer would ideally design for stability with tetrahedral spaceframes, while an HVAC (heating/ventilating/air conditioning) specialist would prefer to make every home a sphere to enclose the largest possible volume with the least surface area to minimize heat loss and promote air flow. Buckminster Fuller's genius combined sphere and triangle as icosahedron via tetrahedron to make the geodesic dome. A tetrahedron's volume is minimal compared to its surface area, whereas a sphere's volume is maximal compared to surface area. Yet for millennia architecture has been based on the cube as volume. Why? Some suggest our opposable thumb. More likely, the intersection of horizon and vertical plumb line forms the dominant right-angled geometry of our local environment. We are upright and face frontally forward. Since architecture concerns the structure of human perception as well as the structures of built volume and atmosphere, there is no perfect form for any structure, but always a balance between at least these three contradictory impulses, which may be why architecture is always geometrically rich. This is especially crucial when creating habitable hollow solids. In Dynamics the question is how to order force and motion to wrap mass around void. As every molecule of every wall and floor is trying to move, architecture requires the stability of firmness as well as the volume of commodity and the harmony of delight. Does not cube imply tetrahedron and sphere?

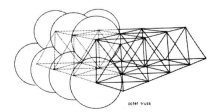

octet truss

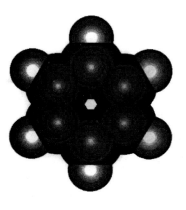

STRENGTH AND WEIGHT

Buckminster Fuller asked "how much does a building weigh?" Before he put it this way, engineers and architects would ask how much beams, columns, roofs or floors weighed, but they did not make weight of the entire structural ensemble a primary concern for the designer of spaces. The important relationships of strength to weight, material to form, and structure to aesthetics, were again raised as legitimate concerns of the architect. Fuller's geodesic dome lifted by a helicopter, shown opposite, is close to the ideal: spherical shape with maximum volume and minimal material.

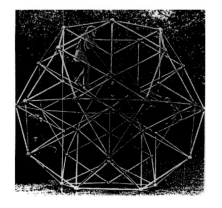

Atoms

Atoms are units of matter identity. The ancient Greeks thought they were the smallest possible units (in Greek *a-tom* means "no cut", "uncuttable"), but today we know atoms are made of even smaller units like electrons, protons, and neutrons (which in turn are made of quarks, which ...) Ernest Rutherford's 1910 experiments showed that most of an atom 's mass is concentrated in its nucleus. Atoms are mostly void, as empty of matter as a solar system. Atoms are more spheres of influence than indivisible "billiard-ball" particles. Electrons whiz far from nuclear protons and neutrons. From atomic to cosmic scale, forces on moving matter determine the shape and structure of volume-- just as they do with rocking chairs and swings. Atoms join by sharing electrons, making chemical compounds of elements. Molecules are the groups of atoms that are units of chemical identity. Common materials are made of huge numbers of molecules. For example a cubic inch of steam would have over 6×10^{20} water molecules!! But any material, even rock, is mostly space. A "solid" desk is actually an array of carbon, hydrogen, oxygen and other atoms held apart by electromagnetic forces. We can equally model molecular structure as close packing sphere-like bubble clusters with electron "skins" or as "tinkertoy" skeletons with mass concentrated at center points. The 20th Century inner space revolution in physics called quantum mechanics, could only explain why negatively charged electrons would not plummet to the positively charged protons in the nucleus by invoking a weird, non-intuitive new world in which an electron must be understood as *both particle and wave*, not a definite thing in a definite place, but a *probability* of finding something somewhere. Einstein rejected this view with his famous "G-d does not play dice" but so far it appears that he was wrong.

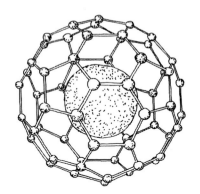

BuckyBalls... Microvolumes

The Nightly News, with its cliché mix of opinion, argument, crime, sports and weather can easily obscure the fact that we live in wonderful times. Science and art continue to merge and reveal marvels. A very contemporary example is the development of a new carbon chemistry based on a hitherto unexpected and unseen form of carbon. Until now, the element carbon was thought to occur naturally in only two forms, graphite and diamond. The nineteenth century saw the discovery of benzene, a six-atom carbon ring, which formed the basis for all organic chemistry industry that has transformed our lives with everything from petroleum to polymers. But now a third basic configuration of carbon has been discovered, consisting of 60 carbon atoms arranged in the same pattern of hexagons and pentagons as the geodesic dome! In honor of the great architect and inventor of these domes, the class of matter has been named buckminsterfullerene (nicknamed "buckyballs"). The fullerene family has a remarkable chemistry, already capable of the highest achieved temperatures for superconductors (materials with virtually no resistance to the flow of electricity), the strongest fibers yet found, and exotic assembly capabilities, like enclosing a uranium atom within its hollow sphere! No mere laboratory curiosity, the development and application of these new materials exploded into business and industry within a matter of months! Buckyballs show that volume even at molecular level is a basic concern in the structure of matter.

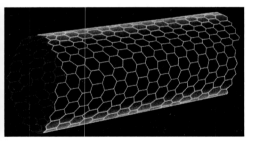

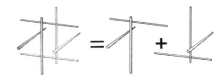

TENSEGRITY

Push and pull drives masses hither and yon, ultimately deriving from the thermal dance of atoms. **Tension**, or stretching, pulls things apart while **compression** tend to push things together. **Structure** is about finding ways to keep "stones" where you want them, whether moving or still. Towers and masts are structures that have demanded utmost ingenuity, since they need to go as far *up* (against gravity) as possible while resisting lateral instability from wind and other loads. Making a tower is like driving a nail into wood, or better, like balancing a pin on its point. A tower is a line into the sky. Is it a line that is stretched or crushed, is it a cable or a column?

Buckminster Fuller found a geometry of structures which resolves individual members into almost all pure compression or pure tension, an equilibrium of push and pull resolved within the structure. He called this **tensegrity**, which he defines as "tension compression integrity", describing a balance of pushing and pulling forces, that is, a tension-compression equilibrium− whose internal force resolution is so strong that it tends to resist any deformation from outside forces or loads. Snelson's *Spring Street* (page 105) is a tensegrity structure. You could actually step on such a tensegrity and flatten it, yet as soon as your foot is removed, the structure would return to its original form. Such a structure has an order which keeps it intact even under external loads. Dynamic loads like vibration can be accommodated and even magnified without unraveling the complex weaving of forces that hold the masses together. This is what violins, clarinets, and drums do.

Fiber: Every Line is Living

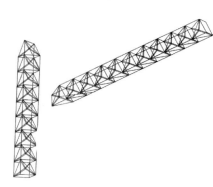

When we pluck the string of a guitar, we apply a force that sets the molecules in its fibers to vibrate not only thermally, but also mechanically. This creates the successive compressions in the air that we hear as sound. Whether pushed, pulled, or plucked, every line in the real world of forces is in motion. While some strings are rigid, like bones, and others stay thin in tension like stretched sinews or skin, eventually even the strongest wire can break, even the toughest rock can crumble. In some sense, the life of a structure is its period of fiber integrity.

A tensegrity like *Spring Street* is robust and long-lasting in its balance of forces, but it is also difficult to build. All aspects of it must be pre-planned. The members must be exact in position, length, and strength, and all must be assembled virtually simultaneously. Its ultimately resolved perfect symmetry is an astounding kind of beauty, but hermetic and closed. Such tensegrity seems to be the very opposite of spontaneous spacial improvisation, but if we recall that construction literally means to "pile things up", then we understand that *every* structure is a tensegrity in which gravity, wind, and other forces always move the parts to an ultimate stability. A pile of rubble can collapse no more-- of course a pile of rubble gives us no room, no volume for human habitation, either. When you take into account all the forces involved in a system, then you will find that every construction is a tensegrity-- the trick is to make it last, and to find the means to sustain its volume.

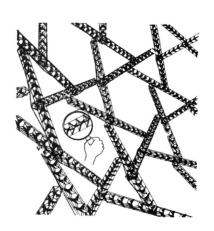

One of the most elegant solutions to the problem of tower is Kenneth Snelson's *Tensegrity Mast*, shown opposite. Snelson, co-inventor of tensegrity with Fuller, has created a structure whose members are either almost entirely squeezed in compression or entirely stretched in tension. The result is a virtually weightless volume, or at least one with a huge proportion of void to mass in the overall structure. The remarkable thing about this form, as Fuller himself has pointed out, is that if you consider the entire mast as a column which mainly resists compression due to gravity, then it should be possible to replace each compression member (the rods rather than the wires) with a smaller version of the whole tensegrity mast. Then each new small compression strut could be replaced by a new miniature tensegrity mast, *ad infinitum*, until the entire form tends toward pure tension only!

Installation view of the exhibition "Three Structures by Buckminster Fuller." The Museum of Modern Art, New York. September 22, 1959 through Spring 1960. Photograph (c) 1998 The Museum of Modern Art, New York.

TENSEGRITY VS. IMPROVISATION

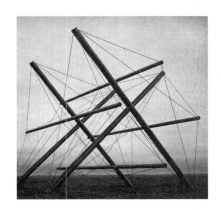

Johann Sebastian Bach (1685-1750) was an excellent improviser. At age 62, he visited son Carl Philip Emanuel Bach and was asked byFrederick the Great to improvise on a theme based on his name (h in German was B flat) Spontaneously, he wove not just the four parts of a fugue, but the many voices of a ricercar, a complex musical form of counterpoint for six or more voices, and created the wonderful *Musical Offering*. However, that was after a lifetime of "woodshedding" at the highest possible levels of musical invention in composition and technical mastery in performance. Bach was said to be the best organist of his day. The play of improvising spacial order may be as natural to the brain as breathing is to the lungs. Who has not arranged restaurant utensils parallel to table edges, marking areas through geometry and rhythmic spacial interval, positioning empty solids of volume? We make a first "move": point a spoon at a glass, align a dish, and organize divide the table. We build inward and out, relating and responding, elegantly joining volumes into interacting areas. Experiment and invention reveal "moves" until an unexpected organization emerges.

On the other hand, there is much to be said for perfect order. Take one cable or rubber band away from a tensegrity and the whole thing explodes. A tensegrity like the cuboctahedron of the frontispiece is **very** hard to build-- all the members must be both the right length and the right strength, and they must all be assembled simultaneously-- externally held in place until every rubber band is properly stretched and attached. Some building plans seem to be as tightly ordered, and preordained, as a tensegrity. Move one window, wall, stair, or column in Ise, the Parthenon, or Villa Capra and the proportional harmonies are destroyed. The perfection of a plan tensegrity seems to be the very opposite of spontaneous improvisation. No wonder Le Corbusier wrote of his "simple" shoebox *parti* for Villa Garches "*tres difficile*"! The stretched strings of a violin are in tension. Its wooden bridge, pegs, and sounding box create a structure whose compression must equal the strings' tension. When played, the vibrating strings move the air and wood of the instruments sound box, which sets the air we hear as sound in motion. Although many parts oscillate, the instrument of course does not break apart-- rather, it makes music. The tightly organized picture planes of certain Purist and Cubist paintings are a kind of visual tensegrity-- balancing forces between painting field and implied three-dimensional space. What distinguishes architectural tensegrity from the more "molecular" tensegrities of Snelson and Fuller is the presence and participation of the site as a necessary part of any volumetric unity.

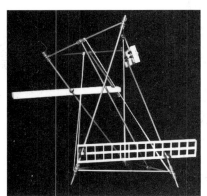

BOB ALBERT

In 1959 the Museum of Modern Art presented a show of Buckminster Fuller's geodesic and tensegrity structures, as shown opposite. What was striking to the thoughtful visitor was that here were all the essential tensegrity "toys" arrayed at full scale for human habitation. The message was clearly not that these were finished structures, but rather the basic elements for a new building kit that someday might well replace current wood frame construction. The plastician's primary needs for defining volumes were satisfied, but at a new scale. Point, line and plane were provided-- but rather than as nail, 2 x 4 framing stud, and plywood sheathing, here they were given as geodesic dome, tensegrity mast, and tensegrity space frame respectively. The possibilities of their linkages and combinations are no less limited than the improvisations of add-on rooms contemplated by every home-owner with a growing family. Here they reveal a new vocabulary of forms that can operate in an additive mode no less that the trabeated orthogonal structure of wood frame construction. These masts, slabs, and bubbles suggest extension and interconnection if we see them not as finished isolated elements but as extensions along many axes of growth. Following this path, architect and inventor Steve Baer has developed Zomes, which permit extrusion along all the implied axes of a geodesic crystalline sphere, and designed and built structures like the playground climber shown on page 123 based on them.

CREATION II

ALISSA FELDMAN

BRAD ANDERSON

impromptu: modeling as spacetime animation

> *"The art of structure is where to put the holes."* Robert Le Ricolais

Modelling solids subject to loads directly in three dimensions is itself is a kind of animation, since mass deforms under load when time is present to permit such motion. Issues discussed in the previous few pages require more than just reading to fully grasp and truly feel their impact. Thus a brief exercise is offered here, not so much a formal "Doing" as much as a kind of finger exercise, perhaps a kind of three-dimensional calligraphy of structure and structural elements, an animation of spacetime phenomena directly in its fundamental medium.

DYNAMICS

Improvise a tensegrity of at least 3 mutually perpendicular planes.

Use your Bag of Tricks to compose the planes into an "air", a unified solid which is mostly void-- a perceptible volume. This space should be essentially equal in extent in all three dimensions and may be conceived either as mass perforated by void, void perforated by mass, or void perforated by void. Your improvisation may be a "temporary" tensegrity, differing from a true tensegrity in that when temporarily deformed (stepping on it) in may not necessarily bounce back and return to its original three-dimensional configuration. If you can rotate your project to a different orientation so that bottom is now top or side, it is to some degree structurally stable independent of its gravity orientation, although not necessarily yet independent of its external load condition. To assure you have made a complete tensegrity, you must balance the forces so that when the structure is moved to any position or orientation, the overall configuration and relationship between elements remains the same.

Use no glue!! Gravity and mechanical connections are the "glue" that hold the parts together. Explore the material, physical, structural, light-modulating and space-making properties in your Bag of Tricks as you work outward from an origin. Be inventive in discovering what each element can do and how they can join together. Consider how a concept of structure informs a concept of space. Consider the spectrum of materials (rigid to flexible), connections (pin/moment), volumes (open-closed, tensed-compressed, horizontal-vertical) you make. See the Appendix for more on improvising structure. THEME AND VARIATIONS: Working quickly, use the same elements in different combinations to make four more variations, for a total of five different structures in all.

ANIMATION

In a sequence of at least five time frames show the assembly of your tensegrity from the first joining of two elements. Indicate the forces that act on the two elements of this first joint through the entire five frames as a set of free body diagrams, showing the magnitude and direction of the forces, and how they balance into equilibrium at each stage. Make your drawings sufficiently careful and accurate that anyone else could reassemble your structure, knowing how to manage the forces on the pieces. Exchange these "working drawings" with another set and build the new project from what you receive. Compare results!

COLOR

1. ***Relative Contrast: Gray Scale***. Place 2 areas of 1 **Color-aid** *gray* on 2 color fields, using relative contrast of hue, value, and chroma, to make the three selected colors appear as four.   See page 463.

2. ***Relative Contrast: Color Pairs***. Place 2 areas of 1 **Color-aid** color, on 2 color fields using relative contrast of hue, value, and chroma, to make the three selected colors appear as four.   See page 463.

MIKE RIZZO

LUIGI CIACCIA

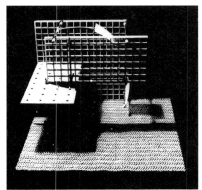

BENJAMIN HURWITZ

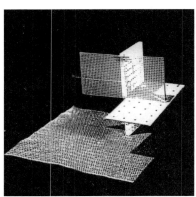

M. CASDIA

CANON

row, row, row your boat, gently down the stream...

Canon in Latin means" measuring line, rule", from the Greek *kanon, kane*, a reed, rod. Canon defines a law or body of laws; any law or decree; a standard used in judging something; criterion. In music, canon is a round; composition in which there are exact repetitions of a preceding part in the same or related keys. The **impromptu** exercise suggests another step, where the emphasis is on void rather than mass, or more precisely, on the creation of volume, bounded solid both empty and filled. This is the exact stuff of space, the "clay" that architects mold to make space a perceptible phenomenon of human experience. Composing directly with volume as the primary material is, in essence, the CANON of architecture. Now we are ready to leap across the canyon to confront architecture on its own terms. Architects are ultimately judged on their ability to orchestrate the interaction of volume.

Defining Volume

How can we see empty solids? Certainly the vertices (corners), edges, and surfaces of a solid must be identifiable, but some may imply others not actually marked by mass. Usually, more than three of the six sides of a cubic volume need to be opaque or otherwise marked, but they need not "outline" the volume-- they may imply it and build it through the boundaries of their own edge conditions and their location inside the volume. Positioned correctly, just two perpendicular sides and an opposing edge may define a cube. Clearly, mass need not completely fill the region, nor need sense of enclosure be absolute for the solid to be present to our perception. An architect may both wrap mass around a void and sustain mass through it to define a single volume or a whole fabric of volumes.

Take a look at the work you have just completed for "Improvised Tensegrity". Notice that each piece is composed of rhythmically spaced little volumes. The eggcrate is made of hollow cubes close together, the pegboard masonite is made of flattish cylinders more distantly spaced apart. Now it should not be a hard leap to reconsider "Improvised Tensegrity" as a study of the resolution of forces not on masses but on volumes. Volume must come to the foreground of your compositional concerns. Architects work directly in the medium of space. This is how to make something from nothing!

Intersecting Planes vs. Intersecting Volumes

Notice that the most three-dimensional, deepest, "neatest" Improvised Tensegrities"-- the most spacial-- usually include a clearly marked or strongly implied intersection of at least three mutually perpendicular planes. Of course this is so! By definition, three dimensions must be exploited in fully plastic spacial works. But it is possible to make the intersection out of volume, primarily, rather than mass. Some of the projects on these two pages are made primarily of the intersections of three mutually perpendicular **mass** planes intersecting, while others are made primarily of the three mutually perpendicular **volumes** intersecting. Can you distinguish which are which? If melody is a rhythmic succession of single tones organized as an aesthetic whole, then perhaps joining three mutually perpendicular volumes may form the spacial equivalent of the triad of tones forming the musical structure called a chord. Like mass, volume can be improvised. First join a few elements in an elegant way. Then build inward or outward from one and then another direction from the first elegant connection of solids, or elegantly join elements onto the first extension. As these steps are repeated to achieve a balanced set of volumes, allow isolated structures of voids to intersect, securing connections into a stable tensegrity of both mass and volume.

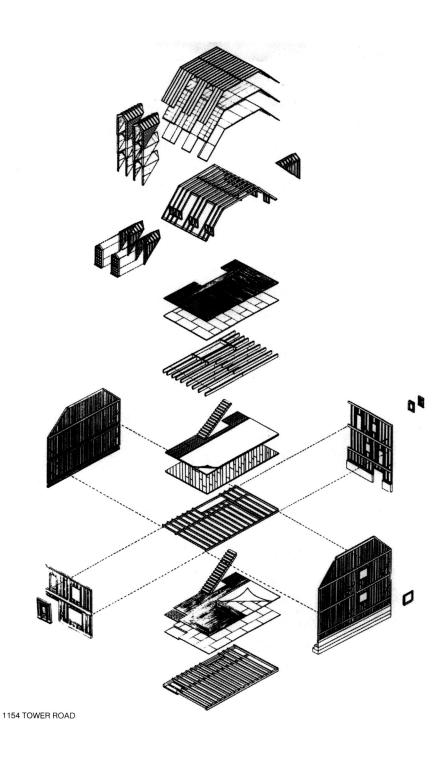

A "volume" from three "fat" "planes"
cubic space from three intersecting volumes--

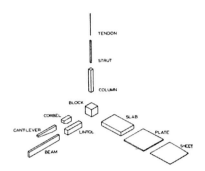

The primary elements of structure belong to a progression which is not only historical, but depends on the nature of the material from which it is made.

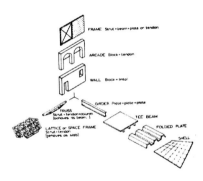

Once the primary elements of structure are understood, the development of skeleton and surface structure from these primary elements is clear.

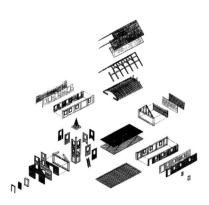

The Little Dutch Church, Brunswick Street

REVEALING VOLUME

Proportioned Solids: "Line", "Plane"...

A solid is a bounded three dimensional figure, filled or empty. Just as a chain is a discontinuous line, so is a space-frame a discontinuous plane. And just as a drinking straw is a hollow line, so is an air mattress a hollow plane. A volume need not literally be enclosed to be present to perception and experience. A floor deck, a wall, and an overhanging canopy may well define an exterior cubic volume as an outdoor room. The proportions of a volume may qualify it as closer to a figure of one or two rather than three dimensions. For example, a corridor is more a "line" and a whole floor of apartment "flats" is more a "plane" than a point-like room. Quotation marks around such terms as "line" and "plane" here indicate solids with such non-solid characteristics. In this sense, volume can be linear or planar. An elevator shaft, like the drinking straw, is a "line," while an air mattress is a "plane."

Extend a cube along one primary axis and get a line-like rod, extend it along two axes to get a plane-like slab. There are two ways of seeing the relationship between a cube and a rod. The first is to see the rod as simply the addition of many square cross-section layers packed in a row, discrete pieces becoming more discrete even down to the molecular, atomic, and subatomic levels. The second is to understand the rod as a cube which has been stretched in one direction, relating cube and rod in a wavelike manner of greater or less frequency. (Is a light-beam a cube stretched to maximum wavelength?) The first is an addition of discrete architectonic "still life" elements; the second is the transformation of a single *dynamic* volumetric entity. These contrasts parallel the particle-wave duality of light phenomena.

... and "Volume"

Geometry in two dimensions still sustains a high degree of abstraction. But in the real spacetime world of three-plus dimensions, thickness is no longer negligible. A thread is mainly linear, yet it still possesses width and breadth. Thickness affects the properties of material and structures it can support. For example, if a slab of mainly planar masonite pegboard is made too thin or wide, gravity or wind will warp the plane. The distribution of mass in space can make a structural element stronger. A spring is part line (coiled spiral), part plane (tube), and part volume (cylinder). An I-beam has the most steel at its edges, an open web joist has almost no steel in the middle. An eggcrate frame is a "plane" that can be lighter while supporting more than a solid slab of the same material. The Eiffel Tower and the Verrazano Bridge show how very elegant can be the distant distribution of mass in space-- each defining volume from masses kept far apart, hardly touching each other.

Architecture can explore fascinating questions of the relationship of plasticity to perception. Must a line or plane be made from a single piece? *Can* a "line" or "plane" be made from a single piece? Can a repetition of oddly shaped elements read as another form. For example, can a series of folded vaults define a "plane"? How do mesh, grid, net, network, and frame differ, and in what sense are they the same? How might volume and "volume" differ? A cube can be the result of three intersecting "planes" or defined by two "lines" and a "plane". The Vertical Assembly Building at Cape Kennedy Florida is a space frame "volume", and Villa Shodan is a "volume" made of a rich mix of "lines" "planes" and "volumes". *We can translate any* **mass** *shape or figure into an equivalent if not exactly congruent* **volume**. And of course, it is possible to to translate any **volume** figure into an equivalent if not exactly congruent set of **masses**.

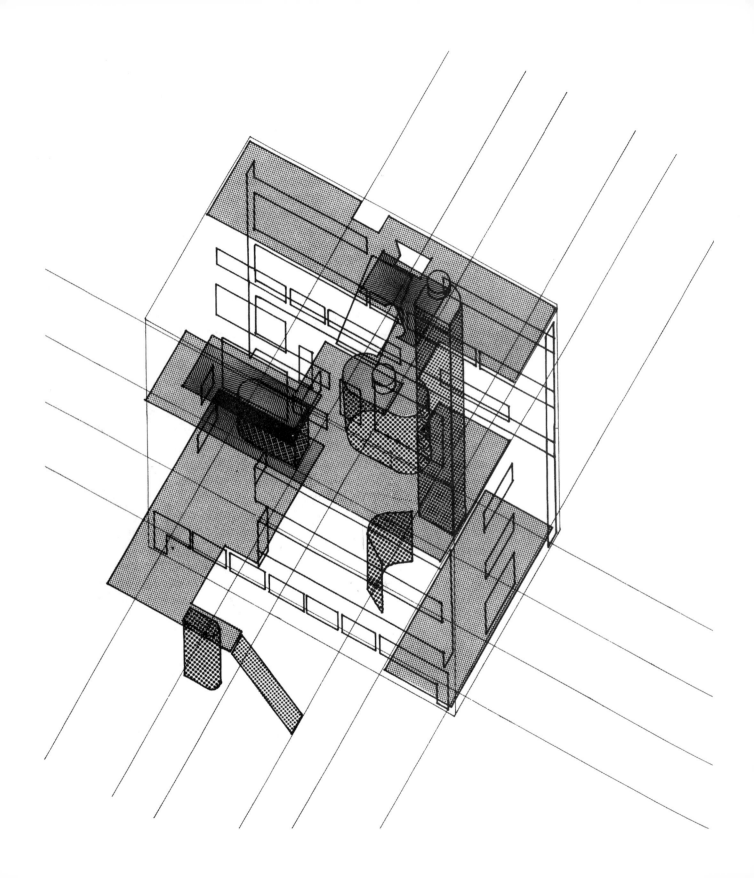

PRECISION

High Resolution and Low Resolution

Once, a near-sighted architect broke one of two contact lenses. For a few days, he walked around with one lens in and one lens out. A curious way of viewing the world emerged-- one eye saw only large fuzzy areas of colored light, while the other eye saw the sharp contours and lines that depict the precise edges of objects. One eye gave spacial information in low resolution, the other provided high-resolution definition. Together, the two fields merged into a complex set of layers of overlapping fields and lines, and the tension between the two induced an extraordinary sense of depth and volume in the mind. A late lithograph by Le Corbusier comes very close to illustrating this experience. Le Corbusier called the Gothic cathedrals "hirsute, arrayed as an army" since the exterior flying buttresses that carried the span thrust of the nave far enough from the walls to admit light made a "hairy" outside massing in order to sustain the smooth "pure" volume of the interior nave.

Marking volumetric boundaries with surfaces, lines and corners is a high-resolution method of defining volume. (A wire frame model in this sense is a high-resolution definition of a volume.) But low-resolution volumes can also exist, like clouds, whose general extent is present as a dense center with hazy edges. There are advantages to both. When we don't want to allow local shapes to interfere with finding overall solutions to combinations of volume, low-resolution definition is often preferable. Many architects will cut out rough areas of colored paper to represent program elements in the early stages of resolving a design problem, to quickly locate program areas, not caring so much about their shapes as much as the relative sizes of the elements. Architects usually sketch volume first in low resolution when locating program elements for solving a *parti*, while engineers often define volume immediately in high resolution, locating structural and skin elements even before programmatic use for a space has been established. Precision in architecture consists of unifying high and low resolution definitions of volume.

The bubble meets the spaceframe

Which is the "best" strategy for the architect-- the designer of both mass structure and hollow volume? For hollow lightweight structures like straws, bird's bones, open-web joists, the eggcrate of the Bag of Tricks, free body diagrams still apply. When solids are mostly, or even completely, empty, they are volume. Are there not forces on these empty solids akin to those on structural mass elements. Zones of volumetric interactions may reveal "a free volume diagram" akin to the free body diagram used to analyze structural loads, as shown opposite in the layered axonometric analysis of Le Corbusier's Villa Garches, built in 1927. Are there still forces that tend to move these free "bodies"? What kind of loads can push or pull volumes? The dynamics of volume is not an engineering problem but an architectural one. The designer may generate a space frame of structural support, or a set of inflatable bubbles of program volumes. For some, the ideal solution requires these to converge, so that one seems to press against the other. Then there will be precision fitting of every solid, so that structure and habitation will support, define, and reveal each other. The space between the steel frame skeleton of a high-rise building is where we live and work. Alignment generates precision and reveals the forces acting betweensolids. For example, a square diagrams the concept of room as brick. But a thickening of its outline suggests void with mass at the perimeterwhich generates the edge and center square -within-a-square diagram we saw in Prelude. We shall find other implications in the pages to come.

FORCES ON VOLUMES

Earlier we saw how considering forces on masses allows builders to create volume. We shall now proceed to a subtle extension of that understanding, and discuss how architects create meaning-ful space through resolving **forces on *volume*.** Empty solids can be treated like filled solids both architectonically and dynamically. Even when masses are mostly empty as in straws or honey-combs, the free body diagram still applies. A heavy weight deflects a beam. Mass-filled solids push and pull each other in fields of forces like gravity or wind. How then do empty solids interact? Consider volumes as free bodies. Can one diagram forces on volumes? If a load can bend or shear a beam, then how may a nearby room bend or shear a beam like a corridor? In such a manner, architects develop "moves", ways to think about shifting volume elements in plastic compositions. Volume transformation is a drama of spacial "forces" which may emerge in the final form as a simultaneously revealed animation. In his house for his parents, architect Charles Gwathmey developed a rich interplay of volumes pushing and pulling each other, yet the space is ultimately in repose. Not only are the structural forces acting on masses resolved into equilibrium, but also are the architectural forces acting on the volumes. This house exhibits a precision in volumetric design, where the low-resolution overall strategies of program organization merge perfectly with the high-resolution order of volumetric definition, even down to the careful choice of visible details like which handrail upstands to make opaque and which to leave open, less visible details like the carefully considered and changing orientation of the resawn cedar siding both inside and out, and the nearly invisible details like the grade elevation of the foundation cap to allow the house to read as a perfect cube delicately poised to meet, not crush, the ground.

How does an architect build with "bricks" of rooms? Is it just a matter of putting one volume next to another, above, below, or side by side, and hope that all goes well? For Architectonics, that is probably a sufficient level of insight. But now we understand that moving matter in fields of forces produces loads on structural elements. Just as taffy stretches, so too may volumes react to forces of spacial organization, of the plan and section. Architects act on the idea that there are *at least* perceptual and organizational forces on the order of the spaces. What kind of loads can push or pull volumes? The methods of locating program elements (rooms stairs, etc.) in plan and section can lead to a structure of activity relationships. "...these rooms are a tight fit, but if I can just squeeze this...." A successful volumetric order will resolve its architectural forces into a kind of tensegrity of plan/section and fully three-dimensional space.

Forces *OF* Volumes

Forces may distort volumes. For example, where a room meets a corridor, proper architecture recognizes this event , adding volume to accommodate the door swing as well as the two very different actions of walking along a corridor and negotiating a door (stopping, turning the knob, preparing to enter or leave one space for another). An inflecting wall, widening of the plan, balcony opposite the door, or a combination of these and more may become appropriate architectural responses. Space is dynamic. We can imagine that void is the tension between masses stretched apart and that mass is the compression between voids seeking the union of complete vacuum. On the other hand, void can be felt as the compression between masses seeking the union of perfect density, while mass may be the tension between voids. Ambiguity results from both readings being present simultaneously. Volume is the sum of mass-void interactions, while architectural **space** is the sum of all solid interactions, both empty and filled. Discussing Gwathmey's work, Peter Eisenman has written, "Pragmatic formalism is defined when the conceptual mechanisms that inform what can be called in this case a formal ordering, i.e. hollowing, rotation, extension, and so on, at the same time informs *vectoring of movement* in the building."

"SPACIAL FORCES"

Charles Gwathmey: Gwathmey Studio and House, Amagansett, New York, 1965-67. Axonometric.

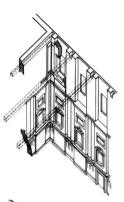

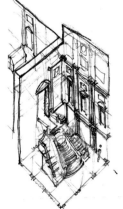

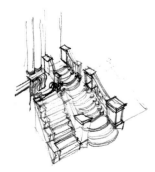

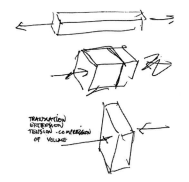

TRANSLATION
EXTENSION
TENSION - COMPRESSION
OF VOLUME

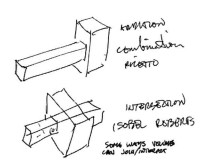

TRANSLATION.
combustion
RICETTO

INTERSECTION
(SOME ROBBERS

SOME WAYS VOLUMES
CAN JOIN/INTERACT

TENSION   COMPRESSION

ADDITION OF VOLUMES

Laurentian library
ricetto vertical volume (ex-)tension and
compression by walls, reading room horizontal volume(ex-)tension and compression in perspective by grid rhythm

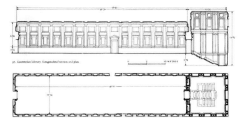

AN EXAMPLE: ARCHITECTURAL FORCE ON VOLUME *(STRETCHING BOXES)*

Michelangelo's Laurentian Library shows how architectural forces can modulate habitable volume. This early nearly-public library of the private Medici book collection, begun in 1524, only 70 years after Gutenberg's use of movable type, is also a psychological drama about the difficult access to knowledge of both the world and the self. Everywhere in this composition, push and pull vie for supremacy, architectural forces distort and deflect solids, stretching and squeezing both masses and volumes, exaggerating dimensions. Loading one volume can often animate neighboring spaces. The Ricetto, or antechamber, stretches vertically and activates its surrounding skin of internal wall surfaces into a writhing vibration of compressing and expanding planar counterpoint. It is a cube pulled taller, while the reading room is a rod pulled horizontally longer. The space made by this sculptor is like both taffy and marshmallow, yielding and resisting to heighten contrast in primary dimensions. These volumes reveal the forces acting on them: in the Ricetto stretched yet turbulent walls culminate in the crushed flattened oozing lava flow stair, while an accelerated perspective rushes the reading room deep into the distance (see page 16, Volume 1). In his letter to Giorgio Vasari, Michelangelo not only suggests the rich plastic world of interacting solids, both empty and filled, that he was creating, but also seems to anticipate the intuitions of Sigmund Freud (1856-1939) about the human psyche, articulated almost 400 years later.

> "Giorgio, my dear friend... Concerning the stairway for the library that I've been asked about so much, believe me if I could remember how I planned it I would not need to be asked. A certain staircase comes to my mind just like a dream, but I don't think it can be the same one I had in mind originally since it seems so awkward. However, I'll describe it to you: first it is as if you took a number of oval boxes, each about a span deep but not of the same length or width, and placed the largest down on the paving further from or nearer to the wall with the doors, depending on the gradient wanted for the stairs. Then it is as if you placed another box on top of the first, smaller than the first and leaving all round enough for space for the foot to ascend; and so on, diminishing and drawing back the steps towards the door, always with enough space to climb; and the last step should be the same as the opening of the door. And this oval stairway should have two wings, one on either side, following the centre steps but straight instead of oval. The central flight form the beginning of the stairs to half-way up should be reserved for the master. The ends of the two wings should face the walls and, with the entire staircase, come about three spans from the wall, leaving the lower parts of each wall of the anteroom completely unobstructed. I am writing nonsense, but I know you will find something here to your purpose. Michelangelo Buonarroti" September 1555

Freud's investigations into the realm of the unconscious include a passage remarkable in its parallels to Michelangelo's letter. It is hard not to think of the Ricetto in terms of Freud's spacial metaphor for exploring human psychology when reading these words....

> "During the period of the technical papers, Freud was guided in his thinking about repression and resistance by conceiving of the mind in terms of a *spatial* arrangement of the unconscious and conscious states. In the *Introductory Lectures*, proposing a "crude" metaphor, he asks the student to imagine a large entrance hall that opens onto a small narrow drawing room. In the large hall (the unconscious), mental impulses "jostle one another" as they try to get past the guard who stands on the threshold of the drawing room, which Freud named the preconscious. The fate of most of these impulses is to be immediately repelled by the guard or, should they slip by him and get into the drawing room, to be dragged back. (The latter are the *repressed* unconscious thoughts.) The few impulses that are allowed into the conscious drawing room are not yet conscious, and may or may not become so, depending on whether or not they "succeed in catching the eye of consciousness". Freud located this "eye" at the far end of the preconscious drawing room. The significant border relationship in regard to repression and resistance was not the one between the preconscious and the conscious but the one between the preconscious and the unconscious. This "topographic" model of the mind was derived from Freud's concept of how dreams are formed, and remains at the heart of psychoanalysis. ("The property of being conscious or not is in the last resort our one beacon light in the darkness of depth psychology," Freud wrote in 1923 in "The Ego and the Id.")

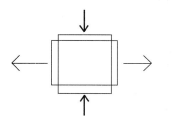

VILLA CAPRA, ANDREA PALLADIO 1516, PLAN

POISSON'S RATIO

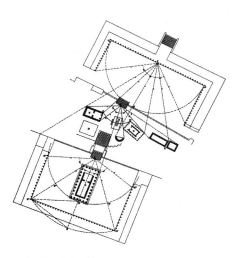

Cos, Ascelpeion. Plan.

STRETCHING A POINT

"Pushing and pulling both produce 90 degree resultants, which we mistakenly call side effects, and vice versa.
R. Buckminster Fuller, Tensegrity

Stress and Strain

We use force to move something. Newton wrote F = ma, indicating that force, motion, and matter are intertwined. What is the relationship between force and volume? How do masses move in relationship to the loads placed upon them? This basic question of civil engineering is also a key to understanding how architects form orders of volumes; how they manipulate positional and proportional relationships in plan and section to accommodate programs of required spaces. When solids resist applied forces they generate **stress**; when solids yield to applied forces, they undergo **strain**. **Stress** is the internal force per unit area on a material. Tensile and compressive and shear stresses can act axially (along the line of the load) or laterally (perpendicular to the load). **Strain** is the geometric deformation of a body under load. Masses compress and tense under external loads, and their internal structure yields to the strain. Cables in tension can be very thin and still strong, whereas any resistance to compression requires some thickness to the member to resist both crushing and buckling. To some degree, stress tells us of forces acting within a free body element, whereas strain tells us of forces that remain outside the free body.

Push the ends of a marshmallow together and the sides fatten. Pull taffy and it thins. **Poisson's ratio** compares the axial and lateral unit strain in a given material. Every pull on mass generates a lengthening strain in the direction of the pull. This increased length comes from a reduction of cross section area, thinning the material into a filament. Stretch a rubber band and it gets skinnier. Every push forces matter away from the compressed zone, fattening the sides. Forces may distort volumes. The plan of Palladio's Villa Capra shows the effects of loading both along and across the major axes of volumes. Although the building is externally symmetrical on all four sides, the plan reveals a "Poisson diagram" in which the entry forces a compressive organization of rooms which then generates an expansion outward perpendicular to the line of that compression. A loaded column takes stress and bulges outward. The exterior escalator tube at the Pompidou Centre in Paris is a "line "-- a stretched balcony "volume" with people in it!

We may extrapolate how this effect may work on a structure of volumes. Let's imagine a parallel condition for an architect who needs to fit 20 row-houses at 400 square feet each into a site only 340 feet long. Each unit is normally 20 feet wide, but that would require 400 linear feet, which exceeds our site by 60 feet. Can we squeeze the unit plan to be only 17 feet wide? But then we must lengthen the unit to 23.5 feet to provide the needed 400 square feet. This taxes our plan-- windows may not get light sufficiently deep into the unit-- can we move closets, stairs, bathrooms into this center dark zone? This is an example how the stress of fitting volumes to a given site can strain a plan and demand ingenuity in the volumetric solution. Le Corbusier's 1952 Unité d'Habitation at Marseilles is a masterful example of resolving such spacial stresses: he minimized the bulk of the building and maximized the number of units per facade by making each double height unit only 15' wide and about 60' deep. The plan includes neighboring children's bedrooms each only 7.5' wide-- a sliding full wall blackboard partition between them offers privacy but also permits a shared playroom 15' wide! He minimized the building's height by developing an ingenious interlocking section around an access corridor located only every third floor. In some rooms walls compress, in others space flies out to the horizon. Ronchamp is a complex volume that plays the plastic emotions of compressing ceiling and opening southeast corner against each other.

RIGGED ALTERATIONS

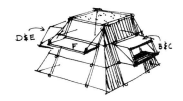

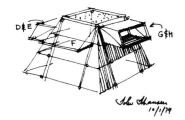

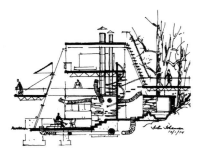

IS THE CUBE A POINT?

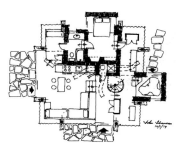

*The point is cosmic, a primordial element.. The primordial movement, the agent, is a point
that sets itself in motion. A line comes into being (genesis of form).
The most highly charged line is the most authentic line because it is the most active.* Paul Klee

Point is related to pungent, puncture, pugilistic, and poignant. Perhaps it is also akin to *poem* in the
Sanskrit root meaning *to make, to construct or arrange.* Is a point solid? Every seedpod is a birth
of volume. Paul Klee suggested a dynamic geometry in which a point in motion generates a line, a
moving line generates a plane, and a moving plane generates a solid. This simple parable of
development from zero to three dimensions suggest a relationship between forms in different
dimensions. A room is like a point compared to a more linear corridor, while a whole floor of
apartment "flats" is more like a plane. What then is a solid in space-- a cube in time? A "room of one's
own" be a "can point of stability" in a fluctuating world. Structural engineers seek to extend points of
mass in three directions, while architects seek to extend volumes. A cube is a right rectangular
parallelepiped solid whose extensions are equal in all three mutually perpendicular spacial dimensions. Architects often seem to favor cubes, perhaps because they suggest spacial fullness, even
roundness. (A sphere is tangent to a cube inside it at all eight corners, to a cube outside it at all six
face center-points.) Other solids alone may become paradoxically less spacial as they grow fuller
along one or two rather than all three dimensions. As volumes thrust first along one dimensional axis
and then another, the original cubic volume gets deformed, and may experience both stretching
and squeezing. In this sense, we may suggest that a tensegrity is an evolution of the origin point.

Dwelling Volume, Elbow Room

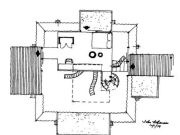

To live in space we must create habitable volumes. To create volumes we must organize an
interplay between mass and void according to the loads and stresses that various forces, both
physical and organization, make present in our field of operation. Architect John Johansen's home
embodies both cave and treehouse: it is like living in an acorn as it pops outward to become living
in an oak. No doubt desiring an economy of means, the architect used and expressed common
material like corrugated siding and flexible ductwork throughout. The curved duct also marks a
gateway dividing one zone of the house from another. The *volume* structure of the house, an
exploded 9-square plan and 27-cube solid, is similar to Theo Van Doesburg's three-dimensional
diagram , but here the scheme is given a literal expression through foldout platforms and balconies.
Three perpendicular axes are developed through the masses of vertical spiral stair, horizontal
ducts, and suspended bed platforms as counterpoint to the axes' volumetric development. Except
for the masonry-enclosed bedroom suite, the house is a single volume throughout. Its space is
continuous, not broken into separate rooms. Upper bedrooms achieve privacy through sectional
isolation without cutting off flow of air or space in this solid.

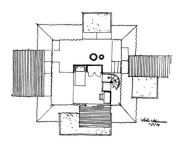

Thus we might identify a means of animation called spacing, in which we improvise the generation
of a "balloon" of space, through the solids that surround and permeate a volume. Spacing suggests
an improvisation of positioning solids, locating things in space and time, like the mental place held
for the next cube in four-dimensional tic-tac-toe. This is similar to working out a sequence of
construction, only for kitchens and living rooms, rather than just for concrete foundations and wood
stud walls. At each scale of intersection and detail, there are important proximity relationships
between the elements. The most immediate become the **tactical** concerns. When tactics must be
ordered globally, **strategy** enters. A doorknob sits in a lockset, which sits in the door frame, which
sits in the wall in the room-- tactics; the position of this room in relation to other rooms-- strategy. At
the scale of a whole city, a house is a cube. Is the cube a point?

GEORGE FIGUEROA

OSCAR HIGUERA

CHRIS BALLANTINE

DOING

Canon defines a criterion or body of laws; in *music*, canon is a round. The following investigation builds on the experience gained in the *impromptu* exercise. Now the emphasis is now on void rather than mass, or more precisely, on the creation of volume, bounded solid both empty and filled. This is the exact stuff of space, the "clay" that architects mold to make space a perceptible phenomenon of human experience.

*D*YNAMICS

Make a space station (a time ship).

Organize mass to define the volume of a 14' cube (+/- 2' in each dimension), at 1/2" = 1' - 0" scale, using elements from the Bag of Tricks. Consider the result as a climbing structure that allows a person to explore three intersecting perpendicular orders of movement (up-down, in-out, left right). Add vertical circulation as needed. Organize the volume so that it reacts to and resolves the architectural forces that result from the program of action of human entry into, circulation through, and exit from the volume. This is at least a dialog between volumes of arrival (stasis) and volumes of passage (transition). You may wish to include a mezzanine at about 7 or 8 feet off the ground.

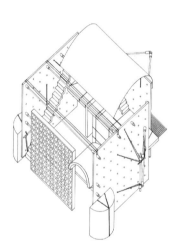

Make your space station/time ship stable in the face of changes due to loads and forces. Use tubes, planes, and space frames. Use lines and joints to transfer loads as needed, but try to keep their forms part of and subordinate to the plastic intentions of the *volumetric* order. Use whatever you need from the complete Bag of Tricks, including stair elements. No minimum or maximum is specified; however, you should use no more than what is absolutely necessary for the order of space and structure. This is called ECONOMY OF MEANS. The construction should touch the ground at no more than three points, or along a line (the edge of a plane) and one other point. Develop your scheme through model and freehand sketches of plan section, axonometric, perspective, etc. Document the final result. Be sure to draw the sections through all perforations that you cut. You might wish to make small-scale paper models to study the architectural and structural forces that animate the space. Locate north and identify the passage of light.

ANIMATION

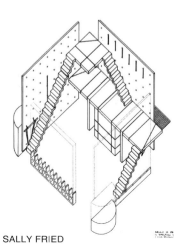

Draw a projection in a sequence of at least three time frames that shows the assembly of your three mutually perpendicular volumetric "planes" from first the joining of two elements. Indicate through color and/or free body diagrams (of the volumes!) the interaction of the volumes that might be generated by any forces they exert on each other.

COLOR

3. **Relative Contrast: Four to Three.**   See page 463.
4. **Collage 1:** Edge contrast between adjacent fields.   See page 463 .

FUNCTION

On graph paper, plot the function $x^2 + y^2 = 1$ with as many points as necessary to enable you to construct a smooth curve in ink.   See page 452.

SALLY FRIED

IN-HABITING

We grow up and enlarge our vision beyond the blocks that frame the dream castles of our childhood. We create vessels of dwelling volume for ourselves and our institutions, no longer simply arranging masses on a tabletop, but also in the world around us. It takes effort to create spaces bigger than ourselves, and ingenuity to arrange surrounding masses to keep them from collapsing in on us. We find ourselves embedded in the spaces we create, not simply observers regarding them from outside. To build structures larger than ourselves we must contend with span and spine, as we make habitable hollows out of the heavy masses that would otherwise crush us. Rooms are volumes bigger than our bodies. It takes effort to place the boundaries of our inhabiting beyond our easy grasp. As void becomes preponderant, free body masses are kept in place by combinations of carefully applied forces, systems which have both space and time dimensions.

Since people need whole rooms, not just walls, engineers have learned to resolve structural forces through a geometry of intersection that balances opposing loads rather than through the simple inertia of heavy stones. It is possible to improvise an order of masses (structure in the common usage) and an order of voids (rooms) simultaneously, or nearly so, and to use the insights gained in one area to inform the development and resolution of the other. To make a single room eloquently, where walls are as much the result of the volumetric idea as the cause of it, has often been the basis for the most daring revelations about architecture. Important examples include the construction of Abbe Suger's 'gothic' scholastic program at Sainte Chappelle, Brunelleschi's Pazzi Chapel, Wright's Unity Temple, Mies van der Rohe's Barcelona Pavilion, Lou Kahn's Trenton Bath House, and Le Corbusier's chapel at Ronchamp. Architecture arises from the continuity of order in the fabric of mass and void and the relationships of volumes it creates.

As we learn to build volumes for our adult realities, we may find in them all the poetry, dreams, and imagination of the 5 year old architect, and thus give voice to the humanity within us all. Architects cultivate imagination through the poetic content of the play between mass and void in the structure of space. In some rooms we sense oppression as the ceiling seems to press downward, as at Ronchamp (*plus bas sil vous plait*); whereas in others a soaring space above us seems to raise our spirits, as at Beauvais Cathedral. In the hands of an architect, space is not passively empty. Rather, space becomes a plastic medium, alive to forces running through and around it. Such forces divide volume into smaller zones or unify it into larger ensembles, making contrasts to mass as well as other voids. Humans animate space by inhabiting it. Architecture animates dwelling by responding to human aspiration. The skylit tiled *chaise longe* in the bath at Le Corbusier's Villa Savoye reveals the human body as subject of the composition, in partnership with light and space. It welcomes our custom to the rituals of daily life, making room for our needs, firmly accommodating us with delight, giving us the precise space we need to dwell in our habits. George Segal's sculpture of lovers beneath the stairs brings to mind Gaston Bachelard's *Poetics of Space*, in which the psychology of the mind is mapped in the topography of a house, from subconscious cellar to superego Apollonian attic garret. The rhythmic washboard staircase carries the mind to promised if as yet unreached heights of erotic power. There is a story in vertical ascent, and a second story above, and so on. Segal's sculpture is as much about the space in people as it is about people in space. This ever-living medium of interaction is the subject of this new course in Dynamics.

*"The healthy heart dances
while the dying heart
can merely march."*

*Ari Goldberger, Harvard Medical School
"Heart at High Risk of Cardiac Arrest",
Omni. p 88 February 1990*

REFLECTING

"Dad, everything is made of atoms except air and songs." Charles Michael Friedman 8/15/93

A dancer in motion is creating space as much as occupying space. Jeff Bottomley's model viewed in animation from three different angles, shows space, mass, and volume in motion. It is a dance of plastic relationships. From point to line to plane to solid-- geometry in motion makes volume. In music a sequence of pointlike note-tones creates a melodic line, which may generate layers of harmony, that leap off the score to fill concert halls with the spacetime phenomenon of music. We breathe a song's notes into melody, vibrating air with standing waves of sound.

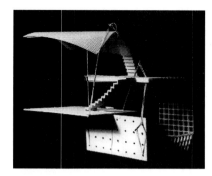

When Cézanne painted trees, he painted the spaces between the branches as dense as the wood itself. Trees are alive! They grow out from the center of the earth. A twig, branch, or tree is an arrangement of living stones (cells) drawn into a span. The forces of gravity pulls on the limb, but the internal hydrostatic forces in the cells of the tree, larger at the lower side of the branch, supply a continuous resistance to the load. As the branch grows out even longer, new cells are added to buttress the increased weight. The branches of a living tree are formed in such a way that their reaction is equal to the loads applied by wind and gravity. If they were stronger than gravity, the branch would take off and fly into outer space! An engineer may see the play of loads and forces in the geometry of a bowl of fruit or branch of a tree, free body diagrams in every branch. An architect may see the play of solid and void in the same geometry. A fallen twig is a free body of a tree's structure. If we see it as the result of the forces that played on it in the tree, the twig becomes a guide to discovering a dynamic world, always in motion, where forces playing on bodies only barely in contact create volume and space itself. There is an intimate relationships between mass and void. If Architectonics is all about the *difference* between mass and void, then Dynamics is all about the *equivalence* of mass and void as volumetric solids.

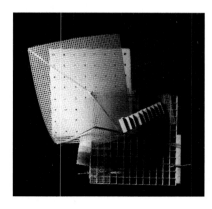

Improvisation is variety against order, the variations of a theme. In volume too there can be improvisation. Other shapes besides cubes also fill three-dimensional space. For example, tetrahedrons and their octahedron duals completely fill any extent of "triangular" space. Architect Steve Baer has developed a system he calls Zomes, a variation on Fedorov's zonohedra and Fuller's geodesic geometry that allows extension along any of the axes of the crystalline structure of geodesic space. The following reading selections include more about the art of improvisation, from the cutting edge ecumenical musical world of our time-- *Keyboard* magazine; and then from Paul Klee's *The Thinking Eye,* a study of graphic phenomena which develops an argument and theory in which motion generates form. We investigate this attempt to relate figures and dimensions with a twist-- that in Dynamics forces applied to dimensions generate further dimension. For example, tension can stretch point into line, just like a rubber band. As Klee has written "if we had a medium... [we could make] an ideal three-dimensional piece of sculpture in space. But I am afraid that is utopian..." That utopian medium is what our Bag of Tricks attempts to approximate. Henri Matisse spoke of *drawing* directly with scissors; so may the Bag of Tricks permit modeling directly in space with structure of mass and void together. In the Prelude studies, plane engendered solid. Now we have the means to transform mass into volume to create architectural space, which in accomplished hands can give rise to plastic e*motion*.

READINGS

Banham, Reyner. *Theory and Design in the First Machine Age*
Davies, Colin. *High Tech Architecture*
Duddington, C.L. *Evolution and Design in the Plant Kingdom.*
Klee, Paul. *The Thinking Eye*, and *The Nature of Nature*
Prouvé, Jean. *Jean Prouvé, Constructeur*
Tafuri, Manfredo. *The Sphere and the Labyrinth: Avante Gardes and Architecture from Piranesi to the 1970s*

JEFF BOTTOMLEY

IMPROVISATION
EXPLORING THE MAGIC OF THE MOMENT

from *Keyboard Magazine*, October 1984

The act of artistic creation takes place in a state of dynamic tension between the opposing forces of freedom and control. When there is too much control and no enough freedom, the results rigid, lifeless. When, on the other hand, there is too much freedom and not enough control, the results are scattered, vague, and unconvincing. In music, control comes first of all the endless hours of practice, and second from written scores, supplemented by theoretical writings. For many musicians, in, fact, these represent nearly the whole of the musical world. The role of freedom in their artistic activities is narrowly circumscribed, extending no further than the license to interpret whatever details of a score were no specified by the composer. Even the act of interpretation is hedged with various controls, in the form of questions about authenticity. That performances prepared from this vantage point are no rigid and lifeless but often vibrant and compelling is due primarily to the freedom exercised first by the composers and second by the creators of the performance tradition within which the music is realized, and only second-arily to the moment-to-moment flexibility with which the performers play.

Alongside the traditions of written music, however, is a another set of traditions that embody a far greater measure of freedom. These are various forms of improvisation. Improvisation has existed in music throughout history; an argument could be made that it was the original form of music-making, of which the written traditions are an outgrowth or refinement. In recent times, as in the past, the two currents have intertwined, feeding one another in myriad ways. As improvising musicians evolve new modes of expression, they enrich the vocabulary of written music, and the theoretical underpinnings provided by written music have enlarged the harmonic and melodic resources available for improvisation. Neither tradition could exist in its present form without the other, and it's probably more accurate to look at them not as opposing camps but as interdependent parts of a system.

Nonetheless, a great deal more is written about written music, which is explicitly structured and subject to analysis, than about improvisation, which seems at first glance elusive, wholly mysterious. What exactly is it that improvising musicians do when they improvise? The process is fleeting, subjective, and almost entirely nonverbal. Thanks to recording technology, we can analyze the results of improvisation exactly as we would any other piece of music. But improvisation itself, the internal process that the impro-vising musician goes through, is gone. It can only be inferred indirectly or examined after the fact through introspection.

Like other acts of artistic creation, improvisation is a form of controlled free association, in which each idea somehow suggest the next. It differs from composition in that the ideas are executed immediately rather than retained in the mind or on paper, and consequently in that there is no opportunity to try several different continuations before settling on one. Igor Stravinsky referred to composition as "selective improvisation, " and this comment underlines the idea that all creativity is improvisatory. Improvisation itself,

however, involves a further step in which the created idea is instantly executed. Thus improvisation places great demands on instrumental tech-nique and the power of concentration. A great improviser must posses, at the very least, these three attributes: a superior technique, the ability to create musical material of high quality, and the ability to focus the mind so that the other two factors can be harnessed on demand.

Some people seem to be born with a native capacity to develop all three attributes to a high degree without apparent effort. But for others, learning to improvise is a struggle. In our culture in particular, there are many talented musicians for whom the process of improvisation is terra incognita. They may never attempt to improvise, or they may become so discouraged by the sound of their first fumbling efforts that they never pursue the matter any further. Our own culture is somewhat unusual in this respect; the tradition of music performance as consisting of nothing but the execution of a score provided by a separate specialist called a composer arose in Europe only at the beginning of the nineteenth century. Prior to this time, the roles of composition, execution, and improvisation were much less clearly sepa-rated, and all accomplished musicians were expected to be adept at all three.

The biographies of the leading composers of the Baroque and Classical eras offer abundant testimony to this fact. Bach, Mozart, and Beethoven were renowned as much for their skill at extemporization as for the quality of their written scores. "Cutting contests " in which several keyboard players would compete, improvising entire fugues and sonatas on themes handed to them, were a popular form of entertainment in the drawing rooms of the nobility. And several kinds of improvisation were common in concerts as well. During the Baroque period, harpsichord accompaniment parts were not notated completely, but were merely sketched out using a system of chord symbols called figured bass. Thus the player might alter the realization of the part from night to night, depending on the size of the ensemble, the acoustics of the room, or other factors. The practice of ornamentation of keyboard parts was also an opportunity for spontaneous elaboration; only later did it become codified into a more or less explicit and uniform tradition. By the late eighteenth century, the soloist's improvised cadenza was a fixture a concerts; it was the excesses of the virtuosos' grandstanding during this unaccompa-nied interlude that finally drove Beethoven to initiate the practice of providing written cadenzas for his concertos. Beethoven, Mozart, and many other performers typically played their own concertos from extremely sketchy sheet music parts (the tradition of playing solos from memory not yet having arisen), and we can be fairly certain that during these performances they experimented with different kinds of passage-work and melodic variation. In other words, they were improvising over a fixed orchestral accompaniment.

Improvisation has long been a vital part of non-European music traditions, the best - known example being the vocal and instrumental ragas of Indian classical music, with their intricate scales and ornamentation. In recent

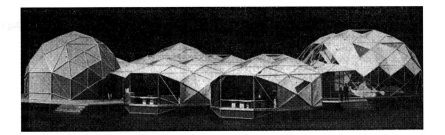

Architect Steve Baer has developed a system he calls Zomes, a variation on Fedorov's zonohedra and Fuller's geodesic geometry that allows extension along any of the axes of the crystalline structure of geodesic space. Architect Peter Pearce has also explored variations on geodesic and crystalline growth geometries for extended structal and *architectural* adaptability.

years it has returned to European/American classical music as well. Composers searching for new means of expression have developed various kinds of indeterminate (non-specific) notation, many of them involving undefined graphic elements, which the performer may feel free to reinterpret spontaneously during the concert. But by far the most important form of improvisation in the twentieth century has been jazz. For many people, "jazz" and "improvisation" are synonymous. From its humble beginnings in the American South in the early years of the century, jazz has swept the world. And because of its emphasis on freewheeling individual creativity, jazz has evolved rapidly into a bewildering variety of styles, from Dixieland and swing to the furthest reaches of the avant-garde. Even rock and roll, in its early years, an outgrowth of a short-lived high-energy form of jazz blues: boogie-woogie. But today, rock music has become a different sort of beast, one dependent almost entirely on tightly controlled arrangements from which the possibility of spontaneity has been resolutely excluded. Young rock players deride what they see as the self-indulgence and pointless of the extended solo. This trend is nurtured by the climate of fierce economic competition among bands; improvisation means taking chances, and few musicians are willing to take chances, when they might lose their audience by doing so. It's safer to put together a tightly constructed show and stick to it. The audiences themselves bear some of the responsibility; having been force-fed an endless diet of three-minute singles and 30-second TV commercials, they are impatient with anything that requires mental effort to listen to, especially when the outcome remains, as it does in improvisation, uncertain. They want their gratification guaranteed, and they want to get it without having to work for it.

The reasons for the trend away from improvisation in rock are understandable, and some of the tightly edited music that is being played is certainly marvelous. Nevertheless, there is something disturbingly reactionary about the lack of instrumental freedom in rock today. A style of music that has been nourished again and again by infusions of social rebellion seems increasing to have become hypnotized by the trappings and poses of rebellion, to the exclusion of the substance. One feels that a real musical rebel, a visionary virtuoso whose playing was lit by the flames of improvisatory fire, would find scant haven in the closed ranks of rock, where everybody marches to the same drum machine. Freedom is a rare enough commodity these days, and if there is no room for freedom in rock and roll, the world is the poorer.

So the purpose of a special Issue of Keyboard devoted entirely to improvisation is not simply to provide information on the subject for those who are already interested in it; we are also hoping, in some small way, to commend it to those who have been neglecting or avoiding it. No matter what level you're operating musically, the process of improvisation can broaden your horizons and enrich your artistic expression. We could easily have filled several magazines this size with material on improvisation. Specifically, we had to hang onto two features originally planned for this month, both of

which dealt with improvisation in classical music (Baroque and pre-Baroque in one case, contemporary in the other). They're still in our files, though, so you can look for them by the end of the year. Even without them, we think you'll agree, this is a very Special Issue. To begin with, we have a conversation with Denny Zeitlin on the psychology of improvisation. Zeitlin is uniquely qualified to discuss the ramification of the topic, as he is both a well-known jazz pianist and a practicing psychiatrist. In addition to providing his professional insights, Denny has provided us with a previously unreleased solo piano improvisation of his own, which you will find on Keyboard's first-ever Soundsheet. Though we did not have space to transcribe the entire solo, more than half of it appears in sheet music form, beginning on page 26.

One of the most perplexing aspects of improvisation is how to begin doing it when you've never done before. A number of prominent educators share the techniques they use with their students, both complete beginners and those who already play the keyboard well but haven't yet taken the plunge into the uncharted seas of free playing. In addition, Keyboard's book reviewer takes a look at a stack of method books that purport to teach beginning improvisation and assesses some of the approaches contained there. Much of the basic vocabulary of jazz and rock improvisation has its roots in an older form of folk music--- the blues. So we asked blues pianist and authority Mark Naftalin to outline the basics of blues piano. If you're into more high-tech music, on the other hand, you'll appreciate progressive rock keyboardist Eddie Jobson's comments on the art and craft of effective rock soloing. To round out the feature section, we have a retrospective on the evolution of jazz styles, with an accent on the contributions made by jazz pianists. And if you still want more on improvisation, thumb through our columns; you'll find a variety of perspectives and techniques provided by Keyboard regulars Dick Hyman, Tom Coster, Richie Beirach, Don Muro, and Bill Irwin. We'd especially like to thank Mark Naftalin and Eddie Jobson for taking time out from their busy schedules to put together such extensive and valuable articles. Thanks are also due to Denny Zeitlin for allowing us to make use of his solo, and to Elizabeth Perry for being so patient when we kept giving her more stacks of musical examples to type up.

When we began planning this issue, we weren't entirely sure what there was to be said about improvisation. We on the staff have been improvising for most of our lives, and the process seems as natural to us as breathing. But as with most often-seen objects, the more closely we examined it the more complex and mysterious it became. We came away with a renewed respect for those artists who have had the courage to make improvisation their livelihood, and a feeling of awe for the seemingly boundless resources of the human brain, which make improvisation possible. Also, we're all a little more enthusiastic about improvising than we were a month ago. As soon as we get the issue sent off the printer, we're going to have ourselves a jam session.

excerpts from **Paul Klee:** *The Thinking Eye.*
Towards a theory of form-production

1. Infinite Natural History   The Living Forces

Causality: the point that sets itself in motion.

What was in the beginning? Things moved so to speak freely, neither in straight nor crooked lines. They may be thought of as simply moving, going where they wanted to go, for the sake of going, without aim, without will, without obedience, moving self- evidently, in a state of primal motion. There was just one thing-- mobility,
the prerequisite for change from this primordial state.
I can't prove that this is how it was; I hope it was; at any rate it is conceivable, and what is conceivable is fact and useful. It is useful as a counterconcept, the opposite of what seems to have happened afterwards, change, development, fixation, measurement, determination.
Moreover, it can be used because it can be formally expressed in terms of contrast.

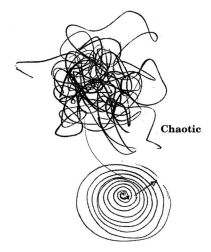

Chaotic

Cosmic (coiled)

The point is not dimensionless, but an infinitely tiny elemental plane, an agent that carries out no motion; in other words it is at rest [1].
Apply the pencil and shortly a line is born [2].

1 , 2

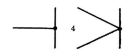

3   4

The point as a primordial element is cosmic. Every seed is cosmic.
The point as an intersection of ways is cosmic [3].
As a point of impact the point is static [4].
Tension between one point and another yields line [5].
Not yet discharged (abstract) [6].
Discharged [7]. The universal cause is therefore reciprocal tension, a striving for two dimensions.

5
6
7

8   9

Two points ideally related in tension to a line. Result: an arc [8].
Given equal velocities, the propagation of points along a line r esults in a meeting in the middle [9].

Other possibilites of   Bending

dividual structure   Breaking

The mode of treatment depends on our feeling about the obstacles we are facing: are they hard or soft?

Combination of the two aggregate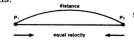
states solid and liquid

Liquid above   solid below   Light murmur above, hard ring below

Slightly obstructed flow
as of water over pebbles
Receptive accent on units made up of higher and lower parts

'Gaseous',
a refinement of liquid
(evaporation). 'Cloudy'

1921/I88: *Recital on the Branch.* Pen Drawing.
[Study for *The Twittering Mavchine*, 1922]

Diagram of the dynamic formation
of the circle.
The radious grows from the inside out
in pure progression

Linear-active

From point to line. The point is not dimensionless but an infinitely small planar element, and agent carrying out zero motion, i.e. resting. Mobility is the condition of change. Certain things have primordial motion. The point is cosmic, a primordial element. Things on earth are obstructed in their movement; they require an impetus. The primordial movement, the agent, is a point that sets itself in motion (genesis of form). A line comes into being. The most highly-charged line is the most authentic line because it is the most active.

In all these examples the principal and active line develops freely. It goes out for a walk so to speak, aimlessly for the sake of the walk.

Another diagram of the dynamic
formation of the circle by radiation.
Radiation comes from the centre
and is ralated to the innermost point.

Dynamic repose

Dynamic movement. The point seen in dynamic terms, as a agent.

Simpler linear motion, self-contained. Free line a -b [1]
Free line a-b; companion line a1 - b1. (The melody in Fi. 1: accompanied) [2, 3,4 , 5,].

A linear figures takes time, and one must travel receptively the same road as one has taken productively. For example, things in motion, things that curve, things one has touched firmly, desultory things, are attached by a strong line and made into one. The longer a line, the more of the time element it contains. The purely linear always remains ideal. Distance as time, whereas a surface is apprehended more in terms of the moment.

A line contains energies that manifest themselves by cutting and by consuming time. This gives the linear element a mutual relation to imaginary space. For space is also a temporal concept. The course of the motor organism is indicated by arrows ("identity of form and the method of its production") Cf. the motor function... and cause and effect of concentric and eccentric forces.

Free line making detours [6, 7, 8, 9]

Two "interpenetrating" lines

Two secondary lines, moving round
an imaginary main line [10, 11, 12, 13]

Dividual-individual,
connected by
rhythmic articulation

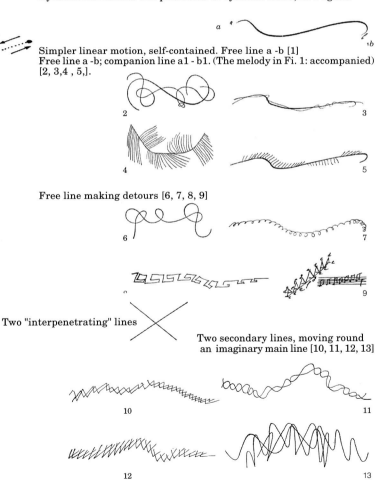

930/ J 7 : *Twined into a group*. Pen and ink drawing.

1. Line: active, middle, passive

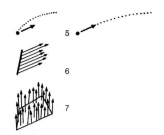

From point to line
The line as element
Linear and planar character

Shortlly after application of the pencil, or any other pointer tool, a (linear-active) line comes into being. The more freely it develops, the clearer will be its mobility [1].

But if I apply a line, e.g. the edge of a black or coloured crayon, a plane is produced (at first and when the freedom of movement is very limited) [2]

If we have a medium that made it possible to move planes in a similar way, we should be able to inscribe an ideal three-dimensional piece of sculpture in space [3].

But I am afraid that is utopian.

For the present then let us content ourselves with the most primitive of elements, the line. At the dawn of civilisation, when writing and drawing were the same thing, it was the basic element. And as a rule our children begin with it; one day they discover the phenomenon of the mobile point, with what enthusiasm it is hard for us grown-ups to imagine. At first the pencil moves with extreme freedom, whenever it pleases.

But once he begins to look at these first works, the child discovers that there are laws which govern his random efforts. Children who continue to take pleasure in the chaotic are, of course, no artists; other children will soon progress towards a certain order. Criticism sets in. The chaos of the first play-drawing gives way to the beginning of order. The free motion of the line is subordinated to anticipation of a final effect; caustiously the child begins to work with a very few lines. He is still primitive.

But one can't remain primitive for long. One has to discover a way of enriching the pitiful result, without destroying or blurring the simple, intelligible plan. It becomes necessary to establish a relation between things of first importance and those which are subsidairy.

Graduated accentuation of the line (lines made stronger or weaker).
Productive growth of selected line with graduated accentuation (flux) [1]. Productive growth of the point (concentric waves). Two dimensional structure emanating from nuclear strata [2]. Linear accent on nerves, or incarnation of the line (the linear body becomes broader in growth). Incarnation : the middle line as skeleton [3]. The line as limit: for progressive growth, flow, inner content [4].

Incarnation represented in terms of casual reality. The constructive propagation of lines strictly adjusted to the threads of construction [5].

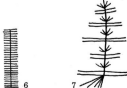

The line articulated in terms of measure or time (growth, motion, divisibility [6]. Structure classified in its essentials [7]

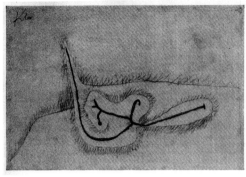

1937/N 3: *Germinating*. Pencil Drawing.

Companion forms, of an absolute converging character [1]. of an effective converging character [2]

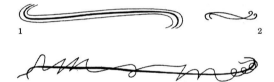

or effectively converging, while the conpanion line retains its independence [3].
Rather like the path of a man with a dog running free.

The laws of statics
translated ↓ plumb-line, ↑ falling counterforce,
building into
pictorial abstraction

All straight lines that run vertically are schemata of the first law of statics (gravitation).

All straight lines that run horizontally are schemata of the second law of statics (horizontals, stratification as consequence of gravitation).

Possible compensation in the case of falling

Possible compensation in the case of building

The compensating diagonals are the ✕ third law of statics.

Area of the rules of material or terrestial statics.

The canon of totality.

This combined diagram permits us to follow the three part movement. The voices come in successively as in a canon. At each of the three main points one voice reaches its climax, another voice softly begins, and a third dies away. One might call this new figure the canon of totality.

MATERIAL STATICS. (gravitational forces in one direction).

From the terrestrial point of view
the parallelism of verticals
and horizontals (really tangents)
is an illusion caused by the
enlargement of the area of the "I".

The centre of the earth
is the centre of gravity.

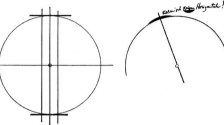

Dynamics is the great, the principal area, the endless area of the cosmos. Statics, by comparison, is an exception, where gravitation kills motion by subjugating it to an alien law. The suction of the stronger. The stronger power is itself dynamically moved and carries the vanished along its orbit. But the vanquished does not perceive this directly; he must accustom himself as best he can to the power and gradually carve out a sphere of motion where, if he manages it skilfully, he can attain a kind of independence.
This is how the plant grows, how man and beast walk or fly.

From a terrestrial point of view: Statics = Gravitational forces in one direction.
Dynamics = energy

From a cosmic point of view: Only gravitation
The forces of gravity come together from all sides.

A theme treated in different ways

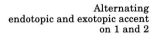

Interpenetration with exotopic

and endotopic accent

The commmon ground
treated endotopically, the individual
ground with exotopic accent.

Interpenetration with alternating
endotopic and exotopic
accent (in relief)

outside-inside   outside-inside

Interpenetration of space and volume:
(variations on the treatment of relief).
Variants: "Meshed or interwined".
Organizations and unification of
variations:
Reciprocal interpenetration, equal
parts unequally accented.

Concentric mesh
in harmonious interpenetration.
Forms generated by the superimposition
and mixing of 1 and 2.
With displacement
(shift of centre)
or change of position
the mixed forms are modified

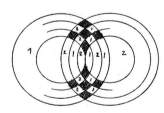

Alternating
endotopic and exotopic accent
on 1 and 2

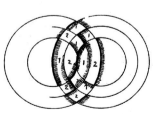

Inner linking of the two in free variation.
Interpenetration of space and body.
Basic possibilities:
Combinations of identical forms,
which are related,
touching,
which interpenetrate,
which are meshed with one another,
one which absorbs the other.
a) In constructive-logical connection.
b) In a party free selection.
(Metalogical, sometimes psychological,
allowing deeper spiritual reaction)

4. Figuration is connected with movement.

I begin where all pictorial form begins: with the point that sets itself in motion.

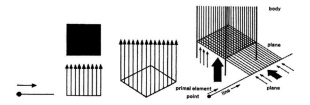

The symbols for pictorial dimensions.

The point (as agent) moves off, and the line comes into being - the first dimension [1].
If the line shifts to form a plane, we obtain a two-dimensional element [2].

In the movement from planes to spaces, the clash of planes gives rise to a body(three-dimensional) [3].

Summary of the kinetic energies which move the point into a line, the line into a plane and a plane into a spatial dimension [4].

Concerning of the development of the point into a line, of a line into a plane, of a plane into a body.

Point. The point as primordial element, all-pervasive.
Line. A point discharges its tension to another point.The casual principle is the will inherent in reciprocal tension. Essence of a dimension. One-dimensional element.
Plane. Essence of two dimensions. Two-dimensional element.

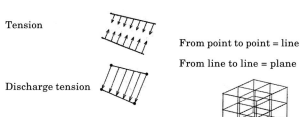

Tension

From point to point = line

From line to line = plane

Discharge tension

Body. The line moves and produces a plane;
The plane moves and the body becomes into being.
Essence of three dimensions. Three-dimensional element.
The cube is balanced synthesis of three definite dimensions and as such the normative symbol of corporeality.

Thre movements summarised:
Characteristic of the dimension behind-in from (the third dimension) is the increasing progression of points, lines, and surfaces. In the point the opposite ends of the pictorial elements are still effective; less so intermediary stages. They need more room before they can be weighed or measured by the eye, or critically appraised.

Forces and Limits

Detail from 1928/k9 : *Overtones*
Pen-and-ink drawing

The dimensional signs

Body , three dimensions

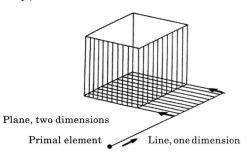

Plane, two dimensions

Primal element   Line, one dimension

Illustrations:

Variant on
"towards the innermost".
Inner dynamic density

Variation of rotation
extension into space

Diagram of the dynamic
formation of the triangle
in a variation
with rotary movement.

Progressively spatial [1].
Progressively pushing from the centre to the limits [2]
Outside and inside in corporeo-spatial combination
(progressively inward and medial) [3]

Stratification is defined by the relation
that outer bears to inner.
Inside and outside, as concepts, are
either relative or limiting.

 1 2 3

1929/n 6: *(Little) jeser in trance*. Oil on Canvas.

Body

body
two-dimensional,
marginal or middle
(body-limit)

Body
two-dimensional
External-material,
active-planar
(outer surface
of a body)

body
three-dimensional
(body-outward)

Spatial

spatial
two-dimensional
encompassing
(activated passive)

exotopic
encompassing
(without body)

spatial
three-dmensional
and transparent

Inward

inward
two-dimensional
(content)

Most-inward
(centre)

inward
two-dimensional,
inward
representation
of outer planes

In contrast
to the inside and
outside of a body

Inward
three-dimensional,
body outside

Purely inward,
body innermost

The inward
plays the dominant part.
The whole inward territory
designated by the word "content"

The Water Mill   First example

1   Main organ: the water. Other organs: two wheels connected by a drive belt, one large, one small [1].

Criticism of figure 1 :

a) Format mistake in the choice of the subsidiary organs. There is no organic three-part gradation relating them in the order of their importance to the principal organ.
b) Mistake in the form of the principal organ. At best its form is a conventional wave structure,"the way you do water", not a striking representation of a principal organ.
c) Mistake of accent: the principal organ, the water, is not treated dynamically enough.

2

Correction to figure 1:   **A**   The appropiate choice of organs: [2]

At this point the incongruity of figure 3 from the point of view of the form and accent must be obvious. The least probable event occurs; namely, that the intermediate organ becomes the most prominent.

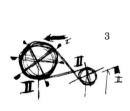   

3   4

Correction to figure 3:
Water wheel and hammer [4].

B   The appropiate formation of organs [with proper functional accent].

I. The water wheel   active
II. The works   middle
III. The hammer   passive

Instead of extending the faulty example [1] downwards by including the hammer in my choice of organs, I can extend it upwards. Then the hammer is omitted, the wheel becomes [III], the water becomes [II], and for my [I] I think of something new, which is all the easier as flowing water is hardly an original inspiration [11] .

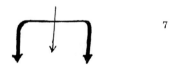

5

We are familiar with
the force of gravity   (towards the centre of the earth).

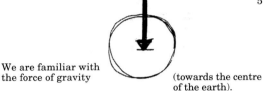

6

We are equally familiar with the horizontal mirror of "still" water [6];

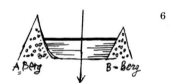

7

without Mountains A and B to hold it in, the water would flow off on both sides [7].

Berg	mountain
hindernde	obstructing
Schwerkraft	gravity
ursprunglicher	original
Wasserspiegel	water-level

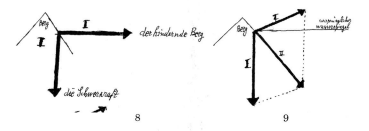

8   9

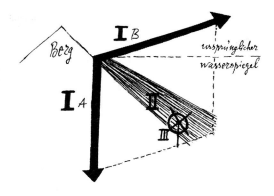

Correction of Fig. 10: the water mill [11]

But if we eliminate Mountain B and leave Mountain A in place, the water flows off only to the right [8]. 1 Here two forces are at work, first gravity, second the obstructing mountain. (The obstructing mountain B' [6] is displaced or eliminated.)

The diagonal in the parallelogram of forces will the force of the flowing water, II [9]

10

With the accent misplaced   this variation looks like this.

C Appropiate accentuation of organs

I   Principal energy

II Middle energy

III Subsidiary energy

The two forces :
IA gravity, IB the obstructing mountain, active
the diagonal of the parallelogram of forces,
the force of the flowing water, II, middle
the wheel that is turned, III, passive

In terms of language :

I.   We drive   active
II. I yield   but with the understanding that [1] is re
                                    sponsible in case anyone should suffer; middle
And as a matter of fact
somebody does suffer:
III. the wheel which says: I am turned, passive, III

1927/D 9: *Difficult Journey Through O.* Pen-and-Ink.

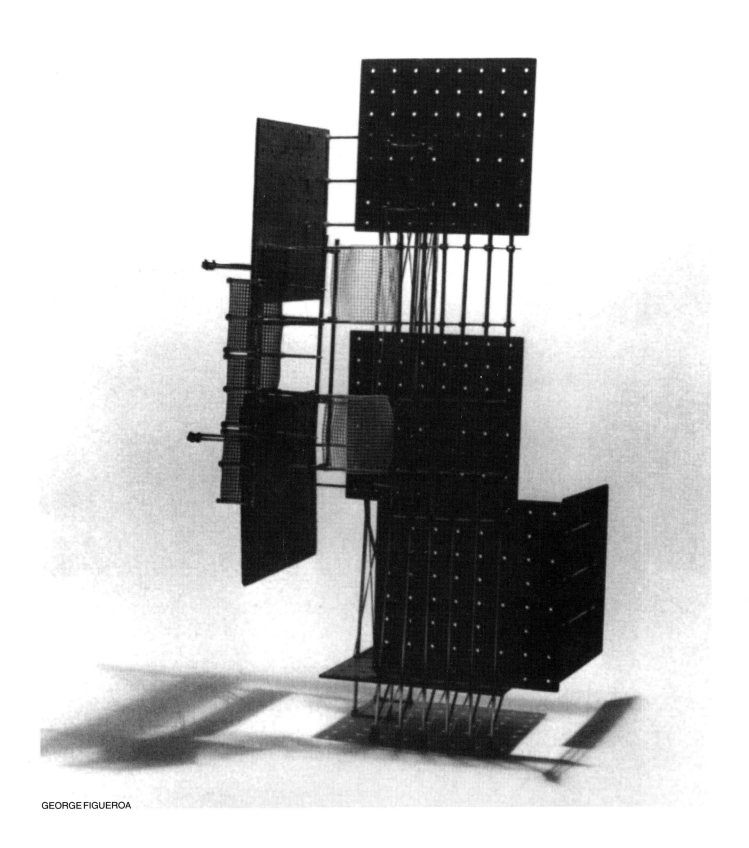

GEORGE FIGUEROA

Harmony means joining, from a Greek carpentry term. Webster: a combination of parts into a proportionate or orderly whole; congruity. 2. agreement in feeling, action, ideas, interest, etc.; peaceable or friendly relations. 3. agreement or proportionate arrangement of color, size, shape, etc. that is pleasing to the eye; a fitting well together. 4. an arrangement of parallel passages of different authors, made so as to bring out corresponding ideas, qualities, etc.... 6. in music the pleasing arrangement of two or more tones in a chord.

Counterpoint (originally said of a plainsong having accompaniment); 1. a melody accompanying another melody note for note. 2. the art of adding a related but independent melody or melodies to a basic melody, in accordance with the fixed rules of harmony, to make a harmonic whole.

2. HARMONY

SPINNING AND GROOVING

HARMONY: *SPINNING*

BEING

"I seem to be a verb." R. Buckminster Fuller

LOW ORBIT

Where do we come from? That is a mystery we have yet to solve. Consider the shell of the chambered nautilus, a mollusc who seems to create the walls of its home from an infinitesimally small origin. How did it begin to make its beautiful form, the logarithmic spiral, whose characteristic is that it is always the same shape, no matter what size it grows to? It takes a leap, perhaps of faith, to grow into the void, to create the reality of such a beautiful seashell. We know that the animal's shell stops growing only when it dies. Somehow the act of living sustains its perfect geometry. That which spins outward "evolves". Evolution means literally "to turn or spin outward". "Volume" comes from the Sanskrit root, "vol"— meaning "to roll". The roots of "wheel" and "circle" include Latin *colere*, Sanskrit *cakras* , and Greek *kuklos* , "to bestir oneself, be busy, live in, cultivate." Carati "he moves," close to *bhavati* "he is" in Sanskrit is the source of phunai, "to be born" in Greek.

Building volume means making space by moving parts. The Latin root of the word "construct" means literally to "pile up [things]". A pile of stones can be a simple yet powerful architectural creation. The Great Pyramids of Gizeh in Egypt are perhaps the most remarkable of such human constructs. But this is a difficult way to create large volumes. The Pyramids, in fact, have only very little volume carved out for burial chambers compared to the great mass of stone needed for the full work. But to create space, to wrap material around a void and keep it there despite all the forces acting on it, is to make a *span*. Both "spin" and "span" derive from the root word meaning in Greek "to pull, or to draw out". A more efficient way of using material to make space than piling up stones is to pull them apart in such a way that they keep space between them. The stones of an arch are kept in perpetual low orbit by the skill of the architect. The stones of Machu Picchu are in a higher orbit than the stones of Venice. We used to be completely anchored to the Earth. Now, however, humankind has succeeded in spanning space not just across the land, but also outward from our planet's center. Bruce McCandless, the astronaut who floated free above the Earth in the Manned Maneuvering Unit was not just "hovering out there in space". His forward thrust kept him falling around the earth as fast as gravity pulled him to the surface. McCandless maintained his position because he was spinning about the center of the earth at orbital velocity, which is 17,000+ MPH. Again, a picture of this astronaut is not only a still life, but also a movie.

A child seeks the corners of the playground, the whole site, moving outward to the world. Eventually the lure of the horizon is too great to resist-- the street and Rubicon are crossed. Imbalance develops with outward thrust. A salient along one radius is greater than another. Soon things become eccentric. When two squares (or figures, for example the images of shell and Saturn opposite) are overlapped, they imply a larger square they do not completely fill. Tie a stone to a string and spin it. The stone leaps outward, balancing its motion to the tension in the string. The circle it describes can be tilted to describe a sphere in space. No literal string ties earth to moon, yet these two free bodies have danced together in dynamic equilibrium of force and motion for billions of years. The moon pulls loose seas from Earth to make tides. Within the mass of earth spacetime is contractile, while outside earth's horizon spacetime is dispersive. Between bodies spacetime curvature is tidal, so loose seas rise moonward. What delicate balance there is in the music of the spheres! Will we as a species attain a permanent presence beyond our planet's surface as grand (yet tenuous) as the rings of Saturn- so suggestive of record grooves or CD diffractions awaiting our attempts to unravel their mysteries?

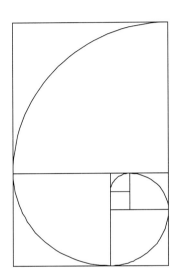

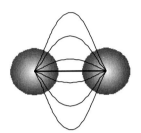

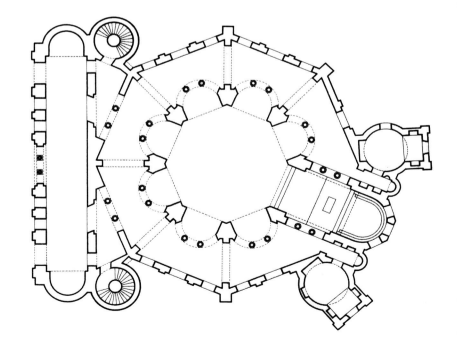

SPACE IN THING
THING IN SPACE

THING IN SPACE
SPACE IN THING

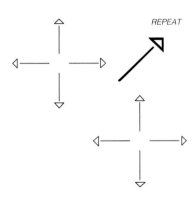

REPEAT

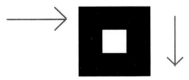

ECCENTRIC LOAD TURNS THE CORNER

TURNING THE CORNER
AND THE FOUR COLOR MAP PROBLEM

THINKING

Translation and Rotation

We build a volume by moving mass to the edges of a solid. This first *action* in space establishes identity, a thing in itself. Two volumes introduce dialog between This and the Other, an *interaction*. As points of solids translate (move along lines) outward, they extend their influence beyond their original centers. Eventually, in a closed universe, the influence of two solids will intersect. When forces meet, a resultant vector occurs. Since the outward spacings from two different solids cannot share the same center, the translational force of one will become an eccentric load on the other. An eccentric load generates spin. Thus for tending-to-move solids, in addition to a momentum of translation, (which pushes one billiard ball from another along a line) there is also angular momentum, (which gives the billiard ball its spin.) Thus, mass at a perimeter generates the tendency to rotate or spin. The earth on its axis spins like a top and gives us day and night.

Turning the Corner

Two planes intersect to form a corner. Any orthogonal solid already suggests an intersection of the forces of two or more translations at its corners. How to resolve these forces while recognizing the identity of each originator? Simple, turn the corner! Thus is the invention of the wheel! Like a reel winding the point-like frames of a film into a curled line around the axle of the spool, rotation added to translation allows us to generate spin in volume. Spin can generate stasis in motion and therefore is both animated and still, like a spinning gyroscope. Some of the greatest architecture, including Michelangelo's St. Peters in Rome, Le Corbusier's Museum in Tokyo, and the Monastery at La Tourette make use of this valuable means of establishing lasting presence in plan.

Two forces acting in opposite directions on the same mass cause it to bend, or if strong and close enough, to *shear* like scissors cutting paper. Shear permits "orthogonal spinning", or turning a corner without losing the integrity of space-filling right-angled geometry. One example of orthogonal spinning combined with growth occurs in a simple way to build the logarithmic spiral, an infinite series which converges on Φ (phi), the golden section ratio of .618... as it approaches infinity. Add a set of squares sized by the Fibonacci series 1 1 2 3 5 8 .... In each draw a quadrant arc of a circle whose center is the corner of the square. The curve will be continuous, tangent at the joining of the next square, and will grow infinitely, with proportions of the figure more and more closely approximating a golden section: $^1/_1 = 1$, $^1/_2 = 0.5$, $^2/_3 = .66$, $^3/_5 = .60$, $^5/_8 = .6125$, $^8/_{13} = 0.6154$, $^{13}/_{21} = 0.6190$, $^{21}/_{34} = .6176$ .... $^{89}/_{144} = 0.61806...$ (Compare with *Architectonics*, page 170.)

Spinning Space

Two solids moving in a straight line may meet and exchange eccentric forces, generating angular momentum. As spacing extends mass to a perimeter to create volume, it also generates the tendency to spin. A volume's center of mass is empty; the density of matter at its edge sets an instability in its inflated skin. The slightest asymmetrical loading can set it spinning An architectural way to say this is that any influence from outside or inside a volume may eccentrically load it with a force. For example at San Vitale, a Byzantine Church in Ravenna Italy, both west entry and south-south-east orientation to a distant holy focus eccentrically load the centralized octagonal plan. Added to the centripetal drive from empty domed center, through concentric screens of columns around the turning polymorphic aisles and galleries, to massive perimeter walls, these plan responses to external demands set the whole space spinning like the wheeling heavens above.

SPINNING SPACE

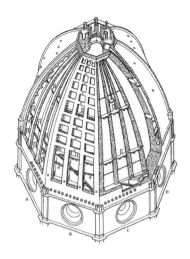

Filippo Brunelleschi (1377-1466), first architect of the Renaissance, found a way to restrain the outward thrust of the Florence Cathedral Dome (1420-34) without resorting to the older Gothic (then called the "International Style") flying buttresses. He set an iron chain in the walls of the drum at the base of the dome (*Il Duomo*) to act as a tension ring, which directed the outward thrust of the ribs radically inward. The armature of ribs and tension ring gave the dome a graceful volume in revolution the way the fingers of a potter form a bowl on a spinning wheel. The painter Paolo Uccello (1397-1475), using Brunelleschi's new system of perspective, spun a frame of lines in space to draw a Chalice of eternal mystery and elegant balance. Both architect and painter created volume through spinning eccentric line. The photo opposite shows that the hills of Florence wheel about the cathedral at the city's center. *Il Duomo's* man-made hill engages the horizon of the surrounding bowl, as any visitor who has made the climb to the lantern atop the dome will learn. Note how the horizon line of the distant hills coincides with the base of the dome's lantern cupola. To surmount this church is to embrace all the surrounding landscape as one's own backyard, which is a perfect expression of the Renaissance ideal of *Uomo Universale*, humankind at home in all the cosmos, both near and far. Thus the center of this city is both gateway and landmark beacon to the edge of its region. When the Dome joined Giotto's Tower (finished in 1359) on the Florentine skyline, it created a parallax that makes this architectural ensemble both clock and compass. When the dome is to the right of the tower, you are looking north. If the dome is shaded on its eastern side, it is afternoon. The architecture can tell you both *where* and *when* you are in Florence.

Mostly Space

No one is foolish enough to sit in the middle of an Interstate highway, because we know that even if there is no car on the road at that exact moment, soon enough another car will fill that space with its 60+mph momentum-energy. Thus although the highway is mostly empty space, it is always filled with the potential for very high energy mass. Physicists find the same condition between atoms and inside atomic nuclei. Any material, even rock, is mostly space. A "solid" desk is actually an array of hydrogen, carbon, oxygen and other atoms in a field of electromagnetic and nuclear forces that hold them together. Enormous energy is released when the nuclear bindings are broken, as atomic bombs have demonstrated. Most atomic mass is concentrated in the nucleus. The nuclei of atoms are relatively as far from each other as are stars in cosmic space What keeps molecules from collapsing into a superdense mass is the vibrational state of the momentum-energy of the electron clouds surrounding their atomic nuclei at a significant distance apart. What maintains the identity of atoms is the tendency for its electrons to stay within a bounded spherical shell around the nucleus. They do not fly off unless excited by additional energy-- rather, they spin around their nucleus centers. Spin maintains identity. Spinning makes us mostly space. Spinning is how far out you can get.

Four columns can mark out the corners of a square and many columns can establish a grid of volumes with much more void than mass. This is an architecturally efficient way to use a little mass to make a lot of space. Such columns in plan are stationary. But a single point set in motion, like a roving guard dog or swinging pendulum can also mark out a region of large volume with even less mass. A well-hit tennis ball, bouncing back and forth, can mark all four corners of the court as surely as four stationary pebbles at those same corners. In architecture, masses don't have to actually move to mark space, they can imply connections over distance through geometric relationships, to set a whole intentioned space in plastic motion.

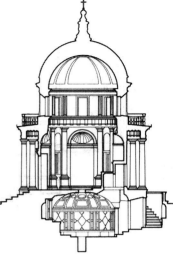

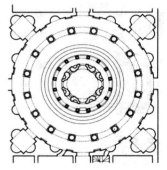

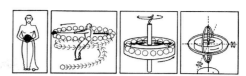

ECCENTRIC SPACE

Leonardo da Vinci's version of Vitruvian Man [Book III, Chap.1] with outstretched limbs may illustrate the Renaissance ideal of *Uomo Universale*. Like *Il Duomo*, Leonardo's drawing also shows us inhabiting a space larger than the mass of our bodies through peripheral development. A ballet swinger creates a volume even larger than the span of Leonardo's man by swinging on a three-dimensional "rocking chair", body dancing to occupy a space even more eccentric than Leonardo's Man. Is not this akin to the orbital energy shells of electrons around a nucleus?

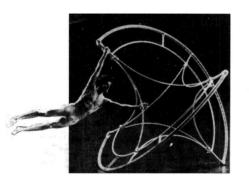

Buckminster Fuller's diagram of a hammer thrower in action, spinning a spherical Olympic "hammer", illustrates the inherent stability of a gyroscope, which tends to balance on a point as long as its rotational motion creates sufficient angular momentum to generate the side effects that overcome gravitational instabilities. What space does the hammer thrower create and occupy while spinning? The still propeller of a windmill marks the terrestrial orthogonals, while the rotating mill generates a circular plane. The Dutch windmill shown opposite is also capable or rotating about its platform base, so that the two perpendicular axes of the windmill's vanes may generate a spherical volume if they are turned completely through all three dimensional rotations.

Solids of revolution

Rotate a square or triangle about an axis to make a cylinder or cone. These are solids of revolution. Some architectural plans are not only circular, but also rotational; that is, they set up volumetric forces that keep the composition in apparent movement and dynamic equilibrium around a central point. This animation of angular momentum generates a push-pull of rotational forces, keeping spaces moving outward from and inward to that center. Bramante's San Pietro in Montorio, built in the generation after Brunelleschi, is a case in point. This diminutive building, also called the *Tempietto* or "Little Church" is vast in its spacial impact. Can a volume be not only vacant in its center, but also seem to be expanding outward equally in all directions. What does this do to the quality of the architectural space created? Can two or more volumes create eccentric space for their inhabit-ants? Can exploring the perimeter be as potent as dwelling in the center? The Tempietto is hollow but denser (spacially more present) at its perimeter columns that at the inner wall around its central room, establishing a tension between centripetal ("to seek the center") and centrifugal ("to flee the center") architectural space, a dialog between implosion and explosion. Satellite means "body-guard"; planet means "wanderer". What is generated in rotation, in spinning, is... span.

Just as moving mass can define a volume, so can moving or tending-to move volumes define a space. Volumes can be inside volumes, internal realms can broadcast their influence, external realms can intersect, and thus the continuity of all space can be expressed. Living in time as well as space, we move through volumes even as volumes move through us. Our ever-changing world, subject to fluctuating fields of energy, generates a daily news collage of separate events whose continuity only emerges in time. We inhabit a dynamic universe, living on a spinning planet in revolutionary orbit around a star whose weather is an ancient massive thermonuclear fire. Change is inevitable and continuous. Cubes move, whether we wish them to or not, in ways which have an important bearing on how things are made. Wind blows things over, gravity makes them sag, and heat causes them to expand or contract, or even change their state and structural properties. Architectonics is about how and why two cubes in mutual relationship define spacial order between them. Dynamics is in part about how and why two *moving (or tending-to-move)* cubes in mutual relationship define spacial order between them. Dynamic architecture is a study in space *and* time.

MICHELANGELO, CUBIST

"If you lived here, you'd be home now"

As architects we carry an internalized reference volume, a moving mental cube akin to an artist's ever-handy adjustable framing square made of the opposing right angles of forefingers and thumbs of both hands. The presence of a frame suggests that this *now* in time and space is one of an endless flow temporarily bounded by consciousness. Between the primacy of here-and-now and the ubiquity of there-and-then lies the architectural conflict of every Site. Which boundary does our center of Being find: front door, wall, fence, property line, or horizon? Between center and edge is every Where. Swing your eyes around a full 360 degree landscape panorama to gain an unobstructed view of the horizon, note a landmark at the boundary, and hike to this new center of sight. Thus does the surveyor mark elevations and a plot site contours into continuously gridded space. But this does not satisfy our sense of place. Two radiating centers will eventually intersect and both centers will vie for our allegiance. So how then can more than one place be an important "center" to any society? If all roads lead to Rome, where is Rome's Christian center-- at the foundation of St. Peter's Church or at the location of his crucifixion, marked by the *Tempietto*? If perspective suggests a unique station point for its truest reading, then spacial unity is broken when two such perspectives are side by side. Raphael's 1504 painting *Marriage of the Virgin* and Bramante's 1504 architectural Tempietto are contemporary plastic masterpieces which attempt to resolve this conflict in two different but ultimately incomplete ways. The temple in Raphael's painting is octagonal, so that the orthogonal paving on the plan can conveniently meet both the frontal order of the picture plane and the same orthogonal order of the horizon with only the 4 diagonal panels of the octagon breaking, but still primarily obeying, the orthogonal meter of the gridded paving. Raphael here proposes a continuous universal space dominating a discontinuous center. The painted temple is rigid, abrupt, and unresolved compared to the graceful curves of Bramante's actual building, where the logic of construction generated pure solids of revolution of cylinder, drum, and dome. At the Tempietto a radiating center predominates over any universal orthogonality. The presence of another strong center like St. Peter's is minimized by opaque walls surrounding a second set of radial columns and the entire courtyard. Bramante's Tempietto does not address the demands of "there", just as Raphael's temple does not really address the demands of "here."

Local and Global

Michelangelo's 1567 designs for Rome's Capitoline Hill reveal how such a conflict was important to this sculptor of space. He made this Campidoglio a place which is both local and global. The orthogonal mapping nods to the inflection of the local center without ripping; the central radial scheme is distorted outward without rupturing. Curtis Taufman has noted that as you climb higher in the Senate building, the star ellipse appears rounder. At the Senate Chamber, the topmost apartment, the ellipse becomes a perfect circle, and There becomes Here! Particular and general often reverse on this site, in a spacial analog to the two-dimensional surface of the cubist picture plane-- a locale which harbors many "pure" frontal views and other confrontations of orthogonal order. This multi-dimensional extension of the Cubist picture plane has many volumes--side spaces, front spaces, top spaces, etc. converging into a space which is somehow more than all of its three-dimensional snapshots, a place which hovers between flat and deep, between cubic and hyper-cubic, between local and global. Iron filings show how radial lines of a magnetic field tend to the orthogonal in a bipolar field. The strength of vision of artists like Michelangelo, Juan Gris, Le Corbusier, and Frank Lloyd Wright, could unify radial and orthogonal realms simultaneously throughout the spaces they created in many dimensions.

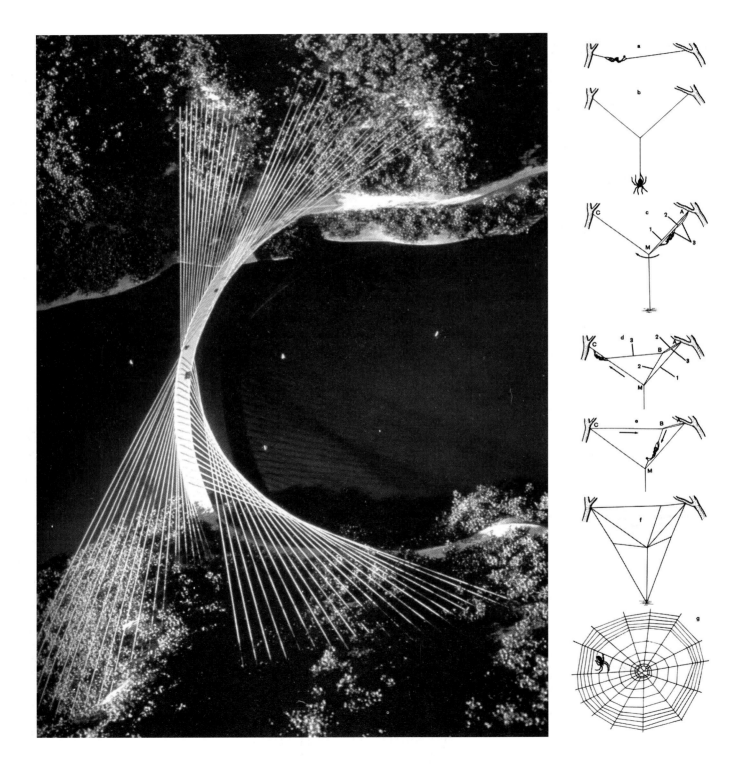

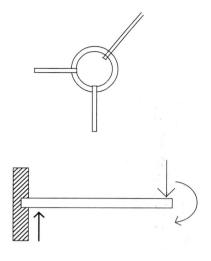

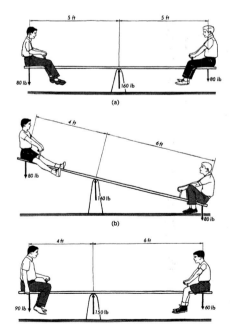

Cantilevered load,
showing rotation and shear

Knife edge fulcrum pin joint
permits free rotation

ANIMATING

Filaments

E-vol-ution means spinning outward, from a starting point. Can a builder throw mass "out there" in such a way as to wrap it around space? A spring in a tug of war rope will stretch, showing tension. Swing a stone on a string around your head, and a spring again shows tension as the moving stone seeks to fly outward. Whenever a string is taut, it is in tension. A spider spins a web of sticky protein filament to span a space to intercept its prey. This web is a (mostly) two dimensional frame of lines spun together in a way that resists great forces in relation to its weight. Wire, hair, and thread are filaments. String, rope, and cable are made of many filaments twisted together. These materials are very strong in relation to their weight and size, because they generally work best when stretched in tension. The Hetch-Hetchy Bridge design is an elegant three-dimensional rotation of tension elements. Joseph Needham has said "biology is largely the study of fibres."

It is clear that a rope or cable in tension cannot bend in the middle or near its joints. Hence connections to cables are pin connectors, which like hinges permit rotation. Cable structures have relatively dense connecting joints at their nodes and relatively thin filaments between them. This makes the planes between the filaments thin (wire frame!) and the voids between these planes sparse, i.e. bubble volumes. If the wire-frame model is a geometer's ideal for defining volume, a cable structure may be an engineer's ideal, because it can describe the largest space with the least material. Spiders are wise engineers, spinning webs of strong filaments around, within, and between volume.

Cantilever: Over the Edge

Placing one solid on another in such a way that its position is displaced in plan with respect to the first mass may create a cantilever. A cantilevered ledge resists rotation by virtue of its moment connection- the support carries both strain and stress. The cantilever is a means of marking void in section, between the overhanging solid and the ground plane below. Modern and very strong materials like steel and reinforced concrete have taken the ancient corbel, at least as old as the Mycenean Lion's Gate, and extended it to dramatic possibility. A Constructivist project for a suspended restaurant, Wright's Falling Water, and skyscraper towers make both structural and architectural use of the cantilever.

Moment's Notice: Resisting Rotation

Push and pull can be directed on a mass from any direction, which is why vectors are needed to describe both the magnitude and direction of forces. But sometimes a force can have an influence on a mass at some distance from its point of application. A seesaw provides a good example. The knife edge fulcrum of the seesaw acts like a pin joint. It permits free rotation at the support. I sit at one end, and the other end rises. It matters both how much I weigh and how far I am from the fulcrum, the central balance, of the seesaw lever. The product of force (weight) and distance is called *moment* and measures the tendency of a body to rotate about a point of support. Unequal mass times unequal distance can produce equal moments. The seesaw creates balance through equilibrium of moment. One child will balance an adult twice as heavy by sitting twice as far from the center support. Some connections tend to resist moment by stiffening the intersection of the members: not surprisingly they are called moment connections. Pin connectors cannot resist the tendency to rotate. If you make two rings with the thumbs and forefingers of both hands, and loop them without touching, your hand-arm-wrists will move freely, without any bending. But if you grasp one wrist with another, and then try to move that right arm, your right wrist will tend to bend to keep the hand/wrist connection steady. These are good models of pin and moment connections, respectively.

"The creative junction and interpenetration of horizontal axes with centralized vaulted shapes was to be one of the major achievements of Byzantine architecture... They abandoned the molding of masses for the composition of spaces." William MacDonald

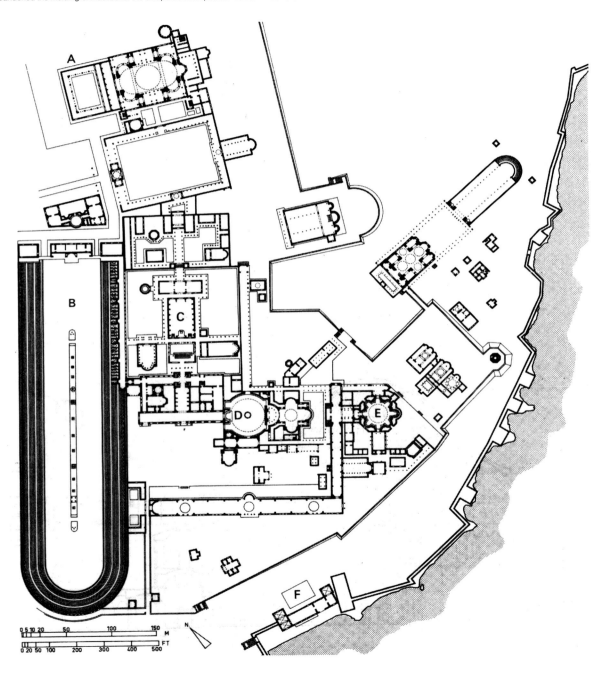

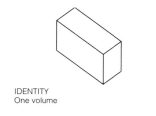

IDENTITY
One volume

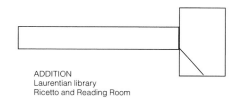

ADDITION
Laurentian library
Ricetto and Reading Room

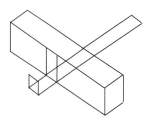

INTERSECTION
two corridors crossing

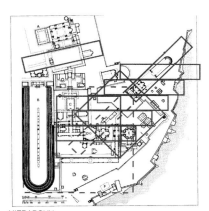

HIERARCHY
analysis of Constantinople plan

INTERACTION OF VOLUME

Dynamics studies forces on solids in space and time. Volumes are mostly empty solids whose presence is as much perceptual as physical. An intellectual reading of volume can reveal the order of architectural space, the relationship between volumes. Volumes appear around, through, and within each other. Some column arrays unite two rooms, others cut them apart. In some rooms walls compress, in others space flies out to the horizon. However, a volume in tension seems stretched only in relation to another which seems compressed. Interaction between volumes is thus close to the phenomenon noted in Josef Albers' formulation of the *Interaction of Color*. Just as Albers argues that what color we see in a figure depends on the color of its surrounding field, so here we argue that what volume we experience depends on its relationship to other volumes. One volume may feel linear compared to a very cubic room, but fairly boxy compared to a long corridor, for example. We suggest that an *interaction of volume* defines form, filled and empty, by relationship. The shade of a tree limb affects the growth of other branches. In a soap foam, the presence of one bubble affects the form of all others. Position, access, and illumination of a room can affect all others in a building. One passing galaxy can actually bend the space of another.

The most basic volume interactions are:

1. VOLUME IDENTITY. To place mass in such away as to make void apparent is the first interaction which manifests the identity of a volume.

2. ADDITION OF VOLUMES. Volumes may be added-- aligned and/or placed in proximity, and individual effects may be magnified by their contrasts. The Laurentian Library's vertically extended, laterally compressed Ricetto seems to be even more compressed by the horizontal reading room. The stairs yield like lava, showing an architectural strain between the stress created by the horizontal push load of the upper chamber and the vertical stretch of the lower one. The stair may also be seen as a resultant diagonal "vector" between these two forces.

Architects act on the idea that there are **at least** perceptual and organizational forces that generate loads, stresses, and strains on the plastic order of spaces. Circulation, light, and view can act as forces on volumes which can spin or push each other, intersect, overlap, etc. Architects often employ, without explicitly referring to it, an interaction of volume as a useful tool for planning for strategic resolution of program elements in three dimensions. Architects animate *partis* at every level of detail to solve program demands in spacial terms: "Move this here, then this can go here, and if you just shove this over here, then there's room to squeeze this in here..." describes the true **action** of architects and architecture. A *parti* is resolved by moving program volumes (breadbox, entry, city hall) until everything fits. "Fits" means right size and place for all volumes.

Simple and complex interactions are revealed in the plan of the Byzantine capital, Constantinople, begun in 330 AD. We can see how careful placing of rooms, colonnades, and courtyards not only unifies separate buildings into a coherent ensemble, but also enables the total plan to "turn the corner". Rotation is facilitated by the hinge **E**, the Chrystoklinos, the Imperial audience hall which unifies the "diagonal" east-west axis of the structures to its east with the "orthogonal" planning of Hippodrome and Imperial Palace **C**. Hagia Sophia **A** (with forum to the southwest) seems random in orientation, but actually is carefully placed to inflect towards Jerusalem. It is rotated more to the southeast than the apse at San Vitale, because Italy is further west of Jerusalem than Turkey!

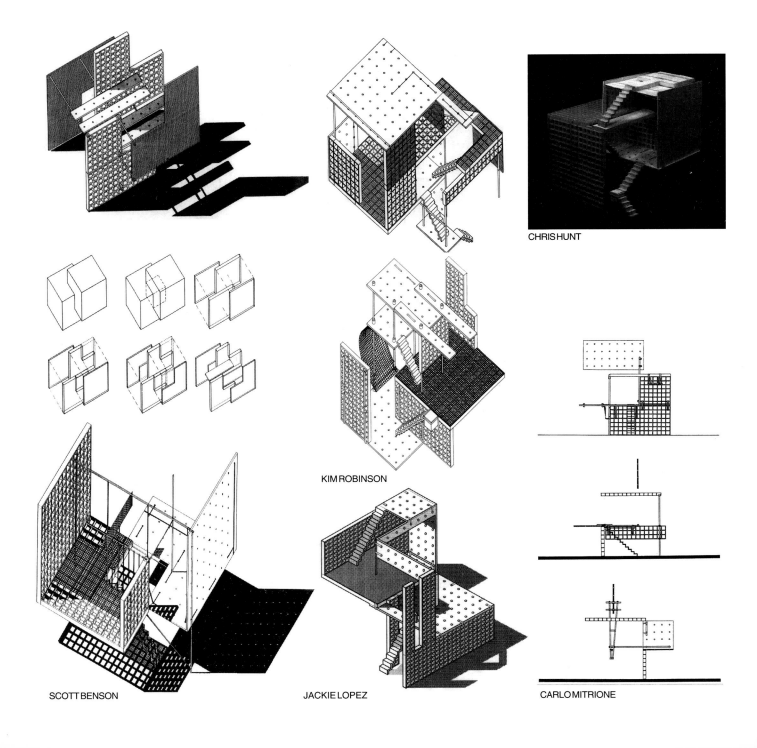

CHRIS HUNT

KIM ROBINSON

SCOTT BENSON

JACKIE LOPEZ

CARLO MITRIONE

DOING -- DYNAMICS *pro-position*

PEACETIME. Two philosophical-political factions seek places where they might clarify their respective positions. The only site available is a 24' cube, which they must share. Each group requires a 16' cube meeting hall, and as much space as possible outside this for impromptu outdoor walks and talks. Each group wants the whole 24' cube site to appear as an extension of their own 16' room. To maintain their individual identities, they wish to make their halls as far and as different from each other as possible. The structural and spacial qualities of your architecture should express the unique qualities of each group and differences between them. (Their individual volumes will still overlap at an 8' cube in the center, according to the plan/section diagram shown on this page.) Needless to say, neither group wants to yield the 8' center cube to the other group: your task here is to make that 8' space part of both larger cubes.

The climate is mediterranean, at around 40° N lat, so you must provide some shelter from harsh sunlight and from rain, but the structure need not be totally enclosed. Both groups desire equivalent (not necessarily the same!) entry to give access to the separate 16' halls; both desire equivalent (not necessarily the same!) view from top of the structure, at the 24' elevation; both wish to take advantage of perimeter views as well. Both groups respect the notion that purely resolved structure, with honestly expressed material properties, can be eloquent and beautiful.

Construct a model of your solution at 1/2"=1'-0" scale, using the Bag of Tricks. You may use as many elements as you wish, although the fewer needed the better: "Less is more". The 45° stairs may be cut and reglued anywhere as needed. Do not use the spiral stairs for this project. Consider how structure and material inform space. For example, eggcrates filter both light and space, separating volumes while generating depth between them. Although eggcrate openings are larger than those in the mesh or masonite, the interval of its perforations, at 1/2", generates a spacial grid actually smaller than that of the masonite. You may also develop your design strategy through paper models to study continuity of volume and surface. (See pages 448, 484, and 490 for suggested working methodology.) Reminder: Program spaces must be well-defined, so that **more than** three of the six sides of a cubic volume are "closed", i.e., opaque or impervious to movement. Second reminder: this is constructed space! Keep it pure, clean, direct! No toilets! No borrowed cliches! Economy of means! Heighten the architectural contrast between the volumes for the two groups. Size and proportion of the major 16' volumes are equal, so these qualities cannot be exploited for contrast. Use architectonic means, such as light, surface and orientation, and dynamic means to activate volumes through structure, material, circulation and plasticity. For example, make the volumes feel expansive (moving outward) or compressive (withdrawing inward), or set them to different orders of tension and compression for volumetric tensegrity.

ANIMATION: Consider your plans and sections as moment diagrams. Show how the volumes tend to generate rotational space (moment and shear) through occupation of the whole site. Show a series of at least 3 successive formal operations how the entire site is occupied through outward evolution of the volumes and user circulation.

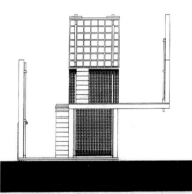

KIM ROBINSON

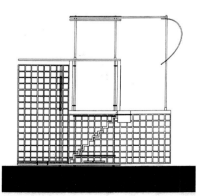

KIM ROBINSON

COLOR: 1. **Tint & Shade of Equal Color: 4 Hues.**   See page 463 .
              2. **Tint & Shade of Unequal Color: 8 Hues.**   See page 463.
              3. ***Collage 2a.*** Explore the illusion of film overlay.   See pages 452 and 458.

FUNCTION: Plot and/or construct a Logarithmic Spiral.   See page 453 .

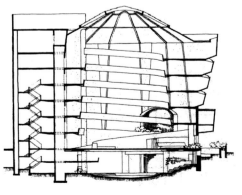

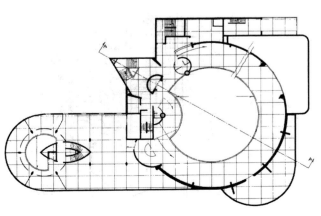

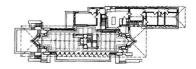

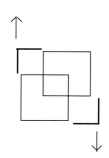

MOMENTOUS VOLUME

"A wheel turns by virtue of its empty center." Lao Tze

Every project in Architectonics involved the addition of solid mass pieces to order space-piling up elements to define volumes between them. The only operational strategy for space-making in such cases is to add discrete elements of mass. But other ways exist for making spaces; for example sculptors carve volume from solid stone; potters shape clay by turning it on a wheel. Volume is a solid in which the preponderance of mass occurs on the perimeter. Could not there be also a kind of space in which volumes are made to occur primarily eccentrically, that is at the periphery of the overall site or spacial figure? As volumes become more empty and materials tend to become less massive, conceptual tools allow architects to compose not only physical structures but complex hierarchies of volumetric order as well. Volumes can not only be added, but also subtracted, united, and intersected. Two intersecting squares can also effectively organize the larger implied square they both inhabit. The intersection of two cubes may also be a sum of their volumes, implying by rotation a still larger volume.

Architectonics suggests a five-year-old child in the midst of still and ancient monuments. Dynamics suggests a young adult in revolution (if not in orbit!) making room to move and breathe in a brand new world. Children make castles with wood blocks in their hands. But as adults, the wood gets heavier or becomes stone, and time's ravages demand attention to maintenance and upkeep. We work to push our own boundaries beyond our easy grasp. How can we use our architectural resources to imply the corners and bring them into the plastic equation that actuates an entire site? We must make *human volumes*, at human scale, for the human body in motion and at rest; then we may find space in motion and space in repose. Is there a special relationship between life, art, and evolving space? Frank Lloyd Wright set the major plan elements in rotation to both turn the corner and embrace the whole site at his 1905 Robie House in Chicago. While spinning volume is literal in the 1926 plan of the Bauhaus at Dessau, Wright's Guggenheim Museum in New York City spins volume more subtly, not only reaching for the edges, but loading the periphery with dense program space, animating the entire architecture the way the hub around an axle permits a wheel to turn.

The Guggenheim Museum is a wonderful example of a human space that is a centrifugal spinning volume, suggesting even the three-dimensional "shadow" of spacetime curvature near a black hole predicted by relativity theory. The plan strategy puts exhibition galleries on the outside of the hollow great heart of the museum, illuminating the volume by a central skylight above. The path through the volumetric sequence is simple but elegant-- an elevator takes the visitor straight up, then a gradual spiral downward facilitates an easy walk while viewing the show, leading back into the gravity well of earth. Arriving at ground level, the visitor moves into the center, to be once again illuminated from above, completing a spacial cycle of down and up. (Restaurant and staff quarters generate further eccentricity as outriggers to the central volume, so that whole ensemble makes a graceful turn at the end of the city block. The volumes are not simply an erosion into the Fifth Avenue edge of Central Park; they also carry the movement of the river-flow traffic around the end condition of the block. Compare this parti with Reitveld's Schroeder House (*Architectonics*, page 83) where a single wall and three exposed edges also form the site. The Guggenheim is a temperamental space: it was hard to show Kenneth Noland's horizontal stripe paintings against its curved wall, but Roy Liechtenstein and late Picasso shows were knockouts. Across the space the small scale images looked like their cartoon and portrait prototypes, while up close the benday dots and brush strokes dominated to reveal abstraction. The space was always animated.

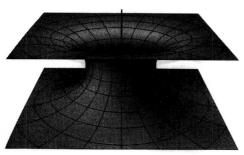

black hole from wheel(er)!

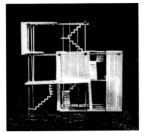

NELSON PARRA

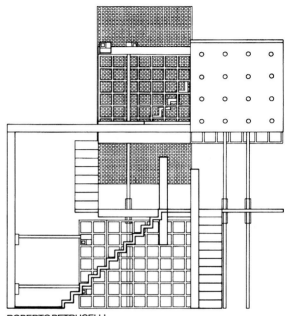

ROBERTO PETRUCELLI

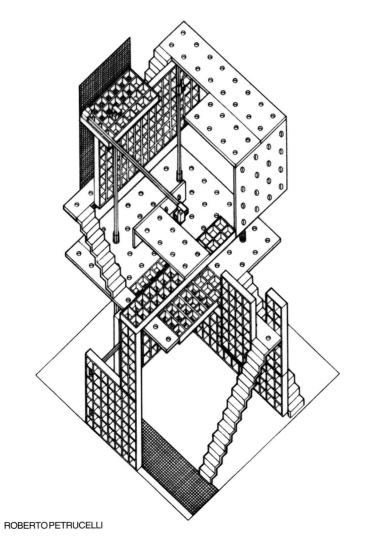

ROBERTO PETRUCELLI

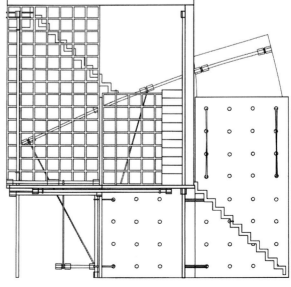

BIL REYMAN

Large α   Small α

Large β   Small β

Large γ   Small γ

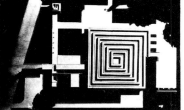

REFLECTING

*"The Constructivist idea in Art... does not separate content from form--
on the contrary, it does not see as possible their separated and independent existence."
Naum Gabo, "The Constructivist Idea in Art" in the 1937 magazine Circle*

The logarithmic spiral is increasingly accurately constructed from whole number square modules based on the Fibonacci harmonic series. Since at least Brunelleschi architects have sought harmony in the order of compounds of volumes, finding rhythm in the relationship of intervals between grid bays, the way a musician combines notes of standard frequency intervals or a chemist combines atoms of elements in exact proportions to get sugar or protein. *On The Plastic* (*Architectonics*, page 30) proposes an architecture composed from basic geometric solids. The question of harmony is always one of relations between elements: their dimensions, shapes, extensions, and interactions. In the first reading selection below Wittkower identifies at least one source for the Renaissance architect and theorist Andrea Palladio's methods of integrating the measures of the volumes of his buildings as coming from musical theory.

The spiral is often a mythic symbol of fertility and evolution. Since the Babylonian Ziggurats and the construction path up the Egyptian Pyramids, the spiral has also been a geometric figure that literally enables growth to occur in architecture. Le Corbusier said "Biology, that's the new word in architecture"; he found in the nautilus shell a key to planning his Museum of Infinite Growth. The interesting question he must have set himself was "What is the logical plan for a building which collects works of art, since the very nature of its program suggests that there will always be a need for more room for new acquisitions. Further, how to make the plan always spacially complete, at every stage of its eternally incomplete growth?" Wright's Guggenheim Museum adds an ironic twist to this *parti*. Its spiral is not simply rotational, but also translational, like a coiled spring, upward, forward, out into time, recalling D'arcy Thompson's studies of shells as diagrams of the forces that generated their forms. A seashell is a cast of a spacetime figure of growth. It is worth studying through freehand drawing. Gabo's introduction to "The Constructivist Idea in Art" in *Circle* makes frequent use of the word *revolution*, referring to Raphael and artistic revolutions, as well as scientific ones like the Copernican Revolution, which established that the earth is not the center of the universe. Why revolution? One who is enlightened is ever returning to the source. The adult beginner is always becoming young. Some easy exercises can also become art at the most advanced level. With a simple piece of music like *Prelude in C* in Bach's *Well Tempered Clavier*, both a child and a virtuoso like Vladimir Horowitz can play the notes correctly, but while the child struggles to simply master the notes, a Horowitz can continue to discover new levels of meaning and human expression in the piece at every recital. The same can be true of the study and practice of architecture. Recall that "plastic" is derived from the Greek root *pla-* like our words flow, play, and clay, and means "capable of being molded". Dutch plasticist Vincent Van Gogh's ecstatic vision *Starry Night* paints a flowing river of energy and mass, light and dark a spinning contour relief map-- of the cosmos! And so we begin, again. And again...

READINGS

Billington, David. *The Tower and the Bridge*
Bruschi, Arnaldo. *Bramante*
Eames and Morrison. *Powers of Ten*
Ghyka, Matilla. The *Geometry of Art and Life*
Schwenk, Theodore. *Sensitive Chaos: The Creation of Flowing Forms in Water and Air*
Thompson, D'Arcy W. *On Growth and Form*
Wittkower, Rudolf. *Architecture in the Age of Humanism*

Villa Godi

ARCHITECTURE IN THE AGE OF HUMANISM
by Rudolf Wittkower

5. Palladio's 'fugal' System of proportion

To the minds of the men of the Renaissance musical consonance were the audible tests of a universal harmony which had a binding force for all the arts. This conviction was not only deeply rooted in the cry, but also-- and this is now usually denied-- translated into practice. It is true, that in trying to prove that a system of proportion has been deliberately applied by a painter, a sculptor or an architect, one is easily misled into finding those ratios which one sets out to find. In the scholar's hand dividers do not revolt. If we want to avoid the pitfall of useless speculation we must look for unmistakable guidance by the artists themselves. Strangely enough, no scholar has yet attempted to do this. Such guidance is not very common, but a careful survey would certainly yield considerable evidence. One must, above all, be able to decipher and interpret the artist's indications. One example may show what we mean.

At the end of his first book Serlio illustrates a geometrical scheme as a guide for the 'right' construction of the door of a church (see Fig. 10). He completes the central bay, in which the door should be placed, into a square [by drawing a line parallel to the base], draws the diagonals (AB, CD) and erects from the two corners of the base an isosceles triangle (AEC). The intersections between the diagonal and the sides of the triangle (FG) mark the height and width of the door. The drawing seems to suggest a geometrical procedure, not very different from the 'ad quadratum' method practised during the later Middle Ages. In both cases the geometric pattern leads to the arithmetically irrational focal points of the design (point F, for instance, divides the 2 diagonal CD as well as the 5 line AE into one part and two parts). But in Serlio's case the geometrical scheme is posterior rather than prior to the ratios chosen for the door. His design was evidently the result of commensurable divisions of the large square. The door itself is a double square, its width and height in the light are related to the side of the square as 1:3 and 2:3, the frame of the door and the height of the pediment are related to the width of opening as 1:3 and 1:2 respectively, and so forth. Thus an interrelated series of ratios of small integral numbers is really at the basis of Serlio's design. 'Medieval' geometry here is no more than a veneer that enables practitioners to achieve commensurable ratios without much ado. But there is material at hand of a much less ambiguous nature.

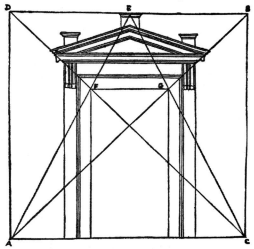

Fig. 10. Construction of a door. From Serlio's First Book.

By far the most important practical guide to a coherent system of proportion known to me is embodied in the illustrations of Palladio' *Quatro Libri*. If properly interpreted, they are no less a key to the problem of harmonic proportion than Alberti's theories. Palladio's second book contains his own buildings in elevation, plan and section, and it is they that must now be considered. The many discrepancies between the plates and the actual buildings were and are usually attributed to careless publication. Yet the plan of the whole work reveals that Palladio did not publish his buildings merely as an autobiographical contribution. He made a statement to this effect in the preface to the *Quatro Libri* with these words; 'In the second [book] I shall treat of the quality of the fabricks that are suitable to the different ranks of men; first of those of a city; and then of the most convenient situation for villas.... And as we have but very few examples from the antients, of which we can make use, I shall insert the plans and elevations of many fabricks I have erected....' In this light many differences between buildings and plates can be explained.

The illustrations were to him a means of expounding his conceptions not only of planning but also of proportion, hence his theoretical measurements could deviate from the executed ones. If this is a right deduction, the hypothesis seems justified that Palladio wanted his inscribed measurements to convey ratios of a general character and of universal importance beyond the scope of individual buildings. In most of his plans ratios of width to length of the rooms are prominently placed and easily readable, while-- with the exception of a few large-scale details-- it is generally more difficult to read them in the elevations. For heights of rooms, which are given only in relatively few sections, he often refers in the text to the method employed. These module, and by a process of multiplication beginning with two all the ratios of the building can be derived.

An organic structure developed from the module, the *regola homogenea*', has no room for incommensurable quantities; however, the application of the module does not necessarily mean that the ratios throughout a whole building must be harmonic. But the systematic linking of one room to the other by harmonic proportions was the novelty of Palladio's architecture, and we believe that his wish to demonstrate this innovation had a bearing on the choice and character of the plates and the inscription of measurements. Those proportional relationships which other architects had harnessed for the two dimensions of a facade or the three dimensions of a single room were employed by him to integrate the whole structure.

The demand that the parts should correspond to the whole and to each other was generally adhered to in churches, for the relation of nave, aisles, and chapels, and here the Renaissance could build on medieval traditions. But for domestic buildings the decisive step was taken by Palladio. He formulated his views on this point in one very important sentence which will add weight to our analysis of two of his villas: "But the large rooms ought to be so related (*compartite*) to the middle ones, and these to the small, that, as I have said elsewhere, one part of the building may correspond with the other, so that the whole body of the edifice may have in itself a certain harmony (*convenienza*) of the members which may make it entirely beautiful and graceful".

A thorough acquaintance with Renaissance ideas on proportion is often necessary to understand the legitimacy of the ratios given by arrangements seem to reveal a definite scheme which we propose to follow by confining ourselves to an examination of some Palladio's plans.

What kind of proportion did Palladio exemplify, with his inscribed measurements? The early Villa Godi at Lonedo (PL. 21c) contains the gist

Villa Malcontenta

of the story in a simple form. Each of the eight small rooms-- four at each side of the hall-- measures 16 x 24 feet, i.e. width:length = 1:1 1/2 which is one of seven shapes of the rooms recommended by Palladio. The ratio of width to length is 2:3. The portico has the same size of 16 x 24, while the hall behind it measures 24 x 36; its ratio-- 1:1 1/2 or 2:3 -- is therefore equal to that of the small rooms and the portico. The use of the same ratio throughout the building is apparent. But beyond this, the equation 16/24 = 24/36 shows that rooms and hall are, one might say, proportionally firmly interlocked. The series underlying the plan as a whole is the progression 16, 24, 36, which we know from Alberti's analysis of the ratio 4:9 as 4:6:9 and which can be expressed in musical terms as a sequence of two *diapente*. Thus, for those who understood the language of proportion, Palladio's meaning was made abundantly clear by the conspicuous inscriptions of measurements in the plans; without them the reader would be left with no key to the architect's intentions. On the other hand, the notation of the measurements as executed would have interfered with the clarity of the harmonic concept, for the depth of the portico is actually 14.9 feet instead of 16 feet and the widths of the two adjoining rooms are15.5 and 17.3 feet.

The ratios of Palladio's later structures are somewhat more complicated as can be illustrated in the Villa Malcontenta (Pl. 45b). The smallest room on either side of the cross-shaped hall measures 12 x 16 feet, the next one 16 x 16 and the largest 16 x 24, while the width of the hall is 32 feet. Thus, the consistent series 12, 16, 24, 32 is the keynote to the building. As if in an overture the first and last members of this series appear in the ratio 12:32 of the portico, which is a *diapason* and *diatessaron* (i.e. 12:24:32). The intercolumniation of the centre (6 ft.) is related to the depth of the portico (12) as 1:2. The smaller intercolumniations are 4 1/2 feet; they are related to the central one as 3: 4 which, incidentally, is the ratio of the smallest rooms. Finally, the diameter of the columns, 2 feet, represents the smallest unit, the Palladio. In the Villa Emo (Pl. 46a) rooms of 16 x 16, 12 x 16, 16 x 27 frame the portico (also 16 x 27) and the hall (27 x 27). the ratio 16:27 can only be understood by splitting it up in the way Alberti has taught us; it has to be read as 16:24:27. i.e. as a fifth and a major tone (2 :3 and 8:9) and similarly the compound ratio 12:27 can be generated from 12:24:27, i.e. an octave and a major tone (1:2 and 8:9). Thus the figures 27, 12, 16, which, written one under the other, strike the reader's eye, are perfectly intelligible by means of the generation of ratios. Ratios of the same order are to be found in the wings; 12 is again the middle term, this time inscribed between 24 and 48. The harmonic character of this series is obvious (2:1:4, 1:4 being two octaves = 1:2:4). The whole building appears now like a spatial orchestration of the consonant terms 12, 16, 24, 27, 48.

The same theme was developed in other structures with different measurements. The Villa Thiene at Cicogna (Pl. 45a) has 4 as module (diameter of the columns) and the rooms are based on the harmonic series 12, 18, 36. In the four corners are square rooms measuring 18 x 18 feet; the flank a double square room, 18 x 36, and this ratio is repeated in the two porticos which flank the hall which is 36 x 36 feet, i.e. four times the size of the corner rooms. The progression 18:18, 18:36, 36:36 is broken between the small squares and the porticos by rooms measuring 12 feet in width, so that the sequence 18, 12, 18 (3:2:3) is repeated four times. Progressions of 1:1, 1:2, 2:2 used in the Villa Thiene occur in other buildings. Rooms of 20 x 20, 20 x 30, 30 x 30 form the core of the Palazzo Porto-Colleoni, and ratios on the series 12, 16, 18, 24, 27, 32, 36 are frequent. All these spatial proportions have their equivalent in the consonances of the Greek musical scale. But we are far from suggesting that Palladio, while planning his buildings, was consciously translating musical into visual proportions. Francesco Giorgio, in his memorandum, did not set out to prove the applicability of musical consonances to

architecture, but worked with them for the design of S. Francesco della Vigna as a matter-of-course procedure.' The rules of arithmetic', said Daniele Barbaro, elaborating Vitruvius, 'are those which unite Music and Astrology: for proportion is general and universal in all things given to measure, weight and number.' We have Palladio's own word for it, that for him the proportions of sounds and in space were closely related, and must have been convinced of the universal validity of one and the same harmonic system. These convictions which belonged to the general intellectual makeup of the Renaissance, and it needed no particular sophistication to translate them into practice.

6. Palladio's Ratios and the development of Sixteenth-Century Musical Theory

It should now be said that ratios based on the small integral numbers of the Greek musical scale (1:2:3:4) are by no means the only ones to be found in Palladio's plans. Palladio showed a predilection for rooms measuring 18 x 30 or 12 x 20, i.e. for a ratio of 3:5. There are buildings with ratios of 4:5 and 5:6 and these are similar ratios occur not only in the proportions of one room but also in the relation of one room to another-- 4:5 in the Villa Valmarana at Lisiera, 5:6 in the Villa Ghizzole, 3:5 in the design for the Palazzo Angarano, 5:9 in that for Count della Torre at Verona, and this list could be considerable extended.

All these buildings present new problems which cannot be understood without considering the fundamental changes in the approach to the proportion during the sixteenth century. In the course of this century ratios became perceptible which were outside the grasp of fifteenth century artists. The development of musical theory during that period, particular in Northern Italy, is a reliable guide. It was Ludovico Fogliano of Moena who, in his *Musica theorica* of 1529, first protested against the sole authority of the Pythagorean consonances; according to him experience teaches that, apart from the five Pythagorean consonances, minor (5:6) and major third (4:5) minor (5:8) and the major sixth (3:5) and the major (2:5), eleventh (3:8), and minor and major sixth above the octave (5:16 and 3:10) are all consonantes. But it was Zarlino, the great Venetian theorist of the mid-sixteenth century who, with his rigorously scientific approach, classified the entire harmonic material which had come down from antiquity. It is a phenomenon which Zarlino calls '*veramente maraviglioso*' (truly miraculous') that the consonances are determined by the arithmetic as well as by the 'harmonic' mean. The arithmetic mean 3 between 2 and 4 divides the octave into fifth and fourth (2:3 and 3:4); the same result, is achieved by the 'harmonic' mean 8 between the extremes 6 and 12 (6: 8 = 3:4 and 8:12 = 2:3). Zarlino could show that the same law applies to the division of the fifth, for 2:3 or 4:6 with the arithmetic means determines the ratios of major and minor third (4:5 and 5:6) and with the 'harmonic ' mean-- as in 10, 12, 15-- the ratios of minor and major third. A further division of the major third is possible; the insertion of the arithmetic mean between 4 and 5 leads to the ratio 8:9:10, 8:9 being the major tone and 9:10 the minor tone, while the 'harmonic' mean 80 between the extremes 72 and 90 divides the series into minor and major tone. Zarlino can now show in a diagram the '*divisione harmonic della Diapason nelle sue parti*' ('harmonic division of the octave into its parts').

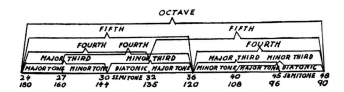

THE CONSTRUCTIVE IDEA IN ART

by Naum Gabo

Our century appears in history under the sign of revolutions and disintegration. The revolutions have spared nothing in the edifice of culture which had been built up by the past ages. Our century appears in history under the sign of revolutions and disintegration. The revolutions have spared nothing in the edifice of culture which had been built up by the past ages. They had already begun at the end of the last century and proceeded in ours with unusual speed until there was no stable point left in either the material or the ideal structure of our life. The way was only a natural consequence of a disintegration which started long ago in the depths of the previous civilization. It is innocent to hope that this process of disintegration will stop at the time and in the place where we want it to. Historical processes of this kind generally go their own way. They are more like floods, which do not depend on the strokes of the oarsmen floating on the waters. But, however long and however deep this process may go in its material destruction, it cannot deprive us any more of our optimism about the final outcome, since we see that in the realm of ideas we are now entering on the period of reconstruction.

We can find efficient support for our optimism in those two domains of our culture where the revolution has been the most thorough, namely, in Science and in Art. The critical analysis in natural science with which the last century ended had gone so far that at times the scientists felt themselves to be in a state of suspension, having lost most of the fundamental bases on which they had depended for so many centuries. Scientific thought suddenly found itself confronted with conclusions which had before seemed impossible, in fact the word 'impossibility' disappeared from the lexicon of scientific language. This brought the scientists of our century to the urgent task of filling up this emptiness. This task now occupies the main place in all contemporary scientific works. It consists in the construction of a new stable model for our apprehension of the universe.

However dangerous it may be to make far-reaching analogies between Art and Science, we nevertheless cannot close our eyes to the fact that at those moments in the history of culture when the creative human genius had to make a decision, the forms in which this genius manifested itself in Art and in Science were analogous. One is inclined to think that this manifestation in the history of Art lies on a lower level than it does in the history of Science, or at least on a level which is accessible to wider social control. The terminology of Science alone plunges a layman into a state of fear, humility and admiration. The inner world of Science is closed to an outsider by a curtain if enigmas. He has been educated to accept the holy mysticism of these enigmas since the beginning of culture. He does not even try to intrude in this world in order to know what happens there, being convinced that it must be something very important since he sees the results in obvious technical achievements. The average man knows, for instance, that there is electricity and that there is radio and he uses them every day. He knows the names of Marconi and Edison, but it is doubtful where he has ever heard anything about the scientific work of Hertz, and there is no doubt that he has never heard anything about the electromagnetic waves theory of Maxwell or his mathematical formulae.

Not so is the attitude of the average man to Art. Access to the realm of Art is open to every man. He judges about Art with the unconstrained ease of an employer and owner. He does not meditate about those processes which brought the artist or the group of artists to make one special kind of Art and not another, or if occasionally he does he never relinquishes his right to judge and decide, to accept or reject; in a word, he takes up an attitude which he would never allow himself to take with Science. He is convinced that on his judgements depend the value and the existence of the work of art. He does not suspect that through the mere fact of its existence a work of art has already performed the function for which it has been made and has affected his concept of the world regardless of whether he wants it to or not. The creative processes the domain of Art are as sovereign as the creative processes in Science. Even for many theorists of Art the fact remains unperceived that the same spiritual state propels artistic and scientific activity at the same time and in the same direction.

At first sight it seems unlikely that an analogy can be drawn between a scientific work of, say, Copernicus and a picture by Raphael, and yet it is not difficult to discover the tie between them. In fact Copernicus' scientific theory of the world is coincident with Raphael's concept in Art. Raphael would never have dared to take the naturalistic image of his famous Florentine pastry-cook as a model for the 'Holy Marie' if he had not belonged to the generation which was already prepared to abandon the geocentrical theory of the universe. In the artistic concept of Raphael there is no longer any trace of the mythological religious mysticism of the previous century as there is no longer any trace of this mysticism in Copernicus' book, The Revolution of the Celestial Orbits. In the work of both, the earth is no longer the cosmic centre and man is no longer the crown of creation and the only hero of the cosmic drama; both are parts of a larger universe and their existence does not any more appear as the mystical and dematerialized phenomenon of the mediaeval age. At that time one and the same spirit governed the artistic studios of Florence and held sway under the arches of the Neapolitan Academy for the Empirical Study of Nature led by Telesio. This tie between Science and Art has never ceased to exist throughout the history of human culture, and we can discern it in whatever section of history we look. This fact explains many phenomena in the spiritual processes of our own century which brought our own generation to the Constructive idea in Art.

The immediate source from which the Constructive idea derives is Cubism, although it had almost the character of a repulsion rather than an attraction. The Cubistic school was the summit of a revolutionary process in Art which was already started by the Impressionists at the end of the last century. One may estimate the value of particular

Cubistic works as one likes, but it is incontestable that the influence of the Cubistic ideology on the spirits of the artists at the beginning of this century has no parallel in the history of Art for violence and intrepidity. The revolution which this school produced in the minds of artists is only comparable to that which happened at approximately the same time in the world of physics. Many falsely assume that the birth of Cubistic ideology was caused by the fashion for Negro art which was prevalent at that time; but in reality Cubism was a purely European phenomenon and its substance has nothing in common with the demonism of primitive tribes. The Cubistic ideology has a highly differentiated character and its manifestation could only be possible in the atmosphere of a refined culture. In fact it wants an especially sharpened and cultivated capacity for analytic thought to undertake the task of revaluation of old values in Art and to perform it with violence as the Cubistic school did. All previous schools in Art have been in comparison merely reformers, Cubism was a revolution. It was directed against the fundamental basis of Art. All that was before holy and intangible for an artistic mind, namely, the formal unity of the external world, was suddenly laid down on their canvases, torn in pieces and dissected as if it were a mere anatomical specimen. The borderline which separated the external world from the artist and distinguished it in forms of objects disappeared; the objects themselves disintegrated into their component parts and a picture ceased to be an image of the visible forms of an object as a unit, a world in itself, but appeared as a mere pictorial analysis of the inner mechanism of its cells. The medium between the inner world of the artist and the external world has lost its extension, and between the inner world of the perceptions of the artist and the outer world of existing things there was no longer any substantial medium left which could be measured either by distance or by mind. The contours of the external world which served before as the only guides to an orientation in it were erased; even the necessity for orientation lost its importance and was replaced by other problems, those of exploration and analysis. The creative act of the Cubists was entirely at variance with any which we have observed before. Instead of taking the object as a separate world and passing it through his perceptions producing a third object, namely the picture, which is the product of the first two, the Cubist transfers the entire inner world of his perceptions with all its component parts (logic, emotion and will) into the interior of the object penetrating through its whole structure, stretching its substance to such an extent that the outside integument explodes and the object itself appears destroyed and unrecognizable. That is why a Cubistic painting seems like a heap of shards from a vessel exploded from within. The Cubist has no special interest in those forms which differentiate one object from another.

Although the Cubists still regarded the external world as the point of departure for their Art they did not see and did not want to see any difference between, say, a violin, a tree, a human body, etc. All those objects were for them only one extended matter with a unique structure and only this structure was of importance for their analytic task. It is understandable that in such an artistic concept of the world the details must possess unexpected dimensions and the parts acquire the value of entities, and in the inner relations between them the disproportion grows to such an extent that all inherited ideas about harmony are destroyed. When we look through a Cubist painting to its concept of the world the same thing happens to us as when we enter the interior of a building which we know only from a distance - it is surprising, unrecognizable and strange. The same thing happens which occurred in the world of physics when the new Relativity Theory destroyed the borderlines between Matter and Energy, between Space and Time, between the mystery of the world in the atom and the consistent miracle of our galaxy.

I do not mean to say by this that these scientific theories have affected the ideology of the Cubists, one must rather presume that none of those artists had so much as heard of or studied those theories. It is much more probable that they would not have apprehended them even if they had heard about them, and in the end it is entirely superfluous. The state of ideas in this time has brought both creative disciplines to adequate results, each in its own field, so that the edifice of Art as well as the edifice of Science was undermined and corroded by a spirit of fearless analysis which ended in a revolutionary explosion. Yet the destruction produced in the world of Art was more violent and more thorough.

Our own generation found in the world of Art after the work of the Cubists only a conglomeration of ruins. The Cubistic analysis had left for us nothing of the old traditions on which we could base even the flimsiest foundation. We have been compelled to start from the beginning. We had a dilemma to resolve, whether to go further on the way of destruction or to search for new bases for the foundation of a new Art. Our choice was not so difficult to make. The logic of life and the natural artistic instinct prompted us with its solution.

The logic of life does not tolerate permanent revolutions. They are possible on paper but in real life a revolution is only a means, a tool but never an aim. It allows the destruction of obstacles which hinder a new construction, but destruction for destructions' sake is when this analysis does not care about the results, when it excludes the task of finding a synthesis, it turns to its opposite, and instead of clarifying a problem it only renders it more obscure. Life permits to our desire for knowledge and exploration the most daring and courageous excursions, but only to the explorers who, enticed far away into unknown territories, have not forgotten to notice the way by which they came and the aim for which they started. In Art more than anywhere else in the creative discipline, daring expeditions are allowed. The most dizzying experiments are permissible, but even in Art the logic of life arrests the experiments as soon as they have reached the point when the death of the experimental objects becomes imminent. There were moments in the history of Cubism when the artist were pushed to these bursting points; sufficient to recall the sermons of Picabia, 1914-16, predicting the wreck of Art, and the manifestos of the Dadaists who already celebrated the funeral of Art with chorus and demonstrations. Realizing how near to complete annihilation the Cubist experiments had brought Art, many Cubists themselves have tried to find a way out, but the lack of consequences has merely made them afraid and has driven them back to Ingres (Picasso, 1919-23) and to the Gobelins of the sixteenth century (Braque, etc.). This was not an outlet but a retreat. Our generation did not need to follow them since it has found a new concept of the world represented by the Constructive idea.

The Constructive idea is not a programmatic one. It is not a technical scheme for an artistic manner, nor a rebellious demonstration of an artistic sect; it is a general concept of the world, or better a spiritual state of a generation, an ideology caused by life, bound up with it and directed to influence its course. It is not concerned with only one discipline in Art (painting, sculpture or architecture) it does not even remain solely in the sphere of Art. This idea can be discerned in all domains of the new culture now in construction. This idea has not come with finished and dry formulas, it does not establish immutable laws or schemes, it grows organically along with the growth of our century. It is as young as our century and as old as the human desire to create.

The basis of the Constructive Idea in Art lies in an entirely new approach to the nature of Art and its functions in life. In it lies a complete reconstruction of the means in the different domains of Art, in the relations between them, in their methods and in their aims. It embraces those two fundamental elements on which Art is built up, namely, the Content and the Form. These two elements are from the Constructive point of view one and the same thing. It does not separate Content from Form-- on the contrary, it does not see as possible their separated and independent existence. The thought that Form could have one designation and Content another cannot be incorporated in the concept of the Constructive idea. In a work of art they have to live and act as a unit, proceed in the same direction and produce the same effect. I say 'have to' because never before in Art have they acted in such a way in spite of the obvious necessity of this condition. It has always been so in Art that either one or the other predominated, conditioning and predetermining the other.

This was because in all our previous Art concepts of the world a work of art could not have been conceived without the representation of the external aspect of the world. Whichever way the artist presented the outside world, either as it is or as seen through his personal perceptions, the external aspect remained as the point of departure and the kernel of its content. Even in those cases where the artist tried to concentrate his attention only on the inner world of his perceptions and emotions, he could not imagine the picture of this inner world without the images of the outer one. The most that he could dare in such cases was the more or less individual distortions of the external images of Nature; that is, he altered only the scale of the relations between the two worlds, always keeping to the main system of its content, but did not attack the fact of their dependence; and this indestructible content in a work of art always predicted the forms which Art has followed down to our own time.

The apparently ideal companionship between Form and Content in the old Art was indeed an unequal division of rights and was based on the obedience of the Form to the Content. This obedience is explained by the fact that all formalistic movements in the history of Art, whenever they appeared, never went so far as to presume the possibility of an independent existence of a work of art apart from the naturalistic content, nor to suspect that there might be a concept of the world which could reveal a Content in a Form.

This was the main obstacle to the rejuvenation of Art, and it was at this point that the Constructive idea laid the cornerstone of its foundation. It has revealed an universal law that the elements of a visual art such as lines, colours, shapes, possess their own forces of expression independent of any association with the external aspects of the world; that their life and their action are self-conditioned psychological phenomena rooted in human nature; that those elements are not chosen by conventions for any utilitarian or other reason as words and figures are, they are not merely abstract signs, but they are immediately and organically bound up with human emotions. The revelation of this fundamental law has opened up a vast new field in art giving the possibility of expression to those human impulses and emotions which have been neglected. Heretofore these elements have been abused by being used to express all sorts of associative images which might have been expressed otherwise, for instance, in literature and poetry.

But this point was only one link in the ideological chain of the constructive concept, being bound up with the new conception of Art as a whole and of its functions in life. The Constructive idea sees and values Art only as a creative act. By a creative act it means every material or spiritual work which is destined to stimulate or perfect the substance of material or spiritual life. Thus the creative genius of Mankind obtains the most important and singular place. In the light of the Constructive idea the creative mind of Man has the last and decisive word in the definite construction of the whole of our culture. To be sure, the creative genius of Man is only a part of Nature, but from this part alone derives all the energy necessary to construct his spiritual and material edifice. Being a result of Nature it has every right to be considered as a further cause of its growth. Obedient to Nature, it intends to become its master; attentive to the laws of Nature it intends to make its own laws, following the forms of Nature it re-forms them. We do not need to look for the origin of this activity, it is enough for us to state it and to feel its reality continually acting on us. Life without creative effort is unthinkable, and the whole course of human culture is one continuous effort of the creative will of Man. Without the presence and the control of the creative genius, Science by itself would never emerge from the state of wonder and contemplation from which it is derived and would never have achieved substantial results. Without the creative desire Science would go astray in its own schemes, losing its aim in its reasoning. No criterion could be established in any spiritual discipline without this creative will. No way could be chosen, no direction indicated without its decision. There are not truths beyond its truths. How many of them life hides in itself, how different they are and how inimical. Science is not able to resolve them. One scientist says, 'The truth is here'; another says, 'It is there'; while a third says, 'It is neither here nor there, but somewhere else'. Everyone of them has his own proof and his own reason for saying so, but the creative genius does not wait for the end of their discussion. Knowing what it wants, it makes a choice and decides for them.

*"Space and time are the only forms on which life is built
and hence art must be constructed."*
Naum Gabo and Antoine Pevsner
The Realist Manifesto, 1920, Moscow

The creative genius knows that truths are possible everywhere but only those truths matter to it which correspond to its aims and which lie in the direction of its course. The way of a creative mind is always positive, it always asserts; it does not know the doubts which are so characteristic of the scientific mind. In this case it acts as Art.

The Constructive idea does not see that the function of Art is to represent the world. It does not impose on Art the function of Science. Art and Science are two different streams which rise from the same creative source and flow into the same ocean of the common culture, but the currents of these two streams flow in different beds. Science teaches, Art asserts; Science persuades, Art acts; Science explores and apprehends, informs and proves. It does not undertake anything without first being in accord with the laws of Nature. Science cannot deal otherwise because its task is knowledge. Knowledge is bound up with things which are and things which are not heterogeneous, changeable and contradictory. Therefore the way to the ultimate truth is so long and difficult for Science.

The force of Science lies in its authoritative reason. The force of Art lies in its immediate influence on human psychology and in its active contagiousness. Being a creation of Man it re-creates Man. Art has no need of philosophical arguments, it does not follow the signposts of philosophical systems; Art, like life, dictates systems to philosophy. It is not concerned with the mediation about what is and how it came to be. That is a task for Knowledge. Knowledge is born of the desire to know, Art derives from the necessity to communicate and to announce. The stimulus of Science is the deficiency of our knowledge. The stimulus of Art is the abundance of our emotions and our latent desires. Science is the vehicle of facts - it is indifferent, or at best tolerant, to the ideas which lie behind facts. Art is the vehicle of ideas and its attitude to facts is strictly partial. Science looks and observers, Art sees and foresees. Every great scientist has experience a moment when the artist in him saved the scientist. 'We are poets', said Pythagoras, and in the sense that a mathematician is a creator he was right.

In the light of the Constructive idea the purely philosophical wondering about real and unreal is idle. Even more idle is the intention to divide the real into super-real and sub-real, into conscious reality and sub-conscious reality. The Constructive idea knows only one reality. Nothing is unreal in Art. Whatever is touched by Art becomes reality, and we do not need to undertake remote and distant navigations in the sub-conscious in order to reveal a world which lies in our immediate vicinity. We feel its pulse continually beating in our wrists. In the same way we shall probably never have to undertake a voyage in inter-stellar space in order to feel the breath of the galactic orbits. This breath is fanning our heads within the four walls of our own rooms.

There is and there can be only one reality - existence. For the Constructive idea it is more important to know and to use the main fact that Art possesses in its own domain the means to influence the course of this existence enriching its content and stimulating its energy.

This does not mean that this idea consequently compels Art to an immediate construction of material values in life; it is sufficient when Art prepares a state of mind which will be able only to construct, co-ordinate and perfect instead of to destroy, disintegrate and deteriorate. Material values will be the inevitable result of such a state. For the same reason the Constructive idea does not expect from Art the performance of critical functions even when they are directed against the negative sides of life. What is the use of showing us what is bad without revealing what is good? The Constructive idea prefers that Art perform positive works which lead us towards the best. The measure of this perfection will not be so difficult to define when we realize that it does not lie outside us but is bound up in our desire and in our will to it. The creative human genius, which never errs and never mistakes, defines this measure. Since the beginning of Time man has been occupied with nothing else but the perfecting of his world.

To find the means for the accomplishment of this task the artist need not search in the external world of Nature; he is able to express his impulses in the language of those absolute forms which are in the substantial possession of his Art. This is the task which we constructive artists have set ourselves, which we are doing and which we hope will be continued by the future generation.

First published in Circle, 1937

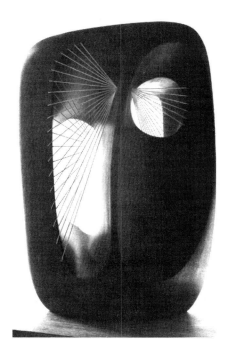

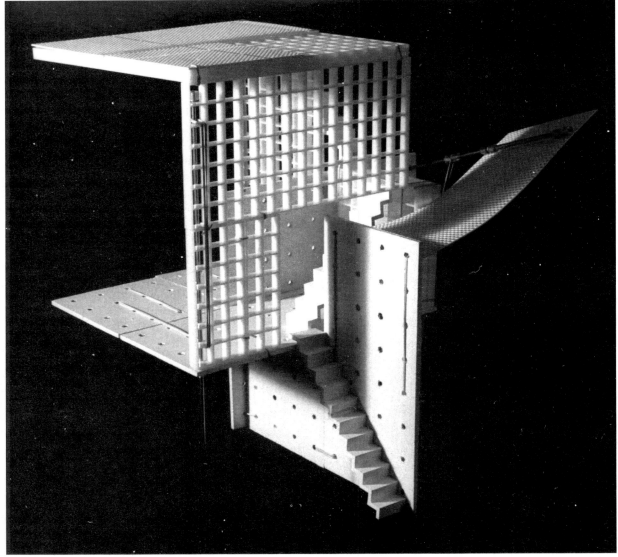

BIL REYMAN

van GOGH, Vincent.
The Starry Night, (1889)
Oil on canvas, 29 x 36 1/4"(73.7 x 92. 1cm).
The Museum of Modern Art, New York. Acquired through the
Lillie P. Bliss Bequest.
Photograph (c) 1998 The Museum of Modern Art, New York.

HARMONY: *GROOVING*

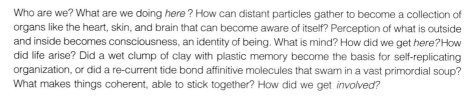

BEING

"Life is just a bowl of cherries" Rudy Vallee

Gathering

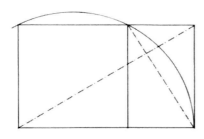

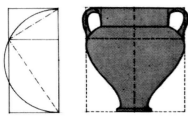

CRETAN KRATER

Who are we? What are we doing *here*? How can distant particles gather to become a collection of organs like the heart, skin, and brain that can become aware of itself? Perception of what is outside and inside becomes consciousness, an identity of being. What is mind? How did we get *here*? How did life arise? Did a wet clump of clay with plastic memory become the basis for self-replicating organization, or did a re-current tide bond affinitive molecules that swam in a vast primordial soup? What makes things coherent, able to stick together? How did we get *involved*?

At both smallest and largest scales of the universe lie enormous spaces between things. The distance between atoms is as vast in proportion to their nuclei as the distance between stars is to their diameter. What keeps all the stars in the Milky Way swimming in the same swarm? What makes wood, diamond, or human flesh and bone seem solid when it is mostly empty space? On the earth and the moon there are craters that are formed from the impacts of meteors and other celestial visitors. The ancient Greek *Krater* was a kind of bowl used especially to mix wine with water. Its linguistic root was *kerannunai*, which meant *to mix*.. We still hear the prefix *ker*- in words connoting impact or the sound of a heavy blow, fall, or collision as in *kerflop* or *kerwallop*, and even in *crush, crash, crumple*. A drop of milk makes a splash when it falls in a pool. When the corona of small droplets subside, the pool becomes smooth as each drop of liquid falls as close to Earth's center as possible. What pulls things inward and keeps them together?

Why are some shells long and thin, others short and fat? Do their growth angles vary according to local ocean currents? Darwin and others argue that we evolve according to natural selection, the survival of the fittest. Taoists suggest a strategy for wise living: be like water (that most plastic medium), filling every depression before flowing on, without thought of one's own form. Who forms a bowl or shapes the container? A species may evolve, but doesn't each individual seek to respond to immediate conditions of the local environment, that is, to get involved? Prairie chickens battle to the death in mating competition, the winner gaining the right to the center of the territory and a harem of mates. Why is it that even in this day of faxes and satellite communications central city real estate is still the most valuable? Why do we so often seek the center? That which turns inward "involves". What is it in the nature of forces and space that makes things collect? If, since the Big Bang, all the universe has been flying apart, why then doesn't the earth shatter into infinitesimal fragments. What holds cherries together when there is no bowl? How do bowls form? Spacetime grips matter, telling it how to move; matter grips spacetime, telling it how to curve (as modern scientists and Adam and Eve suggest). Now COBE, the Cosmic Background Explorer, shows us ripples of matter density in the cosmos. Harold Edgerton's strobe photo shows a drop crashing and splashing into a pool of milk. This is everyone's home-grown lactic galaxy.

There can be two kinds of volumes, one spun and another grooved; two kinds of spaces, one sparse, airy, expanded, the other dense, condensing, contracting. Spinning is how far out you can get. Grooving is how dense you can make the center. This is but one of many sets of how spaces differ in *dynamic* qualities. The most interesting harmonies are those that successfully resolves differences. This section, Grooving, is offered as an "antidote" to Spinning, as another way of looking at the relation of mass to void in making space. Spinning inward, "by devious means we reach the center."

The terrestrial island of Manhattan and the lunar Crater Aristarchus, shown at the same scale. 100 million people could live in spacious apartments with magnificent views along the 12,000 foot interior walls of the crater.

Below: Computer animation showing formation of moon as splash from meteor impact with earth.

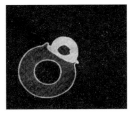

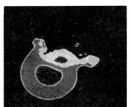

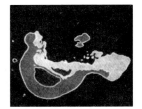

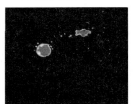

IN THE GROOVE

Billiard balls crash into each other and rebound. Heavenly bodies also sustain elastic collisions. A computer animation illustrates a convincing scenario showing the moon forming from the rebounding debris of a collision between earth and another planetesimal. A similar distribution of lighter elements in both the moon and upper layers of the earth supports this theory. Oxides of silicon, aluminum, magnesium, and titanium are abundant on the moon. Perhaps our Moon was providentially placed, to be a helpful stepladder for us out of our gravity well to the interstellar heavens, offering us lightweight strong metals (the very ones used for backpacks, bicycles, and aircraft)-- and oxygen as a by-product!

If free floating balls rebound from collisions, what keeps earth and moon in a mutual perpetual dance? What is so *involving* about matter? How do rocks and bubbles stick together? What is in the nature of forces and space that collects things? Why don't the planets abandon our sun or shatter into fragments. What gathers the fruit around the pit of a cherry? What holds cherries together when there is no bowl? Indeed, how do bowls form? As mass curves spacetime it sets the path for moving mass. The "string" between earth and moon is gravity. Earth's mass makes a bowl or groove in spacetime that lures the moon ever earthward. The moon makes a similar dimple in its local spacetime, which is why astronauts *walk* on its surface. A motionless Moon would crash into Earth, but its orbital momentum energy, or *spin*, keeps the two bodies apart. Matter falling into a gravity well increases geometrodynamic distortion in nearby spacetime, potentially gathering even more matter. Eventually the pressure of all mass seeking the center releases energy that may lead to thermonuclear ignition and the formation of a radiant star. If enough matter concentrates in a small enough space, gravity becomes so great that even light will not escape, and a massive, invisible "black hole" will form. The center of the Milky Way, our home galaxy, is probably a huge black hole so massive that it keeps all the remaining stars in the galaxy swimming in the same swarm, isolated by light-years of void, balanced in apparent equilibrium between dispersal and collapse.

Keeping Records

Footprints and craters may last for billions of years on the moon, where winds sleep, whereas craters on earth are obliterated by geological upheavals and erosion that make our planet's rocky crust seem oceanic in a cosmological time scale. The view of the full moon shown opposite includes two of the major craters in its upper left quadrant. Bright Aristarchus, also shown lower left at the same scale as Manhattan, is an average sized lunar crater compared to stellated Copernicus, which is 90 km across, larger than Belgium! Lunar craters and record grooves show how gravity draws mass inward to record information about events. In the now historic technology of vinyl records, a recording stylus is pulled downward to dig into the disk's turning surface to leave a linear but inwardly spiralling grooved track of vibrations, to give the playback needle a similar ride to reproduce the electronic signals that bring music to our ears. A diagram of trips in spacetime also suggests record grooves, as each of us describes a spacetime area as we move along the intervals of daily ritual. The eminent philosopher and historian of science, Dr. Sheldon Reaven reminds us that earthquake movements grind rock into microscopic powder along microgroove striations in the fault faces called *slicken slides*. Recent studies of aging in cells have identified *telomeres*-- a kind of genetic clock and counter-- end-condition chromosomes which are sloughed off individually each time the cells divide. When the last telomere is discarded, the cell dies. This final separation of one mass from another, this last fall into the gravity well beyond our genetic continuity, is the root of our mortality.

Silicon as an atomic spacetime groove. The silicon-oxygen tetrahedron is the basic structural unit of the silicates made of the two most abundant elements in the earth's crust. The tetrahedron is the most stable three-dimensional structure. The black central sphere is silicon, larger surrounding spheres are oxygen.

Vinyl record grooves, enlarged over 10,000 times

HUMAN FOOTPRINT ON THE MOON, ABOUT 12" LONG, 4 DECADES OLD

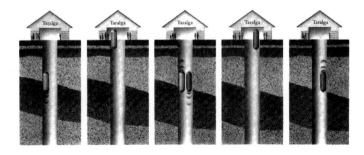

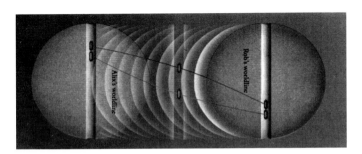

"Two stations are established at the earth-surface ends of a friction free shaft dug through the center of the earth. One station is at Taralga [near Sydney, Australia], the other is at Atlantis, somewhere in the middle of the Atlantic.

The Boomerang Shaft

"Both earthcraft respond to the gravity of the far larger mass of Earth without detectably influencing it or each other. In this sense they serve as *test masses*... At exactly 1 second before 11:18 AM. Rob frees B1 from its mooring and begins zooming past feature after feature of the earth's interior. Alix departs 2 seconds later and pass the same landmarks, always 2 seconds after Rob does... One second before noon Rob is at rest for a fleeting instant at the level of the Taralga passenger platform. Without a jolt he could then and there lock his craft to the wall of the shaft if he so chooses. He doesn't. He wants to keep on longer in free-float travel. At this instant Alix is 20 meters below the platform and still rising fast... She finds her rise to be half as fast at noon itself. Alix is in the final showdown of her own approach to Taralga. At this point, only 5 meters below the platform, rising Alix meets descending Rob. He has already covered the first 5 meters of his return to trip to Atlantis... One second past noon Alix is at the summit of her flight. Rob is descending at twice the speed he had a second ago. He is already 20 meters down... Two seconds past noon Alix herself is 5 meters down, well started on her return trip to Atlantis... A minuet is in progress. The two boomerangs execute its next movement, at 12:42, near Atlantis. There they encounter each other again; Alix is slowing as she rises, Rob gaining speed as he starts downward on a new trip to Taralga... The passage of yet another 42 minutes finds them passing once more, near Taralga... The minuet goes on and on, ever maintaining its 42-minute rhythm, even as the two masses, in free float, zoom through the center of the Earth at the fantastic speed of 7.9 kilometers a second, or 18,000 miles an hour. The 42 minute minuet will continue until they moor at one of the platforms.

Curvature of Spacetime in the Boomerang Shaft

"By the late afternoon, it is clear that the Boomerang Project is a great success. Alix and Rob are fine. The earthships have survived intact. On their next approach to the Atlantis platform, the two boomerangers lock into the moorings and disembark, to the cheers of all, from BI and BII. The amazement of it! We have seen two test masses, both in free float. They were together at high noon, at the point where their paths cross 5 meters below Taralga. As they left the crossing point, they floated apart on the darkness of the shaft. The separation between them every second grew 20 meters greater. Imagine Rob and Alix thus to be parting company in some faraway region of the cosmos where spacetime is essentially flat. Goodbye forever! Within and near the earth, however, spacetime is not flat, nor is it so within the Atlantis-Taralga shaft. Not forever do Alix and Rob continue to increase their separation by an additional 20 meters with each passing second. As the metronome of the minuet prepared to boom out the 42-minute beat, Alix and Rob were both coming up to Atlantis. What is more, Alix was shortening Rob's lead. Each second then, the distance between them was not 20 meters greater, but 20 meters less!

"The Alix-Rob separation increased fast in the first phase of the Taralga-to-Atlantis trip. It decreased fast in the final phase of that journey. Clearly at some place between the two terminals a changeover occurs from slow increase to slow decrease in separation, a place where that separation isn't changing at all-- not changing because it has crested. Crested where? Obviously at the center of the earth. Crested at a separation how great? Sixteen kilometers, according to a bit of figuring that we can skip... roughly only a thousandth of the diameter of the Earth. A peanut distance! Thus we're talking about local physics when we're analyzing the Alix-Rob separation. And Einstein tells us that physics only looks simple when we analyze it in local terms. So no more mention of Atlantis, or Taralga, of the position of Alix and Rob relative to the Earth. Only the distance between the two earthships is relevant.

"The spacetime area responsible for bending the boomerangers' worldlines relative to each other-- from 1 second before their maximum separation-- is bounded by Rob's worldline, Alix' worldline (her tunnel hidden behind Rob's), and the lines connecting their positions in space at the two times. (The diagram is not drawn to scale)."

"The same ball thrown from the same corner of the room in the same direction with the same speed appears to move quite differently when viewed by an observer in the room when it is not in free float (left) and when it is (right), Yet in the two pictures the ball arrives after the same time at the same location in spacetime. Einstein recognized that fall is an illusion. The illusion arises from looking at motion from a reference frame (the room at the left) that is not in free-fall."

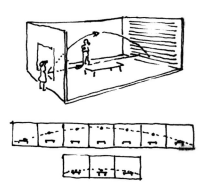

"The tracks of a ball tossed across a room and a bullet shot across the same room appear to have very different curvatures: the bullet seems to follow a much straighter path. When viewed from the side with the naked eye or a movie camera, the tracks of fast and slow balls are very different. That is because we naturally visualize the tracks in three space dimensions and ignore the time dimension. But by plotting the tracks in two space dimensions (up-down and east-west) and one time dimension, we see that in fact the degrees of curvature of the two tracks is identical. The bullet track will fit exactly over the ball track.... Looking head-on as the balls approach, the movie camera records their height at each successive instant in time. To see the curvature of the tracks in spacetime, we cut out each frame and line them up side by side in sequence, placing the fast-ball frames below the slow-ball frames. The tracks of fast and slow balls in two-dimensional up-down, past-future spacetime have the same curvature, as appears in comparison of the identical tracks of the fast ball and the slow ball in the three middle frames. The tracks of the balls curve differently in space but in spacetime the tracks curve the same."

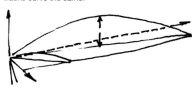

GROOVE THROUGH SPACETIME

The notes on these pages are from John Archibald Wheeler's wonderful book, Gravitation *and Spacetime,* perhaps the clearest, most spacially vivid explanation of the strange world of spacetime and momenergy. Even with Dr. Wheeler's compassionate and imaginative guidance, this subject is not easy to comprehend. The facing page describes a thought experiment about a very deep groove that demonstrates how mass actually bends worldlines in spacetime.

"We must break out of the narrow view of a one-dimensional channel through the Earth. Out of a spacetime of only two dimensions: one of them past-future, the other in-and-out along the [boomerang] shaft. We must somehow sense spacetime in its full four-dimensionality: east-west, north-south, in-out, yesterday-tomorrow. That is the real spacetime around us, through which, minute by minute, all our separate worldlines thrust their way ever further forward. Creating in the mind a single vivid image of four-dimensional spacetime is beyond the picture-making power of anybody I know. But it is it really any easier to capture from one view all the richness of a modern metropolis? That power no single sight possesses. We carry in the memory instead a hundred images. Each registers on the retina from a separate vantage point. In a similar way we can grasp spacetime curvature. And of curvature in a given locale, we need not a hundred but only six views... each of them a two-dimensional slice of the full four-dimensional spacetime...

"A stone, sitting on the ice, makes a painful resistance when we kick it to the far shore. That resistance, that inertia, arises, Newton argued because we accelerate the stone relative to absolute space. No, Ernst Mach reasoned, (c.1900) that resistance, that inertia, arises because we accelerate the stone relative to the masses of the faraway stars and other masses in the universe. Einstein added: "Inertia originates in a kind of interaction between bodies.

A Link between Gravity and Curvature

"Relativity, or the identity of physics in frames of reference in uniform motion, which arose form a question of electrodynamics, proved central to the understanding of electrodynamics. But does frame independence have anything to do with gravity? Let us go from the old space to the new spacetime and compare the tracks of a moving ball and bullet... The curvature of the two tracks, so different when they are depicted in space, turn out to be the same when depicted in spacetime... There it is, a record of motion in up-down, past-future, two-dimensional spacetime! In this two-dimensional spacetime, the tracks of the fast ball and the slow ball can be superimposed: they have the same curvature. Spacetime is the medium responsible for the motion of mass!... This identity of curvature in spacetime was a tantalizing clue. It was clue to a new view of gravity having to do with curvature. Curvature, yes, but curvature of what? Of the tracks? Of the space? Or of the *spacetime*, whatever that means!

The Addition of Time to Space

"Our experiments comparing the paths of balls enable us to visualize the medium of spacetime-- at least a two-dimensional form of spacetime, at least two-dimensional flat spacetime. But how can we grasp the concept of spacetime curvature? Earlier we saw that the curvature of an automobile fender was revealed by the inability to lay down rectangular postage stamps in register on its surface. We can gauge the "imperfection"-- the curvature-- of a two-dimensional space be seeing how perfect pieces, postage stamps or ideal townships, fail to fit. Perhaps the same approach will work with spacetime. In 1908, Einstein recognized that local free-float reference frames are the spacetime equivalent of ideally rectangular postage stamps or ideally square townships; they are, in other words, "perfect pieces of spacetime." ...We are now almost ready to follow Einstein's advance into spacetime curvature. About to start, we suddenly realize that our images of a free-float frame do not yet measure up to what we need. Room cut loose from a cliff-- good. Ball coursing through that room on a course straight in space-- good. But where is *time*, and that unity of time and space that is spacetime? The track of the ball is straight not only in space, but also in spacetime. This straightness signals the flatness of both space and spacetime, at least so far as room-scale evidence goes."

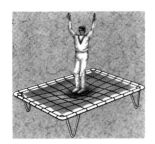

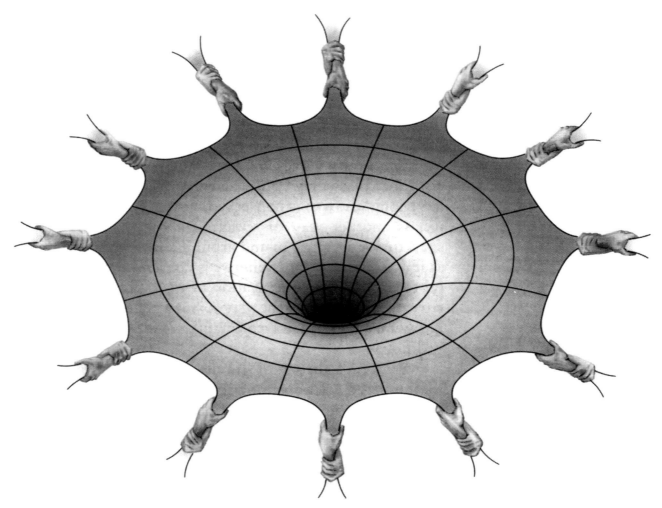

MASS BENDS SPACETIME

Imagine a trampoline. Place a softball in its middle, and then shoot a marble across the surface. The path of the marble will curve as it gets near the softball. Add bowling ball, and both the paths and positions of marble and softball may shift. The elastic fabric of a trampoline surface curves down toward the distortion of a bouncer's foot. Directly under the foot, the fabric forms a bowl. The curvature of four-dimensional spacetime is roughly similar to the two space and one time dimensions of the trampoline model. Inside the boundary of a mass like earth, spacetime is contractile; outside it is non-contractile, or tidal. A drop of milk falls into a pool and creates an impact crater. Splashing droplets explosively scatter from the point of impact. What keeps these new droplets from flying apart forever, themselves becoming new independent drops? Why aren't all masses, from atoms to galaxies, forever bouncing and rebounding away from each other into an evenly dispersed mist throughout space? How is it that the moon falls around the earth rather than zooming past it? Gravity, yes, but what is gravity? Physicist John Archibald Wheeler, the man who coined the term *black hole*, has explained that Einstein's insights radically altered our (Newtonian) understanding of gravity. No longer is gravity just a force. Now we understand it as the interaction of matter and the fabric of space and time. As Dr. Wheeler explains in *Gravitation and Spacetime:*

Matter tells spacetime how to curve

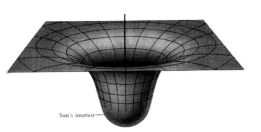

Sun's interior

If spacetime grips matter, telling it how to move, then it is not surprising to discover that matter grips spacetime, telling it how to curve. To understand this corollary notion, let's imagine what free-float spacetime-driven motion would look like if spacetime were not curved. Every object in free float would move in a straight line with uniform velocity for ever and ever. The Earth and the other planets would not enjoy the companionship of the Sun. Each would float away on its own proud, disregarding course. Conceivable though such a universe is, it is not the universe we know. Faced with this difficulty, we could give up the idea that spacetime tells mass how to move. But if we want to retain this idea, despite the observed curvature of planetary orbits and the identical tracks of a ball and a bullet through spacetime, we will say, with Einstein, that spacetime itself is curved. Moreover, this curvature is greater at and within the Earth than it is far away from the Earth. In brief, *mass grips spacetime, telling it how to curve.*

Einstein's Geometric Theory of Gravity

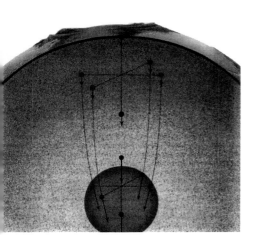

The message of Einstein has two parts: spacetime tells mass how to move, and mass tells spacetime how to curve. If these ideas are correct, all physical phenomena must at bottom be local, and physics only looks simple when it is described locally. But, we protest, the Sun undeniably does hold the Earth in orbit; surely that is not local, that is action at a distance. No, every bit of the physics is local, Einstein will reply. The mass in the Sun curves spacetime where the Sun is. This curvature curves spacetime just outside the Sun. That curvature curves spacetime still farther out, and so on. Thus spacetime even as far out as the Earth partakes of this small curvature. Spacetime there, with that small curvature, acts on the Earth, telling it what to do. That spacetime curvature is so slight that the Earth's track is only slightly curved. That is why it takes so long as 365 days for the Earth to complete one revolution of its orbit.

In brief, distant action arises through local law. Each mass follows its natural state of motion, free float, unless deflected by an electric or elastic force. The elastic force of the Earth on our feet drives us earthbound mortals away from the natural condition of free float. The force acting on our feet is not itself gravitational in character. It originates in solid-state physics and the elasticity of matter. We have only to remove that soil, that elasticity, that solid-state physics to be left in a condition of free float.

1007 The Duke of Normandy, Richard II The Good, who wants to marry the young Judith of Brittany, chooses, in a symbolic gesture, the Mount as the place for the wedding.

1023 Abbot Hilderbert II begins the construction of the Roman Church from the crypt of the *chevet*. This crypt with ambulatory/maze is finished in 1026, when Richard II dies, who is replaced by Robert the Devil or the Magnificent

1031- The Italian disciples of Volpiano, Theodoric and Suppo, are Abbots of the Mount. In order to support the arms of the transept covering the space, lateral crypts [foundations?] are begun (St-Martin to the north, Our Lady of Thirty Candles to the south). The School of Avranches becomes an international University (Lanfranc-St-Anselme). Normans from Guiscard d'Hauteville have conquered middle Italy, Naples, and Sicily.

1048 The priest Raoul of Beaumont erects four master pillars at the cross of the transept, on the peak of the rock. He dies upon his return from Jerusalem.

1060 The priest Ranulphe of Bayeux begins the nave, whose west corner is placed over the pre-Roman church commence (Notre-Dame-sous-Terre, now transformed into a crypt).

1065 William the Conqueror crosses the Couesnon with Harold before his expedition to Brittany. This scene is illustrated in the Bayeux Tapestry, the first stylized representation of Mont Saint-Michel.

1066 Conquest of England. Battle of Hastings. Song of Roland. The abbot sends six ships as reinforcements. Four monks from the Mount become priests of new monasteries of the Outer Channel. St-Michel-de-Cornouailles is given to Mont-Saint-Michel.

1080 Continued construction of the high parts of the Roman nave. Completion of three floors of the eventual structure from north of the nave to the ossuary to the south. The main entry is set at the west. The whole structure completely encloses the old Notre-Dame-sous-Terre.

      Death of William the Conqueror. Quarrels about succession develop between his three sons.

      Henri the First Beauclerc is surrounded and besieged at the Mount by is two brothers.

1100 He succeeds in crowning himself King of England, as well as Duke of Normandy.

1103 The unfinished north side of the Abbot's nave crumbles onto the nearby convent buildings.[?]

1112 Fire provoked by thunder.

1115- Reconstruction of the Ranulphe Buildings by Abbot Roger II (three superimposed stories. Aquilon's Room, walking gallery, and dormitories). Construction is begun on the lower rooms of the future Merveille (Marvel), the priest room and cellar in its first configuration.

1131 Abbot Bernard du Bec, called the Venerable, completes the construction of the nave's north side. He replaces the steeple of the transept. He founds the Priesthood of Tombelaine. After a fire, the first experimental ogive arches are placed in the walking gallery.

1138 A fire is set by the Avranchais during the War of Sucession, provoked by the death of Henry the First Beauclerc. His daughter Mathilde, married to the Count of Anjou, Geoffrey Plantagenet, has had a son, Henry II Plantagenet, future king.

1149- Investiture quarrels between Henry II and the monks of the Mount about naming the new Abbot.

1154 The illustrious Abbot Robert of Torigni, great administrator, historian, builder, and diplomat, erects the two steeples of the high church facade, the library of the "city of books", and west buildings (office, gate-lodge, housing under the great terrace.)

1158 Pilgrimmage to the Mount by the Kings of France, Louis VII and Henry II Plantagenet. One after the other they have both married the same wife, Eleanor of Aquitaine. Through this marriage, Henry II heads a French-speaking empire that extends from the Pyrenees to Scotland.

1161 Torigni is godfather to Henry and Eleanor's daughter, future mother of Blanche of Castile.

1164 Torigni completes the great hostelry-infirmary in the southwest corner. The monastery of Mont-St. Michel is at its peak. William of Saint-Pair. Scriptorium and miniatures workshop are in full activity.

1166 New visit of Henry II to the Mount. Torigni is personal counsellor to the King.

1172 Council of Avranches. Public falling-out of Henry II after assassination of Thomas Becket in Archbishop of Canterbury.

1186 Death of Torigni, succeeded by Furmendi.

1189 Death of Henry II, who is buried at the Benedictine Abbey of Fontevrault. New reign of his sons Richard the Lion-Hearted, followed by John the Homeless.

THINKING

Aspire: Mont St. Michel

If the grip of gravity is so remorseless, how amazing it then is that any work is ever done. How much we must respect the man or woman who does heavy lifting, who breathes upward, who literally *aspires*. The inevitable sentence and judgement of gravity returns all things to their lowest point on or in the earth. How remarkable it is that any stone ever rebounds from a splash. Every stone moved up a hill is the work of a life-time. Every tree records its work in the grooves of its grain, involving energy, evolving mass outward toward the sun. For Einstein, spacetime was "marble" pure and elegant like a temple, whereas the equations describing momentum and energy, were "wood", complex and messy. Now we have learned that fractal geometry and chance can describe tree growth-- and may provide part of the key to uniting Einstein's "wood" and "marble". The pull of gravity means endurance is a grave thing-- survival and achievement requires no waste, an economy of means, to achieve the grace of standing, of stature. Carving is the opposite of assembly. One is subtractive, the other additive. Both are needed for plastic unity. The reshaping of volumes, stone by stone, has taken over one and a half *thousand* years to create the town, school and sacristy of Mont St. Michel! Legend tells that this man-made mountain is a gift from the sea and sky: lightning set fire to the first church erected, and in 709 a tidal wave and earthquake then separated this spit of land from mainland France to create an island. It was clear to Aubert, Bishop of Avranches, and his followers that this was no ordinary site.

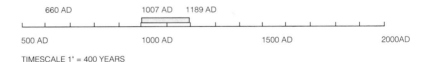

TIMESCALE 1" = 400 YEARS

Mont St. Michel provides room for the full spectrum of humanity, from the gluttony of the crowded busy streets in town to the asceticism of the scholars on high. Whatever is found at the gravity datum-- sea level-- is always a gift. But each stick and stone in a tower (ivory or otherwise) costs work to haul toward heaven. Each piece must be either a necessity, a personally needed "luxury" to make work worthy of any Holy mission (for example Raphael should have canvas and paintbrushes, just as Shakespeare should have a theater and actors), or an indulgence and therefore a dangerous temptation. Work may be physical or mental, communal grain harvest or lonely pursuit of truth. But both must be tested within the demanding context of the collective-- such is the courageous voyage of every human worldline in spacetime, from innkeeper to carpenter, from bell-maker to scribe. Removing a room, carving a cliff, adding a cloister or cantilevered terrace, these are the plastic events of the animation of life in spacetime. Each development is a rebound from gravity's groove. The resulting spaces continue to radiate a belief in an ever living human spirit, from animal to divine.

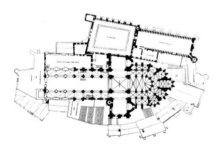

Mont. St. Michel gives us a snapshot in many dimensions; it shows us how to see evolution in volume and in time. What is remarkable is that Mt. St. Michel chronology reads like a yearbook-- '48, '60, '65, '66, '80, '85, '91-- but then we see the notes are for the year 1048, then 1148, on up to now! How long this amazing island utopia dream and actuality has survived! Mt. St. Michel continues to influence the human spirit. Aspiration is expectation and hope, and occurs *now*, the ever-present spacetime event. In the stone refectory La Merveille in Mont St. Michel, where fireplaces are 5 feet tall, 500 year old windows close effortlessly. In that marvellous volume, the large reverberation time makes it possible for one person to sing all four tones of a chord and be in harmony with himself, as well as all those who have sung in this room before. Who cannot hear Gregorian chants and even heavenly choirs in such a setting?

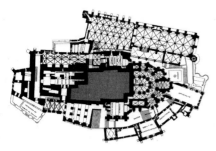

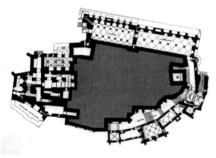

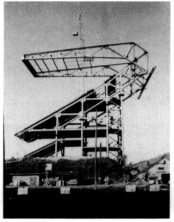

The collapse of the University of Washington Husky Stadium Expansion in Seattle on February 25, 1987 was caused by construction site errors and was not due to the stadium design. The finished stadium today is judged to be completely safe.

No one was killed or injured in the accident, largely because the construction supervisor evacuated about 50 workers from the site an hour before it fell. Despite the setback, the stadium was completed in time for the opening game of the 1987 season.

GRAVITY 1 U.W. 0

These exclusive photos were taken by John Stamets, a photographer who happened to be bicycling past the site when he stopped to snap some pictures. Ten minutes later the structure collapsed. The film was advanced by hand in 12 seconds.   © John Stamets 1987.

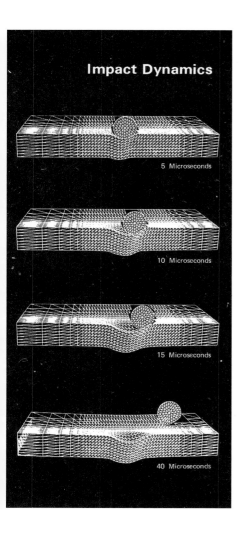

Impact Dynamics

5 Microseconds

10 Microseconds

15 Microseconds

40 Microseconds

HUBRIS

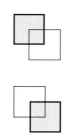

Ozymandias of Egypt -- by Percy Bysshe Shelley

*I met a traveler from an antique land
Who said: Two vast and trunkless legs of stone
Stand in the desert. Near them on the sand
Half sunk, a shatter'd visage lies, whose frown
And wrinkled lip and sneer of cold command
Tell that its sculptor well those passions read
Which yet survive, stamp'd on these lifeless things,
The hand that mocke'd them and the heart that fed;
And on the pedestal these words appear:
'My name is Ozymandias, king of kings:
Look on my works ye Mighty and despair!'
Nothing beside remains. Round the decay
Of that colossal wreck, boundless and bare,
The lone and level sands stretch far away.*

What goes up must come down. How long-lived the monument(al) pyramid! Will today's temporary tower (of Babel) last as long? Archaeology digs down through compacted layers of yesterdays' dust to find the past, while astronomy reaches out to tomorrow's light from ancient stars. We live life in the present, at the boundary, where free body meets gravity mass and joins the surface in foot and footing, the inward pull compresses sand into stone, shells into chalk, and fern into coal. Further heat and pressure cook these stones into metamorphic rock: limestone into marble, coal into diamond. To stand, to attain stature, demands work, courage, and standards. Monuments are means to memory that persist through gravity's crush. The old gain gravity in their words.

A stadium collapses. What goes down comes up. A finite element analysis of impact dynamics presents a wireframe model showing strains linking local deformations geometrically. It also shows that the ball *rebounds*. Society dreams of justice, the reward of the righteous, if even in the future. While we often locate paradise in heaven above as goal for rising and aspiring souls, there is a heaven of truth beneath our feet, awaiting the archaeologist. We may excavate the past to make it present and support our flights of fancy. Physicist Freeman Dyson has noted that since Marconi we are broadcasting humanity to the cosmos at the speed of light. The "Dyson sphere" is now some 100 light-years in radius and ever expanding. Our light-cone, emanating from this here and now defines those events in spacetime which we can influence and which can influence us.

The stop-frame feature on a video camera is like a time microscope. Playing back recorded images one by one, a father may see a year-old-son's expression as he triumphantly crosses the living room in an early lurching walk. The frame-by frame replay reveals an astounding range and intensity of at least a dozen emotional states. While the parental eye registers only an instant blur, the camera catches 24 frames each second, revealing first desire, then fear, then struggle, then surprise... each clearly a feature of personality and character as intense as any in a Shakespearean actor, and all over within a second! How eternal is every instant! How fleeting is every eternity! Which has lasted longer: the Egyptian pyramid inert pile of stone, or the living truth of divinely inspired human light-- for example the Ten Commandments, the Beatitudes, teachings of Buddha and Lao Tze-- the eternally permissible products, those things of true gravity? Yet true architecture can embody both. Recent studies (not the movie!) make a convincing argument that the Great Pyramids at Gizeh not only provided shafts from the Royal Chamber and Queen's Chamber to Orion's Belt and Sirius in the night sky, but also that the whole complex was a careful map of the constellation Orion alongside the earthly version of the Milky Way, the Nile River. Thus did cosmology and architecture coincide in thoughtful order 6000 years ago; thus after millennia does idea recover meaning in form.

The contours of the architecture have been eroded by the elements, the site turned to pasture and farmland... The largest theatre-- probably set into a meteoric crater-- accommodated as many as 60,000 people... Nothing is known about the kind of spectacle performed.

Bernard Rudofsky
Architecture Without Architects

CRATER   DOME/VAULT   TRULLI

DIGGING IN

So are all aspirations doomed? Is there no way to endure gravity's severe decree? One path-- humility-- turning inward, quietly offers itself, and provides a bonus, the blessings of community. Gravity can make space. Gathering mass into clumps leaves places where void predominates. An architecture of subtraction is an obvious and ancient mode. From the caves at Altamira to the first archeological pit houses, the powerful feeling of being *inside* a mass has long protected the human body while supporting the human psyche. Time slows in the trenches. Excavating deepens and anchor flights of fancy. Carving reveals the positive value of negative space. When we move below gravity's boundary at the earth's surface, we dig in.

All over the world, humanity has exploited sites to foster collective identity. The Inca nation dug seats into the natural bowl formed by a meteor crater, and then expanded on the theme. The Greek amphitheater at Delphi, a man-made *krater* human container, provides spatial enclosure even without a roof. The bowl seems to confine the open air itself. This stadium still stands. *Stadios* is Greek for stable or established, from the older *spadion* from *span*, to stretch. Both word and form carry tension and compression. This is clearer in the Roman Colosseum, where interlocking radiating vaults buttress the outward thrust of the seats, keeping the whole structure tight as a drum. The Colosseum was a portable amphitheater, an arena "franchise" exported to towns throughout the then known world of the Roman Empire. Our cities today still aspire to sports franchises replete with stadium as proof of "arriving" in the world community. Pier Luigi Nervi's 1928 stadium in Florence adds a dramatically cantilevered roof, but otherwise retains the ancient basic form. Perhaps we all seek the glory of center stage, what Hannah Arendt calls "the space of political appearance" in her thoughtful study *The Human Condition*. What compression there is when all consciousness is focussed on one point during a drama, speech or sports event! An arena recalls the protective shelter of the womb even as it thrusts humanity into the sky. Entry to the Colosseum suggests the parable of Plato's cave-- we move out of shadowed vaults to seats in full daylight to see action directly, casting off secondhand reports of reality. Like our simian arboreal ancestors, we are perched at the forest roof of the city. Beyond the circle of our concentration there is only the celestial soffit, the realm of angels.

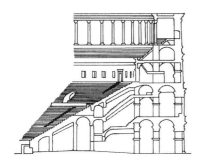

Gathering can launch spirit. Medieval Arles transformed its colosseum into a village. Paolo Soleri's basic *parti* for his arcologies is a city with a hollow heart, a vertical Central Park around which people live on the thin edge between in and out. (See page 365.) Wright's Guggenheim Museum is centripetal as well as centrifugal. Earth's current five billion people would fit into a box a little more than half a mile in each direction. If this box were pushed off the edge of the Grand Canyon, a century later all that would indicate where humanity lay buried would be a little mound densely covered with plants. Solid mass without void eliminates breathing room, both literally and figuratively. We need potential at the center of our body politic for culture to flourish. The New England village green gives birth to democracy precisely because everyone, or rather no one, owns the center. Even the heart is hollow. Cupped hands gather water in a bowl. For a dam the problem is how to hold water *in* (and up), to resist the tendency for the mass of the water to seek the center of Earth's mass. The geometry of the inert mass of the wall holds back the larger inert mass of the water. While gravity tends to pull both to sea level and below, the huge retaining wall of a hydroelectric dam resists sideways motion because it is moving downward so hard that friction (rough surface molecular interaction) keeps it there. *Inertia* is the property of mass to tend to keep still or moving the way it has been. Gravity translates the potential energy of the stored water into the kinetic energy of electric turbines. As John Wheeler says, " Matter gets its moving orders from space, right where it is."

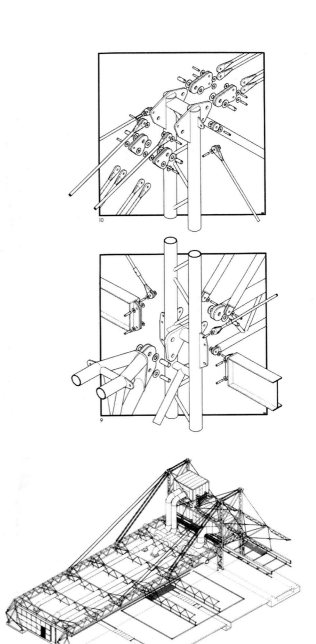

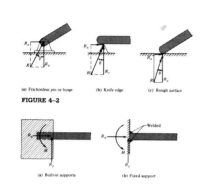

(a) Frictionless pin or hinge   (b) Knife edge   (c) Rough surface

FIGURE 4-2

(a) Built-in supports   (b) Fixed support

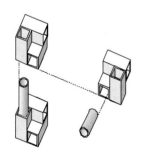

PIN.   MOMENT.

ANIMATING

Joining Free Bodies

The relative immovability of the earth lying inert beneath our feet is its great advantage for builders. It is the *foundation*, the locally "motionless" free body that allows us to anchor other free bodies in a relatively stable configuration. (Earthquakes remind us how relative that stability is!) Footings are the big side of the connector of buildings and a variety of fixed and movable support types give advantage to various loading conditions. But what of other connections throughout a structure? Combining free bodies into a unified structural element requires making a joint. Elbows, knees, knuckles, and hip sockets are wonderful and complex joints in the human body, with geometries capable of taking a variety of dynamic loads in a variety of positions. You may have already noticed that elements of the Bag of Tricks tend to stick together in certain ways better than others. A load applied eccentrically tends to generate a moment of rotation about the points of support, as we have seen. This happens within a structural member as well as along it, and effects how the member will strain, trying to move under load. The geometry of the joints also affect this. There are two main kinds of connectors. When thumb and forefinger loops of both hands link, they form a **pin connection**, when one hand grasps the wrist of the other, a **moment connection** is made. The first allows great movement of one structural member in relation to another without establishing any resistance to that movement-- the pin connector is essentially a hinge. The other resists the tendency of the members to move, and sets up within it stresses connected with bending called moment stresses-- hence it is called a moment connector. You can make **XYZ** Joint moment connectors for your Bag of Tricks that fit nicely into eggcrate voids.

What of other joints, like those almost magical connections between toy Lego™ blocks? Solids hold together at the mesoscale of human activity ultimately by using friction as a kind of glue. Friction is the physical interlock of rough surfaces, resisting motion as the bumps fit in ridges and grooves like cogs in wheels and gears. The Mero™ connectors opposite show what look like many small Delphi theaters that gather the radiating struts into the grooved receptacles of the ball joint connectors. Screw threads increase surface area for friction. The mechanical nature of chemical glue and the chemical nature of mechanical joints are related at the atomic level. Kenneth Snelson's patented atom models suggests motion in all connections from electrons to galaxies.

Joints by Addition: Good Connections

Moment also occurs within structural members. Hold a sponge at its ends and put a stone on its middle and you will see that the top of the sponge will seem to crush while the bottom seems to stretch. In between, there is a line along which the sponge seems to remain unchanged. This is the **neutral axis**. No tensile or compressive stresses occur here. Pulling the mass of a structural member as far as possible from the neutral axis increases its strength, its effective resistance to these internal stresses. Good design of the cross-section of structural elements: means getting the most for least by careful placement of mass in the cross section as well as the span.

Joining structural elements in buildings requires finding not only the best geometry for connecting loads, but also finding a possible geometry for a *sequence* of connection (tab A in slot B, etc.) Details of connection nodes in the Richard Rogers Partnership's Inmos Factory show how beams, struts and fasteners are assembled to take loads and resist unwanted movement. The whole factory is also an assembly of volumes joined in sequence. Not only the extended systems of space frame roof, catwalks, plumbing, and HVAC ducts; but also an assembly of program volumes: the work shed, control tower, lift hoist, etc. For architects there may be an essential unity in the two scales of thinking.

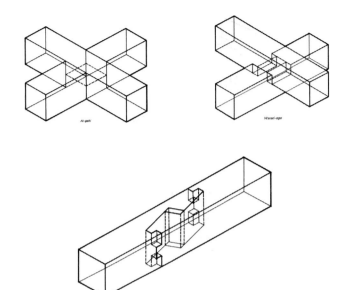

Ai-gaki

Wasari-ago

Kanawa-tsugi

JOINTS BY SUBTRACTION

The rarity of bulk...

When we contemplate the universe, we are struck by how empty of matter it is! Stuff is scarce, while emptiness is plentiful. Within the sphere described by the planets in our solar system (Neptune or Pluto's orbit) there is very little mass and a lot of void. But here on the surface of the earth, there is plenty of matter beneath our feet. Round dense stones are "filled with inertia", compared to long light sticks of lower inertial mass, and in this sense the earth is a very big stone. However, when each piece of stuff is a discrete self-contained tensegrity, as it is in a carefully designed structural assemblage of joints by addition, rather than the continuous lumpy mass of stone or clay, bulk becomes a rare commodity. Tensegrity geometry must then work to resolve all forces into internal equilibrium. Growth and stasis depend on whether outward forces are more or less than inward forces.

The ancient art of carpentry is based on making joints, and in fact, the Greek origin of harmony is *harmos*, from *arthron*, meaning "joint" (as in arm, and arthritis). Nail into wood is crude but effective-- it works by intruding steel (the nail) into the space of the wood, which crushes the fibers of the wood, pushes them out of the way, and then relies on friction between wood and steel to hold the nail in place as the wood fibers try to get back to their original shape through the springiness of their own structure's desire to return to its original form. Hammer and nail make a joint that is effective but crude. Consider this interesting linguistic paradox: the word *cleave* means one thing as well its opposite. From Eric Partridge's wonderful study of etymology, *Origins* we find that **cleave** means both (1) to forcibly part (e.g. by splitting), divide, or pierce; and (2) to adhere. Related words in the first sense include *cleaved, cleft, cloven*; Middle English *cleven* is akin to Greek *gluphein*, to carve, as in butcher's cleaver; in the second sense related words include *cleaved, clave, clove* and *cliff*; Middle English *clevien* relates to Latin *glus*, and Greek *glia*, glue, as well as our word clay.

Carving is negative assembly

Adding pieces by forcing them together, as with a nail into wood, is one way to join elements. Another option is to add pieces by taking mass away! How much more elegant than the joist hanger or toenail are the carved mortise and tenon intersections so carefully planned and planed in cabinetry. The wood joints of traditional Japanese carpentry, like intricate wooden puzzles, raise this elegance to both intellectual and aesthetic refinement. Translation and shear are the moves used to develop lap joints and more complex intersections that allow structural members to pull at each other cleanly rather than push through each other with crushing deformation.

Japanese carpentry joints provide an important lesson for the architect. The art of combining volumes requires balance in many ways. The junction of the volumes should be neither too tight nor too loose. Rather it should act as an integrated structure with many parts acting as one, and also *reading* as one. An intersection of two volumes to make a third one that belongs to both and yet remains distinct in space is central to the Harmony studies. While this is easy to achieve in the realm of intersecting volumes, to make masses intersect is difficult. The lessons of Japanese joinery show that with care and ingenuity, such a trick of being in two or even three places at once may appear to be possible. The *art* of combining volumes suggest an important intellectual resource in many realms of thought. Hegel's notion of synthesis calls for the resolution of oppositions like In and Out, I and Thou, Involve and Evolve, Here and There. Thus shall "the lion lie down with the lamb". Common speech calls mass inside void "outer" space. But architects know that any continuum of nesting void inside mass inside void inside mass etc… is essential to the "inner and outer" space of architecture.

THE EVOLUTION OF THE PLAN OF ST. PETERS

ROBERTO PETRUCELLI

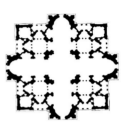

PLAN BY BRAMANTE, 1506

PLAN BY BRAMANTE-PERUZZI 1513

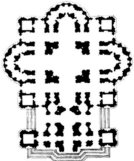

PLAN BY SANGALLO THE YOUNGER, 1539

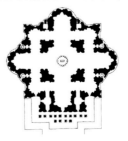

PLAN BY MICHELANGELO, 1546-64

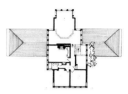

Wright's Isobel Roberts House
an intersection/union *parti*

VOLUMETRIC ALGEBRA

Boolean Operations

ADDITION

Algebra means "the reduction and the comparison by equations". It comes from the Arabic root *jbr* meaning "to *bind together.*" Dynamics suggests the possibility of an algebra of volumes that permit at least the operations of ADDITION, SUBTRACTION, INTERSECTION, and UNION. Addition is the simple combination of two nearby volumes. Subtraction is the result of one volume removed form another. Intersection is the only part of two overlapping volumes that is shared by both. Union is the overall volume formed by two overlapping volumes. These four operations form a special group in logic and mathematics, described by George Boole (1815-1864) in his study of the mathematics of sets, so today they are called *Boolean operations*. Computer aided drafting (CAD) programs now include Boolean operations as valuable modeling tools.

SUBTRACTION

Using the Kit of Parts involved the addition of solids-- the piling up of discrete architectonic masses to define voids between them. But other ways exist for making space; for example sculptors carve volume from solid stone. Manipulating pure "wireframe" volume permits even more compositional strategies. Prof. William Mitchell has shown how a volumetric algebra can guide architectural thinking. For example, one intersection of cube and sphere generates the squinch, an essential device in Byzantine architecture for transition from a cubical space to a spherical dome. Subtracting a small half-cylinder from a larger one produces a vault. The union of four such vaults and squinch creates a crossing of nave and transept. The Pantheon is an intersection of a sphere and a cylinder.

Complex Interactions

INTERSECTION

Alone or combined in complex sets, the Boolean operations begin to describe a means for explicit definition of what happens in the medium that is unique for architecture, space itself. That is why when a client only cares about how many bedrooms there are in a house, an architect will care what order of space the relationships between them can create. This method of thinking is perhaps the most powerful design tool available to architects. To design by moving volumes with, through, and from each other in the mind's eye is to make a *dynamic* of volumetric composition. While Michelangelo's Ricetto may be the addition of two volumes, Wright's Isobel Roberts House is the intersection of two volumes. Wright's Prairie house *parti*, as seen in the Isobel Roberts plan, is an intersection of the major living room volume with the secondary service volume of kitchen, dining, etc. A fireplace often acts as pivot where these volumes cross and reveals itself as the chimney in the exterior massing. In the Isobel Roberts House, the mezzanine and master bedroom suite further articulates this spacial drama. (See also Wright's plans of the D.D. Martin House, and Unity Temple, page 82, in *Architectonics.*)

UNION

More complex polynomial expressions of volume are also possible. The equation $a^2 + by^3 - cz^4 = 0$ is a polynomial expression. Combinations of Boolean operations when applied to three-dimensional volumetric relationships may characterize those very complex, multistage evolving *parti* manipulations and operations that generate most architectural spaces we know. Expressions like **A** UNION (**B** SUBTRACT **C** INTERSECTION **D**) may suggest volumetric order. The evolution of the plan of St. Peters Cathedral, in Rome, reveals to us an ongoing experiment in volumetric algebra. How many operations do the most accomplished works of architecture embody? Does simplicity guarantee intensity of feeling? Will complexity always offer subtlety?

the heart is the joint
of the head and hand

Polygon B overlaps A

Shape A   Shape B

Union   Intersection

A-B   B-A

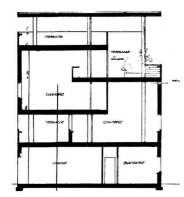

Le Corbusier's proposed villa at Carthage in 1928.

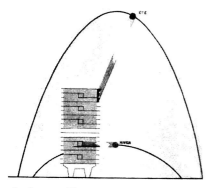

Sun Space and Green
at Le Corbusier's *Unité d'Habitation*, Marseilles, 1952

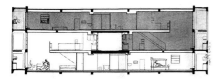

Le Corbusier proposed an ingenious interlocking section for a villa at Carthage in 1928. He used this
discovery to wrap two units around an access corridor
located only every third floor at his *Unité d'Habitation*,
Marseilles, 1952. A masterful example of resolving
spacial stresses: bulk of the building is minimized and
the number of units per facade is maximized by making
each double height unit only 15 feet wide and 60 feet
deep. (See also page 78.)

HARMONY INTERSECT UNION

*The set of all subshapes of the complete bitmap grid, and the operations of shape
union, intersection, and subtraction form a Boolean algebra."*
William Mitchell, The Logic of Architecture

Pythagoras at Chartres

At the base of one side of three arched rings of figure sculptures framing the smallest of the
three entry portals on the West facade of the great cathedral at Chartres, close by where the
most casual and unimportant visitors may pass, modest but essential, compact but intense,
sits the figure of Pythagoras, carved in stone by an anonymous 13th century mason. When we
stop to think of it, this remarkable work is quite self-referential: the stubby monkish hands of
Pythagoras hold a knife for cutting grooves in sand, or on clay tablets-- or is it stone? The
sculptor, carver of this figure-stone, must have thought that sculpture is geometry with a knife!
We know he was not far from truth. The Greek geometers like Euclid, Archimedes, and
Pythagoras are thought to have conducted their investigations of the mathematics of form by
making markings in the sand. Are modern photography, photolithography, or photoengraving,
which all cut figures into plates with light, so far from this earlier art of making grooves? The
photo of Pythagoras opposite is a lesson in how proportion and balance can resolve the union
of divergent forms. A quick diagrammatic analysis shows the same figure of overlapping
squares that describe the condition of the Harmony exercise. Our eye is drawn to the center of
the nine-square field, between Pythagoras' eye and hand. But there is more: we see that the
hand is the center of its own set of four squares, and so is the ear the center of its own set of four
squares. Two important realms in a mason's life-- one is the inward portal for listening to the distant
world and more immediate steady ring of hammer and chisel on stone, the other is the outward
stretch of fabricating fingers, the extremities-- these two meet in the charged (hardly neutral) zone
between them to sustain the timeless poise of this creation. And of course, behind the robes in this
center space, lies the sculptor's heart-- the union of head and hand in intelligence and compassion.

Harmony is a resolution of spinning and grooving, of volume in both tension and compression.
Density and sparsity can create moments (theatrical *and* structural) of high drama. The section
through Le Corbusier's project for a villa in Carthage is an elegant demonstration of how two
volumes can intersect and form a union without losing their individual identities. When this device is
executed well, there can arise a three-dimensional transparency in the composition. The miracle of
good design means making room for *everyone* to fit in. An old architectural triumvirate is restated
here as the union of program (firmness), fitness of use (commodity) and the rhythmic play of contrasting
volumes (delight). Enthusiasm means "to receive G-d". With Open Hand we receive and we share.

For two political-philosophical groups, the idea of Spinning suggests periphery and independent identities, whereas Grooving suggests inward convergence of shared and mutual concerns. The potential for the intersection of two volumes to make a third central space that
belongs to both and yet remains distinct in space in this Harmony project demonstrates a
remarkable thing about the an architecture of Dynamics--it is relatively easy to make such a
configuration with the elements of the Bag of Tricks and the insights of composing architecture
from volume-- but this could only have been achieved with great difficulty, or not at all, with the
Architectonics Kit of Parts. Such an intersection indeed could be implied in Architectonics, but
intersection is the stuff of a new understanding of creation in space. Consider standing in the
8-foot volume where the two 16-foot volumes overlap-- if the architecture achieves its aims, you
will actually be in not only two but three places at once, without even moving a step!

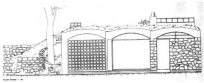

"By devious means we reach the center."
Le Corbusier

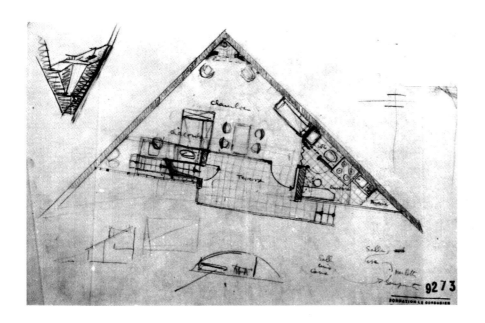

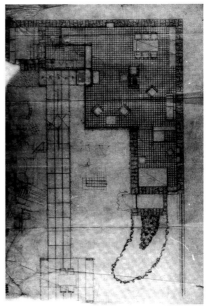

FROM ROUGH TO SMOOTH

You have made a preliminary design, a Pro-position for the Harmony study. It remains for you to re-solve the plastic and architectonic implications of the spacial order you have established. The repeated rearrangement of program volumes and the elaboration of mass/void to articulate desired plastic relationships are the part of an architect's practice called **Design Development**. You are ready to consciously undertake Design Development, which demands both attention to detail and to the overview, *simultaneously* (what astronauts Joseph Allen experienced as an "overview effect", while high in orbit above the earth.) Understanding and mastering this process forms an important stage in the maturation of the student architect. In *Spinning*, you established the primary positions for spaces to accommodate the separate identity of two philosophical groups, their individual volumes, entries, and roof access. Now you must also consider their shared volumes and circulation patterns through the location of structure, walls, stairs and landings. You must find how the spaces join. Now you must re-solve your pro-position.

Pro-position and Re-solution

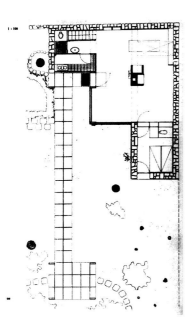

Through Re-solution the designer explores the many interrelationships that arise in *poesis* (the making of things)-- between tension and compression in both space and structure, between logic and plasticity, between movement and emotion, between silence and light. Earlier we suggested that while pro-position implies "something from nothing", re-solution implies "something from something". Mies Van Der Rohe's famous dictum "Form follows function" is only a beginning of the design process-- a Pro-position. To arrive at a complete answer to all needs, plastic, poetic, and programmatic we must pursue Paul Amatuzzo's guide that "form follows form" to encourage reconsideration of ideas and configurations toward a resolution of concerns: Re-Solution. Sketch books and sketch models facilitate the desire to see "how it comes out" by permitting attention to detail and overview concurrently, exploring how ideas may come together at extremes of scale, as well as the middle. The possibility of Resolution makes the invention required for Proposition much easier to undertake: the experienced designer knows that no matter what the first attempt may be, it need not be perfect. After all it is only a start. As Le Corbusier said "by devious means we reach the center."

Le Corbusier spoke from experience. We see in the development of his 1935 Weekend House painful, crude, and ungainly beginnings, only later modulated into a harmonious whole. One vault module replaces two unequal spans. The standard measure simplifies construction and brings order, allowing meaningful variation to surprise and delight. The 9-square grid plan responds to the orthogonal bounds of the site while accommodating the corner better and more subtly than the original klunky diagonal first plan (what is stored in a triangular closet?) But the later plan also needed development: a canopy is added at entry, the bedroom exhedra is eliminated, improving circulation. The outrigger pavilion, reached along the path stretched from 12 to 16 pairs of 3:4 proportioned pavers, not only establishes entry (or rather extension into the landscape, if entry is by car) and even the space between it and the main house, but also helps define the "missing piece of the implied 9-square gestalt" taken from the remaining sawtooth configuration, permitting a variety of Boolean readings-- intersection, union, subtraction and addition-- from inside to outside. See photo on page 481 for the beautiful result. After all, this became the prototype for a house Le Corbusier designed for the mathematician Prof. Fueter (instrumental in the creation of Pavillon Suisse in 1930-32) in Switzerland in 1950. What he wrote about this later scheme reveals much about the Weekend House: "It was a most modest program. Such problems constitute a veritable algebra, a game of chess." Here the architectural solution had such clarity that the humble house in which the old savant had hoped to spend his old age, became dignified. The harmony of mathematics was brought to it by the Modulor."

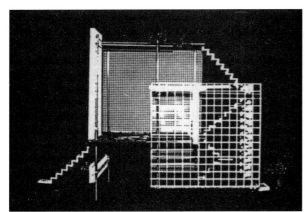

JERRY MAGGIO

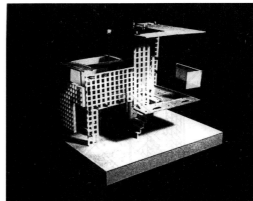

JOHN CUNHA

ENRIQUE PINCAY

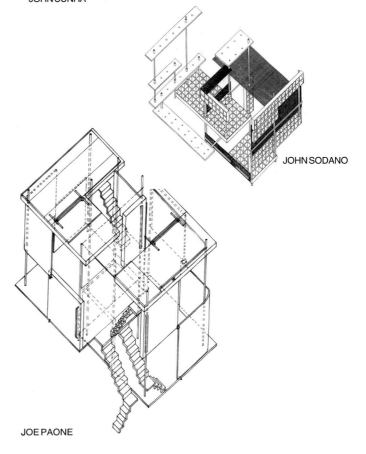

JOHN SODANO

JOE PAONE

DOING: *Re-solution*

PEACETIME. Two philosophical-political factions seek to establish a place where they might meet and mutually settle their differences. The site available is a 24' cube, allowing each of them to make a 16' cube hall for private meetings and an 8' cube for mutually shared negotiations at the intersection of the two larger halls. Any remaining spaces within the site may be used for informal walks and talks. They desire that the structural and spacial qualities of your architecture should if possible express *both* the differences between the two groups *and* their unified resolution. (Compare these notes with those on page 179.)

DYNAMICS

Recall that "form follows form", that pro-position implies "something from nothing", while re-solution implies "something from something". You have made a Pro-position for Harmony. Now you must re-solve your proposition. Note that the two groups must each give up some of their primary 16' volume at the 8' cube overlap. Your design task remains to coordinate all materials, circulation, structural, and plastic elements to make both the central 8' cube and the larger 24' cube site truly joints, harmonious intersections within and without the 16' spaces of both groups, favoring neither one over the other. To succeed, your architecture must encourage turning both outward and inward in spacial and human affairs, expressing both the distinctly separate characters of the two groups and their shared union. The shelter you provide to deflect sun and rain need not be fully enclosed volumes, but you must consider how many corners, edges, and/or faces must be articulated to make a cube present to our perception. Entry and roof access for both groups should be equivalent but not necessarily the same. Circulation through the site and program spaces may help express both individual and shared experience. The relativistic notion of *interval* suggests that movement implies both people moving through spacetime, and spacetime moving through people.

Continue to model your solution at 1/2"=1'-0" scale, using the Bag of Tricks. Use as many elements as you wish, although the fewer you need to resolve the architecture, the better. "Less is more". Purely resolved structure of mass and volume, with honestly expressed material properties, can be both eloquent and beautiful. "Economy of means" and Buckminster Fuller's "How much does it weigh?" suggest a weigh-off at project's end, using a simple balance. The lightest one wins.

ANIMATION
Revise your *pro-position* animation series to show inward as well as outward development of the volumes and circulation, and the relationship between order of volumes and order of movement. Document your Re-solution of Harmony with a complete set of architectural drawings. Include plans, sections, elevations, axonometrics and perspectives as needed, in ink, at full or half scale of model. Use shading, shadows, and collage where appropriate.

COLOR
4. **Transparency**   See page 463.
5. ***Collage 2b***. Free exercise   See page 463.

FUNCTION
Plot and/or construct the cycloid. This curve is also known as the brachistochrone, or curve of least time for a falling bead, and is also a tautochrone, or curve of equal time. See page 453.

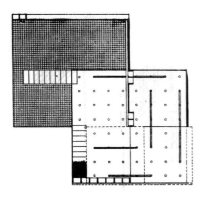

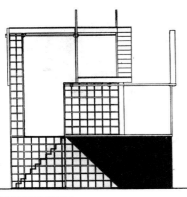

GEOFF FUNSTON

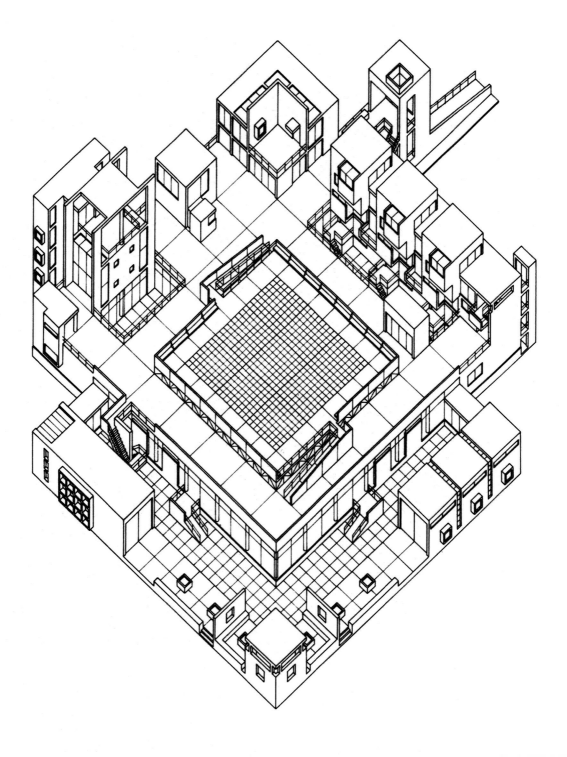

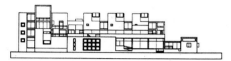

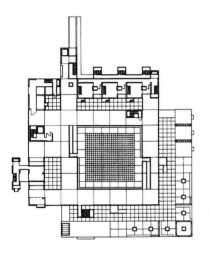

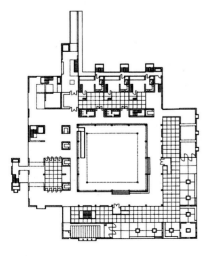

Paul Amatuzzo , Architect
The lessons of a master

Paul Amatuzzo is most eloquent in that most difficult medium, intentional human scale space. He has coined the term *poetic pragmatics/pragmatic poetics* to describe his position vis-a-vis the significance and meaning of architecture. He speaks knowingly about competence in architecture, and is the only architect I know who knows both the building codes and the works of the masters cold. He brings that rarest of combinations, immense intellect, dedicated technical mastery, and unbounded plastic imagination to the practice of architecture. He also is the fastest pen or pencil on the block.

Interrelationships arise in *poesis*, the making of things-- between tension and compression, logic and plasticity, motion and emotion, silence and light. This example shows how to develop the richest architectural possibilities, and the richest architecture, from even (especially!) the simplest *parti!* The following are all the words Paul Amatuzzo needs to set the conditions for and resolution of a work of architecture. They are respectfully reproduced and set in Helvetica Light.

PROJECT NOTES FOR FRIENDS - IN LIEU OF HELVETICA MEDIUM

1)   WISHFUL THINKING - A SCHOOL OF ARCHITECTURE
         FOR 45 STUDENTS AND THREE ARCHITECT/TEACHERS

2)   CENTRAL STUDIO, THREE FACULTY APARTMENTS, EXHIBIT HALL,
         LIBRARY, LECTURE ROOM, SHOP, GARDEN, UPPER PIAZZA

3)   HARMONY - PARTS IN CONCERT

4)   DEFINING THE HEART - THE STUDIO - GLOWING WITH TOP LIGHT.

5)   PERIMETERS, CENTERS, SHARED PERIMETERS, . . .

6)   THE WHOLE IN REPOSE

7)   20' X 20' X 20'

8)   THE RIGHT ANGLE, THE GRID, THE RIGHT ANGLE, THE GRID, . . .

9)   NINE SQUARE, FOUR SQUARE, TRANSPARENT SQUARES, . . .

10)   PLAN AND/OR SECTION AS GENERATOR

11)   CENTRAL SECTIONAL STEEL INSERT - MAKING STUDIO
         AND PINNING TOGETHER UPPER AND LOWER GROUNDS

12)   CONSTRUCTED AND CONSTRUCTABLE

13)   . . . .

REGARDS (1990-1991)

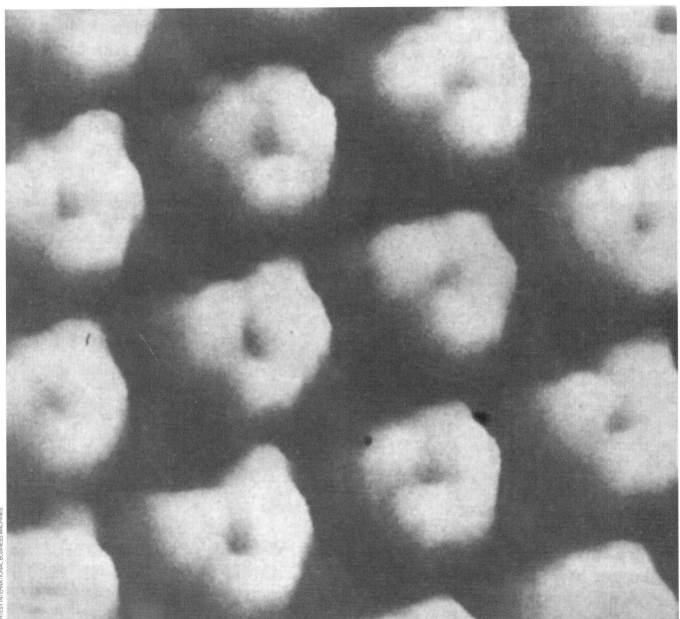

REFLECTING

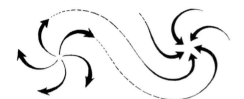

Kekulé, a 19th century architecture student, dreamt of Ourobouros, a mythical serpent who devoured its own tail. Upon waking, he realized the ring form of his dream was the solution to benzene, the first aromatic hydrocarbon to be synthesized, the foundation of industrial chemistry. Carbon is essential to life in part because of the variety of geometric ways it can combine with itself and other materials. Many atoms together may form long chain molecules called olymers. DNA is a complex polymer. The simplest one-celled organisms are great collections of molecules millions of times larger than atoms but still microscopic. The material properties of a cell's membrane wall enables creatures to carry out the necessary biological functions of ingesting, digesting, respiration, locomotion, reproduction, metabolism, etc. Unlike inorganic steel or salt, living organisms have the capacity to change the properties of their constituent materials. Thus we flex our arms to stiffen the fibers and "make a muscle" and our lungs stiffen or sag as we breathe. Benzene has a hollow center. Now buckminsterfullerene "bucky balls" can form a carbon cage around even an atom of uranium.

A black hole is a body so massive and dense that not even light escapes its gravitational pull. There is great likelihood that a black-hole region of spacetime lies at the very core of our Milky Way galaxy. This region is extremely compact, only a tiny fraction of a light-year across, compared to the hundred thousand light-years diameter of our galaxy-- a concentration equal to squeezing 200,000 people into a five foot elevator, instead of spreading them evenly across a continent! Such is the capacity for concentration of mass on a scale we can only begin to comprehend. How rare and valuable, then, is the presence of an empty center! A black hole at the center of the Milky Way may resolve a fairly old puzzle in astrophysics. When we look at the photographs of these galactic swirls, it is not easy to decide whether they are spinning inward or outward. But as suns fall into a black hole and disappear from visibility, their increased mass further increases spacetime curvature, attracting more mass, etc. Why then doesn't the whole swarm of stars condense into one enormous invisible space-bending blob? Because the galaxy is spinning! Cyclones and anticyclones make weather, cooler systems spin inward while warm air systems spin outward. There appears to be a delicate balance between the inward pulling force of mass and the outward pushing force of rotation. No wonder the view of a spiral nebula tantalizes us with multiple readings of inward- and outward-ness.

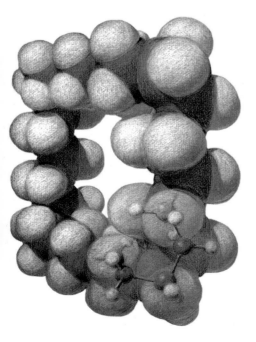

In lightweight structures, mass is a rarity, so stability must be invented configuration as in Gothic flying buttresses, *and Il Duomo's* tension ring. Of course, there is a distinct economic advantage to enclosing much space with little material, but there are times when the very massiveness of a structure has architectural significance. Both Sverre Fehn in the excerpt from "the thought of construction" and Anthony Ames in his *Foreword* to a published collection of his own work entertain the possibility of simultaneous balance between two realms, between fire and brick (light and mass) or between object-space and poché-space, which may well come to the same thing.

READINGS
Arnheim, Rudolf. "Dynamics of Arches" in *Dynamics of Architectural Form*
Fuller, Buckminster, *Synergetics*
Kundera, Milan. *The Unbearable Lightness of Being*
Maidstone, R. "Intuition and the Springs of Structural Invention" in *Via 7*
Mark, Robert. *The Dymaxion World of Buckminster Fuller*
Thorne, Kip. *Black Holes and Time Warps*
Otto, Frei. *Tensile Structures*
Ozenfant, Amedée. *Foundations of Modern Art*
Pauling, Linus. *The Architecture of Molecules*
Wachsmann, Konrad. *The Turning Point of Building*
Wheeler, John Archibald. *Gravity and Spacetime*

**From *The Thought of Construction*
by Sverre Fehn, Architect**

Fire and water have always been the focus for the places where people gather. These elements are opposed in character and are by their very nature social. Outside the city wall woman once washed their clothes. The river brought clean water and took the foul away. The place was social and work was the essential contributory factor. The center of the village was the well and through its reflection wishes could be realized. The periphery of the well was a place for exchanging the latest news; water providing the essential excuse for conversation. From the well one carried water buckets into the house, the water splashing according to the rhythm of the body. This porterage was a service and an act of generosity. The tub could be place anywhere. One could choose to converse with others or select a place of privacy. In the north, the sauna involved bathing in one's own sweat; a renewal of the body in an amiable atmosphere. The bath was not simply a technique but rather part of a ritual.

The sun's shadow belonged to the tree and both withdrew as the day unfolded, the night taking over with a "room" that had

no limit. Its nature was that of silence. The open fire yielded points of light in the night. This point was once the definition of a place, since the fire was a maker of a "room", the creator of private and intimate realms without interior walls. The "room" beyond the light belonged to the night.

In the past the night bestowed distance on everything. Beyond the range of light everything was reduced to mystery. Here the obscure gave way to fantasy, to a myth which permeated the outside darkness as a tale inhabits the soul. The presence of the old was then honored, for they held the key to a story. The light bestowed youth on their performance for the flickering shadow erased the tell-tale signs of longevity. For the children this was the key to the upbringing.

At that time the essence of night was the sound of stillness and one found peace in the room of darkness. All expression was left to the voice at night, for sound had a larger vocabulary. One's dreams became manifest in breathing and in whispering, and the room of darkness acquired a personal scale.

At that time the light one carried defined the "room" around the body, the body participated in the light and was inseparable from its source. As the fire ebbed, the point of light withdrew until the larger "room" was complete and the figure restored to his dreams.

The enemy of night is artificial light. When men conquered darkness the latent generosity of night ceased to exist. In the totality of light the fairlytale disappeared. The night was deprived of imagination. The "room" had no place outside the range of sight. The old were now force to confront their faces, and shadow no longer added distinction to memory. Within the glare of the bulb, age became dishonored and the child lost his interest.

When the oven was separated from the open grate, the light withdrew from the realm of heat. When the water had no restriction as to its source, the pipe distributed it everywhere. These two elements of contrast, abstracted through the diversity of man's relation to nature, became as it were a unity, the source of a single thought.

The open fire gives beauty to experience.

FOREWORD TO *FIVE HOUSES*
by Anthony Ames Architect

The following projects are not presented as proposals for the method of architecture, but rather as a method for an architecture. Their representation is not offered as polemic, but rather as exploration.

In all of the projects, except the first, the Hulse Pavilion, I have made similar assumptions about architecture and urban design, that when applied in a specific manner, form a technique, or method, for creating architectural form, space, and order. For example, rotation and superimposition serve as planning devices that permit certain conditions to exist in plan, and ultimately in three dimensions. As in Val Warke's competition entry for a museum in Dusseldorf (figure 5), the rotations and superimpositions found within the plan are founded upon two separate orthogonal systems such that the pattern generated by one system is superimposed on, and informed by, the pattern generated by the second system. The resulting plan is charged with a dynamism, or tension, that would not exist otherwise because we are asked to "read" both systems simultaneously. "As in the Cubist painting, when the organizational geometries do not reside in the objects themselves, the possibilities of combining various buildings within a system of order, which attributes to each piece a bit of the organization, become almost infinite." By contrast, Paul Letarouilly's engravings of the Vatican (figure 6) illustrate a different conception of rotation. Instead of systems or overlapping patterns that create a transparency, discrete bodies collide, resulting in non-orthogonal adjacencies. The area of collision between both bodies is poche, a dense, thickened wall that allows the integrity of both spaces to remain intact.

The distinction between 'Modern' and 'Pre-Modern' (or as Michael Dennis has observed, Pre-Industrial or Pre-Enlightenment) space has been described as one of opposing traditions. Pre-Modern space is carved, anthropomorphic, 'objectified', as in the Nolli Plan of Rome (figure 7), and Modern space, as in Le Corbusier's Plan Voison of Paris (figure 8) is continuous, infinite, boundless. The relationship between building and datum in the Modern tradition becomes a relationship between object and field. For example, the Uffizi Gallery (figure 9) by Vasari, as Fred Koetter and Colin Rowe have described, defines the exterior space that is circumscribes, and it merges with the existing fabric of Florence. The unite d'Habitation (figure 10) by Le Corbusier floats above a non-differentiated and uninterrupted plane, serving to reinforce the notion that space is infinite, immeasurable, sempiternal. At a smaller scale, the difference between the Villa Madama (figure 11) by Raphael and Guilio Romano, and the house for the 1931 Berlin Building Exhibition (figure 12) by Mies van der Rohe illustrates the difference between Modern and Pre-Modern space. In the Villa Madama, rooms are contained, defined, and carved, becoming Platonic voids that, but

5, 6

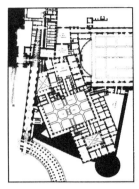

7

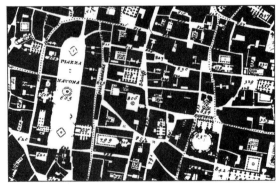

8

Fig. 5. Val Warke. Dusseldorf Competition Entry. Plan. 1975.
Fig. 6. Pontifical Palace. Vatican City, Italy. Detail of Ground Floor Plan. 1882.
Fig. 7. Giovanni Battista Nolli. Rome, Italy. Plan. 1748.
Fig. 8. Le Corbusier. Plan Voisin. Paris, France. 1925.

9, 10

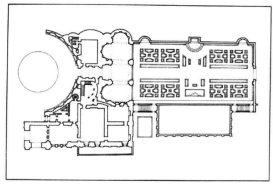

11

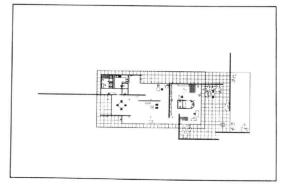

12

Fig. 9. Georgio Vasari. The Uffizi. Florence, Italy. Aerial View. 1559.
Fig. 10. Le Corbusier. Unite d'Habitation. Marseilles, France. Aerial View. 1946.
Fig. 11. Raphael and Giulio Romano. Villa Madama. Rome, Italy. Plan. 1516.
Fig. 12. Mies van der Rohe. House for Berlin Building Exhibition. Berlin, Germany. Plan. 1931.

virtue of the articulated poche defining them, appear as Platonic solids. In Mies' house, space is undifferentiated and formless, continuous and an infinite 'given' for the objects (service elements) that float in this continuous void.

That the Modern tradition in the modern city has absorbed the corporeal presence of the Pre-Modern tradition into an ever widening black hole, is a dilemma we are now forced to confront. However, as has been wisely studied and documented, it is possible to acknowledge these traditions by simultaneously making use of each. As in the case of precedents that have already revealed such enlightenment, the church of Sant'Agnese in the Piazza Navona in Rome (figure 13) by Borromini, is both an object and a space definer because of its centralized plan, and the articulation of the frontal wall facing the piazza. This wall, because of its thickness and profile, is a mediator between two different kinds of space; outside and inside, autonomous and static centralized space and the directional space of the rectangular piazza, requiring the front of Sant'Agnese to reinforce the 'wall' of the piazza. The condition to be found in the north pier of Sant'Agnese illustrates another enlightened possibility to be explored in the development of a coexistence of Modern and Pre-Modern space and has been observed by Steven Peterson. Poche has been typically understood as the 'area inbetween', the thickness of a wall, that separates and independently describes the space on either side. However in the north pier of Sant'Agnese the poche becomes occupied. Peterson also describes the work of Sir John Soane, who in his house at Lincoln's Inn Fields (figures 14,15) demonstrates a clearer understanding of this possibility, and designs an architecture that begins to occupy the wall. As in the case of the thick habitable wall along the front facade of his house and between the parlor and the living room, one experiences both a sense of room, and a sense of uninterrupted continuity as spaces flow together.

Another dichotomy, illustrative of the difference between Modern and Pre-Modern space, that might be fused for a multifarious set of spatial consequences is the definition of center. In a plan of a Pre-Modern castle (figure 16), the service elements as well as different kinds of rooms occupy the poche. However, the hierarchical difference between the central space and those spaces surrounding it, insure the reading of the center as most important. In fact, by virtue of the independence of these spaces, mediated by poche, space becomes very important. On the other hand in Mies' project for a fifty foot square house (figure 17), the definition of center becomes the difference between the massiveness of the service core relative to the undefined and continuous space surrounding it. The transparency of wall here is intended to dematerialize it, unifying inside and outside. The plinth on which it sits, and the roof plane, are the only record of object, however anonymous. Center in this case has nothing to do with 'place-making', but rather with the celebration of function, however abstract.

The simultaneous presence of a defined and dense center, and of center as void, would then become an opportunity to create an ambiguous reading of "sense of place", if placemaking can be associated with closure. In *Forest of Symbols* Victor Turner describes this condition as "liminal", a transition between states. "Undoing, dissolution, decomposition are accompanied by processes of growth, transformation and a reformation of old elements in new patterns. It is interesting to note how, by the principle of economy of symbolic reference, logically antithetical processes of death and growth may be represented by the same tokens...This coincidence of opposite processes and notions in a single representation characterizes the particular unity of the liminal: that which is neither this nor that, and yet both." It is in the sense of orientation through hierarchy and symmetry, that the center as void was and is powerful spatially, and it is in the stimulation of the edges, the transposition of stasis to movement, that the Modern dense center is significant. When both are allowed to coexist in a manner that subtly applies both these phenomena, we can enjoy a sense of closure and psychological 'rest', and a sense of open-endedness and continuity with the exterior environment. Ultimately, the experience of architectural space - Pre-Modern (figure 18) and Modern (figure 19) is heightened through the juxtaposition and simultaneous manifestation of the positive qualities of each.

Different evolutions of poche as principle, articulated by Peterson, Dennis, and others provide the method for achieving the simultaneity of 'solid' and 'void' and in a range of levels that allow for the development of different scales of experience. As Peterson writes: "The architecture of the wall, of negative space, can incorporate another world of intimacy, emotion, and memory. It can contain places which are the equivalent of the attics and basements. Alcoves, window seats, inglenooks, hidden panels and secret passages, can be carved from the 'solid'. The space of the walls can provide new mystery, illusion and surprise."

All the above references have informed the work presented here, but none of these works are direct applications of these allusions and it is with consideration that I present the quotations above as a forward to the work to follow. Each project embodies some or all of these principles, without positing any of them as unique solutions; rather, they are points of departure for a series of investigations that are not linear in development, nor conclusive as a set. Each project, beginning with a small pavilion completed about a decade ago, has only borne more to investigate.

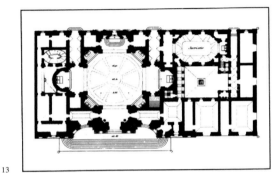

13

14

15

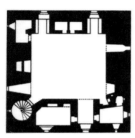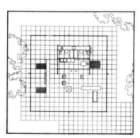

16, 17

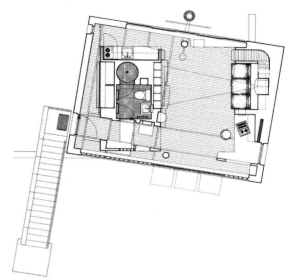

18

19

Fig. 13. Borromini. St. Agnese and Collegio Innnocenziano. Rome, Italy. Plan. 1657.
Fig. 14. Sir John Soane's House. Dining Room. London, England, seen from Library. 1812.
Fig. 15. Sir John Soane's House. The Dining Room. London, England, plan, 1812.
Fig. 16. Medieval Castle, plan.
Fig. 17. Mies van der Rohe. Project for a 50 foot square house. Plan. 1951.
Fig. 18. Carpaccio. St. Jerome in his Study. Oil (56 1/4 in. x 851/2 in,) c. 1502.
Fig. 19. Mies van der Rohe. Gericke House. 1932.

Notes:

1. The first project is based on a Modern aesthetic where the grid has been casually layered in the establishment of an order. Although it lacks the considerations that the others share, it is not wholly dissimilar, and it shares the site with the final project presented here.
2. Schumacher, Thomas. "Contextualism: Urban Ideals and Deformations," *Casabella* 104, 1971, p.87.
3. Dennis, Michael. "Architecture and the Post-Modern City,"*The Cornell Journal of Architecture*, Fall 1981, Rizzoli p. 48.
4. Schumacher describes, at some length, these differences at urban level in the article cited above, and attributes much of his discussion to Colin Rowe's work with graduate students at Cornell between the years 1963 to 1971. Steven peterson discusses the differences between 'space' and 'anti-space' in an article entitled "Space and Anti-Space" in *The Harvard Architecture Review*, Spring 1980. Colin Rowe, in his article: "The Present Urban Predicament" in the Fall 1981 issue of The Cornell Journal of Architecture, distinguishes the 20th century as having the dubious distinction of making little sense of space until Pevsner's An Outline of European Architecture, and Giedion's Space, Time & Architecture appear in the early 1940's; Bernard Berenson, Geoffrey Scott and Frank Lloyd Wright being exceptions.
5. Koetter, Fred, and Rowe, Colin, *Collage City* (Massachusetts and London: The MIT Press, 1978) p.68.
6. Schumacher, p.86.
7. Peterson, p.89.
8. ibid.
9. ibid.
10. Koetter, Fred "Notes on the Inbetween," The Harvard Architecture Review, Spring 1980, MIT Press, p.63.
11. Peterson, p.89.

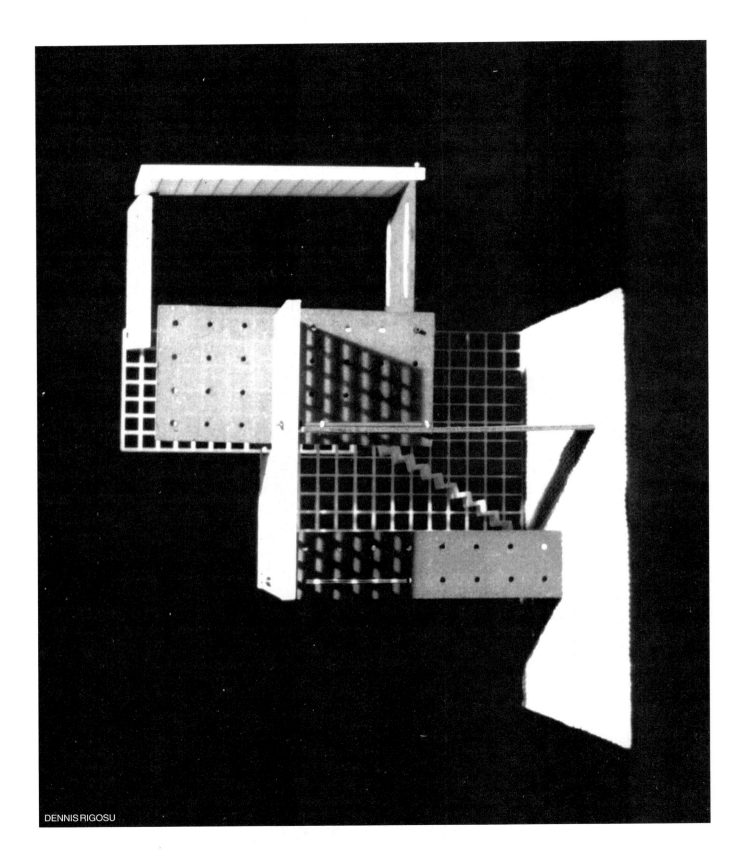

DENNIS RIGOSU

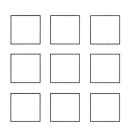

concert - to arrange or settle by mutual understanding; contrive or plan together; devise. a musical performance in which a number of musicians participate. *concerto* - a composition for one, two, or three solo instruments and an orchestra: it is based on the sonata form and has, usually, three movements.

orchestra — in ancient Greek theatres the semicircular space in front of the stage, used by the chorus. Greek *orchesithai* , to dance, from Sanskrit *rghayati* he trembles or is agitated, from *er* - to move, go, come. cf Greek *erkhomai* — I come or arrive.

fugue -- from Latin fuga a flight; (see fug itive).... 1. a musical form or composition in which a theme is taken up and developed by various instruments or voices in succession according to the strict laws of counterpoint. **polyphony** - 1. multiplicity of sounds, as in an echo. 2. in *music* , a combining of a number of individual but harmonizing melodies, as in a fugue, canon, etc. (canon: reed, tube, cannon, canyon); counterpoint: opposed to monodony, homophony.

*The term "**concerto**" is said to have come from a Latin word which means "to fight side-by-side, to compete as brothers-in-arms." This is really quite fitting, as the relationship between the orchestra and the soloist in a concerto is not always a friendly one, nor even one without tension. But the tension can - and should - be a source of excitement and stimulation, and its resolution pure joy.... There are many reasons why tension must exist between the two elements in a concerto - the orchestra and the soloist - rather than being a friendly partnership. In a concerto, if the solo instrument and the orchestra parts blended beautifully, expressed the same musical viewpoint, shared the same sorts of melodic material, and in general, had a relationship where no tension existed for the duration of the work, there would be as much boredom in the concert hall as there would be in a theater where there were no differences, hardships, tension or difficulties between the characters in the play. To make an artistic point as well as to hold the interest of an audience for a long period of time - usually a half hour to forty five minutes - a concerto must build tension and resolve it, often in each movement of a work as well as in the overall design of the piece itself.*

.... Because of their substantial length, most concertos have been written for instruments which are best able to sustain interest with the greatest variety of expression and virtuosity, tone color, largest range of notes and dynamic variety. That's why there are more concertos for violin, cello, and piano than for piccolos, tubas, or harps. Or for recorders, violas, or pianists who play with only one hand. Perhaps the most interesting aspect to listen for in concertos is the nature of the relationship between solo instrument or instruments, and the ensemble. Are they in sympathy, sharing a given mood or emotion? Do they agree on their outlook on life? Are they in opposition, "arguing" through the abstractness of their musical dialogue, with tension building between them? Does one try to dominate the other, and does one win? All of this, the sensitive listener can answer for himself.

Nancy Shear, Introducing "Concertos Diverse and Unusual" program of the New Jersey Symphony Orchestra 1990-91 Broadcast Series

3. CONCERTO

BENDING AND WEAVING

CONCERTO: *BENDING*

Michelangelo, Tabernacle niche, Medici Chapel

| 1 | 2 | 3 |

Archimedes' Theorem: volume ratios of cone, half sphere, and cylinder, all of same height and radius, are 1: 2: 3! Beautiful mathematics!

The four possible intersections of a plane and a cone. The area of a cone's circle increases as the square of its distance from the origin-- like gravity.

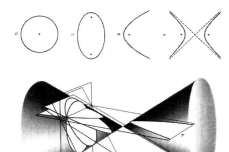

BEING

"The springing flexibility of bamboo allows it to survive, even in the winds of change." I Ching
"Bamboo without mind, yet sends thoughts soaring among clouds." Wu Chen (1280-1354)
"The little Reed, bending to the force of the wind, soon stood upright again when the storm passed over." Aesop
"Man is a thinking reed." Pascal's Pensées

How can we account for *many* forces at once? We become at home in a field. The expert is adept at fielding questions; the ball player at fielding a fly ball, where calculating all the curves of the speed of the pitch, swing of the bat, arc of the flight, and drift of the wind meet at the moment of the catch. How do we master a field? We explore, off the straight and narrow. We meander. All moving mass bends to the curvature of spacetime, which in turn warps in the presence of mass. This is gravity. The bending paths of moving solids are revealed in celestial and earthly structures all around us. Physicist Julian Schwinger tells us that "the rainbow symbolizes the Sun; it was the observed deflection of light passing near the Sun that drew popular attention to relativity and Albert Einstein. And the radio telescope symbolizes modern technology that has produced much more accurate confirmation of the theory of relativity." The parabola is one of the conic sections already known at the Alexandrian Museion, temple of the Muses, whose noted Library contained over 750,000 manu-scripts and scrolls. The four conic sections are obtained by passing planes at various angles through a cone, generating figures with one or two focal points. A parabola has a single focus. Archimedes (287-212 BC) reputedly used parabolic "burning mirrors" to focus the sun's parallel rays on the masts of Roman ships invading Sicily. Johannes Kepler in 1609 found that planets follow elliptical orbits with the sun as one focus. Every 76 years Halley's Comet falls toward the sun, following the path of an extreme ellipse.

Bending: Gravity's Rainbow

Gravity bends flights and structures in a spectrum of distortion, a rainbow of force and motion, along paths of the conic sections of circle, ellipse, parabola, or hyperbola. The carved stone swag in Michelangelo's Medici Chapel niche shows the curve of a sagging cord. The arch above cambers to resist a force like gravity, and creates "invented" space below. The hollow bar between suggests the stress and strain in every beam that spans a gap. In spacetime the shortest distance between two points is a curve of least action, called a *geodesic*. A single stone millions of light years from the nearest galaxy would still free-fall along very slightly curved world-line through spacetime (the effect of gravity decreases as the square of the distance). On earth a thrown stone traces a parabola in flight, *because* it moves through time and space on a path of least resistance. The "force" that throws you back when a car or plane accelerates is the same as the "force" that glues your feet to the floor. In both cases, the free-fall your body would like to take through time and space is deflected-- by geometry! When we stand we cannot tell if our feet are held to the floor by gravity, or because the room is an accelerating elevator or spaceship. Gravity and acceleration produce the same effect, which is to bend the geometry of spacetime. This is Einstein's principle of equiva-lence, what he termed his "happiest thought".

Beams are bent by gravity, just as bamboo is bent by wind. The fibers yield their free-float positions to the curvature mass imposes on spacetime, deflecting each molecule in a path toward the earth's center of mass. Simply-supported beams deflect in the same parabola shape as the ballistic path of a thrown stone. Each molecule in a loaded curved beam is also pulling on its neighbors, so as it deflects, it adds to the deflecting "force" on its neighbors. Pieces try to **shear**, or slide across each other, and to **bend** around each other, generating **moment** like children on a seesaw. The human rib cage not only holds heart and lungs but also acts like an arch to protect these vital organs from any fall or blow from without.

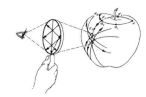

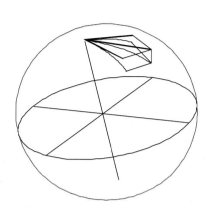

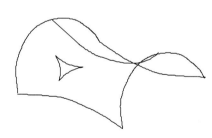

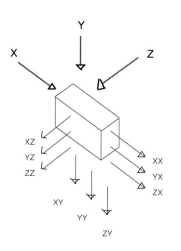

THE "PICTURE" OF A TENSOR

CURVATURE: FORCE = GEOMETRY

Newton's First Law of Motion describes the inertia of a mass: "Every body persists in its state of rest or of uniform motion in a straight line unless it is compelled to change that state by forces impressed on it." The photo opposite shows the Skylab satellite in orbit around the earth. Already far enough from the surface gravity of Earth to be virtually weightless, its thin lightweight structure spans great lengths with almost no deflection. Why then does Skylab curve around the Earth, deviating from its inertial straight line? While Newton described this "force" of gravity that acted on distant objects, pulling apples, baseballs, and spaceships to the ground, Einstein showed that such force was actually a distortion in the *geometry* of space and time. Matter moves in geodesic or least action "straight" paths that bend in spacetime. Inside Skylab, a "weightless" ball flies straight, but the whole ship is a local reference frame whose spacetime path bends in the presence of the mass of Earth. Consider this problem: An airplane at 10,000 foot altitude flies south 400 miles in one hour with a wind blowing east at 300 miles per hour. How *high* will the plane be above the ground after one hour?! Vector addition of the speed and direction of plane and wind shows that the plane will be 500 miles southeast after one hour, but what measures the curvature of the earth below the level-flying plane? The question is equivalent to asking how an ant on an apple can know its surface is curved, when in every local measure it seems flat. In both cases the flat geometry of local space has been changed in a way not immediately apparent to the inhabitants.

The 19th century mathematicians Riemann and Gauss suggested a way to measure such curvature. Suppose our aviator flies from the North Pole to the Equator, turns and flies 6000 miles due east (one-fourth the way around the globe), and then turns due north to return to the Pole. She will find that her three right angle turns describe a triangle with a total of 270 degrees, not the 180 degrees of a triangle on a flat surface. The surface of a sphere has positive curvature. A saddle-shaped hyperbolic paraboloid has negative curvature (less than 180 degrees for the angles of a triangle). Riemann broke the 2000 year old assumption since Euclid that geometry must always be flat. He demonstrated consistent mathematics for non-Euclidean geometry, flat everywhere locally on its surface, but curved in a higher dimension. He devised the metric tensor to describe such curvature. A tensor is a "machine" that tells how any input vector will affect all possible output vectors. Our aviator parable describes the curvature of a two-dimensional surface in a three-dimensional space, but the principle applies as well to the curvature of three-dimensional volumes in a four-dimensional space(time). Einstein, using Riemann's metric tensor, found the mathematics that precisely described the effect of gravity on the curvature of a path that a freely falling body will take. Curvature-- geometry-- is the "force" that determines the sum of the angles of triangle, that is, the variation from flatness in any geometry. Just as an ant walking on an apple may feel a "mysterious force" deflecting it from a straight path, so too do we see a straight flightpath for Skylab deflected by the curvature of spacetime.

Under external load, the free-body molecules of a material give up some of the form of their microscopic structure and *deflect*. Each freely falling chunk of matter is pushed, pulled and twisted by the curvature of spacetime nearby. The way every element of a solid responds to and generates loads in all directions can be described by tensors, a volumetric extension of the vectors used for free-body diagrams. The sum of all those pulls, from every direction on every direction creates the curves taken by deflecting bodies like cables and beams. External load and internal resistance are revealed through the stress and strain in structural materials. Strain is curvature of a "force" (change in metric tensor) made manifest externally through change in shape (stretch, compress, shear, bend), while stress is curvature of a "force" (change in stress-strain tensor) within the material, made manifest in how structures fail. A block of wood maps a stress-strain tensor of all the forces that bent the trunk of the tree in its growth, from instant wind shifts to climate changes that take centuries.

VISIBLE CURVES

The Catenary

Hold a string and hand a weight from its center. Add other equal weights at evenly spaced intervals and you will find that the shape of the structure tends toward a smooth curve called a catenary (from Latin *catena*, chain-like), the shape a free rope or loose chain takes when freely suspended between two points, characteristic of a cord under its own weight. A cable or rope supporting a uniformly distributed hanging load takes the slightly different curve of a parabola. Catenary structures are essentially in pure tension, which makes them very efficient in spanning large distances with little mass. The line of action is essentially the curve of the structure, which is thus in pure tension, with little or no resistance to bending. The catenary is the form of the long cable arc in suspension bridges, as well as the curve of the profiles of the Eiffel Tower. Jacob Bernoulli, who loved the logarithmic spiral, solved the curve of the catenary function.

Long Spans

The central span of the Verrazano Narrows Bridge at New York Harbor is 4265 feet-- wide enough so that the earth's curvature sets the summits of the towers several inches further away from each other than the bases. To carry a highway full of heavy cars and trucks requires a vast pile of matter arrayed so as to support not only its own weight and vehicles, but also the sideways push and pull of wind and water. What structure to choose? A suspension bridge-- two massive pylons that carry cables supporting the beam of the roadway. The great concrete anchor piers at each shore resist the enormous tension loads of the cables. Gravity is the ultimate glue that holds the ensemble in place. The Verrazano Bridge strides across the gateway to the harbor like a Colossus. The whole structure is an exercise in suspension. It is quite musical, tuned like a stringed instrument to a tension-compression equilibrium-- a tensegrity.

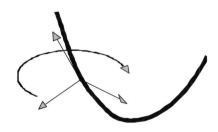

Why aren't the cables simply straight lines across the water (or at least straighter-- like the beams below them)? The inertia described by Newton tends to keep each molecule of the cable moving in a straight line, until it is acted on by an outside force-- in this case gravity. Each freely falling "free body" molecule in the bridge cable pulls and pushes against its neighbors while being be pushed, pulled and twisted by the local curvature of spacetime (gravity). The "free body" molecules of a material give up some of the shape and rigidity of their microscopic spaceframe and *deflect*. The sum of all those pushes and pulls, from every direction on every direction, is the catenary curve of the bridge. Visualizing all the forces acting on each element of each strand of the cable suggests the following: the force of gravity acting downward generates one component load vector in tension tangent to the curve of the cable, and another normal (perpendicular) to this. The vector product of these generates a third force perpendicular to the first two, which creates twisting, or torsion in the cable. Torsion explains why the cable is braided. Unbraided strands will not resist each other's torsion and are thus no stronger than parallel single strands.

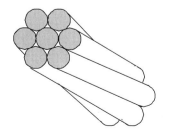

Antonio Gaudi, born in 1856, a year after Gauss' death, was a visionary architect and engineer who found ways to let gravity directly calculate his structures. He built models of cables with suspended weights as upside down versions of the vaulted structures which became the stones of his Sagrada Familia Cathedral in Barcelona, Spain. Frei Otto used similar methods to explore and design lightweight structures for large span stadiums like the one at the 1972 Munich Olympics Stadium.

THE ARCH IN ARCHITECTURE

The Curve of Projectile Motion

The ideal flight of a ballistic projectile like a golf ball has a constant horizontal velocity, which is the speed it has when it leaves golf club face. Thus there is no horizontal component to its acceleration. However, the vertical velocity varies with time. Galileo found that the magnitude of the vertical distance **s** will vary with the acceleration due to gravity **g** taken over the time **t** squared, compactly expressed as **s** = $1/2$**gt**^{2}. Thus at 2 seconds, the acceleration will be four times greater than after one second, and at 3 second s the acceleration will be nine times greater. The velocity vector is tangent to the projectile at every point, while the acceleration vector is directed downward (towards the earth's center) at every point. Thus the path in flight traces a parabola, the curve of the quadratic equation that related the value of one function to the square of another. Since Newton, we have been saying that the "force" of gravity pulls a golf ball to the ground. But since Einstein, we understand that force equals geometry, and say that the ball is traveling in a least action geodesic whose straight path is only bent by the curvature of spacetime caused by the presence of mass.

Keystone

Pile up stones in a carefully shaped curve (using formwork to support them if necessary) and finally add a single wedge-shaped stone in the center. Gravity will pull on this center keystone, whose angled surfaces will push down and outward on the stones supporting it, which in turn push down and outward on those below, and so on. The result is a kind of bending of force into a curve around the space below the stone arch. Arches frame space in such a way that bending is resisted by the geometry of the structure. It was the desire to dispense with the flying buttresses that had been developed to resist the outward thrust of the vaulted span that led Brunelleschi to make his tension-ring double-dome for the Florence Cathedral.

We can see the same curve in a golf ball's flight and in Robert Maillart's 1929 daring and graceful reinforced concrete Salginatobel Bridge in Switzerland, because any particle traversing a span in a gravity field takes the ballistic up-and-down path of a parabola. The parabola describes the path of every stone in an arch as much as the path of a flying golf ball. In both cases, a uniformly distributed load is applied to the span (in the former case, distributed in space, in the latter, distributed in time!) We can see this in the diagram for the moment in a beam. Since the mass of an arch also acts as a uniformly distributed load, the parabola is the most efficient shape for an arch. Other profiles develop additional stresses and strains. In addition to shear stress, a mass element that spans a space exhibits three different conditions of bending stress: compression at its top fibers, tension at the bottom, and no stress at all along its neutral axis. Extrude an arch to get a vault. Rotate an arch about its center vertical axis to get a dome. The photograph on the facing page shows Maillart's elegant cement hall of 1939 in Zurich. The reinforced concrete shell is 16 m wide, 12 m high, but only 6 cm thick. The vault shows a man is standing inside, sheltered from the elements. Bending makes two sides of volume on either side of a structure. Within the 6 cm thick curved sheet of concrete mass itself is a kind of spacial "neutral axis". In addition, there is a kind of spacial compression within the concave volume of arch, vault, or dome and a kind of spacial tension in the region outside its convex surface. We might even suggest that inside a vault volume is denser and more compressed than outside it.

Compression structure alone: a masonry arch wedged into position along line of compression in a reversed catenary curve.

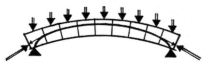

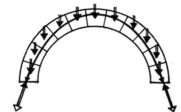

In the semicircular masonry arch the line of pressure does not conform to the shape of the arch and therefore the crown tends to fail while the sides buckle out.

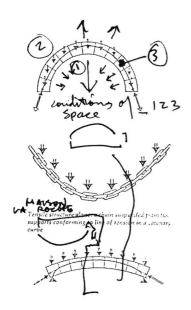

Tensile structure along a chain suspended from two supports conforming a line of tension in a catenary curve

THINKING

For architects, spaces can distort. "Forces" can determine the structure of space. Bending, shear, tension and compression may all be translated into terms not only of structural engineering but architectural composition as well. When an arch is rendered as a plan, three "force" conditions of space are revealed, as shown in the diagram: 1. compression; 2. tension; 3. neutral (neutral axis). Bending makes two sides of space in section *and* plan. A strong curve creates tension against implied orthogonality. Bending and shear provide architects with planning tools for creating dynamic organizations of space. Walls need no longer be passive dividers between inside and outside. The Baroque architects exploited the combination of bent and sheared surfaces and volumes whose "flatness" varied from layered in shear to round in torsion.

Bending Volume

If loading mass generates internal stress, could loading volume also generate stress that distorts the intrinsic form of the volume? We suggest that "loading volume" means simply the distortion from some original configuration according to any architectural need for program, circulation, acoustics, lighting, etc. Just as load may deflect mass, so also may architectural forces strain the volume of architectural space. For example, a room opening onto a corridor creates an unpleasant space unless that corridor "beam" yields to this force, either through bending outward to receive the space, or shearing to permit a punch of volume in the opposite wall to create a balcony or the like. Other dynamic actions-- shatter, shear, explosion, etc.-- may also alter space. Thus we may speak of an architectural "structure" of volume, just as we may speak of the steel frame structure of a building. Just as engineers seek to establish equilibrium within mass to sustain structures, so too do architects establish equilibrium in plan and section *of volumes* to resolve forces in space. Such forces define the quality of a volume. Beyond the addition and subtraction of a volumetric algebra, one volume may stretch or squeeze another. In terms of plan (and section), one volume may be fuller, stiffer, harder to move than another. Spaces can have different sizes, shape, proportion, density, orientation, inertia, stress or strain.

Bending mass suggests bending void. A vault creates a sheltered volume within. Outside, where rain may fall, volume has a different quality. Transforming such a sectional phenomena into plan reveals a dynamic of load and force in architectural space. Rotate an arch 90 degrees to get the colonnades which surround Piazza del Popolo, the plaza in front of St. Peter's Cathedral in Rome, designed by Bernini and completed by 1567. Within the piazza, a vast elliptical urban volume delimited by great bowed colonnades on either side, one senses containment and compression (albeit on a vast scale), while without one may well feel excluded and pushed away. We see in the fragment of the Nolli plan, shown here to the left, that in the plaza lies what Hannah Ahrendt has called "the space of appearance", an arena for civic visibility and public interaction on policies and affairs of the city. The mundane world outside is repelled by the colonnade, convex to urban life, concave to the sacred space of the plaza. Between these two realms, stress and strain animate the volume of the colonnades as much as light and shadow, yet a certain repose along a neutral axis is available to the visitor along the curving path who seeks the balanced between two divergent worlds. The photo opposite is deliberately turned sideways to reveal both arch and cable in plan, suggesting that the stresses of dynamic loading transform the neutral Boolean algebra union of Bernini's central plaza and rod-like avenue into a volumetric tensegrity of expansion and enclosure running from the Portico of St. Peter's to the River Tiber and beyond to Michelangelo's Campidoglio.

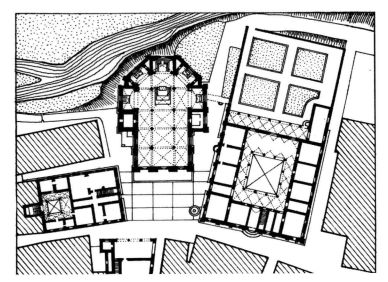

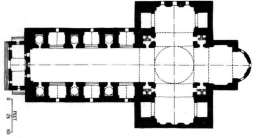

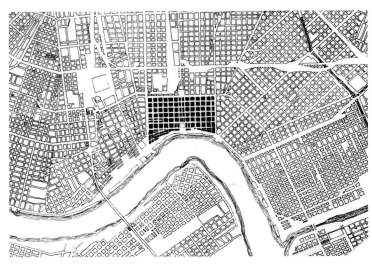

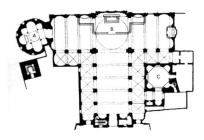

THE CRISIS OF THE RENAISSANCE: THE COLLISION OF "PERFECT" SPACES

Italian Renaissance artists and architects of the 15th and 16th century, from Brunelleschi and Massaccio through Michelangelo and Bernini, had mastered the organization of the visual world on the picture plane with the rediscovery (the Romans knew of it) and application of scientific, geometrically constructed "true" perspective. Before this painters used a rough and ready observed perspective to construct pictorial space. Each portion of such a painting would show diagonals converging in depth, but each zone had its own vanishing point. There was no overall unifying vanishing point or volumetric construction to the implied space. (Cézanne of course rediscovered the liberating capability of such multiple views of a single scene.)

The architects could even exploit perspective to construct spaces within a painting that directly extended the space of an actual room. Leonardo da Vinci used this technique when he painted *The Last Supper*, so that lines of the clerestory windows in the monks' dining refectory at Santa Maria delle Grazie in Milan converge into the lines of the painting. Donato Bramante (1444-1514) used this technique at Santa Maria Presso San Satiro, begun in 1478 in Milan, to complete the interior of a church by extending a wall pictorially when the site would not permit the addition of actual volume. At San Andrea in Mantua, Leon Battista Alberti (1404-1472) developed an elevation for the facade which he repeated for each bay of the church's nave on the interior in attempt to create a unity of spacial experience.

This triumph of human vision in the union of art and science had one small problem, however. The "truth" of the image depended on the position of the viewer. For each perspective construction, an ideal station point for the viewer is implied. Joining pictorial space with constructed volume into one visual unity was convincing only at a single point in space. This was fine so long as the view mattered only to one individual or a single hierarchy, and from the Popes in the Vatican to Louis XIV at Versailles, society supported such political pyramids. However, as is perfectly obvious to any casual visitor to Bernini's Piazza del Popolo in Rome, there is another side to every wall. The problem troubled some architects so much that at the very center of the Christian world of the time, directly facing Piazza del Popolo, where the grand vaults of St.Peter's Cathedral intersected under Michelangelo's heroic and sublime dome, Bernini and later Borromini constructed the writhing twisting supports of the Baldachino canopy directly under the dome. Apparently, the convergence of every set of eyes in Christendom was so loaded with importance that only forms dynamically responding to the conditions could hold its place.

With the powerful tool of scientifically constructed visual perspective, Renaissance artists could propose views of ideal cities in their paintings so accurately that it is possible to draw the plans of such spaces using just the spacial data present in the painting. Such a plan bears an uncanny resemblance to the actual patterns of cities that emerged from separate villages that in time grew into each other as they extended their individual street grids. When large fields of space are organized on a grid, or when buildings are aligned to create a perfect perspective in a public square, any space beyond must be excluded from consideration. When "perfect" fields generated from different origins meet, volumetric collision occurs. The plan of New Orleans reveals that the city developed as independent colonies of French, Spanish, and British settlers who laid out separate grid plans, each orthogonal to the to river edge. Later the extended grids of the French Quarter and the others grew to intersect, but even today they remain clearly rotated against each other. Such street plan collisions are also found in Brooklyn, San Francisco, Paris and many other cities.

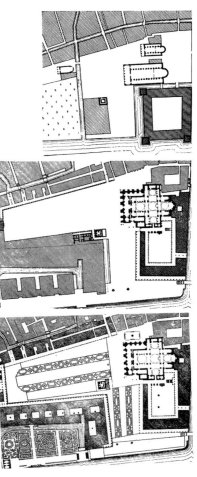

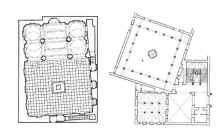

HINGES IN THE CITY

Stress and Strain on Volumes

When rotated orientations meet, they come into conflict, as shown in the plan of the Palace of the Marques de Peñaflor, Andalusia, Spain, 1726, or they generate internal volumetric stresses, as shown in the plan of the Pearl Mosque, Red Fort in Delhi, India, 1638. What are we to make of the volumes that result from such encounters. When one space moves through another does this generate stress in both volumes? Spaces can yield and bend; slip like sliding blocks; or shatter like flying bowling pins, depending on the strength of the programmatic bonds between the volumes and the programmatic and site forces that drive them apart. Alvar Aalto's plan for a high-rise apartment in Bremen seems to be more energetically shattered than the plan of New Orleans shown on the previous page. Aalto is able to give student rooms more private space and window exposure while concentrating circulation close to the elevators to increase public interaction with such a "shattered" plan.

Hinges in the City

Void can be the lubrication between masses. Overlapping orders may push each other in the void, but the encounter is not catastrophic. Thus, two spaces can be in the same place at the same time... but not two masses! Mass encounters generate stress and strain: an urban intersection may resolve two realms without stress, capable of carrying more than one volumetric order within the same dimensions as a stressless bend of two different local frames of reference... in other words, the plan equivalent to a pin joint. Such a space becomes a hinge in the city. One example is Pietro da Cortona's Santa Maria della Pace in Rome, where the circular curve exhedra church portico is the hub for the spokes of all the streets that intersect there. Architectural plans normally abound with volumetric joint conditions. Entries, vestibules, halls, lobbies, and the like all function as connectors between sets of other program volumes.

Properly arranged volumes can act as both lubrication and glue-- holding mass and void in complex plan relationships without compromising individual integrity. One demonstration occurs at the intersection and union of volumes in that masterful urban volume, Piazza San Marco in Venice. We can see in plans of three successive stages of this vital urban space the evolution of the sophisticated resolution of the collision of various spacial orders. It did not all happen at once., yet the progress toward a plastic resolution seems, in retrospect, almost inevitable. The first plan, before 1000, shows two piazzas, one along the water edge and one internal, are almost equal in size and configuration. The campanile is engaged as part of the massing to the southwest of the internal piazza. In the second plan, c. 1100-1200, the piazza is lengthened. The new church of San Marco is still orthogonal to the Doge's Palace to its south, but now the center axis of the church is no longer aligned with the central axis of the internal piazza. The Campanile is separated from other buildings, but still inset to the massing at its corner. The third, and most current plan, shows Jacopo Sansovino's 1536 widening of the internal piazza to the south, to make the campanile free standing. Sansovino's Library wraps the water edge facade into the internal piazza, turning two corners. The campanile is now a true "pin joint". The 1735 paving in the piazza aligns with the center of San Marco, but is parallel to neither side of the internal piazza. The volumes of the piazzas are sheared, displaced, and set in rotation. This is a space in which volumetric bending shear and rotation occur concurrently! Here one can be in many places at once.

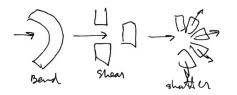

Bend   Shear   shatter

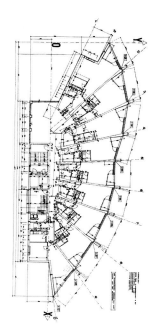

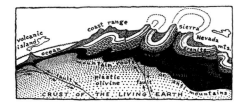

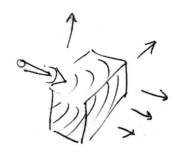

A scalar has magnitude. A vector has magnitude and direction. A tensor has magnitude in all directions to operate on a vector. A tensor responds to the action of a vector in all directions, as a function of both the solid's field (tensor) and the vector's magnitude and direction.

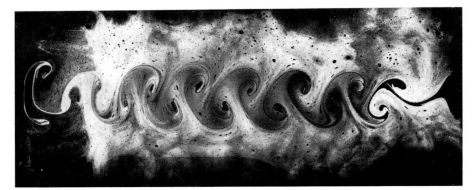

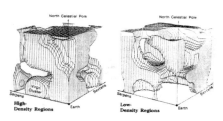

The sponge-like structure of the universe is evident when the observed locations of galaxies (left) and voids (right) are plotted in a cube 100 million light years on a side.

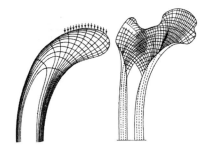

Crane-head and femur. After Culmann and J. Wolff

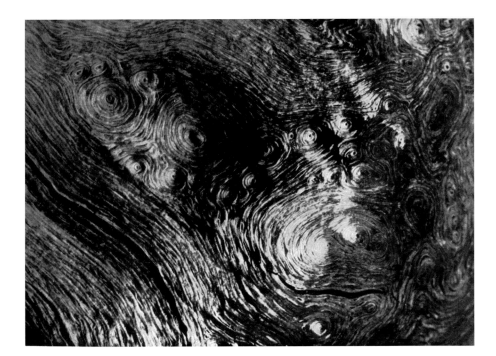

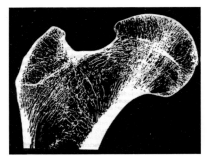

ANIMATING

$e^{i\pi} - 1 = 0$

Hidden Curves

A beam is a straight bar that spans between two supports. It carries its own weight, and often additional loads. But is a beam truly straight? Every load deflects a beam to some degree. (Stand on a diving board.) A beam under load is already bending into a shallow curve. Even more curves lie hidden inside the beam, as photoelastic analysis reveals. The interior of a beam bending under a load experiences at least three tendencies to strain. Along the bottom chord, the particles of the beam would tend to stretch, so here the beam is pulling apart, in tension. At the uppermost chord, bending will tend to squeeze the particles together, putting them in compression. The tension and compression are greatest at the extreme outer fibers, and decrease toward the middle of the cross section of the beam. Thus, there is also the neutral axis, generally near the midline of the beam, which is neither in compression or tension. Loads can deform whole structures: axial loads will bend a too-thin column before it crushes the material, so the column fails in *buckling*, not only compressing but also popping out sideways, like a plastic coffee stirrer squeezed between thumb and forefinger.

Moment and Shear

Moment bends a solid; shear is a kind of punch into it. There is a reciprocal relationship between the two. Consider a row of books held between two hands as a beam. Unless we squeeze tight, the books will tend to slide downward, and the "beam" will fail in *shear*. If the books are tied together around top and bottom edges, the arrangement will sag to maximum deflection at the center, the point of maximum *bending moment* where shear is at a minimum. **Strain** distorts solids. When elements cannot yield completely to applied forces, the external load generates internal resistance, and strain becomes **stress**, or force per unit volume. The elements are *trying* to move, and in part succeed. Stretched rope fibers get thinner, squashed marshmallows bulge sideways even as they shorten. Hooke's Law tells us that strain deformations are proportional to stresses. So the less material per given load, the greater the stress. **Tensors**, operators that transform an input into its multiple and related outputs, describe many phenomena related to bending: there is a stress-strain tensor and moment of inertia tensor, as well as the metric tensor of spacetime. The grain in a block of wood may be an imprint of a tensor. A tree grows at many time scales and directions of stress: in a day it bends with the wind and sunlight, in centuries it torques to the slower push and pull of climate and gravity.

Bending and Shear Stress

A bending beam has maximum compressive stress along its uppermost fibers and maximum tensile stress at its lowest fibers. Shear stress has maximum stress at the neutral axis of a beam, the center of its cross section. Both shear and bending develop characteristic stresses in structural members. The engineer's job is to find the locations of the highest values of these stresses, putting as much material there as possible, while keeping the weight of structural members to a minimum. Thus structural design is a search for the most efficient deployment of mass to resist stress and strain. Bending generates a combination of tensile and compressive stresses. **Moment diagrams** and **shear diagrams** show bending and shear stress for a variety of load conditions, and are essential tools for structural design. They show that bending stress varies as a parabola, which is why the most efficient shape for an arch is a *parabola*. A large span bridge develops stresses similar to those in a beam, so an efficient bridge design seeks to be a direct (and literal!) expression of its moment and shear diagrams.

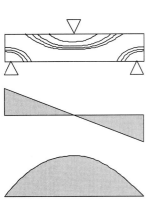

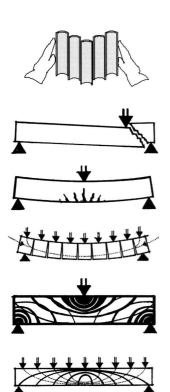

Loads on a beam and stresses in a beam. Each molecule of a beam generates a moment, and their sum yields a parabolic graph across the span.

STRAIGHT CURVES

Plastic and Elastic

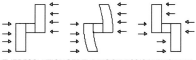

COIL   SPRING

Inside a straight beam lie curves of stress and strain. Most beams will bounce back like a spring after a load is removed-- they are **elastic**. Young's *modulus of elasticity* measures the degree of this resistance to deformation for each material. Steel has a higher modulus of elasticity than wood, just as a rubber band is more elastic than taffy. Materials which tend to flow rather than snap back or recoil are **plastic** rather than elastic. Poured concrete is plastic until it sets and hardens into an elastic synthetic stone. Under the model conditions of your Bag of Tricks, mesh is more plastic than the pegboard. Although the eggcrate is made out of a plastic material, it acts as an (almost rigid) elastic material for your structural models in these studies. You can make the eggcrate more plastic by heating it until it melts, and then using blocks as formwork, set it into simple cylindrical curves or compound surfaces like hyperbolic paraboloids (hypars).

The Constructivist-Purist Dilemma

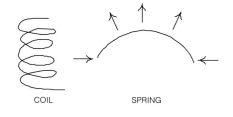

SECTION THROUGH A HOLLOW CUBE UNDER LOAD

Gustave Eiffel designed the supporting armature inside the Statue of Liberty as well as his Eiffel Tower in Paris. Which of the two resulting works is more valid as architecture? This difficult question is at the crux of a fundamental debate about form: an honest assembly of materials according to structural necessity vs. an ordering of perceptions to express formal ideas. Consider a hollow cube whose sides are all of equal material and thickness. Stress analysis will show that the cross plate needs to be thicker than its two side walls to carry its weight and resist bending-- a beam should be deeper than its supporting columns are wide. So a dilemma arises for the plastician: in a gravity field, make either a "pure" form, or an efficient structure, but not both. Purism's goal was the pure cube, whereas Constructivism revelled in articulating every structural variation. Gerrit Reitveld's wooden sideboard and Santiago Calatrava's steel and granite *Toros* (Bull) sculpture are two attempts to respond to this dilemma. Individual elements of stick, stone, strut, and wire are "pure", but the overall compositions reveal the stresses and strains that act on and in a beam. Calatrava's piece, by the nature of its materials and their extreme condition of counterbalance, is perhaps the more visceral, the more Constructivist of the two. If one seeks the superficial "perfection" that hides the guts of a struggle against real forces, then their plastic elaboration offends a reductionist sensibility. But if both works are understood as refined expressions of a beam under load, then the results are very satisfying indeed.

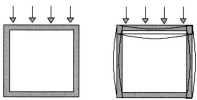

THE RESOLUTION OF BENDING STRESS IS PURE SHEAR.

The Fold: Right Angle Bending

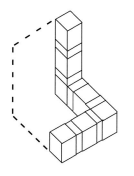

Shear stress occurs when two forces act on a body in opposite directions, but not in the same line. Any non-axial load creates shear stress as a general condition. The resolution of bending stress is pure shear. In a sense, shear is orthogonal bending. The extreme case of a bend is a right angle **fold--** which turns a corner into another dimension. The extension of the boundaries of 3 folded lines or 2 folded planes define a volumetric solid. One approach to the Constructivist-Purist dilemma is to use "pure" geometry to develop legitimate structural solutions. The triangulation at the corner of every wood frame house, where stress-skin plywood walls and floors create a rigid trihedral angle is an example. This sets "pure" planar elements perpendicular to stresses, defining volumes while resisting loads. This is one *architectural* 3-space solution to the conflict between the geometries ideal for architect (square), structural engineer (triangle) and HVAC engineer (circle) mentioned on page 121 above.

Bending stress: see the stretch lines in the stone, not only sedimentary layers laid down over eons,
but then whole set of strata bent in earth upheavels, folding and refolding, actually *bending* the layers of rock...

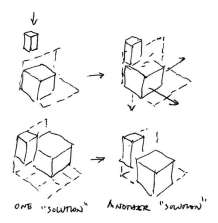

A CAN WIGGLE
B CAN MOVE BUT ONCE IN PLACE SITS "HEAVY"
C ARE VOLUMETRICLLY "LIGHT"

ONE "SOLUTION"   ANOTHER "SOLUTION"

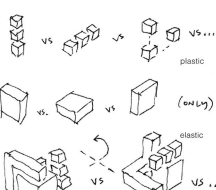

plastic

elastic

(ONLY)

increasingly elastic

VOLUME INERTIA

Archimedes, a great thinker, found deep meaning in everyday situations. Vitruvius tells us that one day while bathing, Archimedes noticed how his buoyant body displaced water. Leaping from the tub, he ran stark naked, shouting "Eureka!" He had just solved the problem posed by King Hiero to determine whether the royal crown was truly gold without melting or cutting it. What he understood in the bath was that the crown when immersed would displace a volume of water determined by its weight per unit volume, what we now call *specific density*. (This is why ships are calibrated in tons). So the rising water level could indicate whether the crown were made of heavy gold or some less dense material. We can extend this principle to the architectural character of volumes. In developing a *parti* or plan, an architect learns that some volumes are "weightier" than others because they are harder to move around for spacial or programmatic reasons. Some stones are harder to move than others. Were stones of space atop the monastery at Mount Athos in Meteora harder to move than those that made the Anasazi city at Chaco Canyon? In one case, people had to overcome inertia in lifting, in the other they relied on inertia for spanning.

Specific Density: Resistance to Change

Kicking a block of rock hurts your foot more than kicking the same size block of styrofoam. Mass has inertia, and resists any change in its spacetime worldline path. To paraphrase Ernst Mach, the rock is held in place by the entire universe. A volumetric equivalent to the idea of inertia in mass suggests that some volumes seem to resist relocation while others are easier to move around in solving a plan or *parti*. Size, importance, or position can all affect the inertial resistance to change, or specific density, of a volume. Such volumetric inertia may be due to orientation requirements (a bowling alley may have the same dimensions and proportions as an elevator shaft, but cannot be set vertically); necessary location within the site (must be near the front, on the roof, sunny view in morning, etc.) and in relation to other volumes (beside the kitchen, away from the children, above the nursery, and so on). Some volumes can stretch or squeeze their shapes to fit available space more easily than others. Some can even wiggle or bend, while others are too rigid in their plastic or programmatic demands-- you can't bend a bowling alley. Furniture and fittings may also limit possible locations-- it is desirable to cluster kitchens near bathrooms to share plumbing stacks. A configuration requirement may lead to location demand (a 90' long volume must fold to fit into a 30' cube site), thereby limiting *parti* options, which increases the specific density or inertia of the volumes. As volume relations or connections increase, so may inertia of the plan: it is easier to move a log than a tree stump whose roots are still embedded in the earth.

Program

An architectural *program* lists specific volumetric needs and qualities to accommodate the actions of the inhabitants of a space. The concepts of inertia and specific density suggest a dynamic interpretation of program. Increasing relational elasticity and consequently decreasing relational plasticity means that there are fewer possible variations or "moves" that "work in solving the positions of program volumes. A program means that people have called for specific volumes to be located in the organization of the site. When program volumes are large compared to the site, distortions that bend shear or fold things may develop. What gives two equal volumes different specific densities is program content-- use, size, position, orientation, proportions, lighting, ventilation, access, and proximity requirements. Must entry always be at ground level? That is a somewhat "movable" program location demand compared to an airport control tower's need to be the highest space for visibility. How to evaluate such program needs when they conflict demands an almost intuitive sense of their "weight" or specific density, but it is a skill that develops with architectural practise.

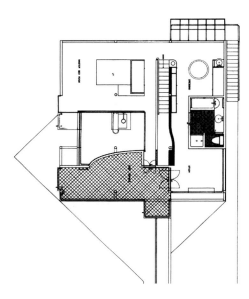

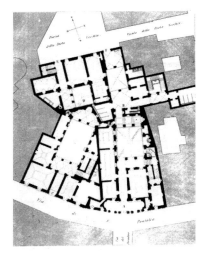

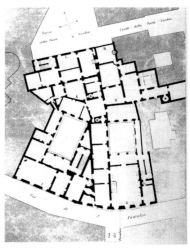

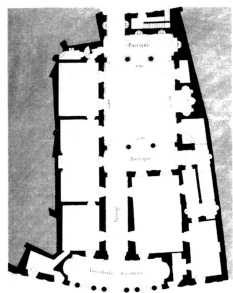

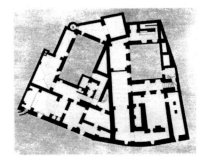

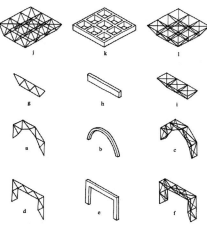

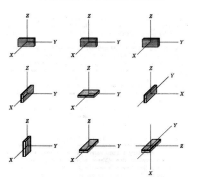

TRANSLATION OF A SET OF 4 STRUCTURAL
SECTIONS INTO FIRST THICKENED LINES
AND THEN INTO SPACE FRAMES

SUCCESSIVE 90 DEGREE ROTATIONS
OF A BLACKBOARD ERASER.
POSSIBLE ORIENTATIONS OF A VOLUME

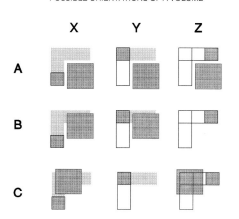

SET OPERATIONS

The concepts of inertia and specific density in conjunction with the Boolean operations of volumetric algebra become enormously powerful planning tools when applied not just to individual volumes, but also to groups of them, or related **sets** of volumes. The set of rotations of a blackboard eraser show how orientation can organize and stress a site or group of volumes. Such a matrix of operations recalls the nature of a tensor, in which the **Y** component of force **Z** in the **X** direction is one of nine similar factors. Operations on sets include rotating, moving, mirroring, scaling, even bending the whole group of elements, making linked relationships within the larger group to rapidly generate many alternative *parti* and plan options that can organize (or stress) an entire site. For example, three small volumes may find many positions in relation to a group of two large volumes, which may be rotated independently of the smaller volumes. Each of these combinations can itself be rotated into a number of positions. How many schemes would have benefited from just turning the plans over before construction! Instantly a garage at the southeast corner can be replaced by a sunny breakfast room without changing any internal relationships! This is the difference between an architect and builder!!

Poché

Spacially dense sets of volumes can "read" as one three-dimensional zone, just as solid elements like lines and planes may define groups of spaces. These zones in turn can be understood in plan or spacially as a conceptual solid. Just as planes can define and intensify the spaces between them, "conceptual solids" can also organize larger spaces. Spaces gathered together into one conceptual solid are sometimes called *poché* spaces-- from the French word for pocket. Peruzzi's plan for Palazzo Massimi (1536) uses *poché* spaces to negotiate the bend in the avenue that generates nonparallel axes for the adjacent houses of Angelo and Pietro Massimi (west and east, respectively). Note how the rooms between the two major courtyards accommodate the bend and allow the major volumes of the courtyards to preserve their orthogonal integrity. Side elements read as walls, which is especially clear in the foundation plan. Note also how the entry vestibule is symmetrical to the exterior facade but generates an asymmetrical load on the interior courtyard. Taken together, the plans reveal how sets of volumes can be organized to resolve even the most complex site conditions.

Invented Space

Consider a typical situation: an opening in an art gallery includes a table with food and drink near the entry. People generally disperse to look at the paintings on the walls, but naturally crowd at the intersection of passage and eating. What is needed is either a rearrangement of volumes or an invention of another space, a vestibule perhaps, to accommodate the additional need of mediating between the two busy areas without disrupting the fabric of the plan. Michael Graves is a master of this kind of "invented space" (a sort of "anti-*poché*"). His plans for the Hanselman House show adroit use of an inflected curve to situate the stair volume within the volume of the hall without an abrupt collision of separate zones. The relative "weight" or importance of different rooms, their varying alignments and connections, and their hierarchy of location needs all generate an interaction of volumes near each other and within an overall plan. Increasingly "elastic" plans arise as fewer possible variations of "moves" are left that "work". "Move this here, then this can go here, and these organize this, and if you just shove this over here, then there's room to get this in here..." describes the true **action** of architects, the essential animation of architecture. Design means resolving a *parti* by relocating program volumes (breadbox, entry vestibule, bedrooms, eating space, city hall) until everything fits. "Fits" means the right size and tight place for all volumes.

  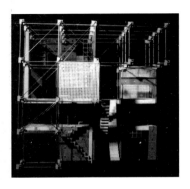

  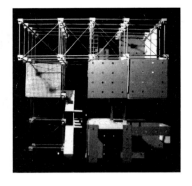

 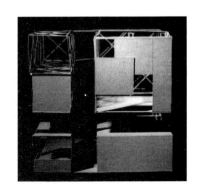 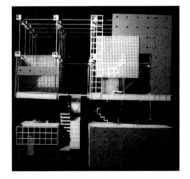

  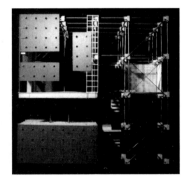

HIROYUKI TORII

DOING: *pro-position*

> *phoenix* -- a mythical bird of gorgeous plumage, fabled to be the only one of its kind, and to live five or six hundred years in the Arabian desert, after which it burnt itself to ashes on a funeral pyre and emerged from its ashes with renewed youth, to live through another cycle of years. Also, a paragon; the palm, a dry tree. (*Phoenicopter* is the flamingo.)
> *Phoebus Apollo* -- from Greek meaning bright, shining. The sun personified. Apollo is the god of light and truth, poetry and music, presiding over the Muses, hence the genius of poetry.

DYNAMICS: RETURN OF THE PHOENIX

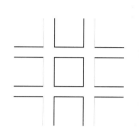

Not far from here people have heard recent reports of the return of the phoenix. Musicians are especially excited, for it is said this fabulous Bird improvises melodies, rhythms, and harmonies of incomparable beauty. Plasticians foresee a joyous spectacle, for since ancient Egypt this red-gold eagle-like solar avatar has been a reputed god of sun, light, and truth. Those who delight in structures (programmers, engineers, storytellers) also eagerly await this genius of poetry. To entice the wonderful bird to visit long enough to share in resurrecting the Muse, people have located a suitable site, a freestanding 30' x 30' plot on a flat grade. Local codes limit construction to 30' maximum height. The 40° N latitude mediterranean climate, demands some shelter from harsh sunlight and rain, but the structure need not be fully enclosed. People wish to modulate the space of the site by composing a set of volumes which will encourage the Bird to fly, people to dance, and all to sing, solo and ensemble, using the whole site to full advantage. Legend and common sense suggest an order of spaces that best encourages harmony between humankind and the phoenix. While only the Bird can fly, people seek a human equivalent to flight, a sense of free movement in all three dimensions. Both straight run and spiral stair may be used. Circulation throughout the site must access all significant spaces, including one entry and another exit from a lookout platform at the +30' elevation.

PROGRAM

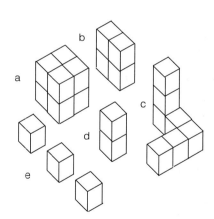

a. 1-   16 x 16 x 16' large chamber where people and bird make music together. light & dark.

b. 1-   16 x 16 x 8' roost for phoenix, vertical or horizontal, mostly dark. connect to **a** and **c**.

c. 1 -   8 x 8 x 90' continuous 3D flight run, well lit. This linear run may be thought of as 3 mutually perpendicular 8' x 8' x 30' tubes intersecting at the corners, bent or folded to fit in site.

d. 1 -   8 x 8 x 16' practice room, horizontal or vertical, for visiting musicians. connect to **a**.

e. 3 -   8 x 8 x 8' visitor galleries, offering a view to the proceedings & privacy to a small group.

f. 1 -   30' x 30' x ?? vertical reference plane to "catch" the attention of the phoenix.

The phoenix is a respectful soul, and will not fly away or pass through any opening less than 4' on a side; thus a 3' wide door and eggcrate are impenetrable to the phoenix. Program dimensions may vary ±15%, but the 30' site boundaries may not be exceeded! Volumes **a** through **e** and the articulated tartan grid still leave at least three 8' cubes left over within the cubic site. These may be useful for entry, arrival, interior lobby, or exterior terrace and patio volumes. Light indications mean *relatively* light or dark, transparent, translucent, opaque, etc. Visitors like to frame their views for cameras and are partial to squares and cubes. The contractor wants to keep insurance down, and seeks diagonals, triangles, and tetrahedrons for stability. Both musicians and the phoenix are partial to cylinders. Document your design through all necessary architectural means.

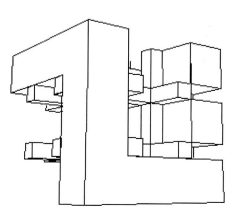

ANIMATION: In an animation of at least three successive frames show how the cube of the site has been transformed by the evolution of your *parti* to locate the program elements.

COLOR: 1. **5 Ugly Colors.** 2.**3 Ugly Colors.** 3. *Collage* ***3a.*** Free exercise. (See page 464.)

FUNCTION: Plot or construct a parabola, $y = x^2$ and a catenary, $y = a/2(e^{x/a} + e^{-x/a})$. (See page 453.)

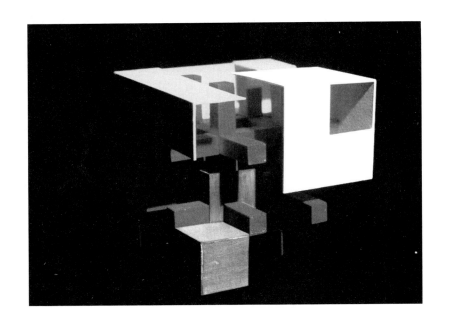

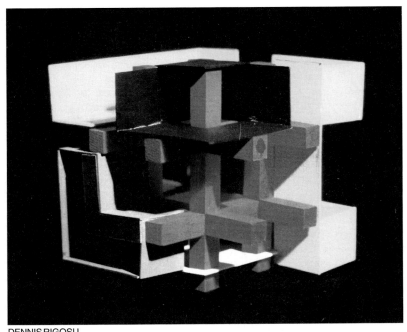

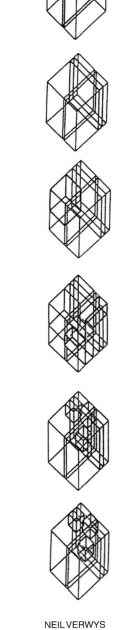

DENNIS RIGOSU

KEVIN MOLNAR

NEIL VERWYS

PROPOSITION: 1. ARRANGING PROGRAM VOLUME TO FIND *PARTI* VARIATIONS

The Return of the Phoenix presents a complex set of architectural issues. Where does a designer begin in attempting to solve them all? Let's *analyze* (take apart) the problem bit by bit to identify plastic means for finding three-dimensional configurations that accommodate all requirements. Note that there is a **Program**. Thus your first design task is to identify volumes by type, and model them at the same scale as the given site. Conveniently, your Architectonics Kit of Parts will model these volumes accurately enough for this first level *parti* study. The 1" cubes can represent the 8' cubes (and their multiples) required here. Thus one cube will equal an 8' visitor gallery, 8 cubes together can represent the 16' cube large chamber, and so on. Make 8 more 1" cubes to add to the 16 you made for the Kit of Parts, for a total of 24, to model all the volumes called for in the program. Note this is three cubes less than a full 3 x 3 x 3 = 27 cube solid. The remaining 3 cubic voids in the site are available for entry, terraces, etc. Using the Kit of Parts blocks to model the **empty solid** program volumes as filled solids at this 1/8" = 1'- 0" scale enables "a quick and dirty" modeling of manipulating already built volumes, moving them around to find promising *parti* variations easily. At this stage of the study you don't need to build the volumes; if volumes are given elements, you can get on with building relationships between them to discover viable *parti* organizations and their implications in plan and section. You may wish to polychrome the blocks according to functional identity.

Use the 1/4" x 1/4" x 3" rods from your Kit of Parts for marking zones of movement between program volumes in your models. The rods thus become circulation "spacers" which enable you to investigate the three-dimensional implications of a variety of rhythmic organizations of tartan intervals (B) between the program volumes (A): ABABA vs AABBB vs ABBAB, etc. perhaps each in a different dimension in the same model! You may prefer to use the rods as markers for major horizontal and/or vertical circulation zones, leaving empty those zones of the tartan which are not yet so important to your scheme.

You need not locate the "first" space first. You don't have to start with entry when designing a house. Le Corbusier suggests working from the inside out in all architecture. In fact the first major problem you face involves BENDING, that is fitting the 90' long flight run into confines of the 30' cube site by folding this linear volume into a form that provides the longest possible exercise run. The relationship between the two major elements, the 16' cube and the flight run, will determine the possible locations for the other program volumes. There is a **hierarchy** of decision making and location strategy: first place the volumetrically more inert (bigger, klunkier, heavier) elements, then smaller ones, and their rotations and echelons. Note that the thickness of element **f** (the plane) is left unspecified. This is for you to determine as an even more dependent variable.

Here is one method to "beat the clock." First, does everything fit? Then, start moving the volumes around (to find possible solutions to proximity demands). Note how varying specific densities of program volumes (some are easier to move, rotate, bend and fold than others) generate varying overall inertias for different *partis*. As *parti* variations arise, document them through sketches, photos, direct xerocopies of models, etc. Keep these records handy to consider the implications and potential of each configuration. For example, what might it mean to make the large chamber (**a**) nested close to the flight run, rather than as far from it as possible? What might it mean to have all the visitors galleries at the highest roof level, vs. all at grade, vs. one each at each of the three major levels, vs. one in the center of each of three exterior sides...?

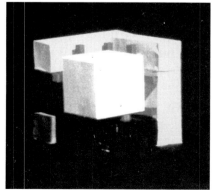

DENNIS RIGOSU

JEFF DRYER

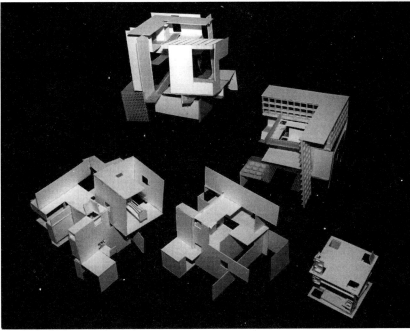

SYLVIA KUMAR

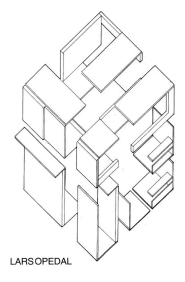

LARS OPEDAL

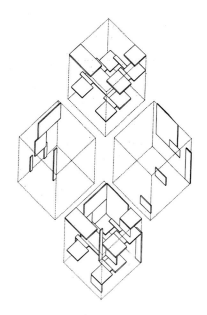

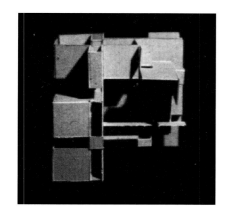

JOHN RICHARDS

PROPOSITION: 2. CLARIFYING *PARTI* THROUGH VOLUME AND SURFACE CONTINUITIES

After you have identified one or more viable *partis* through your Kit of Parts models of required program volumes, you are ready to investigate their spacial implications at another level. Now that you have located the volumes you need, you may consider how they interconnect, by establishing the continuity of volumes (which ones open onto others, permitting visual or circulation connection) and continuity of surface (how and which walls, floors, ceilings connect to others). This revisits the issue of enclosure raised in *Melody*. How many sides and corners are needed to define a volume and make it perceptible? Program spaces must be well-defined. Does this mean that at least (or more than?) three of the six sides of a cubic volume are "closed"-- opaque or impervious to movement? You may wish to model the composition of major volumes with construction paper (as in *Prelude*) in a series of studies to accompany and follow your Kit of Parts investigations. Note that two program elements, the flight run and the 16' double cube may cross the implied tartan: you can now articulate this interval in your planar models in ways that were not possible with just the solid block, either inside or on the surface. Planar models are particularly valuable in developing sectional strategies for light, view, passage and structure simultaneously. Note also that dimensions indicate required volume, not necessarily precise shape. Thus a cube of 8' (= 512 cu.ft.) could instead be a cylinder of about 512 cu.ft., roughly 9' diameter by 8' altitude. However, while first using the Kit of Parts to position *parti* elements, you may certainly consider the cube to be a valid general notation for required program volume.

This is the chance to study **circulation** with even greater detail and care. As you learned in the *Harmony* study, if adequate space isn't provided for getting from one place to another, given program volumes may be compromised. Plastic integrity (an incomplete reading of a cube through the loss of a corner chunk) as well as usable floor area may both be lost. Proportions and any sense of spacial repose may be ruined as one kind of space (the program volume as end condition) is violated by another (circulation space as through condition). Thus there arises the need for space for movement between program volumes, normally called circulation, which may account for about 5 to 30% of a building, depending on location, use, code and safety requirements. A building is considered efficiently designed when no more than about 15% of its total area is given over to circulation in the form of corridors, stair and elevator towers, lobbies, vestibules, etc. In addition to the corridors and stairs provided for literal human movement, this project demands that people encounter the entire site in three dimensions, like a jungle gym. This is the origin of the *poetic* need for circulation. You may wish to continue your polychrome studies for identifying related program volumes and/or surfaces.

Make your planar models to study preferred *parti(s)* at 1/4" = 1'- 0" with stiff file folder or construction paper to identify opaque and transparent planes that define surface and solid continuities/discontinuities (as walls, doors, floors, stairs, etc.) Thus do program solids become void and mass to make volumes. Now consider bending, folding, and shear for planes as well as volumes. Note that folding does not equal rotation. Certain sets of operations are not commutative: that is fold A, then rotate B+C may not equal fold B then rotate C+A. A new round of 3D "beat the clock" may suggest "if this plane goes here, then these voids are left, and if I rotate the surfaces to another orientation around the volume, then entry could be here...." Refer to your paper constructions as a guide for understanding the architectural implications of Cubism and Purism, as in the Prelude studies. Document these new planar *parti* models with architectural plans, sections, elevations, axonometrics, perspectives, as appropriate (freehand but to scale is fine). Consider the results and repeat the entire cycle.

MARK SULTANA

LARS OPEDAL

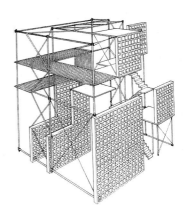

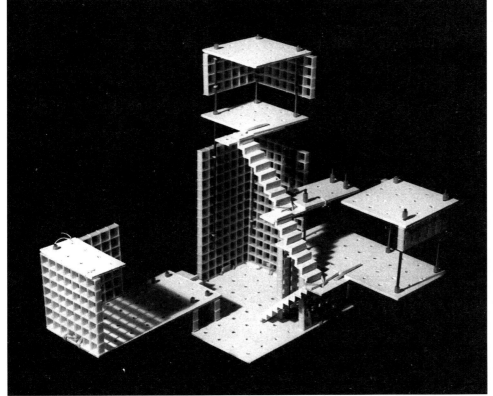

STEVE KRONER

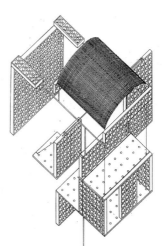

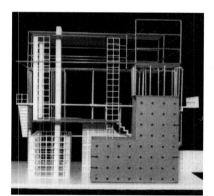

CHARLES WILLIS

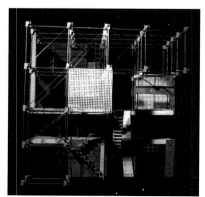

BRIAN MIEDZINSKI

HIROYUKI TORII

PROPOSITION: 3. ORDERING PLASTIC CONTINUITIES BY ARCHITECTURAL MEANS

Now you are ready to use your BAG OF TRICKS to complete your investigation of the implications of preferred *partis* through available architectural means. These in include not only available **materials**, including ABS and brass struts, mesh, eggcrate and pegboard, joints and stairs; but also available **non-material** elements, such as light and dark, proportion, scale, circulation, and orientation. Thus do program solids become void and mass to make volumes; thus do volumes become space. Recall what you learned investigating plastic and elastic masses while improvising tensegrities for *Melody*. You may begin by trying to build outward from floor, ceiling, and wall planes while defining program volumes; but also try to find ways to make coplanar elements and/or sets of volumes as a single design unit. From Kit of Parts cube-and-rods *parti* studies at 1/8" scale, to planar studies at 1/4" scale, and now to the materials studies at 1/2" scale (each to equal 1' - 0"), there is a **hierarchy** of decision making and location strategy. First program solids are located and oriented according to their possible rotations and echelons. Second, perforations for light and movement are located to establish planar and volumetric identities and continuities. Third, details of structure, material, scale, rhythm, interval, and illumination are elaborated, always referring to the studies at the previous stages to evaluate the clarity and direction of the ongoing investigations.

You may make quick diagrams in plan, section, and axonometric, using a code of colors to denote various materials. Note how useful plan and section drawings are in revealing relationships between structure, circulation, and light. You may also wish to develop a "quick axonometric" method for studying the implications of your three-dimensional ideas through drawing. (See the Visual Glossary for more on these.) These are good ways to develop strategies for using the various scales and spacial grids implied by the available materials.

Your means of expression are now orchestral. You can communicate architectural ideas through volume, surface, and material, or any combination of them. You can contrast symmetry in *parti* with asymmetry in material expression, make the flight run and circulation relatively dark, compared to visitor galleries, or make the north side of all public volumes opaque, etc. Now the composition of lines, planes, and joints may help develop an organization of spaces of different conceptual densities, as the plans to the left demonstrate. Of particular interest is the potential contrast between foreground figure and gathered-- between volume as foreground figure and volume as background context. You may wish, via the Bag of Tricks, to explore for yourself the possible role of *poché* in architecture today. Is it possible to reverse perception of mass and void to "enclose" the undefined volumes and leave programmed volumes as "open" space? (See Project 3 in *Architectonics*.)

You will discover in addition that construction assembly can become a major constraint in design, whether calculating how to lift air-handling equipment 60 or more stories into the air, or more directly, figuring out where to find a third hand to hold the two ends of spar while wrapping a rubber band around it and a nearby eggcrate plane. As structural design and construction elements become increasingly lightweight, finding enough inertial mass to anchor a structure against wind, earthquake, etc. emerges as a significant problem in building design. You will discover how valuable friction and inertial mass can be. The truly elegant dynamic architectural solution will reveal an order and sequence of volumes and construction that enhances the programmatic and plastic intentions of the architect. Just as the whole structure might become an instrument, well-tuned and vibrating in harmony with music made here, so too might the volumes work in concert to reveal poetry in even the most ordinary events, like climbing stairs or entering a building.

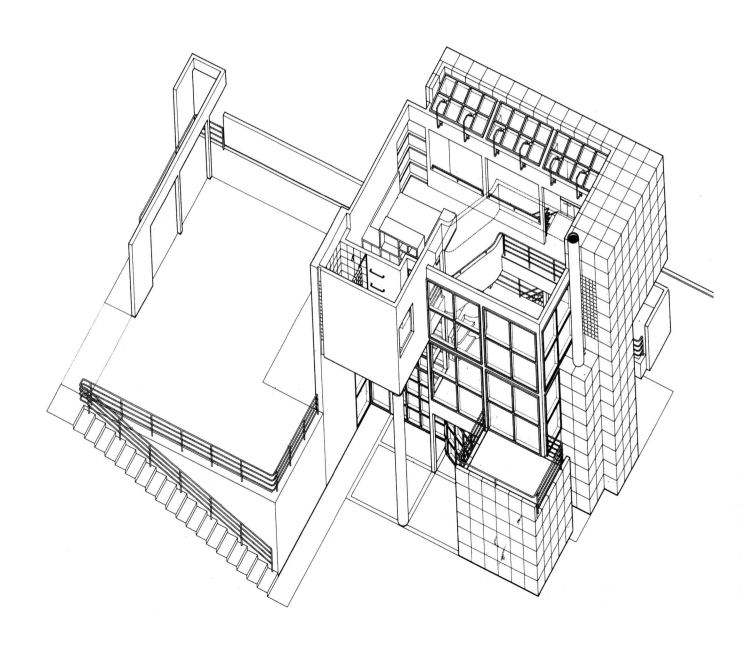

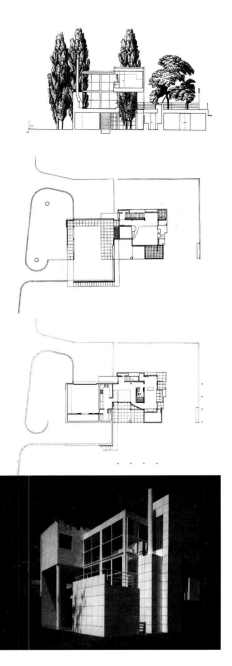

CITY IN A HOUSE

"The audacity of the square moldings; austerity and nobility."
Le Corbusier on the Parthenon

The Gridded Foam of Space

Foam is a form of gridded space, bubbles packed in such a way as to reveal fracture lines through the entire aggregate, but it is a grid by default. One may find a most intense example of orthogonal resonance at Schipol Airport in Holland, that land rescued inch by inch from the North Sea through an ingenious system of dikes of muck placed in the sea to encircle an area of water and isolate it from the whole sea. Windmills atop the dikes are driven by the high sea-land edge air pressure gradient we call offshore breezes. These windmills turn the archimedean screws attached to them in such a way as to slowly lift the isolated water out of the diked zone and pour it back into the open sea. The result of this ingenuity and patience is new land called *polder*-- eventually. In Schipol's vast lobby for arriving passengers, I noted that the structural span was built on a column grid of about 30 to 40 feet. The columns were square in plan. The floor was covered with very small square tiles, less than an inch across. Without fail, the lines of grout of the tiles aligned with the edges of the column faces! Not a square inch was taken for granted in that space! Walking through the city of Amsterdam, one may *feel* and see that same precision in the layers of space between the street curbs and door sills of the many beautifully scaled urban row houses. Each face of stoop, door frame, jamb, and infil panel aligned with whole sets of brick soffits, corbeled ridges, and balconies at upper levels. Mondrian was a naturalist- - a realist painter from the passionate yet cartesian geometry (land measure) of Holland.

Close-packing and orthogonal resonance

Le Corbusier wrote "un maison, une palais". Why then not make a simple house also be a palace in the grandeur of its life, introducing a sense of the sacredness of everyday life through the integrated order of its sunlight, space, and greenery? Look at Richard Meier's Giovanitti House on these two pages, and see how things keep aligning. This sense of nothing wasted when it comes to an economy of means for all necessary masses and volumes is perhaps the greatest measure of the real modesty an essential value of competent architecture. It looks so easy! How easy it is to overlook the tremendous accomplishments of architects like Meier and Palladio, who all too often to the beginning architecture student seem "boring" because nothing is unusual, or wild. Of course not--nothing is out of place! Every solid, filled and empty, is measured, weighed, and balanced in relationship to every other measurable element. Only then can relationships themselves reveals new sets of propositions, balance, harmonies. In this house the bending is not literal but concerns the way the order of the space is folded. The vernacular village architecture of Italian hilltowns or Aegean island towns may have developed as a "loose fit", a tolerance of things sort of lining up, but with a little extra slack between-- not quite square, not quite packed. But as space becomes more densely and intensely developed (more valuable in terms of real estate), we find that the skills of architects as knowledgeable and inspired managers of volumetric combinations become more in demand. This house is a place of many local regions, working up from the inside out-- engaging the opportunities of the terrain and landscape at every level. Levels interlock in double and triple height volumes, modulating the entire structure of the space, ultimately at many scales and all at once. As in the complex volumes of a biological organism, we find here a richness of order and invention, of expectation and surprise, that generates an inexhaustible resonance of echoing and reinforcing proportional and plastic relationships, belying the naive notion that square is "boring."

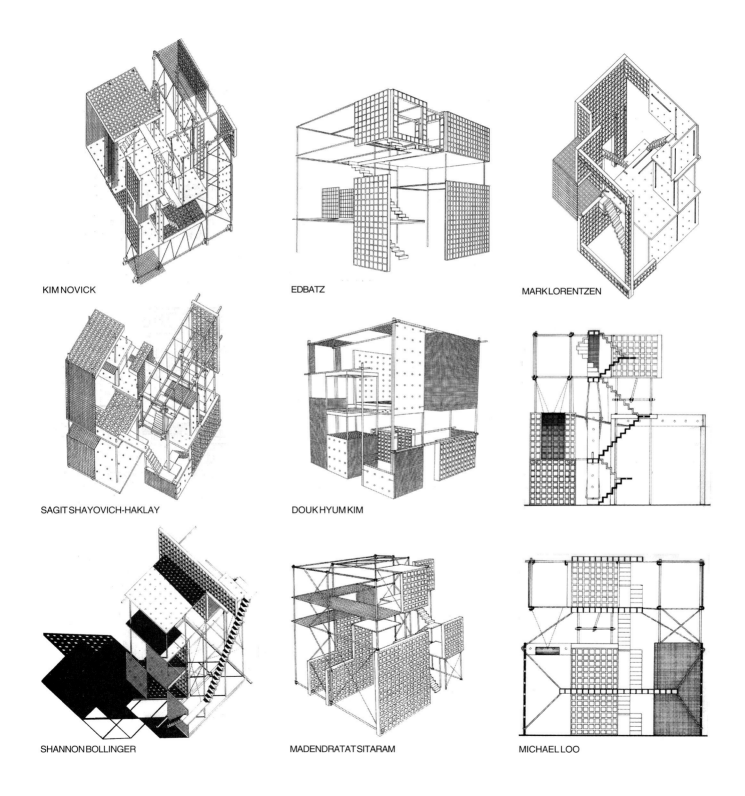

KIM NOVICK

ED BATZ

MARK LORENTZEN

SAGIT SHAYOVICH-HAKLAY

DOUK HYUM KIM

SHANNON BOLLINGER

MADENDRATAT SITARAM

MICHAEL LOO

REFLECTING

"Give me a place to put a lever and I can move the world." Archimedes

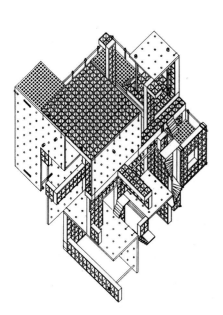

The classical origins of architecture, from Euclid's Elements and Archimedes' studies of hydraulics (eureka!) to Vitruvius' last of his *Ten Books on Architecture* which discusses machines and "the elements of motion", may give us some comfort that the "radical" approach of this work, *Dynamics*, is actually part of a very old and venerable tradition. Thus we are pleased to claim its radical nature-- in the true sense of that word, which means "root." Roots dig deep through unyielding earth, and as they diverge they provide the anchor which enables a tree to grip its place in its forest-high spacetime field, perhaps for centuries.

We move through buildings and landscapes in both straight lines and slaloms. When we are in a hurry we go straight from here to there. When we "take time" to stop and smell the roses, to explore the byways that life has to offer, we "serpentine" (in Peter Falk's immortal words in the movie *The In-laws*.) The complex, multi-leveled plan of Le Corbusier's Carpenter Art Center seems to support such conjectures about the nature of the human condition. The bending or even buckling of the Carpenter Art Center between the orthogonal of the Fogg Art Museum and Quincy Street restates the rotated grid of Mass. Ave, while the warped ramp resolves into a frontal and directly piercing tube of space through the central cube of the building, through "front" facades on both sides of the building. Architect and poet John Hejduk finds many profound speculations in this architecture, as he discusses in his essay "Out of Space and Into Time".

Program is a noun, naming a space; the action of relationship between volumes is a verb; and the quality of a volume is an adjective. Vectors measure the magnitude and direction of a force. Tensors measure how vectors transform volumes and can describe the interaction between stress, strain, and the curvature of space. Tensors, like sets, can be denoted by a matrix of values and operations. Relaxed/tensed, hard/soft warm/cool are qualities learned through comparison of sense impressions. Touch is a phenomenon of both gravity and spirit, anchoring and elevating us. The work of an honest plastician/sculptor/constructor, like Calatrava, Chillida, or Snelson reminds us that what matters in a dynamic order of volumes is not superficial shape, but rather the presence of *sympathy*-- literally *feeling with* the stresses and strains that develop in any organism in a field of forces. For architects, sympathy with and for program volumes can help resolve the order of an inhabited institution. *Harmony* showed how one volume may read simultaneously as part of at least two orders of space. But many harmonies may exist within a site where multiple volume relationships can modulate an ensemble of volumes. A musical concerto builds harmonies between solo instruments and the total ensemble. Purism's shared contours, overlapping layers, and fluid exchange between mass and void suggest the potential for Concerto in plastic terms.

READINGS

Benjamin, Walter. "The Work of Art in the Age of Mechanical Reproduction"
Calder, Alexander. *Calder's Universe*
Deleuze, Gilles. *The Fold: Leibniz and the Baroque*
Hejduk, John. *Mask of Medusa*
Kopp, Anatole. *Town and Revolution*
Le Corbusier. *Creation is a Patient Search*
Rowe, Colin. "Mathematics of the Ideal Villa"
Ryckwert, Joseph. *The Necessity of Artifice*
Wright, Frank Lloyd. *Writings and Buildings,*
Wasmuth and *Wendigen* editions of Wright's early work

ALAN SAUBERMAN

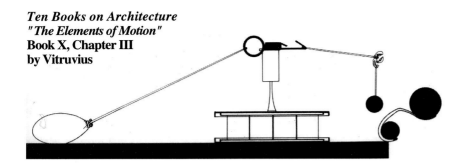

THE ELEMENTS OF MOTION

1. I have briefly set forth what I thought necessary about the principles of hoisting machines. In them two different things, unlike each other, work together, as elements of their motion and power, to produce these effects. One of them is the right line, which the Greeks term *enqeia*; the other is the circle, which the Greeks call *kuklwth*; but in point of fact, neither rectilinear without circular motion, nor revolutions, without rectilinear motion, can accomplish the raising of loads. I will explain this, so that it may be understood.

2. As centres, axles are inserted into the sheaves, and these are fastened in the blocks; a rope carried over the sheaves, drawn straight down, and fastened to a windlass, causes the load to move upward from its place as the handspikes are turned. The pivots of this windlass, lying as centres in right lines in its socket-pieces, and the handspikes inserted in its holes, make the load rise when the ends of the windlass revolve in a circle like a lathe. Just so, when an iron lever is applied to a weight which a great many hands cannot move, with the fulcrum, which the Greeks call *υπομοξλιον*, lying as a centre in a right line under the lever, and with the tongue of the lever placed under the weight, one man's strength, bearing down upon the head of it, heaves up the weight.

3. For, as the shorter fore part of the lever goes under the weight from the fulcrum that forms the centre, the head of it, which is farther away from that centre, on being depressed, is made to describe a circular movement, and thus by pressure brings to an equilibrium the weight of a very great load by means of a few hands. Again, if the tongue of an iron lever is placed under a weight, and its head is not pushed down, but, on the contrary, is heaved up, the tongue, supported on the surface of the ground, will treat that as the weight, and the edge of the weight itself as the fulcrum. Thus, not so easily as by pushing down, but by motion in the opposite direction, the weight of the load will nevertheless be raised. If, therefore, the tongue of a lever lying on a fulcrum goes too far under the weight, and its head exerts its pressure too near the centre, it will not be able to elevate the weight, nor can it do so unless, as described above, the length of the lever is brought to equilibrium by the depression of its head.

4. This may be seen from the balances that we call steelyards. When the handle is set as a centre close to the end from which the scale hangs, and the counterpoise is moved along towards the other arm of the beam, shifting from point to point as it goes farther or even reaches the extremity, a small and inferior weight becomes equal to a very heavy object that is being weighed, on account of the equilibrium that is due to the levelling of the beam. Thus, as it withdraws from the centre, a small and comparatively light counterpoise, slowly turning the scale, makes a greater amount of weight rise gently upwards from below.

5. So, too, the pilot of the biggest merchantman, grasping the steering oar by its handle, which the Greeks call *οιαξ*, and with one hand bringing it to the turning point, according to the rules of his art, by pressure about a

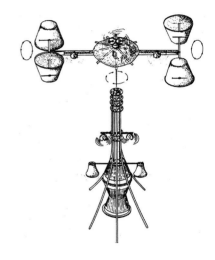

TODD O'CONNELL

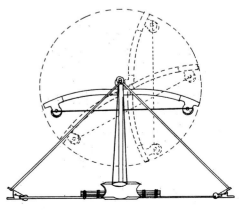

PAUL PELLICANA

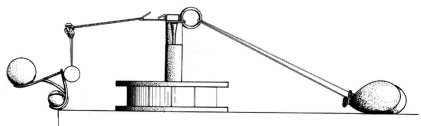

MICHAEL SORANO

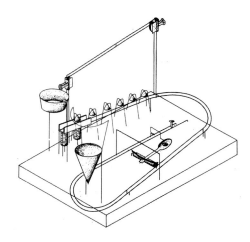

centre, can turn the ship, although she may be laden with a very large or even enormous burden of merchandise and provisions. And when her sails are set only halfway up the mast, a ship cannot run quickly; but when the yard is hoisted to the top, she makes much quicker progress, because then the sails get the wind, not when they are too close to the level of the mast, which represents the centre, but when they have moved farther away from it to the top.

6. As a lever thrust under a weight is harder to manage, and does not put forth its strength, if the pressure is exerted at the center, but easily raises the weight when the extreme end of it is pushed down, so sails that are only halfway up have less effect, but when they get farther away from the centre, and are hoisted to the very top of the mast, the pressure at the top forces the ship to make greater progreess, though the wind is no stronger but just the same. Again, take the case of oars, which are fastened to the tholes by loops, -- when they are pushed forward and drawn back by hand, if the ends of the blades are at some distance from the centre, the oars foam with the waves of the sea and drive the ship forward in a straight line with a mightly impulse, while her prow cuts through the rare water.

7. And when the heaviest burdens are carried on poles by four or six porters at a time, they find the centres of balance at the very middle of the poles, so that, by distributing the dead weight of the burden according to a definitely proportioned division, each labourer may have an equal share to carry on his neck. For the poles, from which the straps for the burden of the four porters hang, are marked off at their centers by nails, to prevent the straps from slipping to one side. If they shift beyond the mark at the centre, they weigh heavily upon the place to which they have come nearer, like the weight oof a steelyard when it moves from the point of equilibrium towards the end of the weighing apparatus.

8. In the same way, oxen have an equal draught when their yoke is adjusted at its middle by the yokestrap to the pole. But when their strength is not the same, and the stronger outdoes the other, the strap is shifted so as to make one side of the yoke longer, which helps the weaker ox. Thus in the case of both poes and yokes, when the straps are not fastened at the middle, but at one side, the farther the strap moves from the middle, the shorter it makes one side, and the longer the other. So, if both ends are carried round in circles, using as a centre the point to which the strap has been brought, the longer end will describe a larger, and the shorter end a smaller circle.

9. Just as smaller wheels move harder and with greater difficulty than larger ones, so, in the case of the poles and the yokes, the parts where the interval from the centre to end is less, bear down hard upon the neck, but where the distance from the same centre is greater, they ease the burden both for draught and carriage. As in all these cases motion is obtained by means of right lines at the centre and by circles, so also farm wagons, ballistae, pressbeams, and all other machines produce the results intended, on the same principles, by turning about a rectilnear axis and by the revolution of a circle.

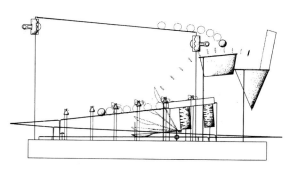

GREG ISOLA

OUT TIME AND INTO SPACE
by John Hejduk, from *Mask of Medusa*

Art has that particular irreverence towards accurate chronological sequence. It hops back and forwards upon the frame of time, playing hide and seek with the Historian's sense of propriety. The perennial stylistic arguments which caused the investigator concern will only bring forth mild amusement to the creator and critic of form. The event is important as a relationship to other events, particular not to time but to space. Le Corbusier's Visual Arts Center at Harvard proves the staying power of a single idea; the idea of cubist space in Architecture.

The very profundity of this piece of visual metaphysics brings into question all that went before. The Carpenter Center can either be liked or disliked-- this is irrelevant: the fact is the proposed ideas can not be ignored; they can be viewed squarely and understood. The questions and arguments become inexhaustible; they are like the major thesis - the thesis of simultaneity. Simultaneity has always been a complex phenomenon with reference to the retina's capability of maintaining hold over kaleidoscopic relationships. The mind may be more prone to accept an ambiguous basis, yet when operating upon single stills, the eye is like a camera: the moment the same image is clicked twice and interposed on the same frame an interesting effect can be obtained although in the process the initial form becomes blurred and might be irrevocably lost.

The human body, its auxiliary senses and the capability of cerebral workings cause architecture to be involved in the movement and dynamics of space. One cannot approach the Center without unleashing the ghosts and spectres of the visual revolution which occurred at the early part of our century. Old doors are forced open admitting Picasso, Braque, Leger, Gris, Mondrian -- all the known protagonists and ancestral impregnators.

To begin with, the disposition of building to site may seem erratic, uncalled for, in opposition to the hierarchical laws of good taste, particularly when the work is tipped and skewed at an acute angle to the sensibility of right-angle relationships of the two streets and two buildings it is enclosed within. Surely, most of the buildings on this street had the good sense to present their best facade forward. Why does the Frenchman insist upon disturbing our puritanical attitudes? Is it effrontery or whimsy? It is neither; it is a reinforcing for all concerned. The sense is on two planes of operation, the external and the internal.

The external ordinarily precedes the internal; here at the Center, they are co-joined to the same organic system.

There might never be a compatibility of Cubist vision wth New England decorum. The problem was not how to relate them, but how to disengage them, permitting each its sovereignty. This is what Le Corbusier has accomplished; not only did he placate his neighbors, he also used them in the scheme of things. A system of coexistence was devised through the skewing of the Center. This was a secondary reason, the primary being involved with a Juan Gris-like disposition of 90 - 60 - 45 - 30 degree griddings and their spatial implications.

A square, when tipped at an angle of 45 degrees, loses its previous static orientation. The four corners immediately become charged and filled with maximum tension. Piet Mondrian was aware of this phenomenon. Le Corbusier is cognizant of the tension ramification. When Le Corbusier turned the major central block upon an angled axis, the corners simply become taut and activated. The attention given to these points fixes the disorientation.

As a scholasticist, Le Corbusier realized it is to simple just to present the thesis. The anti-thesis had to be propagated; thus the curvilinear shapes at the periphery, juxtaposed in shear, act as wingscrews to the central configuration (Figure 1a,b,c). From the exterior these bulbous locks compress the central block and reestablish an implied right-angle relationship to their associates. The split, sheared, turned about mandolin is the external transition between two combatants and smoothes the way for the acceptability of the transient intruder. These are the social soothers of the retina. An observer's eye is constantly ricochetting off the outer surfaces of the Fogg Museum and the Harvard Faculty Club back again to the Center. The eye never attemps to relate the tw-- it never had the time-- it must focus on one or the other, but never on both together.

At first the somewhat agitated contour of the building can come as a shock to the student of our long-ago rationalist. Upon closer look we see the old principle of contained field in operation. The rectilinear figure is completed by implication. The beginning points of the major entry ramp make this necessary completion. The generating nucleus of the

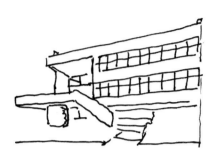

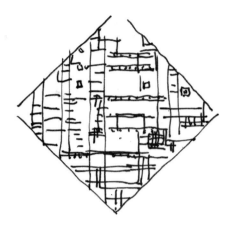

cubist scheme is the inserted Z bar which moves through the center providing for centrifugal acceleration. The ramp is in three-dimensional torque; it is the aorta of the heart upon which the breathing depends. Like a bicycle pedal, when pressure is brought down upon the terminal ends, the whole building starts to revolve and spin. The curved blocks are the governors and screws-- tightening, loosening- the runaway spacial fantasy.

The site is finished off in a network of walks and warped grade planes. The axial views upon the ramp terminate--one to a Jacksonian portal; the other to a Bostonian misfit. The way for the central theme is now prepared.

In order to fully understand the implication of spatial views incorporated within the Center, one must look at the workings of the Cubist canvas; in particular, the synthesization by Juan Gris. The architectural ramifications are answers to the new Center's mysteries. Before entering this sacred field, it is in order to say that the ideas scattered throughout the Center have been encased within a time-bomb set in Paris during the early 1920s, and finally exploited at Cambridge, Massachusetts in 1963. The detonator did not realize that another bomb was fired with a smaller, stronger and more devastating discharge in the form of Le Corbusier's Villa Garches, 1927 (Figure 3), and Mondrian's *Victory Boogie-Woogie* 1943 (Figure 4). Perhaps it is necessary to throw bombs back into time in order to affect a future liberation. Since the first setting, the dialectic has continued with painstaking exercises and fulfillment upon the canvases of Piet Mondrian.

Le Corbusier is well aware of the Cubist and the Neo-Plasticist points of view. His architecture is the pendulum between the two poles of spatial magnetism. Today the weight seems in favor of the Cubist vision, although the seduction of the spartan, flattened, taut shallow depth formulation holds its grasp. Villa Garches was the pinnacle of the Cartesian instigator; it remains the classic contender in the new world of architectural space.

The Cyclops of brute force is again challenging. The stimuli for further spatial conflicts exist.

The composition entitled *Guitar, Glasses and Bottle* by Juan Gris 1914 (Figure 2) will be used as a prototype for investigation. *Violin and Newspaper* 1917 (Figure 5) can be equally viewed as a generator.

The field comes first. As with most Cubist canvases, the field worked upon is usually directional; it either has a vertical or horizontal preference, perpendicular to the observer's vision. In the above paintings the field is vertically disposed. Rarely did the Cubist use a square canvas. The foundation had a priori directional orientation. In contrast, the canvases of Mondrian are usually square, a non-directional field. His first bias is one of equilibrium. The Carpenter Center favors the Cubist vision of the field.

The major planimetric direction of the building is reinforced by the ramp and structural bay disposition. The long bay runs parallel to the ramp; the short bay perpendicular - therefore introducing compressed spacing and tighter penetration. (Figure 1b)

Guitar, Glasses and Bottle, as well as *Violin and Newspaper*, are split through the middle, with a vertical and horizontal axis dividing the canvas into quadrants

The shapes and figures congesting the inner field energize a high concentration of action towards the intersecting axis, compressing the central space. The compression eases off as the eye is lead to the periphery of the canvas. It is as when a stone is thrown into the water - upon disturbance of the surface and depth, the radial forces from the point of contact outwards diminish in intensity with the distance from the nucleus of impact. Le Corbusier's plan of the Carpenter Center is presented in a similar manner, with one important difference. This difference is the edge compressor which imposes itself on the free flow of space regarding the peripheric boundaries. Le Corbusier splits the scheme along the longitudinal axis creating a high concentration of the center of the form through the use of the ramp, the major entry ways and the vertical horizontal circulations. As one moves away from the necessary biological nuclei and organs, the space flows generally uninterrupted until it arrives at the edges where again it is activated through the forms of curved walls, 60 - 30 accordion-like brise-soleil and the horizontal syncopation of the vertical mullions. The peripheric tension is homage and acknowledgment to the Neo-Plasticist contribution. The push-back of the forces to the center establishes the spatial fluctuations.

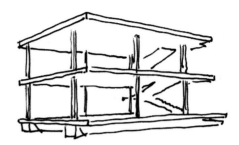

A plan is a section-- and when sections are put together they make space. If Le Corbusier is interested in the phenomenon of the flat plane in plan, it could follow that the vertical sections might operate in a similar way. Upon close look, one finds that they do. Le Corbusier is involved with the coordinates of spatial composing. As the plan, there is a high concentration of elements in the center of the sectional configuration. The elongated slot through which the ramp passes is the locking device for the two curvilinear volumes. (Figure 1c). These volumes act in shear, pulling laterally in opposite directions towards the periphery. These are capped and compressed in a sandwich vise of the upper and lower floors, applying additional pressure to the centralization of space. The same generator works both in plan and section. Given all the necessary plans and sections, the cubic configuration is set into motion driving the whole organism around the field of space.

The constant rhythmical modulation of grid is a stabilizing frame upon which counterpoint is played. It is elemental theme and supporting structure. Painter and architect are forced to recognize the ordering principle of the intersections of grid. Objects relate in various ways to its dictatorial insistence. They can be outside of it, within it, on top of it-- unlimited variance and possibility are inherent about it.

In Gris's *Guitar, Glasses and Bottle*, the use of grid is most pronounced. Two major systems of gridding are incorporated; one at right angles upon the picture plane, the other at 45 degrees. The meshing of the two grids produces innumerable combinations of figure readings. There also is implied a third gridding of 60 - 30 degrees.

The subtle play of the shaded, shaped modulated curves and warps creates the necessary concentrations which explode the initial smaller griddings into larger more central squares and diamonds. The smaller, minor spatial griddings have quite simply expanded into larger, major griddings through the use of curved figure imposition and intensity. One is approaching the realm of the infinite. Le Corbusier does not abandon the three dimensionality of architectural space, but he does insist that the observer become involved with the geometric rules of the game. The visual-cerebral mechanism must be generated for total effect take place. In this respect the intention can be measured as to its validity. The structural frame plays the inquisitor. The Center's col-

umn-slab system of construction was stated in all its purity in the Domino House drawing of 1914 (Figure 6).

Since that inception, Le Corbusier rarely forgets it and continually is the user. As in most pavilion-loft structures, architectural containment of space is at best problematic. Planes encloses space, lines elaborate; planes emphasize, lines dissolve. The structural bay mentioned is directional, yet square bay readings are possible. Every third column of the lateral spacing completes a square with its opposite number. Le Corbusier wants it both ways. The prime longitudinal reading states first direction, but a more subtle secondary central reading of the square exists. Similar readings found upon the Juan Gris canvases are again discovered in architecture-- in a way more diabolical because the idea is running loose in a three-dimensional field.

The shape of the structural columns is round, indicating a centrifugal force and multidirectional whirl. In section the columns are at times caught by the floor slabs, at other times they bypass the slabs and rise uninterrupted through two stories. A piston-plunger, compression-expansion of column lines is affected. Not only are the column lengths modulated, so are their diameters; if the observer takes the same 360 degree course about the columns, he will enter the realm of dynamic and static kaleidoscopic relationships. A 90 degree view parallel to the columns proposes an ordered, static system of space except for the before mentioned peripheric interaction. The observed can now begin the trek of the arc with the next stop at a 60 degree point, then a 45 degree, and finally back to 90 degrees. The spatial views between these fixed geometric points and lines are filled with a conglomerate of fluctuating columnar tensions. First, when one looks into the kaleidoscope, he sees an ordered system. The box is the shaken, the elements move into dynamic relationships and upon deceleration are fixed into a new order. After each shake new spatial configurations take place, the added gifts are the outside walls, bellow-like, compressing and expanding the linear formulation. Still, through this labyrinth one is always conscious of the centralizing aspect of the scheme.

It is hard to believe that anyone could have conceived all these levels of spatial consciousness. It is even harder to believe that they were not so conceived. The above has attempted to explain the technical feats in

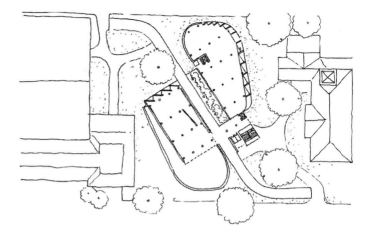

space accomplished by one of the masters of geometric figures. In a way, Le Corbusier has not been able to detach himself from the Cubist tradition; more cannot be expected from one man's vision. Our heritage is shown and our future can only be anticipated. The technical competence and accurate finish needed to strengthen the theoretical arguments are impeccable. The ease with which one floats through the building is like being on a magic carpet. It takes all things possible. Le Corbusier's solution to clear, defined central circulation is classical.

Unfulfilled promises of past drawings haunt the Center's halls. The vast spaces of the Palace of the Soviets (1931) and the grand stair of Rio de Janeiro ministry project (1936) are unveiled in a more modest way. The decorative use of color will only sadden the purest of color structure. One can feel secure that all the other promises have been kept.

Of course the old dogmatic arguments between Van Doesburg and Mondrian are again unearthed with the erection of the Center. One imagines Van Doesburg would have been excited and elated were he to be here, and perhaps Mondrian would be interested, impressed and skeptical. The very placement of the diagonal on the canvas caused the breakup of the two De Stijlists. Mondrian's answer to the diagonal was delivered with the tipping of the maintenance of right angle relationships. This brings up one of the strange feelings of uneasiness upon being lured into the Center. The sense of being twisted and torqued upon the rack of Architecture is a new one. The tension-compression, the push-pull may have therapeutic value to the docile; the question remains, at what point do the harmonic fluctuations crack causing dissolution and failure to the spatial organism?

Mondrian's concern for the spatial-architectural dilemma was prophetic. Painting can be purely abstract expression. In painting reality is established with the limited space of the canvas which can be completely determined by planes. In sculpture and in architecture, the work is a composition of volumes. Volumes have a naturalistic expression. Seen, however, as a multitude of planes, sculpture and architecture can be an abstract manifestation. Moving around or within a rectangular building or object, it can be seen as two-dimensional, for our time abandons the static vision of the past. By moving around, the impression of a two-dimensional aspect is directly followed by that of

another two-dimensional aspect. The expression of the structure, form and color of the planes can have a continuous mutual relationship which produces a true image of the whole . This fact shows the intrinsic unity of painting, sculpture and architecture.

The conception of a mobile viewpoint appeared first in early Cubism. Already in that tendency, the need for a truer and more concrete expression was felt. But this Cubism intended to express volume. Intrinsically it remained naturalistic. Abstract Art attempts to destroy the corporeal expression of volume, to be a reflection of the universal aspect of reality.

Skepticism can cause the martyrdom of an idea; inquiry can cause its liberation. Civilized memory may be preferable to barbaric sensibility. If the ordinary mortal of architectural endeavors had to conceive works in such a complex manner there would probably be fewer buildings-- on the other hand perhaps better ones would be imagined.

It appears that the revolutionary tribunal has relaxed its stringent laws as regards the encyclicals of purism, in favor of a more tolerant acceptance of spatial views. When the laws are not enforced, neither are the forms. Perfect works not only become impossible, they become undesirable. When the pursuit of the ideal is cut off, so is the bloodstream of an organic unity-- where flow the genes of codified space. When everything is permitted, limits are in jeopardy-- objects then enter the realm of the celestial float.

The joy of the remembrance of things past. Fernand Leger returned to painting figures incorporating all the principles of the new spatial discoveries. Braque returned to flowers. Le Corbusier, in a similar way, returns to some of his early triumphs with a more poignant commitment to expanding space. If Harvard Visual Arts Center had arrived prior to Villa Garches, all the armchair historians could rest unmoved, for " this was not the natural order of events ?" The fact that it postdates Garches by some 30 years can only prove the quirks of time. Whereas Garches heralded the promise of things to come, the Center postpones them. Whereas Garches appealed to the proper elite, the Harvard Center appeals to the improper common; it is, to put it bluntly, "as you like it." Some won't, some will.

CHARLES WILLIS

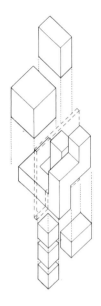

JORGE PORTA

CONCERTO: *WEAVING*

BEING

"I was born by the sea and I have noticed that all the great events of my life have taken place by the sea. My first idea of movement, of the dance, certainly came from the rhythm of the waves." Isadora Duncan

WAVE

Grooving clam shell,
        streaks through marble,
        sweeping down ponderosa pine bark-scale
        rip-cut tree grain
                sand- dunes, lava
                        flow

Wave   wife.
        woman--- wyfman---
"veiled;   vibrating;   vague"
    sawtooth ranges pulsing;
                veins on the back of the hand.

Forkt out: birdsfoot-alluvium
                wash

        great dunes rolling
Each inch rippld, every grain a wave.

Leaning against sand cornices til they blow away

        --- wind, shake
        stiff thorns of cholla, ocotillo
        sometimes I get stuck in thickets---

Ah, trembling spreading radiating wyf
                racing zebra
        catch me and fling me wide
To the dancing grain of things
                of my mind!

        Gary Snyder

Making waves

Once we start, why don't we stop? How do we wake after sleep? What keeps us going? Movement is preserved in a material system as *potential energy*. Like the pendulum that continues to swing past its low point and the roller coaster that drives past the first valley in its track, released masses in any elastic system may carry motion temporarily beyond the resting point. A pendulum bob transfers the potential energy it holds at the peak of its arc into maximum kinetic energy as it falls through the low point of resting stable equilibrium. The kinetic energy, or motion, carries the pendulum on to its opposite peak, where potential energy is again maximum and kinetic energy becomes zero-- and the pendulum actually stops for an instant. The pendulum continues to *vibrate* until dissipative forces like friction bring it to rest. Movement back and forth in a medium makes *waves* and can create a pattern of oscillation or vibration called **simple harmonic motion**. A stone dropped in a quiet pool compresses the water beneath it. But the hollow wake of trailing air bubbles quickly fills with in-rushing water. This alternation of compression and tension creates waves, visible on the surface as concentric ripples radiating from the splash. Newton's Third Law of Motion declares that "every action has an equal and opposite reaction". Applied force not only tends to move a thing, but also creates stress and strain on its internal structure, which reacts by tending to return to its original state. Impact creates recurring rebound until energy is dissipated as waves of sound, light, or heat. The moon stretches the spacetime outside earth, creating the tides which slosh the liquid oceans across the face of the planet in a month-long orbital cycle of yin and yang, of high and low conditions. Together the fluids of sea water and windy air-ocean atmosphere grate against each other as well as against the less yielding mass of the rocky continents to generate the oscillations on the sea's surface we know as ocean waves.

Standing Wave and Fabric

Tie a rope to a wall. Shake its end rhythmically up and down, applying a force in a constant manner. If the ripples thus generated move along the rope and rebound at just the right frequency, the reflection will stay in phase with incoming ripples to create a standing wave that appears not to move at all! A piece of paper can be warped or bent into a "standing wave", a row of arches and sags that will not move. Rows of threads warped into such waves, set out of phase (the peaks of one near the valleys of the other), and placed at right angles create a *weave* of fabric. A rigid fabric of steel beams (grillage) forms footings for the columns of skyscrapers. A fabric of basically plastic elements like string fibers creates cloth, which conforms to the human body without returning completely to its original shape. A fabric of elastic elements like rubber bands can make a geomet-rodynamic trampoline. Reinforced concrete is a fascinating material, because when poured it is completely plastic, but as it sets up around a woven fabric of structurally elastic steel rods, it becomes virtually rigid and will resist any load for which it is designed. John Hejduk, weaving a story, regards architecture as a "fabrication". Woven lines of essentially one-dimensional threads or straws can create essentially two dimensional planes of cloth or three dimensional baskets. What architectural spaces can be made of weaving planes and volumes? From organic architecture's woven fingers to the free plan to a multilayered transportation system that keeps cars and pedestrians as separate as the nerves and blood vessels in our bodies, architecture thrives on the skillful integration of independent networks within the same spacial field.

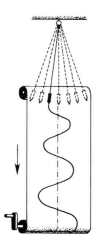

GENERATING WAVES

Calendric architecture revealed rhythmic patterns characteristic of the calendric changes themselves-- the wanings and waxings of the moon, the rhythm of ebbs and tides, of menstrual cycles of the female body... On a miniature scale, the wave patterns of this cosmic rhythm are shared by our heartbeat... Our brain waves are further variations of these rhythms, depending upon our condition-- light sleep, deep sleep, sweating, or the mental disturbances called petit mal and grand mal, for instance. Our breathing has a similar... ongoing rhythm of inhaling and exhaling, and similar fluctuations characterize the physical and mental cycles called biorhythms. Our "inner clocks" allow us to register our own rhythmic patterns of time, called circadian rhythms.

from Power of Limits, by Doczi

Sine Wave, Harmonics and Proportion

A swing, a tuning fork, and a pendulum all move in the same pattern. For each, the position of the moving end plotted against time describes a sine wave. The moving element of swing seat, fork end, or pendulum bob shakes the medium around it in a regular and repeating pattern of vibration, a complex phenomenon which shakes a thing in many different ways at the same time. The amount something vibrates is its *amplitude*, how often it vibrates is called its *frequency*. Vibrating elements in a medium such as air or water can produce pressure on our ears which we distinguish as sound. Particularly pleasing combinations of these vibrations make music.

Stretch a rubber band between two ends of a tube, slightly bent to make a bow. It is a crude musical instrument, with tension and compression elements balancing forces in the structure, like a guitar or violin. Pluck the rubber band and notice its vibrations. Notice that the whole band vibrates back and forth. Now hold the band at its midpoint, and pluck it again. The half-length band will vibrate exactly one octave higher! Other simple divisions give equally clear tones: dividing the band into 2:1 = octave; 3:2 = the fifth (the dominant) and 4:3 = the fourth (subdominant), 5:4 = major third, 6:5 = minor third, 9:8 major second, 16:15 = semitone. The Pythagoreans called this scale "perfect" proportions; musicians today call it "just intonation. "Higher overtones of these notes are always exact whole integer multiples of the basic tone, or first partial. The second partial is octave, third partial is upper 12th, 4th is double octave, and so on. This produces the harmonic series of musical overtones. Combinations of these produce what we call harmony, which we recall comes from the Greek term meaning "joining together or fitting together", as in carpentry. When the original whole string is plucked, it naturally produces these fractional vibrations as well. Thus the whole string will vibrate once, while the thirds will vibrate three times, the fourths will vibrate four times, etc. These are the harmonic frequencies, or whole-number multiples, of the tonic. How these occur gives different musical instruments their distinctive timbres, oboe vs. steel drum, or string bass vs. trumpet, for example.

Shooting the Curl

Harmonic motion generates recurring values at successive multiples of a full clock rotation. Sine and cosine curves reveal an intimate relationship between rotation and translation, between the circle and spiral. To move up and down a spiral stair like Gaudi's stone stair at the Church of Sagrada Familia, shown opposite, is to make both a linear and angular displacement at the same time. Thus a spiral stair is a kind of torsion, a curl of volumetric forces, where rotation and translation are taken together. We find the same pattern of harmonic motion in celestial phenomena. A plot of the March 1991 orbits of Jupiter's four bright Galilean satellites: **I** Io; **II** Europa; **III** Ganymede; and **IV** Callisto is shown as sine curves along the path of Jupiter's own orbit around the Sun (indicated by the center pair of vertical lines.) The horizontal lines mark O^h Universal time on successive dates.

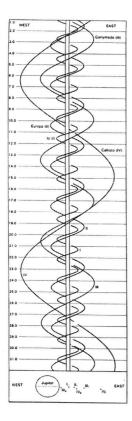

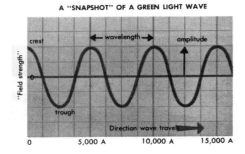

A "SNAPSHOT" OF A GREEN LIGHT WAVE

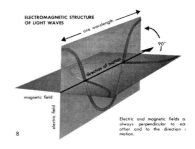

ELECTROMAGNETIC STRUCTURE
OF LIGHT WAVES

one wavelength

90°

direction of motion

magnetic field

electric field

Electric and magnetic fields a
always perpendicular to ea
other and to the direction
motion.

8

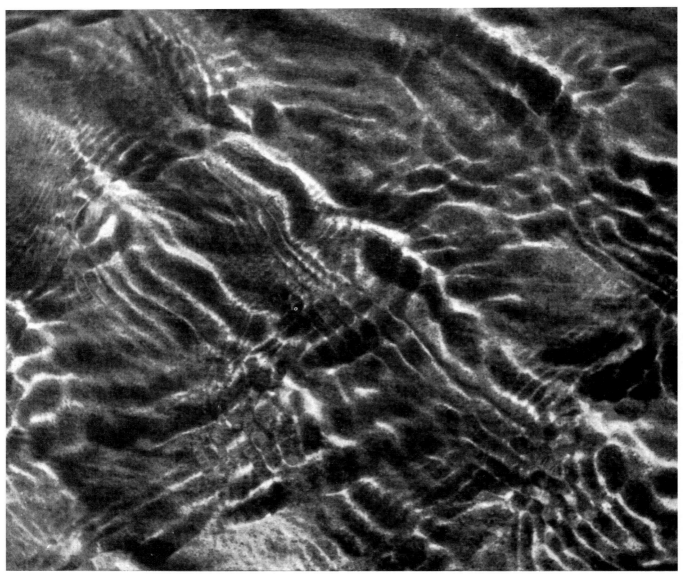

RIPPLES IN THE POND

"The rotating armatures of every generator and every motor in this age of electricity are steadily proclaiming the truth of the Relativity Theory to all who have ears to hear." Leigh Page, 1941

Electromagnetic waves carry energy in all directions through the universe. All objects receive, absorb, and radiate these waves, which can be pictured as electric and magnetic fields vibrating at right angles to each other and also to the direction in which the wave is traveling. All electromagnetic waves travel in space at the same speed, the speed of light. Electromagnetic waves show a continuous range of frequencies and wavelengths. Frequency is the number of wave crests passing a point in one second. Electromagnetic wave frequencies run from about one per second to over a trillion-trillion (10^{24}) per second. For light visible to our eyes the frequencies are four to eight hundred trillion ($4 - 8 \times 10^{14}$) waves per second. The frequency times the wavelength gives the speed of the wave. The higher the frequency, the shorter the wavelength. Visible light is all the frequencies of electromagnetic radiation our eyes can see, but it is a very small fraction of the entire electromagnetic spectrum.

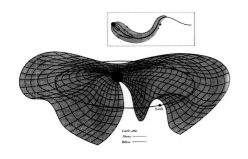

Michael Faraday (1791-1867) was curious about the world, so he experimented. He found in the 1830's that when a current flows through two nearby wires, they move! Currents moving in the same direction make the wires attract; in opposite directions, the wires repel each other. Faraday carefully measured how these effects varied in space and described them as fields-- where what he called lines of flux were comparable to a farmer's plowed rows. He also found that an electric current generates a magnetic field and a moving magnet generates an electric field. He also showed that current moving through wires rotated and translated into a helix coiled like a spiral stair create a solenoid-- a magnetic field within the coil. Modest yet farseeing, he changed the world. When the Prime Minister of England visited his laboratory and asked him what use there could be in his contraptions, Faraday is said to have answered "why some day, Sir, you will be able to raise taxes from them!" Faraday's investigations form the basis for much of what we think of as modern technology. The electric motor is a refined application of his observation that a current through a circuit will cause a magnet to move, and his discovery of the reverse phenomenon, electromagnetic induction, in which an electric current will be induced when a magnet moves is the essential aspect of the electric generator. (Le Corbusier proudly claimed "the plan is the generator!") James Clerk Maxwell in 1873 published the mathematically complete quantification of Faraday's investigations that are the four basic field equations of the electromagnetic force. Maxwell's equations show that periodic oscillations of the electromagnetic field are possible (at the speed of light). Without elaborating the mathematics, they are presented here only for completeness and possible future reference.

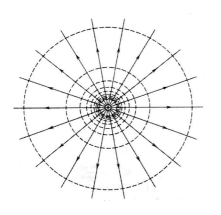

$$\nabla \bullet D = P; \qquad \nabla \bullet B = 0; \qquad \nabla \times E = \partial B / \partial t; \qquad \nabla \times H = J + \partial B / \partial t.$$

Fields are real. At first Maxwell's equations were derided because they predicted nonlinear behavior, which seemed to be outside the bounds of a world view based on Newtonian physics. But then Heinrich Hertz proved that Maxwell was right by making radio waves! Nobel Physicist Richard Feynman's explained how radiation works, how there need be no material medium for propagating light, and other electromagnetic effects over large distances: "Suppose that somewhere we have a magnetic field which is increasing because say, a current is turned on suddenly in a wire. Then... there must be a circulation of an electric field. As the electric field builds up to produce this circulation, then [also] a magnetic circulation will be generated. But the building up of *this* magnetic field will produce a new circulation of the electric field, and so on. In this way, fields work their way through space without the need of charges or currents except at their source. That is the way we *see* each other!" The diagrams on this page show equipotential surfaces (dashed lines) and lines of force (solid lines for a point charge and an electric dipole. The drawings show constant difference of potential DV between adjacent equipotential surfaces. Equipotential surfaces will be relatively close together where E is relatively large and relatively far apart where E is small. Similarly, the lines of force are relatively close together where E is large and far apart where E is small.

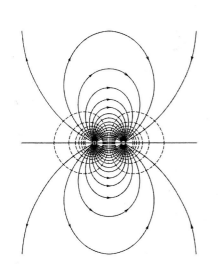

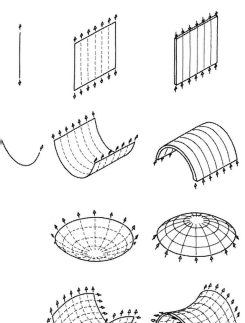

THINKING

Laocoön, a priest of Apollo, warned the Trojans not to touch the wooden horse made by the Greeks. As he and his sons sacrificed to Poseidon at the seashore, two serpents came from the water and crushed them., The Trojans took this as a sign of divine displeasure with Laocoön's prophesy, and took the fabled horse into their city, much to their regret. Subsequent events vindicated Laocoön's judgement, since the horse was filled with Greeks who waited until night and then sacked Troy. A magnificent statue by Polydorus and others, now in the Vatican, shows Laocoön and his sons in their death struggle. This Laocoön sculpture has a fascinating and important history. It was lost in Antiquity and unearthed on the Palatine Hill in Nero's Golden House in 1506. Michelangelo rushed to see this true messenger from the "Golden Age". No doubt he was struck by the plastic expression of its action, the dynamic *contraposto,* or counterpoise of forces revealed in body twists and poses of each figure separately and the whole in ensemble. The father's chest is torqued back and away from the coiled serpents, while his lower *torso* (the part of the human body that can sustain torsion) and legs seem to stretch in agony along an opposite set of vectors. G.E. Lessing's 18th century seminal essay in art theory *Laocoön: or the Limits of Painting and Poetry* noted that in the restrained faces amidst struggling limbs we find an even deeper counterpoint of action and expression.

Multiple Curvature: Inside and Outside

A bay window, bowing out beyond the plane of a wall, presents a curious phenomenon. Standing in that niche, you wonder if you are truly inside or outside the room. John Wood the Elder's Royal Crescent at Bath (1767-75) is a sinuous line of dwellings, like advancing and receding bay windows oscillating between public and private. The green at the Royal Crescent is between buildings yet also part of park beyond them. Alvar Aalto's plan for Baker Dorm at MIT, 1947-48 is able to unify river edge and street side through the inflection of its plan configuration. It creates spaces in plan which are metrically closer to street-side while feeling like they belong to the river edge. Of course, there is also a simple advantage to bending the single loaded corridor scheme. Aside from achieving a number of "leftover" spaces useful for promoting student interaction, as Lou Kahn advocated in his Erdman Hall dormitory at Bryn Mawr College, Aalto is able to increase student rooms per floor in this waveform plan. And like the *villi* in our intestines, this manifold flooding increases the surface area, which has the advantage of getting more river views to more students than a conventionally block-like double loaded corridor scheme would have achieved. Forces can bend the aggregate mass of a structural member. Consider how space itself can seem to bend. The concepts of bending and shear provide architects with a means to create a dynamic organization of space. Walls need no longer be passive dividers between inside and outside or one room and another. The Baroque architects expressed dynamic spacial order through the combination of bent and sheared surfaces and volumes whose "flatness" varied from layered in shear to round in torsion. Today engineers continue to develop surfaces of complex curvature, weaving steel in the concrete to make thin shell structures as bowls and domes, and two way saddles with both hills and valleys.

The plan is the field of action

The plan is the field of action, the intersection of gravity and light. Field derives from the Sanskrit *prathati*, "it widens broadens out." Distant events affect distant elements in a field. When things spin out or groove into other things, they tend to drag nearby things with them, like ripples moving a cork on the surface of a pond. Fields can be distorted. Integrated architecture considers the site and program as intersecting fields. Field phenomena like Interference, diffraction, turbulence, and current can guide planners in resolving the organization of volumes.

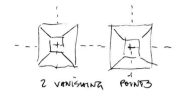

2 VANISHING POINTS

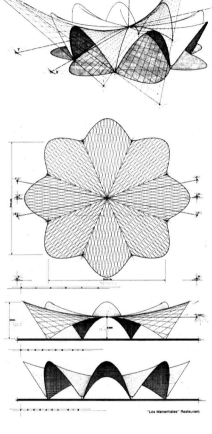

"Los Manantiales" Restaurant

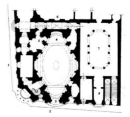

THE OTHER SIDE

The last chapter, Bending, presented a troubling aspect of perspective-- its "truth" exists from only one point in space. How did sensitive architects of the Late Renaissance, who surely must have grasped the difficulty, reconcile the problem when building two different but volumes next to each other? One fascinating work from this period is the church of San Carlo alle Quattro Fontane in Rome begun in 1637 and designed by Francesco Borromini (1599-1667).

Borromini's Dilemma

The dome of San Carlo alle Quattro Fontane is an oval surmounting torqued arches springing from inflected double column supports developed on a paired equilateral triangle plan... so much complexity in that volume! Where does the section sustain the transition from bipolar ground space to centroidal (but of course also bipolar) elliptical attic? No wonder it took Borromini (and the Church) almost thirty years, until 1665, to resolve the spacial proposition in the remarkable facade. There are in-and-out ripples that play in counterpoint between the ground plan and the upper story porch. Volumetric torsion is sustained throughout this very small but plastically immense space. (The whole chapel would fit inside one of the four massive central piers that support the dome at St. Peter's!) Note how the beams made of stones combined to read as rods not only bent into arches but twisted along their length as well.

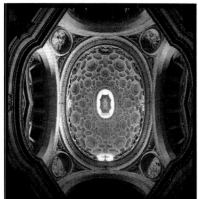

Even more remarkable is to compare this entire chapel space with the apparently completely irreconcilable spacial proposition of the adjoining cloister courtyard, shown in plan in the top right margin of this page. All of the spaces in this plan were designed by Borromini, yet they might as well have come from two different galaxies! Perhaps here is the moment of the recognition of the essentially futile Renaissance search for the "perfect" perspectival central plan space... the notion that "all roads lead to Rome", and that all roads in Rome would lead to the crossing under Michelangelo's Dome at St. Peters. (Recall that Borromini helped complete the Baldachino.) To state the problem simply, when two adjoining rooms are both designed to be the centers of their respective perspectival worlds, observers in them cannot both share the same vanishing point and station point. We now know, of course, that there cannot be a single universal point of view, but that all pluralist versions of truth and vision carry equal relative merit. There may be some connection here between democracy, horizon, and aerial perspective. Thomas Jefferson, after all, observed the Montgolfiers' hot air ballooning over pre-Revolutionary Paris.

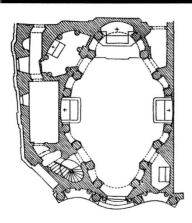

If perspective suggests a unique station point for its truest reading, then spacial unity is broken when two such perspectives are side by side. This may be the reason why the cloister courtyard abutting San Carlo alla Quatre Fontana is so different a space from the chapel itself. It may also be the source of Borromini's architectural anguish. Michelangelo may have been a Cubist before its time, but Borromini was both more and less than that. Felix Candela designed an elegant (15 mm thin!) concrete shell roof for a restaurant in Xochimilco, Mexico, in 1958. It is not hard to see the same preoccupations here as in Borromini's Sant' Ivo della Sapienza, where the ribbed dome of intersecting triangles, alternately convex and concave, project a powerful weave of expansion and contraction to the space below. Where Candela achieves an extreme economy of material in his design, both architects are able develop an embroidery of boundary definition over what are essentially simple central volumes.

MANIFOLD COMPLEXITY

Consider the problems we would have to live with in Flatland or the Planiverse. (See page 89.) We couldn't pass an oncoming person without elaborate detours and mechanisms, we couldn't put a "hole" in anything without making it fall apart, and crossing two wires without making a short-circuit would be impossible. But we live in Flatland all too often. "Cross at the green and not in between" ultimately makes no sense. Why traffic lights at all? Why must 3 MPH pedestrians ever cross through 60 MPH roadways that endanger both walker and driver? Imagine if pushing baby strollers along or across roller coaster tracks were permitted! We separate movement passages for deer and beavers, yet not for people. It is relatively cheap to warp the grade when first building, just bulldoze the cut-and-fill slightly differently. Why not Interstate-style culverts and overpasses everywhere ? We don't put electrical cable in plumbing pipes! Our nervous system does not clog our blood vessels! Is it that too often so-called planners (trained as lawyers?) lacking three-dimensional imagination fail to explore the rich topologies of three-dimensional knots and manifolds? Ply means" to fold or bend" Hence manifold: plait or weaving. *Ply* is the source of all words like complex, multiply, supple, perplex, imply, employ, deploy, replicate, reply, explicit and implicit. Simple is from *simplex,* a single fold; explicate means un-fold, imply means fold in, entangle, involve.

Weaving in Three Dimensions

Andreas Vesalius (1516-1564) was curious about human blood circulation, so he investigated. Despite prohibitions by the Church, he dissected cadavers and published the results. "Venous man" shows the veins of the human body as they appeared in his 1543 *Fabrica.* Anatomy continues to untangle the intricate webs that sustain the living human body. Increasingly subtle explorations of "inner space" enabled a University of Pittsburgh team to create a schematic "map" of a "stiff-armed dancer" that shows how one arm of the enzyme Eco RI wraps around the double helix of DNA before chopping it in two. The universe is complex. Everywhere in biology, from molecular structures to gross anatomy, we find evidence of the most complex volumetric interweavings which get a lot of structure in a little space. Such complexity flies in the face of the decaying "heat-death" implied by the increasing general disorder of entropy. Today people seem to choose political positions that identify either with the "haves" or the... "knots"-- those who recognize that simple-minded answers do not always develop the complex plans needed to arrive at the solutions of true simplicity. Slow people with fast cars in the same space is too simple-- and unnecessarily dangerous.

Paradigms: not only linear...

To see planning (of houses, of cities!) not as zoning of flat areas, but as a truly multi-dimensional volumetric problem, demands a shift in paradigm, the implicit world view in any given realm of study. Thomas Kuhn's seminal *Structure of Scientific Revolutions* notes how Benjamin Franklin's picture of electricity as a flow related hitherto isolated phenomena so well that it has become our paradigm: we still think in his terms of current, resistance, and circuit. Maxwell's equations were at first derided because they predicted nonlinear fields acting at a distance until Heinrich Hertz proved Maxwell correct by *making* radio waves. Since Newton's mechanics were always linear, radio required a paradigm shift. Things *do* behave in nonlinear ways. Two wires with current move together, sideways! Electric fields build magnetic fields build electric fields etc. in a manner described by Faraday through the "right hand thumb rule", which is not simply an addition but a multiplication of vectors. George Chaikin notes that the nervous system behaves logarithmically, non-linearly. Einstein revised Newton's paradigm by explaining gravity as spacetime geometry. Suddenly all the elements of the field make sense together-- everything fits.

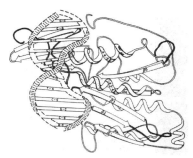

Human circulation in the neck. Gray's *Anatomy*

"The stiff-armed dancer" By solving the three-dimensional structure, a University of Pittsburgh team created a schematic "map" to show how one arm of the enzyme Eco RI wraps around the double helix of DNA before chopping it in two. (J. Rosenberg)

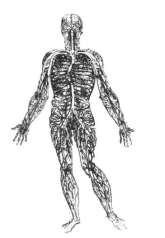

"Venous man": the veins of the human body as they appeared in Vesalius' Fabrica, 1543 edition.

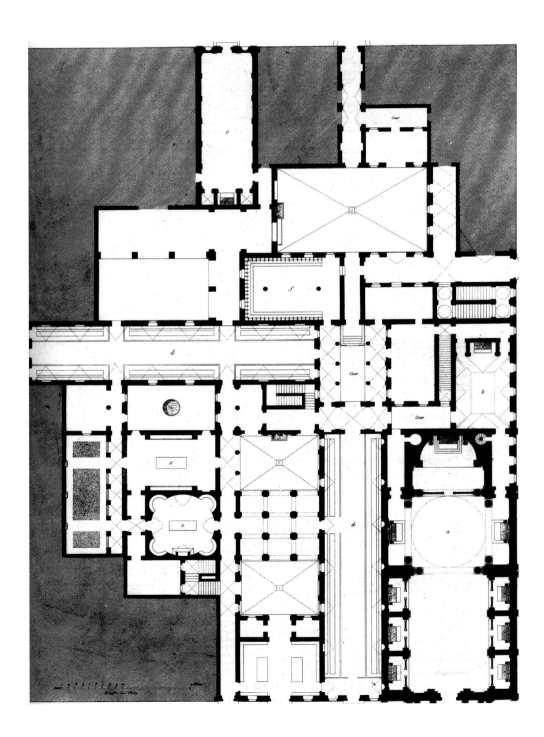

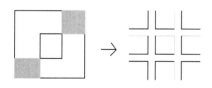

THE FIELD OF ARCHITECTURE

Recall the left over spaces in created around the intersection of the two 16' cubes in your Harmony project. The volume of the 24' cube site includes these volumes: perhaps you were able to exploit them as part of your scheme. But if we focus on the major program volumes only as objects, we miss the opportunity to use them to organize the whole site. These "leftover" spaces can become very important as part of the spacial and plastic equation of the whole ensemble. After all, isn't their architectural context created by the interaction of the other major volumes? Volume plus volume can generate a field greater than the parts. The plan of the seven churches of St. Stevens, in Bologna, Italy shows many volumes placed close together, all connecting with doors, corridors, and colonnades. Is the total a coherent ensemble of architectural space? Not when compared to the more "urban" experience of Palazzo Pellegrini opposite, where the entire fabric is continuous. There are unrealized opportunities of volume relationships in the Bologna plan. Dynamics studies the structure of volumes. A **field** is a concept and tool akin to the Cartesian grid (graph paper) which relates all positions to a set of coordinates measured from a common point reference-- the origin-- thus everywhere in the grid is part of the field. A structured relationship of volumes can constitute a field.

Orthogonal Fields

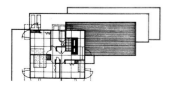

Gravity pulls on beams and bends them. The bonding structure of the steel molecules yields to the gravitational field of earth in the long-span cables of a suspension bridge. Just as masses tend to move in force fields, so too may volumes react to forces in and *of* the field. If a field is large compared to the volume(s) in question, then the stress (resistance to relocation) is low. A small field generates a "high flux", so a volume that is large compared to its field can be moved only with difficulty: it sits "heavy" compared to smaller volumes which are "programmatically light". Thus field can affect "volume inertia", which is a volume's resistance to relocation (in both translation and rotation) within the field. The relative "weight" or importance of different rooms, varying alignments, and clusters of connections within an overall plan, begin to generate interactions of volumes throughout the entire field of plan and section. Some program volumes (like the Phoenix flight run) may have a specified size which may take many different shapes. When such volumes are large compared to the size of the field, distortions like bending and folding to fit things in may develop. In a space-filling configuration of volumes, the boundaries of the field force linear elements into a restricted space-- weaving linear volumes into three-dimensional folds that imply other volumes in and around them. Torsion may crowd the site and stress volumes at their corners. Right angle bending makes a volume inside the corner. This interplay of linear to planar to volumetric phenomena suggests that orthogonal bending is the outcome and thus the plastic equivalent of shear and that the resolution of bending stress is pure shear. If volumetric moment ultimately becomes all shear, then a field of three right-angled mutually perpendicular dimensions may provide the strongest order of close-packing program volumes. Perhaps this is the ultimate architectural three-space solution to the relationship of square/triangle/circle mentioned on page 123.

A Spacial Continuum

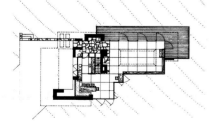

The plan is the field of action,
"the intersection of gravity and light".

Imagine the plan of Palazzo Pellegrini as both plan and section to a complex volume field. Frank Lloyd Wright's 1940 Clarence Pew House shows spaces weaving through each other, creating a whole fabric of related interpenetrating volumes at many scales, and organizing the site into a coherent field tied ultimately to the orthogonal of plumb line and horizon. Architecture can weave orthogonal volume relationships into a spacial continuum. The notion of a volumetric field suggest a beginning of a way to resolve "Borromini's conflict" between "this" side and "other" side of a wall. This is an issue not fully resolved until Einstein showed that only when motion and acceleration were considered in terms of *both* space and time, could they be related independent of their local frames of reference.

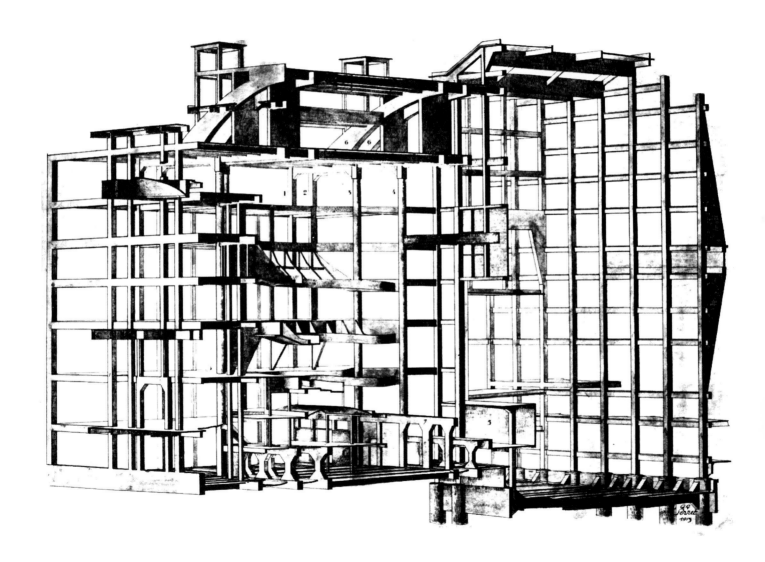

ANIMATING

The steel frame, first developed in Chicago at the turn of the 20th Century, created a three-dimensional trabeated skeleton of minimal mass and maximal habitable volume. Today a fully triangulated three-dimensional truss called a **space frame** is common. The International Space Station (see inside back cover) illustrates the advantage of such an "exploded" mass, carefully perforated with void according to the calculations of structural engineers. Tetrahedral space frames can hold overhead interstate highway signs rigid against the wind or cover entire convention centers in a single flat span. We might go so far as to propose a space frame in which the program volumes of rooms are supported and separated by a structure which is itself entirely volumetric in all three dimensions. This suggests the spacial tartan grid investigated in Concerto.

Moment of Inertia and Structural Sections

The molecular structure of an elastic material is a tightly bound group of solids that interact with each other under load. Their resistance to displacement, especially in bending, develops the tensor called **moment of inertia**, which varies with the *square* of the length that measures the movement of the material away from the neutral axis. Deflection depends more on moment of inertia than anything else, which is why engineers design structural shapes for putting mass as far from the neutral axis as possible. One basic form is the I beam. Maximum compressive stress occurs along its top chord and maximum tensile stress at the bottom. At the neutral axis, only shear stress exists. This is why steel joists can have *open* webs! While not as strong, wood acts very much like steel under structural loads. Wood is a material with many small cells arranged in radial rings across the section of the trunk and in long fiber tubes running along its length, creating a three-dimensional web of fiber grain. Wood resists tension and compression about equally, since shifting winds can stress the same side of a tree trunk first in tension and then in compression.

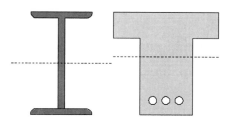

Reinforced Concrete

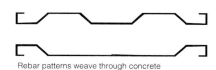

Rebar patterns weave through concrete

Concrete, unlike wood or steel, is made of many small granules of sand, cement, and lime, only loosely joined when mixed. It gradually becomes chemically stronger as it dries and sets. It is a material that resists crushing much more than it resists stretching (so we use concrete to carry a lot of weight as footings, but not as cables). However, concrete is much cheaper per unit mass than steel, so it makes sense to figure out where resistance to compression is most needed and put concrete there, while placing steel to resist the tensile stresses where they are greatest. Bonding between the materials is important, hence the ribs in reinforcing bars. The placement must be precise-- put the steel too high and the beam won't resist the greatest tensile stressses along the bottom chord or too low and the steel will pop out of its concrete matrix. This is the basic theory behind reinforced concrete-- a composite material of tensile fibers embedded in a more massive compressive stone matrix. The principle is not unique to these materials, but also is applied in newer composite structures like carbon fiber epoxy and boron resins used in sports equipment and aerospace design. In theory, a light strong nylon reinforced foam could make houses light enough to lift with one hand. Auguste Perret's 1911 concrete frame design for Theatre des Champs-Elysees shows a tartan skeleton of mass between a field of rooms-- the program volumes. Like a block of wood, a volume can have a grain of orientation and resitance to program and site loads. For example the combined subset of double cube and Phoenix flight run "throw their weight around" and usually determine the conditions for placing the 3 small visitors galleries. Also, the 16' long practice room in the phoenix study may fit vertically into some *partis* and horizontally in others. One this is established, you may find it very difficult to rotate this "long" volume against other constraints, including access and sun orientation.

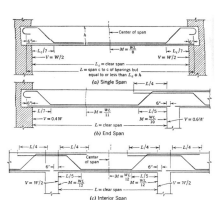

Reinforced concrete beams

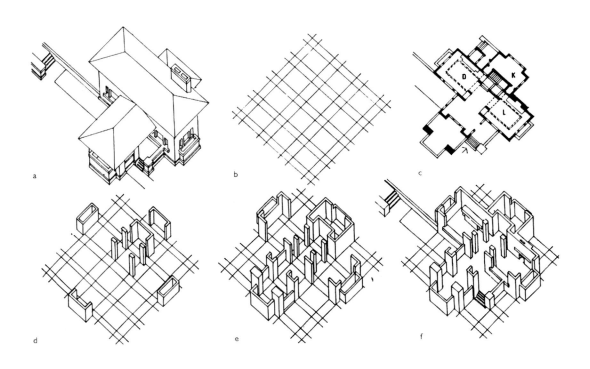

a

b

c

d

e

f

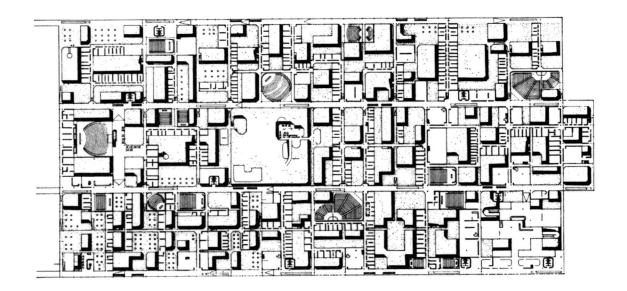

VOLUME FOR CIRCULATION

An order of rooms is not necessarily the order of our experience of them. While we may come in the front door, the vestibule may not be as important as the living room or den that is a center of volumetric order for the inhabitants. However, an order of circulation volume can organize architectural space as much as any other set of program volumes. For example, a dense-packed 24' cube can accommodate all the Phoenix program needs (see page 255), but there would be no way to get to the inner and upper rooms. For access to program volumes, circulation is necessary. Architect Guillermo Jullian de la Fuente calls the space between program elements the "yellow peripherical distinction". Louis Kahn spoke of "servant" and "served" spaces. Circulation space typically is allotted about 15% of the floor area in an efficiently designed building. As in a living organism, the function of circulation is vital. We might call a perfect fit between "negative" circulation solids and "positive" program solids a union of plastic and elastic space. To design by moving volumes within, from, and through each other in the mind's eye is to make a *dynamic* of volumetric composition. This understanding has produced simultaneously functional and beautiful works of architecture. There is a kind of "mega moment of inertia": if the program volumes have been located and "solved" before considering circulation volumes to provide access to them, it is often the case that the program volumes may become much more difficult to move as a group. Is this a case of the tail wagging the dog? On the other hand, if corridors and stairs are placed first, these elements may generate their own spacial order. To make both volumetric systems work together is not always a simple or obvious task.

The Tartan Grid: Loom and Zoom

One structure of circulation is the **tartan grid**, a kind of weaving of access and movement through a field of program volumes, somewhat akin to the wood framing between the rooms in a house or the steel/concrete skeleton in high-rise building. A tartan grid is an extension of multiple and parallel lines of movement in all three dimensions of space, and is a kind of spacial perforation akin to the perforations evident in the eggcrate, tube, and other elements of the Bag of Tricks. In a sense, a tartan grid is a human circulation "equivalent" to flight. You need not articulate every possible element of a tartan, but can imply its extension through markers between and within other volumes, thus reconciling volumes that are larger than and overlap the intervals of the tartan grid. Many tartan variations are possible, from ABABA to AABBA etc. These arrangements can vary in different dimensions within the same field: ABABA in plan, AABBA in north-south section, and ABAAB in east-west section, for example. Manifold issues of overlap, interface, and resonance of volumes thus arise. Tartan grids can structure whole sets of volumes. Diagrams of Wright 's 1903 George Barton House in Buffalo NY show the tartan loom on which plastic events such as rhythmic piers, inflected walls, and modulating soffits are placed.

Interval

Many cities are structured on grids of streets weaving through evenly spaced blocks. Travel from Third Avenue and 27th Street to Fifth Avenue and 30th Street in a city can take many orthogonal paths of equal length. For example, two blocks north, two blocks west, and two blocks north again gets you there in the same distance as one block north, one block west, three blocks north, and one block west again. The distance between the end points is invariant along possible paths. If we add time to the discussion of end points, then the *interval* is invariant in space and time. A leisurely steady stroll from Third and 27th to Fifth and 30th, window shopping along each block for 10 minutes, is an equivalent event, from a spacetime point of view, to sitting still for 55 minutes, and then dashing to Fifth and 30th in the last 5 minutes. Both cover the same distance in the same total time. An event is something that happens at a point in space at a particular time. Between two events is an interval.

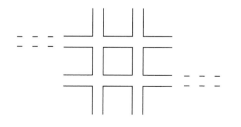

LUBRICATION
"THE YELLOW PERIPHERICAL DISTINCTION"

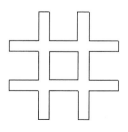

TARTAN FIGURE/GROUND

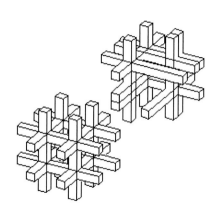

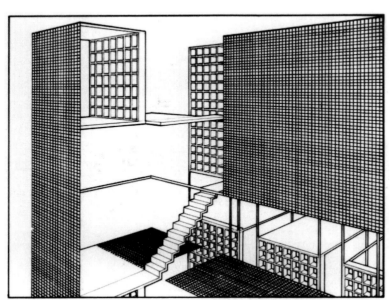

SUSIE PEZZELLA

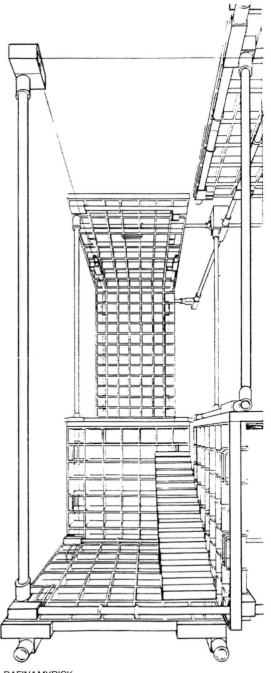

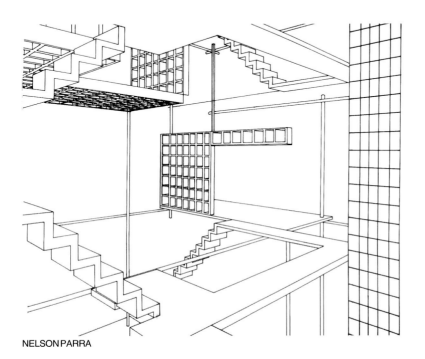

NELSON PARRA

DAFINA MYRICK

PROMENADE ARCHITECTURALE

JOE LIGOURI

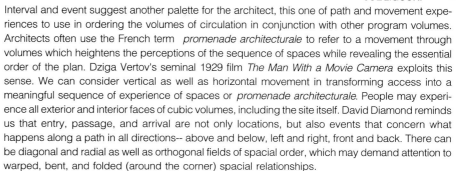

Interval and event suggest another palette for the architect, this one of path and movement experiences to use in ordering the volumes of circulation in conjunction with other program volumes. Architects often use the French term *promenade architecturale* to refer to a movement through volumes which heightens the perceptions of the sequence of spaces while revealing the essential order of the plan. Dziga Vertov's seminal 1929 film *The Man With a Movie Camera* exploits this sense. We can consider vertical as well as horizontal movement in transforming access into a meaningful sequence of experience of spaces or *promenade architecturale*. People may experience all exterior and interior faces of cubic volumes, including the site itself. David Diamond reminds us that entry, passage, and arrival are not only locations, but also events that concern what happens along a path in all directions-- above and below, left and right, front and back. There can be diagonal and radial as well as orthogonal fields of spacial order, which may demand attention to warped, bent, and folded (around the corner) spacial relationships.

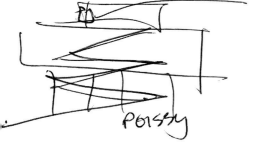

Procession is the act of proceeding, especially in an orderly manner. A number of persons or things moving forward, in orderly fashion toward some destination is also a procession. Visitors will communicate best when an entire volumetric organization is legibly transparent-- that is, required spaces are clearly identified, and any remaining site volume is continuous in flow. *Promenade architecturale* clearly comes into play in a copy of Le Corbusier's sketch proposal for the approach to the Governor's Palace at Chandigarh. While the widening path halfway to the goal permits a gentle shift of axis from center of the facade to the left where the main entry occurs, the entire visual and plastic ensemble invites the visitor into an excursion of more extensive meandering in both plan and section. A tour down the stairs, past the reflecting pools, through a colonnade, invites recollection of realms from marketplace to the lotus of enlightenment. Back up another set of stairs, we might note that as we move closer to the Palace, the Monument to the Open Hand (at the extreme right of the sketch) appears to rise above the ridge line of the distant Himalayas, like a bird in flight, an image explicitly developed by the architect. Le Corbusier exploited the possibilities of *promenade architecturale* in many of his works, including his early Parisian Maison La Roche and illas Stein at Garches and Savoye at Poissy, and later buildings like the Millowners' Building in Ahmedabad and Carpenter Art Center at Harvard.

Pas Perdus

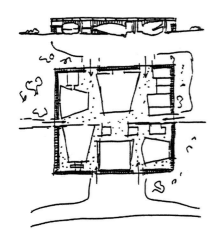

Le Corbusier developed a wonderfully poetic and subtle application of the notion of *promenade architecturale* in his proposal for the lawmakers' chambers at the United Nations General Assembly hall in New York. Taking advantage of the understanding of how politics, that is, the cultivation and enactment of policy, actually works, he surrounded the voting and assembly chambers in his plans with large open zones of columnar halls, and in the drawings labeled them *pas perdus* -- the place of "lost footsteps". One can easily imagine one diplomat putting his or her arms around the shoulders of another and saying, "c'mon, lemme buy you a drink" as they wend their way to lunch after a rancorous session in the Assembly. Perhaps it is in the place of lost footsteps, in the moment of informal exchange, where the real business of government gets accomplished. Once in Venice, this author met a traveler. Together we agreed to go to the main Piazza San Marco, and then talked together intensely about architecture and philosophy. An hour later, we realized that we had not gotten to our destination, but rather had walked through the city and returned to our starting point! Venice, a labyrinthine but continuous pedestrian thoroughfare (no cars, no cross streets, no traffic lights!) is an entire city of *pas perdus*.

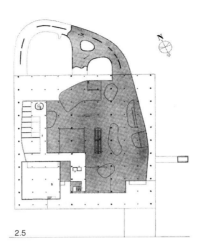

2.5

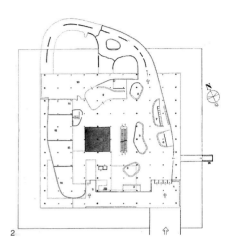

2

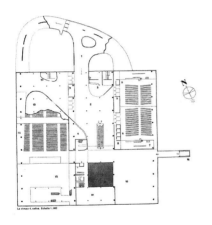

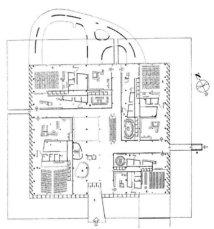

1

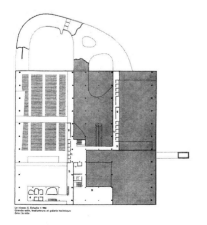

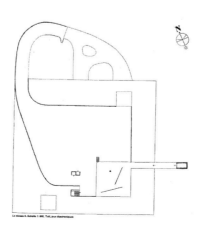

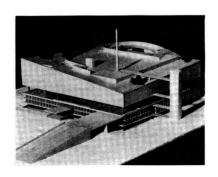

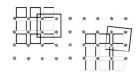

THE FREE PLAN

A tartan grid proposes a circulation volume that permeates a field of program volumes but remains independent of it. What if circulation were not dependent on the order of other volumes or structural elements like walls and columns at all? By 1891 this question had become critical, as The Monadnock Building had pushed masonry construction to its limit. Planning of openings and disposition of elements in this 16 story building were severely contained, especially on the ground floor, where bearing walls were 8' thick. From this problem the modern multistory steel and concrete skeletons emerged. *Architectonics* (page 82) includes Frank Lloyd Wright's proposal to "explode the box", which suggests freer placement of domestic walls. Le Corbusier further articulated this special opportunity in his 1914 steel and concrete Maison Domino system, and presented it in 1926 as the **free plan**, one of his *Five Points of Modern Architecture*. This concept distinguished between load bearing and volume-defining elements within a building or other architectural space, stating a basic rhythm of structural masses that permit well-proportioned architectural volumes to occur independently of the supports. Thus walls, ceilings, and even floors (see Wright's terrace stair at Falling Water) may become screens to modulate light as much as they are stones to stack against gravity. Solving program needs thus becomes free of structural requirements. Le Corbusier's idea of free facade permits a similar treatment of building envelope. The trabeated (treelike) structures of skeleton frame or column and slab remain as an independent volumetric rhythm, working to accent program intervals or play syncopation and counterpoint against them, permitting simultaneous readings of flat and deep, light, and dark, or near and far spaces through the transparent layering of plastic orders.

Weaving walls through and against a column grid develops plan as warp and woof, where space perforates structure as much as structure perforates space. Here Borromini meets Descartes. The intellectual and visual separation of structural and non-structural building elements allowed for space to be defined and articulated in a new way, where the relative inertia of a field of program volumes becomes independent of the relative inertia of the circulation field. The Carpenter Art Center (page 270 to 273), exploits particularly dramatic effects of the free plan. Curved elements set against an orthogonal column grid that is itself rotated against the right angled geometry of the street establish rich transparencies of local and global spacial orders. There is an interior seminar room whose skylight opens to a seemingly random array of beams and an oddly placed column that are eventually revealed as reminders of the original column grid.

Only when we see several plans of the same building can we appreciate the real potential of the free plan. Le Corbusier's 1964 proposed City Hall for Strasbourg, France, shown opposite, is organized in three major layers, each containing several floor levels. Pinwheeling at the base are government functions like town clerks and traffic courts, which may be entered directly on three sides for quick access. The next level recreates the life of a town square, with kiosks for newspapers, travel bureaus, small cafes, and so on loosely distributed through the hypostyle-hall column grid. One reaches this main level via a grand ramp from the south. The volume of the ramp is extended through this level and emerges to the north where it warms in both plan and section, branching once for access to the upper-level theaters. The ramp continues on to the roof, where a small terrace permits a grand view of the entire city. We may see in this scheme Le Corbusier's lifelong love of the Acropolis and its jewel, the Parthenon. The warped ramp propylaea makes the roof an acropolis to the surrounding city. And the plinth-like base, columnar middle level, and pedimented upper boxes (especially when viewed diagonally from the corners!) recreate the plastic scheme of the Parthenon itself. It may not be extreme to suggest that the urban planning diagrams incised onto the upper level theater exteriors recall the heroic battle sculptures of the Parthenon's marble metopes and pediments.

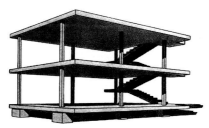

FREE PLAN: TARTAN PERFORATION OF BOTH MASS AND VOUME STRUCTURE

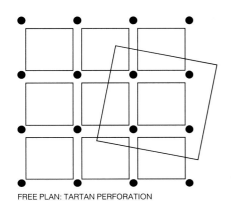

MAISON DOMINO, LE CORBUSIER 1914

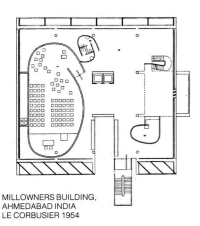

MILLOWNERS BUILDING, AHMEDABAD INDIA LE CORBUSIER 1954

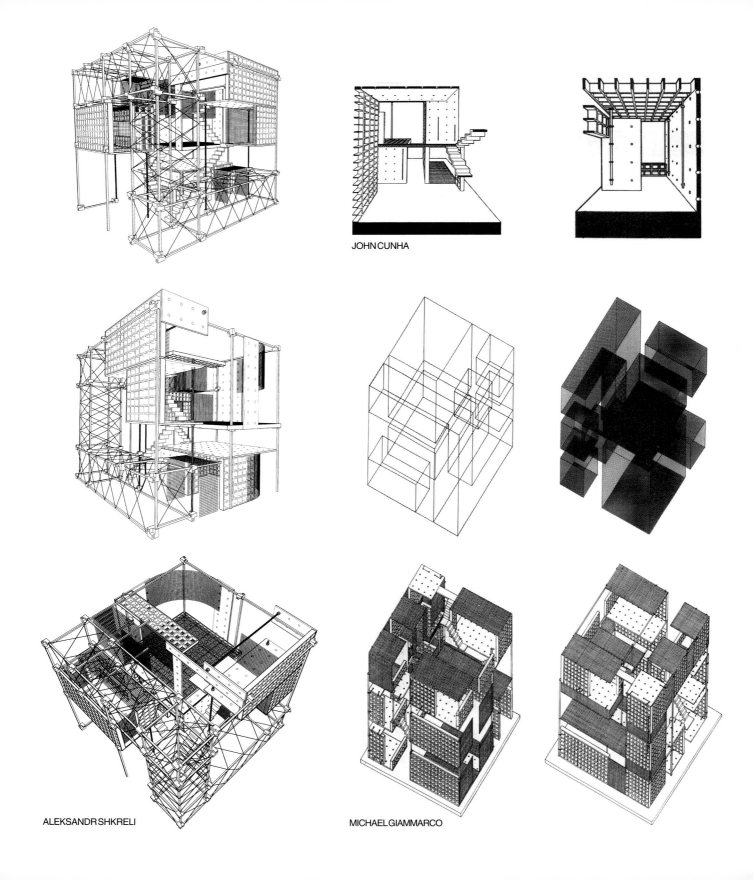

JOHN CUNHA

ALEKSANDR SHKRELI

MICHAEL GIAMMARCO

DOING: *re-solution*

DYNAMICS: RETURN OF THE PHOENIX PART 2 -- SYMPATHETIC VIBRATION

Near here a phoenix has found evidence of the return of human culture. Wisdom, compassion, science, and all the arts have reemerged as the essence of civilization. This fabulous Bird loves to play solo and ensemble music in concert with others. True to its complex nature, it enjoys shade as much as sunlight, and especially likes to fly through the rich fabric of both. The phoenix is eager to share with people its well-developed sense of freedom in space. It knows that a three-dimensional tartan grid of circulation weaving throughout a site can provide a human equivalent to flight, celebrating movement in fully plastic and temporal terms. In addition to accommodating program volumes listed (page 257), the total site volume may be modulated to indicate the following:

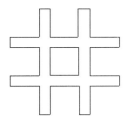

THE TARTAN GRID

approach	A frame of reference for confrontation: the bigger the better for all to see from afar. A 30 x 30' vertical plane may be located anywhere within the site volume.
passage	A means to distinguish without from within, acting as gate and/or portal. The frame of reference may be used for this if punctured with a human-scale door frame.
entry	A place providing a sense of within and preamble to inner arrival.
arrival	The phoenix seeks a roost. The people seek smaller scale spaces for shaded daytime resting. To maximize quiet, visitor cubes may be close to but should not actually touch each other. Both Bird and people seek a place to meet and harmonize together .
procession	The phoenix requires a flight run of at least 64 linear feet to stay happy and healthy. This flight path must maintain a minimum 6' and maximum 12' diameter clearance and may bend and/or twist but must fit *inside* the site, generating a continuous but complex 3D line. The tartan perforation suggests a procession of volumes through space.
ensemble	The site is a 30' x 30' x 30' cube which permits movement through and experience of the whole space and its reverberations. All programmed volume subsets should each read clearly against the others and the whole, even when they intersect.

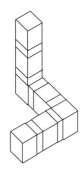

BENDING AND WEAVING IN THE FLIGHT RUN

Now that you have identified and located significant program volumes in the site, you are able to make informed judgements in using the available palette of architectural elements, the Bag of Tricks. With your previous models and drawings as guides, review your Pro-position to identify program and formal issues that require Re-solving. Remember that an architectural solution of the field cannot be merely an additive list of rooms, but must be integrated into a unified whole through light, structure, circulation, and material. An appropriate solution will integrate tartans and programmed volumes so that one set of spaces may read through another set. Seek to make the entire site a volumetric tensegrity. As in the best jazz, spaces should create a balance of expectation and surprise, theme and variation. Document your scheme through a full set of architectural plans sections elevations, axonometrics, perspectives. Collage of *part* forms may be used where appropriate.

ANIMATION: In an animation of at least three successive frames looking outward from within, depict an ordered *promenade architecturale* through the space of your site. Can this journey reveal the development of the cube site as depicted in your animation for Bending (page 255) as well as the events of approach, arrival, etc. [Advanced: In an animation of at least 30 successive frames, depict an hour in the life of the site from the view of the people or the Phoenix.]

COLOR: 4. **Optical Mix 5 Colors** 5. **Optical Mix 3 Colors** 6. *Collage 3b.* See page 464.

FUNCTION: Plot and/or construct a sine curve, $y = \sin x$. See page 453.

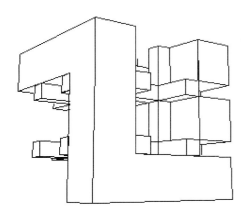

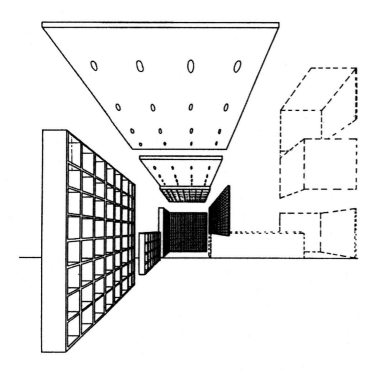

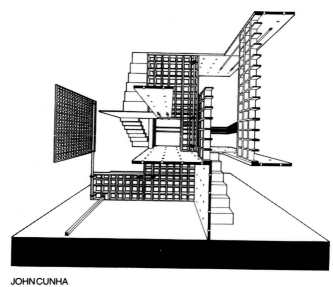

JOHN CUNHA

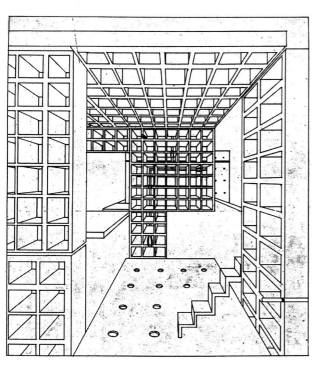

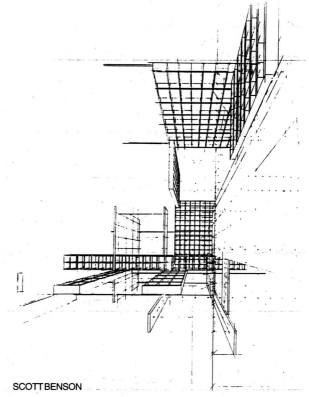

SCOTT BENSON

IN CONCERT

While only the Bird can fly, people seek a human circulation "equivalent" to flight. To facilitate movement and access to inner and upper volumes including the roof, a three-dimensional tartan grid of human horizontal and vertical circulation can weave throughout the site. Note that there are twelve 3' x 3' x 30' tubes intersecting in three dimensions. Of course these tubes are too small to be literal corridors or stair shafts, which may occur in the implied thickened "planes" between them, but the tubes are suggestive in other ways-- as locations for stair treads, railings, clerestory and strip windows, and structure. A 3' x 3' "picture window" incision in a plane can locate a tartan in a volume. The phoenix likes to avoid sharp corners while in flight. The free plan (and free section!) may help in resolving this program need in the context of other architectural concerns.

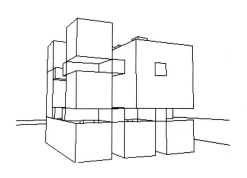

Programmed spaces for Bird (flight run, roost), people (practice, small groups) and both (meeting) are based on multiples of an 8' module while the site is a 30' cube. You must reconcile different orders of spacial rhythm generated by disparate volumetric elements. For example, while the 8' cube visitor galleries can fit neatly between the intervals of an 8-3-8-3-8 tartan, the double volumes will not. Thus the 8 x 8 x 16' volume, and the 16' double cube meeting hall may have a 3' circulation space running through them, while the tartan itself will be intersected by the 16' double cube and flight run. Of course, the flight run will be transected by the tartan grid, no matter what its configuration. Note also that the 3' allowed for circulation is different than the 2' dimension of the actual stair widths. Recall too that elements of the Bag of Tricks imply other modules. Rather than "ruining" a design, this variety of fabrics may make a richer composition of continuous fields superimposed on each other. *Harmony* demonstrated how architects can make one volume read simultaneously as part of at least two orders of space. There can be many harmonies within a single field. Composing different orders of space can modulate an ensemble of volumes as well as single volumes. A musical concerto building on harmonies between solo instruments and the total ensemble suggests a spacial analogy. At each scale of intersection and detail, there are important relationships between elements. The most immediate become tactical concerns. When **tactics** are seen in relationship, **strategy** enters.

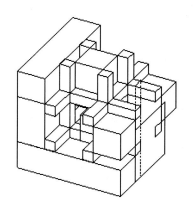

Inhabiting Space

When we inhabit a place we see it from inside out as much as outside in. Like any healthy relationship, we must both confront space and work around it. However, the visual perception of the picture plane is as incomplete as that tactile feel of the sculptural roundness of an object in giving a full account of the volumes we inhabit. You cannot truly see the front and back of a box together. Every "snapshot" single view is but one plane projection, and even a movie film sequence around and through a volume is only a collection of such perspective frames. The dichotomy between frontality and rotation mirrors the ambiguity of two and three dimensional perception. The reciprocal relationship between bending and shear suggests the painter's problem of treating space as either layers of depth or rotation of volume in the round. An architect can feel volume in a plan. We "see" architecture through both plan/section and *promenade architecturale,* which together reveal the plastic intentions of the architect to resolve the continuity of space from the inside out. If plan (with section) is the generator, then the tartan, perforating volume with circulation, is like an x-ray that reveals overlapping and intersecting volumes as an ordered field. Purist devices such as transparency, shared contours, warping, multiple views, and layering make possible the simultaneous reading of multiple volumetric orders. Cubism also suggests a fluid and continuous medium uniting all masses and voids. Like intersecting ripples, different orders of space can mutually coexist to order a field of intersecting volumetric qualities. Inhabiting space in time reveals plan to the mind through all our senses.

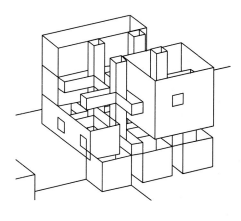

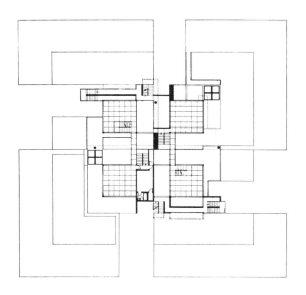

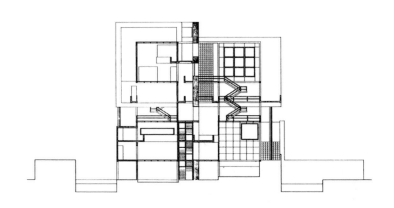

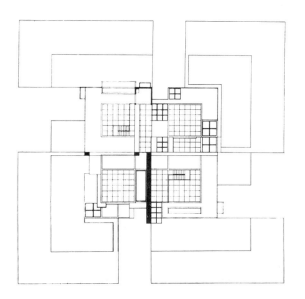

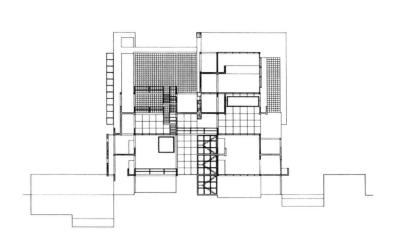

RE-SOLUTION

The e-motion of stationary volumes can create vibrating fields of space. Mike Falco, a fifth-year architecture thesis student, spent a year with Paul Amatuzzo investigating many of the issues raised in *Concerto*. Through numerous models and drawings, he explored how to combine four apartments and four gardens into a single freestanding building. He chose not to settle for obvious orthogonal relationships between elements in the garden-apartment pairs, which can easily lead to fragments, static, or preferentially frontal development of the three-dimensional configuration, but rather find what else might be possible. The twist here is that each garden is diagonally related to its apartment, so that each garden-apartment pair occupies two of the eight- cube half-dimension three-dimensional quadrants. In a sense these dwellings are parts of a double alpha helix, the spiral form of DNA. In Falco's project, there are actually four strands twisted compared to the two that make DNA, recalling Douglas Hofstader's "eternal golden braid" that forms a title anagram to his remarkable book Godel Escher Bach. Falco's four strands spiral up and around the cube site to make rich complex spaces for dwelling. Each unit keeps contact with both ground and sky, at least 3 compass orientations, and a sense of the full roundness of the volume. The modulation of human scale spaces offer ever new combinations to satisfy both the senses and the mind by solving the problem of assuring that all units receive good light, orientation, and amenity. This virtuoso resolution of quadrant (2 x 2) geometry and nine square (3 x 3) geometries in a cube is resolved in two-dimensional plans, sections, elevations, as well is in its overall three-dimensional form. It is a brilliant piece of work.

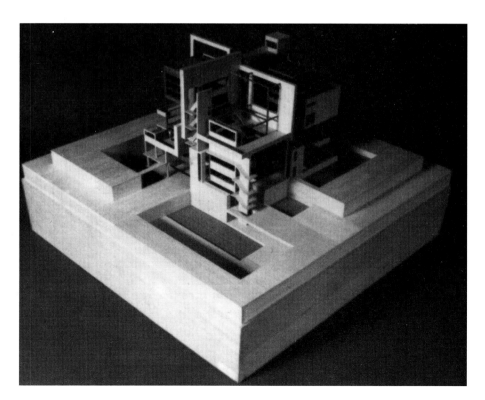

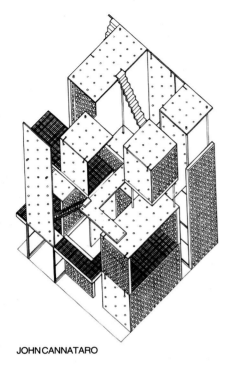

JOHN CANNATARO

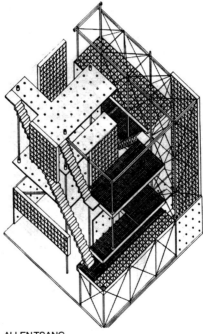
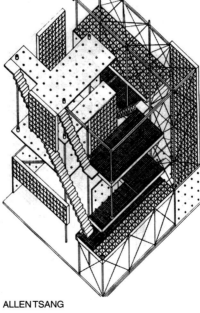

ALLEN TSANG

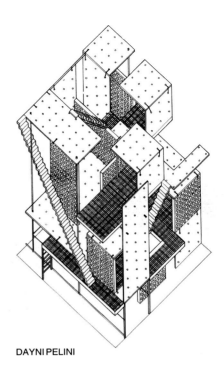

DAYNI PELINI

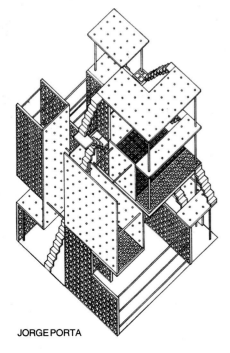

JORGE PORTA

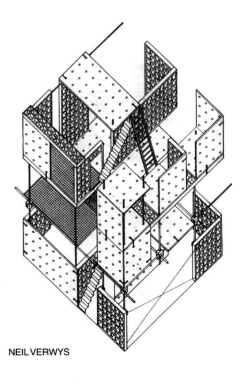

NEIL VERWYS

REFLECTING

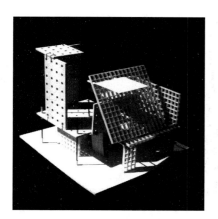

The deep mythology of the phoenix, at least as old as Egypt (*pharaoh*), embodies the essential formal principle of contrast. As Igor Stravinsky expresses in *Firebird Suite,* his ballet-concerto (for bodies and orchestra!), we embody life's conflict between moral and action choices of what Nietzsche has identified as the the explorative, impulsive, intuitive, libidinous promptings of Dionysian spirit and the upright noble "straight and narrow" Apollonian spirit. We live in constant predicament halfway between angels and beasts. The eagle soars the heavens like an angel, the serpent often symbolizes the lowest of beasts. Apollo is the sun while Medusa had snakes for hair. Rudolf Wittkower explores these themes in the notes that follow from his essays on the "Eagle and Serpent" in *Allegory and the Migration of Symbols.* A student may find a theme. With effort, it might even be elaborated. How much more can be made from that simple theme in the hands of a master? John Hejduk, poet, architect and teacher, is a master of play-- in Latin *magister ludi.*

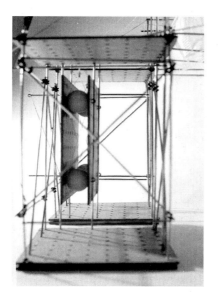

The rich fabric of woven development is best expressed musically in the fugue. Herman Hesse's account of a novice's first introduction to the possibilities of the full flowering of an art form is appropriate as a culmination of the complex study of the Return of the Phoenix. But as the master later reminds the novice,"Try once again to track down the music; pay attention to the figure. But don't force yourself; it's only a game. If you should fall asleep over it, there's no harm." Release a stretched spring and it will gradually subside. A spring is a coiled torsion bar that stores energy by deflecting when loaded, and that "springs back" to its original shape when the load is removed. The spring's harmonic oscillations reveal the elasticity of the molecular structure of the material. There are architectural volumes which act as "levers" or "springs" to an entire spacial fabric, and there are architectural fabrics which seem to generate a kind of volumetric harmonic oscillation. "Reading a wave" from Italo Calvino's *Mr. Palomar On the Beach*, explores the possibilities of harmonic motion in plastic media-- from liquid to spacetime. But Mr. Palomar takes it easy, and enters the play.... In this spirit, consider an advanced version of the Concerto project: *suppose the phoenix is a beam of light.*

Moving things can agitate each other into a chaotic swirl. Vortices in smoke rings or a boat's wake result from turbulence, generally describable but locally unpredictable. While Jupiter's Great Red Spot, larger than several Earths, has survived for centuries, the weather around it changes rapidly and violently, driven by Jupiter's incredibly fast ten-hour rotation period. Every atom of that weather seeks the easiest place to be, and the result is a grand scale turbulence of the kind that blows hats away and wrecks umbrellas. Where is there any sense of spacial resolution in such random agitation? In a similar way, the demands of an architectural program often seem in conflict-- every volume wants the middle, the best light, and so on. What resources can the architect bring to settling these riotous demands, as rooms seem to jockey for position on the drafting table, oscillating back and forth into and out of space? Like Cézanne, great architects learn to accept the inevitable, and allow the whole spacial structure of a *parti* to move all at once. How to make space "move"? We already know how to develop a volumetric algebra for such spacetime events as one space intersecting with another. Accumulations of such operations on sets and subsets of volumes suggest a means for weaving space. Great plans reveal how multiple orders of spacial coherence may permeate the same physical volume. Weaving space is one of the great gifts of architecture-- to be able to create more than one space in a single place, and to do so throughout a site.

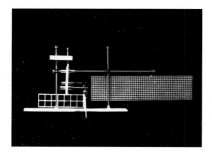

READINGS:

Amatuzzo, Paul.*HomeAge*
Feynmann, Richard. *Lectures on Physics, Volume 2*
Le Corbusier. Ouevre Complet, 8 volumes
Leonardo Da Vinci, *The Notebooks*
Meier, Richard. *Richard Meier Architect*
Palladio. Four Books on Architecture

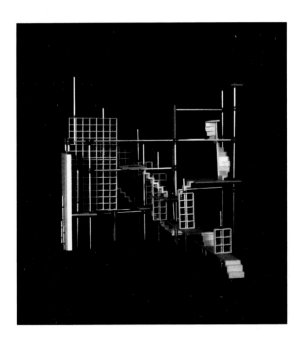

from **ALLEGORY AND THE MIGRATION OF SYMBOLS**
by Rudolf Wittkower

EAGLE AND SERPENT

The passage of the Psalm on which both rejuvenation tales comment must be an adaptation of the old Egyptian legend of the miraculous Phoenix which renews its youth every 5000 years....

The Greek Physiologus, *a collection of animal tales with Christian allegorizations probably brought together in Egypt in the 2nd century AD, contains the following story about the eagle. When he grows old, his flight becomes heavy and his eyesight dim. He first seeks a pure spring of water, then flies aloft towards the sun, burns off his old feathers and the film over his eyes. Finally he flies down to the spring, dives into it three times, thereby renewing himself and becoming young again. This curious story is used as a simile for man: when the eyes of his heart are grown dull, he should fly aloft to the sun of righteousness, Jesus Christ, and rejuvenate himself in the ever flowing spring of penance in the name of the Father, the Son and the Holy Ghost. "This is meant as an interpretation of the words of the psalm mentioned above: "so that thy youth is renewed like the eagle's."*

The Physiologus *story of rejuvenation is made up of at least three different main motifs: the preliminary flying towards the sun, the fall and rebirth, and the "pure spring". The Water of Life is one of the universal myths familiar in the Near East for thousands of years. Fall and resurrection-- for the rejuvenation of the* Physiologus *is a spiritual resurrection--has also a long history in the East. We may call to mind the Etana myth where this motif occurs in another setting. But the whole idea is a direct offshoot of the pagan designation of the eagle as the bird of resurrection....*

In treating as synonyms the Lone Tree, the Dry Tree and the Tree of the Sun, Marco Polo fused different traditions, and it would require a special paper to try and disentangle them.

In all the versions of the Alexander romance the Tree of the Sun and the Dry Tree are kept apart, and connected with separate events. Alexander was taken to the oracular Trees of Sun and Moon, which were capable of human speech and prophesied his early death at Babylon. Before seeing these Trees, he visited the Dry Tree, in whose branches perched the bird Phoenix.

Now according to Early Christian tradition, the Phoenix sits on a palm tree. The Greek word phoenix *means the bird as well as the palm tree, and representations of the bird on a palm tree are common on sar-cophagi and in mosaics. In some of the Alexander manuscripts the two scenes of the Phoenix in the Dry Tree and the Trees of Sun and Moon are combined in one picture. But they also appear singly, as in the early Leipzig manuscript, for instance. The first picture represents the old priest guiding the King and pointing to the Bird in the Tree. The artist, however, did not show the Tree withered -- 'nec folias nec fructus habens', as the text says-- but followed the Early Christian tradition.*

The next page with the talking trees is rather ingeniously devised. Alexander is placed between the trees in whose branches appear the symbols of Sun and Moon. These symbols had, of course, a long pedigree.

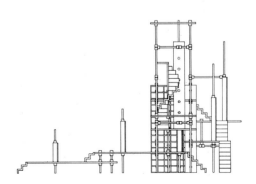

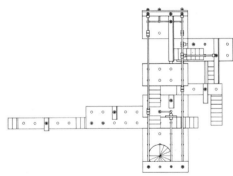

FRANK BIH

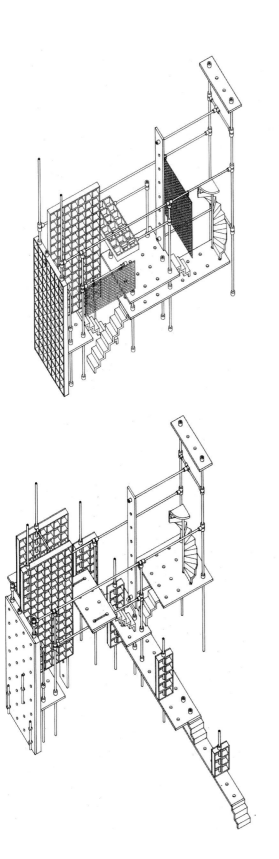

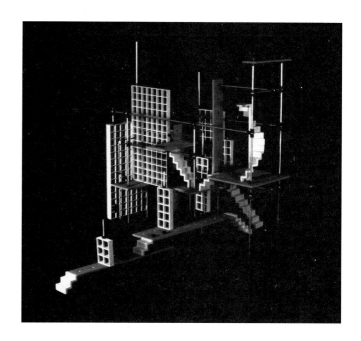

from **MAGISTER LUDI**
by Herman Hesse

The gaze of those eyes might have been frightening, but they were serenely cheerful as well as penetrating, neither laughing nor smiling, but filled with a calm, quietly radiant cheerfulness. He shook hands with the boy, nodded, and sat down with deliberation on the stool in front of the old practice piano. "You are Joseph Knecht?" he said. "Your teacher seems content with you. I think he is fond of you. Come, let's make a little music together."

Knecht had already taken out his violin. The old man struck the A, and the boy tuned. Then he looked inquiringly, anxiously, at the Music Master.

"What would you like to play?" the Master asked.

The boy could not say a word. He was filled to the brim with awe of the old man. Never had he seen a person like this. Hesitantly, he picked up his exercise book and held it out to the Master.

"No," the Master said, "I want you to play from memory, and not an exercise but something easy that you know by heart. Perhaps a song you like."

Knecht was confused, and so enchanted by this face and those eyes that he could not answer. He was deeply ashamed of his confusion, but unable to speak. The Master did not insist. With one finger, he struck the first notes of a melody, and looked questioningly at the boy. Joseph nodded and at once played the melody with pleasure. It was one of the old songs which were often sung in school.

"Once more," the Master said. Knecht repeated the melody, and the old man now played a second voice to go with it. Now the old song rang through the small practice room in two parts.

"Once more." Knecht played, and the Master played the second part, and a third part also. Now the beautiful old song rang through the small practice room in two parts.

"Once more." And the Master played three voices along with the melody. "A lovely song," the Master said softly. "Play it again, in the alto this time."

The Master gave him the first note, and Knecht played, the Master accompanying with the other three voices. Again and again the Master said, "Once more," and each time he sounded merrier. Knecht played the melody in the tenor, each time accompanied by two or three parts. They played the song many times, and with every repetition the song was involuntarily enriched with embellishments and variations. The bare little room resounded festively in the cheerful light of the forenoon.

After a while the old man stopped. "Is that enough?" he asked. Knecht shook his head and began again. The Master chimed in gaily with his three voices, and the four parts drew their thin, lucid lines, spoke to one another, mutually supported, crossed, and wove around one another in delightful windings and figurations. The boy and the old man ceased to think of anything else; they surrendered themselves to the lovely, congenial lines and figurations they formed as their parts crisscrossed. Caught in the network their music was creating, they swayed gently along with it, obeying an unseen conductor. Finally, when the melody had come to an end once more, the Master turned his head and asked: "Did you like that, Joseph?"

Gratefully, his face glowing, Knecht looked at him. He was radiant, but still speechless.

"Do you happen to know what a fugue is?" the Master now asked. Knecht looked dubious. He had already heard fugues, but had not yet studied them in class.

"Very well," the Master said, "then I'll show you. You'll grasp it quicker if we make a fugue ourselves. Now then, the first thing we need for a fugue is a theme, and we don't have to look far for the theme. We'll take it from our song."

He played a brief phrase, a fragment of the song's melody. It sounded strange, cut out in that way, without head or tail. He played the theme once more, and this time he went on to the first entrance; the second entrance changed the interval of a fifth to a fourth; the third repeated the first an octave higher, as did the fourth with the second. The exposition concluded with a cadence in the key of the dominant. The second working-out modulated more freely to other keys; the third, tending toward the subdominant, ended with a cadence on the tonic.

42 Book One

Prelude 11, F Major

Fugue 11, F Major

The boy looked at the player's clever white fingers, saw the course of the development faintly mirrored in his concentrated expression, while his eyes remained quiet under half-closed lids. Joseph's heart swelled with veneration, with love for the Master. His ear drank in the fugue; it seemed to him that he was hearing music for the first time in his life. Behind the music being created in his presence he sensed the world of Mind, the joy-giving harmony of law and freedom, of service and rule. He surrendered himself, and vowed to serve that world and this Master. In those few minutes he saw himself and his life, saw the whole cosmos guided, ordered, and interpreted by the spirit of music. And when the playing had come to an end, he saw this magician and king for whom he felt so intense a reverence pause for a little while longer, slightly bowed over the keys, with half-closed eyes, his face softly glowing from within. Joseph did not know whether he ought to rejoice at the bliss of this moment, or weep because it was over.

The old man slowly raised himself from the piano stool, fixed those cheerful blue eyes piercingly and at the same time with unimaginable friendliness upon him, and said: "Making music together is the best way for two people to become friends. There is none easier. That is a fine thing. I hope you and I shall remain friends. Perhaps you too will learn how to make fugues, Joseph."

He shook hands with Joseph and took his leave. But in the doorway he turned once more and gave Joseph a parting greeting, with a look and a ceremonious little inclination of his head.

Many years later Knecht told his pupil that when he stepped out of the building, he found the town and the world far more transformed and enchanted than if there had been flags, garlands, and streamers, or displays of fireworks. He had experienced his vocation, which may surely be spoken of as a sacrament. The ideal world, which hitherto his young soul had known only by hearsay and in wild dreams, had suddenly taken on a visible lineaments for him. Its gates had opened invitingly. This world, he now saw, did not exist only in some vague, remote past or future; it was here and was active; it glowed, sent messengers, apostles, ambassadors, men like this old Magister (who by the way was not nearly so old as he then seemed to Joseph). And through this venerable messenger an admonition and a call had come from that world even to him, the insignificant Latin school pupil.

Such was the meaning of the experience for him. It took weeks before he actually realized, and was convinced, that the magical events of that sacramental hour corresponded to a precise event in the real world, that the summons was not just a sense of happiness and admonition in his own soul and his own conscience, but a show of favor and an exhortation from the earthly powers....

... [later] the Magister turned on his chair and placed his hands on the piano. He played a theme, and carried it forward with variations; it seemed to be a piece by some Italian master. He instructed his guest to imagine the progress of the music as a dance, a continuous series of balancing exercises, a succession of smaller or larger steps from the middle of an axis of symmetry, and to focus his mind entirely on the figure which these steps formed. He played the bars once more, silently reflected on them, played them again, then sat quite still, hands on his knees, eyes half closed, without the slightest movement, repeating and contemplating the music within himself. His pupil, too, listened within himself, saw fragments of lines of notes before him, saw something moving, something stepping, dancing, and hovering, and tried to perceive and read the movement as if it were the curves in the line of a bird's flight. The pattern grew confused and he lost it; he had to begin over again; for a moment his concentration left him and he was in a void. He looked around and saw the Master's still, abstracted face floating palely in the twilight, found his way back again to that mental space he had drifted out of. He heard the music sounding in it again, saw it striding along, saw it inscribing the line of its movement, and followed in his mind the dancing feet of the invisible dancers. . . .

It seemed to him that a long time had passed before he glided out of that space once more, again became aware of the chair he sat on, the mat-covered stone floor, the dimmer dusk outside the windows. He felt someone regarding him, looked up and into the eyes of the Music Master, who was attentively studying him. The Master gave him an almost imperceptible nod, with one finger played pianissimo the last variation of the Italian piece, and stood up.

"Stay on," he said. "I shall be back. Try once again to track down the music; pay attention to the figure. But don't force yourself; it's only a game. If you should fall asleep over it, there's no harm."

MR. PALOMAR ON THE BEACH
by Italo Calvino

Reading a wave

The sea is barely wrinkled, and little waves strike the sandy shore. Mr. Palomar is standing on the shore, looking a wave. Not that is lost in contemplation of the waves. He is not lost, because he is quite aware of what he is doing : he wants to look at a wave and he is looking at it. He is not contemplating, because for contemplation you need the right temperament, the right mood, and the right combination of exterior circumstances; and though Mr. Palomar has nothing against contemplation in principle, none of these three conditions applies to him. Finally, it is not " waves " that he means to look at, but just one individual wave: in his desire to avoid vague sensations, he establishes for his every action a limited and precise object.

Mr. Palomar sees a wave rise in the distance, grow, approach, change form and color, fold over itself, break, vanish, and flow again. At this point he could convince himself that he has concluded the operation he had set out to achieve, and he could go away. But isolating one wave is not easy, separating it from the wave immediately following, which seems to push it and at times overtakes it and sweeps it away; and it is no easier to separate that one wave from the preceding wave, which seems to drag it to shore, unless it turns against the following wave, as if to arrest it. Then, if you consider the breadth of the wave, parallel to the shore, it is hard to decide where the advancing front extends regularly and where it is separated and segmented into independent waves, distinguished by their speed, shape, force, direction.

In other words, you can not observe a wave without bearing in mind the complex features that concur in shaping it and the other, equally complex ones that the wave itself originates. These aspects vary constantly, so each wave is different from another wave, even if not immediately adjacent or successive; in other words, there are some forms and sequences that are repeated, though irregularly distributed in space and time. Since what Mr. Palomar means to do at this moment is simply see a wave-- that is, to perceive all its simultaneous components without overlooking any of them-- his gaze will dwell on the movement of the wave that strikes the shore until it can record aspects not previously perceived; as soon as he notices that the images are being repeated, he will know he has seen everything he wanted to see and he will be able to stop.

A nervous man who lives in a frenzied and congested world, Mr. Palomar tends to reduce his relations with the outside world; and, to defend himself against the general neurasthenia, he tries to keep his sensations under control insofar as possible.

The hump of the advancing wave rises more at one point than at any other, and it is here that it becomes hemmed in white. If this occurs at some distance from the shore, there is time for the foam to fold over upon itself and vanish again, as if swallowed, and at the same moment invade the whole, but this time emerging again from below, like a white carpet rising from the bank to welcome the wave that is arriving. But just when you expect that the wave to roll over the carpet, you realize it is no longer wave but only carpet, and this also rapidly disappears, to become a glinting of wet sand that quickly withdraws, as if driven back by the expansion of the dry, opaque sand that moves its jagged edge forward.

At the same time, the indentations in the brow of the wave must be considered, where it splits into two wings, one stretching toward the shore from right to left and the other from left to right, and the departure point or the destination of their divergence or convergence is this negative tip, which follows the advance of the wings but is always held back, subject to their alternate overlapping until another wave, a stronger wave, overtakes it, with the same problem of divergence-convergence, and then a wave stronger still, which resolves the knot by shattering it.

Taking the pattern of the waves as a model, the beach thrusts into the water some faintly hinted points, prolonged in submerged sandy shoals, shaped and destroyed by the currents at every tide. Mr. Palomar has chosen one of these low tongues of sand as his observation point, because the waves strike it on either side, obliquely, and, overrunning the half-submerged surface, they meet their opposites. So, to understand the composition of a wave, you have to consider these opposing thrusts, which are to some extent counterbalanced and to some extent added together, to produce a general shattering of thrusts and counterthrusts in the usual spreading of foam.

Mr. Palomar now tries to limit his field of observation; if he bears in mind a square zone of, say, ten meters of shore by ten meters of sea, he can carry out an inventory of all the wave movements that are repeated with varying frequency within a given time interval. The hard thing is to fix the boundaries of his zone, because if, for example, he considers as the side farthest from him the outstanding line of an advancing wave, as this line approaches him and rises it hides from his eyes everything behind it, and thus the space under examination is overturned and at the same time crushed.

In any case, Mr. Palomar does not lose heart and at each moment he thinks he has managed to see everything to be seen from his observation point, but then something always crops up that he had not borne in mind. If it were not for his impatience to reach a complete, definitive conclusion of his visual operation, looking at waves would be a very restful exercise for him and could save him from neurasthenia, heart attack, and gastric ulcer. And it could perhaps be the key to mastering the world's complexity by reducing it to its simplest mechanism.

But every attempt to define this model must take into account a long wave that is arriving in a direction perpendicular to the breakers and parallel to the shore, creating the flow of a constant, barely surfacing crest. The shifts of the waves that ruffle toward the shore do not disturb the steady impulse of this compact crest that slices them at the right angle, and there is no knowing where it comes from or where it then goes. Perhaps it is a breath of east wind that stirs the sea's surface against the deep drive that comes from the mass of water far out to sea, but this wave born of air, in passing, receives also the oblique thrusts from the water's depth and redirects them, straightening them in his own direction and bearing them along. And so the wave continues to grow gain strength until the clash with contrary waves gradually dulls it and makes it disappear, or else twists it until is confused in one of the many dynasties of oblique waves slammed against the shore. Concentrating the attention on one aspect makes it leap into the foreground and occupy the square, just as, certain drawings, you have only to close your eyes and when you open them the perspective has changed. Now, in the overlapping of crests moving in various directions, the general pattern seems broken down into sections that rise and vanish. In addition, the reflux of every wave also has a power of its own that hinders the oncoming waves. And if you concentrate your attention on the backward thrusts, it seems that the true movement is the one that begins from the shore and goes out to the sea.

Is this perhaps the real result that Mr. Palomar is about to achieve? To make the waves run in the opposite direction, to overturn time, to perceive the true substance of the world beyond sensory and mental habits ? No, he feels a dizziness, but it goes no further than that. The stubbornness that drives the waves toward the shore wins the match: in fact, the waves have swelled considerably. Is the wind about to change? It would be disastrous if the image that Mr. Palomar has succeeded painstakingly in putting together were to shatter and be lost. Only if he manages to bear all the aspects in mind at once can he begin the second phase of the operation: extending this knowledge to the entire universe.

It would be suffice not to lose patience, as he soon does. Mr. Palomar goes off along the beach, tense and nervous as when he came, and even more unsure about everything.

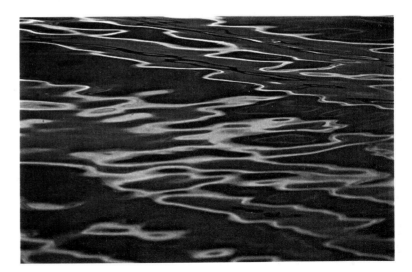

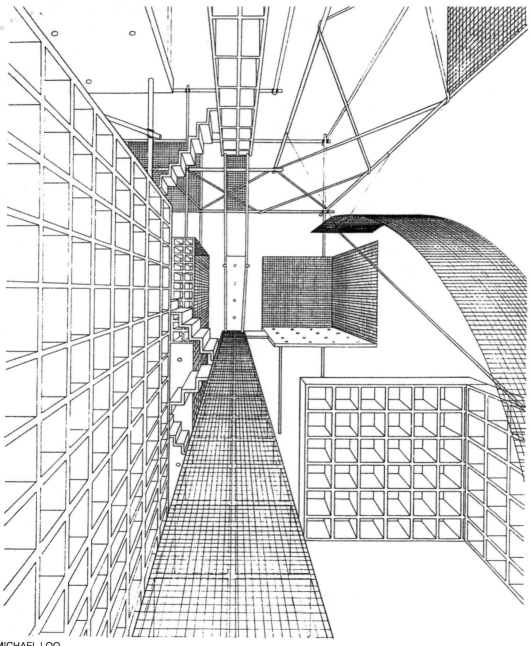

MICHAEL LOO

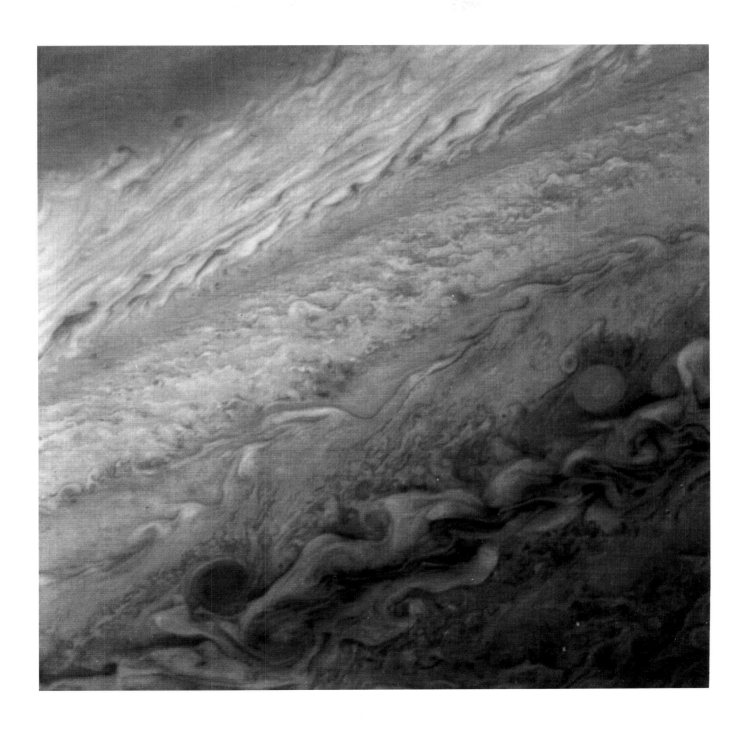

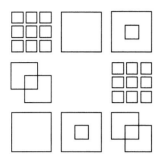

Symphony   comes from the Greek *sym* - together + *phone* - sound. Webster: 1. harmony of sounds, especially of instruments. 2. harmony of any kind especially color. 3. anything, as a picture, character-ized by harmonious composition. 4. in music an extended composition in sonata form for full orches-tra, having several (usually four) movements related in subject but varying in form and execution.

Orchestra   in ancient Greek theatres the semicircular space in front of the stage, used by the chorus. From the Greek *orchesithai* , to dance, and from the Sanskrit *rghayati*   he trembles or is agitated, from *er -* to move, go, come. See the Greek *erkhomai* — I come or arrive.

Music   in Greek myth there were nine goddesses presiding over song, poetry, the arts, hence E. *muse* esp. in poetry…. from IE base, perhaps mendh- to direct ones mind towards something.art of the Muses (lyric poetry set to music).

Mind   from the Greek *mends* -mind, intention, force; and from the Sanskrit *mnasthai*- to remem-ber (as in monastery!), *manas* - mind, spirit; *manyate* - he thinks. Mathematics means ultimately to learn about intelligence, to learn about learning. Mathematics is the *feel* of the mind at play.

4. SYMPHONY

RESONANCE AND RADIANCE

SYMPHONY: *RESONATING*

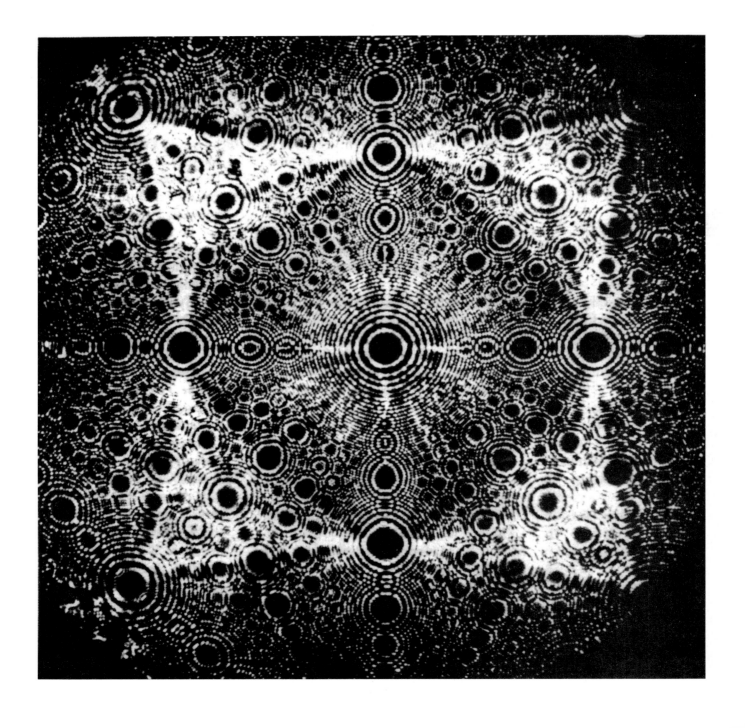

BEING

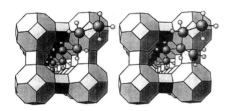

A physical system is said to exhibit a resonance if it can exist in a well-defined state for a time much longer than the period for internal motion for that state. Encyclopedia of Physics

Shout "hello" into the air at a scenic lookout, and you may hear a returning echo "hellooo... hellooo..." The first echo is your call reflected off the distant mountain face. Later tones are sounds bouncing back and forth between the ramparts, reverberating in a great outdoor echo chamber. A concert hall is designed to enhance this effect, so that a single vibrating string can fill a whole room with its sound. A child "pumps" a playground swing at just the right interval to drive it higher in its arc, adding the momentum of the child's shifting body weight to the harmonic motion of the swing, forward as it rises, back as it falls, amplifying its oscillation. The pumping motion is in *resonance* with the natural frequency of the swing motion. Similarly, sound (vibrating air that strikes sensitive nerves in our ear) resonates when vibrating strings on a guitar or violin shake the air inside the wooden sound box. Properly matched vibrations can enormously amplify the original signal. The sound emanating from the instrument projects into the listening room to shake ears, air, and walls. If these sounds reflecting from back, seats, and sides match those coming from the stage, its reverberation ("re-vibrating") can transform a simple room into a resonant concert hall.

Acoustics, the study of design for sound in human spaces, seeks to match echo, sustain, vibrato, etc. to a room's shape, structure, and materials to create sonic resonance. Resonant electrical circuits permit the greatest flow of current of a certain frequency. There is also a kind of "spacial acoustics", in which spaces resonate as volumes reinforce ideas at every scale of detail. A chamber can re-sound or resonate not only in what we hear, but also in what we see or feel. Clarity and proportion in organizing plan and section can make a whole room feel unified and complete. Architectural resolution is achieved by allowing the spacial moves and forces to work on each other until three-dimensional relationships are consistent throughout a volume. It is as if the volumes are allowed to bounce back and forth through each other until there is no more noise, until they are all revealing the same spacial order, in harmony, in tune, singing the same spacial song. Music develops form through theme and variation, in layers of readings of the notation of tone and timing. Musical dynamics express emotions through the colors, the nuances "between the keys": warm/cool, loud/soft, fast/slow, *crescendo* and *descrescendo*, and the bending of the "blue" note slightly off $b3$ or between major 7th and minor seventh $b5$.

The means for sustaining space through time may be spare and simple or florid and ornate. Both complex and simple phenomena are revealed in the remarkable field-emission ion photomicrograph of an iridium crystal shown opposite, where we see the terraced structure of closepacked spherical atoms like ripples in a rain spattered pool magnified about 10 million times. X-ray light strikes these atoms like a hammer and sets them vibrating. Shadow is the back end of the impact summed over all possible histories, as Feynman notes in *QED*. We see a range of steep and shallow gradients of motion into solid, light into dark, and momenergy into the mass of spacetime. How evenly spaced and timed raindrops would have to be to make this pattern! The zeolite molecule model reveals a higher frequency version of the iridium's vector equilibrium geometry, which is again projected in an early study for placing steel bars to reinforce concrete. The wonder of nature is that its spareness, its essential economy of means, generates all the richness of the cosmos. The sacristy of the charterhouse in Granada, Spain, a vigorous example of that special form of Baroque excess called *rococco,* seems almost hallucinogenic in its relentless animation of every repetitive line and surface. How complex are a room, a house, a city, yet how simple can their integrations become.

PARSING SOME NUMBER FACTORS...

$9 \cdot 6 = 54$ $3 \cdot 9 \cdot 8 = 216$
$3 \cdot 3 \cdot 3 \cdot 2 = 54$ $3 \cdot 3 \cdot 3 \cdot 2 \cdot 2 \cdot 2 = 216$

            $3^3 \cdot 2^3 = 216$

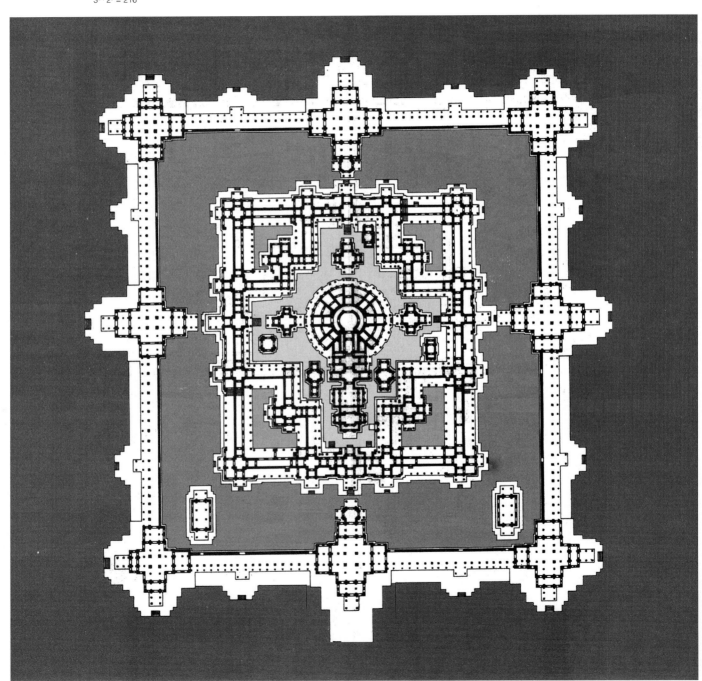

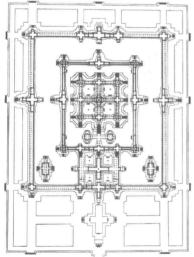

CARVING SPACE

THINKING

Sustaining Emptiness

An empty swing is idly pushed and its momentum describes an arc in space, carving a volume. The same solid is carved by the pumping swinger, but now it is a more energetic volume. The pumped swing moves faster and carries more mass, developing greater **momentum,** carving space more sharply like the chisel of a great sculptor. "Minesweeper", a computer game, rewards carving safe "unmined" zones from a grid of unknown potentially dangerous squares. If nature abhors a vacuum, the stress around a void must be sustained. Securing volume in a hostile environment is not so different from the suburban job of mowing the ever-growing lawn. Nor is it far from at least one architectural concern evident in the plan of the great Bayon Temple at Angkor Thom, Cambodia, whose increasingly central courtyards are nested like the petals of a lotus flower. The plan of Angkor, jungle city of perhaps a million by the 15th century was built of dikes and lakes to catch floods for later irrigation. This 13th Century Khmer Buddhist shrine is the most complex building on the Angkor site. The 54 satellite towers bear a total of 216 faces. The concentric perimeter walls make good sense when we realize the site context is a jungle! Beyond the site's built edges, space is not passive void, but rather filled with life, which if left unmanaged, will engulf the site in vines, trees, and animals, as overgrown "lost" temples around the world reveal. Often human space must first be carved and then *maintained.*

Precincts: *every Where is the middle*

The drive to the center and the simultaneous drive to the edge that is part of every sense of space (claustrophobia vs. agoraphobia) creates a spacial resonance of the first order. Every animal senses the need to mark arrival at the center and the equally strong atavistic desire to "secure the perimeter". The *promenade architecturale* elaborates the journey between them. Thus insides and outsides are always related, and there is always stress at the border. The gnomon mandala plans of Khmer temples hint at the richness of this sustained theme. To reach the center of the 12th century Angkor Vat, a person completes a complex journey inward: the visitor must take a causeway across a moat along a 235 m. wide propylaea portico with towers; proceed along 350 m. long axial avenue raised and paved, cut by twelve stairways and pools; cross a two-level cruciform platform on the first terrace; pass a gallery of bas-reliefs on the first enclosure; enter a cruciform courtyard, past small libraries; move onto galleries of the second enclosure; then to the body of the third enclosure with galleries open both inward and out, and finally arrive at the main shrine-- a tower rising 65 m. above the plain surrounded by four secondary towers. Of course jungle plants need only loft their seeds on the wind to fly across the rings of walls.

District, ward, and neighborhood are each a kind of precinct, a sacred space. The space most sacred for each individual may be the home, while the most sacred for the collective is the abode of the Deity, whatever sustains the life of the community beyond the scope of each individual. No person can guarantee certain intensely personal events-- birth, death, and marriage. A secret marriage has no meaning to society. We do not consciously preside over our own births and cannot truly guarantee that our wishes will be carried out at our funeral. These are the essential tasks of religion, whose etymological roots, *re-lig-ios,* mean tying together again, re-binding. Each collective society needs to enshrine its continuity by making the secular sacred, and engenders the architectural strategy of precincts within precincts, the creation of "holy of holies". Buddhist and Hindu religious tradition celebrates a cosmology of many lives and many deities, and its architecture often elaborates every surface of plan, section, and elevation to reveal the infinite variety manifest in the spirit of life.

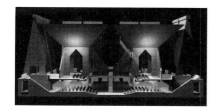

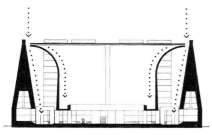

CONVINCING THE WIND

Valves and doors

Void perforates all mass; mass perforates all void. Then how can things be closed? Most architectural models (including the ones you have made for Harmony and Concerto) pretend to keep the inside in and outside out, but their implied windows could not convince the wind. Volume may be shrink-wrapped like a package, but such skin must be punctured to guarantee continuity between indoors and out. Inhabitants must be protected from the weather, but visitors must also find a way to enter. For every architectural volume, you must determine the desirable balance between enclosure (impermeability) and a continuity of inside and out. You must explode the box, but not too much. A room without a window or doorway is not accessible, a room without any walls, floors, posts, or other boundaries or markers is not identifiable as a unique volume. Thus all architecture, from vapor barrier to birdcage, has some degree of openness, and some degree of closedness. The amount of closure, and the coincidence of the marking of closure through the location of other masses like columns, wall, floor, and ceiling planes, and furniture, is one measure of the skill of the architect to develop all necessary functions of habitable volume with a pure economy of means.

A spectrum of perforation

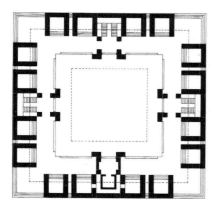

We may conceive of a spectrum of perforation for architectural volumes, ranging from completely impermeable (a totally sealed bag or wrapper) to completely permeable (the "ideal" massless cube of Euclid) offering no hindrance to any thing or force seeking passage through it. This conception has of course a practical application: weatherproofing is an important concern to inhabitants. Designing enclosure to keep a room warm and dry in cold wet weather, and cool in hot weather raises legitimate concerns of how to properly locate such materials as insulation, vapor barrier, and shading devices. But it is possible to understand these concerns on another level as well. The degree of enclosure needed to make volume present as an architectural space creates what some designers refer to as a "sense of place". Here we more precisely locate such feeling by identifying what distinguishes musical instruments like violins and guitars from just any old wooden box. Musical instruments are tensegrity volumes which have been developed, tested, and refined over centuries to produce maximum **resonance** to make a sounding box that can magnify the original sound source to fill a whole concert hall. The concert hall is a continuation and magnifier of the resonating sound box of the instrument. We know how much more difficult it is to hear an outdoor concert (without electronic amplification) than an indoor one-- that is why the concert hall was built in the first place!

Degree of enclosure is a new issue in an architecture of geometrodynamic solids, balancing the integrity of the skin against the continuity of site and program in plan and section. An isolated vessel increases the predictability of placement of things inside a volume. The weather is a chaotic phenomenon and therefore can never be fully predictable. Cladding is the skin and clothes around a room. Doors and windows are valves controlling the flow of light, air, people, water, etc. in and out of volumetric vessels. Architectural space results from forces exploding and imploding through boundary conditions. To carve habitable space from a possibly hostile exterior requires keeping the membrane between them elastic. This permits the plan to be plastic-- modifiable within its protected zone. Spacetime is geometrodynamic, elastic and plastic together. Carpentry may be the first practical skill an architect, if fortunate, will acquire. But learning to carpenter plan into geometrodynamic cabinetry quickly helps the student begin to master space. Lou Kahn's design for Hurva Synagogue, shown in both computer simulation and wooden model, is an orchestration of controlled perforations by light, air and people. Direct and indirect access of all these forces keep this space a lively arena of change.

DRUM AND BUBBLE

Building Envelope and Vapor Barrier

"Good fences make good neighbors." Robert Frost.

Take a deep breath. Inflate your lungs. That's how to make volume. Of course, you had help from the elastic tissue comprising your lungs, as well as from your diaphragm, rib cage, and muscles that sustained the vacuum your local zone of airocean atmosphere rushed to fill. Antoine Lavoisier (1743-1794), father of modern chemistry, discoverer of oxygen and identifier of it as the agent of combustion, was also the father of modern thinking about ventilation and air conditioning. Another Frenchman, Sadi Carnot (1796-1832) showed that in a gas pressure and heat are related, and both are a function of volume. His 1824 ideal cycle of reversible pressure and volume is the basis of both steam and internal combustion engines. Their important work contributed to the formulation of a kinetic theory of matter and thermodynamics, the study of the motion of heat. The flight of a group of hot air balloons (see page 12) can serve as an image of a "gas" of rooms not yet coalesced as decisive plan and section. Hot gas released in one direction is a jet, a thermodynamic demonstration of Newton's Third Law of Motion of action and equal and opposite reaction. A jet can drive a balloon across a room or a rocket across a galaxy. Boundaries reinforce intensity. The thermal and moisture skins that are such an important part of every dwelling must now also be considered as design issues . It would have been impossible to heat any of the projects you have designed so far, although certainly areas in direct sunlight would be warmer than shaded areas. While discontinuity between inside and outside is usually necessary for human comfort and survival, too much separation is a liability. Without holes, not only can't you get fresh air, but also you can't escape! The essential membrane of modern buildings that determines permeability or impermeability is the vapor barrier, the plastic sheeting that is usually found in every opaque exterior house surface.

Floating on Air, Walking on Water

Ant Farm and other experimental architecture groups of the 1960's and 1970's went so far as to use only a building's vapor barrier for its structure, which they inflated with household fans passing over heaters. They noted that as much as half of the structural cost of contemporary buildings goes to hold up the air-handling equipment-- the ducts, fans, vents, heaters, and condensers that comprise a modern large-scale HVAC air supply system. They eliminated this and all other columns and beams by making the entire structure from just the vapor barrier. To hold up the floppy piece of plastic, they inflated the space! They sealed the plastic into a pillow, attaching fans and heaters directly to build a slight interior pressure on the inside. It was fun: on a 50' pillow, scores of people on the roof could see their friends inside 20' directly below them while riding and rolling on an undulating surface carnival of ever-shifting mass and feedback stress. It was cheap, beautiful, and the acoustics were magnificent. These architects had designed and built building-sized drums-- skintight resonators. Cutting flaps for entry doors leaked out only a little air: inside pressure was still positive. In fact the biggest problems with these auditorium pillows was their lightness. The whole building acted like a wing or sail and tended to blow away in the wind unless firmly anchored to the ground at crucial points. At about the same time, Graham Stevens in England made structures that enabled people to literally walk on water. Alone they turned large tetrahedrons like pointed paddle wheels to help them move, together they could walk or ride small hovercraft for miles from shore to deep sea liners or off-loading cargo freighters. For any one person to sink, all of the air in the bubble tube had to remain under water, and as Archimedes showed, like a hull the tube displaces far greater mass of water than its volume of air weighs. Eureka *and* hallelujah!

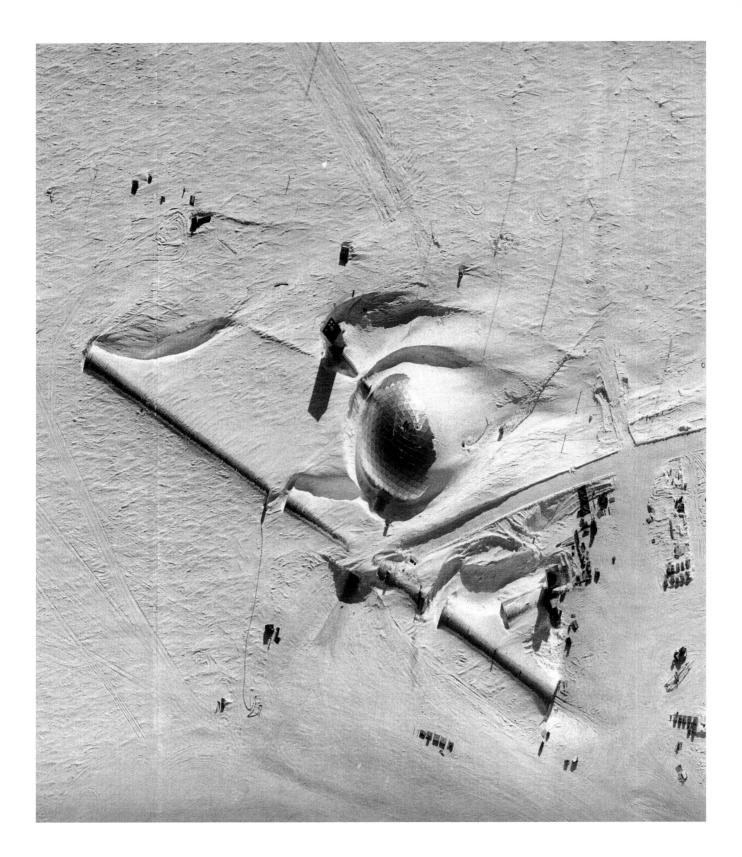

BIOPHYSICS

"Order is." Louis I. Kahn

Entropy

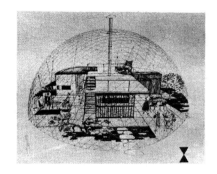

The coldest place on earth is Antarctica. The aerial view opposite of the geodesic dome built to be directly over the South Pole in the year 2000 (the ice drifts!) makes clear how fragile we humans are. We need to keep our bubble warm (not hot) or soon we die of hypothermia. Humans need a very specific range of local conditions: we are only comfortable if the air around us is in "the comfort zone", roughly 68° to 72 °F at 30-70% relative humidity. To maintain this atmosphere the walls, roof, floors, and doors that comprise the skin-clothing of the room must insulate heat loss or gain to the outside beyond, for warm always seeks to move to cool. The ultimate hostility of any environment is not an active malevolence, but rather disorder at the border. Mix bags of red and blue marbles together and pour the results into two piles. The statistical chance that the system will return to its original degree of order, one pile all red, the other all blue, is vanishingly small. The same is true when a hot fluid is allowed to mix with a cold one: inevitably the result is a lukewarm mixture in both containers. Theoretically, the few hottest molecules in the cold fluid could migrate to the hot fluid, making the hot one hotter and the cold one colder, but statistically this never happens. (Separate coffee and cream after they have been mixed!) An important principle in thermodynamics, the study of heat, tells us that pockets of difference tend toward ever-increasing sameness. Ever-growing disorder in the universe is called **entropy**. In the largest scale, increasing entropy appears to be inevitable. But life, culture, and architecture sustain at least temporary pockets of order. The architect must sustain the identity of a volume, a chamber both fluid and stable, in the face of ever-changing environments, and must maintain difference in the face of increasing entropy. Thus the warm-enough human bubble at the South Pole is *always* too warm for the air around it. Its skin must be maintained, insulated, and supplied with heat. To keep space habitable **costs!**

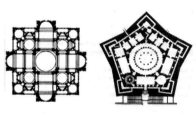

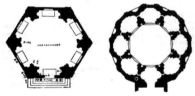

Integrity: The Nature of the Cell

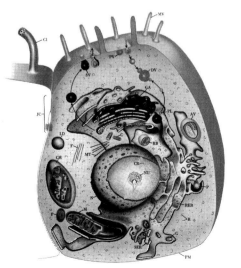

A single-celled creatures like the amoeba is nothing less than a miracle. Its cell wall is an osmotic membrane that allows flow without losing the essential order of the pressure, temperature, and volume of the animal, not in static but thermodynamic equilibrium with its surrounding environment. A living cell is a kind of standing wave in general resonance, reverberating like a violin at all frequencies. The eukaryotic cell, with a nucleus and complex organization, is indeed a remarkable wonder. The nucleus is the means for the cell to know itself. It sends instructions throughout the cell to help it maintain constancy and identity without being destroyed, and receives information from the world beyond it that help it formulate these instructions. Inside the nucleus, DNA, the molecule of inheritance, generates a cell's identity and its posterity. The cell's ability to transform the materials in its environment into what it needs requires a complex resonant metabolism to survive and reproduce. What a design problem: (bio-)mechanical systems that must work millions of times for billions of years! Compare that with the problems of making a safe and working nuclear reactor! Osmotic membranes maintain thermodynamic equilibrium. To sustain an internal atmosphere, punctures of the skin must be controlled by very precise valves. (One thinks of that marvelous fountain in Captain Nemo's submarine living room, bubbling quietly just a few feet away from the tons of water pressure that would occur at "twenty thousand leagues under the sea." What a precise valve that fountain must have had to keep all of the ocean at bay except for the slight burble of the fountain!) Architectural valves like doors and windows help control the passage of air, light, moisture, and people. We seek to make habitable bubble volumes with as little mass as possible, but must make valves especially strong when the difference between inside and out is large. The South Pole settlement includes not only rooms inside the central geodesic dome, but extended quonset huts, an air landing strip, radio and control towers. Through these the cell maintains its inward needs and engages the outside world in constant feedback.

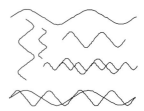

STANDING WAVE: *THE ETERNAL EVENT*

Biology! That's the new word in architecture! Le Corbusier, in *Radiant City*

Le Corbusier's Modulor Man in a volume proportioned to the human figure suggests that we can inhabit harmony, and even further, that the volumes of our rooms can resonate with the volumes of our bodies. His collage showing a room of light in the midst of the black void of space is eerily similar to the image of Apollo 15 astronaut David Scott saluting the American flag on the Moon in front of his mobile dwelling outpost, the Lunar Excursion Module, or LEM. The walls around the Modulor box seem to quiver into resonant space-- and this is quite close to the truth when we consider that the astronaut can only survive in a *thermodynamic* volume, a solid that is properly heated, humidified, and pressurized to something near the conditions of earth's atmosphere. In "outer space" habitable volume **costs, a lot!** And to hold against the vacuum of the void, it must be sealed! Here on earth "outer space" exists too-- right on the surface, the weaving edge between spinning and grooving. Every Where costs to maintain as constant in a dynamic universe. Any habitable volume, from LEM to Noah's Ark, from biological cell to the whole Earth itself, is a **standing wave**, a vessel of relatively constant condition in an ever changing field, packets of energy woven into resonant volume.

Volume in thermodynamic equilibrium

Figure-field resonance creates oscillating forces of both explosion and implosion, so any geometric figure tends to be a *moving* figure, creating a field the way a stone breaking the surface of a pond creates ripples. (Movement within a figure, like human circulation through a building, also generates spacial fields. A breeze through a window can slam shut a door.) Thus does an architect order *moving* fields in space and time. The architectural version of the biological problem of an organism's identity is to maintain the structure and form of a volume through varying environments. This concerns the human-scale mechanisms that act as osmotic membranes for habitable space: skin, valves, and filters. Through these we may engage space beyond the membrane. Until now, a program volume in Dynamics could carry relative inertia, but without a skin it could not sustain a pressure differential. A skin is needed (even if non-material, like air-doors at banks and shopping malls) to modulate relationships between volumes through controlled pressure differentials.

Outpost and Insight

Le Corbusier's plan for the legislature Assembly Building at India's capital, Chandigarh, shows how one vessel or volume can sit inside and interact with another. The Senate Chamber, a skylit hyperbolic paraboloid made of straight spars torquing around a central axis of revolution is based on the structure of a contemporary cooling tower, oriented due north. It creates the integrity of the meeting space like the nucleus of a living cell or a fetus attached to the placenta of the womb. The Chamber is inserted into and distorts the column grid of the hypostyle *pas perdus* court, in turn surrounded by perimeter filters moderating inside to outside: offices to northeast and northwest, *brise-soleil* sun shades to the southwest, and deep fins along the portico to the south east. Each zone has its own acoustic, thermal, lighting, and circulation properties. Volumes meet and intersect through vestibules, lobbies, forecourts, landings, and so on. These transitions between zones create a programmatic equivalent to both vector and thermodynamic equilibrium-- resonance of architectural spaces vibrating with and through each other. Together the program volumes generate their own "weight" to anchor this complex human institution in place.

Our bubble of light air and water...

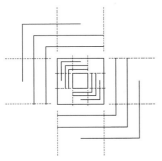

resonance: a *moving* figure creates a field oscillating implosion and explosion.

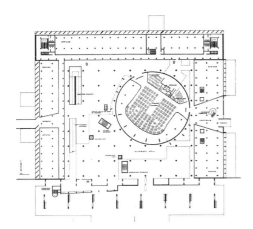

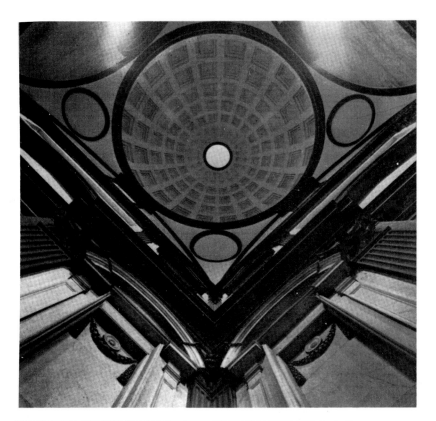

20. Medici Chapel

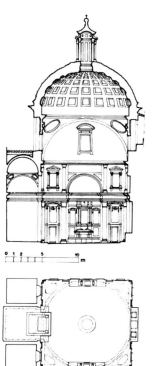

GREAT ROOM

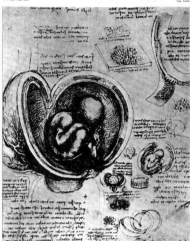

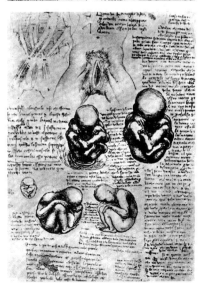

Every beauty which is seen here below
by persons of perception
resembles more than anything else
that celestial source from which
we all are come...
My eyes longing for beautiful things
together with my soul longing for salvation
have no other power
to ascend to heaven
than the contemplation of beautiful things.

MICHELANGELO

Beauty all around me, with it I wander
With beauty all around me, may I walk.

NAVAJO SONG

There are some small places, complete worlds unto themselves, which yet extend far into the world beyond. A simple volume becomes a complex space as each element is kept "in tune" to harmoniously work with the whole. Brunelleschi's Pazzi Chapel, Borromini's San Carlo alla Quatre Fontana, Wright's Unity Temple, Le Corbusier's Chapel at Ronchamp and the Tea House at Katsura Villa are all simply rooms. But they are "Great Rooms" of deep and moving sanctity because of their resonant order, clarity, and unity. Their volumes become spaces of endless dimension, without limit, filling our hearts with emotion and reverberating in our minds because of their *architecture.* They are spaces where offspring come into being...

One example of such a space is Michelangelo's Medici Chapel in Florence. Themes of birth and death are explored in this "womb with a view". Here conception equals both resonance, as "reinforcement of a musical tone by a vibrating body" and the origin of life: in and out through the birth canal, a multigenerational vibration. Michelangelo's Laurentian Library *Ricetto* is no more than a place to pass from the monastery to the library beyond. Yet the elements of that place are arranged to reveal a dynamic of volume, a sense of space ever in flux. Here at the Medici Chapel too mass and volume surge to animate space, but in a more subtle manner. Do not the paired pilasters (framing river gods!) support the uterine dome like great feminine thighs? Do not circle and square, cube and sphere pulsate against each other everywhere in this space? Do not the captive studies of Michelangelo parallel Leonardo's anatomical dissections in their metaphysical quest for birth of vitality-- from rock and flesh together? Here is where organization meets organism.

Order and Proportion: Resonance and plasticity

The Classic orders of Greek, Roman, and Renaissance architecture are based on the proportions of how the parts of column, entablature and arch systems go together. The Ionic order is more slender than the Doric order, and the Corinthian is more ornate than both. Behind all the theory about their use, profiles and proportions, we may find that they are derived from rules of thumb and discoveries about how common and standard elements and materials could go well together in making space of mass sturdily constructed and void well proportioned to human scale, where all parts were in harmony. The perception of space and structure simultaneously can contribute greatly to a sense of architectural resonance. A smallest volumetric interval, or module, can be established which relates to the materials available, method of construction, and human scale all at once. The Egyptians found the cubit, based the length from the elbow to the tip of the hand, which turned out to be almost exactly equal to one fourth the height or armspread span of the person measured! The Romans based their measurement on the foot, which was about one sixth the height of a tall man. (Together the Egyptian and Roman systems yield 4:6 or 2:3 proportions!) The Greeks found modules and proportional systems based on geometric relationships, and applied them to their bowls, pottery, music, and sculpture as well as every interval and curve of their temples. Today we use [nominal] 2x4 lumber and 4x8 plywood in the same way. Le Corbusier 's MODULOR (in French a pun on "module of gold") relates square and golden section to human dimensions. The values of this wonderful system form the Fibonacci series which appears throughout the natural world of living things.

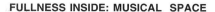

PERIOD

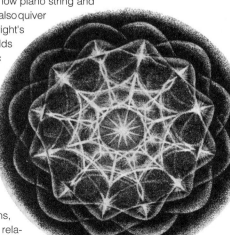

RESONANT LOAD

FULLNESS INSIDE: MUSICAL SPACE

*Space has tonality, and I imagine myself composing a space lofty, vaulted, or under a dome,
attributing to it a sound character alternating with the tones of space, narrow and high,
with graduating silver, light to darkness.* Louis Kahn, Between Silence and Light

At *la merveille*, the monk's stone dining hall at Mont. St. Michel, fireplaces are 5' high and 500 year old windows still close effortlessly. Sounds persist for minutes. In its reverberant chamber, you can sing all four tones of a chord, piling one tone on another like a Gregorian chant. Musical resonance is the reinforcement of a musical tone by a vibrating body (resonator) attached to or near the source of a sound. In the xylophone, for example, each key has its own resonator, a metal cylinder suspended below the key. The sounding board of the piano and the belly of the violin are *general resonators*, reinforcing all sounds produced on the instrument. A violin body is a sound box perforated with holes to let sound out, whose volume vibrates in resonance with the strings. Violin bodies have natural modes of vibration which strengthen certain tones sounded by the strings to help them resonate. Ernst Chladni (c. 1800) devised a method for revealing resonance in a space, showing how a violin vibrates. He put sand on a violin-shaped plate of brass and bowed it at various points. The sand concentrated along quiet nodes between vibrating areas. Low tones produce patterns of a few large areas, while high tones produce many small areas. Poor violins accentuate squeaky top notes. Can the reinforcement of such patterns be one reason why the fan vaults of King's College Chapel in Cambridge England produce such marvelous acoustics? Like *la merveille*, the Chapel is a dynamic resonator that magnifies reverberation; a tensegrity which organizes volume, skin, and bones into a vibrating whole; stones as well as the organ pipes make the structure a built musical instrument to inhabit. This phenomenon is not only acoustic, but plastic as well.

How can we modify space to reinforce desired vibration frequencies? Mandala patterns are created in liquid by harmonic vibrations. A monk bell-puller creates a resonant load. Hit a low piano string and all the tonic and dominant tones above will also quiver in sympathetic vibration. Frank Lloyd Wright's plan for the Friedman House shows two fields concentrating along the nodes of public hearth and private master bedroom. Portoghesi and Gigliotti's plan for a 1967 weekend house, *Casa Andreis*, illustrate their theory of architectural fields, of spacial influence. A physical system may resonate and thus outlast the original forces that set it in motion. For architecture, the time a space exists outlasts its effort to construct it. Does this have something to do with the proportions and reinforcing effects of all the small decisions, like the size and placement of a door in relation to a window or structure for the ceiling?

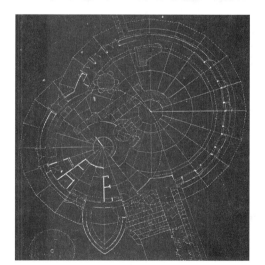

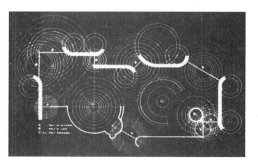

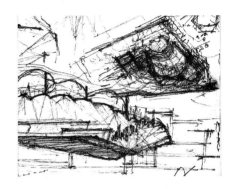

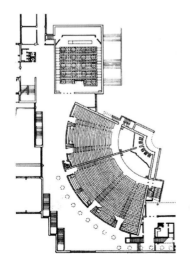

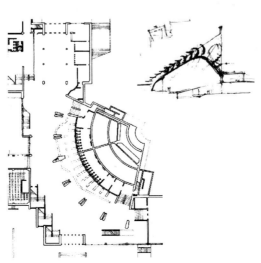

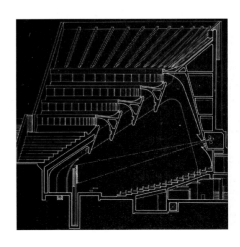

FROM ALL ANGLES

Whole number multiples of vibration are resonant frequencies to the original or fundamental mode of oscillation. At a piano, hold the sustaining pedal down to lift the felt dampers off the strings, and whistle near the strings. After you stop whistling, you will hear a ghostly persistence of the note that you have whistled, which dies away with time. The piano strings act as resonators.

> A taut piano string can vibrate at more than one frequency. The simplest, or fundamental, mode of oscillation can be regarded as sine waves traveling along the string with a constant velocity, and being reflected repeatedly at the ends of the string to generate the resonant frequency f_o. The next three resonant frequencies, $2f_o$, $3f_o$, $4f_o$, have the patterns of vibrations shown in parts B, C, and D, respectively.... Plucking or striking a stretched string excites many of these vibrations and produces a complex sound wave made up of many harmonics. The length, mass, and tension of the string determine the periodicity and pitch of the sound that is produced, but do not determine the exact waveform. The relative strengths of the various harmonics depend on whether we pluck or strike a string, and on where along its length we pluck or strike it. We can hear the difference in the sound quality or timbre. For example, the plucked string of a harpsichord sounds quite different from the struck string of a piano. When we excite a string by bowing it, we get a persistent sound of yet another character, even though the resonances of the string may be the same... The vertical metal tubes under the wooden bars of xylophones and marimbas, and the bamboo tubes under the brass bars of gamelans, act as resonators that intensify and prolong certain of the partials generated by striking the bars, specifically, the partials that correspond to notes of the scale."
>
> *The Science of Musical Sound*, John R. Pierce

The volumetric architectural instrument resonates to both inside and outside forces. For example, the modern architect Alvar Aalto, designing a new college campus at Otaniemi, Finland, responded to two apparently different program demands for a concert hall and an outdoor public arena by integrating them into a single plastic configuration. Aalto was closely in tune with the intoxication of the pure sensation of volume. For him, the fashioning of space was ever contingent, ever sculptural, ever surprising, ever active. He shaped space from inside out and from outside in. At Otaniemi, he curved the ceiling ribs of the auditorium to magnify sound waves, in a manner similar to the way ribs stiffen the sound-box of a concert grand piano. The shape and spacing of these ribs also permit clerestory bands of glazing between them that suffuse the interior with a soft indirect natural light. The biology of this special space goes further, for outside the sound chamber the ribs frame and enhance the effect of the lower concentric seats for a small outdoor stadium. Aalto's sketches show concern for overlapping intersecting fields of rhythm, keeping in mind both the movement of sound waves and movement of people through space in plan and section. His incredibly lively (drunken!) lines are like the living fibers that form the chambers of heart, stomach or lung, pushing and pulling as they perform their bodily functions, responding to both internal and external stresses in several resonant modes like musical strings. Perhaps this is one reason for the Cubist fascination with guitar and violin-- bodies simultaneously flat and curved, hollow boxes empty of mass but filled with energy, living tensegrities of expansion and contraction. For space to resonate, it must find a way to intensify its order. It must concentrate its effects so that they build on each other.

The rigid rib cage skeleton reifies the elastic volume of the heart-lung organs in our bodies. It makes room for that which is within as much as it protects from that which is without. But what are the right sizes for such structures-- does size of heart demand a given rib size, or the other way around? Clearly, both are part of life's subtle complex design equations. It is tempting to speculate about necessary intervals of resonant design that distinguish species and establish their successes. How did bird genes know to make feathers and lightweight bones at the same time? Perhaps the self-standing volumes of each individual suggests a Noah's Ark resonant scale of life.

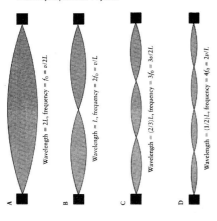

"A violin string is an example of a distributed parameter resonator, since kinetic energy and potential energy are both distributed along the entire length of the string."
The Encyclopedia of Physics

A. Wavelength = $2L$, frequency = $f_o = v/2L$

B. Wavelength = L, frequency = $2f_o = v/L$

C. Wavelength = $(2/3)L$, frequency = $3f_o = 3v/2L$

D. Wavelength = $(1/2)L$, frequency = $4f_o = 2v/L$

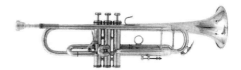

DWELLING INSTRUMENTS

The Art of Dwelling

To dwell is human. Wild beasts have nests, cattle have stables, carriages fit into sheds, and there are garages for automobiles. Only humans can dwell. To dwell is an art.... The human is the only animal who is an artist, and the art of dwelling is part of the art of living. A house is neither nest nor garage. Most languages use living in the sense of dwelling. To put the question "where do you live?" is to ask for the place where your daily existence gives shape to the world. Just tell me how you dwell and I will tell you who you are. This equation of dwelling and living goes back to times when the world was still habitable and humans were in-habitants. Then dwell meant to inhabit one's own traces, to let daily life write the webs and knots of one's biography into the landscape. This writing could be etched into stone by successive generations or sketched anew for each rainy season with a few reeds and leaves.

Ivan Illich

Taking it all with you...

Recall that an instrument, unlike a tool, is designed to perform complex combinations of actions without limit (*Architectonics*, page 7). Whereas a hammer is designed to complete repetitive and predictable tasks, a clarinet, trumpet, violin, or piano permits limitless pattern invention and variation. An instrument is the means for expressing the subtlest phenomena-- love, joy, tragedy, ecstasy. While Le Corbusier's famous "*a house is a machine for living in*" reminds architects that function could formulate volume with the precision of a machine, we should also note that to pursue Illich's "art of dwelling" demands no less than dwelling instruments-- precise, elegant, no more massive than required for liberating life and re-humanizing our whole planet. Thus, along with issues of Environment, Ecology, and Energy ("the three E's"), housing is a problem of dwelling instruments. In this information age, machines need not be repetitive to standard form but rather can be programmed to every given task. Already robot cutters can tailor cloth to the order of each client as easily as a person composes type on the computer screen. With software, the machine is already an instrument. A complex of multi-cultural dwelling instruments can make harmony in diversity of extended more-than-nuclear families who live in walking-scale neighborhoods that recapture the sense and satisfaction of living in community. Extended to a pluralist urban and region scale may engender a symphony of societies, an orchestration of compassion and common sense.

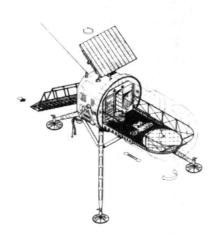

Outfitting Vessels for the Sea of Spacetime

The first step is a decent place to live. Despite the 1980's misconception that "first there is food, clothing, and shelter, and then when you get rich there is cuisine, fashion, and architecture", let us recall that the primary task of architecture is not homes for the rich, but *housing for all*. Perhaps the most fruitful time for such investigation (after the Heroic period from 1890 to 1940, from Wright's Prairie houses to Le Corbusier's Villa Savoye and Garches, and Mies' Tughendat House) was the 1960's and early 70's, especially with Archigram and other groups like Ant Farm, Jersey Devil, and NASA. We must recapture the spirit of willingness to seek ways to hear both birds and Bach in the woods, to experiment with materials, program, and technique to solve human problems, and follow the plastic implications of such experiment. The Lunar Module was a home for humans voyaging in the void, leaping from one world to another. Other outposts, all shown here, include offshore oil rigs, Coop Himmelblau, Mike Webb's Cushicle, David Greene's Fully Applianced House, Dallegret's Envirobubble, Bakewell and Jantzen's Autonomous Dwelling Vehicle, Kaplicky's Earthome and of course the MMU. But don't all these seem elaborate when compared to Inuit igloo or Aboriginal string bag and atl-atl? We still and always will have much to learn about dwelling, to achieve the elegant simplicity of Tokugawa *tatami* rooms, eloquent in their emptiness of implements, filled with *space*.

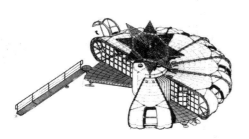

SUSIE PEZZELLO

VINCENT MUIA

ARET LERIAN

J. NAGLE

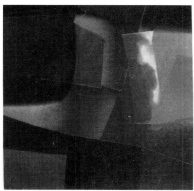

J. NAGLE

JOHN CUNHA

COLLAGE AND BRICOLAGE

An ideal engineer would seek to manage every phase of a design project. To make a chair, the engineer might *a priori* describes everything needed say to make a chair, from mining ore and constructing factories, to ergonomic research for exact dimensions for perfect posture, to careful estimate of market share. On the other hand, a jack-of all-trades handyman may search through a pile of discarded junk, find an old tractor seat, a broken barrel stave, some bricks, and perhaps some baling wire to hold the whole thing together, adjust the seat angle and *voila*-- a chair!

> [There is an activity],,, commonly called 'bricolage' in French. In its old sense the verb 'bricoler' applied to ball games and billiards, to hunting, shooting, and riding. It was however always used with reference to some extraneous movement: a ball rebounding, a dog straying or a horse swerving from its direct course to avoid an obstacle. And in our own time the 'bricoleur' is still someone who works with his hands and uses devious means compared to those of a craftsman... The 'bricoleur' is adept at performing a large number of diverse tasks; but unlike the engineer, he does not subordinate each of them to the availability of raw materials and tools conceived and procured for the purpose of the project. His universe of instruments is always closed and the rules of his game are always to make do with 'whatever is at hand', that is to say with a set of tools and materials which is always finite and is also heterogeneous because what it contains bears no relation to the current project, or indeed to any particular project, but is the contingent result of all the occasions there have been to renew or enrich the stock or to maintain it with the remains of previous constructions or destructions. The set of the 'bricoleur's' means cannot therefore be defined in terms of a project (which would presuppose besides, that, as in the case of the engineer), there were, at least in theory, as many sets of tools and materials or 'instrumental sets' as there are different kinds of projects). It is to be defined only by its potential use or, putting this another way and in the language of the 'bricoleur' himself, because the elements are collected or retained on the principle that 'they may always come in handy'. Such elements are specialized up to a point, sufficiently for the 'bricoleur'; not to need the equipment and knowledge of all trades and professions, but not enough for each of them to have only one definite and determinate use. They each represent a set of actual and possible relations: they are 'operators', but they can be used for any operations of the same type.
>
> ...Consider him at work and excited by his project. His first practical step is retrospective. He has to turn back to an already existent set made up of tools and materials, to consider or reconsider what it contains and, finally and above all, to engage in a sort of dialogue with it and, before choosing between them, to index the possible answers which the whole set can offer to his problem. He interrogates all the heterogenous objects of which his treasury is composed to discover what each of them could 'signify' and so contribute to the definition of a set which has yet to materialize but which will ultimately differ from the instrumental set only in the internal disposition of its parts. A particular cube of oak could be a wedge to make up for the inadequate length of a plank of pine or it could be a pedestal-- which would allow the grain and polish of the old wood to show to advantage. In one case it will serve as an extension, in the other as material. But the possibilities always remain limited by the particular history of each piece and by those of its features which are already determined by the use for which it was originally intended or the modifications it has undergone for other purposes..."
>
> The Savage Mind, by Claude Levi-Strauss

Architect Hans Hollein acted as *bricoleur* when he combined two photographs to propose Carrier City. The juxtaposition between aircraft carrier and mid-continent farmland suggests a new composite form, and thus the unusual idea that a manufactured town or city might be a fruitful strategy for inhabiting the land. The question of housing is always more important than preconceived theory. To find solutions, we must search beyond fences. To live well we must find lifeboats, and in a storm, any ship is better than none. Hollein used montage-- the graphic method of careful cropping to create a convincing illusion. The technique is even more powerful when exploited without illusionistic goals. The collision of hitherto unrelated elements is called **collage**. Careful consideration of the resulting relationships in collage opens the mind to finding new plastic relationships that are born in two dimensions but quickly leap into three, as the graphic works on these pages suggest. Collage a useful tool for the improviser of both structural and volumetric relationships.

ANIMATING

Construction Geometry

Complex figures can be made precisely with just the tools of compass and straightedge, with perhaps protractor and dividers added. Construction geometry is and art as well as science. Contractors are rightful heirs to Euclid and Pythagoras-- it is they who cut and measure pieces to just fit to make built volume strong and stable. The smooth flow of ink or pencil line as the hand turns the compass makes a *perfect* circle curve. Descartes' method of plotting points from an algebraic formula is equivalent to a raster scan on a computer screen-- it generates many points, but there is no internal sense to their connection. It is plotted, but not constructed. Whereas a circle drawn with compass is a vector curve-- it is a *line*--with purpose, continuous, and constructed. The act of construction is both an intellectual exercise, a form of mathematic study, and a physical exercise of the whole body or just the hand. In both cases it involves the feedback of nerves to brain and back again, the interplay of internal and external intelligent skin.

Construction is piling up, in time....

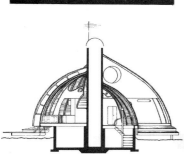

The client for the Snail House was a university steamfitter named Smitty, who approached the Jersey Devil, a group of design-builders led by Steve Badanes and John Ringel, about building a home for his family near the Jersey shore in the states's Pine Barrens region. The Jersey Devil and their construction crew promptly moved on location and started work. The idea of the house evolves as much from thinking about construction as any other issue. This is a house of ready-made elements-- concrete manhole casings stacked into a mast that supports the off-the-shelf barn bents of many sizes. The skin is insulating foam sprayed over cedar boards, then coated with exterior paint. The sprayer attached his rigging to the chimney to pivot easily around the shell. In addition, the shape is due to practical considerations regarding sunlight, ventilation, and privacy. To allow natural light while maintaining privacy, the curved ribbon windows spiral from east to west, catching the sun as it moves across the southern sky. Natural ventilation through the house is aided by the hollow central core, which acts as a gigantic flue, drawing cool air from the basement. The shape also reduces the volumes of the house by 40 per cent (you can enclose more space with less material with a dome form), allowing it to be built on Smitty's slender budget. But the Snail House isn't exactly a dome, hence its name. As you walk around the house it appears more like an exploding, overturned grapefruit half, detonated by a stick of dynamite that rises from its center. In plan it resembles the expanding volutes of a snail's shell, which unfold as you move from the south entry, through the living room and dining area, finally culminating in the bedroom and loft above. In section the house expands as well faithfully replicating the unfolding of the plan." John got the idea of putting the tower in the center and just increasing the sections in size," says Steve, " so it becomes a spiral in both plan and section."

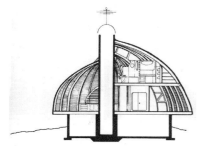

A later Jersey Devil project on a mountain ridge near the California coast continues this tradition of calculated *bricolage* (see previous page) for taking advantage of materials and site in new and untried ways. In the hands of these on-the-site designers, problems of construction become opportunities for making space. The house is dug into its site, earth sheltered to the north and on its roof, so the ceiling is a fan of double bow-shaped open web joists that carry the weight of sod and help withstand the coastal winds. The arc in plan acts as a beam to help this strength and minimize the length of retaining wall on the leeward side. The roof drains into a cistern that forms the garden in the middle of the deck. The plan here too reveals the happy marriage of the compasses of geometer and surveyor. The building constructs is landscape as much as it fits into it.

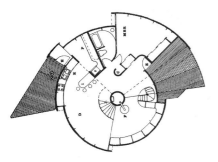

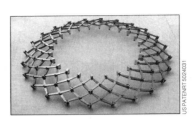

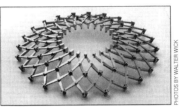

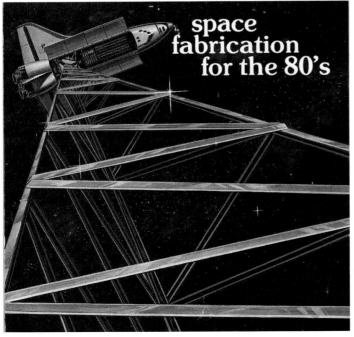

space
fabrication
for the 80's

BEAM BUILDING

Construction begins with arranging mass into structural components. After identifying loads and calculating their effects on individual members, architects and engineers often complete their structural designs by selecting appropriate cross-sections from a wood or steel manual. This presumes that a manufacturer is available to supply members of the specified dimensions, and generally this is true. But the improvising (and enterprising) builder can often make the most efficient beams and columns out of any available materials by following a simple rule of thumb: *put the mass where the action is*, and its corollary, *get rid of mass where it isn't needed*. Action in this sense refers to the loads on members and the stresses they develop. Often, the more you can distribute mass to extremities of elements, the stronger you can make them. Thus, you may make a beam with an efficient "**I**" cross-section out of wood flanges and a pegboard web properly glued together. And you may make a rough-and-ready "retaining wall" out of empty cardboard boxes taped together and carefully placed stones for inertial mass.

Golden Junk

After Apollo 17 left the moon in 1972, the year the Snail House was completed, physicist I. Kistiakowsky discussed NASA's lunar program by recalling the Golden Junk expeditions during China's Tang Dynasty (600-800 AD). Fifty years of research and development produced an ocean going prototype, the Golden Junk. Three of these enormous ships sailed all the way to the Arabian peninsula and returned with tales of new creatures like the giraffe. They were on the verge of discovering Africa and perhaps a sea-route to medieval Europe before 800 AD. How different might have been world history! However, Confucians and Taoists fought like Republicans and Democrats before the Emperor, claiming that this expensive exploration program with no visible direct economic return was something that China could no longer afford. So China turned its back on reaping the riches of the unexpected, after investing in the advanced technology needed to produce ocean-going vessels, after actually landing on an alien shore, after accomplishing the hard parts! Rather than pursue the growth of human spirit into an ever more accommodating cosmos, they quit-- just like us after Eagle and its brethren landed on the moon. We may have saved a few dollars for extra hardware (unable to amortize development costs over use of many vehicles), but we lost priceless resources in allowing the infrastructure of knowledge communications to unravel and disintegrate. A web of working people and thinking minds networking, inventing solutions to problems every day could produce this likely scenario in the NASA design heyday of the 1950's and 60's: in Florida someone asks" who knows about high temperature effects on silicon?" "Oh, check with Jack in California, he know's who's been looking into nonmetals." A call to Jack, who says he doesn't know himself, but knows Fred in Boston who's been trying to solve nuclear reactor glass-melt problems, which after all involve high-temperature silicon... etc. A year of this and all the experts are connected at least 5 phone calls deep. Shut down the program, fire these guys, and that timely and irreplaceable knowledge is lost. No wonder we have not yet revisited the moon!

Grumman designed and manufactured the Lunar Module, the LEM. Its proposal for "Space fabrication for the 80's" seems poignant today. The Beam-Builder is an elegant idea, an almost literal expression of a standing wave. It is a measure of how much culture and courage we have lost that these images, visionary but realizable in the 1970's, in the 1990's seem too difficult, almost beyond our reach and abilities. A related story tells that after the tragic Challenger explosion, NASA engineers sought to reassemble original plans of Saturn rockets to find a way to reuse its "old" technology from the 1960's to replace the shuttle program. This sounds like nostalgia for a mythic "golden age". Why didn't the designers repeat the spirit of the 60's, itself a legacy of the WW II design/production triumph of organization, honesty, and intelligence? Why not just sit down, start from first principles, identify the need, and do it right, rather than copy the "magic" shape but not the content of the works of ancestors?

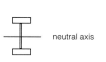

neutral axis

STRUCTURAL SECTIONS
moment of inertia...
skin = thickness with depth

COMPOSITE FIBER GIRDER

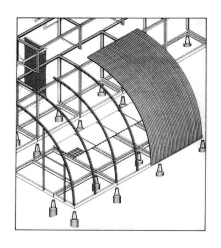

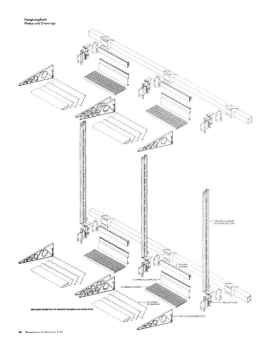

Hongkong Bank
Photos and Drawings

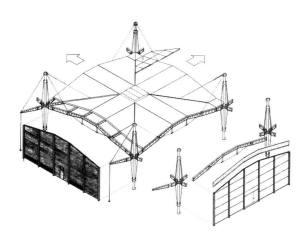

COMPONENTS AND ASSEMBLY

"god is in the details" Mies

Assembling solids

A bridge is a beam of beams, and a skyscraper is a column of columns, both in terms of masses and of volumes. Such complex structures involve joining whole assemblies of components. As you may have already discovered through your construction of models with the Bag of Tricks, the **order of assembly** of solid elements is often critical. Structural components must be shaped facilitate the stages of assembly as well as to meet demands of loads and stresses. Putting the pieces together to make a volume requires thinking about the when as well as where they go into place. Paul Amatuzzo notes that today most office buildings are designed in terms of the way panels are lifted by hoisting cranes and hooks to the upper floors, a clear example of how construction and assembly can drive other design parameters. Assembly is the opposite of carving. (carving is negative assembly). Assembly is additive, carving is subtractive. Plastically, both operations seek unity, and both are needed for unity. We might argue that together carving and assembly create tensegrity. Architectural tensegrity is the coincidence of program, light, and structure. Every design project, whether table or office tower, can aspire to the elegance of finely carved elements carefully assembled into a seamless revelation of space. Pre-fabrication can occur at every scale of design. We see on these pages the attention given to making it easy to carve and assemble masses is evident in the care in design of the volumes. The elaboration of elements around the window frames in Foster Associates' Hong Kong Bank show attention not only to sun control and structural efficiency, but also to simplifying washing the windows.

Strong Straight Square Great

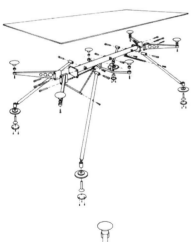

This is a good time to recall the three concerns that seek balance in a building to achieve an architectural tensegrity. Now you know enough to pro-pose ways to let a volume resonate with the many frequencies of their multiple geometries, and you can begin to think about re-solving them as architect, structural engineer, and environmental control specialist *simultaneously (or* at least concurrently). These varying geometries are most efficient in resolving different needs. The skill of the comprehensive designer consists in finding forms that resolve most appropriately and efficiently all constituent needs.

1. Orthogonal: the *architect* can maximize close packing volume integrated with human movement and vision in the perpendicular planes of gravity, horizon, and zoom depth.
2. Tetrahedral: the *engineer* can maximize strength with minimum mass through three intersecting shear planes to triangulate structure.
3. Spherical: the *environmental controller* can minimize surface area and local skin stresses with continuous, perhaps inflated, bubble-like enclosures.

Whole interval resonance

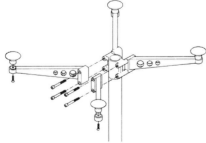

The elevation opposite of the Hong Kong Bank shows us what we might call whole interval resonance. Structure coincides with and articulates the volume. Note how the angle of the stair coincides with the outside diagonal bracing trees, and how the number of stories in these multilevel vierendeel trusses increases with increasing height. As the load increases in the lower floors the depth of the truss increases from 5 to 6 to 7 to 8 floors for each fourth of the height. While volumetric algebra suggests relationships between volumes-- one might be architecturally more rigid or harder to move than another-- integrating them into a whole fabric of relationships requires solving volumetric equations-- not just as volumetric algebra, but as a volumetric resonance into a total plastic and spacial unity.

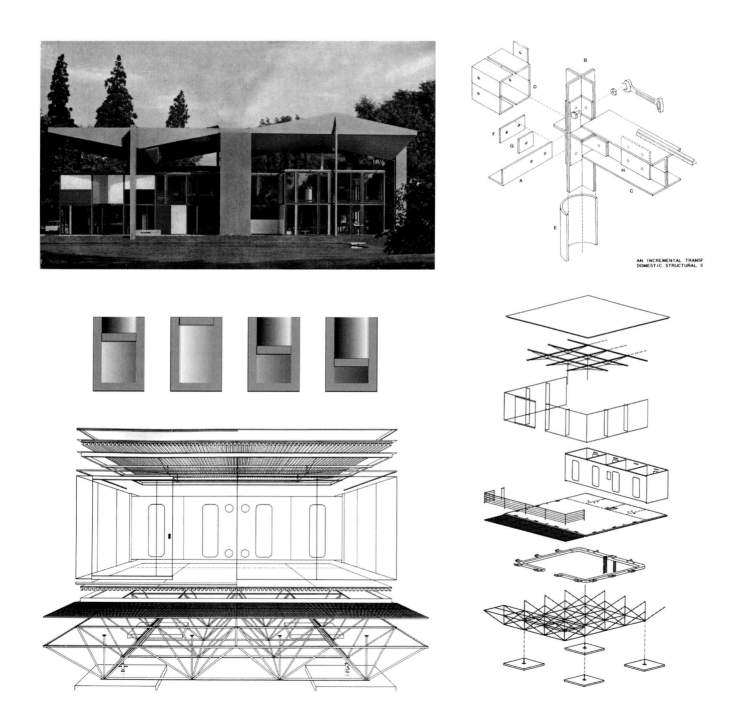

AN INCREMENTAL TRANSF
DOMESTIC STRUCTURAL 5

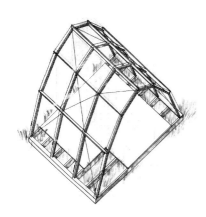

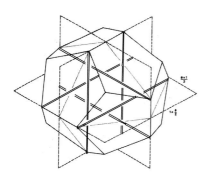

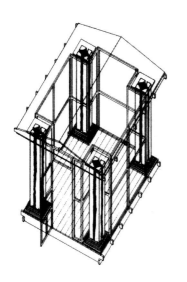

A PORTABLE ROCK

Foundation stone in zero gravity

"Strong straight square great" recalls the foundation stones in the great cathedrals, deep underground but carved most true to set a local origin as reference system for all subsequent orthogonals. The stone has high inertial resistance; gravity is the glue that holds the massive stones together. However, in zero gravity (see Skylab photo p. 234) the foundation stone must also BE the glue-- the thing that other things glue to, in any extended construction. A weightless "foundation stone" must be not only the origin of a local frame of reference, but also the local origin of tensegrity. Temporary construction is a "special case" of zero gravity on earth, where the short duration time of installation does not give the foundation a chance to grow roots. In a spacetime sense, temporal impermanence is equivalent to weightlessness. To build something temporary but sturdy, you must establish a local vector equilibrium that will withstand external forces that may tend to distort it. The greater its internal stresses of tension and compression, the greater the external load it can withstand.

Stone of Foam

To make the largest volume with the least material and highest possible rigidity one must take advantage of moment as well as tensegrity. The most momentous volume will distribute its mass and void to the perimeter as much as possible. A more general extension of *putting mass only where the action is* means that volume has its greatest inertial resistance when it is most hollow, most rigid, and most extended. A carefully jointed room is essentially an "inflated cube". Placing structure, skin, holes, etc. as far apart from each other as possible makes it strong. Internal and external pressures involves the organization of set of elements into whole assemblies of these components to make volumes, full of void, as empty as possible of mass. HVAC designers (heating ventilation and air conditioning) seek resonance of implosion and explosion to sustain the cellular organism of habitable volume. Both skin and bones must balance inside (room) and outside ("the great outdoors"). Change also creates differential pressures: Le Corbusier's Zurich Pavilion has a hypar roof which provides a permanent frame for the demountable cubes of the temporary exhibit volumes inside it.

A foam of pressured volumes...

Architectural space is a fabric of pressured volumes. Architectural pressure is different than inertia (see page 251); it is more a question of the energy each volume contains, plastically and programmatically. For a volume of minimal mass, inertia depends on the distribution of mass to (and containment of mass at) the extremities, hence volumetric inertia depends on pressure. A stone fixed inside a box becomes a rock; it does not roll. The Carnot Cycle shows how pressure and heat vary in a closed but changing volume like the cylinder of an automobile piston. Program volumes often need isolation to function-- a kitchen in the bedroom makes sleep difficult-- but degrees of enclosure-- how much surface to seal and how much to perforate-- is an important issue in planning as well as construction. Every habitable space, even the pressurized cabin of a jet transport, must be perforated somewhere sometime for human use-- even a coffin must be nailed shut. The order of facades and placing doors and windows are obvious concerns of the pressure of architectural space. More subtly, the number and location of entries, porches, columns, and screen walls also define the osmotic membranes that control pressure relationships between program volumes in a plastic architectural version of thermodynamics. A volume of momentum and energy becomes momenergy in each four-dimensional block of spacetime. Imagine a speeding oil truck crashing and exploding even more when filled and moving fast than when it is slow and empty of petroleum. The design of exitways for a colosseum must manage the rapid exiting of patrons at the end of a ball game much differently than a free-access town park.

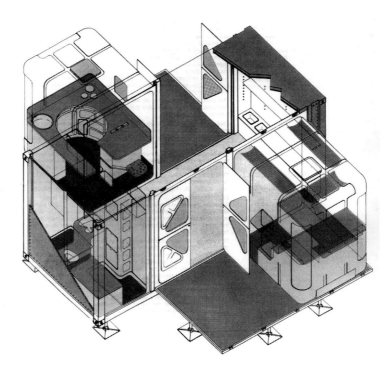

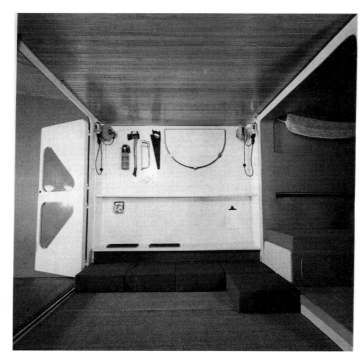

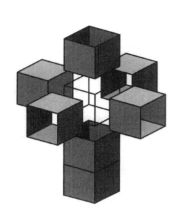

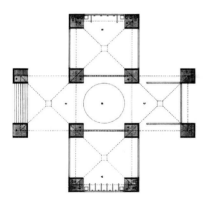

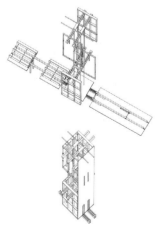

POPCORN

"Big things come in small packages" Anonymous

What a miracle is life! Together we have the capacity to replicate ourselves in our children, to the tiniest detail of eyelash, fingernail, or habit of laughter, and yet with enough flexibility to adapt to new conditions and evolve into new potentials. The means for transmission from one generation to the next is the smallest package, the seed-fertilized egg, the zygote. A simpler problem is how to design a package which can be compact in one mode and deploy to full extension in another mode. Campers, backpackers, travelers, tourists and astronauts have faced this problem since the Israelites took flattened bread into the desert, since Apaches transformed teepee homes into drag sledge moving vans. How is it possible to pack into one place all the masses needed to pop into the required volumes at some other place and time? We solve this question every time we pack a suitcase. Pressure on a package is released through popping-out deployment.

"Deployment" describes the military maneuver of extending the front and reducing the depth, increasing the density of the perimeter at the expense of the center-- enlarging the "volume" of a site! Deployment requires the distribution of elements to occupy, inhabit, and engage a site. There are some compact yet eminently deployable volumes. Hot air balloons, parachutes, and life rafts are packed until needed to expand and fill the space around them. Valves, ripcords, or similar devices expose package contents to a pressurizing force that drives innards outward. What if a whole house could be a "magic" package folded up into a briefcase until needed? How wise are the turtle who carries her home with her and the bird who scavenges bits of straw to make a nest! The space program has forced us to be adept at packaging artificial environments that can completely sustain human life as they move beyond the protective bonds of our home planet. At the simpler level of habitation within our native atmosphere, what do we need to pack to take all our living needs with us wherever we go? Architecturally, how can we de-volumate space into condensed mass for transport, to be re-deployed at its destination, the way we de-hydrate foods until use when we "just add water"? Could we use such insight to ship habitations to those in need from the haves? (It has happened before: tents and camps in wars, conestoga wagons, the Mayflower.) What are minimum needs for a world citizen camper? Food, for how long? All of Bach's music? A winter's fuel supply, an axe, or solar cells-- or all the above, and the knowledge and judgement of when to use each appropriately?

Every oak, every fox, every member of any species is "related" to all the rest, but all are different. A simple mechanical analog of this biomolecular marvel is popcorn, in which every kernel starts the same, but after popping no two are ever exactly alike. Can some similar evolution through unity and variety exist in architecture? Palladio's villas, Wright's Prairie Houses, and indigenous housing around the world all support such a suggestion. They are identifiable to their species, but develop in healthy and apparently inexhaustible variety. A corn kernel, hard and compact, is the same material as the cluster it becomes after popping; adding heat changes only the shape and dispersal of the material. The agitated molecules of the corn moved so fast as to burst beyond the bounds of the skin of the kernel hull. You might think of a piece of popcorn as the exploding air in a popped balloon made visible, or a sculpture of a supernova. In 1972, architect Emilio Ambasz, as Curator of Design for the Museum of Modern Art in New York City, organized a wonderful exhibition called *Italy: The New Domestic Landscape*, which commissioned, as part of the show, designers to propose *and build* solutions to the given challenge packing dwelling inside a standard cargo shipping container. One of the most elegant works was Marco Zanuso and Richard Sapper's pop-out volume shown opposite. Like an old steamer trunk, when this in-transit dwelling box arrives, its reinforcing sides fold down into porches and the kitchen, bathroom, and sleeping volumes, fully appointed, and ready to roll, slide out like drawers on either side. What remains where those boxes were is--room, the very thing we're looking for! Here is a space-ship *and* a time-ship.

ORTHOGONAL RESONANCE: THE POEM OF THE RIGHT ANGLE

*"I have for 50 years been studying the chap known as "Man" and his wife and kids...
to make home the temple of the family, to introduce into the home the sense of the sacred;
A cubic centimeter of housing was worth gold, represented possible happiness."*
Le Corbusier, Oeuvre Complet, Volume 8

With the architecture of Aalto, Borromini, inflatables, and flexible mesh it seems that at last we can escape the "rigid tyranny" of an architecture of cubes and squares. Why then a throwback to "reactionary" praise for the right angle!? When architecture is most essentially concerned with spacial issues, it must close-pack its volumes, with no space left over. To an engineer, triangulation may solve structural problems, but to an architect, the diagonal is often "noise". Orthogonality, the intersection of three mutually perpendicular planes, organizes volume into cubes and stretched variations. It is one of the few geometries (tetrahedron and octahedron is the only other set of two or less of the five Platonic solids) that completely fills any given spacial extent with no waste. Unlike a cube full of cubes, a sphere full of spheres has lots of little gaps between the volumes. In orthogonal space, all volumetric elements are commensurable with each other as a seamless spacial fabric. Compare this with the squinches overhead in Michelangelo's Medici Chapel (page 328), which occur when the sphere of the dome intersects with the cube of the room.

To coordinate all plastic and volumetric elements is a task requiring the consummate skill of the architect. To "retreat" from the complexity of the tartan field of Concerto to the "simplicity" of a single volume also seems to be a step backward, but the complex volumetric relationships generated by the placement of even a single door and window, shelves, a chair, a table, and a light projected across and through the space, and beyond into the outer world reveal that the room and the phoenix tartan multiple volume of many rooms, galleries, stairs, etc. are the *same* problem. They both demand a resolution of the intersection of all spacial orders projected from two dimensional surface into three dimensional volume relationships and beyond.

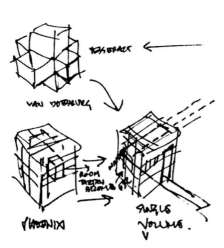

Chamber music

Architects Judith Sheine and Lionel March recently elucidated the profound work of the architect Rudolf Schindler. Among other insights, they have recovered the brilliant idea of the Schindler Frame and have showed how he used it in his work. Quite simply, the Schindler frame is a proportional insight that unifies human space with standard residential construction techniques and materials to yield valuable results in the ordering and illumination of space. Schindler's basic module was the 4 foot cube, which he proposed dividing into 16" thirds, both horizontally (the standard stud frame interval) and *vertically*. (Later 12" intervals were added.) He had all the studs cut at 6-8", a standard door height, to leave a 16" clerestory space above. All windows were hung from the 6-8" line and plank and beam construction was to be used throughout to help minimize floor and joist thickness. Proportions of 1:2:3:4:5:6 were then readily visible in all sections and elevations.

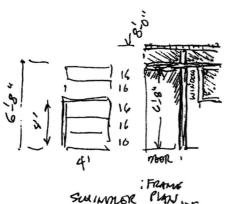

Schindler worked as his own contractor-- an early modern design/build architect. Like Brunelleschi he was architect and engineer at the same time. Early in his American career, he supervised construction of Frank Lloyd Wright's important Los Angeles design for Aline Barnsdall, the Hollyhock House. Schindler called himself a space architect, concerned with more than just structure and sculpture. In his desire for the primacy of interior space he sought to build in much of the furniture as part of the architecture. All these concerns are visible in the image of the interior of his Lovell Beach House on the facing page, an example of what Lionel March has called his "musical space". Resonance between all individual elements and the totality of the space is thus achieved.

Chamber music: 2 views of the hypercube

Dwelling:
inhabited by designers Bill Means and David Reinah.
A journey of a thousand miles begins with the first step.

☐ ENDURANCE

△ TIME

◯ TEMPO

the three friends

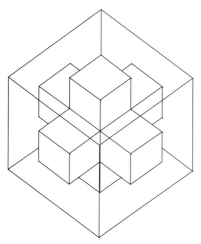

Shadow of a tesseract:
8 cubes: 6 + 1 inside + 1 outside.

THE SHADOW OF TIME

A pachysandra vine in a garden by a children's swing seeks light by growing up through grooves in the bark of nearby maple trees. What we call nature-- the intersection of the global biological field with the local individual-- may also be seen as an infinite fractal struggle of beings to maximize the interface between matter and energy by maintaining space in time. In this sense, phasing is architectural "pressure" in time. The plan, *in all dimensions*, is the generator! We **participate** in the creation of architectural space and time, dancing **with** (as well as **in**) the space we inhabit. If volume is the sum of solids in time, then space is the sum of volumes in time. We compose the flow of architectural space by cultivating the flowering of spacetime chronogeometry.

Mindfulness

An empty room is full of space and time. The Tea House of Shugakuin Palace is shown opposite with its sliding *shoji* screens both closed and open. These two time frames give as vivid an impression as is possible in a book of the solidity of spacetime, of the shadow of time in space. These two views, one empty of all distraction, the other intimate with the landscape, recall the Zen aphorism: *Before enlightenment, mountains are mountains, rivers are rivers, trees are trees. During enlightenment, mountains are rivers, rivers are trees, trees are mountains. After enlightenment, mountains are mountains, rivers are rivers, trees are trees.* Similarly, as Dave Kindred has observed, Michael Murphy's 1972 *Golf in the Kingdom* suggested that a mythical character named Shivas Irons could hit a feathery with an Irish shillelagh 200 yards into the hole while teaching mere mortals that the secret of golf is the secret of life: "true gravity," defined as "the joining of awareness, delight and life-embracing force." The aware person dwells in the mountains of the mind, contemplating pan-orama in all directions, left/right, in/out, up/down, and then/now. To hold such dualities in the mind is to maintain the unity of the most basic multidimensional polyrhythm. Life is always a contingent completion. Plan is the intersection of radiant energy and gravitating matter. Architecture, ever contingent, is the union of momenergy and spacetime.

Hypercube

The architectural problem of a single room appears at first to be a retreat from the complexity of the tartan-permeated field of volumes found in *Return of the Phoenix*. Yet to realize and resolve all volumes which penetrate a chamber in spacetime (recall 4D tictactoe, page 31) is to understand that one room and a multi-volume program are the *same* architectural problem-- the symphonic resolution of the intersection of all projected spacial orders from surface to solid and beyond, from 2D into 3D into 4D. Like sliding drawers in a cabinet, perforations of all "surface" conditions in a room, windows, doors, furniture, lighting, insulation, ventilation, circulation are projected across and through the space, and beyond into the world outside. A hypercube or tesseract is the four-dimensional version of the 3D cube. Some of its 3D shadows are shown on this page. Where a cube has 6 square faces, a tesseract has 8 cube "faces". The spectrum of color light cohabiting our rooms reveals the tesseract. One unified space is a miracle. It is a chamber both fluid and stable carrying volume through ever-changing spacetime, a vessel like a glass of water or ship on the ocean. Fascinatingly, such exploration of dimension suggests that 5 or even more dimensions may provide a means to envision a solution to the "many worlds interpretation" of quantum physics. If 2D plans and sections are "many worlds interpretations" slices taken through the unity of one 3D volume, then why not a 5D "house" as the unity which explains the "many worlds" interpretations of 4D spacetime quantum events?

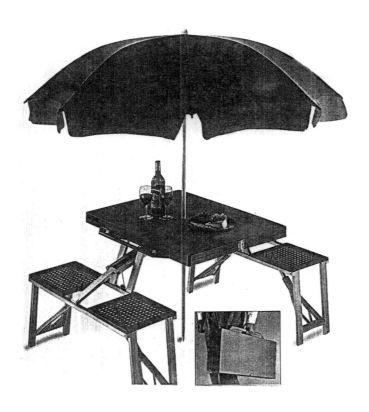

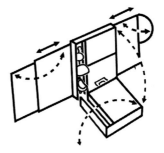

HOW TO PACK YOUR HARTMANN 747 OVER SUIT-O-MATIC®

Arrange suit jacket and trousers on hanger. Remove all items from pockets.

STEP 1.

Pivot hanger hook down and slide on trolley on Suit-O-Matic® and lock into place. Lay suit and frame face down on bed or other surface.

STEP 2.

Unbuckle strap on frame and fold suit over bottom of frame (as shown).

STEP 3.

Fasten buckle strap down tight.

STEP 4.

Fold tail of suit back over buckle strap and insert suit and Suit-O-Matic® frame into ANY pocket you wish on your 747 CM3/FCM3 (there are three compartments with full opening, easy access).

Note: Be sure to fasten down your packed Suit-O-Matic® with the web straps provided in all THREE compartments of this OVER.

Place side with coat tail at the bottom of case.

STEP 5.

by hartmann

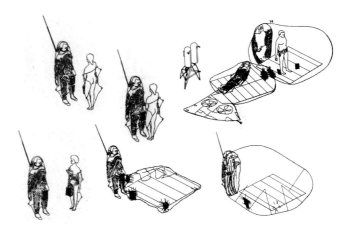

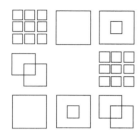

DOING pro-posing :

SPACE IN A SUITCASE

Build a station in space and time. Design and construct a human scale habitation, a volume measuring **7'-0" ± 12"** in each of three dimensions. Establish and maintain boundary conditions and perforations. Extend plastic implications of openings and closures both inward and outward. Consider access to and movement through volume as the means to create a *promenade architecturale*. When the space is complete, you will have designed and constructed your first intentional architecture.

Four dimensions is our reality. We can't see spacetime, because we are **in** it (like a fish in the ocean) but we can **make** it. To do so we must take building action. Extending volume into one or more dimensions can make a space station in time, and a time station in space. You may orient your volume and its extensions either horizontally or vertically. (If the extension forms a second **7'-0" ± 12"** volume, then 2 people may work together to make a single double-cube project. Design elements may then help locate a third intersecting cube within this double-cube that helps develop the transition between interior and exterior.) The palette of suggested materials is a BIG BAG OF TRICKS (see next page),

PROGRAM: Organize a sequence of volume events that create experiences of entry, journey, and arrival to provide at least 3 degrees of enclosure.

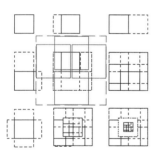

1. Create a **central volume** of human scaled habitable space, to be **7'-0" ± 12"** in each of three dimensions. This gallery is a place that intensifies the experience of JOURNEY.
2. Create an **outer volume** that welcomes and encourages the casual visitor to enter your habitation cell. Extend the central volume outward (up to **14'-0" ± 12"**, or twice its original size) into one dimension to create a forecourt, or into two dimensions to define a precinct of semi-private/semi-public transition. In this space develop a portal to mark ENTRY.
3. Create an **inner volume** that encourages the visitor to focus attention on the design work you have developed throughout this study of *Dynamics*. Extend the central volume inward to define a display area, **2'-0"** in each dimension, a most deeply nested inner zone of ARRIVAL.

The spaces and structure must be designed to be erected, inhabited and demounted within the last $3\frac{1}{2}$ hour studio session of the course. The structures must be able to be erected on any grassy field, and should be self-leveling (within 15% slope). They must withstand normal wind and rain loads, have appropriate acoustics, light and ventilation, and keep the interior space dry and protected from the sun. The design should resolve the continuity between interior and exterior space. All elements for this structure must fit into a container no larger than a normal suitcase. The "suitcase" must be part of the final structure.

Document your scheme with the architectural drawings, model and construction photos needed to plan, build and evaluate the space. Draw your space as if you were inside it, from many points of view, indicating how light might help to define the resonance of volumes you create. Include at least one projection showing shade and shadows cast by the scheme at the time of its erection. Use color as appropriate. Diagram the loads, present the cost and weight of the structure, as well as details of at least two significant joints, drawn at (4:1), four times actual size.

ANIMATION: (Warm-up: Draw three whole kernels of popcorn exploded, 10x actual size-- you will be amazed at what your eye will teach you.) Prepare at least one exploded assembly drawing that shows the sequence of deployment and order of assembly of the elements that create your spaces.

COLOR: Collage studies continued. See page 465.

FUNCTION: Plot a sine curve with multiple frequencies. Do the Fourier addition. See page 453.

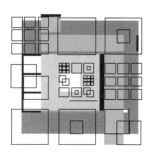

A JOURNEY THROUGH NESTED VOLUMES
INTERACTING AT ALL SCALES

JEFF GALLO/JERRY SALDUTTI

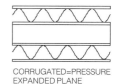

CORRUGATED=PRESSURE
EXPANDED PLANE

BIG BAG OF TRICKS

WORLD'S LARGEST SUITCASE??

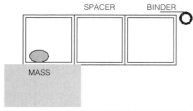

SPACER   BINDER

MASS

THE ELEMENTS OF INERTIAL VOLUME ORIGAMI
MAKIING A CANTILEVER

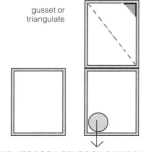

gusset or
triangulate

STONE INTO ROCK: DENSIFIED CARDBOARD
INCREASED MOMENT OF INERTIA

MODEL INFLATABLE: MASS ELEMENT
ZIPLOC BAG + STRAW   ZIPLOC BAG + WATER

pint a pound the world around
62.4 lb/cu.ft

PRESSURE VOLUME

The Big Bag of Tricks is a full-scale dry-assembly plastic medium whose structural principle is *expanded volume*. Corrugated cardboard is an expanded plane, a pressurized solid. An open web joist is an expanded beam; eggcrate is expanded frame. Slab is expanded plate, roof is bent or folded plane. A spring is a pressurized volume. The elements of an "inertial volume origami" are **spacer** (bar or box), **binder** (tape) and **mass.** To "explode the structural box" each structural element and part must be placed where they are most effective. Carefully placed stones or water bags inside reinforced cardboard boxes joined with duct or strapping tape can make columns, beams, storage walls, even houses. From this approach, structure is thus pressurized volume, a fabric of fiber and foam. Thus SPACE can be LIGHT WEIGHT.

The scale of this project is *Human Scale*. Using the actual Bag of Tricks at full scale brings closure to abstraction and concretion. Thus may perforation become doors or windows, and inner volume may be defined by the intersection of entry along one axis and window or skylight along another axis. Every site is asymmetrical, by virtue of morning sun vs. afternoon heat, ground vs. sky, and light vs. shade. Keep the budget for the entire project to the minimum. Economy of means means economy! Display the projected budget and actual expenditures prominently in the shelter. As much as possible, use the Bag of Tricks to model your proposal and to analyze loads and explore characteristics of necessary materials. Elegance of detailing and structure is vital, but even more important is an elegance in the spacial proposition and solution-- an economy of means in terms of structure, construction, assembly, weight, and cost (at least). The work may be (will be) polychromed.

BIG BAG OF TRICKS: a palette of suggested materials
(This list is per person. If one project requires two people, figure twice this list of materials.)

$10.95	1- 4 ' x 8' masonite pegboard 1/4" sheet, tempered
$5.95	1- 4' x 8' masonite pegboard 1/8" sheet.
$7.84	1- 2' x4' diffuser eggcrate panel... (polyethylene at this price, not acrylic!)
$3.88	2- 9' x12' clear, white, and/or black plastic sheeting--2 mil. (2 x 1.94 ea)
$1.94	2" +/- wide industrial plastic tape, 55 yd
$2.48	50' +/- nylon rope 1/8" @ $0.07/ft
$2.70	1 -2" "x 4' x 8' kiln dried douglas fir...
$2.02	1 - 10' length x 1" dia. pvc pipe or aluminum tube
$37.76	total hardware (all prices Home Depot, 12/97, only 23 cents more than in 1993!)
and:	boxes, cardboard, all sizes-- with duct and/or strapping tape
	ziploc bags with water, and or/stones

Elements may be cut and recombined into sub-assemblies before Deployment Day. Glue is permissible for cutting and recombining only: otherwise joints are to be invented or made from *demountable* standard connectors like nuts, bolts, and turnbuckles as needed-- the fewer the better. Use any spare parts from both the Kit of Parts and Bag of Tricks, even one stick or stone. You may wish to choose one of your visitor galleries from the phoenix study as a starting *parti* for this project. Model possible *parti* strategies for using paper at 1/2" scale. This will magnify flimsy conditions during design, which is to your advantage. Use the Bag of Tricks at 1" = 1'-0" scale to study construction and connections. Skin may be structural, as in inflatables. (You can model literally inflated volumes using ziploc bags and a soda straw. Zip up a bag until almost closed, insert straw and blow into bag, remove straw while still blowing and seal bag quickly. You can also inflate a bag inside a bag...)

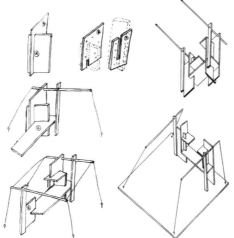

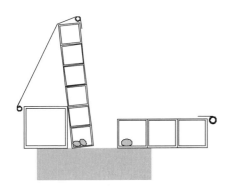

Strong Straight Square Great.
Work with gravity and balance.
Make structure true,
plumb vertically and level horozontally.

YU-CHI YANG

JOEY BRUSCA

Remember, *plastic* is related to *play*.
a place to start-- "the joint is jumping".

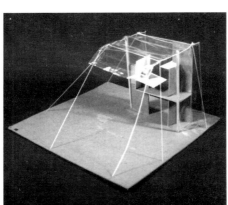

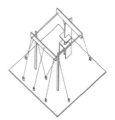

ELLEN SANTOS

MARVENE WORRELL AND HENRY K. CHIN-HONG

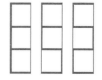

TOKONOMA VARIATIONS

RESONANT SPACE

The carpenter's Secret: Sound

Sound has two basic meanings: audible tone or strongly built. A carpenter, like a musical instrument maker, seeks to make a **sound** box. When three perpendicular planes form a rigid corner, its hidden "chamfer" forms a triangulated structure. The fabric of any well-built container must be resilient enough to sustain amplify, and resonate sound. This is true for music boxes, living rooms, and concert halls. A fabric of boxes at many scales allows the builder to start small and build outward, maintaining stability into a tensegrity of volumes. Boundary closure creates pressure. Volumes filter circulation and structure of both air and people to inform strategy decisions in both plan and section.

Until now, your architectural models have been made on a tabletop, fashioned to the scale of your hands. You can see above and around them, and pick them up or turn them over. You can make the "roof" first, if you want. However, once you enter "the great outdoors" to create volume at human scale, you must locate blocks of space larger than (and all around) you with precision. Use a plumb line and level to establish true vertical and horizontal in the field, working with gravity and balance to make things true. Thus even the most casual arrangement becomes deliberate when needed and work can be strong, straight, square, great. The minimum "skin and bones" needed to define volumes must also withstand normal wind and rain loads and keep interior space dry and protected from the sun. Invent a lightweight tensegrity "foundation stone" to anchor and provide rigidity to your volume and its extensions. Erect the volumes in no more than an hour. Demounting too should take no more than an hour. Allow at least $3\frac{1}{2}$ hours altogether. (Use free remaining time for dwelling and visits.)

Origami Furniture

As an added exercise, you may wish to consider the 12-panel sheet you used for your *impromptu Prelude* origami study (see page 81) as a model for furniture, perhaps at the scale where each of the 12 squares equals about 1 foot. To build it full scale, you may find or make reinforced (triple layered) cardboard, and fold it into a triwall origami furnishing that will enable you at least for a moment, to sit still, so you may travel at the speed of light, through time! The French term for furniture is *meuble*, meaning movable. Hence furniture has a dynamic as well as functional sense. If furniture is what moves in a volume, then for Space in a Suitcase, the whole structure is "furniture". Can origami be generalized as a principle of space-making for your complete Space in a Suitcase?

Tokonoma

The *tokonoma* is a storage and display space, a volumetric filter and important element of the Japanese house (*see Architectonics,* page 37). In a field of pure volume, like a room empty of all but *tatami* mats and sliding *shoji* screens, the placing of objects requires a mediating set of volumes. You can make an inexpensive *tokonoma* as a wall of boxes that will serve both plastic and structural needs. Put a stone in a cardboard box and bind it together with other boxes to make a kind of "densified cardboard" as a cheap way to magnify moment and locate inertial resistance. Weatherproof the cardboard with polyethylene wrap or other, to keep them from losing their stability in case of rain. The *tokonoma* can become a foundation tensegrity giving vector equilibrium to the space, a kind of standing wave of visual acoustics, magnifying the reverberations of the multiple geometries of orthogonal spacial order, triangulation, and environmental control. Carefully placed reinforced boxes made of binder, spacer, and mass can be joined into a fabric of increasing stability while making endless volumetric tokonoma variations.

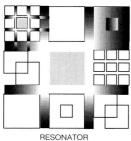

RESONATOR
MASS AND VOID RIPPLE
THROUGH EACH OTHER

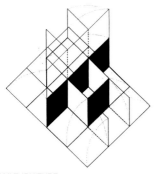

ORIGAMI FURNITURE
IMPROMPTU PRELUDE PROJECT
@ 4 : 1 =ORIGAMI FURNITURE +/-
@ 6 : 1 =ORIGAMI FURNITURE +/-

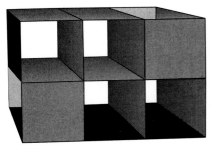

A FABRIC OF HABITABLE *TOKONOMA* MAY MAKE
VOLUME WHICH MAGNIFIES THE VIBRATIONS OF
YOUR SOUND AND LIGHT.

COMING TO THE POINT

A plane is a tetrahedron of macro base and micro altitude.
Buckminster Fuller, Synergetics (vol. 1) p. 571

To arrive, one must make a point. You must not only establish tensegrity as an internal condition of volume to make the self-contained space vessel of *Space in A Suitcase.* You must also extend the evolution of the origin point of the tensegrity to meet its field and establish attachment to the site. You may do this by spreading the load wide enough for the site to carry it, as the hull of a sailboat does in displacing water. Or you may make an incision in the supporting surface, and drive a spike into the ground. Ivan Leonidov designed a huge mast (or is it cantilevered column?) to suspend on a single point the spherical auditorium of his 1928 Lenin Institute proposal, shown on the facing page. Frank Lloyd Wright placed a chimney in the center of his Prairie Houses, anchoring the home to the site like the Golden Spike of the transcontinental railroad. Gravity is often sufficient as connector. But when the field shifts, as in an earthquake, a settler must learn from boats in the sea. Light structures like feathers and inflatable shelters must be anchored against lifting by the wind. Indeed, all structures must be triangulated with the ground plane for stability against both catastrophic change and the slower but more inevitable creep of gravity. To settle widely, one must survey the site to locate deployments. Surveyors mark station points in the measuring traverses they make of land form, and to insure accuracy, they triangulate their positions both in plan and elevation.

Life Boats and the Ship of State

Like a golf ball and a tee, the combination of point and sphere describes the range of possible puncture pressures in the rock or soil as a function of geometric shape. The ball produces the shallower curve and less concentrated stress. It is gentle on the landscape, but also likely to roll along. On the other hand, the tee is sharp, cutting into the soil with the least damage to the surroundings. Timing of the swing of the hammer is where to begin to solve this issue as a planning problem-- how heavy a hammer, how fast a swing, how wide a head? As with a calligrapher's brush, momentum applied to the tools of settlement, whether hammer for boundary stakes, mower for the lawn, or dam for fresh water determines the firmness of the connection to the site. To Fuller the tetrahedron with minimum altitude is a plane but we may still picture it as a mast anchored to the ground through triangulated guy wires. Local conditions, including topography, bearing strength, frost heaves, and house rules, determine the curvature and frequency of anchoring applications.

Yes, well it is nice to draw a plan of ordered space on a nice flat drawing board. But how do you actually build it? When the site is variable, without marked reference boundaries, you must apply a transit from a known station point to match the drawing to the existing ripples of earth swells: the hills and valleys, large and small. But to match the drawn sections to the existing gradients of the landscape, you must establish a **datum**-- a horizontal reference level. To accomplish this over a large site, for many isolated structures, you may employ an old trick of soft landing: fill an extended garden hose with water. Keep it open at both ends. No matter what the intervening contours of the land, the water level at the two open ends of the hose will be at the same elevation, since the air pressure is equal in both cases. Making space is an evolution of weighing, balancing, counterbalancing, testing, etc. until a moment of rest arrives, that is, a moment of no motion relative to the local frame of reference. You can resolve forces by locating solids to find repose, as in no place else to fall; or equilibrium, as in no place else to be without it all coming apart and losing its poise, or tensegrity, as in no place else to go that doesn't return you to where you already were. The "you" in all these formulations is the stone, the stick, the rubber band, a person, or the vessel of volume itself. On Earth, trees grow out, not up.

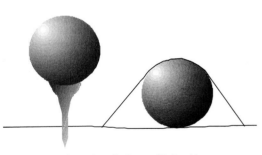

Sailing free in the breeze: hydraulic space. A round hull displaces the most water, as Archimedes explained. Too pointed a hull would sink the sailboat.

Anchoring: point and sphere, golf ball and tee.

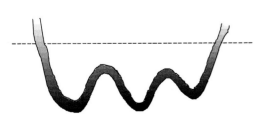

A soft contact. An extended hose can act as level, following contours of the ground. Open ends make equal air pressure, showing equal elevation.

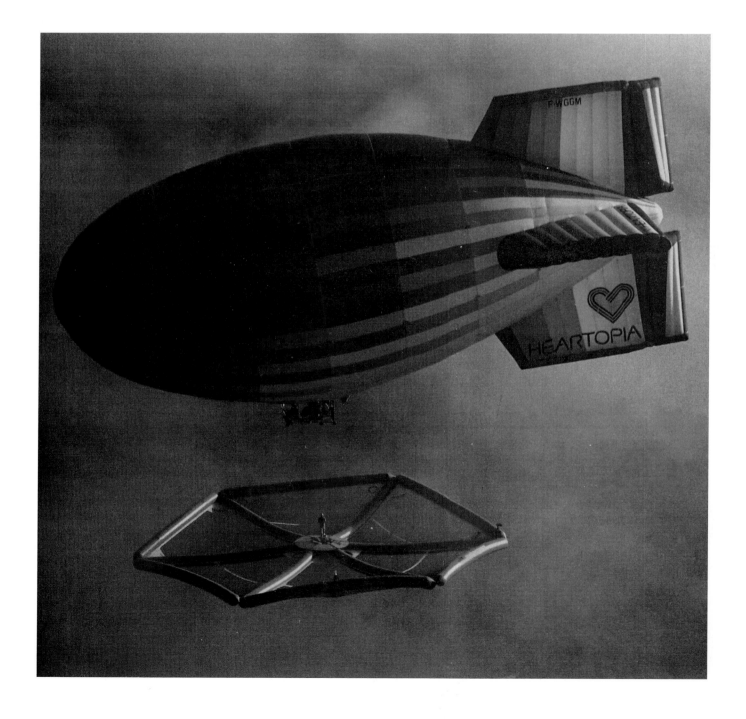

A FRIENDLY REMINDER: *WHERE'S THE HAND??*

"Luckily, we have no money!" Le Corbusier

Modeling a combined spacial, plastic, and structural proposition for a habitable human scale volume on a table top, for example with the Bag of Tricks, is very useful for discovering 3D conditions not necessarily envisioned through drawing. For example, to model wind loads on a Bag of Tricks model connected with rubber bands etc. just push sideways on a wall with your finger. But this method of experiment has certain limitations that demand a vigilant imagination. For example, it is easy to move the model around on the table, and simply put the roof pieces on top of the walls, step back, and admire your cleverness and incredible sense of beauty. But when you get outside and are ready to build your real structure in the real world, you may be shocked to find that there is no longer a friendly hand above the walls of your structure to carry your roof. Such magic skyhooks don't exist, although standard cranes substitute very well. You must consider the means and sequence of construction as well as the structure of your design. A design is *always* experimental. As Le Corbusier said, "Faults are human: they are ourselves, our daily lives. What matters is to go further, to live, to be intense, to aim high, and to be loyal!"

Le Corbusier translated this understanding into a clever visual montage to communicate the organizing principle he adopted to insure privacy in his 350-family high-rise invention of 1947-52, the *unité d'habitation*, or Unity of Habitation, in Marseilles. A hand is shown sliding a single apartment volume into a concrete frame "bottle-rack", an orthogonalized version of the standard wine bottle storage system, to show that these elements were conceive as isolated structures. Lead pads between them would further enhance acoustic and thermal isolation-- so that vibrations within one apartment would not be transmitted to another via the frame of the whole building.

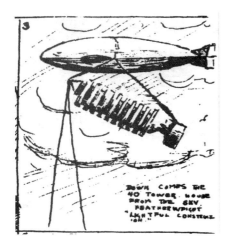

Buckminster Fuller created his *Dymaxion Air-Ocean 4D Timelock* vision in 1927, the same year that Lindbergh crossed the Atlantic Ocean in solo flight. He proposed that a dirigible, carrying a 10-story light-metal high rise building, could drop small bomb to create a crater as foundation, and then lower the tower into ground as if it were a living a plant. Thus could we create a settlement anywhere on earth, requiring no roads. This idea led to geodesic domes, and ultimately to places like Drop City. Later in his life, Fuller realized one result of the relationship between scale and dimension. When a one inch cube is doubled to become a two-inch cube, the surface area is increased four-fold ($2L \times 2L = 4L^2$) and the volume is *eight* larger ($2L \times 2L \times 2L = 8L^3$). As the size of a solid increases, the proportion of area to volume *decreases*. Fuller observed that a sealed greenhouse geodesic sphere large enough could be heated even 1 or 2 degrees by the sun would make the internal volume sufficiently lighter than the exterior cooler denser air that the weight of the dome's skin and even all internal elements would be negligible. He calculated that if the dome were a mile or two in diameter, it would contain enough light air that it could become a floating city! To further challenge our imaginations, he depicted the floating cities (not so) high above a snowy and forbidding mountain range.

A close relative to Fuller's floating city-- an incredibly poetic concept and fitting successor to Jacques Cousteau's kind of holistic vision-- is the French invention and application of a raft atop the rain forest, a web of nylon mesh and inflatable tube hexagon that is dropped onto the forest crown, directly at the horizon of the treetops, recalling the holy platforms of Mayan and Aztec pyramid temples. This technical and imaginative triumph enables environmental and ecological research to take place with minimum damage and in a new way-- from the top down.

GEOFF FUNSTON, TRACY KOSAR, PAUL KURKLEN, RICK LEPIC

MICHAEL GORDON

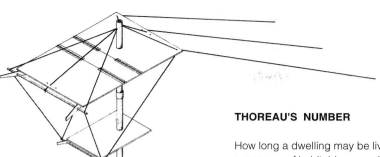

THOREAU'S NUMBER

How long a dwelling may be lived in compared to how long it takes to produce that dwelling is a measure of habitable space in terms of human time. This proportion may give an indication of the value of spirit in a particular culture, because clearly it is to a person's advantage to spend as little time as possible in erecting a shelter as there are many other things to do, especially in cultivating body, mind, spirit-- which are endless and ever-rewarding humane pursuits. These might include some defense against marauding armies, community celebrations, or specula- tion, wonder, and discovery. It is in honor of this last possibility that we choose to call the proportion Thoreau's Number, and represent it by the last letter in the Hebrew alphabet, Taf.

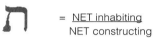

$$\mathbf{ת} = \frac{\text{NET inhabiting}}{\text{NET constructing}}$$

when N = number of people, E = energy, and T = time. By this formula, for Thoreau himself:

$$= \frac{\text{1 man (60 years lifetime)}}{\text{1 man (3 months salary + 3 months construction)}}$$

$$\mathbf{ת} = 120$$

using Thoreau's own reckoning that by spending only \$28.12 $\frac{1}{2}$ and 3 months of his own labor he demonstrated how to produce a "shelter for a lifetime at the expense of one's annual rent."

A typical American wage earner might work 10 years of his or her life to pay for a mortgage on house that might last 30 years for spouse and children. In this case:

$$= \frac{\text{4 people (30 years)}}{\text{1 person (10 years salary for mortgage)}}$$

$$\mathbf{ת} = 12$$

Thus, for every our of free time the wage-earner has, Thoreau might expect 2 $\frac{1}{2}$ hours. But even Thoreau seems to devote far too much effort to the problem compared to the elegant solutions of the Congo Pygmies:

$$= \frac{\text{2 people (up to 10 months)}}{\text{1 person (}\frac{1}{2}\text{ day or .0167 month)}}$$

$$\mathbf{ת} = 1200!$$

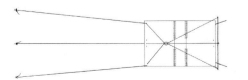

GREG ISOLA

In terms of dwelling, Pygmies emerge as true philosophers, for they have learned to live simply.

...Columns are bound like captives in the rock. Volumes surge from the walls, floor, and ceiling into and through each other.
They collide at corners, collapse between consoles, bulge behind false windows. The walls seem alive.... Compare with the Laurentian Library, see pages 115 and 140.

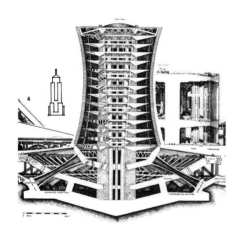

REFLECTING

*The house derives reserves and refinements of intimacy from winter; while in the outside world, snow covers all tracks, blurs the road, muffles every sound, conceals all color. We feel warm because it is cold out-of-doors. Behind dark curtains, snow seems to be whiter."*Gaston Bachelard, *the Poetics of Space*

Music is "the science or art of pleasing, expressive or intelligible combinations of tones; the art of making such combinations, esp. into compositions of definite structures and significance". Listening to music engages our mind as well as our ear, we meditate on the order we find in the composer's work, perhaps with our whole body, even as we dance to the beat. Can architecture be musical when the spaces we create make volumes of definite structures and significance? To **muse** means to meditate or ponder, to maintain mindfulness. *Music*, along with *museum* and *amusement*, comes from the Indo-European root *mendh-* meaning "mind". A museum is a place for all-sense meditation. At an amusement park, the body meditates on and in space as it moves through one volume or another on ferris wheel, roller coaster and the like. Can architecture echo with meaning by encouraging a mind and body to experience its order, its structure and significance through the modulation of resonant volumes? How can a volume become a space? What would it be like to live inside a musical instrument? To find a place to make and listen to music which itself makes a music of volumes? To be in a place which dances as much as the people inside and around it? To see a visual order in the volumes, structure and details which in itself would be a source for stereometric meditation? What would it be like to create and inhabit a musing place? An artist's studio is as sacred as a chapel. What constitutes the membranes for such spaces? In Springs Long Island, the floor of Jackson Pollock's studio is a palimpsest of perimeter spatters and a continuation of his *action painting*. It is a kind of Sistine Floor to mirror Michelangelo's Sistine Ceiling at the Vatican. Thus do the questions of a muse on architecture echo.

Henry David Thoreau said: "I have travelled much in Concord." The following sections on Architecture and Economy from his book *Walden* are quite appropriately illustrated with Le Corbusier's own cabanon, a plastic manifestation of the beauty of simplicity. Thoreau wrote "Near the end of March 1845, I borrowed an axe and went down to the woods by Walden Pond nearest to where I intended to build my house, and began to cut down some tall arrowy white pines..." Le Corbusier simply said, "I work with light." What a privilege it is to be able to occupy space-- even more to be able to inhabit one of your own devising and construction! A space which has been planned with intelligence and insight can resonate with the enlightenment of courage and experience. Find someone who has done this, and chances are you will have found someone who illuminates the world. The study in this chapter and the next gives you at last the chance to work with your own architectural canvas. As architect Bernard Maybeck is reputed to have said to his carpenter and mason friends during the Depression of the 1930's, "You have no money, I have no money, so let's build a house." This nicely amplifies the Sufi proverb: "You have leather, you have tools? Why don't you make yourself a pair of shoes!?" Who today gets the satisfaction of making one's own home? Will the building trades of the future be replaced by a home component store like today's electronics outlet? Will the owner become architect-as-assembler to inhabit an instrument of dwelling volumes?

READINGS:
Ambasz, Emilio. *Italy, The New Domestic Landscape.*
Ant Farm *InflatoCookBook*
Brand, Stewart, ed. *The Whole Earth Catalog*
Defoe, Daniel. *Robinson Crusoe* (and Johann Wyss' *Swiss Family Robinson*)
Isaac, S. *How to Build Your Own Living Structures*
Le Corbusier, *Le Modulor*
Nilsson, Lennart. *Behold Man*
Ryckwert, Joseph. *On Adam's House in Paradise*
Scientific American Series, *The Physics of Music*
Turnbull, Colin. *The Forest People*

from **WALDEN**
by Henry David Thoreau

"Near the end of March 1845, I borrowed an axe and went down to the woods by Walden Pond nearest to where I intended to build my house, and began to cut down some tall arrowy white pines...

At length, in the beginning of May, with the help of some of my acquaintances, rather to improve so good an occasion for neighborliness than from any necessity, I set up the frame of my house. No man was ever more honored in the character of his raisers than I. They are destined, I trust, to assist at the raising of loftier structures one day. I began to occupy my house on the 4th of July, as soon as it was boarded and roofed, for the boards were carefully feather-edged and lapped, so that it was perfectly impervious to rain, but before boarding I laid the foundation of a chimney at one end, bringing two cartloads of stones up the hill from the pond in my arm. I built the chimney after my hoeing in the fall, before a fire because necessary for warmth, doing my cooking in the meanwhile out doors on the ground, early in the morning: which mode I still is in some respects more convenient and agreeable the usual one. When is stormed before my bread was baked, I fixed a few boards over the fire, and sat under them to watch my loaf, and passed some pleasant hours in that way. In those days, when my hands where much employed, I read but little, but the least scraps of paper which lay on the ground, my holder, or tablecloth, afforded me as much entertainment, in fact answered the same purpose as the Iliad.

It would be worth the while to build still more deliberately than I did, considering, for instance, what foundation a door, a window, a cellar, a garret, have in the nature of man, and perchance never raising any superstructure until we found a better reason for it than our temporal necessities even. There is some of the same fitness in a man's building his own house that there is in a bird's building its own nest. Who knows but if men constructed their dwellings with their own hands, and provided food for themselves and families simply and honestly enough, the poetic faculty would be universally develop, as birds universally sing when they are so engaged? But alas! we do like cow birds and cuckoos, which lay their eggs in nests which other birds have built, and cheer no traveller with their chattering and unmusical notes. Shall we forever resign the pleasure of construction to the carpenter? What does architecture amount to in the experience of the mass of man? I never on all my walks came across a man engaged in so simple and natural an occupation as building his house. We belong to the community. It is not the tailor alone who is in the ninth part of a man; it is as much the preacher, and the merchant, and the farmer. Where is this division of labor to the end? and what object does it finally serve? No doubt

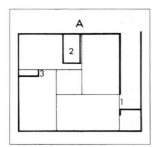

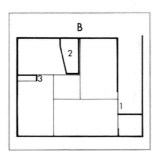

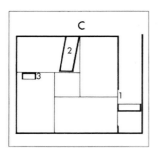

another may also think for me; but it is not therefore desirable that he should do so to the exclusion of my thinking for myself.

True, there are architects so called in this country, and I have heard of one at least possessed with the idea of making architectural ornaments have a core of truth, a necessity, and hence a beauty, as if were a revelation to him. All very well perhaps from his point of view, but only a little better than the common dilettantism. A sentimental reformer in architecture, he began at the cornice, not at the foundation. It was only how to put a core of truth within the ornaments, that every sugarplum, in fact, might have an almond or caraway seed in it, - though it hold that almonds are most wholesome without sugar,- and not how the inhabitant, the indweller, might build truly within and without, and let the ornaments take of themselves. What reasonable man ever supposed that ornaments were something outward and in the skin merely,- That the tortoise got his spotted shell, or the shell-fish its mother-o'-pearl tints, by such a contract as the inhabitants of Broadway their Trinity Church? But a man has no more to do with the style of architecture of his house than a tortoise with of its shell: nor need the soldier be so idle as to try to paint the precise color of his virtue on his standard. The enemy will find it out. He may turn pale when the trial comes. This man seemed to me to lean over the cornice, and tidily whisper his half truth to the rude occupants who really knew it better than he. What of architectural beauty I now see, I know has gradually grown from within outward, out of the necessities and character of the indweller, who is the only builder,- out of some unconscious truthfulness, and nobleness, without ever a thought for the appearance; and whatever additional beauty of this kind is destined to be produced will be preceded by a like unconscious beauty of life. The most interesting dwellings in this country, as the painter knows, are the most unpretending, humble log huts and cottages of the poor commonly; it is the life of the inhabitants whose shells they are, an not any peculiarity in their surfaces merely, which makes it picturesque; and equally interesting will be the citizen's suburban box when his life shall be as simple as agreeable to the imagination, and there is as little straining after effect in the style of his dwelling. A great proportion of architectural ornaments are literally hollow, and a September gale would strip them off, like borrowed plumes, without injuries to the substantials. They can do without architecture who have no olives nor wines in the cellar. What if an equal ado were made about the ornaments of style in literature, and the architects of our Bibles spent as much time about their cornices as the architects of our churches do? So are made the belle-lettres and the beaux-arts and their professors. Much it concerns a man, forsooth, how a few sticks are slanted over him or under him, and what colors are daubed upon his box. It would signify somewhat, if, in any earnest sense, he slanted them and daubed it; but the spirit having departed out the tenant, it is of a piece with constructing his own coffin, - the architecture of the grave,- and "carpenter" is but another name for "coffin-maker." One man says, in his despair or indifference to life, take up a handful of the earth at your feet, and paint your house that color. Is he thinking of his last and narrow house? Toss up a copper for it as well. What an abundance of leisure he must have! Why do you take a handful of dirt? Better paint your house your own complexion; let it turn pale or blush for you. An enterprise to improve the style of cottage architecture! When you have got my ornaments ready, I will wear them.

Before winter a built a chimney, and shingled the sides of my house, which were already impervious to rain, with imperfect and sappy shingles made of the first slide of the log, whose edges I was obliged to straighten with a plane.

I have thus a tight shingled and plastered house, ten feet wide by fifteen long, eight-feet post, with a garret and a closet, a large window in each side, and trap doors, one door at the end, and a brick fireplace opposite. The exact cost of my house, paying the usual price for such materials as I used use , but not counting the work, all of which was done by myself, was as follows; and I give the details because very few are able to tell exactly what their houses cost, and fewer still, if any, the separate cost of the various materials which compose them:—

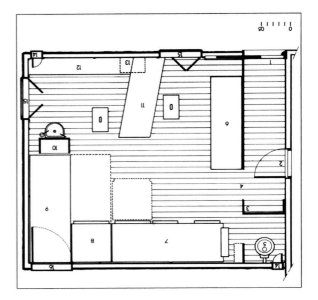

Boards	$8 03 ½,	mostly shanty boards
Refuse shingles for roof and sides	4 00	
Laths	1 25	
Two second-hand windows with glass	2 43	
One thousand old brick	4 00	
Two casks of lime.	2 40	That was high.
Hair	0 31	More than I needed.
Mantle-tree iron	0 15	
Nails	3 90	
Hinges and screws	0 14	
Latch	0 10	
Chalk	0 01	
Transportation	1 40	I carried a good part on my back.
In all	$28 12 ½	

These are all the materials, excepting the timber, stones, and sand, which I claimed by squatter's right. I have also a small woodshed adjoining, made chiefly of the stuff which was left after building the house.

I intend to build me a house which will surpass any on the main street in Concord in grandeur and luxury, as soon as it pleases me as much and will cost me more than my present one.

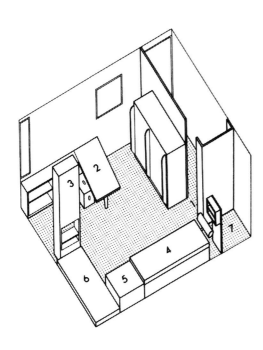

I thus found that the student who wishes for a shelter can obtain one for a lifetime at an expense not greater than the rent which he now pays annually. If I seem to boast more than is becoming, my excuse is that I brag for humanity rather than for myself; and my shortcomings and inconsistencies do not affect the truth of my statement. Notwithstanding much cant and hypocrisy,- chaff which I find it difficult to separate from my wheat, but for which I am as sorry as any man,- I will breathe freely and stretch myself in this respect, it is such a relief to both the moral and physical system; and I am resolved that I will not through humility become the devil's attorney. I will endeavor to speak a good word for the truth. At Cambridge College the mere rent of a student's room, which is only a little larger than my own, is thirty dollars each year, though the corporation had the advantage of building thirty-two side by side and under one roof, and the occupant suffers the inconvenience of many and noisy neighbors, and perhaps a residence in the fourth story. I can not but think that if we had more true wisdom in these respects, not only less education would be needed, because, forsooth, more would already have been acquired, but the pecuniary expense of getting an education would in a great measure vanish. Those conveniences which the student requires at Cambridge or elsewhere cost him somebody else ten times as great a sacrifice of life as they would with proper management on both sides. Those things for which the most money is demanded are never the things which the students most wants. Tuition, for instance, is an important item in the term bill, while for the far more valuable education which he gets by associating with the most cultivated of his contemporaries no charge is made. The mode of founding a college is, commonly, to get up a subscription of dollars and cents, and then, following blindly the principles of a division of labor to its extreme,- a principle which should never be followed but with circumspection,- to call in a contractor who makes this a subject of speculation, and he employs Irishmen or other operatives actually to lay the foundations, while the students that are to be are said to be fitting themselves for it; and for these oversights successive generations have to pay. I think that it would be better than this, for the students, or those who desire to be benefited by it, even to lay the foundation themselves. The student who secures his coveted leisure and retirement by systematically shirking any labor necessary to man obtains an ignoble and unprofitable leisure, defrauding himself of the experience which alone can make leisure fruitful. "But", says one, " you do not mean that students should go to work with their hands instead of their heads?" I do not mean that exactly, but I mean something which he might think a good deal like that; I mean that they should not play life, or study it merely, while the community supports them at this expensive game, but earnestly live it from beginning to end. How could youths better learn to live than by at once trying the experiment of living? Methinks this would be exercise their minds as much as mathematics. If I wished a boy to know something about the arts and sciences, for instance, I would not pursue the common course, which is merely to send him into the neighborhood of some professor, where anything is professed and practised but the art of life;— to survey the world through a telescope or a microscope, and never with his natural eye; to study chemistry, and not learn how his bread is made, or mechanics, and not learn how is earned; to discovered a new satellites to Neptune, and not detect the motes in his eyes, or to what vagabond he is a satellite himself; or to be devoured by the monsters that swarm all around him, while contemplating the monsters in a drop of vinegar. Which would have the most at the end of the month,— the boy who has made his own jackknife from the ore which he had dug and smelted, reading as much as would be necessary for this— or the boy who has attended the lectures on metallurgy at the Institute in the meanwhile, and had received a Rodgers penknife from his father? Which would be most likely to cut his fingers?... To my astonishment I was informed on leaving college that I had studied navigation!— why, if I had taken one turn down the harbor I should have known more about it. Even the poor student studies and is taught only political economy, while that economy of living which is synonymous with philosophy is not even sincerely professed in our colleges. The consequence is, that he is reading Adam Smith, Ricardo, and Say, he runs his father in debt irretrievably.

As with our colleges, so with a hundred " modern improvements;" there is an illusion about them; there is not always a positive advance. The devil goes on exacting compound interest to the last for his early share and numerous succeeding investment in them. Our inventions are want to be pretty toys, which distract our attention from serious things. They are but improved means to an unimproved end, and end which it was already but too easy to arrive at; as railroads lead to Boston or New York. We are in great haste to construct a magnetic telegraph from Maine to Texas; but Maine and Texas, it may be, have nothing important to communicate. Either is in such a predicament as the man who was earnest to be

introduced to a distinguished deaf woman, but when he was presented, and one end of her ear trumpet was put into his hand, had nothing to say. As if the main object were to talk and not talk sensibly. We are eagle to tunnel under the Atlantic and bring the Old World some weeks nearer to the New; but perchance the first news that will leak through into the broad, flapping American ear will be the Princess Adelaide has the whooping cough. After all, the man whose horse trots a mile a minute does not carry the most important messages; he is not an evangelist, nor he comes round eating locusts and wild honey. I doubt if Flying Childers ever carried a peck of corn to mill.

One says to me, " I wonder that you do not lay money; you love to travel; you might take the cars and go to Fitchburg today and see the country." But I am wiser than that, I have learned that the swiftest traveller is he that goes a foot. I say to my friend , suppose we try who will get there first. The distance is thirty miles; the fare ninety cents. That is almost a day's wages. I remember when wages where sixty cents a day for laborers on this very road. Well, I start now on foot, and get there before night; I have travelled at that rate by the week together. You will in meanwhile have earned your fare, and arrive there sometime tomorrow, or possibly this evening, if your lucky enough to get a job in season. Instead of going to Fitchburg, you will be working here the greater pert of the day. And so, if the railroad reached round the world, I think that I should keep ahead of you; and as for seeing the country and getting the experience of that kind, I should have to cut your acquaintance altogether.

Such is the universal law, which no man can ever outwit, and with regard to the railroad even we may say it is as broad as it is long. To make a railroad round the world available to all mankind is equivalent to grading the whole surface of the planet. Men have an indistinct notion that if they keep up this activity of joint stocks and spades long enough all will at length ride somewhere, in next to no time, and for nothing; but though a crowd rushes to the depot, and the conductor shouts " All aboard!" when the smoke is blown away and the vapor condensed, it will be perceived that a few are riding, but the rest are run over,— and it will be called, and will be, "A melancholy accident." No doubt they can ride at last who shall have earned their fare, that is, if they survive so long, but they will probably have lost their elasticity ad desire to travel by that time. This spending of the best part of one's life earning money in order to enjoy a questionable liberty during the least valuable part of it reminds me of the Englishman who went to India to make a fortune first, in order that he might return to England and live the life of a poet. He should have gone up garret at once. "What!"

exclaim a million Irishmen starting up from all the shanties in the land, " is not this railroad which have built a good thing?" Yes, I answer, comparatively good, that is, you might have done worse; but I wish, as you are brothers of mine, that you could have spent your time better than digging in this dirt.

Before I finished my house, wishing to earn ten or twelve dollars by some honest and agreeable method, in order to meet my unusual expenses, I planted about two acres and a half of light and sandy soil near it chiefly with beans, but also a small part with potatoes, corn, peas, and turnips. The whole lot contains eleven acres, mostly growing up pines and hickories, and was sold the preceding season for eight dollars and eight cents an acre. One farmer said that it was "good for nothing but to raise cheeping squirrels on." I put no manure whatever on this land, not being the owner, but merely a squatter, and no expecting to cultivate so much again, and I did not quite hoe it all once. I got out several cords of stumps in plowing, which supplied me with fuel for a long time, and left small circles of virgin mould, easily distinguishable through the summer by the greater luxuriance of beans there. The dead and for the most part unmerchantable wood behind my hose, and the drift wood from the pond, have supplied the remainder o my fuel. I was obliged to hire a team an a man for the plowing, though I held the plow myself. My farm outgoes for the first season were, for implements, seed, work, etc., $ 14.72 1/2. The seed corn was given to me. This never cost anything to speak to unless you plant more than enough. I got twelve bushels of beans, and eighteen bushels of potatoes, beside some beans some peas and some sweet corn. The yellow corn and the turnips were to late to come to anything. My whole income from the farm was

	$23.44
Deducting the outgoes	14.72½
	————
There are left	$ 8.71 ½

beside produce consumed and on hand at the time this estimate was made of the value of $ 4.50,— the amount on hand much more than balancing a little grass which I did not raise. All things considered, that is, considering the importance of a man's soul and of today, notwithstanding the short time occupied by my experiment, nay partly even because of its transient character, I believe that was doing better than any farmer in Concord did that year.

The next year I did better still, for I spaded up all the land which I required, about a third of an acre, and I learned from the experience of both years, not being in the least awed by many celebrated works of husbandry, Arthur Young among the rest, that if one would live simply and eat only the crop which he raised, and raise no more than he ate, and not exchange it for an insufficient quantity of more luxurious and expensive things, he would need to cultivate only a few rods of ground, and that it would be cheaper to spade up that than to use oxen to plow it, and to select a fresh spot from time to time than to manure the old, and he could all his necessary farm work as it were with his left hand at odds hours in the summer; and thus he would not be tied to an ox, or horse, or cow, or pig as at present. I desire to speak impartially on this point, and as one not interested in the success or failure of the present economical and social arrangements. I was more independent than any farmer in Concord, for I was anchored to a house or a farm, but could follow the bent of my genius, which is a very crooked one, every moment. Beside being better off than they already, if my house had been burned or my crops had failed, I should have nearly as well off as before.

I am wont to think that men are not so much the keepers of herds are the keepers of men, the former are so much the freer. Men and oxen exchange work; but if we consider necessary work only, the oxen will be seen to have greatly the advantage, their farm is so much larger. Man does some of his art of the exchange work in his six weeks of haying, and it is no boy's play. Certainly no nation that lived simply in all respects, that is, no nation of philosophers would commit so great a blunder as to use the labor of animals. True, there never was and is not likely soon to be a nation of philosophers, nor am I certain it is desirable that there should be. However, I should never have broken a horse or a bull and taken him to board for any work he might do for me, for fear I should become a horse-man or a herds-man merely; and if society seems to be the gainer by so doing, are we certain that what is one man's gain is not another's loss, and the stable boy has equal cause with his master to be satisfied? Granted that some public works would not have been constructed without this aid, and let man share the glory of such with the ox and the horse; does it follow that he could have accomplished works yet more worthy of himself in that case? When men begin to do, not merely unnecessary or artistic, but luxurious and idle work, with their assistance, it is inevitable that a few do all the exchange work with the oxen, or, in other words, become the slaves of the strongest. Man thus not only works for the animal within him, but, for a symbol of this, he works for the animal without him. Though we have many substantial houses of brick or stone, the prosperity of the farmer is still measured by the degree to which the barn overshadows the house....

TODD WRIGHT AND MIKE CUTITA

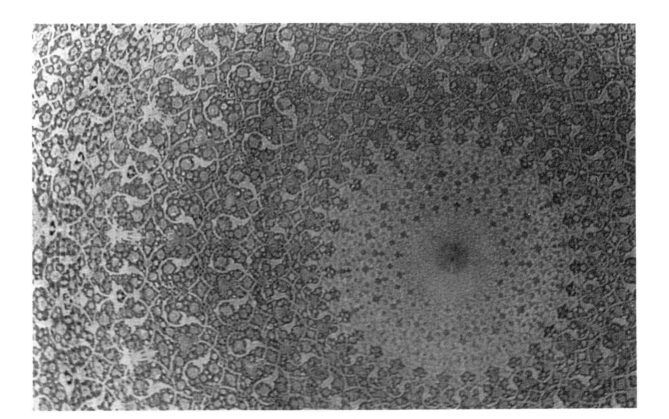

SYMPHONY: *RADIATING*

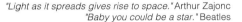

BEING

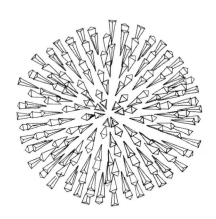

"Light as it spreads gives rise to space." Arthur Zajonc
"Baby you could be a star." Beatles

A "cylinder detector" made so a square-sectioned cylinder could pass through a circle in plan and a square in section is perfectly understandable in three-dimensions. But how could a two-dimensional Flatlander account for such weirdness? Something like that confronts us when we consider light. Quantum mechanics, the very accurate and successful working model that describes how matter and energy interact at the smallest scales of the subatomic world, is... weird.

What is light? To date there is no single clear answer, and certainly no adequate picture or description. Light exists in discrete packets of energy called *quanta* and acts both like waves and particles, but at different times. When light is directed through a narrow slit, photons pass like well aimed bullets or remain outside the opaque gate. But if two slits are made, each photon seems to know how to behave as if it were a wave, and the scatter pattern produces a wave-function of probable positions. Also, each of a pair of photons (quantum light particles) seems to know just how its partner is doing--instantly-- even if they are years of light travel apart! Our explanations of such phenomena, demonstrable in labs, are not really explanations in the common sense of the term-- but rather descriptions of seemingly incompatible evidence which we simply cannot picture, with such names as "the many-worlds interpretation" which suggest that at each choice a quantum particle can make, new universes develop for *every* possible outcome! But nonetheless, light exists, and its energy is the means for mass and void to organize itself into life. Rudolf Schwarz envisioned:

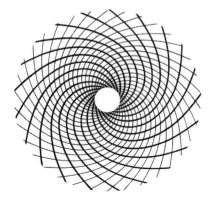

> "... a dome of sheer light. The building consists of light, light breaking in from all sides, light shining forth from all things, light fused with light, light turning to face the light, light the answer to light. The earth is transformed into a star, her stuff afire, she is a monstrance of rays about the child in the center, her altar as flame, the people a sea of fire and each one of them a star. All the land and all the nations spread out without end within the universe. The vault of the world is a pellucid infinitude, clear and transparent like an evening sky high in the mountains, ethereal and incorporeal, a golden effulgence where the heavenly beings are hovering motionless in bliss. Heaven is everywhere, earth everywhere, the one melting into the other.... The eternal joy comes at a late time when it is no longer hoped for and it comes, not in a gradual development, but in a flash. At the very beginning when the closed form breaks open and light falls into the darkness this joy seems near." *The Church Incarnate*

Repeated and superimposed vibration cycles generate resonance. Some bodies resonate so much that they transform their matter into pure energy and *radiate*. These are called stars. The sun, our local star, is a solid of momentum/energy. So is the earth and so are we. Each inhabits weather systems of pressure cells of hydrogen, lava, or blood, fluids flowing from dense to sparse. The sun burns 5 million tons of hydrogen each second. It has done this for perhaps 5 billion years, and should continue for at least as long. Although the earth receives only a billionth of the sun's total radiation, this still amounts to about 10^{14} kilowatts, or 5 million horsepower per square mile. When energy encounters inert mass, there is no telling what can happen. Even life, intelligence, and spirit can arise. Which brings us full circle from the gift of the mystery of the acorn and the spiral to the gift of an ever bountiful cornucopia. The world is filled with an interplay of energy and matter. The cosmos is a cobweb of vector equilibria, a swirling foam of galaxies. After winter, life springs into rebirth. Light and dark make waves of ice and fire that flow in time to earth's complex dance around our solar beacon. Crashing ocean waves create surf between beach and sea, violently mixing water and air to create a foam of bubbles. The temporary symbiosis creates new space of gas-filled liquid spheres unlike what either formed alone. Might one such chance communion be our most remote and humble ancestor?

forest flower flowing in spacetime

THE KEY

The key is light
and light illuminates shapes
and shapes have an emotional power.

By the play of proportions
by the play of relationships
unexpected, amazxing.

But also by the intellectual play
Jof purpose:
their authentic origin
thier capacity to endure,
structure,
astuteness, boldness, even temerity, the play
of those vital abstractions which are the essential qualities
the componbents of architecture.

$$\frac{4}{6}$$
56

cap
martin
LC

the (blue-) green house

'CATCHING THE LIGHT"

"see the mind is capacious" Benny Golson

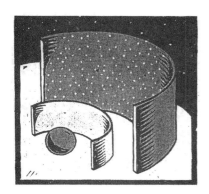

The Olbers paradox asks: why is the night sky black? Ultimately, because the speed of light is finite and the universe's age is finite, perhaps less than 20 billion years old. Looking at the black night sky, you see the birth of the universe. A supernova explodes most of its matter in an instant. What remains is one giant atomic nucleus, perhaps as big as Manhattan and rotating thirty times a second. A cubic inch of the remaining neutron star weighs as much as a mountain range on earth. Matter is even denser in a black hole, a star that collapsed under the inward pull of its mass until its concentrated gravitational field bends spacetime so much that even light cannot escape. Nearby light beams may escape oblivion only to be warped into cosmic hairpin turns. Light is a beam, gravity acts like a load on light that can deflect it!Light glows! Light is the skin which radiance becomes on meeting gravity.

The (blue-) green house

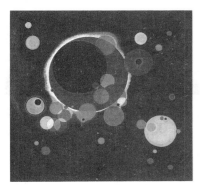

Here in the comparatively vaporous and torpid spacetime of Earth, mass is too dispersed to significantly bend light. But plants and animals have developed subtle strategies to unravel light and catch and rebind its energy into the molecular structures that feed us. Plants use photosynthesis and we eat plants and plant eaters to weave the light into sugars, vitamins, and protein. A leaf is like the mirrored prisms that can split laser light into separate beams-- a lens and spectrum sorter converting solar light by photosynthesis into the molecular bricks of life. A plant turns light into matter, energy into mass. Plants propagate across the planet. Why not factory plants across the stars? Dr. Robert Frosch, former NASA Administrator and Vice President of General Motors, has argued that it is feasible to develop solar-powered lunar self-replicating factories:

> "Such a factory could mine the extra-terrestrial (e.g. lunar) material under it or next to it... and make and assemble the parts for another factory identical to itself, including the solar energy plant. The new factory would proceed to do the same, the result being a machine pseudo-biology, with factories growing in numbers at an exponential rate.... The time required for a solar cell to collect enough energy to make another solar cell in this fashion appears on the order of several days. Thus the replication time is sufficiently short that-- starting with one machine and assuming that there are no accidents, no catastrophic wear, and no hardware or software "mutation"-- more than a million machines could be provided in twenty years... A machine versatile enough to replicate itself is clearly a general purpose factory. A number of such machines, "living" on solar energy and local materials, would represent a general purpose industrial base-- a base for whatever the human race cares to do in the solar system where such local materials are available in sufficient density... the return appears to be beyond obvious bound."

Vital Dust

Space is an embroidery of weaving waves, resonating at all frequencies. Energy becomes concrete as it cools into matter. Gas as dust is born and condenses into stars and planets. *Dust is the first fossil.* Dust is made again as fractal rocks chipped off ever-cooling matter into ever smaller masses by the sharp chisel point of hot bright light. Dust is a rain of fractal stones. If gravity is the seed of matter at densified ripples of spacetime, then is light the agent of space? Are there fractal voids too? Are fractal hollows carved by local increased pressure of momentum/energy as the universe expands? Why isn't the cosmos one gray smear of sameness? Is life the agent of increasing order that balances the heat-death of increasing entropy? The eponymous Louise B. Young believes that life and mind are part of the evolution of the universe into inevitable complexity. Every child is an interplay of energy and matter in a new and irreproducible branching of the tree of the family of man. Every offspring of every spectral weaving is another opportunity for the Universe to come to know itself.

DAZZLE

'Space is everywhere: light just travels." "Space is the only thing faster than light."
Charles Michael Friedman

Wrinkles in time

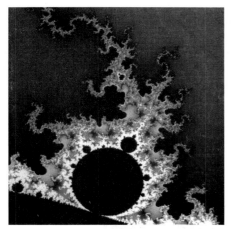

About 15 billion years ago in all directions, there was a singularity. As it exploded, the Big Bang made more material, more time, and more space. **Space itself is expanding!** The evolution of the universe allows us to extrapolate back to its original infinite density. In 1992, George Smoot and colleagues found "wrinkles in time", slight variations in the background energy radiation of the cosmos on the order of one part in a million, against the 30 degrees Kelvin temperature right after (300,000 years) the Big Bang itself, some 10 to 20 billion years ago. Stephen Hawking called the discovery of the relic radiation structure of the Big Bang thermal spectrum, the "holy Grail of cosmology", "the most important scientific discovery of the century, perhaps of all time." Smoot calls the infrared/microwave variation map (shown faintly in very dark red on the cover of this volume) a "baby photo" of the universe showing the moment when the universe was cool enough to allow matter to de-couple from energy, so that the universe became transparent to light. If the universe is now in its "middle age" like a 40 year old person, then the "baby photo" is equivalent to the picture of a human fertilized egg **5 hours** after conception! The map shows that structure in the cosmos was imprinted right at the time of creation. Even larger structures than the galaxies, clusters, superclusters, and Great Attractor visible today may eventually form. If the universe were a perfectly symmetrical and even distribution of all matter space and energy at its birth as a point, or singularity, then what accounts for the vast complexity we see today, where some regions of the cosmos are crowded with stars, while others are empty desert bubbles of volumes perhaps billions of light-years across? Without the variations this map shows, then gravity alone would need to account for all the structure in the universe. This is very difficult to demonstrate in terms of what we currently know about forces.

A mathematical object: a computer generated portion of the fractal Mandelbrodt set, No, it is not an astronomical photo of the side view of a solar flare.

An eternally self reproducing cosmos?

It is easy to mistake the top left image on this page for a solar flare, but in fact, it is just another part of the fractal Mandelbrodt set shown opposite (see also page 454.) The Mandelbrodt set is a plot of the formula $f(z) = z^2 + c$, where z is a complex number including $i = \sqrt{-1}$, an imaginary number. The formula is deceptively simple, the figure is self-similar without limit-- and currently is the most complex figure ever devised by humankind. The graphic figure on the facing page is dazzling, and suggestive of so many readings and so many incarnations of the universe we see from the smallest to the largest scales. If we read the white as fractal radiation and the black as fractal gravity it is hard to resist speculating that an infinite figure-ground recursion is the fabric of our world. Fractals are noted in *Architectonics* (page 84) and since that book was published have played an increasing part in theories of the structure of the cosmos, providing a means for matter, space, and time to fluctuate in expansion and contraction within the overall expansion of the cosmos since the Big Bang. Andrei Linde of Stanford University believes that fractals can help describe the possibility of an eternally self-reproducing cosmos. He has proposed that instead of being an expanding ball of fire, the universe is a huge, growing fractal which consists of many inflating balls that produce new balls, which in turn produce more balls, *ad infinitum.* Dr. Linde helped devise the concept of "inflation" which suggests that soon after the Big Bang, the very tiny dense hot universe experienced a huge growth spurt before settling down to its current relatively slow growth rate. He recently suggested that since quantum mechanics requires that space never be completely empty, chaotic and fractal fluctuations of energy in the vacuum could rapidly grow into new universes. This may help to explain Hubble Space Telescope's recent observation that indicates that the universe may only be 8 billion years old, despite the fact that we know some stars must be at least 16 billion years old!

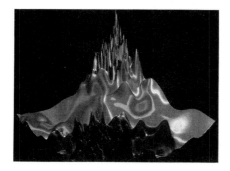

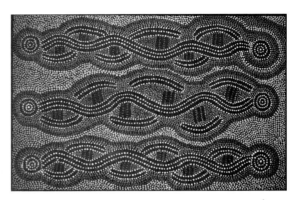

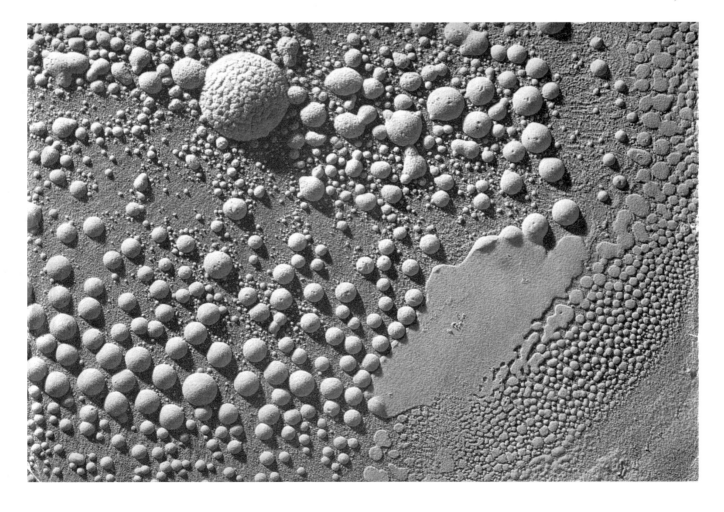

OUTBACK SONGLINES

"He doesn't always go at the speed of light: he knows how to use his time and space to his advantage." Benny Golson

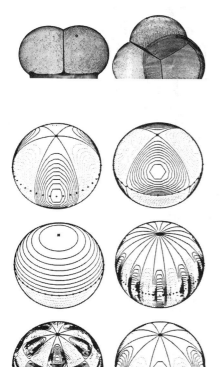

RESONANT OSCILLATING MODES OF THE SUN

LAMINATED LATTICE PACKING

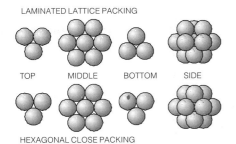

TOP   MIDDLE   BOTTOM   SIDE

HEXAGONAL CLOSE PACKING

TWO MODES OF CLOSE-PACKING SPHERES

The sun, our local star, rings like a bell. The drawings to the left show contour plots of selected modes of oscillation of the sun. The solid lines represent zones of expansion; the dotted lines, contraction. Only six of thousands of possible modes are shown. The selection of modes illustrates progressively complex oscillatory motions from left to right and top to bottom. Oscillations occur with periods ranging from minutes to at least hours. The longer the period, the deeper the origin of the vibration in the sun. How do these resonant modes affect us here on earth? Earth is the instrument that plays the sun's harmonic music-- the acoustic chamber that resonates to the suns energy spectrum fluctuations and vibrates into the increasingly complex molecules of life and human intelligence.

When a landscape is muted both in contour and vegetation, the slightest bump shows up in high relief. The Outback of Australia is very *empty*; there may be one blade of grass every 10 feet, one shrub every 100 yards, one tree every mile, or less. There is a 200 mile (300 km) stretch on the Kalgoorlie Railroad to Perth, which runs absolutely *straight*! On the four-hour drive from Pimba to Andamooka, only the late afternoon shadow of the 4" high mound of same-colored red earth pushed aside by the road construction grader reveals the road through the trackless space. The slightest perturbation in the sun's spacetime, rippled this part of Earth's ground plane landscape... just a bit. Australian Aborigines, who have made this space their home since perhaps the Stone Age, have developed an aesthetic very much in tune with the arid and attenuated atmosphere of their homeland. Their stories may sound elusive to our ears, but to the post-Cubist eye their paintings are direct and comprehensive visions. One painting tells the story of Tingari events at a place called Nakinga, south of Lake Mackay, in Western Australia. One of the roundels represents a Desert Oak tree, while the other is a soaking waterhole. They are located among sandhills. Charlie Tjapangati is relatively young among [aboriginal] artists, being at most in his early thirties when he painted this. He was born in the desert however and was one of the last to emerge.

Another artist, Dick Patimatju Tjupurrula, of the tribe Luritja, notes: "In this oft represented tale, the Rain-Dreaming, or Kalipimpa Story (since that is where the storm set out, way west of Alice Springs), the mother and father of all rain storms started out in the west during the Dreamtime. It blew eastwards, setting the pattern of all future storms which blow up in the desert. The sinuous lines represent the path of the storm or running water or lightning or all three at once since they are so closely associated. The short bars are clouds and the curved ones rainbows. In the main story, the storm ended up at Watulpunya, just west of Central Mount Wedge. Thence subsidiary storms dispersed to give rise to secondary mythologies."

These people are sensitive to even the subtlest variations in their landscape. Their Songlines are interval/event oral maps and travel guides, that link all places across this emptiest of continents. Lycopodium spores form a powder that clumps when vibrated on a plate. The resulting Chladni patterns suggest community. In human history, resonant modes generate self-sustaining configurations: we call them populations and generations. People make culture by fine-tuning their senses to take advantage of their space. It is said that Aborigines can smell and hear a rain storm coming 40 miles away. It is said that Inuit Eskimos have 50 words for snow. Claude Levi-Straus recounts bringing a native of the rain forest to the city and asking him what he thought of all the tall buildings. "What tall buildings?" the Amazonian replied. "But I see that here you have very little sky..."

Digital Weather Readout: The Blizzard of '93-'94, TV polaroid photo taken by the author. A single high pressure clear cold air mass holds at bay all clouds along the United States continuous continental shelf front! The clouds outline the continent!

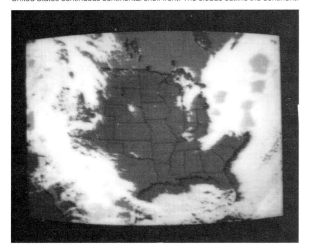

A cabbage is a big bubble to worms and insects.

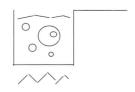

one view of global warming: big bubbles!

's High Temperatures and Precipitation

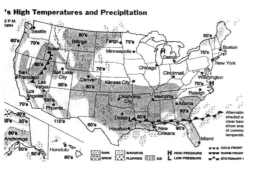

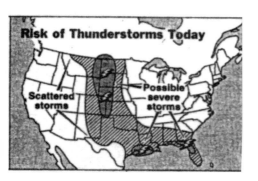

WEATHER IS PRESSURE SYSTEMS

Boiling Big Bubbles

In recent decades it seems the earth's weather is becoming more violent: longer hotter heat waves, faster winds in hurricanes, deeper snows, bigger floods, sharper drops between one day's record heat and the next day's record cold. One dynamic explanation of these phenomena is this: increased global warming from fossil fuels and the greenhouse effect resulting from the alteration of the upper atmosphere's CO_2 and ozone content means that there is more overall heat added to the earth's airocean fluid. When a pot of water is boiled on a stove, it first forms little bubbles like ginger-ale, but then bubbles get bigger in a rolling boil. Perhaps the high and low pressure systems of our planet's weather are becoming bigger bubbles.

Electric Sky

Chaos theory suggests that when a butterfly in Tahiti flaps its wings, it will change the weather in New York a week from now. Chaotic systems give nonlinear response to linear input. We cannot predict exactly *how* but we can predict *that* a small change in original conditions of such a system will produce a large change in the outcome. Will one more summer sprinkler in Montana cause a blizzard in Kyoto the following spring? (Is it true that for every acre of rain forest destroyed, the antidote to the new virulent microorganism thus released is forever lost?) Taking any long view of human settlement it is remarkable how an easy choice to set up camp by a stream of fresh water, with firewood, things to eat, and shelter from predators may yield perhaps 10,000 years later a metropolis that seems more inevitable and eternal than the few weeds from the original ecosystem that still break through its sidewalk cracks. How remarkable is the self-sustaining aspect of whole human settlements that are cities. The Parthenon has been a civic center for three millennia. People continue to remodel homes built into the Justinian walls of Istanbul. Jericho and Matera have been continuous cities for perhaps 10,000 years! Since in any chaos system-- weather, fire, or history-- early minor shifts can radically affect the outcome, what happened at that first urban instance? How did mental lightning strike? What did the original settlers bring to the site, both in intelligence and material goods, tools and devices, not the least of which was the decision to stop *there* rather than somewhere else! What was in their "suitcase" that would be the very things needed to spawn a city, sustain it, and keep it thriving ten millennia hence? That is the first and basic question in an art of Planning.

Microclimates

The people of Gavriotis, a new community growing in the altiplano of Bolivia now since the 1970's, have invented a new kind of pump in which the piston is stationary and the cylinder moves. It is much lighter than the old kind, so children are able to pump water from deep wells while playing on their seesaws! Every body in our cosmos is warmer than absolute zero (zero degrees Kelvin), so every body radiates. Heat is motion and generates light. In Gavriotis they have also planted Caribbean pines that have survived and provided shade. The trees have generated beneath their leaves a relatively cool and damp microclimate that has fostered the growth of plants whose seeds have waited centuries for such fortuitous conditions to return. The Gavriotans will allow these new plants to overtake the pines and continue to climax growth, becoming... rain forest! While the rest of the world is cutting down the jungle, Gavriotis is *creating* rain forest! Another plan to prompt arid desert air to yield its rare but present moisture by condensing is an inflatable artificial cloud. Surely with such human ingenuity, we cannot yet dispense with hope for the flowering of our home.

TAO

THE AIR OCEAN LAND SEA.

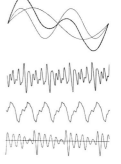

BREUGHEL'S HUNTERS IN THE SNOW

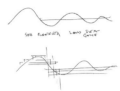

SETTLING

"My grandparents had to live their way out of one world and into another, or into several others, making new out of old the way corals live their reef upward. I am on my grandparents' side. I believe in Time, as they did, and in the life chronological rather than the life existential. We live in time and through it, we build our huts in its ruins, or used to, and we cannot afford all these abandonings." Wallace Stegner

Animated landscape

Gaston Bachelard in *Poetics of Space* notes that a cabin feels more cozy and its fire more intense when it is deep in snowy woods. Breughel's *Hunters in the Snow*, on the facing page, celebrates the spirit of indigenous inhabitants, native-born, who are adept at living *in* and with the landscape, not against it. They try to learn to take advantage of their world without destroying it, collecting wisdom from ancestors who won it through observation, wit, and trial-and-error. It may take generations to discover and cultivate, and it may not make for easy life, but the Garden all around us is Edenic, and welcomes us with its abundance. For successful conservationists, homes are dwelling instruments, not the dwelling weapons brought by thoughtless invaders of any culture and/or ecosystem.

For buildings **grade** denotes the landing or footing on the site, the place of the foundation. **Gradient** is the slope, the degree or flatness or steepness of the land. To make a building as Wright advised "of the site, not on it" is to locate volume in the land as if it were the work of nature. A wise builder may find guidance in the spacial resonances of the site, the multiple frequencies of waves of landscape that ripple and overlap. Setting a foundation requires a kind of intuitive (if not literal) Fourier analysis of the factors of surface drainage, percolation, water table, frost heaves, subsoil structure, on down to bedrock. If resonance is a consonance of parts and intervals, then proper planning requires fitting dwelling into the shaping of the larger space of site from center to at least horizon's rim. Near Earth's surface, gravity makes spreading out easier than spreading up. Panorama is an all-around view, in which the horizon encompasses vision as seeing eye and roving body meet in mind.

Intimate Immensity

The Chinese term for landscape is two characters: mountain and river. One builds up the terrain, the other cuts it down. It is all you need. We might make a set of blocks to play the game of landscape, and call it "cut and fill", to teach the site engineer's goal of seeking to get cut equal to fill; to make the amount of excavation on a site be equivalent to the amount of soil that must be imported to complete the grading. Dwelling inhabits a landscape of consciousness, where the terms *terrestrial*, *terrain*, and *territory* intersect. The essentials theories of Chinese landscape painting are based upon the ideas of Tao, tradition of ruralism at Chinese culture's highest intellectual levels. TAO the character depicts a hairy head on moving feet, meaning "walking on the way", and ultimately "path". TAO suggests that no man (or any other creature) is an island in nature. The great masters of Chinese landscape painting like Fan Kuan, Ni Tsan, Kuo Hsi, or Hsia Kuei found relationships between natural land forms and forms of human thought. For them the landscape was perhaps more the actor and main character than any human figure. Breughel's hunters dominate the foreground of the scene. When we compare it to Tai Chin's landscape at the left, we may see by proportion another sense of man's importance in the world. The lodge at the mountain pass is radiating correct response to the all-encompassing *ch'i*, the pervading spirit and breath of the landscape that must be allowed to breathe free, to flow through everything without hindrance or opposition. How far the common landscape of middle ground suburbia, with its power lines, commercial strips, muzacked malls, and airport highway interchanges, is from such a comprehensive healing vision of the world!

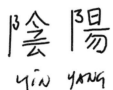

Yin and Yang
the shady and sunny sides of a hill
no ambiguity--no debate

RETURNING LATE FROM A SPRING OUTING. ATTRIBUTED TO TAI CHIN C. 15TH CENTURY.

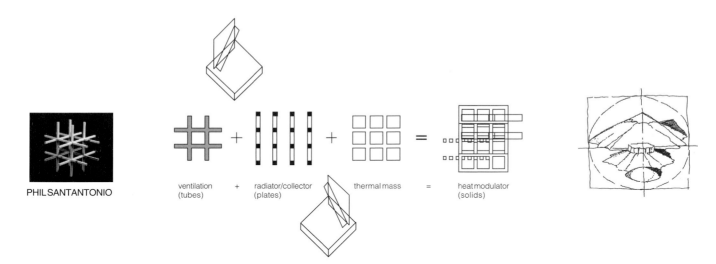

PHIL SANTANTONIO

ventilation + radiator/collector + thermal mass = heat modulator
(tubes) (plates) (solids)

CATCHING THE HEAT

Heat Modulator

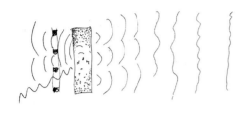

Conduction is the transfer of heat from one body to another by direct contact. **Convection** transfers heat through circulating fluids; warm fluids are lighter than cool ones, and thus rise. Bodies emit heat energy as electromagnetic **radiation**; blue light is hotter and more energetic than red light. By adjusting the rates of these three means of heat transfer, the skin of a volume can control and modify the energy in a volume, cooling it or trapping heat inside. The total volume becomes a wave diffractor of heat energy. If only conduction is at work, the center of mass will usually have a different temperature than the edges. However, perforation of the thermal mass with convection plumbing can accelerate the distribution of heat throughout. Our 98.6° Fahrenheit temperature is maintained by blood circulation-- the human body is a water-cooled engine! Heat is moved rapidly by the tartan matrix of blood vessel pipes ventilating the body mass connecting to the heat exchanges of lungs and skin. The large ears of an elephant, the spinal plates of a stegosaurus provide large surface area for moving air to cool a lot of blood quickly. They are like solar collectors in reverse. A network of ventilation (tubes) joining radiator/collector (plates) through a thermal mass (solid) constitutes a **heat modulator**. Whole volumes can form the filter surfaces to a larger volume. In the Phoenix Study, (page 257) the three visitor galleries could act as shadowing sun-breakers (*brise-soleils* in French) to the entire 30' site volume. Similarly, by carefully cladding the large music chamber with insulating opaque walls to the north and glazing to the south, you could make it the major heat collector for the whole building. Such strategies are often effective in plan as well as section.

Greenhouse and Atrium

TAO suggests that no man or place is an island in nature. Akin to the spirit of the great Chinese landscape masters, William Morrish' elegant book *Civilizing Terrains* seeks relationships between natural land forms and forms of human thought. C.C. Wang's *Mountains of the Mind* is also sugges-tive in this regard. The greenhouse effect is a phenomenon, like fire or gunpowder, that can be a tool for good rather than a threat. Very energetic sunlight bombards the earth in the ultraviolet (UV) range. Much of it is filtered by the ozone in the upper atmosphere, but enough reaches the ground to agitate surface molecules-- to warm them. The heated rocks and plants radiate back their newly gained energy, but less violently than the sun, as long infrared waves. These are more easily absorbed or blocked by matter than the UV waves, so the sunlight that passes through the glass walls of a greenhouse heats brick floors and is trapped inside as heat. Romans understood this and aimed the rare glass used in their public baths toward the south to heat their *caldaria*. The Chinese sages were wise in their simplicity, expressing the basic *Yin-Yang* duality they discovered in the cosmos in direct and common terms: literally, *yin* is the shady side and *yang* is the sunny side of a hill. There is no ambiguity in this geographical perception. Paolo Soleri's arcologies and the traditional Indian *haveli* show volume strategies for taking advantage of solar gain, both in heating and in cooling (a chimney or atrium effect in shadowed courtyards promotes convection for cooling) and provide lessons that may apply to suburban settlements and other dwelling patterns. Why not make a city as a means to minimize energy consumption? Sunlight is always raining down, and uranic warmth is always welling up from within the earth. *There is no energy crisis! Rational* use of available resources will guarantee abundance! Architecture and city planning can shape light and shade to catch the heat and promote the cool. It is just a question of organizing the abundance of energy in the best way! Shadowed roof plans and shadowed cut-through sections become studies in economy. As biologist Lynn Margulis says in *The Creativity of Symbiosis*, "Natural selection is the editor, not the author."

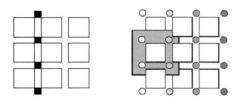

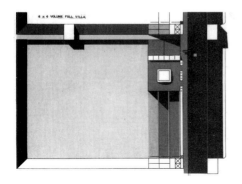

6 x 6 VOLUME FULL VILLA

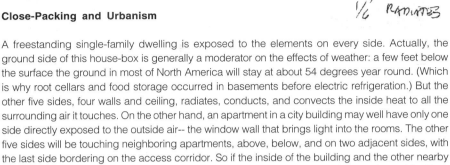

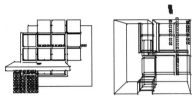

"...every cubic inch was golden." Le Corbusier

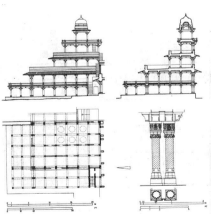

HOLDING THE HEAT

Close-Packing and Urbanism

A freestanding single-family dwelling is exposed to the elements on every side. Actually, the ground side of this house-box is generally a moderator on the effects of weather: a few feet below the surface the ground in most of North America will stay at about 54 degrees year round. (Which is why root cellars and food storage occurred in basements before electric refrigeration.) But the other five sides, four walls and ceiling, radiates, conducts, and convects the inside heat to all the surrounding air it touches. On the other hand, an apartment in a city building may well have only one side directly exposed to the outside air-- the window wall that brings light into the rooms. The other five sides will be touching neighboring apartments, above, below, and on two adjacent sides, with the last side bordering on the access corridor. So if the inside of the building and the other nearby apartments are heated, they will act as both heater and insulation to the first apartment. The Taos Pueblo has been a collective urban dwelling for hundreds of years, and remains in continuous inhabitation today. There is a distinct energy advantage to close-packing. This is why relative to its weight, an elephant needs less food and eats less often than a mouse. Both must maintain a warm-blood internal temperature, but the mouse has proportionally far more surface area than volume. A simple act of imagination demonstrates this fact: imagine an elephant filled with mice and you will see how much more skin of mouse there is inside than the single outside wrapper of elephant hide.

Resonance into Radiance

When homes or bubbles are isolated, separate, far apart from each other, they an each afford to attain their full spacial destiny, unencumbered by boundary demands from any neighbors. But as any backyard gardener knows, good neighbors ultimately need good fences. When bubbles get close to each other, they eventually begin to share borders. When this happens, new geometries engender new biophysical demands. The play between circle and square is once again revealed, once again reinterpreted. Gerster's aerial view on the previous page of an African kraal shows the loose fit between the circular rooms curved paths and fences, and occasional orthogonal grana-ries. But the air view opposite of another, more densely settled kraal village shows how orthogonal-ity begins to emerge even from groups of essentially circular plan elements. As bubbles share borders, their boundary surfaces resonate the plan grouping into orthogonal foam.

Brunelleschi's San Lorenzo Church in Florence, opposite, like the subtle and beautifully resolved paintings of Giorgio Morandi on this page, keeps aligning volumes until the whole field becomes a unified space. We find again such integrated spacial fabrics in the structures of Fatepuhr Sikri (1569-1580), Akbar the Great's administrative capital of Mughal India. We have encountered such plastic resonance earlier in this book, in the Cubist and Purist paintings of Gris and Le Corbusier, and in Schindler's Lovell House and Meier's Giovanitti House. This sense of nothing wasted when it comes to an economy of means for all necessary masses and volumes is perhaps the greatest measure of the real modesty which is an essential value of competent architecture. It looks so easy, but it is so hard to resolve the spacial fabric for everything to have its place with nothing out of place! Every measured thing is balanced in resonant relationship to every other measurable element, revealing new sets of propositions, balance, harmonies. Everything is measured, every opportunity seized. No mass seems out of control, no volume is a fragment, left over, or lost. "Static noise" recedes. Brunelleschi's space of the "holy spirit" seems to glow, recalling the essential discovery of Thomas Edison, that the glow of a resistance coil could be magnified in brightness and duration when placed in a vacuum-- sustaining the spark into the steady glow we now take for granted as "electric light".

THINKING

Creating in the mind a single vivid image of four-dimensional spacetime is beyond the picture-making power of anybody I know. But is it really any easier to capture from one view all the richness of a modern metropolis?
John A. Wheeler

Critical Mass

An early film on atomic energy showed an empty room with two pingpong balls sitting on a mousetrap in the middle. Another pingpong ball was tossed into the room and the viewer watched as its bouncing dampened and then became a roll across the floor. Eventually all motion stopped. The same room was shown again. This time its floor was covered with pingpong ball and mouse-trap sets. Another ball was tossed into the room, bounced once, and then landed on a mousetrap. It triggered the release of the two balls sitting there. They each landed on another trap, releasing four more balls into the air. Within seconds, the volume was a fizzing whir of snapping traps and flying balls. This demonstration illustrated in vivid terms the concept of critical mass for atomic power. A few atoms of fissionable material kept apart will stay stable, but bring a lot of them together and you will get a nuclear explosion! The sun burns not by fission, but by fusion, and its billion years old thermonuclear fire demands that all mass seek to get as dense as possible. So long as the focus maintains a critical mass of heat and pressure, solar fusion of hydrogen into helium persists.

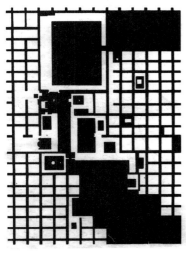

Incandescence

The same is true of human culture. When human interaction attains a critical mass of interaction, it glows with incandescence and becomes... a city! (Subways run because, on average, some stations have some passengers.) When our ancestors huddled together in caves or grasslands around campfires for warmth and safety, they also concentrated their perceptions and cultivated thought. Just as an apartment insulated on five sides reduces the cost of heating space, so too do the groves of academe shelter students from the labors of survival long enough to enable them to speculate on improvement, and advance our general welfare on every human front. The stoa is an urban *brise-soleil*. Perhaps the figure-grounds of the ancient Hellenistic city of Miletus (c. 150 BCE) may serve as source and inspiration for plans and sections for Soleri's ArcCube, a solar heated incandescent arcology city for 3 million souls. The artist Deborah Huff (1954-1995) suggested that the interplay of energy and matter created a third condition of radiating organism-- the city.

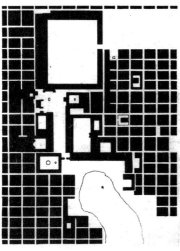

Black bodies radiate when heated. Glowing coals at a fire's center are incandescent, shining solids bathed in a field of interacting radiant heat. The biggest rocks store the most heat and fattest logs take the longest to burn. Pull apart the glowing embers and a fire will go out. *City* is the critical mass of culture, the place of maximum anonymity, variation, and individuation. (How many different kinds of northern afghani kosher all-night take out restaurants can one find on the *West Side* of New York?) A city is a lens for mental focussing of every vision. Coming to the middle, everyone seeks the center. This generates critical mass, interaction, and radiating waves of culture. City is the home of the good-neighbor policy. Out-of-towners are surprised when citizens are often friendly but for collective urban survival, everyone must try to get along. City is the means for a region to act in resonance, to attain a consonance of parts and intervals. Jane Jacobs' important book *Economy of Cities* suggests a new interpretation of the theory of region and city-state, arguing that the success of the hinterland depends as much on its focal city as much as the city depends on it. While one grows food, the other provides both market and consumers. When one preserves tradition, the other invents (which is which?) Together the city and its region become the realm of inevitable complexity. "We are gods, we might as well get on with it." wrote the *Whole Earth Catalog*. The city is an organism, a collective of both individual and community dwelling cells, capable of creating a landscape of consciousness. Le Corbusier said " light is the key". No wonder he called his urban vision *Radiant*City!

ROOM ENOUGH FOR EVERYONE!

And what of the unity of the result? *Citizen, civic, civil, civilization, polite, policy politics* all carry significant connections. *Polis* is a community of people. Just as a community of cells becomes tissue into organism. Early attempts to confront the modern problems of human habitation made urban places that looked like stars. They radiated in the geometric sense, if not in the geometrodynamic sense. How to combine unities of integrity, i.e. houses for individuals (or groups) into a community, without compromising the integrity of either individual or collective is the solvable but "indissoluble binomial." Is it a collage of wholes becoming parts, or a pre-planned organism requiring specialized participants? From Plato's *Republic* and Thomas More's *Utopia*, whose frontispiece of 1516 is shown opposite, to the latest techno-dream, the paradigms have been many. All are incomplete. The city-home phenomenon is a unique relationship that can inform our thinking about evolution, art, and information as much as the other way around. In this sense, architecture remains a branch of practical philosophy. A useful political distinction might be made between those who hold that human beings, and life, is intrinsically valuable and adds wealth to the cosmos, and those who hold that life, both collective and individual is a negative drain on the limited resources of an already overcrowded world.

Since trees produce more acorns, pinecones, and apples than are strictly needed for survival of the species, it appears that creation is essentially fruitful and bountiful. Increasing complexity seems to be the dividend of diversity, and provides the incredible richness and variety of the abundance of nature and the cosmos. The most complex space we know of is the human brain. It is likely that each and every unique human mind has something valuable to offer us all. Any institution which magnifies interchange between minds is especially vital to the ongoing inevitably growing wealth of existence. We need only take advantage of the opportunities offered in such institutions by attending to their overall planning as well as all small significant details to insure an integrated working organism. The most important institution of human invention for the purpose of valorizing and optimizing the interactions between all forms of Mind is the City.

It is time to return to the call of the "heroic" period of architecture that opened this century-- when the collective opportunities of new materials, new social visions, new philosophical insights, new ways of seeing, new understandings of the cosmos inspired many generations to articulate in clear terms the problems and opportunities that faced everyone, and that called architects to their best capacities. It is time for us to reject the condescension that has plagued the public's perception of architecture in these last decades of this century. Is architecture just decorated shelter for the rich? What a perversion of the nobility of this profession. There are real problems of human habitation, both at the scale of the individual or family and at the larger scale of groups-- cities, regions, even planets-- that demand the spacial configuration skills which lead to true working plans of position *and* action. Le Corbusier concludes *Towards a New Architecture* with the question *architecture or revolution?* The pressing problems of our time: global poverty, overcrowding, traffic, pollution, and depletion of ozone, rain forest, natural resources wilderness, solitude, privacy, silence-- all demand and can be solved by *architectural* solutions, and these problems can be solved through the opportunities of *our* time: new materials, new technologies, new means of communications, not just of data but of true human value messages, exchanges of ideas and intentions, new vistas and powers to manipulate nature at the edges of the very large or small, the very hot or cold. We now perhaps begin to see "peace breaking out all over". Production has been solved. Now remains the problem of fair sharing and distribution of humanity's ever-increasing wealth. When the opportunities of our times are balanced by the eternal wisdom of enduring human values that foster individual and collective growth and by technical solutions that cultivate, not diminish, cultural diversity, then perhaps we shall evolve into a species that truly merits the term civilization.

MEXICO CITY PLAN, 1556

This plan shows the Aztec City Tenochtitlán soon after its conquest by Spanish conquistadores. The city is an artificial island permeated with canals in the middle of a lake surrounded by mountains. Cortez entered the city in 1519, only 3 years after the publication of Thomas More's Utopia.

TENOCHTITLÁN

> *"We were amazed, and we said that it was like the enchanted things related in the book of Amadis because of the huge towers, temples, and buildings arising from the lake, and all of masonry. Some of the soldiers even asked whether the things we saw were not a dream. You must not wonder that I write of these things in this way, for it beggared all description, since we were seeing things which had never been heard or seen before, not even dreamed about."*
>
> *Bernal Diaz del Castillo, conquistador*

"Hernan Cortez, writing to Emperor Charles V, called it "the most beautiful city in the world", and so it was. There was a radiance about it, a shining splendor. It shone fiercely in the light of majestic blue skies, snow white mountains, a calm blue lake. There was about this city, built on an island in the lake, an astonishing air of unreality, because it was too perfect, too beautiful, too richly decorated. Not Venice, nor Paris, nor Isfahan, nor any of the rose-red cities of India had such sumptuous elegance and soaring grace. As the early morning mist rose over the lake, the city seemed to shimmer and flash with all the colors of the rainbow. The green forests came down to the lakeside, the canoes were rushing about like so many brilliantly colored water beetles, the smoke rose from the temples, and there was that subdued quivering sound which comes when thousands upon thousands of people are going about their business..."

THE LOOM OF TIME

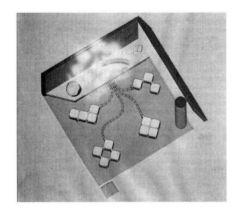

Everything wants to connect with everything else, without losing its own continuous line of connectivity. Our everyday experience of this: standing at the corner watching and waiting for the light to change, so that you can walk across while the ton of steel and rubber that is the car coming toward your crosswalk must now be the one who stops. Buckminster Fuller once observed that America is a place where at any given moment you have 20 million horses straining to move while idling at intersections. What a waste! Isn't there a better way? Of course: the third dimension! Weaving over and under allows complete separation of vehicles and pedestrians, just as the three dimensional networks in our bodies intertwine blood vessels with nerves without intersecting them, just as our houses have networks of pipes and wire that never need to cut through or into each other.

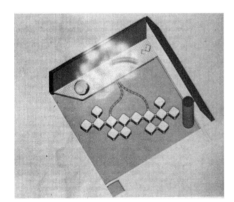

Amsterdam and Venice each solved the apparent contradiction of two-dimensional conflicts, accommodating two incompatible networks of circulation, slow (by foot) and fast (vehicular.) They both did it with intertwining networks of streets and canals, which heightens the tension and contrast between water and land in the most elegant ways, and provide a true measure of civilized life, that is life in a city without compromise of essential human values of peace and quiet, light, and air. Both cities remain lessons to us all. I personally can attest to meeting someone in Venice, agreeing we should go to another place in the city we both knew, and getting so involved in conversation and thinking that an hour later we found ourselves back where we started... not because we couldn't find our way, but because we could lose ourselves in the vivid exchange of human concerns without once having to break a train of thought to accommodate a rude interruption by traffic, fumes, noise, or all the myriad calls to our attention and reminders to survival that usually confront the urban driver or pedestrian. Intrusive signals of *Stop! Walk! Don't Walk! No U Turns!* were just not needed.

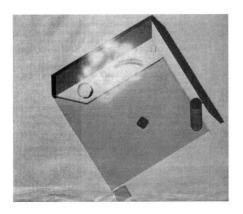

There was also such a place in the New World. It was the great capital of the Aztecs, Moctezuma's Tenochtitlan. The floating gardens of Xochimilco in the midst of the lake that was the home to these people provided food that could be cultivated and marketed by boat directly at the center of the city. Since the Aztecs made this lake their home, they naturally must have had superiority in "sea power", so that they could protect their food supply and urban life in such a way to make them virtually undefeatable by attack or siege. Sadly, this site is now engulfed by the dry, choking, and crowded metropolis of Mexico City. Emilio Ambasz' scheme for a computer research facility in Xochimilco recalls the elegance of the original urban system that preceded the European arrival in the Western Hemisphere. Ambasz suggests that the facility could eventually be replaced by home electronic offices, so that each of these floating/anchorable office/labs could become "ultimately a flower barge." How much change should we design our cities to accommodate? How much should our rooms and buildings be dynamic, floating on waves, or how long should they be static (with their ballast blown?) The issues of change, interval, phasing, and deployment raise questions of the human relationship to the warp and woof of space in time.

There is a sad irony in the history of the quest for Utopia. Europeans encountered a paradise lost and found. Cortez entered Tenochtitlán in 1519. By 1521 the Aztec civilization was destroyed. The 1556 map depicts a figure-ground reversal of More's *Utopia* frontispiece of 1516 (see page 394). In a sense it was historically also a figure-ground reversal. Cortez found a wonderful urban system, that sustained food production, ceremony, commerce, and defense. He initiated a process that paved over its lake (a symbol of joy in China), and began the settlement that filled the bowl between the mountains with modern Mexico City and the worst air pollution in the world. Paradise was found and lost before the seekers knew it.

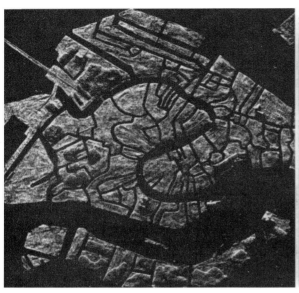

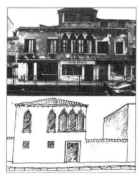

16. Lista di Spagna:
casa rinascimentale
con corte
17. Campo N. Sauro
casa a corte laterale

18. Presso S. Stae:
corte intasata da casa
a schiera di
«tabernizzazione»
19. Campo N. Sauro
casa a corte laterale
con addizione di casa
di «tabernizzazione»

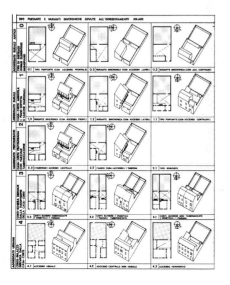

ANIMATING

"I think that a plan is a society of rooms. A real plan is one in which rooms have spoken to each other. When you see a plan, you can say that it is the structure of spaces in their light." Lou Kahn

Tempo and Duration

Van Den Berg distinguishes between these two modes of experiencing time in his phenomenological study called *Things*. Tempo for him is about the conscious rhythm of the passing of time, like a beat, meter, or parade march, whereas duration is about the longevity of the persistence of existence that also is a property of things. Cities must balance tempo and duration in their continued development, reification, and realization. How much can we tear down and yet preserve the character of a place? How long can we tolerate outdated facilities when we must make sure our settlements work? What is needed in such cases is not simply a plan in the physical sense of a plat, but further a plan in the sense of a strategy or directive for action. Ideally, such a plan should take into account the beauty, ease, and facility of elements at every scale from smallest to largest. Every urban dweller expects both a "nice apartment" and trains that run on time. Place and circulation the very set of needs of every living organism -- both the cells and the organs an the whole creature (and the species) should be designed in such a manner as to thrive.

The city of Venice, according to Paolo Maretto's book, *La Casa Venezia nella Storia della Citta*, reveals a system of order which permits growth and change without destroying its overall fabric, which in fact included this possibility from the beginning. Manhattan, Philadelphia, Charleston, Savannah, all were developed on patterns of grid and house-type infil that generated and supported the unique character of each of these cities. In Venice, the basic house-type of the Roman Atrium plus garden was generalized to a double square in plan. The garden was kept more or less empty, as was the center of the atrium square, which allowed first one and then subsequent rooms to be added to the homestead in an orderly but nonuniform fashion in such a way to provide a good mix of sunlight and shade, privacy and community, and collective and individual identity. Hence, as David Diamond has noted, the Venetians could tolerate asymmetry in their public facades because both their cities and homes were always becoming and because the boundaries of their places were firm enough to control the whole composition without artificially generated symmetries. (We only have one heart, and it is not in the center of the chest). The drawings on the opposite page show the "before" of the "after" photographs paired with them. Note how different orientations to the sun generated different lot proportions and infil patterns. The bonus in urban terms to such a strategy is to be found in the remarkable surprises and wonderful spaces of the "leftover" zones, the streets, alleys, piazzas, bridges and canals that serve these settlement cells and neighborhood tissues, and provide the nutrients and remove the wastes from this whole urban organism.

Venice shows how to close-pack individual cells and keep them healthy in long and short-term time. Despite apparent lack of order, Venice is an example of a method-- infil a plot toward the ancient Roman atrium prototype, keeping programmatic and plastic flexibility for the cell as it evolves through time while maintaining the unit module as an element of the larger urban organism. The module can be modified for both internal and external planning, according to the major axis orientation east-west or north-south, and to take advantage of the local opportunities of water and canal edge. The neutral mediating walls between the cells insure the plan to be both individual and collective urban strategy that permits independence within each cell and growth without destroying the total fabric. This "ugly" city is beautiful, full of life at every scale. After all Piazza San Marco is the whole city's central atrium -- or should we say that each home has its own local family piazza?

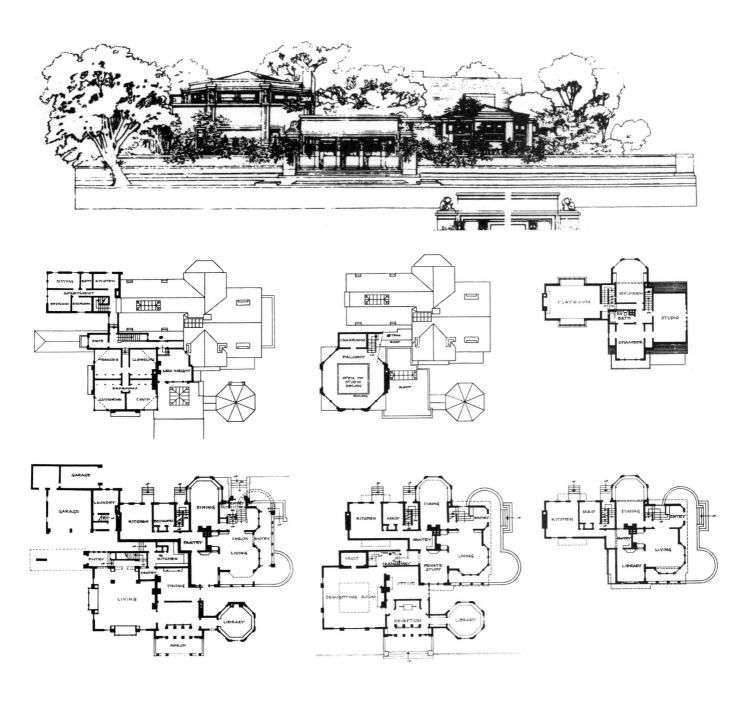

1911   FIRST AND SECOND FLOOR PLAN   1898   FIRST AND SECOND FLOOR PLAN   1895   FIRST AND SECOND FLOOR PLAN

WRIGHT, FRANK LLOYD.
428 FOREST AVENUE, OAK PARK, ILLINOIS. 1889.
PHOTOGRAPH COURTESY, THE MUSEUM OF MODERN ART, NEW YORK.

PHASING

"A building is not something you finish. A building is something you start." Stewart Brand

Pressure on volume pushes for expansion. As the cells of a zygote grow into embryo and fetus, the womb swells to make room. The domestic space adequate for a couple experiences pressure when a child is born. One response to pressure is growth. Frank Lloyd Wright, never one to hide his light under a bushel basket or to shrink from opportunity, took the matter of volumetric growth and mastery of the space of personal domain into his own hands. In 1889, a 22-year-old Wright started his own practice and bought a house in the new suburb of Oak Park, near Chicago. Six years later, in 1895, the year of his pioneering design of the Winslow House, he added a playroom, moved the kitchen, and expanded bedrooms and dining room to accommodate his growing family. He continued to add to his home over the next sixteen years, incorporating his staff and studio while he completed turning the corner of the site. For Wright clearly rooms are the true bricks for building a house. In the course of two decades, his suburban site revealed its potential as its early concentrated shelter evolved into the complex and extended field of a small city.

What is most interesting is how the early developments in plan seem to cleverly anticipate later moves even when they appear at first as surprising and unexpected exploitations of existing conditions. Where the unimaginative planner might see the northwest exterior stairway in the 1889 plan as an obstacle to further growth, Wright takes advantage of it as a secondary service circulation and adds a kitchen/playroom wing beyond it to the northwest. The original kitchen becomes dining, extended in the 1895 renovation, while the original dining area evolves into a library and then private study. By 1898, an entire office wing is added to the southwest, and the library is given its own octagon. Entry to the business wing is off a different street, turning the corner and now entirely separate to the domestic space. Yet the whole remains well integrated, even to the point where Wright's children could (and did!) leave the playroom to harass the draftsmen below from the second story balcony. These evolving plans show a poignant struggle in the architect between the deep herd instincts for species survival through family growth and the equally deep drive for accommodating the isolation of the lonely struggle of the single creative individual whose limitless capacity to imagine, invent, and understand is bounded only by the constraints of animal mortality. Wright's concern for this lifetime plans for a house was later developed in his Usonia owner-built system of cast block and rebar fabric, and in the plans of his Prairie Style and later Usonian houses. Above all, the ongoing love so many of his clients and their children still have for their homes is a powerful testament to his interest in designing durable and evolving homes for generations.

In an age of speed and change like ours, we often overlook the fact that every move is a disruption. Imagine just packing and moving from your house... and then moving right back into it! Packing, unpacking, setting up furniture, hanging pictures, reloading drawers, etc. would wreak havoc on everyday routine and cause traumas of indecision. The value of re-solving things once and for all, of getting settled, of settle-ment, is too often overlooked in planning (and in politics!) The unfolding of volumes in Wright's Oak Park home is a miracle of packaging in reverse. We might well ask what was the spacetime shape of the first zygote-cell in Wright's home/studio plan evolution? Structured energy is information, meaning in the human-cosmic discourse. Through the world-lines of our lives we paint our own portrait, not just as a nice contour line, pretty picture surface, or solid sculptural pose, but as a dance of ethics and morality through action in four dimensional spacetime. From the perspective of change, what Wright did in Oak Park was to allow the field (the whole site) to move through time but not space, to age, to mature, "to arrive". Wright might agree with Thoreau, who said that he had "traveled much in Concord."

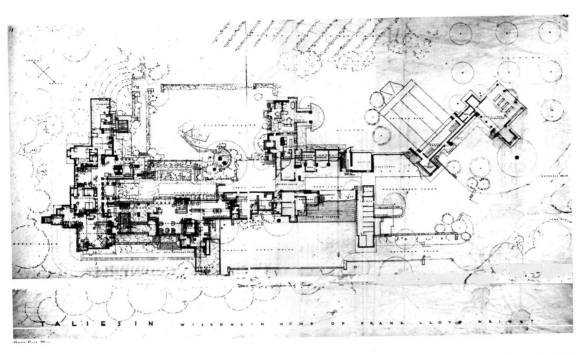

TALIESIN   WISCONSIN HOME OF FRANK LLOYD WRIGHT

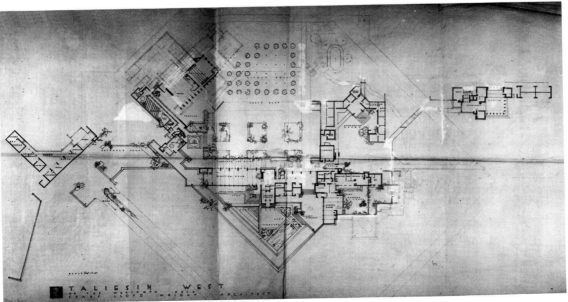

TALIESIN   WEST
FRANK LLOYD WRIGHT   ARCHITECT

DEPLOYMENT

Frank Lloyd Wright was an American original, a major personality figure in the culture of his time. His reputation as a wizard was confirmed in the Tokyo earthquake of 1922 when his Imperial Hotel was one of the few major civic building to survive. His claim of designing it to survive such disasters by floating it on a pad of piles in the spongy subsoil, and by using the reflecting pools as fire protection were born out by the remarkable results. But celebrity is fickle, and many people in America claimed he got his "just desserts" when Taliesin, his country home and workers' colony in Spring Green Wisconsin, was burned down by a deranged servant who axed many people to death. Among the murdered was Wright's lover, a woman who had traveled with him to Japan, which scandalized "society", since at the time both were married and had children. But who can account for the workings of the human heart? And who can say what is another person's justice?

Wright's vision was romantic, and Romantic, following Utopian Americans from the Pilgrims through Thomas Jefferson, westward settlers and their offspring who made intentional communities, Robert Owen at New Harmony Indiana, Amana, Shakers, Amish, Joseph Smith in Salt Lake City. It still goes on today. Wright formed a community of architects, who also managed their own self-sufficient farm, who designed works for outside clients (Wright built over 500 houses, all across the country!) and traveled to the job sites to oversee construction. As he got older, he found a way to avoid the winter cold by moving his whole operation to another "wilderness" on the undeveloped acres outside Phoenix Arizona that became Taliesin West. Wright first moved there in 1938 in the midst of a Depression, after worldwide fame, and then fifteen years of hardly any work, from the age of 50 to almost 69. Most practitioners in architecture, most professionals and professors had dismissed him, saying his career was finished and he could offer nothing new. And then he designed, in 1936 Falling Water, and other astonishing works, like the Marin County Civic Center, and the Guggenheim Museum (construction began when he was 92!).

Annual migration

Migration is an ancient human art, well developed in the New World since at least the Bering Land Bridge 100,000 years ago. Riding the wind has been the strategy of the dandelion floater, the milkweed, all flying seeds. The arctic tern is a bird who performs an annual global migration, flying from Arctic to Antarctic and back each mating season. The Northwest Haida Indians lived in the sheltered Douglas Fir forests of the Cascade slopes in the winter building lodges with five-foot wide planks of these 400' tall noble trees, and camped at the banks of the Columbia for the spring salmon spawning, and lashed the planks together to make rafts to float downriver to the Pacific coast for their summer homes, where once again the planks became the basic elements of their seashore lodges. Homes for each season, like the privileged classes today, yet with few material goods or mortgages. How simple, how elegant! Wright embraced the Jeffersonain vision of democracy, both in his designs for Broadacre City, and in his own migration habits. Even the serial expansion of his Oak Park home couldn't contain his dreams. Perhaps it was his recollection of growing up on the land, or the understanding that almost all Americans are immigrants and nomads, but pursuing his dream of living "*of* the land, not on the land" drove Wright to "up the ante" in the struggle between collective participation and splendid isolation, and to construct Taliesin West. Ironically, the one architect who was able to join him in Arizona without surrendering his own radical individuality had to leave Taliesin West after only 6 months of his apprenticeship. He moved even further into the desert to build his own dome-home. This man was Paolo Soleri, and his plans evolved into Arcosanti and the brilliant arcologies he continues to design and build. And so the thread of rugged individuals continues. It is a difficult path, not for the many, certainly not for those who only seek to follow.

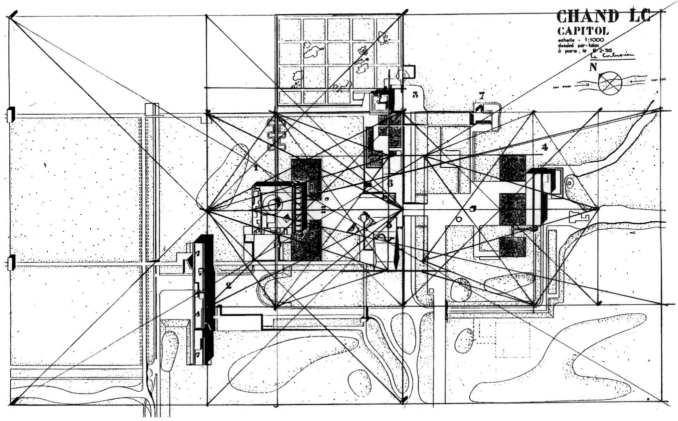

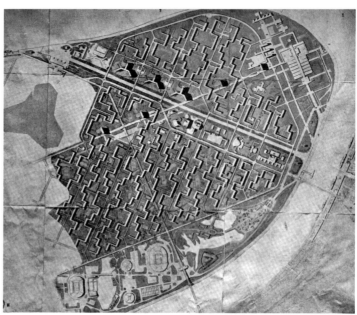

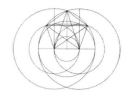

PLAN WEAVING IN TIME AND SPACE

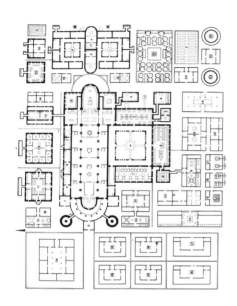

Giambattista Nolli's 1748 Plan of Rome shows public and private realms, and the space in between, through graphic means of black (unavailable to the public), gray (accessible to the general public-- gridded columnar spaces of churches and other sacred or official building interior), and white (public street or piazza). The resulting integument is a rich variety of inside and outside spaces, of large and small places, and of long and short paths opening onto wide spaces or confronting opaque walls. Such a plan was serviceable for the millennia before mechanical high-speed vehicular traffic. But now, as Joseph Ryckwert has noted in *The Idea of A Town* there is a significant difference between the space of a street and that of a road. One is a place for public appearance and political interchange, the other is primarily a thoroughfare, a means to get to some other place quickly. But how are people to accommodate cars capable of moving at 60 plus MPH with people and other animals that move no faster than 4 or 5 miles an hour at a walking gait? The obvious solution continues to elude the vast number of so-called "planners" whose training is often in policy and law rather than architectonics and dynamics. These planners see maps of cities or other geographical regions and think they tell the whole story. In fact, what such maps mask to those without eyes, to the unimaginative, is that gravity distorts a three-dimensional spacial reality at the boundary surface of a planetary sphere. It appears to these blinded professionals that north-south and east-west are the only directions available to solve conflicts of proximity and connection.

But the genius of urban design has identified a means to completely circumvent this apparent conflict-- and this insight has arisen more than once since the Renaissance. Both Leonardo Da Vinci and Le Corbusier have identified the solution-- design cities as layers capable of interweaving as well as intersecting. The magnificent fabric of Le Corbusier's 1930's plan for the city of Anvers (Antwerp) solves many urban concerns simultaneously, taking advantage of the lesson of Venice as an organism. As in Tenochtitlan and Amsterdam, in Venice pedestrians are clearly separated from vehicles. (In Holland, the master who set the water level of the canals thus composed the form of the community.) In Anvers, Le Corbusier went even farther, and proposed a complete separation of high speed automobiles and pedestrians, thus returning the natural grade of the landscape to direct, safe, and unbounded human use for walking, so that people in their daily lives can truly touch the earth. At Anvers, networks of subways, private car roads, highways, bus routes, pedestrian paths, and housing *redans* patterns are so distributed as to enable every citizen to be no more than 400 yards or meters from any means of public transport, which means no one need walk more than 800 yards total to get to anywhere else in the whole city!

The plan for the Capitol area of Chandigarh shows in detail how cars and people may coexist in harmony. Unlike New York and other modern cities, the emphasis here is on public space for gathering, what Hannah Ahrendt has called "the space of human appearance" and the essential arena for a true polis, a group of humans who meet to form policy-- what politics can and ought to be. How different is such meeting space, recalling the town square and village green that is the birthplace of American democracy, from the current rush hour commute of individuals trapped in isolated cars who consume nightly news but feel far from their own history of making news. The City and its hinterland is the instrument which is self-replicating in human space. The city as a self perpetuating construct suggests a means to consider the idea of reproductive architecture. Le Corbusier's **Radiant City** is an idea based on a building system of volumes, of totally integrated grid rather than simply additive lots and or parcels. At least in local terms, a well-designed, well-working city is the human artifact most evidently anti-chaotic and anti-entropic phenomenon in our universe.

CUBES	1	2	4	8
JOINTS	8	12	18	27
EDGES	12	20	32	52
(OUT)SIDES	6	10	16	24
JOINJTS/CUBES	8/1	6	4.5	3.375
EDGE/CUBE	12/1	10	8	6.5
(OUT)SIDE/CUBE	6/1	5	4	3

HOME ECONOMICS
CITY IN A SUITCASE

E PLURIBUS UNUM: FROM MANY, ONE.
IS CHEAPER THAN SPACE INA SUITCASE.

HIROYUKI TORII

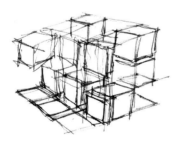 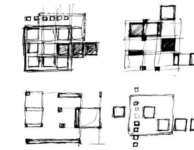

BEYOND 2 X 2, INTERNAL ACCESS
REQUIRES A TARTAN GRID PERFORATION.

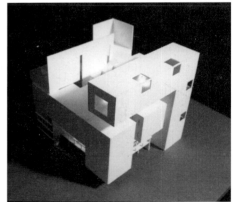
KUNCHUL CHANG

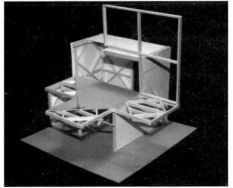
SCOTT SEPELA

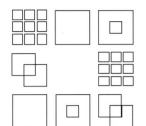

ORDER AND VARIETY
THE INDIVIDUAL AND THE COLLECTIVE

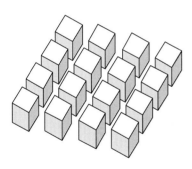

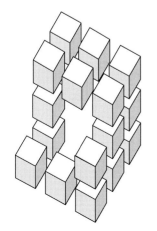

E PLURIBUS UNUM-- FROM MANY, ONE

DOING: re-solution

CITY IN A SUITCASE

Design a temporary community in which to place your full-scale spacetime station. Work with other members of the studio group to coordinate and locate all individual cells in a "climbing sculpture" configuration which creates a well-defined internal urban public space. At this new urban scale, each gallery precinct is a brick. Just as individual linear and planar elements in the Bag of Tricks combine to form volumetric ensembles, so too can individual dwelling cells combine to form a plan for collective settlement, like houses around a village green, apartments around a hotel atrium, or buildings around Piazza San Marco in Venice.

Home Economomics

An array of many free standing separate volumes uses more materials for structure, siding, and joints than the same number of volumes combined into an integrated three-dimensional complex. (See chart to the left). Collectively you can make more space with less cost if you combine your gallery precinct with others into a unified ensemble. This takes work and care, but is the true source of an architectural economy of means. Seven double cube volumes can define a full 3 x 3 x 3 (27 cube) volume if you carefully arrange the programmed solids to define the non-programmed voids, as you learned in the Volume study (*Architectonics*, p. 63.) As in Concerto, you may create a 3D tartan fabric in which the intervals between program volumes can be structure and/or circulation.

The Means: Spirit in Materials

To plan a city, *develop site plans and site sections!* Be sure that models and drawings of all cells are at the same scale, and then join together to take advantage of the unique formal properties of each gallery precinct. Some may help turn corners or function as entry gateways, others may be linear connectors. Some vertical ones can be double-height (without floors). Groups of three or more may form urban *tokonomas*. Consider site access and context construction methods, and solar orientation. Greenhouse and atrium effects can modulate the atmosphere(s) of the whole site. For construction of your gallery and precinct, your materials are the Big Bag of Tricks (see page 355). For building a city, the best things in life are free. Le Corbusier wrote "the elements of architecture are sun, space, green, steel, glass, and concrete, in that order." The materials of a city are :

site: grade: flat/sloped; contour: warp/wave; landscape: mountain/river
orientation: light = north/south; time = east/west (dawn/dusk); gravity = up/down
weather: sun, wind, rain, cloud, temperature, sky, earth, moon, stars

Document your work through full architectural means, including site plan, section, axonometric and perspective projections, videotape, photography. You have made the birth of a city!

ANIMATION: In a sequence of at least three frames, show access to your gallery, from outside the community, then within the shared central public space, and finally entering your own gallery precinct. Choose your views to reveal any intentional *promenade architecturale*.
COLOR: 3. Space: Color Field. Collage 4a. Critical Faculty. **Collage 4b.** Compelling Fragment
FUNCTION: Construct or plot a lemniscate or an analemma. (See page 453.) Advanced: construct or plot an N-leafed rose to make a rose window. Computer options: plot a fractal solar flare and/or generate a self-replicating "Game of Life" configuration. (See *The Recursive Universe*, page 426.)

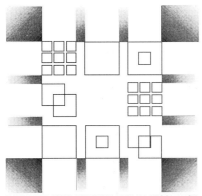

RADIATING: PROPAGATING INTERNAL RESONANCE
BEYOND BOUNDARY MEMBRANE INTO THE FIELD

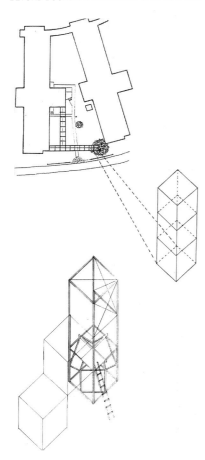

MAKING COMMUNITY

If successful, your community will become an oasis of pressurized time in space. (Of course it is also a unique space in time.) It will transform the energy of inert matter into a spirit manifest in carefully organized materials. To build energy(!) consider how your individual scheme might best help to order the collective "city plan", which itself becomes a **precinct** requiring some enclosure. As an element of this city, your own scheme's primary task is mediating the inner public court with the total site of the overall landscape field. In section, your cell must help to mediate ground and sky. It also projects outward, ordering site and field from the *parti* cues of the gallery within. Arrayed on grade, all the cells will make a "flat" city plan. But if you fold the configuration up into a fully three dimensional form, the resulting concentrated space will be a much more urban solution. Precincts may be mutually defined by galleries as shared walls. Consider collage as a guide to taking advantage of the idiosyncrasies of each separate gallery. "This one already turns a corner, this one should be opposite the gate..." Note the collision of two fields may transform both of them and the dense/sparse relationships of all program elements. Integrate your gallery precinct with both its internal contents and the total group form. Xerocopy plans and sections of each individual gallery and precinct to the same scale, and using scissors and tape combine into a workable organization, using montage as a technique to locate individual cells and to organize collective site plans and sections. Use these as aids for making quick model studies of the whole collective scheme. Include significant contours. Agree on an organizing grid and rearrange for best effects.

Deployment

Make a tensegrity between the collective community form and the landscape. Anchor point and sphere with the ground and build out from a first vector equilibrium to extend stability in plan and section throughout the structure. Before construction, survey the actual site. Use surveyor's transit to stake out the precise location of all plan and volume elements in the field, or substitute compass and triangulate stakes with string and measure equal diagonals of a square to establish a right angle corner. Mark off each precinct with stakes measured from that "cornerstone." Use a long hose filled with water and open at both ends as a field level to establish elevation controls for your collective scheme on the site. Such careful on-site layout will help the entire group to take advantage of mutual alignment and controlled volume intervals between individual projects. You will find that the resulting sum is much greater than the parts, that is, a well-planned and well-executed collective community will have a greater volumetric presence than you might expect from a group of individual cells.

Production and Re-pro-duct-tion

It is one thing to produce something. This takes leadership. (*Dux* is the Latin word for leader or chief, as in our word *Duke*. Hence productive means "to lead forward".) It is quite another thing to produce the means to produce viable and useful institutions, human orders that maintain their integrity while responding to change. This is the awesome and holy task of re-production, and engages the full human spirit of adventure, excellence and compassion in urban affairs as much as in biological ones. While the individual galleries might be constructed indoors as warm-up, the essence of this study requires anchoring community to an outside meeting ground. In part and in whole, the total project should resolve Le Corbusier's equation of "the indissoluble binomial, the individual and the collective"? The form of this community space is as important as the design of the individual cells. If your gallery works in concert with your neighbors to achieve this, you will have given form to community! For any community to survive, it must beget and nurture offspring. Beyond the beginning, we now seek cultivation, the flowering of the fruit, the recreation of another generation.

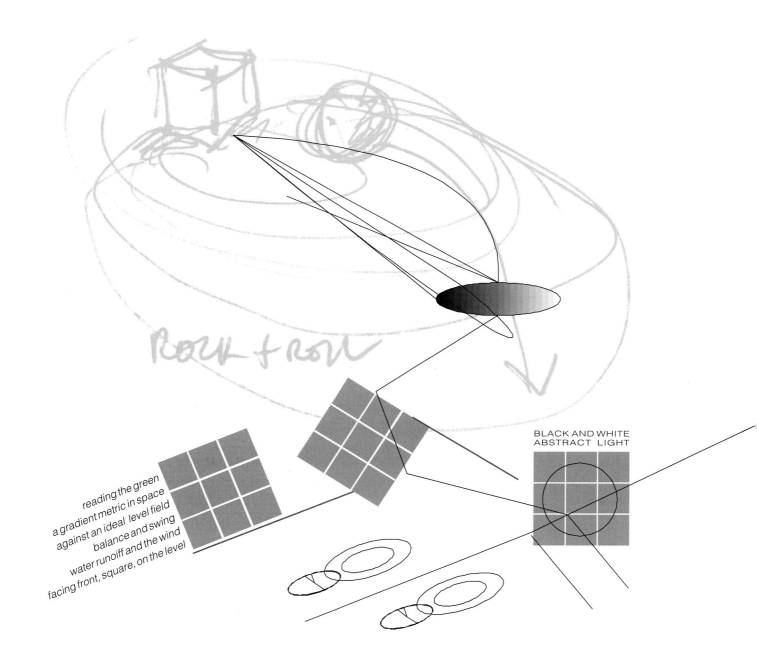

reading the green
a gradient metric in space
against an ideal level field
balance and swing
water runoiff and the wind
facing front, square, on the level

BLACK AND WHITE
ABSTRACT LIGHT

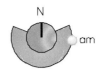

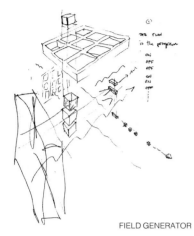

FIELD GENERATOR

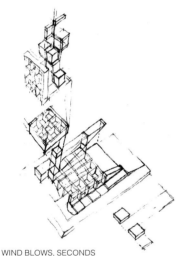

WIND BLOWS, SECONDS
TREES GROW, CENTURIES

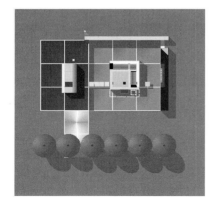

GOLF LESSONS: THE COLOR OF ENERGY

Architecture takes planning. The delayed gratification of foreseeing problems, considering options, and careful calculation can lead us to desired ends. But building is action. How can architects live in the here-and-now, the spacetime moment, the unique event as it comes around? Recall that your first Sticks and Stones study asked you "make something you like", and your naive "just do it" impulse seized the day, *carpe diem*. The next question was "why?" Thus did the creator meet the critic. Unity of plan and construction demands *both* the Apollonian reason of Daedalus and Dionysiac ecstasy of Icarus, a meditation rhythm that partakes equally of the states of mind of worship and workshop. Implacable reality tests our goals in every field. Seeking light, feeling wind, treading earth, I have sought to unite thought with action, and have learned from the collective wisdom of fellow-suffering mentors Neil, Ray, Peter, Howie, Ken, Todd, Henry, Rick, Greg, Nadia, Jeremy, and others-- all in the surburban zen test of a round of golf. To them I offer thanks and a hearty "nice pants"!

Swing. The only action you control in golf is the swing. To swing is to animate stature, to set the stance in motion. To develop a golf swing rhythm, allow body and club to join together in a smooth gravity metronome time pendulum. The sure swing of a carpenter's hammer drives the nail cleanly home. To keep the golf swing reliable in every new situation, you must practice, like a jazz player "woodshed-ding" on your musical "axe" until you have your chops down, until you attain your personal best. The architect's "axe" is a (conceptual) field generator, a comprehensive instrument for plastic relationships.

Transit. The ball flies off into the wild blue yonder. Once the golf swing (or architecture plan) is executed, the resultant ballistic trajectory enters an objective realm beyond intention. Wind can modify flight, dampness in the landing area affects the roll, and all-too human errors in the swing can spin the ball into tragic consequences. Here the hunter's virtures of patience and aim are rewarded. The potential energy of "here" is launched into the kinetic energy of "there". As we walk the fairway to follow the ball, our mental survey links landscape to the meaning of our movements, sensing in our footseps the slope and repose gradient tune of the earth, readying us for the next swing. *Look, listen... the universe is lonely, and it wants to play with us....*

Glory. Eventually the ball attains that once-distant goal, the green. But here the game begins anew, requiring refinement, finish, precision. What was objective becomes subjective, and there is a new objective, the hole. Of all the angles, how to choose which one is best, of all the speeds and strengths, how to know exactly how hard to stroke the putt? You calibrate, using an inborn sense of balance to estimate level and gradient, and read the green. You may also learn from others ("go to school on that putt") but in the end remains an implacable physical reality: the ball rolls in the cup or stays out. Bingo! or bust, both are engagement. The golfer (or architect!) does not stand aside as a spectator but is a participating actor, both cause and result of the world. And sometimes-- in golf, music, or architecture-- the ball goes in, the music is beautiful, the space is *alive*!

Monday. In golf, as in architecture, there is always the day after. No one will ever achieve golf's perfect score of 18. "Up to par" is a competent score of around 72, four times perfection (and even great players miss par often), so there is lots of room for mistakes, and enough compassion for all to share. So go at it if you want. Practice until action is guided by both insight and foresight and learning is the critical evaluation of hindsight. "Woodshed" towards spontaneity, not rote repetition, to be able to move easily between subjectivity and objectivity. Prove your prowess and improve luck. Conquer chance and gravity to get a small sphere into a very small hole in a very large field. Is this so different from properly setting a home's foundation stone in just the right place or finding the best spot to settle a tribe along a riverbank? Children of the next generation will help the living site evolve.

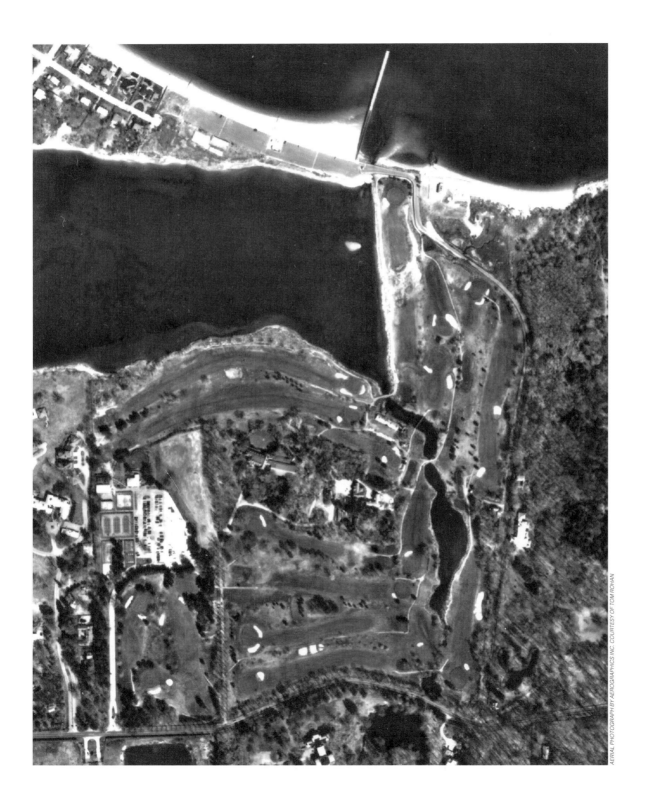

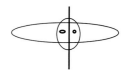

GETTING YOUR BEARINGS

There is a spot on a public golf course on the north shore of Long Island which seems particularly blessed. It is a hillside, facing south. Further south is the highest local elevation, a hill of some hundred feet in height. Just to its north, is the lowest local elevation, where the watershed draw from this terminal moraine meets the tidal estuary of the Long Island Sound further north. This spot is also a corner, a right angle along the edge of forest and field, the end of a natural wind-tunnel inlet off the Sound. Thus there is always a fresh breeze blowing here, bringing not only sea air, but the first delivery of any polar arctic Canadian air that might come. From this spot, the land climbs again, just as the water level drops back to sea level. In short, there is more topographic contrast and action here, it seems, than in most other nearby places. Close to marsh but well-drained, shaded by oaks and maples to the south and pines to the north, it gets early spring and late fall sun, moderate winters, and stays cool and moist in the summer growing season. This spot, the tee-off to the particularly difficult seventh hole, is a frequent source of four leaf clovers. In just a few rounds, this author found more than a half-dozen of these rare specimens (their finding did not necessarily improve the tee-shots, but no doubt were a factor in averting the water hazard!) Perhaps it is the fortuitous meteorological and topographic conditions which fostered their growth may be the basis for the legendary link between four-leaf clovers and good luck.

Why are some sites blessed for prosperity? How can we find the right place to build a house or found a city? We must bring to every site the same basic tools for measuring spacial potential, the traditional surveyor's transit, level, compass, plumb line, and tape of geometric inertial guidance. Our informed awareness can make us organic gyroscopes, measuring gradient as we move. In short, to get your bearings, you must put yourself in space, both as object and subject, matching landscape curve to the orthogonal origin of frontality. An aerial photo is a kind of ecstasy, an out-of-body experience. The house/urban planner considers runoff, drainage, water supply, fresh air, proper sunlight and ventilation, shelter from cold winds in properly locating all spaces. These are also advantages to the golfer-as-hunter, who must gauge wind speed and direction, slope and condition of the ground (the ball bounces less and rolls more slowly on wet earth than dry), and who must prove his or her prowess by improving luck, conquering chance and gravity to get a small ballistic sphere into a very small hole within a very large landscape/field. Is this so different from properly setting a home's foundation stone in just the right place or finding the best spot to settle a tribe along a riverbank?

Rock and Roll

The golf lessons of the terrain reveal the contours and gradients of every dynamic physical system, from weather to earthquakes. A rock stays put on a hillside because its corner edges are outside its centroid axis, while a golf ball will roll off the same slope. The faster the ball moves, the shallower the grade needed to send it rolling further down the hill. Tensors tell how gradient modifies vectors in a field. Cool air will sink as warm air rises; streams act as natural air conditioners in the summer. The earth's ground swells are in fact very slow waves of soil and subsoil creep, ripples making hills and valleys, large and small. Structure emerges from mass-positioning, an evolution of balance counterbalance until repose arrives. Surveyors use transit and triangulation to precisely locate plan elements in the field, marking precincts with stakes measured from the station point "cornerstone". Like the golf flags sitting in the center of each green, boundary stakes are extensions of the cornerstone, widening the precinct, extending and valorizing the ground plane. Surveying is not only a practical art, it is also a philosophy for planning moves in space to last a very long time.

ROCK AND ROLL
TENSOR, VECTOR AND GRADIENT

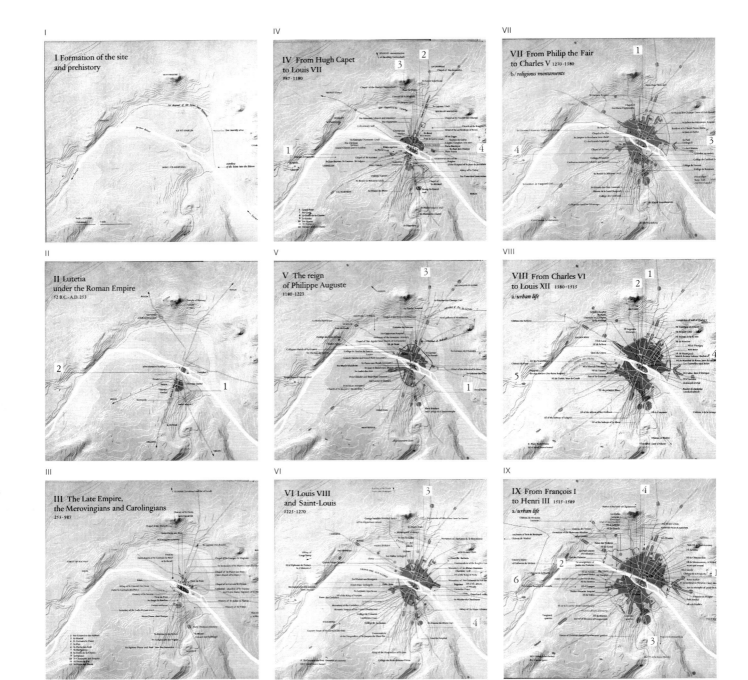

I

I Formation of the site
and prehistory

IV From Hugh Capet
to Louis VII
987-1180

VII From Philip the Fair
to Charles V 1270-1180
b/religious monuments

II Lutetia
under the Roman Empire
52 B.C.–A.D. 253

V The reign
of Philippe Auguste
1180-1223

VIII From Charles VI
to Louis XII 1380-1515
a/urban life

III The Late Empire,
the Merovingians and Carolingians
253-987

VI Louis VIII
and Saint-Louis
1223-1270

IX From François I
to Henri III 1515-1589
a/urban life

Paris Through the Ages
(opposite: read top to bottom, left to right)

behind the garage, by artist Marilyn Turtz
from the simplest home vast realities grow

THROUGH THE AGES

If buildings are bricks then a city is a volume, a single room or field of rooms. Building a city suggests a higher degree of abstraction than one home, but also confronts enormous and inescapable realities, like water supply and garbage disposal. Couperie's wonderful *Paris through the Ages* documents the 2000 year evolution of this City of Light. Urban plans, building photos, and historical narrative **is** the "plan/section" of the city. Why this site? Who first in prehistory saw the physical advantages of a bowl around a river bend, the south facing slope of Montmartre, defensible islands in the river? How did Paris come to grow, wane, and evolve like a phoenix rising from ashes, into an Eternal City, like Rome, Beijing, or Jerusalem? A brief account of the flavor of this city's rich history...

Parisii Celts using iron, conquered Neolithic settlements. In turn, they burned their cult site and fortress in a failed attempt to stop invading Romans, who rebuilt Lutetia as a Roman city after 52 BCE . Entry from the Empire to this outpost was along the southern ridge, the future Rue St Jacques. A 10 mile aqueduct brought fresh water to the forum, set on high ground near the river. Thus the invaders could oversee the locals below. While Rome held a million people at this time, there were only 10,000 living in Lutetia. Barbarians ravaged the upper town in 253-280, but the wall and river around the island of La Cité saved the town. It became a strategic crossroads that prospered as implosion concentrated settlement on La Cité. The upper forum became a citadel. The town was called Paris by 360. When Roman Empire collapsed, Franks conquered the region in 508; Clovis built churches and monasteries. Paris thrived until Danish Viking raids pillaged it in 886, and then returned to weeds. From Hugh Capet to Louis VII (987-1180) there was growth to north of Isle. A wall, fortifications at Chatelet bridge, and Porte de Greve docks were added. Abelard brought intellectual renown from earlier powers Chartres and Laon. By the reign of Philippe Auguste (1180-1223) Paris was already outstanding in finance. 3.3 mi of walls protected by Louvre castle enclosed 620+ acres into a unified town, protecting against possible attacks by Richard the Lionhearted. This circle beyond La Cité included Les Halles markets, which attracted commerce and population which could create Notre Dame nave and facade (1225).

This describes only the first **five** of the eighteen panels shown opposite and on the following page! We stand in awe of human persistence in confronting, solving, and re-solving the problems of our own creation. Every three-dimensional model is a "snapshot" in time. Computers are already providing time-and-space slices, animated models of urban space (the author has helped developed such an interactive four-dimensional model for Princeton University's 250th anniversary). However, the graphic plans we see here are compelling indeed. The historical frames of development show an animation of extension, aggrandizement, and perforation, as forces driving growth and connection map the life of the city. Like a living cell the city extends arms, engulfs territory, builds protective walls in alternating phases of expansion and consolidation. Already the Roman Forum provides the needed urban void that ventilates and relieves congestion, anticipating Place Royale and Place Vendome, "Hausmanization" and the great Parisian parks today. The implosive urge to be at the center of a city, in a "prime mid-town location", helps ignite the critical mass of a city toward its ongoing fusion. But without breathing room at the heart of the matter, the city will eventually strangle. To continue the Paris biography...

[VI] In the 13th Century, a sewer is built to relieve the piles of refuse at the gates as settlement expands beyond the walls. Northern hill villages bring produce to Les Halles. The Sorbonne makes Paris an intellectual and diplomatic center. Paris, not Lyon, is the hub of a road network. **[VII]** The Black Death (1348-50) killed perhaps 40-45% of the people. But by 1356, Charles V created a moated wall 26-33 ft high with 6 bastilles (small fortresses) almost doubled the protected enclosure of the city, from 650 to 1084 acres, with 80,000 people including 10,000 students, at 74 per acre. The Louvre inside but at the edge of the walls, was a royal "escape hatch". Many hôtels (town houses), of urban powerful appear. **[VIII]** Paris is recognized as capital of kingdom in 1415 but economic recovery and new growth beyond the Left Bank fortifications came only after 1450. Paris was under siege for 30 years: a generation did not leave city until adulthood. **[IX]** From Francois I to Henri III 1515-1589, medieval 16th century Paris faced crisis, too small for its population, too vast for its defense, too crowded for sanitation, too torturous for traffic. The city was stifled within its walls and reached its physical limit, the swamps to the east and north. Even dumps became building sites. The newly built protection of Tuileries Palace outside the wall opened up western extension. Bois de Boulogne was enclosed. The King sold the right to collect rents to the city. The rise of Protestantism ended religious unity.

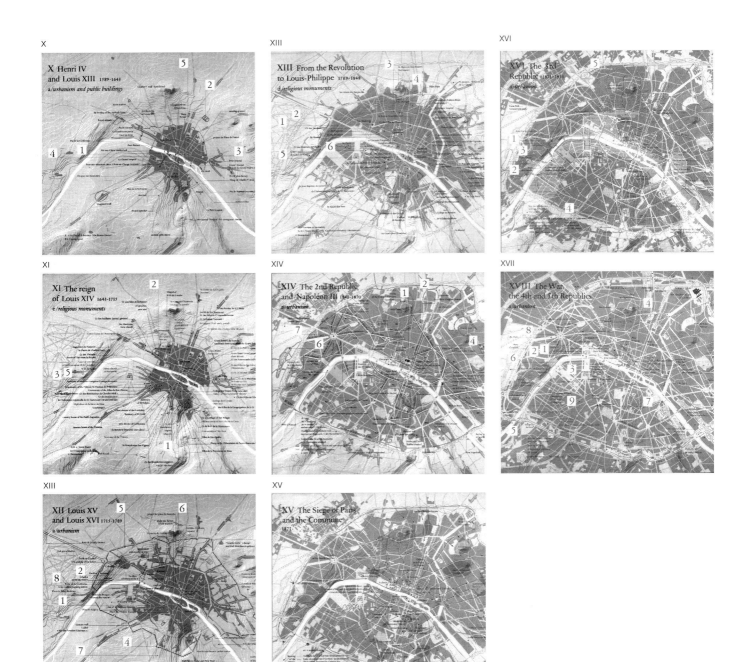

X

X Henri IV
and Louis XIII 1589-1643
a/urbanism and public buildings

XIII

XIII From the Revolution
to Louis-Philippe 1789-1848
d/religious monuments

XVI

XVI The 3rd
Republic 1871-1918
a/urbanism

XI

XI The reign
of Louis XIV 1643-1715
c/religious monuments

XIV

XIV The 2nd Republic
and Napoléon III 1848-1870
a/urbanism

XVII

XVIII The War,
the 4th and 5th Republics
a/urbanism

XIII

XII Louis XV
and Louis XVI 1715-1789
a/urbanism

XV

XV The Siege of Paris
and the Commune
1871

The structure of Paris continues to evolve:

[X] By 1643, Paris demolishes Charles V wall and grows to the new fortifications of Louis XIII, adding 1/3 more land and doubling population to 400,000. Pont Neuf and Rue Dauphine give Parisians a view of the Seine. Place Royale (Place des Vôges) 1612, is an intentional urban void, a sheltered promenade for the aristocracy. King builds 33 new streets on Left Bank to balance 35 new ones on Right, but also joins Louvre to Tuileries, a half-mile barrier along river. Refuge of persecuted English Catholics, Paris grows radially, creating 60 new monasteries, and whole religious districts. **[XI]** During Louis XIV's long reign 1643-1715, the Cours, peripheral boulevard planted with trees, unites perimeter extensions. It is now easier to go around city than through it. Grand projects include rechanneling sewer, grading Mont Parnasse, Champs Elysées, Place Vendôme (speculative venture at urban edge), 123 new streets, paving and lighting (Roemer discovers speed of light at new Observatory, 1676). Pont Royale connects Tuileries to St Germain suburb. Houses reach 10 stories. King moves to Versailles to stop uncontrolled growth of urban "monster". **[XII]** By 1715, half a million people live in Paris. Growth beyond perimeter boulevards requires 14 miles of Encient, Customs Walls by 1785, a toll barrier surrounding the city, with gates by Le Doux. From Place Concorde, 1753, an essential link between new districts, highway extends west past regraded butte at Etoile to 2nd Porte Maillot. Supplying Paris is a national problem, emptying provinces of talent and capital. **[XIII]** French Revolution 1789 brings chaos: high cost of living, workers live in slums, *les Miserables*. Upper class flees during Reign of Terror, 100,00 leave by 1801. Church hospitals, royal parks, gardens closed or in ruins. Napoleon creates Rue de Rivoli, rebuilds quays, sewers, triumphal avenues to Vincennes, L'Ourcq canal to east. Gaslight 1819 brings night life. By 1842 six railroad lines converge on Paris. New 37 mile defense ring keeps artillery 1 mile from Paris.

[XIV] By 1848, population 1 million; disorders bring unemployment, cholera. Napoleon II orders unhealthy impenetrable slums opened up. Hausmannization: triangulated thoroughfares open core, link all Paris, converge at radiating circles of Place Republique, Chaillot (l'Etoile) and d'Italie. Rue de Rivoli/St-Antoine is first major EW avenue. Louvre extends to Tuileries by 1857, is largest palace in world. NS corridor opened, Blvd. St Michel/ Strasbourg/Sebastopol? with "infinite" persepective, extending to Observatory. Blvd St Germain EW on left bank completes inner circle of Blvds. Belt RR (19 miles, 27 stations, 3 trains per hour) along 1839 ramparts surrounds Paris with transportation. Circulation becomes protection? Water system makes spring for private use, river for sanitation. 200 miles of sewers built from plan to completion 1856-1870. City limits expand to 1839 battlement boundaries, annexing 18 towns. New parks and squares increase green space 10x. Bois de Vincennes to E. Tram from Bois de Boulogne in W to Place de la Concorde in 1854. These projects employ 70,000 people, raise price of land 12x. High rents drive new workers to outskirts, where slums reappear. Industrial zones surround Paris. 2 world expositions. Cast iron and glass umbrella construction for Les Halles, Gare du Nord. 2 million people by 1870. **[XV]** German Siege of Paris, Autumn 1870. Congested streets make defense difficult (80,000 troops take 2 days to go from Neuilly to Vincennes). Governement moves to Versailles and rich abandon city to the poor, middle class apart from proletariat. Revolt and proclamation of Commune in March 1871 lead to new seige by govt troops who retake city in May, fighting through gardens, narrow streets, and roofs.

[XVI] Population is 2.8 million in 1911. Paris reaches its saturation point (?!) as dense core begins to decrease around 1890. Unplanned growth beyond 1839 ramparts: while city grows 70%, suburbs grow 500%. Seine boats carry 25 million commuters, and buses trains, cable cars carry 330 million passengers in one year. Metro is opened in 1900 (by 1937 extends beyond city), but no railway connections across city to continent. L'Etoile turns corner of lower Seine development with 6 new bridges and Palais du Trocadero facing 984 ft Eiffel Tower and Gallerie des Machines, 1889. Reinforced concrete and elevators make possible high rise, flexible floor plan apartments. Electric light and cinema. World War moratorium on rents end construction growth. **[XVII]** After 1914, the Paris region draws provisions from as far as Poland and Morocco. Density, 148 per acre, is 6x NYC. Depression, fascism, refugees. By 1938 a million vehicles create intense traffic. LC's Voisin Plan would accomodate cars and provide 60 story "Cartesian skyscrapers". "Red belts" of communist/socialist worker communities surround right-wing center. **[XVIII]** After WW2, Paris takes 20 years to regain 1939 level of service. Decontrolled rents in 1948 foster construction. By 1956 cost of living doubles and rents aree 6x 1948 levels. Population increases to 3 million by 1960, with 8 million in Greater Paris. Expressways along Seine and a 36 km Boulevard Peripherique are built, but by 1963 there are over 1.7 million cars for 330,000 parking spaces. As of 1970, Autoroute South is city's link to Orly Airport. La Defense, extension along main West East axis, is as far from L'Etoile as L'Etoile is from Ile de La Cité. New university at Nanterre. New market replaces Les Halles. There is chronic scarcity of water, energy, and fuel.

Is the contemporary Greater Paris Agglomeration the start of a new scale of structure.? Will it look as simple and primitive to our descendants in the Fifth Millennium as the first Roman plan seems compared to Paris today? As in Merovingian and Capetian Paris (frames III and IV), we see the same scatter-shot pockets of development, not yet linked. Will unity always vie with diversity? Will center always contend with hinterland, no matter what scale the site, be it region, state, planet, or galaxy?

XVIII

XVIII GREATER PARIS AGGLOMERATION. A NEW SCALE

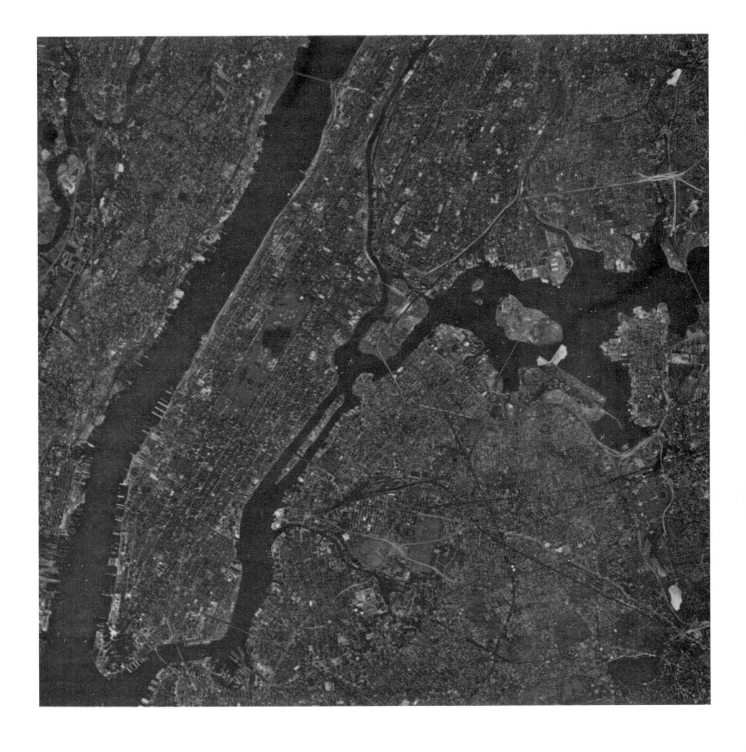

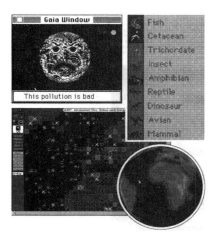

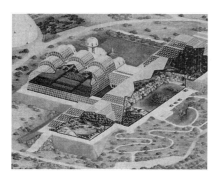

REALITY AND SIMULATION

What music is to the 20th century architecture may be to the next millennium. Since Edison and Marconi music has become ubiquitous. We all have access to high-fidelity sounds. In our cars we hear Bach's music perhaps better than he ever did. Because the audience is global, musicians can be full-time and well-trained. Public tastes can be precise: do you choose west Bulgarian choral jazz on period instruments? The audience for our own ideas in music is just as vast. A lucky tape and anyone can make a hit. When 3D computer modeling with CAD and CD-ROM in real time becomes as common as radio is today, a culture of space ideas may well emerge. Already one CD-ROM advertises "worlds of Ancient Architecture" and another offers a complete museum on a single disk. Today we understand that music sells soap but also can express deep emotions. Similarly, people may come to value architectural forms as *ideas* of pure plastic event, for the thoughts and feelings they express beyond utility. Just as Bach's B-Minor Mass may move us whatever our religion, so too may architecture exploit all modes and styles of volumetric expression to become a cross-cultural continuum . Then the essence of architecture as spacial invention and imagination will emerge and be valued, and those that need to see such ideas translated into dwelling and community will invent, discover, research, and carry from tradition the means to do so.

Computers and Cities

The architect is surprised to hear lawyers describe themselves as planners, since architects are the only professional group whose major medium of communications *is* plans. But accompanying physical plans are often rules for action like building codes and zoning laws. Policy "planners" may be unaware of the spaces such rules create. Sim City, a computer game, allows a player to establish zones for housing , industrial and commercial development. After these zones are linked with roads and electric power, the computer *animates* the plan, solving the matrix once a "month" to plot areas of growth and decay. As the Sims move in and out, they bring wealth, traffic, and pollution. The player must manage resources, adjusting tax rate and funding for police, fire, and roads, to keep the region healthy. Once a "year" the matrix is updated, revenues and budget are adjusted, and the people tell the mayor "how'm I doin?" With feedback, policy and plan interact. These sophisticated simulations presage a future where we may plan our complex cities with the same intelligence and beauty as our best collective works, from Mykonos to Manhattan, from Paris to Sperlonga. As Sim City's guide observes, all surviving populated cities are winners. But today some need help." From satellite photos, once-healthy cities look dis-eased: inner-city heart attack, suburb cancer spreading. Urbanism can heal the earth's wounds. Architecture is *external* medicine.

The Limits of Simulation

Ceci n'est pas une pipe. The facing image is not Manhattan, not a photograph, but rather a digital satellite spectral map. It could easily be animated! We could study it like the valuable patient it is to nurse it back to health. Buckminster Fuller once proposed one dome to cover midtown Manhattan. Biosphere 2 built a similar hermetic world in the desert. Such a marvelous conception, our first potential starship, demands our admiration, but it has abandoned the gift of earth, the volume continuity of in and out. We may yet revive our home without embalming it. Architecture necessarily engenders hope. It takes time to build what can be destroyed all too easily in a flash. The true architect resists war as much as possible. To find and make order is so valuable yet so fragile in the face of mindless chaos that we must do wall we can to preserve and promote visions of organic wholes. Reality cannot be simulated. It is fractally infinite in all dimensional configurations. Reality can be selectively modelled as simulation, but building a model does not provide a roof over the head any more than a recipe nourishes a hungry body.

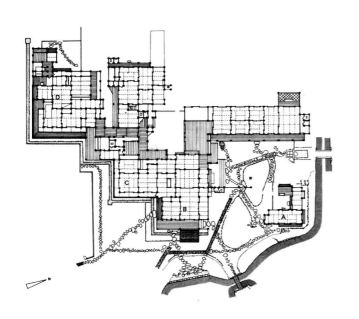

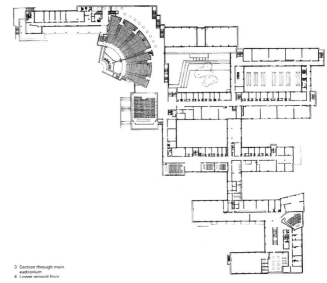

3 Section through main
   auditorium
4 Lower ground floor

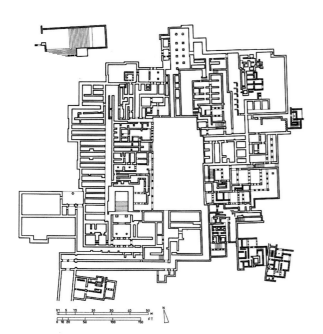

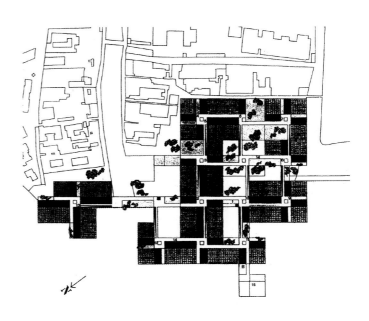

15

HETEROTOPIA

If Utopia means "nowhere", then heterotopia means "other or different where", and by extension, many different wheres, as Dmitri Porphyrios suggests in an essay on Alvar Aalto. Revisiting Aalto's Otaniemi theater (see page 334) through the plan of the entire ensemble, we find that it turns the corner inside the building in a surprising manner not predicted by the orthogonal layout of the rest. The exterior of this theater produces an even more surprising internal corner to the site. It is not only the roof of the concert hall, it is also stadium seating for a large outdoor field. Le Corbusier's and Jullian de la Fuente's Venice Hospital plan establishes a regular order of wards of patients pinwheeling around nursing stations, linked by corridors measured by the length of interfloor ramps. Just when we "get" the logic of the plan, its regularity is broken. The maternity ward is pulled across the canal and the chapel seems alone. Yet such surprises are in keeping with the serendipity of Venice. The Palace at Knossos appears to be a maze-- in fact it is the origin of the Labyrinth myth. The Imperial Villa at Katsura Japan is made of equal and standard 6' x 3' *tatami* mats, yet they are combined in a tremendous variety of configurations, producing unexpected volumes and vistas at every turn. In architecture, through an empty arch, up a hidden stair, lies the surprise of the unexpected, the pleasure of discovered space-- *Heterotopia*.

Individual and collective

Jazz musician Anthony Brown has noted that a unique aspect of jazz as a musical form is that it is a *collective* improvisation. Jazz may then well be a lesson for how a society may thrive. The elastic rhythms of swing and bebop generate momentum through polymeter, laying off the downbeat before returning to a unified pulse. This suspends and compresses time against the regular meter, and provides the percussionist with freedom to explore alternate interpretations as much as enharmonic voicing allows the horn soloist to improvise the melody. According to Darwin, it is to each species' advantage (and to life in general) that there be some variation from individual to individual. In time, environment changes. If there is not variation within a group, there may be no one with a propensity to thrive or survive as climate, food, etc. alter. While all maple leave share the same basic form and structure, on any tree no two leaves are *exactly* the same. To establish order in variety and variety in order in a comprehensively enfranchising society, every individual needs access to completely unique and flexible domestic space. This is no less than Italian hill town dwellers, rain forest Pygmies and Arctic Eskimos have. Note that this does not mean homes might not share essential aspects of their form in response to materials, customs, and climate (see Amos Rapaport's *House Form and Culture*), but that as dwelling needs change-- children arrive, grow up, leave, guests come and go-- inhabitants will be able to alter their spaces, both in physical and technical terms (the spiritual will take care of itself if these are met). Studies suggest that this ability to order one's own space inside the house and within one's community is an important reason why so many people live to great longevity in the mountain communities of Georgia in the Caucasus, Hunza, in Pakistan, and in the Andes. This is common in many developing societies, where the craft of home-making is one of the rites of passage into adulthood, and in rural communities in developed countries, where there is room enough to add on another room to the saltbox farmhouse, and carpentry skills etc. are part of what one learns to maintain a self-sufficient farm. However, so many people in the world now live in urban and suburban conditions that we need to make clear that accessibility to changing ones home is an important right and need. Not just Home Depot and its kin, but a whole new way of thinking about and making homes and communities. We can envision a system of home space components and local suppliers who help upgrade through trade-ins. Wright's Usonian houses and the Pessac experiments of Gropius, Oud, Mies, and Le Corbusier are other visions in this direction. Le Corbusier's proposal for Algiers includes a fascinating suggestion to sell high-rise homestead property, with the means to construct to suit the owners in all variety of styles and spacial configurations.

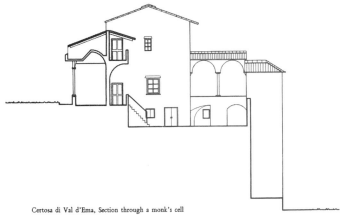

Certosa di Val d'Ema, Section through a monk's cell

THE HEART OF THE MATTER...

"Thirty spokes unite at the wheel's hub; it is the center hole that makes it useful." Lao Tzu

A center is a focus, the measure and goal of the periphery. Everyone seeks the center, so the wise planner keeps it empty. This insight is the basis of the microprocessor, whose supports and inputs may be hard-wired, but whose center is programmable. Modern urbanism began in the 14th Century when the citizens of Siena agreed to establish common facades around the piazza and maintain the emptiness of their central space. Home of the world-famous *palio* horse race, the great piazza is the essence of the freedom of the city. How lucky New York is to have Central Park! Even the heart is hollow. Does the citizen seek the arena of political action or the studio of private reflection? The monastery at Ema Italy addresses this ancient dilemma directly. Each monk's cell, with a double height space, a garden, and view to the horizon, emphasizes the isolation of the individual. But even further inward lies the empty space of the collective courtyard, the cloister. Only when there is general societal approval for and recognition of the necessity of what we as architects are trained to do, will our cities once again be homes for the people, full of sunlight, greenery, and space. The best most elegant architecture produces the most with the least resources-- and, if everyone gives up just a little, the town square, the hollow heart, is free!

Home: inflatable radiant spirit

"When you live closely to individual dramas you marvel that we do not have continuous war, knowing what nightmares human beings conceal, what secret obsessions and hidden cruelties.... I knew the origin of war, which was in each of us, and I knew that our concept of the hero was outdated, that the modern hero was the one who would master his own neurosis so that it would not become universal, who would struggle with his myths, who would know that he himself created them, who would enter the labyrinth and fight the monster. This monster who sleeps at the bottom of his own brain.... The wars we carried within us were projected outside." Anais Nin

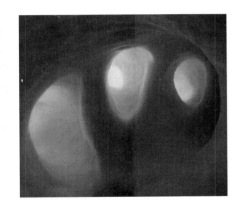

The city is a modulated structure of modulated volumes, finally at many scales. Biology's ubiquitous evidence of cellular organization suggest that working up, from the inside out, is the way to make public spaces which is appropriate for Arendt's space of appearance and is also the result of individual dwellings. A healthy city is always under construction. Like DNA maintaining a species through succeeding generations, a city copies itself (with changes) as it removes the old and inserts the new. We can imagine self-replicating factories fueled by solar energy on the moon, so then why not make such long-lived structures here on earth as well? Of course we do, and we call them cities. Culture and city are self-replicating phenomena. Consider colonization in the New World. Spain created New Spain, now Latin America; France created New France, once all of the Louisiana Purchase and most of Canada, still extant in New Orleans and Quebec; and England created New England, New London, and New York. Cities are the artifacts that humans have created for preserving and transmitting culture to their offspring and posterity, and sometimes it works. This very alphabet and language base came in large part from a city and its culture 2000 years ago-- Rome. All it takes is time. As Dr. Julio San Jose has said of the ambitious post World War II public housing program in England, "because there was a future, we built housing". Time is of the essence for architecture. Post-Modernism was too often architecture without time-- built out of dryvit but made to look like the stones of Egyptian pyramids-- this was an architecture nervous about its lack of the dimension of time. Deconstructivism was also uneasy with time-- its most radical expositions demanded a form of suspended animation as its structural scaffolding. Neither of these eclectic forays accepted the simple reality-- architecture takes time. Your final work in the complete set of *Architectonics* and *Dynamics* studies is ambitious, but it is only a beginning. Your next work, whatever it may be, will commence another cycle, flowering and bearing fruit, to create another generation.

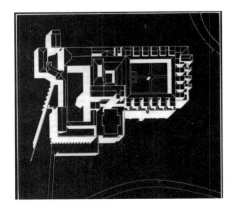

REFLECTING

"She would rather light a candle than curse the darkness."
Adlai Stevenson on Eleanor Roosevelt

Endurance

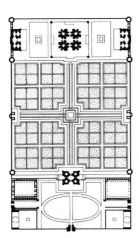

The Church Incarnate passage on page 377 could be speaking of the Taj Mahal, often called the most beautiful building in the world. This voluptuous monument to love is also lustrous, reflecting its reflection through glass and water inside and out, illuminating the inner world through a glowing clarity of order, proportion, and harmony with the sparest materials, yet the fullest light. A struck match ignites, radiates, burns its fuel, and then goes out. But the sun, ringing to its thermonuclear symphony, radiates for billions of years! A violin makes a simple note on a single string and its amplifying sound box fills a concert hall with song. A seedpod sends out roots, stem, leaves and branches. In due season fruit supplies a new seedpod with the means to carry on. Life observes itself, both symphony and orchestra, and conscious wonder brightens the darkest holes with disinterested self-reflection. Trace the moving sun's reflection on a white paper and discover a rainbow. Architecture, well-timed space, ennobles even the simple rituals of daily life with harmony, proportion, light.

Reflecting on Reflecting

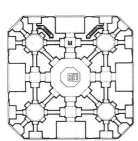

The curious ever seek what is truly new yet always present, and therefore relevant, by breaking out of stereotypes and habits. The wakeful eye looks at looking. Learning to reflect, the mind begins to see. We say "*I see....*" The invention of the city-- the "civilizing terrain" for and of the human condition-- is a miracle, no less than the invention of democracy or the American Constitution, which *sanctions* permanent peaceful revolution once every four years. Society regards itself, and *votes*. Let us imagine such global enfranchisement-- a democrasphere! In the readings that follow Poundstone develops legible diagrams eloquent in a language without word, while Thomas Paine's observations on *Declaration of the Rights of Man* and Lewis Thomas's *Lives of a Cell* are illuminated by figure-ground diagrams of real city forms, taken from Fred Koetter and Colin Rowe's *Collage City*. The evidence of the most enduring works of man, "eternal cities" like Rome Jerusalem, or Bejing shows that even though elements within may change, structure and overall character can endure, just as our bodies slough off dead skin cells while we retain our personalities. Architecture is not only timepiece but also peacetime. Earth seen from halfway to the moon is a simple sphere mostly white and blue, yet it is a complex organism. It reveals to the curious observer weather at all time scales, from wispy clouds to churning seas to migrating continents to roiling magma at the core. All of us dance to the balance and rhythm of these opposing counterpoints. Carl Sagan wrote in *Cosmos* that from a thousand miles up, no evidence of human beings can be seen from space, not even the Great Wall of China. But now astronauts see smoke from the clearcut destruction in the Amazon and Sarawak rain forests. Will our first cosmic marks be our last, or will we be able to create a cloak and mantle suitable to make our home planet radiant throughout the cosmos?

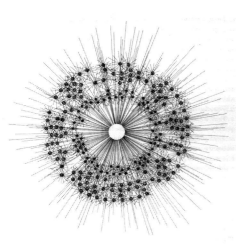

READINGS

Benevolo, Leonardo. *The Origins of Modern Town Planning*
Gerster, Georg. *Grand Design*
Manuel, Frank *Paths in Utopia*
Michener, James. The Source
Morrish, William. *Civilizing Terrains*
Mumford, Lewis. *The City in History*
Ryckwert, Joseph. *The Idea of a Town*
Soleri, Paolo. *Arcology*
Le Corbusier. *Radiant City*
Young, Louise B. *The Unfinished Universe*
Zajonc, Arthur. *Catching the Light: The Entwined History of Light and Mind*

THE RECURSIVE UNIVERSE, *excerpt*
by William Poundstone

The rules of Conway's game of Life are shown at right.... There are no other rules. Conway's game of Life compares the growth of patterns to the growth of populations of living organisms--say, bacteria in a culture. At any rate, the analogy may help you remember the rules. An on cell with fewer than two neighbors dies of isolation. A cell with four or more neighbors dies of overpopulation. Two or three neighbors are just right. If an empty niche has three neighbors, trisexual mating occurs and a new cell is born.

In most games, players make decisions throughout the course of play. In Life, the player's role is almost nonexistent. Life is a sort of spreadsheet program in which each cell's action is dictated by its neighbors. (The game is sometimes played on financial planning software.) The player merely decides what cells are on at the offset-- at time 0. Even the role may be abdicated by electing a random assortment of on and off cells. From then on, the inexorable rules of Life determine everything.

BLINKERS, BLOCKS, BEEHIVES, AND GLIDERS

The best way to get the feel of Life is to use a checkerboard or a sheet of graph paper. Conway and colleagues played black and white checkers. The black checkers marked the on cells. Conway identified cells due for a birth and placed a white checker in each. A second black checker marked on cells due to die. When all births and deaths had been identified, the double black checkers were removed from the board and the white checkers were replaced with black checkers. The process was repeated for each generation. To play on graph paper, make a new diagram for each generation.

Try some simple configurations. If the Life universe starts out empty -- no checkers or no cells at all -- every cell has zero neighbors. By the rules of Life, every cell remains empty in the next generation and next and the next. Nothing happens. Take the opposite approach. Start with every cell occupied, an infinity of on cells in every direction. Then every cell has eight "live" neighbors and must die. The Life plane is empty as above a generation later.

Creation must be more subtle. Try a single live cell in an empty universe. Now there are two cases to be considered. The cell has zero live neighbors, so it must die. Each of the neighboring empty cells has the one live cell for a neighbor. That still isn't enough to make any difference. The configuration dies. Two adjacent cells also die. Three live cells is the minimum for survival in the Life universe. Try three in a row. The center cell has two live neighbors and survives. The two cells have just the center cell for a neighbor and die. Above and below the center cell are empty cells that have all three live cells for neighbors. Both cells experience a birth. The result is a column of three cells.

By the same reasoning, the column of the three cells reproduces the row the generation after that. The triplet oscillates between the two configurations indefinitely. Conway dubbed this object the "blinker". Blinkers turn up frequently in Life. It isn't necessary to start with a blinker to end up with one. Not all triplets create a blinker. Three cells in a L shape form a two-by-two square, the "block". Unlike the blinker, the block never changes. Each of the four cells has three neighbors, so all survive. None of the surrounding empty cells has more than two live neighbors, so there are no births. Conway's term for such stable pattern is "still life." The block is the commonest still life. A row of four cells produces a different type of still life. The two end cells die but

*The rules for the **Game of Life**, invented by John Conway*

If, for a given cell, the number of on neighbors is exactly two, the cell maintains its status quo into the next generation. If the cell is on; if it is off, it stays off.

If the number of neighbors is exactly three, the cell will be on the next generation. This is so regardless of the cell's present state.

If the number of neighbors is zero, one, four, five, six, seven, or eight, the cell will be off in the next generation.

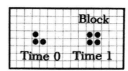

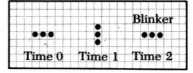

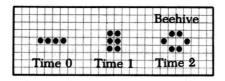

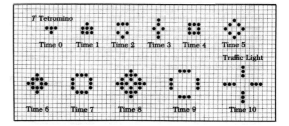

Glider

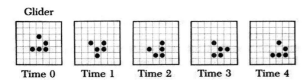

| Time 0 | Time 1 | Time 2 | Time 3 | Time 4 |

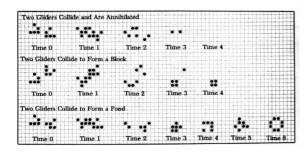

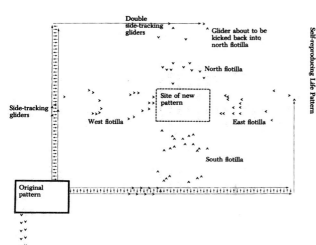

Block encoding description of pattern
is manipulated via glider flotillas

four new are born. The result is a two-by-three rectangle. The rectangle is not stable. It in turn changes into a "beehive. "The beehive is a stable hexagon of six cells. Every live cell has two neighbors. The empty cells outside the beehive all have less than three neighbors. The two empty cells inside the beehive each have five neighbors, too many for a birth.

There are many other starting patterns of four cells. The most interesting is called the *T* tetromino. *Tetromino* is an invented word patterned after *domino*. It refers to any pattern of four squares connected by the edges (as the two square halves of a domino are). Both the row of four cells and the block qualify as tetrominos. The T tetromino is the T-shaped arrangement of four cells.

GLIDERS AND SPACESHIPS

One of the first surprises was the discovery that some Life patterns move. While following a complex pattern, one of Conway's colleagues noticed that a five-unit cell was "walking". The moving unit was named the "glider". The glider creeps something like an amoeba or hydra, changing its shape as it goes. It assumes four different phases. Two phases are the shifted mirror images of the other two. Any phase is exactly reproduced four generations later. By then, the glider has moved one cell diagonally.

A SELF-REPRODUCING LIFE PATTERN

Given enough time, a Life computer can produce the four glider flotillas necessary to replicate itself and have them zero in on any desired location in the (otherwise empty) Life plane. Conway had to invoke many gimmicks to prove that this is so; let's see how they fit together. First of all, what would a self-reproducing Life pattern look like? It would be big. Certainly it would be bigger than any video screen or computer in existence could encompass. It would also be mostly empty space. Design considerations dictate the use of very, very sparse glider streams. If you examine a portion of the interior of the computer closely, you would find only an occasional glider and rarely, a gun or an eater.

There is no way of saying what the grand overall shape of the self-reproducing pattern would be. At large scale, it could assume any shape, if only you chose to design it that way. The pattern would have at least one type of external projection. A special set of blocks would reside at various distances outside the pattern's computer. From time to time, the computer would fire small flotillas of two or thirty gliders at the blocks to change their distance from the computer. The blocks are the pattern's external memory registers. At least one of the blocks is special: It is the blueprint of the self-reproducing patterns.

More exactly, it is the number represented by the distance of this block from the pattern that is the blueprint. How can a single number represent the blueprint for a complex structure? One need only describe unambiguously every part of the structure in any convenient language (English, Spanish, FORTRAN, the machine language of the pattern's internal computer). The symbols of the language can all be encoded as numbers, and the numbers can be joined together into one big number. The block is placed this number of units from the zero position of the register. Of course, if the blueprint is encoded in English, then the pattern's internal computer would have to be so sophisticated that it understands English-- which is an unnecessary complication.

DECLARATION OF THE RIGHTS OF MAN AND OF CITIZENS BY THE NATIONAL ASSEMBLY OF FRANCE
written and reviewed by Thomas Paine, 1789

The representatives of the people of France, formed into a National Assembly, considering that ignorance, neglect, or contempt of human rights, are the sole causes of public misfortunes and corruptions of Government, have resolved to set forth in a solemn declaration, these natural, imprescriptible, and inalienable rights; that this declaration being constantly present to the minds of the members of the body social, they may be ever kept attentive to their rights and their duties; that the acts of the legislative and executive powers of Government, being capable of being every moment compared with the end of political institutions, may be more respected; and also, that the future claims of the citizens, being directed by simple and incontestable principles, may always tend to the maintenance of the Constitution, and the general happiness.

For these reasons the National Assembly doth recognize and declare, in the presence of the Supreme Being, and with the hope of his blessing and favour, the following sacred rights of men and of citizens:

I. Men are born, and always continue, free and equal in respect of their rights. Civil distinctions, therefore, can be founded only on public utility.

II. The end of all political associations is the preservation of the natural and imprescriptible rights of man; and these rights are Liberty, Property, Security, and Resistance of Oppression.

III. The Nation is essentially the source of all sovereignty; nor can any individual, or any body of men, be entitled to any authority which is not expressly derived from it.

IV. Political Liberty consists in the power of doing whatever does not injure another. The exercise of the natural rights of every man, has no other limits than those which are necessary to secure to every other man the freeexercise of the same rights; and these limits are determinable only by the law.

V. The law ought to prohibit only actions hurtful to society. What is not prohibited by the law should not be hindered; nor should any one be compelled to that which the law does not require.

VI. The law is an expression of the will of the community. All citizens have a right to concur, either personally or by their representatives, in its formation. It should be the same to all, whether it protects or punishes; and all being equal in its sight, are equally eligible to all honours, places, and employments, according to their different abilities, without any other distinction than that created by their virtues and talents.

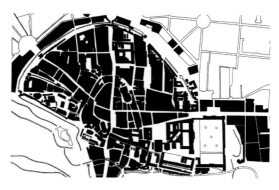

MUNICH, RESIDENZ, FIGURE-GROUND PLAN

VII. No man should be accused, arrested, or held in confinement, except in cases determined by the law, and according to the forms which it has prescribed. All who promote, solicit, execute, or cause to be executed, arbitrary orders, ought to be punished, and every citizen called upon, or apprehended by virtue of the law, ought immediately to obey, and renders himself culpable by resistance.

VIII. The law ought to impose no other penalties by such as are absolutely and evidently necessary; and no one ought to be punished, but in virtue of a law promulgated before the offence, and legally applied.

IX. Every man being presumed innocent till he has been convicted, whenever his detention becomes indispensable, all rigour to him, more than is necessary to secure his person, ought to be provided against by the law.

X. No man ought to be molested on account of his opinions, not even on account of his religious opinions, provided his avowal of them does not disturb the public order established by the law.

XI. The unrestrained communication of thoughts and opinions being one of the most precious Rights of Man, every citizen may speak, write, and publish freely, provided he is responsible for the abuse of this liberty, in cases determined by the law.

XII. A public force being necessary to give security to the Rights of Men and of citizens, that force is instituted for the benefit of the community and not for the particular benefit of the persons with whom it is intrusted.

XIII. A common contribution being necessary for the support of the public force, and for defraying the other expenses of Government, it ought to be divided equally among the members of the community, according to their abilities.

XIV. Every citizen has a right, either by himself or his representative, to a free voice in determining the necessity of public contributions, the appropriation of them, and their amount, mode of assessment, and duration.

XV. Every community has a right to demand of all its agents an account of their conduct.

XVI. Every community in which a separation of powers and a security of rights is not provided for, wants a Constitution.

XVII. The right to property being inviolable and sacred, no one ought to be deprived of it, except in cases of evident public necessity, legally ascertained, and on condition of a previous just indemnity.

DRESDEN ZWINGER, FIGURE-GROUND PLAN

Observations on the Declaration of Rights

The first three articles comprehend in general terms the whole of a Declaration of Rights; all the succeeding articles either originate from them or follow as elucidations. The 4th, 5th and 6th define more particularly what is only generally expressed in the 1st, 2nd, and 3rd.

The 7th, 8th, 9th, 10th and 11th articles are declaratory of principles upon which laws shall be constructed, conformable to rights already declared.

But it is questioned by some very good people in France, as well as in other countries, whether the 10th article sufficiently guarantees the right it is intended to accord with; besides which it takes off from the divine dignity of religion, and weakens its operative force upon the mind, to make it a subject of human laws. It then presents itself to man like light intercepted by a cloudy medium, in which the source of it is obscured from his sight, and he sees nothing to reverence in the dusky ray.*

*There is a single idea, which, if it strikes rightly upon the mind, either in a legal or a religious sense, will prevent any man, or any body of men, or any Government, from going wrong on the subject of Religion; which is, that before any human institution of Government was known in the world, there existed, if I may so express it, compact between God and Man, from the beginning of time; and that as the relation and condition which man in his individual person stands in towards his Maker, cannot be changed, or any-ways altered by any human laws or human authority, that religious devotion, which is a part of this compact, cannot so much as be made a subject of human laws; and that all laws must conform themselves to this prior existing compact, and not assume to make the compact conform to the laws, which, besides being human, are subsequent thereto. The first act of man, when he looked around and saw himself a creature which he did not make, and a world furnished for his reception, must have been devotion, and devotion must ever continue sacred to every individual man, as it appears right to him; and Governments do mischief by interfering.

The remaining articles, beginning with the twelfth, are substantially contained in the principles of the preceding articles; but in the particular situation which France then was, having to undo what was wrong, as well as to set up what was right, it was proper to be more particular than what in another condition of things would be necessary.

While the Declaration of Rights was before the National Assembly some of its members remarked that if a Declaration of Rights was published it should be accompanied by a declaration of duties. The observation discov-

VIENNA, HOFBURG, FIGURE-GROUND PLAN

ered a mind that reflected, and it only erred by not reflecting far enough. A Declaration of Rights is, by reciprocity, a declaration of duties also.

Whatever is my right as a man is also the right of another; and it becomes my duty to guarantee as well as to possess.

The first three articles are the basis of Liberty, as well individual as national; nor can any country be called free whose Government does not take its beginning from the principles they contain, and continue to preserve them pure; and the whole of the Declaration of Rights is of more value to the world, and will do more good, than all the laws and statutes that have yet been promulgated.

In the declaratory exordium which prefaces the Declaration of Rights we see the solemn and majestic spectacle of a Nation opening its commission, under the auspices of its Creator, to establish a Government, a scene so new, and so transcendently unequalled by anything in the European world, that the name of a Revolution is diminutive of its character, and it rises into a Regeneration of man. What are the present Governments of Europe but a scene of iniquity and oppression? What is that of England? Do not is own inhabitants say it is a market where every man has his price, and where corruption is common traffic at the expense of a deluded people? No wonder, then, that the French Revolution is traduced. Had it confined itself merely to the destruction of flagrant despotism perhaps Mr. Burke and some others had been silent. Their cry now is, "It has gone too far:-that is, it has gone too far for them. It stares corruption in the face, and the venal tribe are all alarmed. Their fear discovers itself in their outrage, and they are but publishing the groans of a wounded vice. But from such opposition the French Revolution, instead of suffering, receives an homage. The more it is struck the more sparks it will emit; and the fear is it will not be struck enough. It has nothing to dread from attacks: Truth has given it an establishment, and Time will record it with a name as lasting as his own.

Having now traced the progress of the French Revolution through most of its principal stages, from its commencement to the taking of the Bastille, and its establishment by the Declaration of Rights, I will close the subject with the energetic apostrophe of M. de la Fayette - May this great monument, raised to liberty, serve as a lesson to the oppressor, and an example to the oppressed!**

**See page 18 of this work. N.B. - Since the taking of the Bastille, the occurrences have been published; but the matters recorded in this narrative are prior to that period; and some of them, as may be easily seen, can be but very little known.

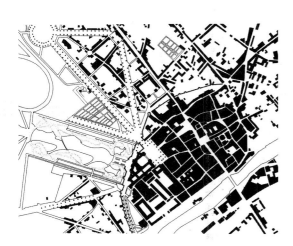

COMPIÈGNE, TOWN AND CHATEAU, FIGURE-GROUND PLAN

THE LIVES OF A CELL
by Lewis Thomas

We are told that the trouble with Modern Man is that he has been trying to detach himself from nature. He sits in the topmost tiers of polymer, glass, and steel, dangling his pulsing legs, surveying at a distance the writhing life of the planet. In this scenario, Man comes on as a stupendous lethal force, and the earth is pictured as something delicate, like rising bubbles at the surface of a country pond, or flights of fragile birds.

But it is illusion to think that there is anything fragile about the life of the earth; surely this is the toughest membrane imaginable in the universe, opaque to probability, impermeable to death. We are the delicate part, transient and vulnerable as cilia. Nor is it a new thing for man to invent an existence that he imagines to be above the rest of life; this has been his most consistent intellectual exertion down the millennia. As illusion, it has never worked out his satisfaction in the past, any more than it does today. Man is embedded in nature.

The biologic science of recent years has been making this a more urgent fact of life. The new, hard problem will be to cope with the dawning, intensifying realization of just how interlocked we are. The old, clung-to notions most of us have held about our special lordship are being deeply undermined.

Item. A good case can be made for our nonexistence as entities. We are not made up, as we had always supposed, of successively enriched packets of our own parts. We are shared, rented, occupied. At the interior of our cells, driving them, providing the oxidative energy that sends us out for the improvement of each shining day, are the mitochondria, and in a strict sense they are not ours. They turn out to be little separate creatures, the colonial posterity of migrant prokaryocytes, probably primitive bacteria that swam into ancestral precursors of our eukaryotic cells and stayed there. Ever since, they have maintained themselves and their ways, replicating in their own fashion, privately, with their own DNA and RNA quite different from ours. They are as much symbionts as the rhizobial bacteria in the roots of beans. Without them, we would not move a muscle, drum a finger, think a thought.

Mitochondria are stable and responsible lodgers, and I choose to trust them. But what of the other little animals, similarly established in my cells, sorting and balancing me, clustering me together? My centrioles, basal bodies, and probably a good many other more obscure tiny beings at work inside my cells, each with its own special genome, are as foreign, and as essential, as aphids in anthills. My cells are no longer the pure line entities I was raised with; they are ecosystems more complex than Jamaica Bay.

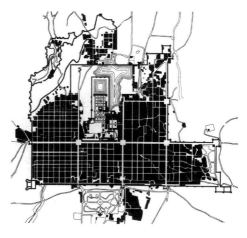

JAIPUR PALACE, FIGURE-GROUND PLAN

I like to think that they work in my interest, that each breath they draw for me, but perhaps it is they who walk through the local park in the early morning, sensing my senses, listening to my music, thinking my thoughts.

I am consoled, somewhat, by the thought that the green plants are in the same fix. They could not be plants, or green, without their chloroplasts, which run the photosynthetic enterprise and generate oxygen for the rest of us. As it turns out, chloroplasts are also separate creatures with their own genomes, speaking their own language.

We carry stores of DNA in our nuclei that my have come in, at one time or another, from the fusion of ancestral cells and the linking of ancestral organisms in symbiosis. Our genomes are catalogues of instructions from all kinds of sources in nature, filed for all kinds of contingencies. As for me, I am grateful differentiation and speciation, but I cannot feel as separate an entity as I did a few years ago, before I was told these things, nor, I should think, can anyone else.

Item. The uniformity of the earth's life, more astonishing than its diversity, is accountable by the high probability that we derived, originally, from some single cell, fertilized in a bolt of lightning as the earth cooled. It is from the progeny of this parent cell that we take our looks; we still share genes around, and the resemblance of the enzymes of grasses to those of whales is a family resemblance.

The viruses, instead of being single-minded agents of disease and death, now begin to look more like mobile genes. Evolution is still an infinitely long and tedious biologic game, with only the winners staying at the table, but the rules are beginning to look more flexible. We live in a dancing matrix of viruses; they dart, rather like bees, from organism to organism, from plant to insect to mammal to me and back again, and into the sea, tugging along pieces of this genome, strings of genes from that, transplanting grafts of DNA, passing around heredity as though at a great party. They may be a mechanism for keeping new, mutant kinds of DNA in the widest circulation among us. If this is true, the odd virus disease, on which we must focus so much of our attention in medicine, may be looked on as an accident, something dropped.

Item. I have been trying to think of the earth as a kind of organism, but it is no go. I cannot think of it this way. It is too big, too complex, with too many working parts lacking visible connections. The other night, driving through a hilly, wooded part of southern New England, I wondered about this. If not like an organism, what is it like, what is it most like? Then, satisfactorily for that moment, it came to me: it is most like a single cell.

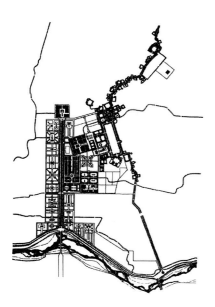

ISPHAHAN, PLAN

"Viewed from the distance of the moon, the astonishing thing about the earth, catching the breath, is that it is alive. The photographs show the dry, pounded surface of the moon in the foreground, dead as an old bone. Aloft, floating free beneath the moist, gleaming membrane of bright blue sky, is the rising earth, the only exuberant thing in this part of the cosmos. If you could look long enough, you would see the swirling of the great drifts of white cloud, covering and uncovering the half-hidden masses of land. If you had been looking for a very long, geologic time, you could have seen the continents themselves in motion, drifting apart on their crustal plates, held afloat by the fire beneath. It has the organized, self-contained look of a live creature, full of information, marvelously skilled in handling the sun."

Lewis Thomas
in *The Lives of a Cell*

JONATHAN HERDES

EARTH POPULATION IN ORBIT
SOME FACTS ABOUT OUR SITE

$S = 4\pi R^2$

EARTH'S SURFACE AREA = **200 MILLION** SQUARE MILES.
OF THIS, ABOUT **50 MILLION** SQUARE MILES ARE LAND.

THERE ARE NOW ABOUT **5 BILLION** PEOPLE ON EARTH.

WHICH ALLOWS **1.12 MILLION** SQUARE FEET PER PERSON
OR **25.9 ACRES PER PERSON** OF LAND
OR **100 ACRES PER PERSON** OF LAND AND SEA SURFACE

"We were like the men who had been fired off in rockets to take up life on another planet. ... We were now face to face with raw nature so grim and stark that our lives could be snuffed out in a matter of minutes... So in a physical sense we at the Pole were 18 men in a box. Only with the aid of our box could we survive, yet it bound us in... Men in a box; that was what we were."

Dr. Paul Siple, 90° South, 1959

"An age is called dark not because the light fails to shine, but because people refuse to see it. " C. W. Allen. Shown below, NASA photo of Earth taken from Apollo 17, December 1972.

APPENDIX

DYNAMICS

1. Bag of Tricks: A New Medium
   - a. Specifications
   - b. Details
   - c. Stairs
   - d. Utopia, a Footnote

2. Spectrum: beyond Graphics
   - a. Evolving Three-Dimensional Ideas
   - b. Design Development
   - c. Function
   - d. Between Dimensions: fractals
   - e. Computers and Architecture
   - f. Collage
   - g. Color
   - h. Music
   - i. Musical Scales
   - j. Modeling at all Scales

3. Visual Glossary

   Solid
   Volume
   Space

   A. Chronogeometry of Solid Animation
   B. Chronogeometry of Volume Development
   C. Chronogeometry of Composing Space in Time

   0. Prelude
   1. Melody
   2. Harmony
   3. Concerto
   4. Symphony

THE BAG OF TRICKS: A NEW MEDIUM

Space is the medium of architecture. The material for this course in the architectural study of Dynamics is space. Space is the order of void and mass in time. Or to say it another way: space is the order of gravity (mass) and light (all radiation, all void) in time. Each *étude* demands the designer to order volumes. Volumes cannot be perceived as only void-- they require mass to make them manifest. But **the mass must be minimal**-- located only where force is concentrated, either through its point of contact (vector transfer free body diagram) or through interaction with local mass (stress and strain, load distribution, moment diagram). If the ratio of mass to void exceeds a certain threshold, then the solid will appear to be filled, opaque-- "solid". But when a solid is mostly void, we may read it as a volume. A fabric of volumes creates architectural space.

We cannot model space directly. We can't cut and paste pieces of space-- or pieces of void, for that matter. We can only cut and paste pieces of mass. So a medium for modeling architecture requires some refinement.

We seek to find a means to bring time into our architectonic research. One obvious maneuver is to set all geometric elements in motion. Rounding the corners of squares into circles and cubes into spheres will "get the ball rolling." Where energy and force vary, either in space (as in the hills and valleys of a landscape) or in time (as in the waves and troughs of a seascape), wheels become clocks and clocks become wheels. A moving wheel develops torque, while a still wheel is unstable. So a moving bicycle stays upright more easily than a still one. To sustain volume, motion must become equilibrium . Perhaps we may yet see an architecture of pure motion resolved into spacetime. But for now we must model motion and stasis to investigate the structure and organization of habitable volume.

The **Kit of Parts** used in Architectonics presumed no particular material, weight, or strength. But to understand how to make space as a fabric of volumes, where geometric distortion of materials in force fields contributes to the architectural order created, we need a new modeling medium. The new set of elements for an architectural study of Dynamics is called the **Bag of Tricks**, where the emphasis is on modeling habitable volumes with deformable elements. Now glue is replaced by mechanical connections and the weight and stiffness of each structural member is important to the overall design. Elements can now model forces, properties of materials, and the foam-like nature of mass-void perforations. In Architectonics, careful joining of two cubes with rubber cement could minimize the joint lines and unify them into one perceptual mass. Now void must be both glue and lubrication between volumes. How to make volumes and masses read as unities with the relatively smaller and disparate pieces of the **Bag of Tricks** is a much more difficult (but possible) challenge.

Two basic assumptions made for Architectonics investigations are no longer maintained in the architectural study of Dynamics. They are:

1. All geometric elements in the Kit of Parts are made from ideal "pure stuff" whose mass is negligible. The weight of one piece sitting on top of another is not sufficient, compared to strength of the wood or paper the part is made of, to distort or deflect the shape of the overall composition in any noticeable, significant way.

But *different materials respond to forces in unique ways. For example, a 1" cube of alabaster (white marble) sitting on a 1" white urethane foam will partially crush the foam cube. All structures carry the loads of at least their own weight, and deflect accordingly. Structures depend on the geometry of their shapes and dynamic properties of their materials.*

2. All connections between elements can be adequately made through the use of the "ideal "glue" of rubber cement. Pieces which can be stuck together will hold their relative positions without any further elaboration of their connection joint.

But *forces developed by gravity and other loads create such large stresses in buildings that substantial mechanical joints like nuts and bolts and rivets, or strong chemical bonds like welding or mortar are necessary to assure secure joints and structural stability.*

The **Bag of Tricks** models forces on mass and void to study the structure of space, and to discover how the interaction of line, plane, and volume create the material of space. Elements have been selected to create as broad a range of forces and motions as possible. Composite materials, common in wood frame, stressed skin, masonry and concrete construction, may also be modelled as beams, slabs, walls, etc. Tensegrity-- an equilibrium of tension and compression forces resolved within a structure-- is relevant to these studies. The basic tools are ruler and clock. From these we can derive weighing scales, strain gauges, thermometers, and all other measures of interactions of matter and fields.

Studio time is still reserved for architectural composition, not technical preparation. The challenge is not easy: to make space (plastic volumetric relationships) out of these flimsy sinews, skins, and bones. The variety of perforations make a wide range of spacial and lighting transparencies and opacities possible. Although this new set is not an exact replica of common configurations of steel, concrete, and wood, it has the virtue of isolating and clarifying basic structural issues like connection, material, and assembly sequence, while exploring architectural issues like light and movement in the design of human-scaled habitable space.

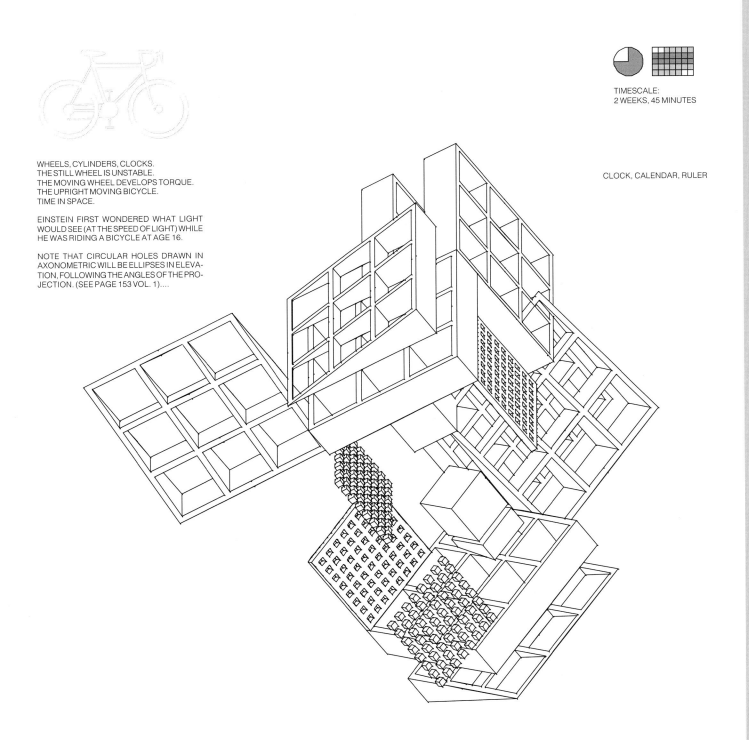

WHEELS, CYLINDERS, CLOCKS.
THE STILL WHEEL IS UNSTABLE.
THE MOVING WHEEL DEVELOPS TORQUE.
THE UPRIGHT MOVING BICYCLE.
TIME IN SPACE.

EINSTEIN FIRST WONDERED WHAT LIGHT
WOULD SEE (AT THE SPEED OF LIGHT) WHILE
HE WAS RIDING A BICYCLE AT AGE 16.

NOTE THAT CIRCULAR HOLES DRAWN IN
AXONOMETRIC WILL BE ELLIPSES IN ELEVA-
TION, FOLLOWING THE ANGLES OF THE PRO-
JECTION. (SEE PAGE 153 VOL. 1)....

TIMESCALE:
2 WEEKS, 45 MINUTES

CLOCK, CALENDAR, RULER

SPECIFICATIONS

Specifications are instructions an architect supplies to the builder that make explicit all construction requirements not completely identified in the working drawings. They may include standards of quality, details of assembly, schedule requirements, conditions of sources, site, and workers. Specifications apply to details as well as larger assemblies. Zoning laws and building codes are a form of specifications for cities.

BAG OF TRICKS: SPECIFICATIONS

The diagrams on the facing page indicate four 8" squares of each planar material. Get more than 24" square of each to allow for cuts (tret).

A. Plane
basic (9-square) 8 x 8, 8 x 4, and 4 x 4 inches.
fine (3-Square): 8 x 2, 8 x 1, 4 x 2, and 4 x 1 inches.
1. elastic "masonite" pegboard slab 1/8" thick, holes at 1" o.c. Paint white.
2. plastic white plastic needlepoint mesh , 1/16" thick, 1/16" holes @ 1/8" o.c.
3. brittle white plastic diffuser eggcrateframe,about3/8" deep, 1/2"openings

B. Line
1. elastic rubber bands (may be cut, or knotted together to extend length)
2. plastic 12-ABS rods(1/8" outside dia.) in 12,8,6,4 and 2" lengths,as shown
   1- 24" length of string or key chain (may be cut into smaller lengths)
3. brittle 12 brass tubes(1/8" outside dia.); 2,4,6,8 and 12" lengths,as shown

C. Point
see pages 444-445 on JOINTS

D. Mass Three Friends
all of same material and volume, thus all of equal mass:
1. block: 1.00" solid cube = 1 cubic inch
2. wedge: 2.04" tetrahedron = 1 cubic inch
3. ball : 1.24" dia. sphere = 1 cubic inch

E. Stair see pages 446-449 for details
Total length may be cut and recombined as needed. Paint white.
1. straight:
   45 degree folded plate: 1" wide,1/8" thick plate, 3/8" risers and treads.
2. spiral:
   2" diameter, 12 steps in 3/4 circle per 4" rise, last quadrant to be1"square landing, 3/8" risers and treads, white. made to fit over 1/8" outside dia. brass tubes. only in full floor intervals (8')...

F. Footing
one 12" square of Novamat, as non-skid foundation,Novamat, about $2, from Nova Scientific, Beverley MA, or from Home Depot as Grip-Hold or equal.

RULES

1. **Use no glue!**
   Connections are made with rubber *bands* rather than rubber *cement*. All joints to be mechanical, neat and capable of disassembly.
2. **No cutting!** Use elements only in available dimensions!
   No extra holes in the middle of any pieces! Do not violate the integrity of each element. (No new cuts or holes beyond what is already there.)
3. **"Less is more." "How much does it weigh?"**
   No limit to number of elements used, but the fewer the better. Use only given elements, in given dimensions. When not specified in an exercise, assume that the kind and amount of each element is limited by the rule: "Economy of means."
4. **Develop prototypes!**
   Solve conditions as prototypical wherever possible. Thus a horizontal plane to vertical plane connection might become standard, and be the source for both continuous edge and corner joints.

NOTES

1. Cut parts so edges are smooth, not serrated. Cut plane elements between openings, not across them.
2. All dimensions are nominal. Eggcrate elements will be slightly larger than nominal dimensions, since perforations are 1/2", but walls have thickness. Thus a 2-square eggcrate with 1" nominal width may actually be 1-3/16" wide. Note that eggcrate walls are thick on one surface and thin on other, making 1/2" openings slightly wedged, making a good friction connection for xyz joints. Keep pegboard holes 1/2" from edge.
3. All elements either come as white or to be painted white.
4. Three Friends may be wood, plaster, or sand-filled. Sphere may be ping-pong ball, filled and sealed, golf ball, or? The 3" cube, cylinder halves, and pyramid from the Kit of Parts may be added to the Bag of Tricks.
5. Floors: Slab (pegboard) is considered "rigid" and may be used alone as floor. Neither mesh nor eggcrate alone can be used as floor (Mesh is too floppy, and a foot could fall through the eggcrate). However, mesh over eggcrate is permissible as flooring. Also, when mesh is warped to stable form, it may be used as (unlevel) flooring.
6. Optional additions: (a) 3 medium springs; (b) 5/16" o.d. (7/32"i.d.) necklace clasps; (c) 3/4" long screw eyes (self-tap inside 1/8" tubing for pin joints); (d) small turnbuckles; (e) small gasket O-rings (1/8" to 3/4" i.d.)
7. Tools: Use Architectonics tools, especially X-acto razor saw and mitre box. Add length of wire to pull rubber bands through tubes, and crotchet (afghan) needles for moving elastic through masonite.
8. Exceptions:
   a. only string, plastic tubing, and stairs may be cut.
   b. glue may only be used for recombining stair lengths
   c. only ABS, brass tubes, and rubber bands may be left non-white.

LINEAR ELEMENTS: CROSS SECTIONS

all cross-sections shown actual size

ABS PLASTIC ROD

1   ST-8 (1/4" x 1/4" x 15" 1/4")

1   ST-6 (3/16" x 3/16" x 15 1/4")

10 ST-4 (1/8" x 1/8" x 15 1/4")

BRASS TUBING

12   1/8" diameter x 12" hollow

3   3/32" diameter x 12" solid

2   3/64" diameter x 12" wire

BETWEEN DIMENSIONS

NOVAMAT
NON-SKID SURFACE

GRIP-HOLD. OR
ANOTHER BRAND

PLANAR ELEMENTS

Cut pegboard, grid, and mesh to following sizes:

| 4 - 1" x 4" | 2 - 2" x 4" | 1 - 2" x 8" |
| | | 2 - 1" x 8" |

| 4 - 4" x 4" | 2 - 4" x 8" | 1 - 8" x 8" |

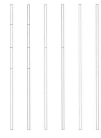

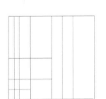
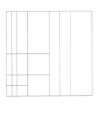

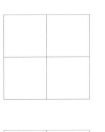

DETAILS

JOINTS are "zero dimensional" intersections of linear and planar elements. Actual joints are of course three-dimensional, but it is often useful in structural design to think of joint connectors as points. Any volume intersection is also a joint. Joints for the Bag of Tricks come in two major types: pin connectors like ready-made **O**-rings or rubber bands (shown here in isometric view), and moment connectors, which must be fabricated. (These notes and drawings have been prepared with the help of Prof. Russell Jordan, AIA.)

Making XYZ Joints

Moment connectors that hold structural members along 3 mutually perpendicular axes under load are herein called "XYZ joints." Three different sizes of XYZ joints and their connectors can be made from ABS plastic and brass in the following dimensions:

ABS plastic:

You have used 12' of the original $15\frac{1}{4}$" length of each of these to make the needed rods for the Bag of Tricks. (See previous page). Now use the remaining $3\frac{1}{4}$" of each of these to manufacture your XYZ joints.

> $\frac{1}{4}$" x $\frac{1}{4}$" ABS hollow square tube with $\frac{1}{8}$" x $\frac{1}{8}$" square center hole
> $\frac{3}{16}$" x $\frac{3}{16}$" ABS hollow square tube with $\frac{3}{32}$" diameter center hole
> $\frac{1}{8}$" x $\frac{1}{8}$" ABS hollow square tube with $\frac{3}{64}$" diameter center hole.

Brass:

1 $\frac{1}{8}$" diameter hollow brass tube as indicated in the Bag of Tricks.
2 $\frac{3}{64}$" diameter x 12" long solid brass wires.
   They will slip snugly into the $\frac{1}{8}$" x $\frac{1}{8}$" ABS plastic tubes.
3 $\frac{3}{32}$" dia. x 12" long solid brass rods, cut into (24) $1\frac{1}{2}$" lengths. These should slip snugly into the $\frac{1}{8}$" diameter brass tubes and into the $\frac{3}{16}$" x $\frac{3}{16}$" ABS plastic tubes, allowing no "wobble".

Tools needed include an X-acto mitre box with fine bladed X-acto back saw and an X-acto knife with plenty of #11 or # 24 blades. A piece of glass about 8" square makes an excellent work surface, since the cement will not bond to it and it provides a true flat surface for squaring up the joints. A small 6" metal straightedge graduated in 64ths of an inch is also very helpful. *Do not use plastic triangles or scales*, as you will ruin them and quite possibly glue them to the joints.

Cutting and Assembly

Refer to the diagrams on the facing page. Visualizing the position of all the parts while making right and left-handed pairs of joints can be confusing. Working assembly line fashion has several advantages. It allows the cement to set as you work on each unit sequentially, and it allows you to visualize the opposing geometries more easily, which is useful in using the joints in the design studies. The steps below apply to making both the mini-joints and mid-joints. Make *at least* one set of each, for a total of eight joints. The following techniques are suggested:

1. First cut ALL the pieces needed for all four joints. Remove all burrs and shavings left by the saw with your X-acto knife. This is important: if loose shavings wedge in the cement weld the joint will not be square or strong. Fit all pieces using a sample piece of the eggcrate grid. Notice that the grid openings are slightly wider on one face than on the other. A perfectly cut piece will slip easily into the grid and wedge there, so that you cannot push it all the way through. (A possible maxi-joint requiring a double opening of the eggcrate must also allow for the thickness of the intervening grid walls.)
2. Assemble X and Y axis arms for both right-handed joints as shown in the drawing. Set them on your work surface in the same orientation.
3. Assemble the X and Y axis arms for both left-handed joints and set them down in exact opposition to the right handed joints on the work surface. See diagram #1.
4. Now add the Z axis arms to all four assemblies. See diagram #2.
5. Add reinforcing blocks in the orientations indicated in the drawings.

Solvent Welding

ABS plastic is easily welded together with liquid plastic model cement. Do not get tube-type plastic cement, as it will make a huge mess out of your pieces. Liquid cement is made by several manufacturers such as Testors, Pactra, and Microweld, which seems to be the neatest to use. Simply wet both surfaces to be joined and wait 15-30 seconds. The cement will appear to dry on the surface but it is really softening the plastic below the surface. Now re-apply cement to both surfaces and press together immediately. Hold for 10 seconds, then allow to dry for several hours. The pieces will appear to be fully joined after the initial 10 seconds, but the weld is not yet fully cured and can break under force. You may however continue to cement additional pieces to the first two during this curing period. Use the cement sparingly and in a WELL VENTILATED AREA. This stuff is flammable and toxic-- do use near heat or flame, do not inhale, do not smoke. Neatness will come with practice, but as a word of caution, never handle and wet-cement surfaces or you will leave permanent fingerprints on the plastic.

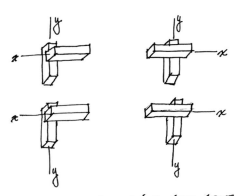

1 - ASSEMBLING X + Y AXIS ARMS

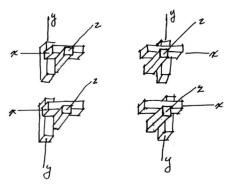

2 - ADDING Z AXIS ARM TO
X + Y AXIS ARM ASSEMBLY

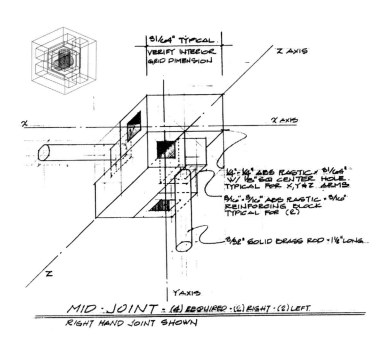

81/64" TYPICAL
VERIFY INTERIOR
GRID DIMENSION

Z AXIS

X AXIS

1/4"·1/4" ABS PLASTIC × 81/64"
W/ 1/8"SQ CENTER HOLE.
TYPICAL FOR X,Y&Z ARMS

3/16"·3/16" ABS PLASTIC · 3/16"
REINFORCING BLOCK
TYPICAL FOR (2)

3/32" SOLID BRASS ROD · 1 1/2" LONG

Y AXIS

MID · JOINT - (4) REQUIRED · (2) RIGHT · (2) LEFT
RIGHT HAND JOINT SHOWN

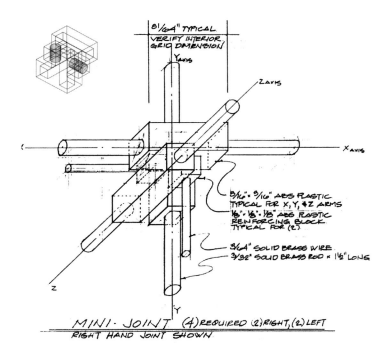

81/64" TYPICAL
VERIFY INTERIOR
GRID DIMENSION

Y AXIS

Z AXIS

X AXIS

3/16"× 3/16" ABS PLASTIC
TYPICAL FOR X, Y, & Z ARMS
1/8"·1/8"·1/8" ABS PLASTIC
REINFORCING BLOCK
TYPICAL FOR (2)

3/64" SOLID BRASS WIRE
3/32" SOLID BRASS ROD × 1 1/2" LONG

Z

Y

MINI · JOINT (4) REQUIRED (2) RIGHT, (2) LEFT
RIGHT HAND JOINT SHOWN

STAIRS

In Dynamics, stairs are volumes for human movement, corridors of passage with both vertical and horizontal extension. The structure is part of the volume, unlike stairs in Architectonics, where supporting mass was assumed to sustain the treads. Now only the tread shell is built, without the mass below. A straight stair creates an inclined block, and a spiral stair creates a cylinder of volume in space. Both are at your disposal in the Bag of Tricks. Actual stairs like these are built in materials ranging from wood and metal to reinforced concrete.

Straight stair

To build a straight stair at 1/2" = 1'- 0" scale, make riser tread pairs from stock x 1" wide by 3/32" x 3/8" trimmed to 1/3" x 1/9". Assemble 6 riser/tread pairs into one 45 degree folded plate half stair, 12 into one full stair. First make **three** flights and landings. Use them to make straight or stacked runs. Later add scissor stairs and double landings. Runs maybe cut and recombined as needed.

Spiral stair: Develop only in full-floor intervals.

To draw a spiral stair in plan and section/elevation:
1. Draw a circle of required diameter. Divide it into 12 or 16 sectors. Use only three-quarters of the circle for plotting treads, reserving the last quadrant for a landing at each level. Normally you can't make more than one full (3/4) turn per level, or there will not be proper headroom.
2. Calculate the riser to run ratio by dividing the total elevation by one more than the number of tread intervals you use.
3. Project central column support and vertical riser intervals up in elevation.
4. Count around the circular plan and up across the elevation grid to match location of riser to tread. Note that this pattern develops a sine curve in elevation. Then... connect the dots!
5. Locate vertical height for railing above each tread in the projection, and connect the dots to make it continuous.

To draw a spiral stair in axonometric projection:
proceed exactly as above. In addition, be sure to draw all edges of each tread, and carry the arc of each tread's circular perimeter up to it.

*How to **build** a spiral stair is almost the same as drawing it!*
To build a spiral stair at 1/2" = 1'-0" scale, draw a 2" diameter plan circle. Divide three quadrants into 9 or 12 sectors for treads. Draw a 1/4" circle around the central column to locate spacers between treads. Draw tangents to the 1/4" circle from the end points of one tread's arc to generate a cutting template for the treads. Drill 1/8" holes for the brass central column shaft. Measure the thickness of the tread, and subtract it from the riser height to find the height to cut support spacers. Glue spacer and tread together. Stack the set onto the brass rod to complete the stair. Glue them into proper rotation, or leave treads loose for mirror runs.

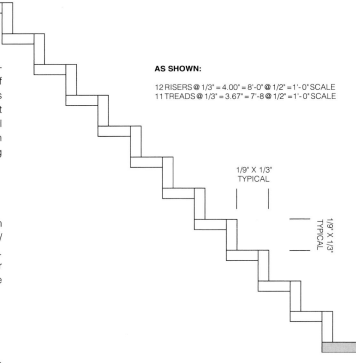

AS SHOWN:

12 RISERS @ 1/3" = 4.00" = 8'-0" @ 1/2" = 1'- 0" SCALE
11 TREADS @ 1/3" = 3.67" = 7'-8 @ 1/2" = 1'- 0" SCALE

1/9" X 1/3"
TYPICAL

1/9" X 1/3"
TYPICAL

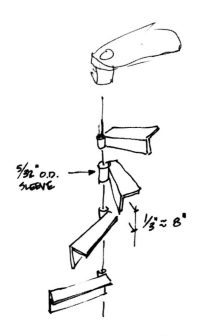

5/32" O.D.
SLEEVE

1/3" ≈ 8"

SPIRAL STAIR

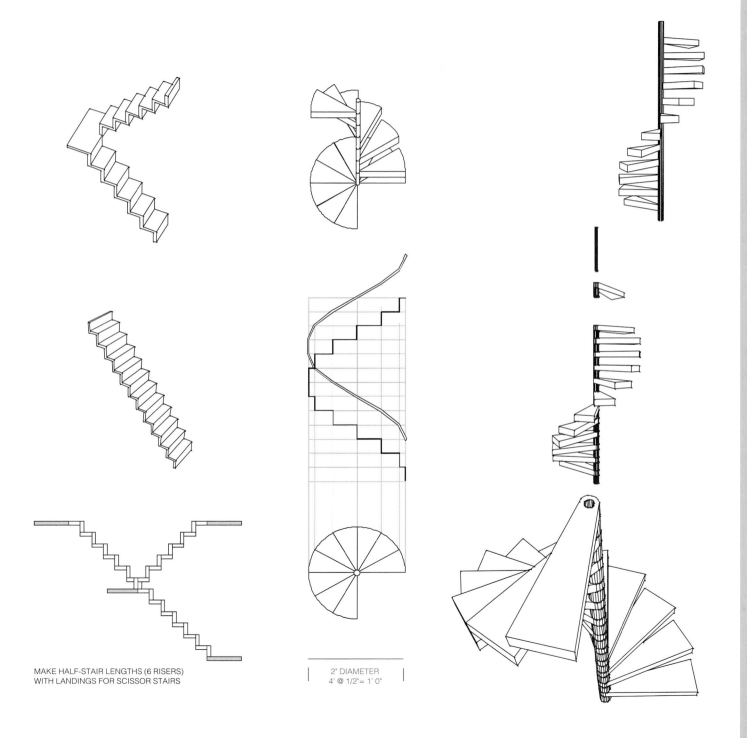

MAKE HALF-STAIR LENGTHS (6 RISERS)
WITH LANDINGS FOR SCISSOR STAIRS

2" DIAMETER
4' @ 1/2"= 1' 0"

UTOPIA, A FOOTNOTE

The Kit of Parts permits direct modeling of architectonic issues by additive arrangement of masses in void. Dynamics seeks to model the energy inter-action between elements. To see void in mass, modeling must be indirect. To give primary reading to light and space before matter, the Bag of Tricks is a collection of perforated and deformable elements. These reveal an essential topology of the interactive duality of our world, like lights at night and shadows in the day. Who has not felt that a frame house under construction is more spacious before its sheet rock is installed? Isn't this why Frank Gehry re-moved walls in his frame house? Isn't this what Le Corbusier sought in the free plan, and what Frank Lloyd Wright sought in "exploding the box?" In architec-ture such honeycombs are often sheathed-- plywood over joists and stud walls, I beams boxed in, lath and plaster fabric over brick and mortar fabric, the hollows in cinder blocks, hung ceilings below open web joists. To empha-size a plasticity of light and volume rather than of mass, the Bag of Tricks makes sheathing additive, rather than subtractive. Openings for windows, doors, and stairwells must be consciously eliminated from this kit of roughly non-opaque elements.

The Bag of Trick is an ad hoc arrangement at best. Our intention is to make this a readily available standard kit of off-the-shelf items. But some-times life changes faster than good intentions. When this work was first conceived, the cost and availability of stock in local building supply, hardware, hobby, and craft stores partially determined the composition of the Bag of Tricks. This required some compromise-- the continuum of rigid to flexible is not equally or smoothly represented in linear and planar elements. The color of materials plays a subtle factor in volumetric com-position-- ideally all materials would be monochrome, and of a uniform modulus of elasticity, so the thickness and amount of perforation of a material could reveal structural loads and deflections. The Bag of Tricks seems to favor orthogonal structures. To encourage other geometries, it would be good to develop angled joint hubs of uniform diameter to connect existing rods and tubes into tetrahedrons, cuboctahedrons, dodecahedrons, space frames, geodesic domes, zomes, and so on. Such a palette of available structures is suggested in Googolplex and other building toys, but these are relatively expensive and inaccessible.

You can introduce warped surfaces into your Bag of Tricks models in two simple and both rather crude ways. You can twist or pull corners of the needlepoint mesh in different directions until it warps into hyperbolic paraboloid (hypar) curves. You also may be able to melt eggcrate over a mold (using the vaults and half cylinders of your Kit of Parts if they are made of wood) in an oven. Be careful not to burn the plastic or wood. Ideally, a material that at model scale would be a slightly elastic thin sheet could enable modeling of tent and inflatable structures, as well as other deformable surfaces with curvature in more than two dimensions.

A further note. When these studies first were tried, all acrylic and polysty-rene eggcrate light diffuser available in Home Depot and similar stores came with a nominal one-half inch opening between plastic ribs. In fact, they were actually tapered on one side to slightly less than that, to about 31/64" in each dimension. This assured a snug friction fit for the XYZ joints and made 3D modeling of the Bag of Tricks especially elegant. Unfortu-nately, this eggcrate has now become very hard to find. Now the nominal one-half inch opening is the smaller dimension. The opening on the larger side has increased by about 1/64th inch in each direction, which means that the XYZ joints slide through too easily. No doubt the change reflects a more efficient design-- the same span with larger holes means less material and more profit for the manufacturer. We have been able to locate the manufacturer for the original mold, who is sadly out of business. We hope to find or rebuild the original mold and recast this material to our own specifica-tions. That will also allow us to produce eggcrate of varying depth, i.e.. 1/16", 1/8", 1/4" etc. to provide a variety of deflection resistances.

With such an improved Bag of Tricks, it would then be fruitful to evaluate all designs for structural and spacial efficiency by simply weighing them. The lightest would also be the one that uses the least material.

So...

We make do with what we can. We discover new ways of using the same old materials and given elements or we rediscover/recycle old methods to solve new problems (which may come to the same thing). As soon as we accept that "there is nothing new under the sun", we may be fortunate to discover the world anew at every turn. At least the Bag of Tricks is a limited palette, which is actually an advantage. After all, in basketball, the cleverest fall-away jumper from the bleachers is still out of bounds.

Donato Bramante built an unusual spiral staircase for the Belvedere in the Vatican. (Leonardo da Vinci had sketched the idea, and someone, per-haps Leonardo, built it for the King of France at Chambord.) This is the double or alpha helix, the form of our genetic DNA. It has the unique feature of coiling two completely separate but entirely nesting spirals around each other. Thus in the Belvedere stair, two flights start and stop on each floor, permitting completely independent circulation for up/down, public/private, or servant/served users. Four hundred years later, architect Jose Oubrerie found a new use for this form apparently awaiting his inspired revisit. For his French Consulate in Damascus, he needed to provide a visible and important public stair through the main lobby to the upper administrative offices. At the same time local codes demanded a completely enclosed fire stair. He made a brilliant synthesis by uniting both into an alpha-helix double spiral stair, with the open flight immediately above and below the closed fire stair.

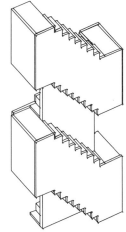

AN INTERESTING VARIANT:
OUBRERIE'S DAMASCUS STAIR
A STRAIGHT SPIRAL DOUBLE HELIX
OPEN PUBLIC AND FIRE STAIR TOGETHER.

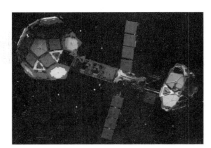

GOOGOLPLEX ™, A MODERN BUILDING TOY

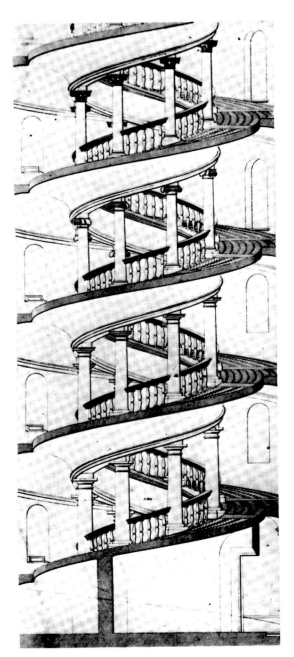

LETAROUILLY'S CUT-AWAY VIEW OF THE SPIRAL STAIRCASE
AT THE BELVEDERE, ROME. NOTE THAT IT IS AN ALPHA-HELIX.

EVOLVING THREE-DIMENSIONAL IDEAS

The human brain normally depends on the eyes for 80% of its sensory input. Recent studies suggest that the brain sweeps the outlying surface of the cerebral cortex thousands of times a second, feeding the record back into the intralaminar nucleus and thalamus for integration. We count on the continuity of this input to transform the sequential perspective images our eyes transmit to the optic lobes into their underlying spacial reality. Perhaps for those with autism or other pervasive development disorders, these inputs seem to be infrequent or discontinuous, as if a moviegoer sees only one of the 24 frames projected each second. In such fragmented perception, spacial information may become a distracting static noise, rather than a smooth flow of changing but related views. For an architect, continuity of vision depends on the continuity of space, which in turn depends on the consistency of plastic ideas (from all angles!) Reality cannot be simulated. Fractally infinite in all dimensions, reality can only be selectively modelled. Building a model does not provide a roof over the head any more than a recipe nourishes a hungry body. However, modeling in both two and three dimensions is still the best way to master composing architectural space.

Working Models and Working Drawings

Copy machines can record our design sketches on paper. But how can we copy a model before changing it? We may photograph and sketch the models we build, but this method of recording often takes as much if not more time than the creation of the original. How can we have the courage to contemplate changes if we can't be confident to be able to return to what we already have? Cinema, holography, and now computer-aided design (CAD) are the current technical means for this. Until 3D xerography is common (or its digital enhancement, a 3D scanner-printer for recording and modifying spacial ideas), we must find other ways to foster the evolution of three-dimensional ideas.

Models are direct renderings of an idea in as many dimensions as required. We need to add time to permit change to volume, so any evolving spacial model is at least four-dimensional. A working model is the set of plan/sections evolving in space. A working model is not a finished model. Changes are not only permitted but also visible: tears, rips, cuts, folds and notes made with pencil, pen, scissors, tape, and glue are all welcomed and vital to map the evolution of thinking in 3D. Working models can test structure, study *parti* alterations, and explore refinements of plastic expression. As in *Return of the Phoenix*, architectural space is often best modeled in at least three interacting stages: 1. **solid block models**, establishing *parti* arrangements of scaled program elements. 2. **planar paper models** defining enclosure, lighting, and circulation, solving volumetric intersections, investigating economy of means. 3. **available material models** (like the Bag of Tricks), incorporating details of grids, joints, etc.

For architects, drawing at work (rather than just posing for pretty pictures) means modeling on paper, in compressed dimensions. To keep an idea alive in the brain-- draw it honestly and continuously, as if completely seen and understood, even when it isn't. Nothing replaces the napkin sketch for speed of notation during rapid inspiration. Pen and ink or pencil and paper are still (always) the best!! Diagrams can be a shorthand for noting essentials. Quick diagrams using graphic or color codes can denote opacity, translucency, and/or various materials. Learning from Cubism, we may use simultaneous and multiple views. Thumbnail sketches in plan, section, and axonometric, and evocative "twisted" perspectives can be diagrammatic; reducing detail often reveals larger issues. Plans and sections provide excellent "x-ray vision" views slicing through space. Plan and section drawings are especially useful in revealing relationships between structure, circulation, and light. Refine ideas through plan/section studies, both sketches and hard-line, as well as freehand to-scale.

Drawing/Modeling Dialog

Increasing complexity in the Architectonics sequence made it increasingly hard to change the model. In Dynamics, only mechanical connections are permitted, so it gets even harder to make quick alterations to any structure or volume configuration. Tracing paper can be the "poor man's computer." Using graph paper if needed, freehand sketch plans/sections to scale, show wall thickness, etc. On a new tracing paper overlay, trace areas of study, shifting the page to examine new plan or section locations for *parti* and/or detail revisions. A **quick axonometric method** enables you to study the implications of three-dimensional ideas through drawing. (See page 492 for more.) This can work independently, or as part of the **quick modeling method** shown opposite. Enter the loop anywhere, alter sequence as needed, repeating the process over and over. Any means of study which gives primacy to the three dimensional reality is relevant. Developing and evaluating spacial ideas works best through a **dialog** between drawing and modeling. (In fairness we should add Chris Chimera's observation that "you can make one hundred drawings in the time it takes to make one model.")

Too many designers mistakenly believe that model-making comes only after drawing plans, a demonstration of ideas already solved. We may just as easily understand that even a finished building is still a model for a Platonic prototype that may be further developed in the next commission. The works of many great architects may be seen in this light: Bernini's churches, Wright's Prairie Houses, Aalto's libraries. Living architecture maintains the freshness (and avoids the staleness) of time by cultivating invention and criticism equally. Every proposition may be built, and yet every building is temporary. Essential ideas are truly plastic, materially present, yet full of potential for development. For both body *and* mind, only evolution is immortal.

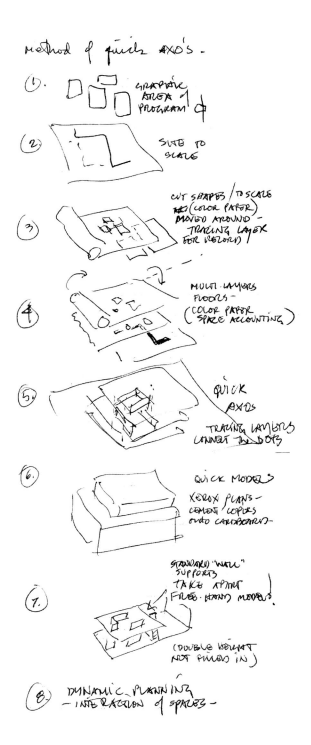

Method of quick AXO's.

(1). GRAPHIC AREA of PROGRAM

(2). SITE TO SCALE

(3). CUT SHAPES / TO SCALE (COLOR PAPER) MOVED AROUND - TRACING LAYER FOR RECORD)

(4). MULTI-LAYERS FLOORS - (COLOR PAPER SPACE ACCOUNTING)

(5). QUICK AXOS TRACING LAYERS CONNECT THE DOTS

(6). QUICK MODELS XEROX PLANS - CEMENT COPIES ONTO CARDBOARD -

(7). STANDARD "WALL" SUPPORTS TAKE APART FREE-HAND MODELS! (DOUBLE HEIGHT NOT FILLED IN)

(8). DYNAMIC PLANNING - INTERACTION of SPACES -

A **WORKING** MODEL!!!

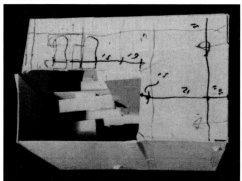

CHRISTINA HALVORSEN

A DESIGN DEVELOPMENT METHODOLOGY (TRICKS OF THE TRADE)

This method enables a designer to create space and modify the model as simply as possible without sacrificing the chance to affix three dimensional ideas with a fair degree of permanence. Document *parti* variations with sketches, photos, and direct on-the-glass xerocopies of models as plan or section. Keep records handy to consider the potential in each configuration. Dialog between volume defining mass and mass defining volume can be efficiently explored through a dialog between drawing and modeling:

1. Transfer program areas into graphic equivalents on colored or graph paper.
2. Develop plan and section of site to scale.
3. Using cut paper shapes, develop alternate partis *of program and record each on a tracing layer.*
4. Develop all plans using multi-layers of trace, cutting program areas and pasting as needed. On new tracing paper overlays, freehand sketch study areas, showing wall thickness, doors, etc. Then trace areas and reorder, shifting page for detail study and parti revisions.
5. Create "quick axonometrics" by shifting tracing paper layers of plans and then "connecting the dots." (See page 492 for more on the **quick axonometric method**.*)*
6. Xerocopy plans developed in step 4.
7. Create **quick** *take-apart freehand model, by rubber cementing xerocopied plans onto thin (1/16" maximum) cardboard. Cut standard height walls and columns from cardboard strips. Glue them to plans using white glue. Stack plan/wall model levels. Modify through direct cutting with scissors (to make double height volumes) and direct drawing with pen and pencil.*
8. Repeat the process to generate new studies and refine the scheme....

DESIGN DEVELOPMENT

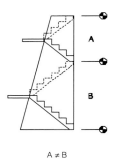

A ≠ B

Anthony Roccanova is an inventor of form and plastic craftsman of impeccable facility. He once designed a stair that had to reach two levels of different heights. As this was an important and highly visible exterior stair, he sought and found a plastic solution that maintained the same riser to tread proportion and angle of inclination while varying the total length of each flight. As shown here, he shaved one side of the central support to just the right degree. A wonderful invention and beautiful solution!

Christopher Chimera is both a practising architect and practising intellect of the highest order. He has extracted from his professional experience useful concepts that help the beginner and more advanced student clarify just exactly what the *action* of architecture is. Where Roccanova is often intuitive, relying on a highly developed painter's eye to find otherwise hidden possibilities of plastic relationships, Chimera attempts to be more explicit. To illustrate the sequence on the facing page, Chimera offers the following suggestions:

1. design from the general to the specific- large scale decisions to small scale decisions
2. generate alternatives with essentially different characteristics and evaluate
3. use simple fully understandable elements
4. place them in particular easily understood relationships
5. organize solid elements, some with voids within vs. voids between the solids.

Plastic and Elastic Thought

If plastic means that a capacity for change (deformation) is always present, then perhaps elastic means that forces may limit and fix the degree of change available. This can apply to plan, and even thought. We may see in the sequence on the facing page the development of plan relationships from a plastic to a more elastic interaction. In the beginning, anything is possible: all relationships are loose, amorphous, as yet unrefined in concept. By the last iteration elements become fixed in a convincing and "correct" (not necessarily the only correct) manner. This is perhaps what Chimera has meant by his use of the term "synthetic inevitability". Note how Chimera's contour (like a spring) becomes increasingly tensed as architectural concerns (program placement, orientation, access, light) are incorporated, until the whole ensemble of site and program becomes the plan equivalent of a vector equilibrium. It is interesting to note that in the hands of

a good form-maker, the more elastic the relationships between elements become, the more that plastic potential is revealed. Roccanova's stair is elegant in itself, it is even more elegant in its suggestion that there are many more solutions to stairs than we may have thought.

Proposition and Resolution

The repeated rearrangement of program volumes and the elaboration of mass and void to articulate desired plastic relationships is the phase of an architect's practise called **Design Development**. (See also pages 47 and 215 for more on Design Development.) In the study of Dynamics, major études are each presented in not one but two chapters. The first permits the exploration of an initial proposal-- a Proposition or Pro-position. The second permits reworking of the "loose ends" and conflicting arrangements revealed in the earlier studies towards a resolution of concerns-- a Re-solution. To study the implications of a design decision at all scales simultaneously, from smallest detail to largest overview, sketch books and models are indispensable. A book of sequential sketches and a series of sketch models make it easy to keep a record of the development of ideas. Design development often proceeds from gathering relevant data for operational modeling to scaling and ordering program space sizes according to proximity, use, lighting, etc. This is the time for program color diagrams, bubble spacial diagrams, etc. Then often a "wild stab" configuration gesture is the first attempt to organize all elements and issues into a form: the pro-position ("something from nothing"). Next is a time for investigating alternative locations for areas by use and according to the architectural implications of the *parti*, which may well lead to the creation of other *partis*. Evaluating the results leads to new possibilities, as form follows form ("something from something"). From the choices created, perhaps one path emerges as most promising. This is selected for detailing, overview, and feedback into the original concerns. The design is now becoming developed. Alternative partis and detail ideas are kept to compare results. Those that best solve the original and subsequent problems become the means to a re-solution, a Resolution.

Professor Chimera suggests that *parti* is not only a noun, but also a verb. To *parti* something implies that *parti* occurs at all scales. One finds the *parti* for the arrangement of rooms in a house, and then one finds the *parti* for the arrangement of fixtures in a bathroom, and there is yet a *parti* for the arrangement of handles and faucet on a sink, etc. This view implies that subsets of order may be rearranged as they emerge into focus. The possibility that a subset *parti* reveals conflicts in an earlier decision of course remains. Thus, the corner of a building and the corner of a city exhibit similar formal concerns. A critical moment in many an architect's office occurs when a window detail reveals a major conceptual error in the organization of the whole building or site.

GENERAL TO PARTICULAR: GENERATION AND EVALUATION OF ALTERNATIVES
by CHRISTOPHER CHIMERA

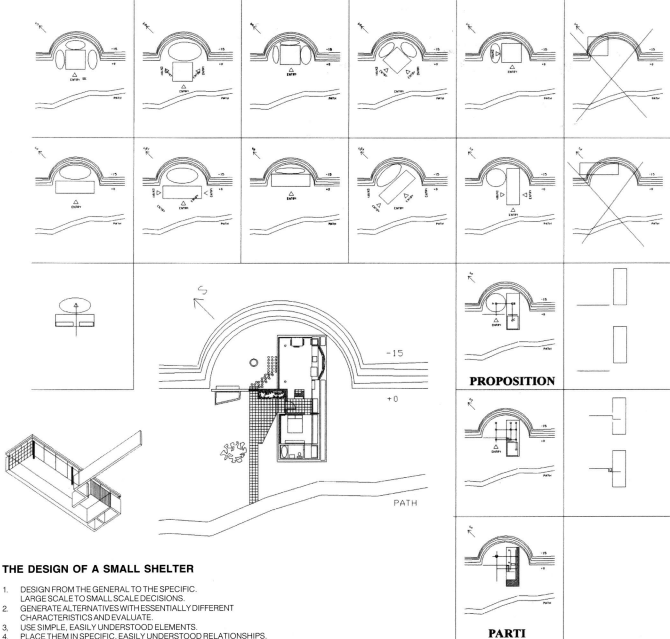

PROPOSITION

PARTI

THE DESIGN OF A SMALL SHELTER

1. DESIGN FROM THE GENERAL TO THE SPECIFIC.
   LARGE SCALE TO SMALL SCALE DECISIONS.
2. GENERATE ALTERNATIVES WITH ESSENTIALLY DIFFERENT
   CHARACTERISTICS AND EVALUATE.
3. USE SIMPLE, EASILY UNDERSTOOD ELEMENTS.
4. PLACE THEM IN SPECIFIC, EASILY UNDERSTOOD RELATIONSHIPS.
5. ORGANIZE SOLIDS AND SOLIDS W/ VOIDS WITHIN VS. VOIDS BETWEEN THE SOLIDS.

FUNCTION

To sharpen artistic vision a student must be able to distinguish the differ-ence between a power line's catenary, a teardrop's parabola, a sea shell's spiral, or the sine curve of an ocean wave or spiral stair. Not until a designer has courage to draw and build whatever shape a form de-mands will the palette be complete. What values must be plotted for a breast's curve, a child's arm, or hood of a car? Architectural space is a function of structure, vision, and human emotion. Structure is a function of the forces, material and geometry that make a space. FUNCTION is a term well known to modern architects. Louis Sullivan first formulated the phrase "Form follows Function". Architects usually take function to mean use, activity, or more generally, program. Function can also refer to structure, material, acoustics, mechanical systems, cost, lighting, or en-ergy considerations. Filling precise relationships between these elements has taken centuries and still occupies the minds of some of the best architects, mathematicians, engineers, and physicists.

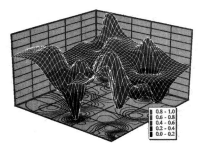

In a world of forces the difference between a curve and a straight line can be simply one of relationship or function. While we in the West use either straightedge or compass-and-protractor to delineate shape, traditional Japanese carpenters would generate the gentle curves of their house roofs by easing the tension in the ink-marking line (equivalent to our chalk line). For them a "straight line" was one extreme of a continuum of curves, and line was function of tension. A point in a plane can vary in two dimen-sions, in a volume it can very in three dimensions. When values in one dimen-sion depend on values in the other, one is a function of the other. A graph can plot the coordinates of such a relationship. Thus, $y = x$ is a straight line halfway between two perpendicular axes, while $y = x^2$ is a parabola. $Y = (f)x$ is a general way to indicate that Y is a function of x. Making a circle using a compass creates a locus of points equally distant from a center. René Descartes showed that a circle could also be described as the graphic plot of the function relationship $x^2 + y^2 = 1$. FUNCTION means a relationship of variables.

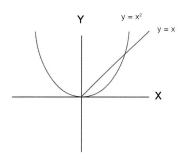

Y $y = x^2$ $y = x$ X

Cartesian coordinates

ρ   θ   initial ray

polar coordinates

FUNCTION PLOT EXERCISE

Each exercise concerns a particular mathematical function and gives two ways of graphically plotting it. The first is based on constructive geometry, while the second depends on analytic geometry, which plots the values of variables according to an algebraic formula. So for ex-ample, a circle may be drawn by a compass, describing all the points equidistant from its center. Or a circle may be plotted on graph paper according to the formula $x^2 + y^2 = 1$ in rectangular coordinates, or $\rho = \cos\theta$ in polar coordinates. In both cases the function should be drawn plot-ted on 8 squares to the inch 8 1/2 x 11" non-photo blue graph paper and the curve should be drawn in ink using rapidograph, compass (with appropriate technical pen attachment), straightedge, and other drawing tools. Be sure that all parts of the curve are smooth and tangent.

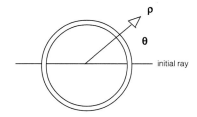

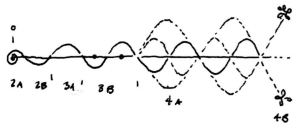

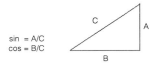

sin = A/C
cos = B/C

FUNCTION PLOT EXERCISES

SPACING

Plot the function $x^2 + y^2 = 1$ in rectangular (Cartesian) coordinates, on square-grid graph paper. Plot the function $x = \rho \cos \theta$, $y = \rho \sin \theta$, in polar coordinates, where $\rho = 1$, on polar graph paper. With a compass whose point is at the origin, draw a circle with radius 1 on both graphs.

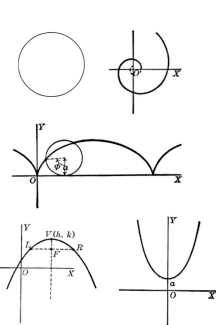

SPINNING

Use a set of squares that grow according to the Fibonacci series (0,1,1 2, 3, 5, 8...) to construct tangent quadrant arcs to form an approximate Logarithmic Spiral function, whose equation in polar coordinates is $r = e^{a\theta}$. e is the natural logarithm base, or 2.7182818284... a fundamental relationship, like Pi, $\Pi = 3.14....$ Sketch freehand first if necessary. Be sure that all parts of the curve are smooth and tangent. What curve is described when square and golden rectangle form the first two elements?

GROOVING

Plot a cycloid, the curve of one point on a circle that rolls along a line, like the path in space that a valve on a bicycle wheel takes as the wheel rolls along. The exact shape of this curve is called a *cycloid* and can be plotted according to the formulae $y = a(\theta - \sin \theta)$ and $x = a(1 - \cos \theta)$. Use a protractor plot values for x and y when θ varies from 0 to 360° (and 720°) in 30° intervals. The vertical mirror image of this cycloid is both a brachistochrone (curve of shortest falling time) and a tautochrone (curve of same falling time)! Construct this curve by attaching a pencil or pen to the edge of a wheel (a coin like a US quarter will do) and rolling the assembly along a straight edge.

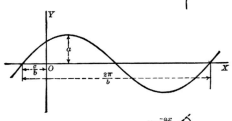

BENDING

Plot a parabola, $y = x^2$ in Cartesian coordinates. Construct a catenary by taking a piece of string and hanging several weights at equal intervals along the string. As you increase the number of weights, decreasing the spaces between them, the curve the string makes approaches the shape of a pure catenary. Plot a catenary according to the function $y = a/2(e^{x/a} + e^{-x/a})$.

WEAVING

Plot the sine curve $Y = \sin x$, and the cosine curve $Y = \cos x$, in Cartesian coordinates. How are these related to the circle? Construct an axonometric projection of a spiral staircase from its plan and section.

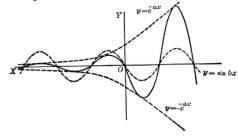

RESONATING

Draw a sine curve with multiple frequencies. Do the Fourier addition-- that is, add up the **Y** values of all overlapping curves at each point along the **X** axis, and plot the new curve that is the function of the sum of the values of all other curves.

RADIATING

Plot the locus of a point which moves so that the product of its distance from two fixed points (foci) is constant. This is the Lemniscate of Bernoulli, not shown here. Its rectangular coordinates are $(x^2 + y^2) = a^2(x^2 - y^2)$. This is expressed in polar coordinate as $\rho^2 = a^2 \cos 2\theta$. Plot the three-leafed rose, $\rho = a \cos 3\theta$, or the four-leafed rose, $\rho = a \sin 2\theta$.

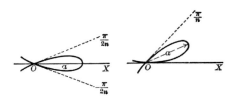

BETWEEN DIMENSIONS: FRACTAL GEOMETRY AND NATURE

A few years ago I was looking at a cover of *Scientific American* magazine and on it I saw what I thought was a close-up of a solar flare, dramatic image of one of our new powerful ground-based or space telescopes. (Check it for yourself on page 381.) The image was no such thing, but rather a geometrical construct of remarkable complexity. I was fooled. I thought it was a real solar flare, an image of the natural world and working of the universe, but in fact I saw a human invention, a figure closer to Pythagoras' triangle or Euclid's square. It was a fractal detail of the Mandelbrodt set, a figure between dimensions that makes possible excursions and travels into an infinite form.

The Mandelbrodt set is the most complex function known to date. It may be to our time what Euclid's square and right triangle were to the Greek World of Socrates, Plato, and Aristotle, giving us a way to calculate and generate figures that seem remarkable akin to what we have heretofore considered those aspects of nature beyond constructible geometry-- the detailed shapes of trees, mountains, islands, fire, even the variety of snowflakes. But the Mandelbrodt or Julia set plotted on the Argand plane, is generated by an amazingly simple formula, of endless iterations of $z \leftarrow z^2 + c$, where z is complex variable multiplier of the square root of minus one , $\sqrt{-1} = i$, an imaginary number.

The Menger Sponge (p. 84, volume 1) is a fractal structure. This kind of geometry now may describe the reality of the living world, of the chaotic play of forces that generate the endless variety of life, as truly as the circle described the disc of the moon and shape of the wheel in Euclid's time. For the Greeks, the cube was the undisputed space-filling and gravidly inert "atom" of earth, that most immovable of elements. But now change and variation enter into the calculus, making the geometry of rivers, forests, dust, and weather, visible, where before they were all invisible. Andrei Linde has even postulated an infinitely fractal set of universes. Fractals can model what before appeared as chaos. The "solar flare" is not a photograph, it is a plot of a formula as much as $x^2 + y^2 = 1$ yields a circle.

Nature's Geometry

The Mandelbrodt set can be iterated into finer and finer detail iterated without limit. We can investigate its figures with the aid of a computer graphic plot. We need only find a site and set the number of iterations to find something new. The explorations presented here show an infinitesimal sample of the truly infinite variety awaiting us in the Mandelbrodt Set. Yet amazingly an almost exact replica of the original whole figure is also present in every image, at every level of magnification. Who knows, this may well be the tool of the new millennium that enables us to model the spacetime structure of our universe with enough accuracy to allow us to broadcast ourselves any and everywhere as easily as we send sounds and images across to each other and into the cosmos today.

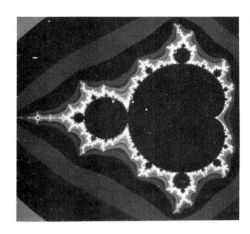

The Mandelbrodt set is generated by an amazingly simple formula, taking endless iterations of

$z \leftarrow z^2 + c$ *where z is complex variable and c is a fixed complex number.*

A complex number has both real and imaginary components. The square root of minus one, $\sqrt{-1} = i$, is an imaginary number, thus $1 + 3i$ is a complex number.

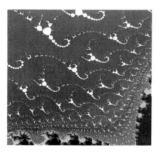
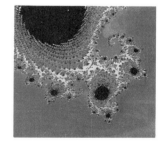
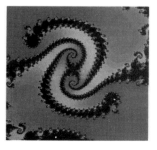

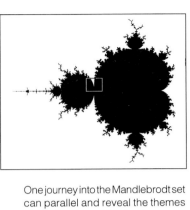

One journey into the Mandlebrodt set can parallel and reveal the themes of the chapters of this book.

Spacing

Spinning

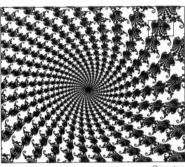

Grooving

Bending

Weaving

Resonating

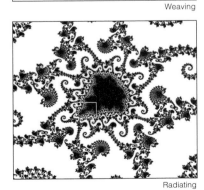

Radiating

COMPUTERS AND ARCHITECTURE

"Every active Glass Bead Game player naturally dreams of a constant expansion of the fields of the Game until they include the entire universe. Or rather, he constantly performs such expansions in his imagination and his private Games, and cherishes the secret desire for the ones which seem to prove their viability to be crowned by official acceptance. The true and ultimate finesse in the private Games of advanced players consists, of course, in their developing such mastery over the expressive, nomenclatural, and formative factors of the Game that they can inject individual and original ideas into any given Game played with objective historical materials. A distinguished botanist once whimsically expressed the idea in an aphorism: "The Glass Bead Game should admit of everything, even that a single plant should chat in Latin with Linnaeus".

Hermann Hesse, Magister Ludi, or The Glass Bead Game

The State of the Art

Computers are by now essential to the practice of architecture. A client may want to move the stair in a high-rise building say 3 inches to the south. That simple spacial request may require changing a hundred working drawings, including plans, sections, elevations, electrical, mechanical and structural sheets, as well as reworking specifications and cost estimates. What may have taken weeks to complete twenty years ago can now be performed in a single keystroke. Multilayered vector structures linked to management databases rapidly rendered on the CAD (Computer-Aided Design) screen is the current coin of the realm, both in terms of production and hiring architecture graduates (replacing the old interview question "Can you letter?" with "Do you know Release 14?") From the time this book was first outlined until its eventual publication date, computer graphics has notably proceeded from its wireframe infancy through solid-modeling toddlerhood to its texture-mapped ray-traced animated adolescence. Who can yet predict what or when its maturity might be?

Herman Melville's story *Bartleby the Scrivener* describes the lonely life of a man who, before the era of typewriters, carbon paper, and xerography, earned his living by making longhand copies of legal briefs and official documents. Just as the practice of law without technical automation is by now unimaginable, so too the practice of architecture without routine computer assisted drafting is becoming equally unimaginable. Simple drafting has as little to do with the real practice of architecture as penmanship has to do with the practice of law. Making precise drawings that describe one's spacial ideas, on the other hand, is as necessary to architects as a command of the language is to lawyers. Since computerized drafting systems already do much of the automatic work needed to translate a spacial idea into a building including dimensioning, rendering, detailing, cost control, specifications, and energy calculations, the question arises, "what does the architect really do?"

Limitations

With all the worshipful rush to incorporate computers in architecture, it is important to keep clear what computers cannot do. An architecture student faced what he thought was an impossible deadline: he needed CAD files plotted *tonight!* and the hidden-line removal was taking much too long. He came to see that keeping these lines would give a unique "x-ray" view through the whole scheme. Human flexibility and invention turned a machine problem into an artistic insight. (See page 43.) A deeper problem concerns what ease of computer modeling obscures. It is easy to crumple a sheet of paper to instantly create a complex space that would take very long indeed to model in CAD. A student modeling a theater in CAD showed all seats correctly drawn, arrayed as "blocks" from a standard file, but all in the wrong place. His theater was a rectangular shoebox! No thought for acoustics, sight lines, or wide spans; no sense of *modeling* the volume!

Pencil and Pixel

The pencil will always be more supple than the pixel (the picture element, or individual electron dot on the computer monitor.) Light is continuous while data is digital. However small, there are always gaps in digital media. But the astonishing improvements of computers let us continue to dream. New computer programs to visualize complex molecules or detailed anatomy use the **voxel**, or volumetric picture element, which carries spacial data directly to the screen. Voxel modeling eliminates the projection computations needed for each pixel, saving huge amounts of time. While pixel modeling is like constructing a single perspective rendering, voxel modeling is more like building a working model, allowing quick study from an infinity of views. The most recent memory device may store up to a trillion bytes, equal to 200 CD's (ten *days* of continuous music) in a tiny holographic cube. Scanning interferometric apertureless microscopy, with resolution now at 5 times the width of one atom, may soon store the equivalent of 30 movies on a diskette the size of a penny. What might architects do with such tools?

A New Vision: Multi-Media Virtuoso Reality?

Just as Impressionist and Cubist painters had to find new roles for art after the advent of photography, so too must we penetrate to the essence of architecture stripped of its superficial aspects. To make space well, one must cultivate vision, the ability to foresee events in a multidimensional world and act on that prescience. Will the world of the Third Millennium allow us to build an inhabit our children's play architecture, correcting for energy efficiency and climate control? Will the Box and Bin conjure up every material need from raw quark, transforming all garbage, including last night's bed or yesterday's villa into pure energy? Will our homes be a card in our wallet, remotely deployable and programmable, or will we live gently with the land? Will we at last be able to live in pure space?

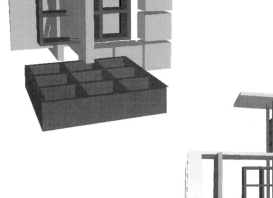

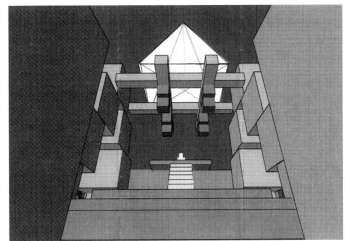

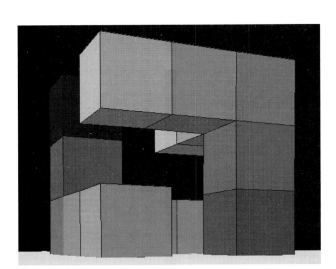

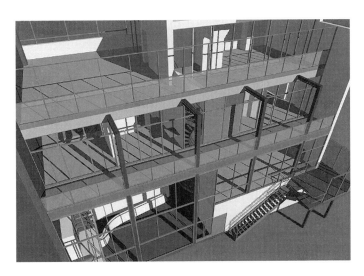

COLLAGE

Many of the early Cubist paintings by Braque, Picasso, Gris and others could be entitled "Daily News Times at the Breakfast Table." They often included **montage**, borrowing imagistic elements and inserting them whole into a new context (bits of newspaper or shelf paper patterned like chair caning). Later these painters fixed pieces directly onto the canvas not as visual quotations but rather as formal compositional elements on their own. This unprecedented new art form came to be called **collage**.

Bricolage and Assemblage

We can imagine that the mind of an engineer seeks to organize all facets of a work, prescribing *a priori* everything needed in a project. To make a chair, for example, the conscientious engineer would plan the mining of the ore and its smelting into usable metal, the construction of factories, ergonomic research into the precise dimensions of the seat for comfort, consideration of assembly, shipping, market demand and so on. On the other hand, the junkman (or as Levi-Straus describes in French, the *bricoleur*), may simply walk into the back yard, search through a pile of old discarded useless things, find an old tractor seat, a broken barrel stave, some bricks, and perhaps some baling wire to hold the whole thing together, adjust the seat angle and *Voila*-- a chair! **Bricolage**, the work of the *bricoleur*, is spiritually close to collage. **Assemblage**, the combination of three-dimensional elements for figurative effects (who has not seen "cute" animals made out of nuts and bolts?) is more akin to montage.

Collage and Dynamics

Collage is an important part of dynamics, not only as a graphic technique, but as a guide to structure, material and construction of solids. Collage is an alternative to computers uniting pencil and pixel, a useful tool not only for the improviser of structural engineering (forks on the tabletop!!) but also for the improviser of volumetric relationships and configurations. Le Corbusier's early still life drawing studies on the facing page reveal a compositional spirit akin to collage as much as architectural planning. They use the same given elements, rearranging them into new juxtapositions, employing systems of regulating lines to establish proportion and geometric order between otherwise unrelated graphic elements. The alterations between the drawings are also illuminating: note how the hat becomes a stack of plates, how the book is opened, how the violin case is reduced to shadow as container. Note also how the curve of the book merges with the cross section of the bottle. Richard Meier published a series of collages, two of which are shown opposite. They too explore themes of plan arrangement, transparency, marrying contours, and layered spaces. They are less pictorially literal than Le Corbusier's drawings, but it is clear that text still dominates the upper collage. Turn the page sideways or upside down to see that space, not object, sets the tone in the lower collage.

Professor Christopher Chimera has articulated a cogent and challenging set of guidelines, rules, or criteria that distinguish collage from any other form. It is not at all easy to obtain these in a two-dimensional field, let alone any higher order of dimensions. Perhaps collages should be identified only by number and key like music, or simply entitled "untitled". We offer the following as it was first presented to students, text centered rather than justified. Herewith are Chimera's Criteria for Collage:

CHIMERA'S **Color Assignment # 9**   *(Week 16)*

COLLAGE: EMPHASIS

No. 7

Use critical faculty to:
Suppress recognition of Text, Image and Shape

Avoid all conventional ordering strategies

Suppress recognizable characteristics of
individual pieces or shared by groups of pieces

Utilize juxtaposition, association and serendipity
to generate complex field and transform materials

No. 8

Find compelling fragment of No.1 and transform
through enlargement or otherwise relate second to first

Architecture and Collage

It would be a mistake to seek a direct translation of collage into architecture. Collage is a unique medium, younger than cinema. Yet like film, collage has had an enormous effect on architects. It may not be possible to control all aspects of a design. The vigilant architect keeps an open eye for happy surprises, collisions which provoke careful consideration of the encounter between hitherto unrelated elements. Surely Gaudi's multi-patterned broken pottery facing on the sinuous concrete seating in Parc Guell in Barcelona anticipates collage. The plan collages found in Alvar Aalto's work (Otaniemi, page 333) may be recognized in the exploration of sectional collage in Frank Gehry's recent architecture. Le Corbusier used the free plan to collage program spaces: see Strasbourg City Hall and the Millowners Building at Ahmedabad (page 294-296.) The cut-and-paste serendipity in Le Corbusier's Modulor collage is akin to his insertion of a cooling tower as Senate chamber in the Assembly Building at Chandigarh, both shown on page 327. The Zurich Pavilion's bolted frames permit an ever-improvised spacial order within the fixed frame of the hypar roof (page 344.)

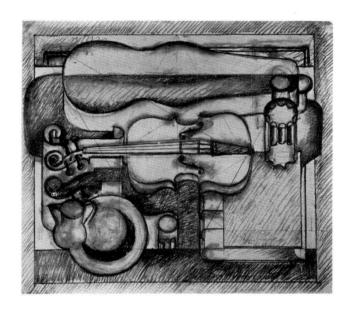

COLOR AND DYNAMICS

Spectrum is a range of possibilities: black and white reveals (structure), whereas color modulates. There is a relativity in the study of color. Just as perception of a dense space requires a less dense one for comparison, the perception of a color depends upon what is around it We may say that color is collage refined to the point where all figuration is ultimately eliminated.

The color exercises closely follow the course outlined in the required text by Josef Albers, *The Interaction of Color* (Yale University Press, 1963, paperback). Each color exercise gives page references in this book, which includes examples in color of the issues considered. Color exercises may be documented on 35 mm slides, or as prints. The least expensive color reproduction methods available are Cibacrome™ "C-Prints", or color laser print xerographic-type copies. Another valuable book for the study of color is Johannes Itten's *The Elements of Color*. Just as the Kit of Parts and the Bag of Tricks explore relationships of arrangements of given spacial elements, so too will color be a study of the relationships of given chromatic intervals, using a "Kit of Color". *Do not mix paints to make your colors!*

All color work in this course is to be done with **Color-aid** paper. Use the new set of 314 colors, with better range balance, choice of hues. It now comes in many sizes and sets-- standard 6 x 9", also 4 x 6", and single 9 x 12 and larger sheets. (These last may be likely, albeit flimsy, substitutes for construction paper.) The set of 6 x 9" color sheets is widely available, may cost about $30, and will last a student's lifetime. The 4x6" set may be more economical for students. The new ColorAid set was developed by the dedicated scholar and researcher and artisan, Kim Vlaun who based it on the European Natural Color System from Sweden, which is built on *four* (4) primary colors, red, blue, yellow, and green! This seems to be right. All work is to be mounted on board (Foam-Core is OK) with rubber cement. For the best effect, razor cut all sheets on glass to get the cleanest edge, and paint the entire surface with rubber cement before removing it with the rubber cement pickup. This last will assure that the whole color area carries an even tone.

Yale University Press has recently made available on CD-ROM Josef Albers' *Interaction of Color*, for $125, which buys an awful lot of ColorAid paper. The obvious advantages to exploring color interaction on a computer is ease, rapidity, and precision of color replacement, experimentation and substitution. The disadvantage, not at all obvious, is that any digital version of the infinite continuum of the spectrum of light loses an infinite number of intervals of variation between the digital locations.

Architects and Color

Polychrome is a method of applying color to the surfaces of masses which emphasize volume relationships. Architects must deal with color in different ways and for different motives. David Diamond has identified strategies for thinking about color that fall into three general categories:

1 - LOCAL COLOR. Local color refers to the appearance of physical context, surfaces, and light. Natural and fabricated materials have color and their arrangement in light and space is a condition of any built or found environment. Representation, depiction, and rendering rely on the recognition of local color to communicate information about a designed or seen spaces.

2 - CARTOGRAPHIC: Cartographic color refers to the use of color to relate a code or system wherein a particular color or range of color tone denotes a category of data. On a road map, yellow can refer to federal highways, red to state parkways, and black and white to local roads. Other colors may represent topography, political boundaries and population density. The use of color allows the presentation of multiple monochrome layers of data simultaneously. Layers of information may correspond to architectural and spatial issues such as continuity and discontinuity of space and mass, form, closure, structure, program, etc.

3 - METAPHORIC: The metaphor of color structure (color relationships which we will investigate), can serve an analogic role in exploring other types of spatial, organizational, and expressive relationships. In the bipolar system of values available with black & white graphics, black and white represent the only absolute contrast. In Munsell's quadra-polar color system, black and white represent opposing value contrast, while red/green, blue/orange and yellow/violet, each represent pairs of absolute color contrast.

Depth, "Literal and Phenomenal"

It is not possible for us to see two or more color areas in our field of vision without attempting to "resolve" their relative distances from us. When other cues like atmospheric perspective, size relationships, or the parallax of binocular vision are absent, we resort to the information of color to reveal the apparent depth of things. And on the other hand, it is not possible to observe any interaction of colors on a two-dimensional picture plane without ultimately attempting to resolve them as fields at at least two different levels of depth. Perhaps this is a result of the intrinsic neurophysiological mechanisms of color and space perception in the eye and brain. *Dimensional Color*, Lois Swirnoff's recent book, presents investigations and exercises exploring color relationships to depth perception and illusion. Professor Russ Jordan suggests constructing an apparatus as shown in the diagrams to the right to investigate color in space.

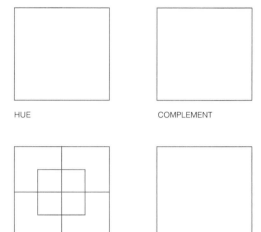

HUE   COMPLEMENT

VALUE: TINT AND SHADE   CHROMA

COLOR DEFINITIONS:
MAKE YOUR OWN EXAMPLES FOR THESE FIELDS

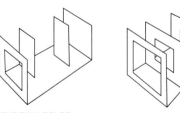

DIMENSIONAL COLOR.
PROF. SWIRNOFF''S SIMPLE APPARATUS FOR FINDING THE
SPACIAL EFFECTS OF COLOR AND THE EFFECTS OF COLOR
ON SPACE PERCETION. THESE EXPERIMENTS GIVE ANOTHER
INSIGHT INTO ALBERS' *HOMAGE TO THE SQUARE* STUDIES.

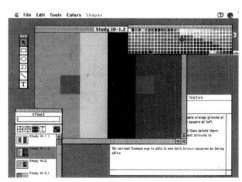

Josef Albers' *Interaction of Color* on CD-ROM

IMPORTANT COLOR DEFINITIONS

HUE is the name of a color (*red* or *blue*, or *red orange* rather than brown).

COMPLEMENT is the opposite color on a color wheel (yellow to violet, red to green). Physiologically, the complement is created when the retina tires of looking at a color and responding to its light wave. If you then close your eyes, the after image you will see is the complement— thus after looking at red, the eye will see the not-red range of the visible spectrum, or green.

VALUE is the relative lightness or darkness of a hue, as in a scale from white through gray to black. Value determines the tint or shade of a color.

TINT is the addition of white to a hue (pink is a tint of red).

SHADE is the addition of black or the complement to a hue (black + yellow = green, but violet + yellow goes toward a neutrality, looks like a darker yellow, that is, a *shade* of yellow).

CHROMA is the brightness or intensity of a hue. Like the brightness dial on a TV, pink can be made bright or dull— same hue and value, varying chroma.

SIMULTANEOUS CONTRAST is the tendency of the eye to spontaneously perceive the missing half of a complementary pair to a color, even if it is not physically present.

EXTENSION is the balance of colors of contrasting brilliance through porportional areas in a composition (a small patch of yellow will balance a large patch of violet).

POLYCHROME is a method of applying color to the surfaces of masses which emphasize relationships of volumes. An example of this is the Reitveld chair.

DEPTH is is the spacial effect of color, the trendency of colors to appear to advance or recede in the picture plane. For example, against a black background, a yellow area will appear to be in front, and a blue area will seem to be far back.

Johannes Itten, in *The Art of Color*, describes seven color contrasts which account for most or all color interactions. Not surprisingly, they include most of the basic terms above. They are 1. Hue; 2. Light/Dark (value); 3. Cold/Warm; 4. Complementary contrast; 5. Simultaneous constrast ; 6. Saturation (chroma); and 7. Extension.

Color Reproduction

Traditionally (in the last hundred years!) color has been much more difficult and expensive to reproduce well, i.e. accurately, than black and white material. However, recent technical developments including the Cibachrome color print process, color laser copiers, and now CCD still cameras linked to popular software including the newer versions of PageMaker, CorelDraw, Photostyler, and Quark Express make color multiples an ever more accessible medium to the design student. But this will not be an automatic thing. Color is subtle, and is of infinite combination and subdivision. It always requires an eye. An extraordinary xerographist once explained how he got such wonderful color copies out of a common model of copier, saying "I understand color". No doubt soon we will be unhappy with the quality and cost of easy inexpensive "3D-xerox" multiple model reproduction!

THE COLOR STUDIES

These exercises are inspired by the writings and paintings of Josef Albers and Robert Slutzky. Other painters whose works reveal the chromodynamic universe include: Fabritius, Vermeer, Matisse, Gris, Seurat, Mondrian, Picasso, Klee, Kurt Schwitters, Burgoyne Diller, Braque, Cézanne, Léger, Poons, Olitsky, Morris Louis, de Kooning, Georgia O'Keefe, Milton Avery, and Fairfield Porter. There are many others.

Use ColorAid for all color assignments except collages. Collect a file of opaque papers (including typography) from trash, magazines, newspapers, etc. to use for all collages. Refer to indicated templates as guides. Unless otherwise specified, the standard format is a 3" square color field centered on a 6" square white illustration board. For collage, recall Professor *Chimera's collage criteria* on page 458. The series is based on a standard 16 week semester time interval.

PRELUDE: *Value, hue, chroma*

Value. From your **Color-aid** set select **3** neutral grays (neither warm or cool), with even intervals between. For each gray, select **2** additional colors of matching value to the gray. Using a 1" square of each, arrange them into a 9-square grid in rows of equal value. *(Week 1)*

Pre-collage: From your collage file, using black, white, and grays only, cut out **9** 1" squares that range in even steps from lightest to darkest value. As in the previous exercise, try to keep these as even, neutral tones. Arrange these into a nine-square grid to create a gray scale. Use the same format as described above. *(Week 1)*

Hue: Select **2** two hues. Arrange them so that one partially overlaps the other. Select a third color which might be the transparent intersection of the two initial colors. The value of this color must be between those of the parent colors. Arrange the colors as in template #0 to create the illusion of film transparency. Try this with adjacent hues in the spectral cycle red, orange, yellow, green, blue, indigo, violet, red, etc. *(Week 2)*

Chroma: Select **2** two complimentary colors. Arrange them so that one partially overlaps the other. Select **1** color which might be the transparent intersection of the two initial colors. The value of this color must be between those of the parent colors. This color should be equidistant from each parent color. Arrange the colors as in template #0 so that one color field appears to overlap the other, and their intersections create the illusion of film transparency. *(Week 2)*

Collage 0: Explore the intersection of two fields. *(Week 2)*

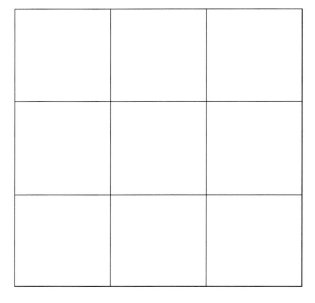

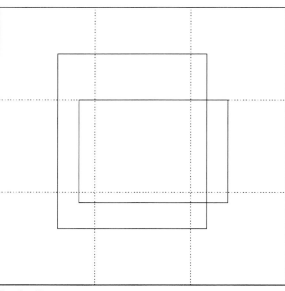

Template #0

MELODY: *Relative Contrast*

1. **Gray 3 to 4**. Select **1** gray sheet from your **Color-aid** set. Experiment with pairs of background colors that influence and change the color appearance of the initial gray. Using relative contrast of hue, value, and chroma, the three selected colors should appear as four. Use template #1 as a guide. Seek maximum color transformation, not merely value change. *(Week 3)*

2. **Color 3 to 4**. Select **1** color from your **Color-aid** set. Experiment with pairs of background colors that influence and change the color appearance of the initial color sheet. Using relative contrast of hue, value, and chroma, the three selected colors should appear as four. Use template #1 as a guide. *(Week 3)*

3. **Four to Three**. Select **2** colors from the **Color-aid** set that you will try to make appear as one and the same. For this exercise, they should be as dissimilar as possible. Experiment with pairs of background colors that influence and change the color appearance of the initial color sheets. Using the relative contrast of hue, value, and chroma, the four selected colors should appear as three. Use template #1 as a guide. *(Week 4)*

4. *Collage 1*: Explore the relative appearance of colored areas by manipulating the edge contrast between adjacent fields. *(Week 4)*

HARMONY *Tint, Shade, and Transparency*

1. **Tint & Shade of Equal Color:4 Hues** Combine **4** 1½" squares of different colors to make one larger square of specific contrast relationships of light intensity (**value**) and color intensity (**chroma**). Transfer these relationships to a higher key (**tint**), and a lower key (**shade**), within 2 groups of equally large squares. The inner squares should measure ½" and create the illusion of a milky overlay and a dark shadowy overlay respectively. See template #2. *(Week 5)*

2. **Tint & Shade of Unequal Color: 8 Hues** Combine **4** 1½" squares of different colors to make one larger square. Transfer specific **value** relationships only, to a higher key (**tint**) and a lower key (**shade**), within 2 groups of equally large squares. The inner squares should measure ½" and create the illusion of a milky overlay and a dark shadowy overlay respectively. See template #2. *(Week 6)*

3. *Collage 2a*. Explore the illusion of film overlay. *(Week 6)*

4. **Transparency** Select **3** colors (A, B, & C). Arrange them as on template #3 (see next page) so that all possible overlaps occur. At each overlap, select the color which will give the illusion of film transparency. There will be a total of 7 colors in all: A, B, C, AB, AC, BC, ABC. *(Week 7)*

5. *Collage 2b.* Free exercise. Refer to Chimera's collage criteria. *(Week 8)*

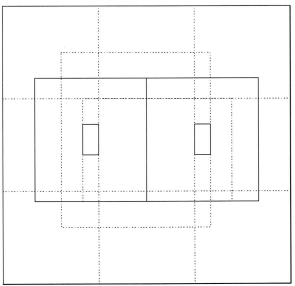

Template #1

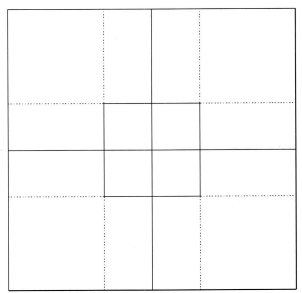

Template #2

CONCERTO: *Color Intervals, Transformation, Optical Mix*

1. **5 Ugly Colors.** After studying the effects of relative contrast, tint and shade, and collage, design a composition that is harmonious in both color and geometry. Choose **5** unstable and discordant colors from your **Color-aid** pack. Saturated primary colors tend to be stable, not easily influenced by adjoining color fields. Unsaturated, muddy, tertiary colors are less stable. Use template #4 as generating lines to design your own plan. Balance the brilliance or intensity of chroma by varying the relative quantities of each color. Use all the techniques you have used to date: control the respective areas and edges of each color field, color changes, color subtraction, simultaneous contrast, flat space/deep space ambiguities, transparency, etc. *(Week 9)*

2. **3 Ugly Colors.** Choose **3** unstable and discordant colors from your **Color-aid** pack. Use template #4 as generating lines to design your own plan. Balance the brilliance or intensity of chroma by varying the relative quantities of each color. Use all the techniques you have used to date: control the respective areas and edges of each color field, color changes, color subtraction, simultaneous contrast, flat space/deep space ambiguities, transparency, etc. *(Week 10)*

3. ***Collage 3a.*** Free exercise. Refer to Chimera's collage criteria. *(Week 10)*

4. **Optical Mix 5 Colors**. Use optical mix to study intersecting and overlapping color fields. Use the plan/section of your Harmony project as a plan. Generate variations in brightness (chroma), hue, and value, to create a composition that is harmonious in color and geometry. Color fields may be defined with densely spaced colored strips or dots. In order for this exercise to work, the areas of color must be quite thin and repetitive. They may vary in size according to the effect you wish to create. No white areas may show within the frame. Craft must be impeccable! Choose **5** unstable colors. Use all the techniques you have used to date: control the respective areas and edges of each color field, color changes, color subtraction, simultaneous contrast, flat space/deep space ambiguities, transparency, etc. Work within a 6" square frame centered on a 12 " square white illustration board. *(Week 11)*

5. **Optical Mix 3 Colors.** Follow the above assignment with **3** colors. Use a frontal projection of your harmony project as a plan. Consider both the transparencies of intersecting volumes and the transparent view through volumes overlapping in space. Work within a 3" x 6" vertical frame centered on a 6" x 12 " white illustration board. *(Week 12)*

6. ***Collage 3b.*** Free exercise. Especially seek non-figurative fields as means to optical mix. Refer to Chimera's collage criteria. *(Week 12)*

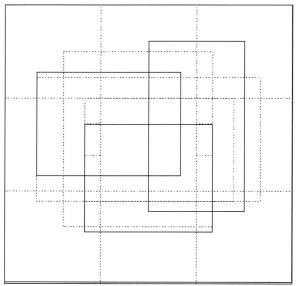

Template #3

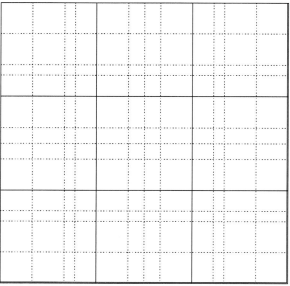

Template #4

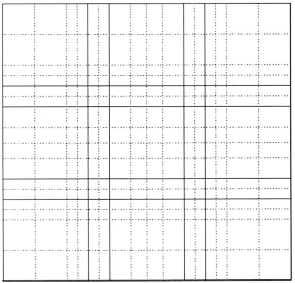

Template #4, alternate

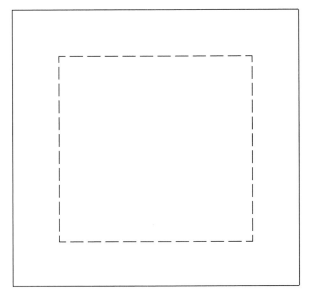

SYMPHONY: *Color Surface, Volume, and space*

(Lois Swirnoff's investigations in her book *Dimensional Color* may be particular helpful for this series, as might be your earlier Cubist/Purist studies.)

1. **Tile: Color Surface** Use color relationships to key space and program relationships in your Concerto project. Cut one section parallel to each of the coordinate axes. Reduce these sections to 3" square centered on a 6" square. Use each of these as a tile template, as in Architectonics, to generate a composition which describes the tartan geometry of the cubic site and the particular geometries to each of the program spaces in your solution. *(Week 13)*

2. **Volume: color cube**. Cut 2 sections parallel to each of the coordinate axes. Reduce these **6** sections to a 3" square. Use each of these as a template to generate a color composition that describes the tartan geometry of the cubic site and the particular geometry to each of the program spaces that are cut through. Mount each study on a 3" square of thin cardboard. As these will be assembled into models, both sides of each tile will be visible. Therefore, you must complete the reverse side of each tile with the appropriate colored papers. Assemble the sectional "x-rays" into a study model of your Concerto project. Recall your origami and cubist studies moving between two and three dimensions. *(Week 14)*

3. **Space: Color Field.** Develop a frontal projection of your Concerto project as a plan. Consider both transparency of intersecting volumes and transparent views through volumes overlapping in space. Use all the techniques you have learned to date: control the respective areas and edges of each color field, color changes, color subtraction, simultaneous contrast, flat space/deep space ambiguities, transparency, optical mix, etc. Work within a 3" x 6" vertical frame centered on a 6" x 12 " white illustration board. *(Week 15)*

4. **Collage 4a**. Use critical faculty to: suppress recognition of text, image and shape; avoid all conventional ordering strategies; suppress recognizable characteristics of individual pieces or shared by groups of pieces; utilize juxtaposition, association and serendipity to generate complex field and transform materials. *(Week 16)*

5. **Collage 4b.** Find compelling fragment of Collage No. 4a and transform through enlargement or otherwise relate second to first. *(Week 16)*

Note: the templates included here on pages 464-467 are shown as full scale three-inch squares. You may wish to reduce them by 66% to get small scale two-inch sketch pieces, which will use only half as much ColorAid.

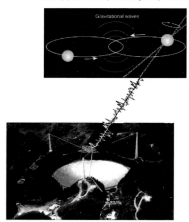

The Pythagoreans believed that the heavenly spheres, as they revolved, produced harmonious sounds. Shown above is the music of the planets imagined by Kepler.

Today's version of this faith: variations in binary pulsars may reveal gravity waves

"My dreams are (still) bigger than my memories.... if you pull back to the macro, there is no time, it is all compressed.... The music happens, there is no time." Saxophonist Charles Lloyd

MUSIC

"The whole point of composing is to sound inevitable" Aaron Copland

Music cannot be embodied in a few words or images. Nonetheless, music has contributed to the conception, structure, and execution of this work in a very deep way. It is possible to imaginatively hear representative musical selections for each chapter. Among many many others, they might include:

0. PRELUDE   *Lush Life,* Billy Strayhorn; *Prelude in C,* from the "Well-Tempered Clavier", J. S. Bach
1. MELODY   *Theme from Black Orpheus,* Louis Bonfa; *Kinderscenen, op. 15,* Robert Schumann;
2. HARMONY   *Kind of Blue,* Miles Davis, John Coltrane, et.al.; d*er Rosenkavalier,* R. Strauss; *Quintet in A, op. 114, "The Trout",* Franz Schubert; *Satch and Josh,* Count Basie and Oscar Peterson, et.al.
3. CONCERTO   *Musical Offering* (6 part ricercar), J. S. Bach; *Rhapsody in Blue,* George Gershwin
4. SYMPHONY   *Ninth Symphony in D Minor op. 125,* Ludwig Van Beethoven, *Missa Luba,* Les Troubadours deu Roi Baudouin; *Live at Carnegie Hall 1938,* Benny Goodman, Count Basie, Lester Young, Walter Page, et. al.

The 88 keys of a piano are all a pianist has to communicate music. Miraculously, they are more than enough to bring forth both Mozart and Ray Charles. Combinations of arrangements are the only means to communicate emotions in both music and architecture. So the problem for the composer is to find necessary and moving relationships of combinations. Composing animates both music and architecture. Compose derives from Latin *ponere* "to place or put aside", Greek *epi* upon, and ultimately Sanskrit *apa* away. To pose "to put, place, set or position something" is the basis for compounds suggestive to both musical and spacial imagination. **Compose** means to place with, suggesting interaction. Propose means to place *forward*, suppose to place *under*, impose to place *in*, expose to place *out*, dispose to set *apart*, depose to put *down*, superpose to place *above*. Related words include juxtapose, oppose, interpose, purpose, repose, composure. Posture holds a pose. Composite is formed of parts. These positional varieties are the expressive "notes" of architecture whose combinations can be infinitely elaborated. Composing in space and time is this book's theme, an idea that yields many variations. The relationship of movement in mind to movement in body shows itself in each study. **0** *Prelude* is the Awakening of vision in many dimensions. **1** *Melody* is the Dance between mass and void that creates volume. **2** *Harmony* is the Drama of volume interaction. **3** *Concerto* creates the Poetry of a fabric of spaces. **4** *Symphony* reveals the Compassion of living and evolving space. In each case, architecture can create resilient space, responsive to changes from without while sustaining its form through time.

Music of the Spheres

Johannes Kepler, following the Pythagoreans, believed that the heavenly spheres, as they revolved, produced harmonious sounds. He believed he saw in the proportions of the planetary orbits evidence for the vibration between celestial bodies that must create a resonance of music in the heavens on a cosmic scale. He thought he found a near-perfect fit of nesting Platonic solids that would "explain" the orbits of the known planets. Believing in a "music of the spheres", he even imagined appropriate scales for each of the planets. Today astronomers listen in via radio telescope to the minute variations in the signals from binary pulsar stars to find evidence of gravity waves. Perhaps Kepler was not so far from the essential truth. The geometrodynamic equilibrium of spacetime depends on a multidimensional polyrhythm of give-and-take between mass, energy, and motion. To master the flow of architectural space in time means to preserve the freshness and avoid the staleness of time. Exploiting the medium of space in the available time, both efficiently and eloquently (economy of means!) produces the pure clarity of *quality*, the economy of time. Music is the essence of the living flame of truly plastic ideas, ever malleable but always tending toward excellence. Weight is the *feel* of mass in a gravity field-- the interaction of one body (subject) with another (object). Music reifies the density and weight of emotion: for example the loving recollection of beloved forebears. Music is for this author a *yartzheit, a remembrance*. Twelve years Charles Friedman, father, of Blessed Memory; forty-five years Joseph Friedman, grandfather, of Blessed Memory.

"Music is the electrical soul in which the spirit lives, thinks, and invents." Ludwig van Beethoven

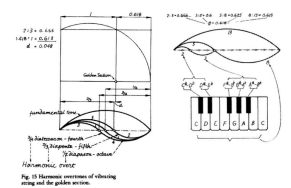

Fig. 15 Harmonic overtones of vibrating string and the golden section.

MUSICAL SCALES

"The wave patterns of cosmic rhythm are shared by our heartbeat...
Our breathing has a similar... ongoing rhythm of inhaling and exhaling ."
Doczi, *The Power of Limits*

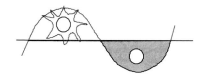

THE 24 HOUR SOLAR DAY

Wave functions carry our emotions through the chromatics of tone as well as light. The time cycles that order our lives may well be the basis for music's power to express our deepest emotions. But the tones of songs and symphonies were brought into harmony only through the careful adjustment of the proportions of vibrational waves to make scales of sound relationships. Pythagoras and his group discovered that certain fractions of a whole length string produce sounds that fit very well with the original tone, called the tonic. These combinations produce what we call harmony, from the Greek term meaning "joining together or fitting together", as in carpentry. A whole string will vibrate once, while the thirds will vibrate three times, the fourths will vibrate four times, etc. These are the harmonic frequencies, or whole-number multiples, of the tonic. A stretched string, when held at its midpoint and plucked, will vibrate exactly one octave higher than the whole tone of the open string! The "perfect" proportions of the Pythagorean or **just intonation scale** are 2:1 = octave; 3:2 = the fifth (the dominant) and 4:3 = the fourth (subdominant), 5:4 = major third, 6:5 = minor third, 9:8 major second, 16:15 = semitone. The scale of C major in just intonation is shown below. The upper numbers indicate the frequency of each note in cycles per second; the lower notes are the frequency ratios between successive notes.

264		297		330		352		396		440		495		528
	9:8		10:9		16:15		9:8		10:9		9:8		16:15	

Later these intervals were adjusted to make the twelve notes of the **equal-tempered scale**, a set of tones that permitted playing in all scales using all tonalities with the same notes. J. S. Bach's *Well - Tempered Clavier* exploits this remarkable property. It consists of two sets of 24 preludes and fugues, one for each major and minor key in chromatic order, C major, C minor, C# major, C# minor, D major etc.... Here the equal semitones in an octave have a frequency ratio of the twelfth root of two to one, $^{12}\sqrt{2}$: 1 or about 1.059463094359. The frequencies for this scale are shown below:

	279.70	**313.95**		**373.55**	**419.07**	**470.39**	
264	296.33	332.62	352.40	395.55	443.99	498.37	528

which shows the pattern of black and white keys on the modern piano. The upper figures, in bold type, are the black keys, the lower are the frequencies of the white keys. Note 528/264 = 2:1, the octave.

	277.18	**311.13**		**369.99**	**415.3**	**466.16**	
261.625	293.66	329.63	349.23	392.00	440	493.88	523.25

The modern equal tempered scale, shown above, is based on the same value $^{12}\sqrt{2}$: 1, but proportioned from A= 440 cycles per second, the standard international frequency basis for music today. Note 523.25/261.625 = 2:1, the octave.

Doczi pairs color and musical scales. It is remarkable that they are so close. Architecture too is a spectrum of plastic volume vibrations. Le Corbusier's Modulor is one attempt to bring harmonic proportions to geometric volumes. Chandigarh's plan is symphonic in its multiple layers of spacial relation-ships. Paul Oliver finds an improvisation of plastic relationships in the facade of the Secretariat at Chandigarh (shown on facing page) akin to jazz, recalling Slutzky's description in *Apres le Purism* of the "shimmering" improvisational surface of the Cubist canvas, where things emerge and disappear. Like an elaborated scale, a theme provides a framework on which to build and variations of melodies, harmonies, voicings, syncopation, other rhythms, without destroying the essential cadence. The simultaneous arrival of jazz and Cubism to Europe is perhaps a first theme of an expanding yet converging truly global World Music.

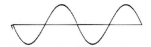

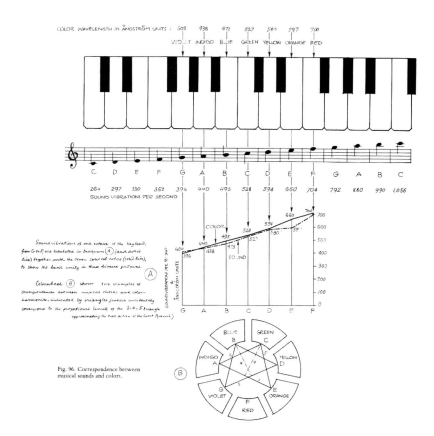

COLOR WAVELENGTH IN ÅNGSTRÖM UNITS : 405 438 473 527 580 597 700

VIOLET INDIGO BLUE GREEN YELLOW ORANGE RED

C D E F G A B C D E F G A B C

264 297 330 352 396 440 495 528 594 660 704 792 880 990 1,056

SOUND VIBRATIONS PER SECOND

Sound vibrations of one octave of the keyboard, from G to F, are tabulated in diagram (A) (dash dotted line) together with the seven spectral colors (solid line), to show the basic unity in these diverse patterns.

Colorwheel (B) shows two examples of correspondences between musical chords and color-harmonies, indicated by triangles (which incidentally correspond to the proportional limits of the 3:4:5 triangle approximating the cross section of the Great Pyramid.)

Fig. 96. Correspondence between musical sounds and colors.

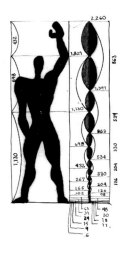

MODELING AT ALL SCALES

Tuning the music of architectural space eliminates the noisy static of bad proportions. When parts and the whole are *in scale,* the melody and attendant harmonies of the architecture emerge clearly and vividly. City design must combine unities of integrity: homes for individuals into a community, without compromising either, like an organism of living cells, a collage of wholes that become parts. The city-home relationship can inform our thinking about evolution and art and information as much as the other way around. In this sense, architecture remains a major branch of philosophy. There is an interesting relationship between the elements of your Kit of Parts and those of your Bag of Tricks, which emerges most clearly in the *parti* investigations for the Concerto studies. The 1" cubes of the Kit of Parts can represent the 8' practice studios at a particular scale, which is **1/8" = 1' - 0", or 1: 96**. When you have arrived at a possible order of program spacial relationships, you might then double the scale of the model, to **1/4" = 1' - 0", or 1:48,** and you can conveniently model planar cuts, folds, and continuities. Double the scale of the model again, to **1/2" = 1' - 0", or 1:24,** and the Bag of Tricks can be used to reconstruct your *parti* and planar organizations while investigating details like connections, material types, relationships of grids, *promenades architecturales*, and other architecturally expressive developments. For Symphony studies, modelling *parti* strategies using paper at 1/2" scale will magnify flimsy conditions, which is to your advantage. You may then use the Bag of Tricks at **1" = 1' - 0", or 1:12** scale to study joints and construction before going to the **full, or 1:1** scale of dwelling. When space clarifies structure, an architect can become the builder's friend. There are of course an infinite number of scales, each of which may be an appropriate zoom in or out for a particular micro or mega study of the space at hand.

A NOTE ON USING SCALE MODELS FOR STUDYING FORCES AND STRUCTURES

Why do a violin, cello, and double bass, all roughly the same shape, make different sounds? Because the size of the vibrating air chamber varies. But must the thickness of the strings also vary? Architects build scale models of their designs to study the spacial relationships they propose. But structural properties change with the size of an object according to some very curious physical facts that depend on the number of dimensions each element requires. Each side of a 1" cube has an area of 1 square inch, while its volume is 1 cubic inch. Each side of a 2" cube has an area of 4 square inches (2^2), while its volume is 8 cubic inches (2^3). Each side of a 10" cube has an area of 100 square inches (10^2), while its volume is 1000 cubic inches (10^3). Note that as the size of the cube increases, its ratio of area to volume actually decreases! This phenomenon affects all the natural world, including the shapes and habits of living things. For example, a mouse eats the equivalent of its body weight, several ounces, in food every day. An elephant, which is also warm blooded, eats far less in proportion to its body weight. Note that the larger sized animal actually has a smaller surface area in proportion to its body, so heat has less chance of escaping. (Another way to visualize this: imagine an elephant filled with thousands of mice. Where does all the extra internal skin go?) The leg bones of elephants are much thicker than those in horses, because if the elephant is twice as tall as the horse, the load increases eightfold, which requires four times the surface area in the cross section to take the stresses on the bone cells while the length of the elephant's leg bone (femur) will only double. By the same reasoning structures cannot be directly modeled without using correct dimensional transforms. Moment of inertia varies as the fourth power of a linear dimension, so a bridge ten times larger than its model will develop moments of inertia 10,000 times (10^4) greater. Deflection is the result of bending stresses, measured in pounds per square inch. This is the second power of the linear dimension, so a structure twice as large as its model will have stresses (and deflection) four times greater. When building a larger scale version of a study model, remember that not all proportions and structural characteristics will exactly correspond. To see how forces will affect a larger structure, magnify the effect of gravity, wind, etc. in your model by pushing at the critical load points with your finger.

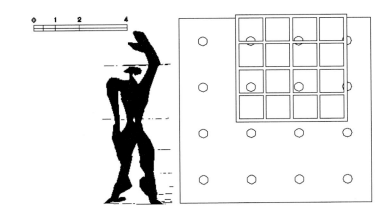

VOLUME FORCE AND SPACE; SCALE MODELS, ARCHITECTURE AND STRUCTURE

Multiple Scales

1/8" = 1' - 0" or 1 : 96
The **Kit of Parts**
Design Fundamentals 1: Architectonics.
Phoenix *parti* mass-as-volume models using cubes as room volumes for location relationships, etc...

1/4" = 1' - 0" or 1 : 48
Paper models, approximately file folder stiffness
Phoenix *parti* development/resolution models.
Study opaque/translucent/transparent, structural strategies, (dis)continuity of line, plane, volume also: Prelude, using color paper (no scale)

1/2" = 1' - 0" or 1 : 24
The **Bag of Tricks**
Design Fundamentals 2: Dynamics
especially Melody, Harmony, Concerto studies
perforation, hues of grids, structural tactics

1 " = 1' - 0" or 1 : 12
Bag of Tricks working models for Symphony
reveal issues of structures, construction, fabrication, detail, texture, material, inhabitation, perception, light

12 " = 1' - 0" or 1 : 1
Big Bag of Tricks
Symphony structures. full scale.
deployment. assembly.
construction vs. structure.
(where's the hand?)

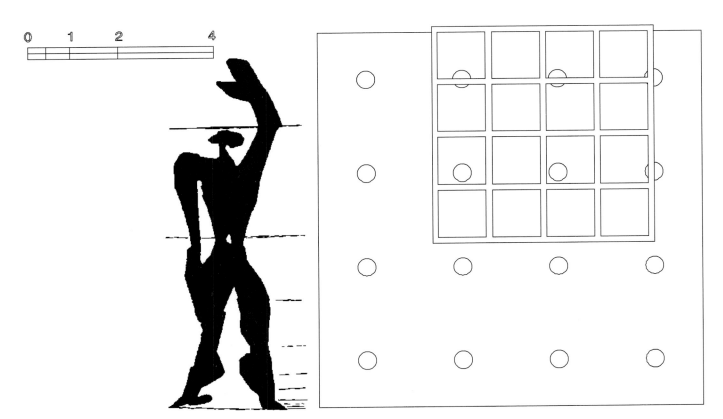

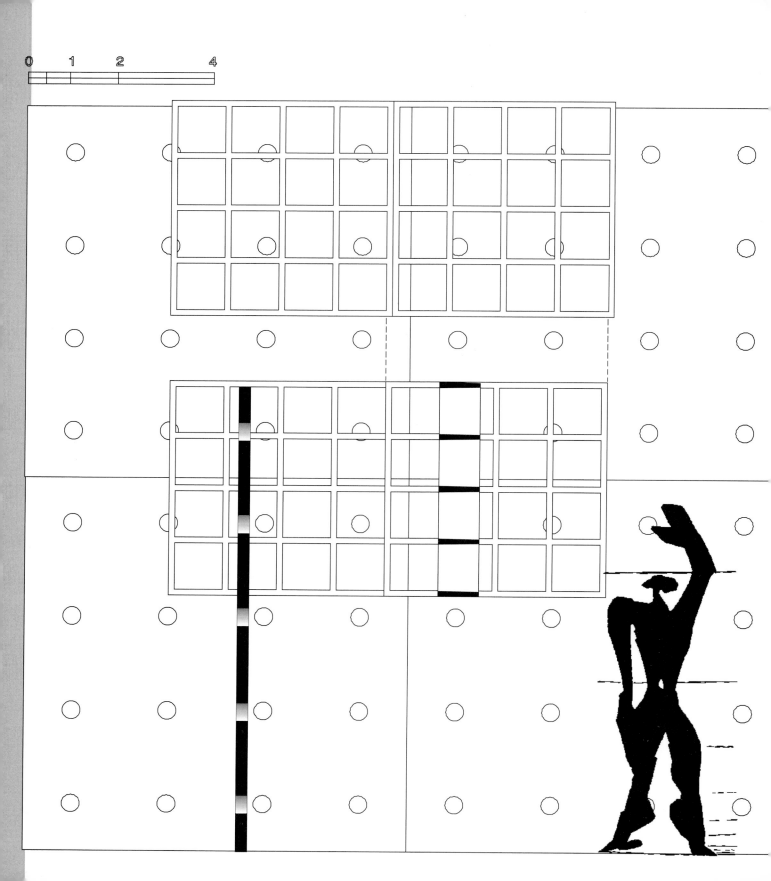

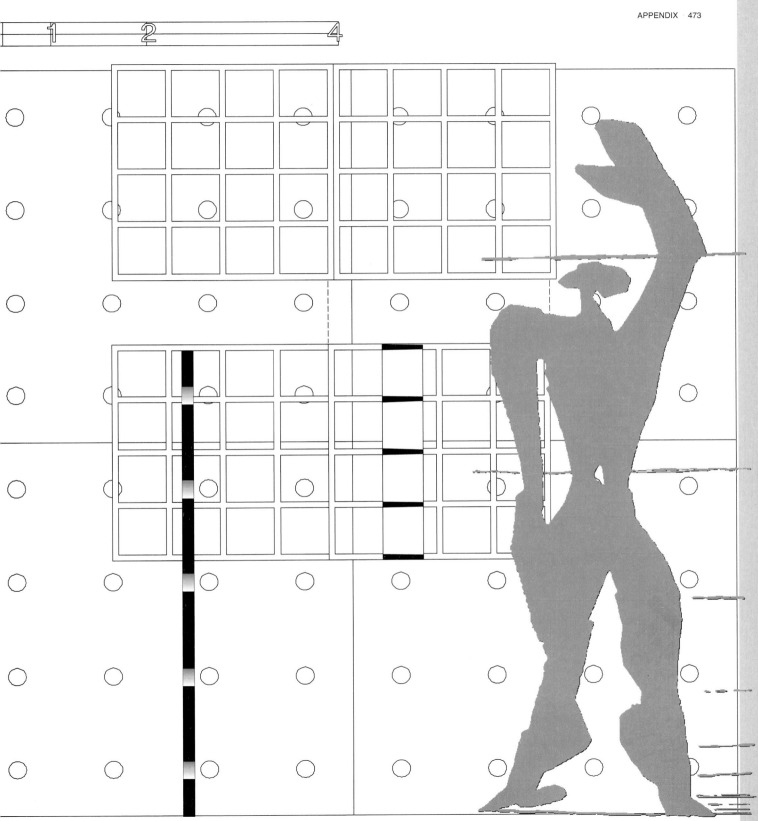

VISUAL GLOSSARY
(3 into 4)

CHRONOGEOMETRY

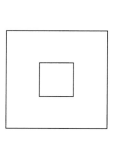

A. Solid Animation

Animation is the extension of three dimensional projection systems into a means to document changes in time of solids in space. Techniques from cinema and kinematics reveal relationships that are important to architectural design. The units M = mass, D = distance, and T = time can describe how motion, momentum, force, work, heat, power, and momenergy relate to solids.

B. Volume Development

Solids, moving and still, must be set in equilibrium to make volume. Volume is solid which is mostly empty. It is the essential element of architectural design, as opposed to the design of structures or construction. Rooms are volumes. Multi-roomed buildings, like cabinets, are collections of many volumes.

C. Composing Space in Time

The composition of space in time recognizes the mutual relationship between the perceiver and creator in the realm of human-scaled habitable volume, or architectural space in time. Realization of space, with all its variables, enables us to understand how architecture feels, and how we find a means of expression through the medium of space to convert plastic relationships into human communication with both intellectual and emotional content.

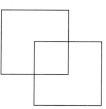

ARCHITECTURAL DYNAMIC ETUDES

0. PRELUDE
0A Motion in Vision
0B The Invention of Volume
0C Awakening: Vision in Many Dimensions

1. MELODY
1A Solids in Motion
1B Defining Volume
1C Dance and Sing

2. HARMONY
2A Forces Between Solids
2B Volumetric Algebra
2C Drama and Humor

3. CONCERTO
3A Solid Fields
3B Volume in Concert
3C Poetry

4. SYMPHONY
4A Pressurized Solids
4B Volume Integrity (Integral Volume)
4C Compassion

CHRONOGEOMETRY: FORM IN SPACE AND TIME

A modern equivalent to classical education: the trivium and quadrivium reconsidered. From classical times through the Renaissance, a scholar of higher education was expected to have mastered the three elements of the TRIVIUM: grammar logic rhetoric; and the four components of the QUADRIVIUM: arithmetic geometry astronomy music. In addition, there were the 7 LIVELY ARTS: painting sculpture architecture dance drama poetry music. What follows below suggest a modern interpretation applied to one of these arts, architecture. But given here a modern musical form, syncopation, and the polyrhythmic polymeters of 4 against 3, and 3 against 4.

A new Visual (and temporal) Glossary

The unique medium of architecture is space. But space is a subtle matter: an order of volumes, a fabric both empty and filled. The volumes in turn are formed from solids, generally massive elements in three dimensions. The organization of all these in time is the unavoidable path to architecture. The instruments are (1) the positioning of solids (2) the disposition of volumes, and (3) the composition of spaces... all with proper timing.

FOUR: Time is the primary material of architecture. Do not waste it! (Yours, or anyone else's-- this is the essence of the economy of means in planning.) This course ought properly be entitled GEOMETRODYNAMICS, not just DYNAMICS. Dynamic geometries concern moving parts and spaces including us and all our physical and visual world. In addition to the zero dimension of the point, there are at least four dimensions for an architect to consider:

1 D	2D	3D	4D
numeric	graphic	plastic	dynamic
linear	planimetric	volumetric	spacetim-ic
melody	harmony	concerto	symphony

THREE: Time amplifies ARCHITECTONICS. Given time, projection becomes *animation of vision*, fabrication becomes *development of invention*, and organizing principles become *idea relationships* of *creation* in space.

ANIMATION has many meanings: 1. it is the recognition of motion in the visual and physical world. 2. it is the development of form through modulation of mass and void. 3. it is the soul, anima, animals, the action, the quickening of life, the conscious organization of light and energy from one generation to the next. The first of these meanings pertains to SOLID; the second to VOLUME, the third to SPACE, all as they are subject to change through forces in time. The suggested animation studies focus on means to indicate the formal development and resolution of architectural ideas. Other issues for animation might include diagramming loads and deflections, mapping movements through spaces, showing the evolution of a phased project over time, or organizing a sequence of assembly and construction.

Why do children love animation? Part of the appeal is the luminous field of bright saturated color shapes that comprise TV or movie cartoons. Cartoons are moving shapes decoded as pictures, figures in a picture plane whose depth layers appear to be clear and simply organized. Yet that simplicity holds the surprises that allow cartoons to entertain us. The wizardry which drove earlier generations of children to peek "behind the scenes" to discover the magician's trick is present in the visual pun, spacial joke, and temporal contradiction of cartoons-- Wile E. Coyote frantically climbing a tightrope in mid air after the supporting ledge breaks off, or from an earlier style, Wily Willy disappearing behind a tree too narrow for his body. These are the clues to the ambiguous migrations our mind's eye takes between two, three, and four dimensions. Now wonder children love cartoons. They love to build!

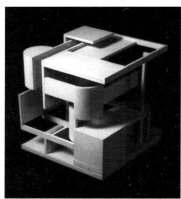

KEVIN FUNG

SOLID

Solids are three-dimensional figures, defined by nodes, edges, and surfaces at their boundaries. We usually think of solids as massive, like a stone or mountain, but an empty "wireframe" cube is still a solid. The three-dimensional blocks of architectonics are *idealized* solids. Outside of time, they do not change. Just as an equilateral triangle, a plane figure, is *always* an equilateral triangle, so too is the geometric solid **cube** *always* a cube. However, in the real world, every material solid is subject to forces which tend to change it over time. Physical stasis only occurs at absolute zero temperature.

Solids in time

Water flows into any given mold-- it is plastic; while ice (the same chemical, H_2O, but cooler) resists such deformation-- it is "rigid". The molecular structure of ice is like a lattice network of connected gently bouncing springs. All solids are intact crystal structures-- they hold their shape when a small part is removed. Removing too much mass can cause catastrophe: wind and gravity tug at the ice and rock of mountains, causing avalanches and rock slides. A solid may be shaped through carving or assembly of united sub-solids. The Architectonics study shown here at left is solid-- carving does not destroy its "plastic unity." It is plastic in the architectural sense, it has synthesized from separate elements a three dimensional unity which could be organized into a continuous human-made crystalline continuity that maintains the integrity of the whole, and that suggests in its very configuration many alternate possibilities. It is a solid pregnant with possibility-- alive to change. Like ice ready to melt, it awaits only the slightest additional energy to become something new. Can you find the Juan Gris-like rotated cube removed from the mountain face in the photo at the right?

Time in Solids

Time flows through materials. Heat is the dance of molecules. The higher the temperature, the more flowing the material. When warm enough, rubber and even steel will flow like viscous water, but under normal temperatures they are ***elastic,*** returning to their original shapes after flexing under load. The chemical bonds of an elastic material are stronger in maintaining the molecular structure than the external load is in distorting it. When too much load is added, a material exceeds its elastic limit and exhibits ***plastic*** behavior. It can no longer spring back to its original shape. Bending a paper clip once is a plastic deformation. Bending it many times causes the material to reach its plastic limit and break apart, or *fracture*. Rubber is mainly elastic, although minor plastic deformation does occur before it snaps; modeling clay is mainly plastic; and minerals like flint and obsidian are mainly brittle. A very brittle material can be dangerous in a structure since it gives little warning prior to failure. **Rigid** is "elastic" with very small amplitude of deformation, brittle is "elastic" with NO amplitude. *Strength* is a measure of the ability of a material to resist elastic deflection or plastic deformation under the force of an external load. *Ductility* measures how much a material will plastically deform prior to rupture, and is an important property in fabrication and safety. (At room temperature, clay is ductile but not strong, glass is strong but not very ductile.) *Durability* describes how a material remains strong over time, and depends on *corrosion resistance*, the ability to withstand oxidizing (rust) or other chemical exposure; *temperature resistance,* the ability to maintain strength as temperature varies; *toughness,* the ability to resist surface abrasion (diamond is the hardest, most scratch-resistant material); and creep, the plastic deformation caused by a small force applied for a long period of time. A steel ball bearing set on a piece of clay may leave no immediate impression. After some time it may displace and sink into the clay. Metal, plastic, and glass are subject to such creep. The Bag of Tricks permits a study of how materials emerge as solid form in time.

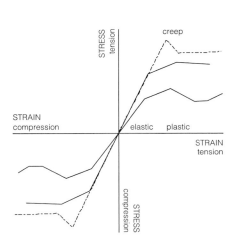

The "wave function" of human scale meso-structures...
meso= not macro or micro but mid, close to us, near at hand...

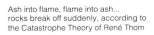

Ash into flame, flame into ash...
rocks break off suddenly, according to
the Catastrophe Theory of René Thom

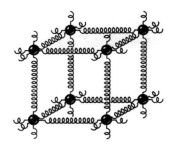

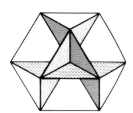

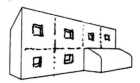

VOLUME

A volume is a solid which is bounded but (mostly) empty, a hollow solid, an empty fullness. Architects define volume plastically. Volume requires at least three mutually perpendicular planes, which themselves may be "filled", perforated, or empty. These may be skew (passing without touching) or intersecting, and may be located within the volume or at its boundaries. Keeping masses apart and in place in the void means ordering them into relationships that will resist the forces that tend to set them in motion. Thus, *volume is solid plus time.* For a builder, a brick is a brick. For an architect, a room is a "brick". For architects, volume is generally plastic; throughout a design, volume has the capacity for change. When a scheme "arrives", and volumes answer both the needs of the site and the program equally well, we might argue that only then does volume become "elastic".

punched openings

Structure: Volume in Time

Time organizes solids into structure. Force moves mass through tension (pulling), compression (pushing), and moment (bending). Stable structures must keep these forces in equilibrium. *Tensegrity structures* typically find the most efficient use of each material to resist each force, creating truly elegant structures. **Structural shapes** like I-beams and corrugation are designed to resist deflection and failure by putting mass where it is most stressed. The Bag of Tricks requires the assembly of solids to develop volume-- just as most buildings are made today. Castles and the Pyramids were essentially massive stone sculptures of great weight and lateral stability, but now we rarely carve caves. A major structural problem of modern lightweight construction is how to carefully load and configure each element to resolve forces to provide lateral stability in place of mass alone. Now a wall might *look* like it is built of stone, but may well be a plane of thin masonry veneer supported by the cage of a steel frame rising hundreds and even thousands of feet.

ambiguous

Time in volume: Perforation and Frames

In architecture, rooms are volumes, as are boxes and cabinets. Just as there is a structure of mass, there is also a structure of volume. The ground floor of a high rise building is both in volumetric compression from the floors above, and in volumetric shear from its intersection with the slab of the street and block. A multistory high rise building is not only an aggregate of separate room volumes, but may also be thought of as one larger single volume **perforated** by sets of solids, some void, some filled with mass. Thus light and proportion become major design issues. Almost all elements of the Bag of Tricks are perforated, which means that each of them, unlike the Kit of Parts elements, is both mass and void, from the very first instance. Thus, each part is a volume! Rubber bands, brass tubes and plastic tubing are topologically equivalent single loop volumes, already hollow mass around void, like a corridor, stair tower, or elevator shaft. The eggcrate, masonite, and mesh all allow many loops through them and are more topologically complex, like a pretzel. The architect Douglas Kelbaugh applied a subtle understanding of perforation and volume structure in the design of a beautiful and intelligent solar heated home in Princeton New Jersey. He selected the Trombe-wall system for passive solar heating of the house. Until Kelbaugh's design studies, most architects had dismissed the architectural use of the Trombe-wall to residential design for what appeared to be a simple reason: the concrete thermal mass had to face south, which meant that any Trombe-wall house would get no direct sunlight in its interior. Kelbaugh the architect modified an engineer's predisposition for 100% efficiency. He saw that if each nine-square area of the wall were perforated with a central "empty" square, every room in the house could be flooded with light, while the Trombe wall would operate with 8/9, or 88% efficiency. Literally and figuratively Brilliant!

frame

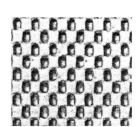

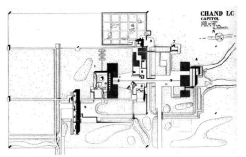

"...but you have not touched my heart..." Le Corbusier

This plan of Chandigarh, Le Corbusier's design for a new Capitol for India, is shown at the same scale as the aerial view of lower Manhattan, right. See page 404 for a larger version of this plan. What will Chandigarh look like 400 years from now?

SPACE

As we visually float over lower Manhattan, our feeling of space is visceral. We have not **yet** fallen! Space is volume with the weight of time: a span of endurance, literally or as idea. Space in time is an awesome breathtaking presence we don't often stop to experience, but the plan rotated into all dimensions engulfs us, moving through us as we move through it. The Brooklyn Bridge spans 1595 feet between its towers. The World Trade Center is 1368 feet tall, almost exactly the same as the 400 meter unit of Chandigarh's plan. That is all the "up" we can build so close to grade. (The first vertical inch is the hardest for a rocket's lift-off.) Truly we have only just entered space. The earth's surface transforms infalling energy into gravity and re-radiates longer waves as heat. Plan and section map the *union of space and time,* the meeting place of dimensions. In all dimensions the plan is the generator. The **plan is the intersection of gravity and light**.

Composing in space and time

Volume is an entity, a solid made of mostly void. But **space** is a medium, a continuum of all possible volumes, from completely filled to totally empty. A plan is a plot for action. We are **participants** in the creation of architectural space and time, dancing **with** (as well as **in**) the space. Space is composed in time, like music. Com-pose, from the Latin *ponere* (to place or put aside) means to place with, suggesting *interaction*. Other variations on this root are suggestive: propose, to place forward; impose/expose, to place in/out; suppose, to place under. Consider also repose, dispose, juxtapose, interpose, purpose, posal (a puzzle). All invoke the musical structure of architecture as a relationship of places in time. The forces that operate on locating program volumes to clarify a *parti* interact with the forces that organize solids to make volumes, either in coincidence (the same location order: column grid or bearing walls also organize the rooms) or in counterpoint (opposition and variation: the free plan). Structure of solid and volume conditions the architecture of spaces. A roof plane defined by a truss will create an entirely different space than the same span defined by an arch or tensile structure. The decision as to **which** wall of a room will be open to light or entry is not only a structural decision. It is one based on the dynamic loading of the volume itself-- and recognizes that each and every solid in the architectural composition may be filled or empty, depending on the totality of the design solution. The fabric of an architectural order is composed not of volume, but of space.

The Shadow of Time

Space is the *union* of gravity and light, embracing all matter and radiation through time. Architecture is the structure and rhythm of energy, where light is the key, and rhythmic number is the notation. Time flows through a deflecting beam. But if a volume does not change the form and evolution of other volumes that encounter it, including the complex volumes of people, then it is limited only to the narrow here and now of abstraction. If volume doesn't cast a "time shadow" into both future and past, then it isn't space. The interplay of material and geometry goes beyond the interaction of volume, because when real materials meet ideal geometries, the true interaction of space and time becomes poignant: the presence of a brick in its mortar, or a drill hole in its steel column bring to both mind and body all the drama and passion of the long arc from conception to actuality that is human architecture. The vivid reality of fresh paint and the smell of shaved wood and curing concrete evolves into another "now", a reality of cooking smells, crumbling rock, summer breezes, decay, and eventual rebirth. As Le Corbusier says, nothing is transmissible but thought. Only the idea persists beyond mortality, but every presence carries space forward out of the staleness and into the freshness of time. Space is volume with a worldline through time.

ANIMATION OF SOLIDS

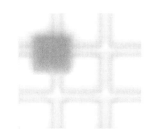

0. MOTION IN VISION

SEEING is drawing with the eyes, tracing and discovering the construction of a perception of the world. Vision is the reconstruction of possible worlds through seeing. About 80% of the human brain is devoted to processing optical information, so to a large degree, the music of the mind is essentially the play of vision. While reading is a controlled linear scan of the eyes across a page, graphic and pictorial perception allows (encourages!) the eyes to roam all over. Motion vision sees change-- either in the position of objects or in the observer's relation to the visual field. A newborn infant opens its eyes, sees a **BLUR**, gains **FOCUS,** eventually learns to move the head, the body, and ultimately walk. Mastering binocular vision and parallax, a toddler wonders: what's on the other side? We must *move* to grasp completely three dimensions beyond still-life illusion. If the picture plane is the surface of all projections, then space becomes the solid of all chronogeometric stereo vision animations. As we learn new optical skills, we increase our vision, until at last the moment of self-consciousness meets awareness of the world beyond, and we exclaim, for the first time, "Oh, I see!"

Moving through Space

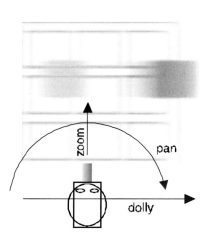

MOTION is distance through space in time. Speed, or **VELOCITY** measures the magnitude of motion, or the rate of distance in time. Where D = distance and T = time, velocity= D/T. Motion itself can be in motion. This is called **ACCELERATION**, or the rate of change of motion. In the same units, acceleration = D/T². **TRANSLATION,** spacial displacement along a line, and **ROTATION**, angular displacement around a point or axis, describe **objects in motion**. Cinema and movie techniques describe ways a **subject** like human eye or camera can be **in motion**. **PAN** is swinging the point of view from a single point, hence the word *panorama*. **ZOOM** is the motion of the field of vision, **in** to magnify a detail, **out** to embrace a wider visual field. **DOLLY** is the motion of a viewer or camera in space, forward or back, left or right, up or down. Note the inherent ambiguity of the relation of the vision field to the point of view in camera or mind's eye. In demonstrations of these motions, it is impossible to tell whether it is the object in the field or the viewer who is actually moving. Without any frame of reference, it would not be possible to sense any motion or change of position between views. There are **combinations of motions**: i.e. dolly left while panning to the right can keep an object in view while the camera moves. Zoom in while panning down can show a distant car driving toward us on a mountain lookout.

Moving through Time

When a frame of reference is spacial, we detect displacement. A chessboard measures the moves of the pieces. When a frame of reference is temporal, we can detect change in time rather than space. For example, stop action movies reveal the otherwise invisible slow-motion walk of a starfish or unfolding of a flower. Film presents the illusion of motion by showing 18 or more slightly different still images each second, which the human eye sees as continuous motion. Editing, the art of plastic temporal composition, exploits the possibilities for non-continuous time, reordering **FRAMES** of events using **CUT/PASTE** and **COPY/DELETE** to order strings of frames into expectation and surprise, elaborating into boredom or thrill, suspense or resolution. Lens effects used for transitions include **WIPE, FADE** (to black or white) and **DISSOLVE/FOCUS**. It is not always easy to distinguish objective from subjective motion. For example, if a background object translates while a foreground object is stationary, the camera is panning. Motion helps resolve depth cues, to distinguish when bigger image means closer rather than actually larger object. **Multiple pathways** of both viewer and object allow **SEQUENCE** and **SIMULTANEITY** to integrate separate "subjective" views into "objective" comprehensive plan/section stereovision.

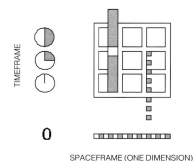

SPACEFRAME (ONE DIMENSION)

0

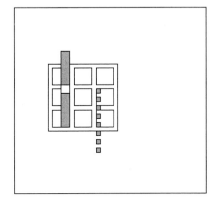

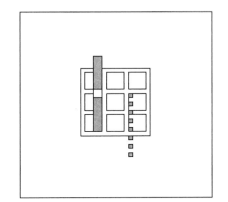

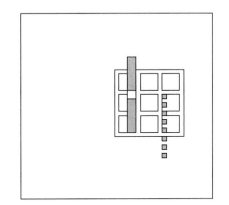

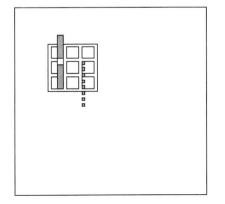

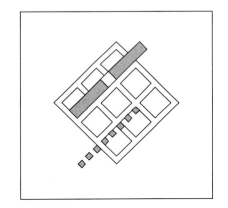

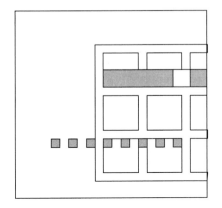

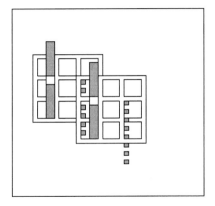

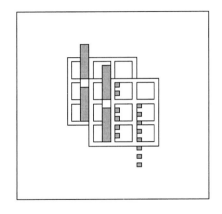

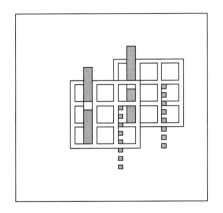

DEVELOPMENT OF VOLUME

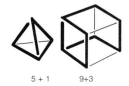

FOLD LINES

STIFF LINES

5 + 1   9+3

CORRUGATION

STIFF LINE
FOLDED PLANES
IMPLIES VOLUME

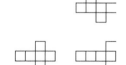

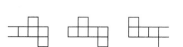

THE SIX UNIQUE WAYS TO SKIN A CAT
FOLD SIX CONTIGUOUS SQUARES INTO A CUBE....
NO MIRRORS OR ROTATIONS

PERFORATION = PUNCH AND SHEAR

0. THE INVENTION OF VOLUME

ADDING DIMENSION. Seeing is an active mode, not passive. It requires searching, exploring, testing, inventing possibilities of meaning. Architects need to be able to move freely in the mind's eye between and through dimensions. **VOLUME** in 3D can arise from its one- and two-dimensional precedents. This is how bridges and cabinets are assembled and built. We must see the potential for section in plan and for plan in section; we must imagine the possibilities of a north elevation from an axonometric taken from the southeast, and so forth. Architects must be able to visualize how line engenders plan engenders solid engenders spacetime, both literally when cutting plywood or models, and more strategically when aligning rooms along a corridor or organizing buildings to form a city square. One way to develop this skill is to practice moving between dimensions. Buckminster Fuller noted that tracing a line into a triangle will not completely close in spacetime-- the origin will have moved in time by the time the pencil returns!

Line into Volume

Not all solids can be made from a single continuous folded line. While a cuboctahedron can be built from a single strut folded 12 times to rejoin its origin, for a tetrahedron a cut must be made to create at least one edge distinct from the other five. Interestingly, while a cube may not be made from 12 continuous folded lines, it can be made from 6 continuous folded planes. To remain sturdy under load, a wire frame cube (lines connecting pin joints), must be triangulated. Moment connections at vertices may replace triangulation to make square faces and cubic solids strong.

Plane Into Volume

CUTTING AND FOLDING planes is a direct means for discovering 3 dimensions in 2 dimensions. One practice that forces moving between dimensions is the game of *"origami spaceframe"*, which can transform a planar surface into a set of frames defining cubic volumes. The repetition of frame permits many 3D variations from any given 2D "plan". The frames are volumetrically apart, and can be experienced in many different orders. Any fold other than 90°, will produce a weaker volume-defining effect.
1. Take a page and fold it orthogonally several times along one axis, then along the other. This generates lines of equal squares for cutting and folding. (**ORIGAMI** is the Japanese art of paper folding.)
2. Then, more or less arbitrarily, make a "plan, of cuts as solid lines and folds as dotted lines
3. Explore the resulting volumes and volumetric relationships that are created.

Solid Into Volume

Unlike a blank paper surface, the articulated picture plane of any confronted image field is loaded with cues to depth as well as plane. Thus the picture plane is a surface as much solid as planar. Part of the enormous power paintings have on vision and our minds comes from the fact that the **picture plane** carries cues to depth-- it is a rendering of solid space. Cubist and Purist painting especially supports seeing the picture plane as a total world view. When there is motion in vision, every side is equally the "front". The eye always confronts, and always seeks to "look around", and through imaginative projection discovers space between and through solids, whether filled or empty. **LAYERING** of planes in space reveals three dimensions in the cues to solids in two dimensions. **PERFORATION** is a kind of "3D folding" where the extreme fold most perpendicular to another dimension is equivalent to shear, a kind of punch through **solid into volume**. The continued relation between a punched hole and its displaced circle of paper can establish the presence of a mostly empty solid, or volume. Perforation can be either additive or subtractive in developing volume.

0

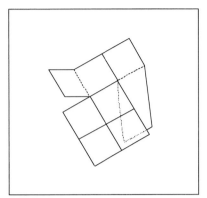

CUT AND FOLD

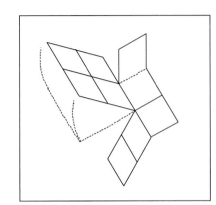

MULTIPLE CUT AND FOLD

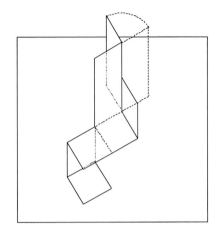

SEQUENCE OF CUTS AND FOLDS

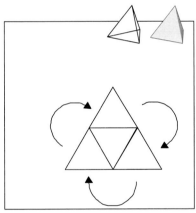

PLANE INTO TETRAHEDRON

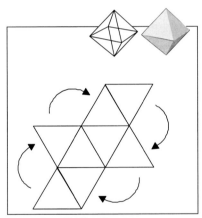

PLANE INTO OCTAHEDRON

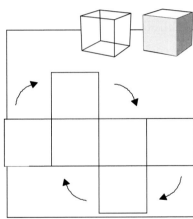

PLANE INTO CUBE

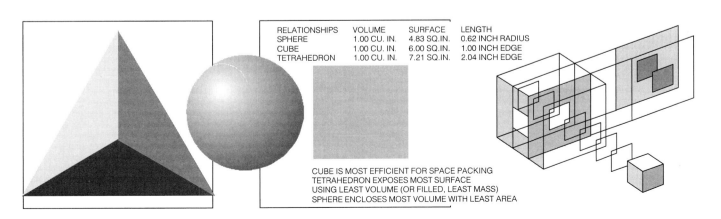

RELATIONSHIPS	VOLUME	SURFACE	LENGTH
SPHERE	1.00 CU. IN.	4.83 SQ.IN.	0.62 INCH RADIUS
CUBE	1.00 CU. IN.	6.00 SQ.IN.	1.00 INCH EDGE
TETRAHEDRON	1.00 CU. IN.	7.21 SQ.IN.	2.04 INCH EDGE

CUBE IS MOST EFFICIENT FOR SPACE PACKING
TETRAHEDRON EXPOSES MOST SURFACE
USING LEAST VOLUME (OR FILLED, LEAST MASS)
SPHERE ENCLOSES MOST VOLUME WITH LEAST AREA

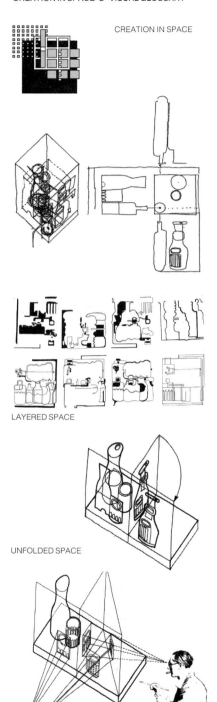

CREATION IN SPACE

LAYERED SPACE

UNFOLDED SPACE

PROJECTED SPACE

O. *AWAKENING*: SPACE IN MANY DIMENSIONS

A baby looks but does not always see. Innocent, a child looks at a fire and touches it--hot! Knowing, a child sees fire and does not get burned. What knowing is needed to **SEE** space? And how to learn such knowing without losing the innocence of the listening mind that reveals intuition, often a key to design? Open any window, or wander through the infinite layers and paths of a book. Explore the dimensions of the picture plane in any visual field. Let the eye travel in, on, and out of the picture plane, into space. Seeing engenders vision, through the ambiguities inherent in 2 dimensions that suggest alternative configurations in 3 dimensions. **VISION** is multiple seeing, that is, the ability to hold relationships from two or more views or projections in the mind at the same time. Examples include the ability to understand that a change in plan may create a change in section, or to see the front and the side as one, or to see both the "before" and "after" of a change together. Vision reveals space, which unites all subjective and objective volumes into a continuity through time.

The Habit of Invention

Space can be music for the eyes, an endless story of the invention of the picture plane, a conversation between multiple dimensions. Invention depends on seeking patterns, building patterns of patterns, taking risks. Roving vision is like moving multiple cameras in all dimensions. It is a pilgrimage through the eye's mind (and mind's eye), shine a light of curiosity into space. The translation from 2 to 3 dimensions helps develop alternative realities for a given field, each valid in surface *and* depth, in graphic clarity *and* volumetric ambiguity. The *origami spaceframe* exercise helps the student to learn to invent dimension in construction. Cubism and Purism depend on skill of multiple seeing. In these works of art subtle changes of lines suggest movement of elements forward and back in depth as an entire configuration moves across the visual field. The variation of repeated and superimposed frames develops meaning an through evolution of form following form. Architectural space is a continuum of energy modulating volumes, where consciousness is both planner and participant in a range of objective and subjective experience. Mind and universe permeate each other, everywhere. Growing awareness means increasing abstraction, increasing concrete-ness, increasing realism.

Exploring Purist Space

PURISM is an outgrowth of Cubism, distinct in its insistence on the equality, if not the primacy, of the picture plane in structuring space. Purism, even more than Cubism, demands the ability to hold both the actuality and the potentiality of all dimensions concurrent in one's vision. Transparency and layering can create depth without perspective and light without shadow. Multiple and simultaneous views create ambiguity. One possible working method for exploring Purist space is:
*1. Build a model to the proportions of the selected Purist or Cubist work which explores the contrast between object and structure. Consider problems of composition, form, and meaning as you move between representation and abstraction. Develop volumes **between** as much as volumes **of** objects.*
2. Build further models, perhaps in color, which within the structure already discovered, explores perceptions of depth. Locate/mediate foreground, middle, and background, using clues consistently interpreted from the given painting. (overlapping, color/light contrast, oblique views, etc.
*3. Explore ambiguities of structure and depth, and polarities within the work-- flat/round, black/white, complimentary contrast (red/green). Keep turning the model to be able to see it from all **six** (plus!) sides. Concentrating only on the "front" view, will leave the other sides undeveloped and unrelated to the whole. Remember, the model is a plastic 3D construction, **not** a picture.*
4. "Folding solids" into cubism is a <u>hint</u> about discovering a dimension perpendicular (⊥) to 3D space.

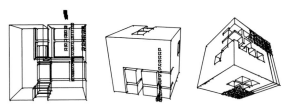

"Gravity is only temporary". Eric Owen Moss, Architect

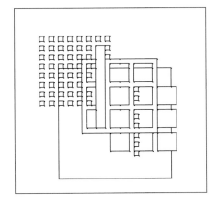

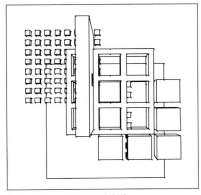

PLAN INTO THREE DIMENSIONS

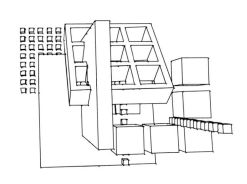

TRANSLATION AND ROTATION INTO DEPTH

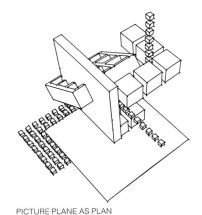

PICTURE PLANE AS PLAN

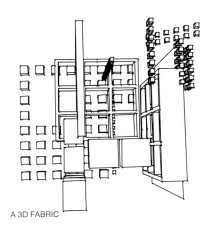

FOLD, EXTRUDE,
DISPLACEMENT

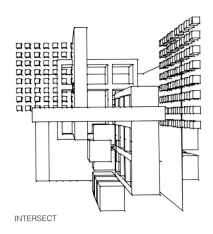

INTERSECT

PERFORATE PLANES, FIND CONTINUITY

A 3D FABRIC

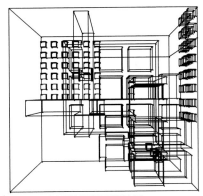

SIMULTANEOUSLY DEEP AND FLAT

ANIMATION OF SOLIDS

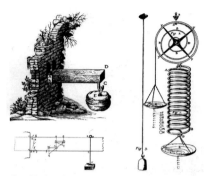

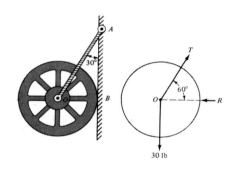

Ernst Mach on inertia: "the reason a rock hurts when you kick it is that you are trying to move the whole uiverse."

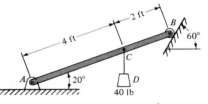

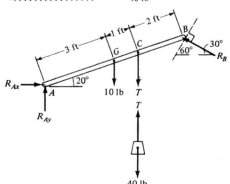

1. SOLIDS IN MOTION

A **SOLID** is an entity in three dimensions, the logical extension in the series point, line , plane.... Matter appears to us as solids of mass. (At the atomic scale solids are mostly empty space between dense concentrations of matter in the nucleus and fields of moving electrons keeping them apart.) Isaac Newton noted that matter tends to keep still or to move in a uniform way unless it is acted on by an outside agent. The quality of this persistence in state is **INERTIA**, a thing's resistance to changing its position if at rest, or velocity if in motion. Inertia is measured in units of **MASS**, expressed as M. Vision alone, without the weight of experience, cannot tell us the mass of solids. In a Biblical movie epic Samson hurls "weightless" capitals made of styrofoam, not marble! Moving mass carries **MOMENTUM** = M D /T, the product of mass and speed we can feel on impact. A one ton truck moving at 10 miles per hour hits a wall with as much momentum as a quarter-ton pickup moving at 40 miles per hour. Whereas speed describes motion of a body in space, it does not specify direction. To do this a new kind of measuring tool: we must make our ruler into an arrow to make a **VECTOR**. Vectors indicate both magnitude and direction. Vectors are added both numerically and geometrically. **VELOCITY** is speed with direction; it is a vector value.

Rock and Roll: Solids Keep Still

The geometry of structures affect how **LOADS** of solids seeking motion are resisted, so strength depends on both the properties *and* arrangement of materials. A round stone will roll on a slope, a rock of equal mass sit still. **COMPRESSION** pushes a solid together, **TENSION** pulls a solid apart. A solid can also be twisted or bent in moment. A rope is virtually a pure tension member: you can't "push a rope". Solids find **REPOSE**, as in no place else to fall; or **EQUILIBRIUM,** as in no place else to be without it all coming apart losing its poise, or **TENSEGRITY,** as in no place else to go that doesn't return the structure to its original condition. While repose and equilibrium depend on gravity as glue typically using one material to resist both compressive and tensile loads throughout , often leading to redundancy of material (stone beams), tensegrity can be independent of gravity. Tensegrities typically assign a particular material to resist each force in the structure based on the most efficient use of the material involved, making them truly elegant. We might say that tensegrity is the evolution of the origin point.

The Free Body Diagram

Many loads on a solid will tend to make it move in different directions. But these loads can be combined to establish equilibrium and keep the body in place. Each element in a structure is held in place by the loads acting on it. A **FREE-BODY DIAGRAM** is a sketch of the body to be analyzed, that uses vectors to show the magnitude and direction of loads exerted on the body, as well as all significant dimensions and angles. A free-body diagram can help in designing a structure by locating exactly how much push and pull is needed to resist and control the motion of its solids. Correct solution of a statics problem depends on the successful completion of the free-body diagram. All external forces and moments that act on a body must be shown in the free-body diagram. These forces and moments may include:
1. *The weight of the body: The weight of a body always acts vertically downward through the center of gravity of the body. The center of gravity of a body is the point of the application of the resultant weight of the body.*
2. *The contact forces from other bodies: These represent the forces exerted by the bodies that are in contact with the isolated free body.*
3. *The reactions from the supports: These are the constraining forces exerted by the supports on the free body. Often they must be calculated from the other loads when designing structural elements.*

1

M = MASS
D = DISTANCE
T = TIME

MOTION = DISTANCE IN TIME = D/T
ACCELERATION = CHANGE IN MOTION = D/T²

1.	MOMENTUM	= M D/T
2.	FORCE = MA	= M D/T²
	NEWTON *(DYNE!)*	
3.	WORK (JOULE)	= M D²/T²
	HEAT (JOULE)	
4.	POWER (WATT)	= M D²/T³
	MOMENERGY	= M² D³/T³

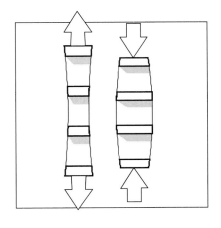

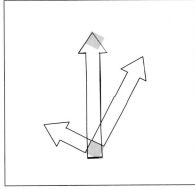

ADDING VECTORS

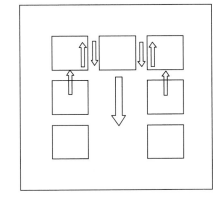

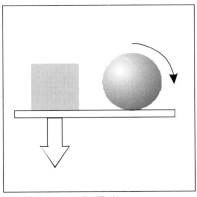

MASS, INERTIA, AND FRICTION

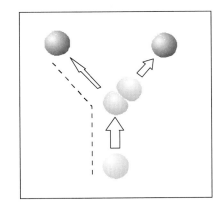

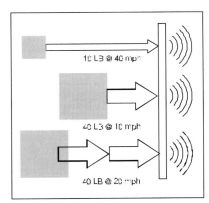

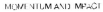

MOMENTUM AND IMPACT

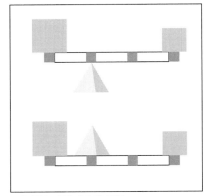

EQUILIBRIUM AND REPOSE

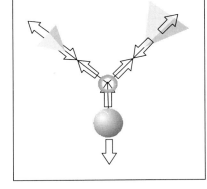
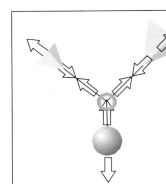

DEVELOPMENT OF VOLUME

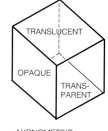

OPAQUE

TRANSLUCENT

TRANSLUCENT

OPAQUE

TRANSPARENT

TRANS-PARENT

PLAN/SECTION

AXONOMETRIC

LIGHT MODULATING MATERIAL CONVENTIONS
IN PLAN AND AXONOMETRIC

Red	rigid line	brass tubes
Orange	plastic line	ABS rods
Yellow	elastic line	rubber band
Green	plastic plane	needlepoint mesh
Blue	rigid plane	masonite pegboard
Violet	rigid frame	eggcrate

ONE COLOR CODE TO DENOTE
MATERIALS IN BAG OF TRICKS

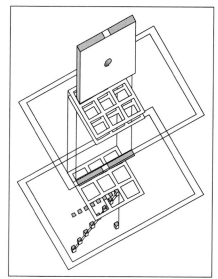

QUICK AXONOMETRIC METHOD

1. DEFINING VOLUME

A **VOLUME** is a solid which is bounded but (mostly) empty. Solids may be filled with any combination of mass and void. **VOID** is the absence of matter. A volume is a hollow solid, an empty fullness. Volumes are vital to architecture: rooms are volumes, as are boxes and cabinets. A multistory high rise building can be understood as not only an aggregate of separate volumes (rooms), but also as one larger single volume perforated by sets of solids, some void, some filled with mass. Architects define volume plastically. How many corners, edges, and/ or faces of a cube are needed to make the volume of the cube present to perception through line and plane? Can one more be taken away? Is there a minimum number? Volume requires at least three mutually perpendicular planes, which themselves may be filled, perforated, or empty. These may be skew (passing without touching) or intersecting, and may be located within the volume or at its boundaries. Solids defining a volume need not be actually touching-- imagine them in orbit with laser controlled thrusters (let's call them Zagorski Coils) to keep them from drifting apart.

Structuring Mass to Make Volume

Structure is a factor in defining a volume made of actual materials. Improvising the position of masses (like playing with forks on a tabletop) helps to get a feel for how forces may define volume. Direct modeling in space and time requires spontaneity balanced by calculation balanced by feedback from forces in the field. Here is one way for **IMPROVISING MASS INTO VOLUME:**
1. Make one elegant joint of two or three mass elements.
2. Build outward in each direction from that first elegant connection.
3. Secure connections of isolated elements into a perceptible volume and stable tensegrity.
4. Resolve into elegant simplicity. Search for and eliminate structural redundancy, etc.

Documenting Volumetric Design

Two-dimensional methods are needed for rapidly recording spacial ideas (and will be, even after the advent 3D xerocopying). Graphics and color conventions can identify materials in plan and section and thus imply force conditions in a volume. Keep sharpened prismacolor pencils handy to sketch ideas. You need not "fill in" the planes nor draw their grid perforations-- simple outlines of the relevant color/material will note your design strategy. Other elements (joints, stairs) can be indicated in simple black and white outline. A "**QUICK AXONOMETRIC**" **METHOD** is a good way to explore three-dimensional ideas on paper. Along with quick modeling techniques, (see page 448), it is one of the best ways to explore the program interactions of **FREE VOLUME DIAGRAMS. IT** is also helpful in developing strategies for using the various grid intervals implied by materials available in the Bag of Tricks.
1. Sketch freehand plans to scale on trace over graph paper, showing wall thickness, etc.
2. Tape tracing paper plans over each other at the correct axonometric rotation and vertical interval.
3. On a clean tracing paper overlay, "connect the dots", freehand, to get a quick view of volume implications of plan and section and see relationships between structure, circulation, and light.
4. Augment with intuitively "twisted" (a la Cézanne) perspective sketches to study joints etc. in detail.
5. Alter model in accordance with drawing discoveries; repeat process over and over...

Exploded assembly

Shift subassemblies along axonometric {or isometric} axes to develop an exploded view of mass elements. Such a view is a time-honored tradition in model building, and is especially useful for developing a guide to the sequence of construction. These may be combined with "twisted" views.

1

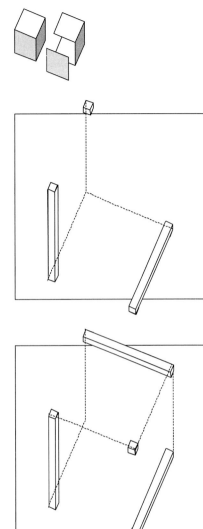

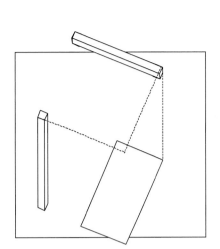

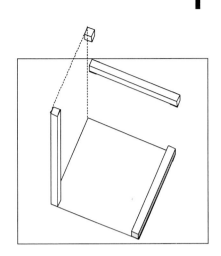

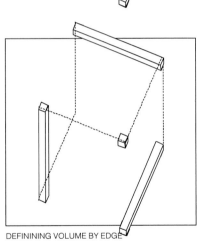

DEFININING VOLUME BY EDGE

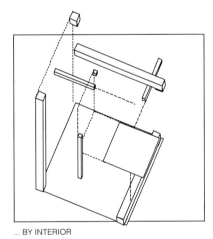

... BY INTERIOR

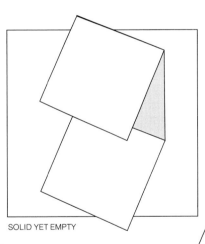

SOLID YET EMPTY

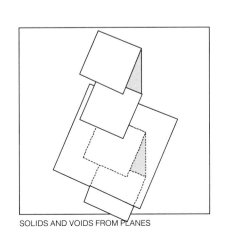

SOLIDS AND VOIDS FROM PLANES

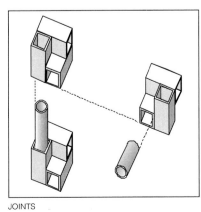

JOINTS

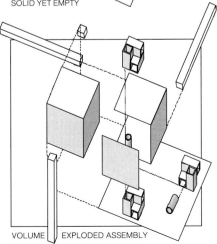

VOLUME | EXPLODED ASSEMBLY

CREATION IN SPACE

1. DANCE AND SING

Volume is an entity-- a solid made of mostly void. But space is a medium. **SPACE** is the continuum of all possible solids, from completely filled to totally empty. Space is the union of gravity and light, embracing all matter and radiation through time. Space is volume with the weight of time-- a span of endurance, literally or as idea. While Le Corbusier's Strasbourg City Hall was never realized, its volume is well documented, so the cues are there for us to imagine its space and the living spirit of a city in it (see page 294) Just as volume is a dynamic development of the still-life of architectonics, so too is space the dynamic development of volume. A room is a volume. Its floor, ceiling and walls are made of masses that experience the dynamic stress and strain of structural forces on them. But the decision as to **which** wall will be open to light or entry is not only a structural decision. It is one based on the dynamic loading of the volume itself-- and recognizes that each and every solid in the architectural composition may be filled or empty, depending on the totality of the design solution. The fabric of an architectural order is a function of the design not of volume, but of space.

Architectural forces in Space

Each volume is a spacetime free body. A "**free volume diagram**" may show how *architectural* forces may distort a volume, creating program stress and strain on spacial relationships which may deflect, shear, or shatter volume. If a load can bend or shear a beam, then a room along a corridor may bend or shear that "line". Architects develop "moves", ways to think about shifting volume elements in plastic compositions. Because we ourselves and all radiation fields are part of a spacetime continuum, we cannot separate objective from subjective experience when we seek the realization of space. Thus consciousness is both the planner of and the participant in architectural space. When we change plan, we alter perception. Not just to see in the space, but to **be** in the space involves all senses, from vestibular to "common sense". We may be able to stand outside a volume, but we can never stand outside of space. Space is the intersection of the dance between body as figure and body as field, between perception and invention.

Architecture is made of space and time

Human bodies are free bodies. The human body dwells in motion or repose, inhabiting space which is also in motion or repose. For architects to design space, filled with all range of radiation, from levity (light) to gravity (matter), is to design both inside and outside ourselves, *simultaneously*. Architecture is made of space and imprints the mold of local spacetime into a fabric of ever-contingent mass and void. The presence of space depends on perception as much as physics. Human movement distorts "pure" volume, as the design evolution of a plan inevitably reveals (see plans of St. Peters in Rome, page 210). To find an architectural order of circulation, a *promenade architecturale*, (first walk up a stair, then along a corridor, look to the left, enter a cube, find a window, move to the light, turn a corner, descend a ramp across a plane, etc.) consider the relationship of the order of movement to the order of the composed volumes. Here is a possible order of study of these issues in developing your Melody project. When you master this, you will be ready to apply it to the more complex programs of the later Harmony, Concerto, and Symphony studies.

1. Establish a simple movement, i.e.. up a stair, across a narrow catwalk.
2. Extend this into path and sequence through volume(s), considering views and orientation.
3. Establish a second simple movement perpendicular to the first. Allow them to intersect.
4. Repeat for a third perpendicular to both the first two. Use all three to help define the order of volumes.
5. Resolve into a unified space of elegant simplicity; search for and eliminate redundancy, etc.

1

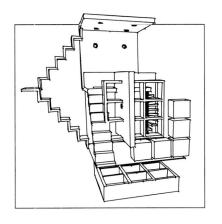

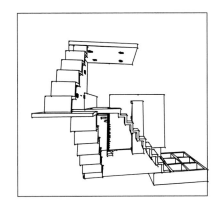

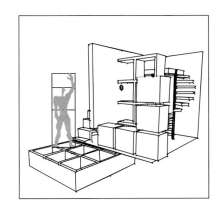

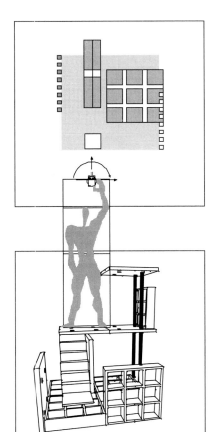

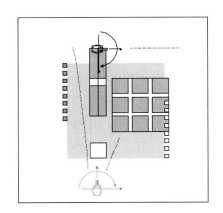

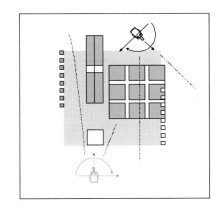

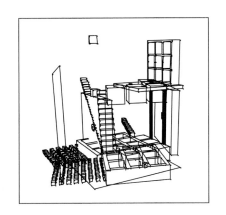

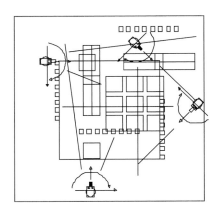

ANIMATION OF SOLIDS

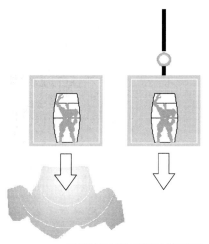

THE RELATIVITY OF TWO VOLUMES

Einstein's principle of Equivalence: acceleration or gravity depends on the spacetime frame of reference. Outside of a gravitational field, a "weightless" person feels no downward force.

PIN AND MOMENT JOINTS: A DEMONSTRATION

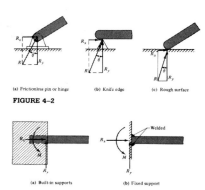

(a) Frictionless pin or hinge   (b) Knife edge   (c) Rough surface

FIGURE 4–2

(a) Built-in supports   (b) Fixed support

TYPES OF SUPPORTS

2. FORCES BETWEEN SOLIDS

Inertia keeps bodies persisting in their current state of rest or motion. **FORCE** is the agent that changes this persistence by altering the speed and/or direction of a solid. Newton's Second Law states that force is the product of mass times acceleration, or **F = ma**. Force is a vector: a load with both magnitude and direction. Einstein noted that we cannot tell if the force we feel on our feet in an elevator is the result of the car accelerating upward or an acceleration downward due to the "force" of a gravitational field. He called this "happiest thought" the principle of Equivalence. Whether we call the event a force on a body or an acceleration of a body depends on the choice of our **frame of reference** in both space and time.

Since masses extend as solids in three dimensions, interactions between objects cannot take place at exact centers. Thus forces between solids must occur eccentrically in at least one or more dimensions. (Although for free body diagrams and load analysis, forces are often assumed to act at a solid's center of mass.) Spacing between the application of forces on a solid generates eccentric loads. **MOMENT** is the product of force and distance. Two people of unequal mass on a seesaw may generate equal moments if they adjust their distances from the fulcrum (moment arms) accordingly to create a balance in equilibrium. Interaction between earth's mass and the extended mass of a **CANTILEVER** like a diving board or balcony creates a bending moment in the solid. Tension and compression forces combine to create bending moments which determine loading on **COLUMNS** and **BEAMS**. A seesaw's lever and fulcrum is one of the basic simple machines: the others are the inclined plane and pulley(a wheel is a special case of lever and fulcrum). Machines are vector benders! Loads act to create both rotation and shear in solids. Why are rotation and shear such important effects? This is how galaxies are made!

Joining Forces

When free body solids meet they act on each other. A **JOINT** is needed to combine free bodies into a configuration that acts as one structural element. A hinge or **PIN JOINT** allows great movement of one structural member in relation to another without establishing any resistance to that movement, while a **MOMENT JOINT** resists the tendency of the members to move. Moment connectors create bending and shear stresses within the connecting members. Two hands grasping through finger loops permit rotation and create a pin connection while one wrist gripping another is closer to a moment connection. Pin joints yield, moment joints resist. Joints can be created through addition of solids, like Tinkertoy™ and struts and hubs, or by subtraction of one solid from another, like classical Japanese carpentry. Lego™ pieces create a **FRICTION JOINT** combing both addition and subtraction. There are many special kinds of kinds of **SUPPORTS** or connectors that sustain the force on one solid through another. A **FOUNDATION** is the supporting joint between any free body configuration and the planetary solid of Earth. Different types of supports include frictionless pin or hinge, knife edge, rough surface, built-in and fixed (welded) supports. Loaded members may sit on one or more rollers, a rocker, a smooth "frictionless" surface, or they may hang from a cable or be linked between supports. Joining solids at the scale of human construction depends on both the mechanical nature of chemical glue and the chemical nature of mechanical joints. Welding steel, laying mortar, nailing wood all depend on both the mechanical roughness of surfaces and the chemical rigidity of the interacting materials. Construction design seeks not only the best geometry to keep loaded solids still, but also the best possible **SEQUENCE OF CONNECTION** ("this goes in first, then this, tab A in slot B...") because building is *always* an animation. Time counts. Literally, a mechanical joint is a harmony machine".

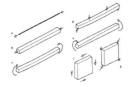

2

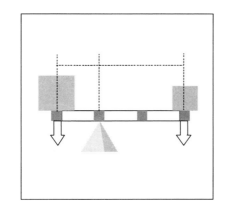

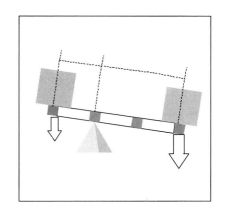

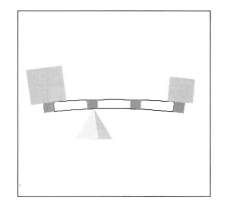

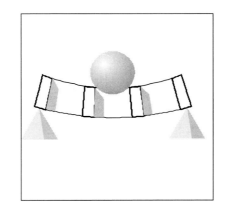

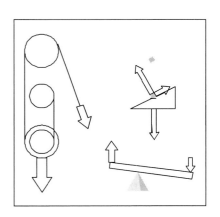

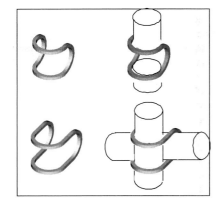

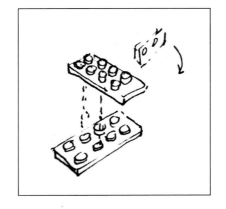

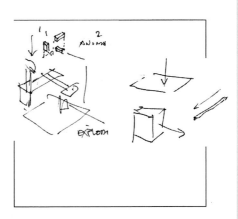

DEVELOPMENT OF VOLUME

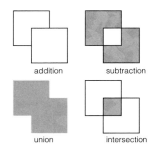

addition   subtraction

union   intersection

BOOLEAN OPERATIONS

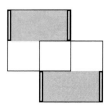

VOLUME JOINT
BOOLEAN OPERATIONS COMBINED
HARMONY:
UNION AND INTERSECTION TOGETHER

OVERLAY AND TRANSPARENCY CAN HELP
INVENTION OF NEEDED ZONES OF SPACE.

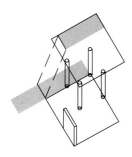

LAYERS OF MODEL AND LAYERS OF TRACE--
DIALOGUE BETWEEN DIMENSIONS

2. INTERACTION OF VOLUME

Boolean Operations

Virtually every project in Architectonics involved the addition of masses to define volumes between them as the only operational strategy for making spacial order. But other ways exist for making spaces; for example sculptors carve volume from solid stone. Even more strategies are available to architects, who conceive of manipulating pure volume. The boundaries of a solid make a distinction between its inside and outside, creating a first interaction between volumes. Volume always exists in interaction with other volume, like Albers' *Interaction of Color*. A volume is a **SET** of solids treated as a plastic unity. Set **BOOLEAN OPERATIONS** are especially apt in developing volume interactions. **ADDITION** is the simple combination of two nearby volumes. **SUBTRACTION** is the result of one volume removed form another. **INTERSECTION** is the only part of two overlapping volumes that is shared by both. **UNION** is the overall volume formed by two overlapping volumes. Computer aided drafting (CAD) programs now include Boolean operations as basic modeling tools.

Free Volume Diagrams

In solving program requirements for architectural space, the designer soon discovers that the mass and position of one volume relative to another generates a load or force on nearby space. Hence we may consider a **FREE VOLUME DIAGRAM** to help determine interactions between volumes to arrive at an equilibrium of locational forces. Just as movement can be a "load" on volume, so too may volume configuration be a "load" on movement. An entry will "compress" or "shear" a room and distort its perfect geometry; long distances between goals will "tense" a corridor, site boundaries may compress program volumes so strongly as to force a Boolean intersection or union. Shifting volumes generate forces which create stress and strain on other volumes and require a dynamic mode of design: shove this, squeeze that, break these apart, pull some up here.... Consider the arrangement of seats in a small theater. The same 36 seats can be planned so as to throw everyone close to the speaker, but at the expense of distortion of view at the extreme sides, or made long and narrow to emphasize the processional of arrival. Circulation is itself a volume which may need to go through or collide with other given volumes. For example human movement through the site of the Harmony project "ruins" the perfect geometry of the major meeting hall volumes. Good design finds the balance between volumetric forces to keep rooms "believable" in response to program forces.

Volumetric Algebra

Algebra, "the reduction and the comparison" by equations, comes from the Arabic root *jbr* meaning *"to bind together."* Combing "free volume diagrams" with Boolean operations develops a kind of **VOLUMETRIC ALGEBRA**. This method of thinking is perhaps the most powerful design tool available to architects. To design by moving volumes with, through, and from each other in the mind's eye is to make a *dynamic* of volumetric composition. Complex interactions and combinations of Boolean operations when applied to three-dimensional volumetric relationships may characterize those complex polynomial expressions of volume, the multistage evolving *parti* manipulations and operations that generate most architectural space. Expressions such as **A** UNION (**B** SUBTRACT **C** INTERSECT **D**) may suggest volumetric order. Symbolic spacial logic leads to *feeling*. The *Spinning* study identifies the separate volumes of the two groups, exploring the possible ADDITION and SUBTRACTION of volumes, emphasizing perimeters of both site and meeting halls. *Grooving* reveals how the two major volumes may create a third between them through INTERSECTION and UNION of volumes. A volumetric union is like a 3D moment joint, whereas an intersection is more like a volumetric pin joint.

2

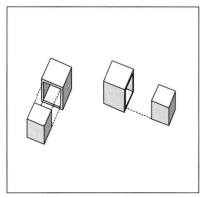

SUBTRACTION OF SOLIDS CAN CREATE VOLUME

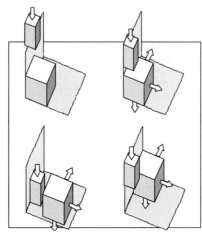

A PUSH IN ONE DIRECTION
CAN STRESS ALL 3 DIMENSIONS

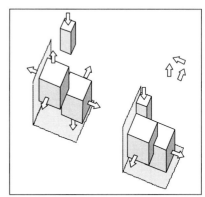

VOLUME STRESS RESOLVED BY BOOLEAN OPERATIONS

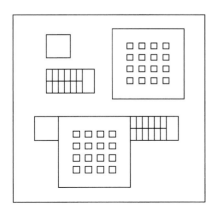

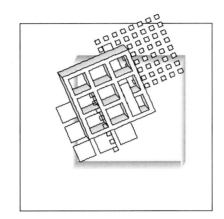

ENTRY AND LIGHT LOAD A VOLUME

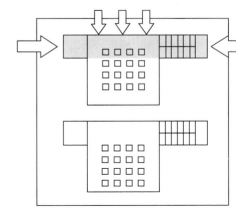

ADDED LOADS ALTER RESULTANT (SEATING)

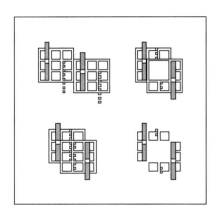

CREATION IN SPACE

THREES	FOUR FOURS
$1 + 1 + 1 = 3$	$\dfrac{4}{4} + \dfrac{4}{4} = 2$
$1 + 2 = 3$	$\dfrac{(4.4 - .4)}{\sqrt{4}} = 2$
$2 + 1 = 3$	$\dfrac{(4^{\sqrt{4}})}{4} - \sqrt{4} = 2$
$4 - 1 = 3$	$\dfrac{4}{4}! - (\sqrt{4})^{\sqrt{4}} = 2$

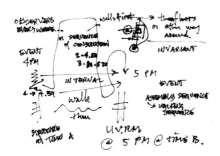

INTERVAL: MOVEMENT VARIATIONS OF OBSERVERS EVERYWHERE. SOME SEE WALLS BEFORE FLOOR, OTHERS SEE THEM IN REVERSE. INTERVAL ALSO SUGGESTS VARIATIONS IN THE SEQUENCE OF CONSTRUCTION.

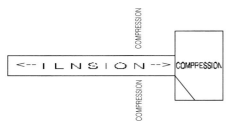

DRAMA BETWEEN VOLUMES
LAURENTIAN LIBRARY

READING ROOM HORIZONTAL VOLUME (EX-)TENSION AND COMPRESSION IN PERSPECTIVE BY GRID RHYTHM, *RICETTO* VERTICAL VOLUME WITH HORIZONTAL COMPRESSION BY WALLS, CREATING VERTICAL (EX-)TENSION.

2. DRAMA and humor

When a body moves beyond stretching, it must act to encounter the world beyond the immediate. Drama means to *act*, to make, in the sense of doing. Drama has meaning only in context: in art at least, there is no absolute happy or sad, but only "happier than" and "sadder than". Generating alternatives makes contrast by comparison possible. To have the courage to experiment, to find out "what if...?", one must play. Adding can arrive at three many ways. Consider too a game of Four Fours-- *express all the whole numbers from 1 to 80 using exactly and only four fours with any possible mathematical notations like square root, factorial, plus or minus signs.* Shown are four ways to express the number two using four fours. Each is correct and elegant in its own way: there is no single right answer. The form is *plastic*. Ode, the Greek word for song or lyric, is the root of both *comedy* and *tragedy*. In emotion as much as in physics, for every action there is an equal and opposite reaction. In slapstick humor, someone gets hit, there is pain, and then laughter. To make any art vivid, we need contrast **with** internal consistency. In *Interaction of Color*, Albers argues that what color we see in a figure depends on the color of its surrounding field. The architectural interaction of volumes is analogous, where our experience of one volume depends on its relationship to other volumes. In relative terms, opaque from one direction may be open and transparent from another viewpoint. While preserving topological relationships like proximity and connection, the architect still has endless opportunities to qualify the character of volumes, so that they have meaning in relationship to others. The continuous interaction of volumes creates actions in and of space, an ever-evolving fabric of space.

Gravity and Levity...

"To err is human." Mistakes lead to insight as well as laughter. Humor is human and humane. Possible void becomes possible mass and shifts back again. Space is capacity; it cannot be fully realized without experimenting with alternatives. Volume transformation is a drama of spacial forces on "free volume diagrams". Qualifying volume generates these spacial forces by shaping proportions, boundaries, and sense of enclosure. Relationships between volumes, i.e. larger than, stiffer than, heavier than, can be heightened through contrast, exploiting expressive qualities of all available means: material solids, program volumes, and their derivatives-- a palette of modulated light, structure, position, orientation, circulation, ventilation, temperature, sound, smell, comfort, and so on.

If an architectonic volume is an ideal "pure" box, without gravity, weather, or population, then dynamic loads will distort the volume, stretching the box. How you move and what you see as you get to where you are going makes movement a spacial force on volume relations, as much as volume configuration is a "load" on movement. The interval between two places in time and space allows for many circulation variations. As volumes intersect, overlap, etc. one room may feel linear compared to a very cubic room, but fairly boxy compared to a long corridor, or one volume in tension seems stretched only in relation to another which seems compressed. In some rooms walls compress, in others space flies out to the horizon. Michelangelo's Laurentian library is a study in spacial compression and tension (as well as shear). The complex volumes of Le Corbusier's Ronchamp generate plastic emotions by lowering the ceiling and opening the southeast corner to contrast vertical compression with horizontal tension in another way. Using volumetric algebra to find alternatives to spacial solutions suggests that *dialectic* is a means to unity. As Taoist masters of Yin and Yang understood, contrast is the essence of completeness. If some volumes seem heavy, then others must seem light by comparison. If we put the heavy volumes on top of the lighter ones, we heighten that sense of contrast and increase a feeling of compression, by playing against our normal expectations of structural support in a gravity field. As Marcel Duchamp said, "only those who play can be serious..."

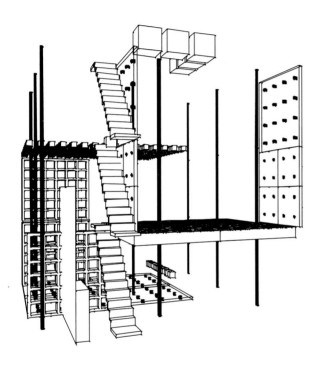

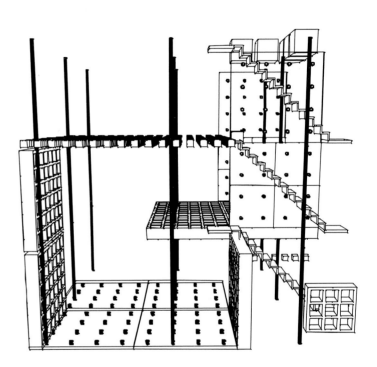

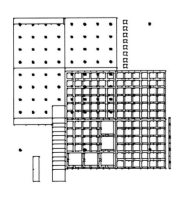

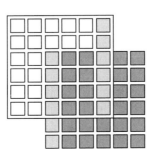

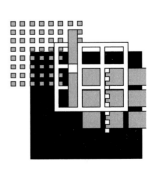

ANIMATION OF SOLIDS

3. SOLID FIELDS

"the words "honeycomb" and "egg crate" may have given some feeling for the geometry that goes with electrodynamics." Misner, Thorne, and Wheeler, in Gravitation

SCALAR FIELD MAPS MAGNITUDE

High heel spikes on the shoes of a hundred pound person may damage a floor where the wide sneakers of a two-hundred pound person won't. This is because the force of the former is concentrated over a smaller area, so the **STRESS**, or force per unit area, is much higher. While a swinging hammer may dent a piece of wood, a nail will concentrate its force into a higher local intensity and cut right through the wood fibers. Stress causes **STRAIN**, or the deformation of a solid per unit of its length. Young's **MODULUS OF ELASTICITY** measures the stiffness of a material, the ratio of stress to strain. Columns flex and beams bend: solids develop tensile, compressive, shear and bending stresses (a combination of the other three) as they resist deflection. **POISSON'S RATIO** shows how stress in one direction can develop strain perpendicular to it: squeeze a marshmallow and it gets fatter at the sides. As a **BEAM** deflects downward under load, its upper fibers are compressed and its lower fibers are stretched. These strains cause stresses in the material as it seeks to restore its former internal equilibrium. A **FIELD** is a region of related values. There are both scalar and vector fields. A beam is a field of varying values of stress and strain, a function of the magnitude and position of all the force vectors on the free body diagram. Polarized light through a treated plastic model reveals a field of stress distribution in a beam under load, like ripples in a pond radiating outward from concentrated load and support points. **MOMENT DIAGRAMS** show distribution and magnitude of bending and shear stress in solids. **TENSORS** describe simultaneous and mutual interaction of forces in fields in many perpendicular dimensions. **MOMENT OF INERTIA**, a tensor, varies to the 4th power (I^4). Proper design and shape of structural sections locates the mass of a beam where stress, strain, and/or moment of inertia are greatest.

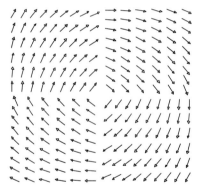

VECTOR FIELD MAPS MAGNITUDE AND DIRECTION

WORK is force acting over a distance. Thus sliding a box across a frictionless floor is *not* work, whereas lifting that same box up (against gravity) *is* work. The physical units of work are F x D, or **ma** x D, so work = $(M D/T^2) D = M D^2/T^2$, expressed in **foot-pounds** or **joules**. A seesaw lifts its riders, first one up, then the other, with only the gentlest push of toes to keep the rise and fall going. It is a lever doing work against the force field of earth's gravity. The falling mass of one body lifts the rising mass of the other, which in turn transfers its potential for doing the work of lifting into the motion of falling. **ENERGY** *is the ability to do work*-- so we say that the high rider has **POTENTIAL** energy which will become the **KINETIC** energy of falling as it changes its position in the gravity field. Energy and work are measured by the same dimensions: Energy = $M D^2/T^2$. Release a stretched spring or the pendulum of a child on a swing and they too oscillate in cyclic alternation of potential and kinetic energy. A beam also flexes and recoils as its external load is transformed into internal stress and strain. Like the plot of a spiral staircase, a clock hand and Jupiter's moons trace the **HARMONIC MOTION** of a sine curve as they move through space and time.

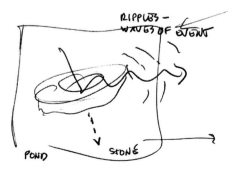

A STONE DROPPED THROUGH THE ELASTIC SURFACE OF A POND CREATES OUTWARD RADIATING **WAVES** OF EXPANSION AND CONTRACTION.

FIELDS are real, even when the solid is devoid of mass, where solids are made of spacetime itself. The effects of electromagnetism depend on the relationship of fields and motion. Michael Faraday observed that electric currents flowing in opposite directions attract and cause neighboring wires to move toward each other, and that currents flowing in the same direction cause the wires to repel each other. He also established the principles of the electric motor (a current flowing through a wire will cause a magnet to move) and the generator (a moving magnet induces a current in a wire). After careful measurements, Faraday was able to draw the lines of force of the electromagnetic field. By 1873, James Clerk Maxwell generalized Faraday's observations that electric current generates a magnetic field and a moving magnet generates an electric field into four basic equations for electromagnetism. Periodic oscillations of the electromagnetic field occur at the speed of light. Indeed, light of all frequencies **is** the electromagnetic spectrum.

3

CONCENTRATED AND DISTRIBUTED LOADS ON A BEAM

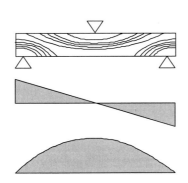

BENDING AND SHEAR STRESS DISTIBUTION IN A BEAM

STRUCTURAL SECTIONS RESIST MOMENT OF INERTIA

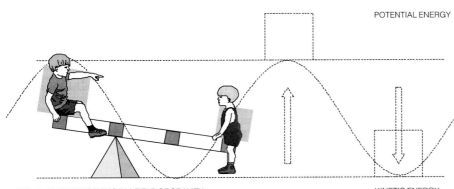

POTENTIAL ENERGY

KINETIC ENERGY

WORK: A LEVER WORKING IN A FIELD OF GRAVITY

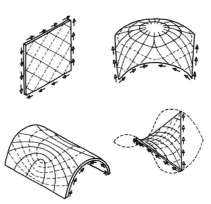

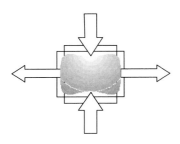

STRESS AND STRAIN ON A ,MARSHMALLOW
SHOWING POISSON'S RATIO AND
YOUNG'S MODULUS OF ELASTICITY

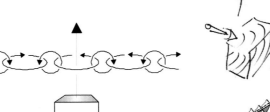

$$\nabla \cdot D = P \qquad \nabla \cdot B = 0$$
$$\nabla \times E = \partial B/\partial t \qquad \nabla \times H = J + \partial B/\partial t$$

MAXWELL'S 4 EQUATIONS FOR ELECTROMAGNETISM

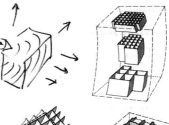

TENSOR MACHINERY

DEVELOPMENT OF VOLUME

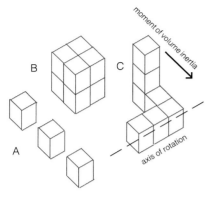

moment of volume inertia

axis of rotation

A ARE VOLUMETRICLLY "LIGHT"
B CAN MOVE BUT ONCE IN PLACE SITS "HEAVY"
C CAN WIGGLE, DEVELOPS VOLUME MOMENT

A = VOLUME INERTIA OF 1 (3 TIMES)
B = VOLUME INERTIA OF 8.
C = VOLUME INERTIA OF 7,
AND MOMENT OF 3 X 2 X 3 = 18

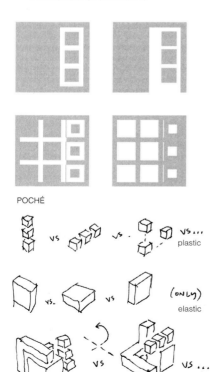

POCHÉ

plastic

elastic

increasingly
elastic

3. VOLUME IN CONCERT

Just as mass resists change, so too does volume. Not only in the literal sense of the skin of walls and floors stiffening against forces, but in the realization of its place in the volumetric fabric of a program. **VOLUMETRIC INERTIA** is the resistance to change in position or orientation; it can vary depending on geometry, size, proximity, access, and importance of volumes. There can be more than one "center of gravity" in a field of volumes. A big concert hall is harder to shift in a constricted site than many small practice rooms. Groups of volumes can be organized so that they "read" as one three-dimensional conceptual solid. Just as planes can define and intensify the volumes between them, "conceptual solids" can also organize larger spaces. **POCHÉ**, from the French word for pocket, describes sets of volumes treated as conceptual solids.

Fields and Set operations

Fields lend themselves to set operations. Sets of volumes act in concert. **SET OPERATIONS** on volumes arraying Boolean operations, moving sets within sets, rotating whole *partis* are not only handy in CAD but are also essential in all 3D design. Resolving the program is first a kind of mental "blockout" computer puzzle fitting game, rotating while translating volume subsets, maintaining shape and proximity as needed, allowing one space to "move through" another. (This is how a hall "enters" a dining room.) A circulation tartan can be a volume set. There can be **VOLUMETRIC MOMENT OF INERTIA**: for example in Concerto studies, rotating the flight run has more effect on other program solids than does rotating the concert hall-- the former is linear and wiggly, the latter more spherical-- thus less volumetric moment of inertia. A set of volumes *(poché)* has higher inertia than the same volumes unconnected. Tensors can describe set operations on a field.

Polychrome Volume

Volumes are the fluid notes of space. When there are many program volumes, volume becomes the primary compositional concern, while locating masses around and through them is secondary. Polychroming program volumes makes it easy to improvise in space and generate many *partis* in 3D. Coloring solids by function helps keep track of program relationships. Using the Concerto study as an example, yellow cubes could indicate all 3 visitor galleries, or human spaces only, or tartan only; later yellow card could denote all flight run, north, or eggcrate walls. **POLYCHROME** for program volumes can suggest more subtle relationships, as in the color studies: 3 as 2, like with like or set in contrast. As program volumes are located, the *parti* evolves from "plastic" to increasingly "elastic" form. First everything can move, but later, as some elements become fixed, there are fewer options for the remainder and the *parti* begins to "set". Here is one method for modeling complex programs:

1. Develop parti using (polychromed) mass solids. (The Kit of Parts can model the Phoenix program volumes perfectly at 1/8" scale! The 1" cubes model practice rooms alone or larger rooms in groups, and the rods serve as tartan spacers to study access needs and movement.) Then, "Beat the clock," mix'n'move the elements within the site. Does everything fit? Reposition volumes to solve proximity demands. Note that some volumes and sets are easier to move and rotate than others.
2. Rebuild the selected parti as a paper or cardboard model at a larger scale (1/4" scale works well here) to study surface and volume distinction and continuity, enclosures and intersections.
3. Rebuild selected paper studies with the Bag of Tricks (at 1/2" scale) to articulate plastic intentions through available materials. Develop dialog with all study modes, using grids generated by details of structure, perforations, and joints. Refine through drawing and model, both "hard-line" and freehand.

3

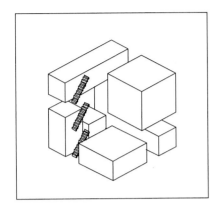
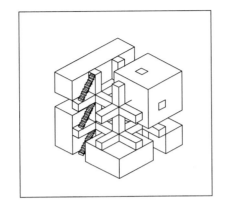
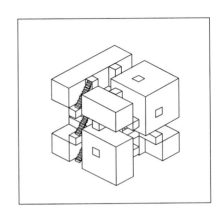

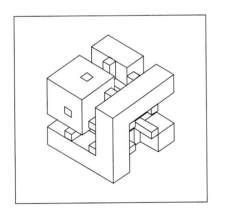
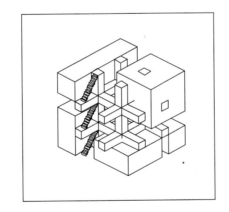
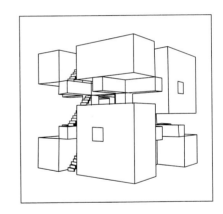

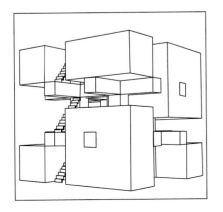
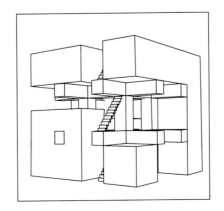
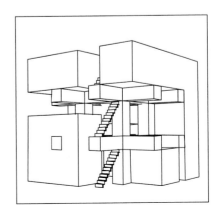

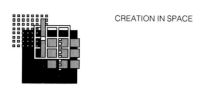

CREATION IN SPACE

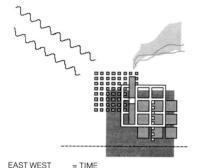

EAST WEST = TIME
NORTH SOUTH = LIGHT
UP DOWN = GRAVITY

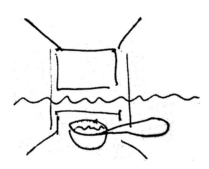

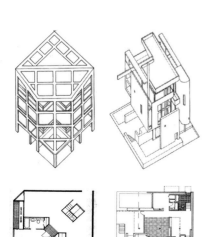

3. POETRY

"Poetry is not a turning loose of emotion; it is not the expression of personality, but an escape from personality. But, of course, only those who have personality and emotions know what it means to want to escape from these things."
T.S. Eliot, Tradition and the Individual Talent

Poetry is *making*. Poetry finds a "hole in the language" between words and invents relationships that link hidden ideas and feelings, sometimes condensing into one potent figure a whole complex of multiple meanings. For architects, a **POETRY OF THE SITE** can express forces in the field: time, light, gravity. Direction is not symmetrical in each of the three spacial dimensions: across the horizon right does not equal left (morning to afternoon), into depth front does not equal back (sun to shade), and along the vertical up does not equal down (ground to sky). Space is a plastic medium, bending around and weaving between volumes. The rituals of everyday life suggest a **POETRY OF THE PROGRAM**. Washing hands, cooking food, eating breakfast, reading a book, each demand volumes with appropriate light, scale, access, acoustics and so on. The eloquence of simple events can illuminate life. For example, a person must remove the shoes before entering a traditional Japanese house. Slippers are provided at the entry, floors are kept free of tracked-in dirt. The architect has a palette of path and movement experiences to use in ordering the volumes of circulation in conjunction with other program volumes-- the tartan is but one. Architects can modulate space to indicate procession, approach, passage, entry, arrival and create a *promenade architecturale* of vertical and horizontal movement through space.

A Prince asked a Zen Master Gardener to build his best garden on land blessed with magnificent views of the sea. When at last it was complete, the prince was disappointed: boulders, a fence, even a pile of debris somehow obscured each great view. Finally, as the Prince lowered his head to drink from the ladle at the tea-house entry, he saw through a slit in the screen before him... the magnificent sea!

Space flows past us as much as we move through space. We not only respond to local cues but also re-create and re-compose an order of simultaneity through the sequential spacial clues we encounter. In the story above, drinking water and ocean are united in profound vision as life-giving liquid.

Composing A Fabric of Spaces

Consider **VARIATIONS** of just the three Concerto visitor galleries: in a vertical or horizontal row, through the center or along an edge, holding three corners. What might these mean? Three galleries set diagonally through the site will oppose the flight run; human complements bird. What might it mean to make the large chamber nested close to the flight run, rather than as far from it as possible? It is crucial to develop *parti* in plan and section together. Levels are stories, where volume meets other fields. Should the ground plane remain intact? Can the roof become a garden terrace connection to the sky? Can entry be at a middle layer? Silence is as important as sound in composing music; void is as important as mass in composing architecture. Architecture is a fabric of interlocking spaces, whether loose or tight fit. Once you see program implications in a *parti*, you may rework the proposal through design development toward resolution. For example, a more advanced student project (house and garden for a potter) is shown here both before and after design development: the difference is not in style but in articulation of the poetry of site and program together. Entry is not wasted space but a sequence of revelations. Morning light greets rising and work, afternoon light greets study. Knowing play of unity and variety makes interesting rhythm rather than dull repetition. The realization of an architectural vision from program to *parti* of articulated volume to a fabric of spacial continuity to expression via material and structure and finally into a composition of modulated light is a cycle from pure idea to matter to pure energy, a poetry not just of things but of interacting relationship itself.

3

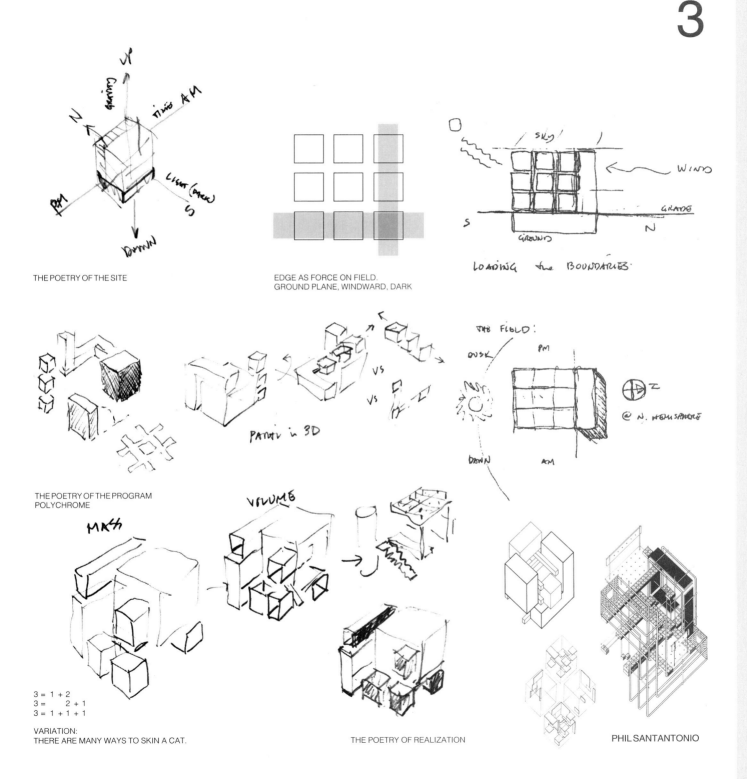

THE POETRY OF THE SITE

EDGE AS FORCE ON FIELD.
GROUND PLANE, WINDWARD, DARK

LOADING the BOUNDARIES.

THE POETRY OF THE PROGRAM
POLYCHROME

3 = 1 + 2
3 =   2 + 1
3 = 1 + 1 + 1

VARIATION:
THERE ARE MANY WAYS TO SKIN A CAT.

THE POETRY OF REALIZATION

PHIL SANTANTONIO

ANIMATION OF SOLIDS

4. PRESSURIZED SOLIDS

Boundaries

Solids, including fields, have boundaries. An inflated balloon is a field of air molecules. When the moving solids of the air molecules meet the rubber skin, the molecules stretch the skin and then rebound. Solids in motion in a bounded field create **PRESSURE,** or stress per unit volume. Hydraulic pressure sustains the forms of plants: tree branches develop their great cantilevers by growing larger cells at the lower part of their branches, generating an upward pressure to counteract gravity. Pressure depends on both the density of solids in a field and their temperature, that is, how fast they are moving. The molecules in a gas are like little springs, vibrating according to their energy. In a gas, temperature *is* pressure! Solids are boxes of heat, or energy. A gas may be treated statistically as a single elastic solid. Liquid is a plastic solid: its shape may vary but its mass is constant. A jack-in-the-box is a pressurized solid; open the top and the compressed spring flies out. Compression and tension are the positive and negative pressures of a solid under load, like a beam or column.

Tensegrity

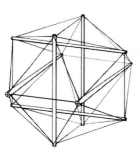

TENSEGRITY is an equilibrium of tension and compression, an elastic structure under internal pressure and thus independent of external loads. Step on a tensegrity and it bounces back. Trees are living tensegrities, sustaining the pressure of ever-outward growth in the face of external loads like wind and gravity. To last, even ad-hoc jury-rigged, structures can be (must be!) tensegrities. Tensegrity can help solve the problem of how to provide enough inertia to resist outward forces in lightweight construction. To make roll-resistant "portable rock" build outward from any available vector equilibrium, transforming flexible solid into more rigid volume. The greater the extension, the more "momentous" the volume. This is the basis for the success of the arch in architecture, from Stonehenge lintel to gothic vault to geodesic domes.

Moving Heat

Heat flows from a warm body to a cool one, bringing both to equilibrium. This inevitable smoothing out of energy fluctuations, of increasing **dis**-order, is called **ENTROPY**. While a fireplace creates local warmth by resonating the flame of a match into a full blaze, eventually room and fireplace will come to the same temperature. Solids expand as they get warmer (water-ice is a rare exception), so expansion/contraction joints are needed in structures to prevent buckling and cracking. The **CARNOT CYCLE** describes how pressure and temperature of a gas vary in an enclosed region. It is the basis for the internal combustion engine in a car. Increasing pressure increases the temperature, until a spark ignites the gas which expands to drive the crankshaft that turns the wheels. Valve openings and closings must be timed to build up pressure and exhaust spent gases as needed. The amount and energy of the gas (octane), as well as the speed of the cycle, determine the rate of delivery of energy to move the car. **POWER** is the rate of change of energy, expressed in **horsepower** or **watts**. Power= $M D^2/T^2/T = M D^2/T^3$. When energy itself moves, its impact with mass can cause radical change in the system. A truck at 60 MPH crashes into a brick house and demolishes the living room. A truck filled with ***gasoline*** crashes into a brick house and demolishes the neighborhood-- the chemical energy of the gasoline is released by igniting the compression of impact. The momentum $M D/T$ of moving energy $M D^2/T^2$, also called momenergy $M2 D^3/T^3$, is the rate of impact of packets of energy. According to Einstein's $E = mc^2$, mass is energy contained. The universe is a solid of void pressurized by the Big Bang of radiance meeting the ubiquitous boundary contraction of gravity.

PISTON MOVING IN A CYLINDER
PRESSURE AND HEAT RELATE
CARNOT CYCLE

HEAT WILL CHANGE A SOLID.
THE QUANTITY OF HEAT **Q** NEEDED TO PRODUCE
THAT CHANGE EQUALS THE PRODUCT OF MASS **M**,
SPECIFC HEAT **C**, AND CHANGE IN TEMPERATURE **ΔT**,
THAT IS **Q = M CΔT**.

4

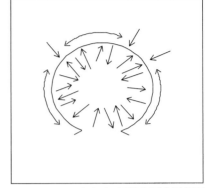

A CLOSED JACK-IN-THE-BOX IS A TENSEGRITY
AN INFLATED BALLOON IS A TENSEGRITY

PLAN IS THE INTERSECTION OF GRAVITY AND LIGHT

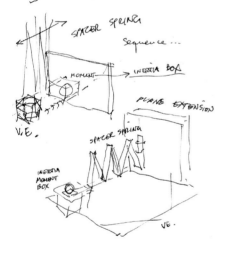

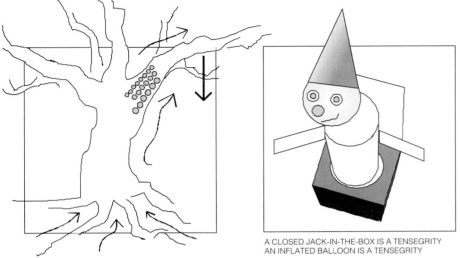

BUILD OUTWARD TO INVENT MASS INTO VOLUME INTO SITE
EXTEND SPACER SPRING INTO VECTOR EQUILIBRIUM

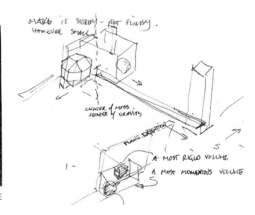

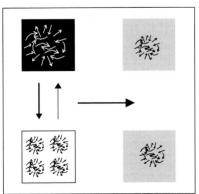

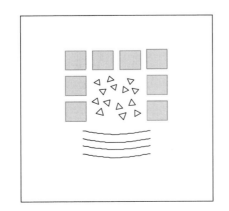

DEVELOPMENT OF VOLUME

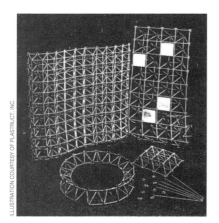

SKIN AND BONES

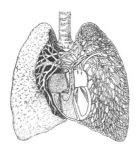

LUNGS ARE LIVING RESONATING VOLUMES

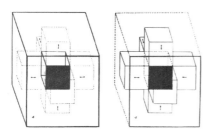

VAN DOESBURG:
ENERGY INERTIA-- "LIVING ROOMS"

4. VOLUME INTEGRITY

Filters

Architetcure is a plastic medium. bending between and weaving around volumes, the fluid notes of space. Sun shades (*brise soleis*) and windows regulate the flow of sunlight, vents and chimneys regulate the flow of air, and doors regulate the flow of people through a building. These valves modulate volume through controlled opening and closing, maintaining perforation without collapse. Many such valves close together act as a **FILTER**. Filters are perforated boundaries, wavelength selectors. The frequency of perforation and size of opening determines what passes through, transparent, translucent, opaque. Walls are opaque, not only to light but also to movement. Volumetric filters in plan and section are vital to architecture: column grids, banks of doors or windows, and circulation tartans provide permeability with varying degrees of enclosure. A good plan is sufficiently permeable for light, air, water, heat, people, and vehicles to sustain an appropriate in-and-out equilibrium. The **FREE PLAN** is perhaps the extreme form of permeability. Different frequencies of perforation generate many orders of spacial rhythm to reconcile. In the Concerto studies, while the 8' cube galleries may fit neatly between tartan intervals, the 16' double cube hall will not. The tartan will be intersected by the 16' double cube which in turn may be pierced by a 3' circulation space. Each filter may create its own module: eggcrate, masonite, mesh. Rather than "ruining" a design, this variety of fabrics may make a richer composition of continuous fields superimposed on each other.

Trading Places

A porch screen lets air in but keeps bugs out. A sealed balloon is an integral volume, but a single pin prick expands it explosively. How to keep volumes distinct but continuous is a difficult and subtle art: we do not want the heat of a sauna to melt a nearby freezer, but we want to feel they are part of the same house. The skin and bones of walls and columns are pressurized volume fields which respond to forces. Lungs filter, ribs support, and heart pumps: joined by elastic muscles together they make the human torso. Lungs are "living rooms": a moving diaphragm varies pressure to exchange carbon dioxide for oxygen in the vast surface area of the capillary tubes that weave through the alveoli sacs clustered like grapes along the bronchii. To define and construct inhabited enclosure, we build different atmospheres. Integral volume requires integrity (*in-teger* means un-touched, whole) but architecture demands resolving the continuity of inside and out through permeable and/or insulating boundaries to keep internal and external volume pressures in equilibrium.

Modulators

Heat moves between solids in three basic ways: **CONDUCTION** direct contact, **CONVECTION** exchange via moving fluids, and **RADIATION**. Volumes through volumes become **HEAT MODULATORS**: tubes can form tartans of convectors, planes can become radiators and condensers which modify the flow of heat through thermal mass. When the sun's short wave ultraviolet light passes through glass and heats brick which radiates energy back as long wave infrared light that cannot penetrate glass, heat builds up in a **GREENHOUSE EFFECT**. An opposite heat-losing **CHIMNEY** or **ATRIUM EFFECT** occurs where a central vertical tube allows cool air to enter from below, which rises as a cooling vertical breeze of lighter warmer air taking heat with it. A dwelling volume with holes in 3 dimensions can be a managed heat flow tensor; a machine for directing vectors of heat gradients. Good design considers cycles of heating and cooling to modify and store energy. If volumes are packet of energy, then Van Doesburg's diagrams of expansive and contractive volumes suggests that beyond the literal pressure of heat there may be architectural program forces that modulate volumes within a field of volumes.

4

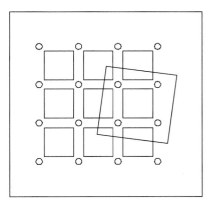

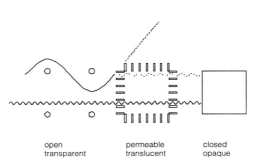

open   permeable   closed
transparent   translucent   opaque

FILTERS

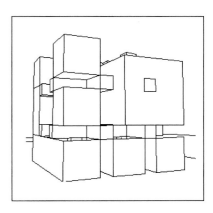

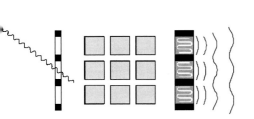

A field is a set of volumes; a volume is a set of fields.
Volumes are packets of energy. A **TRANSDUCER** is
a form that changes one form of energy into another.

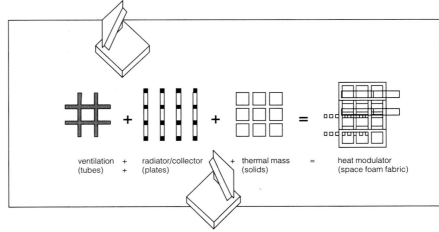

ventilation   +   radiator/collector   +   thermal mass   =   heat modulator
(tubes)   +   (plates)   +   (solids)   (space foam fabric)

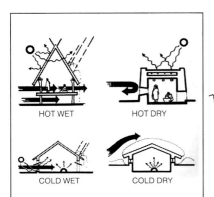

HOT WET   HOT DRY

COLD WET   COLD DRY

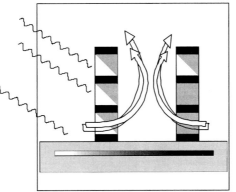

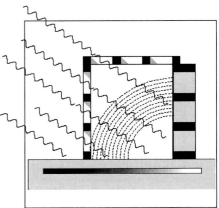

CREATION IN SPACE

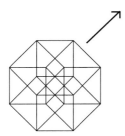

HYPERCUBE

INSIDE AND OUTSIDE TOGETHER.
EXPERIENCE LETS US **BE** IN BOTH.
ALL CUBES TOUCH IN FOUR DIMENSIONS.

A ROOM IS A BOX OF SPACETIME HEAT FLOW.
A MANAGED HEAT FLOW TENSOR,
A MACHINE FOR DIRECTING VECTORS.

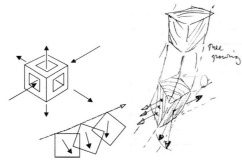

THE GRAIN IN A BLOCK OF WOOD IS THE RESULT-
ANT MAP OF ALL FORCES AT ALL SCALES AFFECT-
ING THE SHAPE OF THE GROWING TREE. WOOD
GRAIN REVEALS THE GRAIN OF SPACETIME.

4. COMPASSION   *sacrifice and offering*

A refrigerator moves heat from inside to out, but requires extra energy to do so. While local sameness may decrease, the entropy of the Universe as a whole *always* increases. Order decreases as entropy increases. Architecture sustains the pressure of the present, persistence in the face of entropy. Whereas volume is a phenomenon of the present, architectural space must account for the order of both past and future, of time beyond now. To "build for the ages" demands the persistence of intention: in the face of impersonal chaos, order survives and prevails through the ongoing gift of the present. If volume is solid in time, then **SPACE** is volume sustained in the flow of time through a box of still space (a room with a clock) and the passage of space through a box of time (a car traveling).

Endowing Autonomy

The heat death of increasing entropy is not so different from our own biological death. Without the spark of life, our body returns to its disorganized constituents, just a lump of atoms without order. So we have learned to prevail through endowing autonomy to our progeny. This demands not only sacrifice but also compassion. **Empathy** means to feel with, to feel inside, imaginative projection of one's consciousness into another being; empathy establishes resonance and compassion begets radiance. **RESONANCE** is the fit of all pressure volumes into a mutually reinforcing ordered whole. In plan, movement within the field creates growth inward, establishing resonance between and within program volumes. **Compassion** means to feel (pain) with; to suffer with, to *endure*. The ultimate pain perhaps is not death but mortality, the consciousness of time passing. But sacrifice heals. We can offer the reserves of our lives to our children, for example. Compassion gives and takes, building future independence on the strength of the past. A personal cycle of birth, marriage, procreation, and death parallels a cultural cycle of create, release, launch, and recede. A new child travels with an older parent for a while, but eventually each will find its own way. **RADIANCE** sustains expanding volumes beyond the boundaries of a site in space and time. The breathing volumes of plants and animals are radiant in the give and take of life. Where **TENSEGRITY** meets **SITE** implosion and explosion create moving fields of growth. A **CITY** is the meeting place of many local fields; civilizing fusion in the melting pot makes a *radiant* city. Cities are where the intersections of local geometries are interesting, where energy and matter interchange. Cities phase volume pressures from temporary to permanent, and weave plans of independent systems into unbroken urban fabric. Cities plan status, yet change through phasing, maintenance, and evolution.

The Heart of the Matter

The heart of matter is energy, and it is empty! The hollow town square or village green is the most plastic field of an elastic plan. Essential emptiness is music for the soul. Mortality makes room for the next generation. The space of possibility engenders freedom. Space creates space through the umbilical that links one generation to the next. **PLAN** is the intersection of gravity and light, the union of space and time. As mass and energy interchange, potential evolves through actual into speculation in an eternal dance of resonance and radiance. Spacetime and momenergy interact, modifying worldlines in plastic-to-elastic alternation. We cannot see the realm of four dimensions, we can only feel it and be in it. (A fish does not go beyond the sea.) Four dimensions is always loss and gain: managing balance by increasing local order is **LOVE**. First is intuition (or divine intervention), inspiration, breathing life into things. Then comes the integrating sensuality and sensibility of a whole mind tuned in to all input, information, and integration. The cycle is a feedback process. The shape of the standing multidimensional wave cycle and its intimate and correct union with meaning **is** art, which reverses all signs easily, turning *worst* into *best*. The fabric of architecture and the creation of space is love becoming plan and plan becoming love.

4

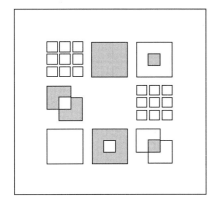

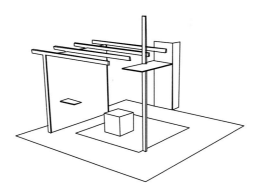

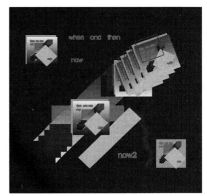

3 DEGREES OF ENCLOSURE

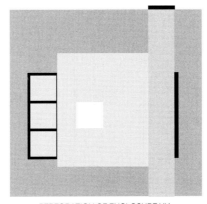

PERFORATION OF ENCLOSURE VIA
CIRCULATION AND STRUCTURE

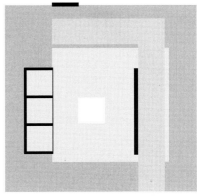

CIRCULATION AND STRUCTURE
INFORM STRATEGY DECISIONS

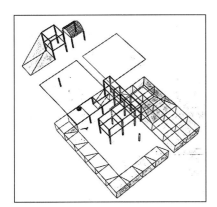

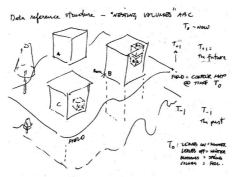

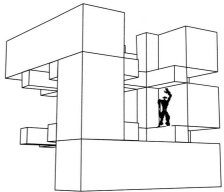

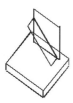

"Architecture, Pure Creation of the Mind

Profile and contour are the touchstone of the architect.
Here he reveals himself as artist or mere engineer.
Profile and contour are free of all constraint.
There is here no longer any question of custom, nor of tradition, nor of construction,
nor of adaptation to utilitarian needs.
Profile and contour are the pure creation of the mind; they call for the plastic artist.

The Engineer's Esthetic and Architecture-- two things march together and follow
one from the other-- the one at its full height, the other in an unhappy state of retrogression.
The Engineer, inspired by the law of Economy and governed by mathematical calculation,
puts us in accord with universal law. He achieves harmony.

The Architect, by his arrangement of forms, realizes an order which is pure creation of his spirit;
by forms and shapes he affects our senses to an acute degree, and provokes plastic emotions;
by the relationships which he creates he wakes in us profound echoes, he gives us the measure
of an order which we feel to be in accordance with that of our world, he determines the various movements
of our hearts and of our understanding; it is then that we experience the sense of beauty."

Le Corbusier, *Towards A New Architecture*

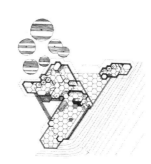

FROM THE BOTTOM UP

What of us, O Lord, what of us? What becomes of our work, our space, our time,
our hopes, our dreams, our life? Reading this page from the bottom up, we may
learn how a shaft of hope can build on a foundation of mortality's despair. Above,
we find inspiration for elevation and section: the entasis of a column, the proportions of a facade, the drama of a flying buttress. The true architect also knows that
the power of these words apply to plan, to volume, to all the dimensions of space
and time. Thus does the loving spirit take flight and triumph through living work.

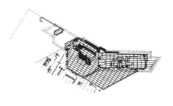

Decay adds... an involuntary beauty, associated with the hazards of history, which is the result of
natural causes and of time. Statues so thoroughly shattered that out of the debris a new work of art
is born... a bent knee which contains all the speed of the footrace; a torso that has no face to prevent
us from loving it; a breast or genitals in which we recognize more fully than ever the form of a fruit or flower....
A curve which is lost here and re-emerges there can only result from a human hand, a Greek hand, which
labored in one specific spot during one specific century. The entire man is there-- his intelligent collabora-
tion with the universe, his struggle against it, and that final defeat in which the mind and the matter which
supported him perish almost at the same time. What he intended affirms itself forever in the ruin of things."

The Mighty Sculptor, Time. by Marguerite Yourcenar

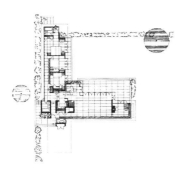

The art of man is able to construct monuments far more permanent than the narrow span of his
own existence: yet these monuments, like himself, are perishable and frail; and in the bound-
less annals of time his life and labours must equally be measured as a fleeting moment."

Edward Gibbon, *Decline and Fall of the Roman Empire*

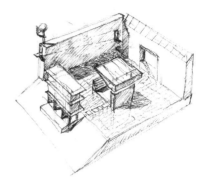

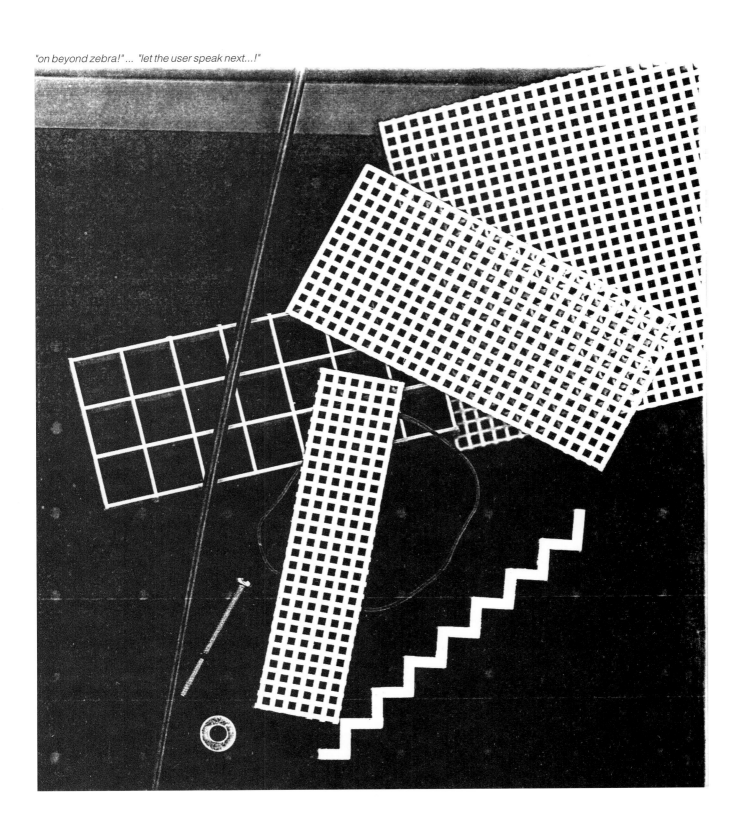

"on beyond zebra!" ... "let the user speak next...!"

BIBLIOGRAPHY

Notes:
1. Historically important books are shown with date of first publication indicated in brackets. i.e. More, Thomas. *Utopia*, Random House 1992 {1516}...
2. State of publisher omitted where obvious.
3. U = University, P = Press; UP = University Press, as in Princeton UP...
4. Museum of Modern Art = MOMA
5. * = *books already listed in Bibliography of CIS Volume 1: Architectonics*

-1. SWING

*Allen,Joseph.*EnteringSpace:anAstronaut'sOdyssey.*Stewart,Tabori&Chang,NY1984
*Arnheim, Rudolf.*Dynamics of Architectural Form*. U. Cal Press, Berkeley, 1977.
Barr, Stephen. *Experiments in Topology*. Apollo Edition, 1972.
Boorstin, Daniel. *The Discoverers*. Random House, NY, 1985
*Boys, C.V. *Soap Bubbles*. Dover, NY, 1959.
Cahill, James. *Treasures of Asia: Chinese Painting*. World Publishing, Cleveland, 1960
Chillida. Maeght editeur, Paris, for the Museum of Art, Carnegie Institute. 1979.
Darius, Jon. *Beyond Vision*. Oxford University Press, Oxford, 1984.
Fanelli, Giovanni.*Brunelleschi*. Scala Instituto Fotografico Editoriale, Firenze, 1980
Ferris,Timothy.*SpaceShots:TheBeautyofNatureBeyondEarth.*RandomHouseNY.1984.
Ferris, Timothy. *The Whole Shebang*. Simon and Schuster, NY, 1997
Green, Michael B. "Superstrings" *Scientific American*. September 1986.
Halliday, David and Resnick, Robert. *Physics for Students of Science and Engineering. Combined Edition*, John Wiley & Sons, NY, 1960. Also in CD-ROM.
Heath, Robert. *Animation in Twelve Hard Lessons*. Heath Productions, Islip NY 1972.
Hey, Tony and Walters, Patrick.*The Quantum Universe*. Cambridge U. Press, NY, 1987.
*Hildebrandt+Tromba*MathematicsandOptimaForm*ScientificAmericanLibraryNY1985.
Jencks,Charles.*ArchitectureoftheaJumpingUniverse*. Academy Editions, London. 1995.
Jencks,Charles. *Le Corbusier and The Tragic View of Architecture*. Harvard U.P.1973.
Kline, Morris. *Mathematics in Western Culture*, Oxford University Press, London, 1953
Laan, Dom H. van der. *Architectonic Space: Fifteen Lessons on the Disposition of the Human Habitat*. E.J. Brill, Leiden, Holland. 1983.
Laeser, Richard, McLaughlin, William, and Wolff, Donna. "Engineering Voyager 2's Encounter with Uranus."*Scientific American*. November 1986.
Malin, David. *A View of the Universe*. Cambridge U. Press. 1993.
*Monkhouse, Richard and Cox, John.*3D Star Maps*. Harper and Row, NY 1989
Munevar, Gonzago. *The Dimming of Starlight: An Introduction to the Philosophy of Space Exploration*. in manuscript. no date.
Murchie, Guy. *Music of the Spheres: The Material Universe-from Atom to Quasar, Simply Explained. Vol 1 and 2*. Dover. NY. 1967.
Parker, Barry. *Chaos in the Cosmos*. Plenum Press. NY 1996.
Penrose, Roger. *Shadows of the Mind: A Search for the Missing Science of Consciousness*. Oxford University Press NY. 1994.
Rothstein, Edward.*Emblems of the Mind: The Inner Life of Music and Mathematics*, Times Books, NY, 1995
Sagan, Carl. *Cosmos*. Random House. NY. 1980.
Thomas and Johnston. *Disney Animation: The Illusion of Life*. Abrams NY 1981.

In addition-- selected readings on the geometry of space and time

Banchoff, Thomas. *Beyond the third dimension*. Scientific American Library NY 1990.
Chiao,R.,Kwiat,P.andSteinberg, A. "Faster than Light".*Scientific American*. August 1993
Epstein, Lewis Carroll.*Relativity Visualized*. Insight Press. San Francisco CA. 1992
Feynman, Richard. *QED: The Strange Theory of Light and Matter*. Princeton UP, 1985.
Hawking, S. and Penrose, R. *The Nature of Space and Time*. Princeton UP. 1996.
Morinigo,F.andWagner,W.*FeynmanLecturesonGravitation*. AddisonWesley.NY. 1995.
SciamaD.W.*ThePhysicalFoundationsofGeneralRelativity*. Doubleday, NY 1969
Schwinger, Julian. *Einstein's Legacy: The Unity of Space and Time*. Scientific American Books, NY. 1986.
Wheeler, John Archibald. *A Journey Into Gravitation and Spacetime*. Scientific American Library NY 1990.
Zee,Anthony.*AnOldMan'sToy:GravityatWork&PlayintheUniverse*.MacmillanNY1989

0. PRELUDE

READINGS

*Abbott, Edwin. *Flatland: A Romance in many Dimensions*. Dover, NY. 1952.
*Dewdney, A.K. *The Planiverse*. Poseidon Press, NY, 1984.
Huizinga, J. *Homo Ludens*. Routledge, NY, 1098.
Ingersoll, R. *Le Corbusier: A Marriage of Contours*. Princeton Architecture P. NY, 1990.
Konig, H. G. "*The Planar Architecture of Juan Gris.*" in *Languages of Design. Volume 1, Number 1, September 1992*. Elsevier, Amsterdam.
Le Corbusier. *New World of Space*. The Institute of Contemporary Art. Reynal & Hitchcock, NY, 1948.
*Loran, Erle.*Cézanne's Composition*. University of California Press, Berkeley, 1963.
*Matisse, Henri. *Jazz*. Brazillier, NY, 1983 (reprint of 1947 edition).
Rosenblum, Robert.*Picasso and the Typography of Cubism*.
Rubin, William.*Picasso and Braque Pioneering Cubism*. MOMA, NY, 1989.
*Rowe, Colin and Slutzky, Robert. "Transparency: Literal and Phenomenal", *Perpsecta 8*. Yale University Press, New Haven. 1965
*Slutzky, Robert. "Transparency 2." *Perpsecta 13-14*.Yale U.P. New Haven, 1974.
Slutzky, Robert, et.al. *cHUbE cHrOME*. Architekturmuseum in Basel. 1988.
Slutzky, Robert. *"Apres Le Purisme" Assemblage No. 4, Oct 1987*.
Slutzky, Robert.*"Color Structure Painting"* Modernism Gallery Catalog, SF, 1984.

ADDITIONAL SOURCES

*Arnheim, Rudolf.*The Genesis of a Painting: Picasso's Guernica*.U. of California P. 1962.
Besset, Maurice. *Le Corbusier: To Live With The Light*. Skira Geneva, 1987
Blau, E. and Troy, N. *Architecture and Cubism*, MIT Press, Cambridge, 1997.
Burger, Dionys.*Sphereland*. Crowell NY, 1965.
Calatrava, et. al., *In the Footsteps of Le Corbusier*. Rizzoli, NY, 1989.
Cooper, Douglas. *The Cubist Epoch*.Phaidon Press Limited, London, 1971.
de stijl.' *The Museum of Modern Art Bulletin*. 1952.
de Vries, Vredeman.*Perspective*. Dover, NY. 1968.
Diamond, David. *The Architectural Lesson of Cubism*. in manuscript. 1997
*Dubery, F. and Willats, J. *Perspective and Other Drawing Systems*. VNR, NY. 1972.
Ellington, Duke. *Controversial Suite*. RCA 1951
Everitt, Anthony. *Abstract Expressionism*. Thames & Hudson, London, 1975.
Everdell, William. *The First Moderns: Profiles in the Origins of Twentieth-Century Thought*. University of Chicago Press, 1997.
Flam, Jack. et.al.*Henri Matisse: Paper Cut Outs. St Louis Art Museum, St. Louis MO, 1977*
Gray, Christopher. *Cubist Aesthetic Theories*. Books On Demand, Ann Arbor MI 1953.
Gifford,Don.*TheFartherShore:aNaturaHistoryofPerception*. AtlanticMonthlyP.NY 1990.
Harbin, Robert. *Secrets of Origami*. Octopus Ltd. London, 1971.
Izzo, A.and Gubitosi, C.*LeCorbusier. Disegni Dessins Drawings*. Officina, Rome, 1978.
Jencks,Charles.*LeCorbusier and the Tragic View of Architecture*. Harvard UP. 1973
Jordan, Jim. *Paul Klee and Cubism*. Princeton University Press, NJ 1984.
Krauss, Rosalind. *The Picasso Papers*. Farrar, Straus, & Giroux, NY, 1998.
*Kepes, Gyorgy. *Language of Vision*. Paul Theobald, Chicago, 1974
Kepes, Gyorgy. The *Nature and Art of Motion*. George Brazillier NY 1966.
Le Corbusier. *Fifty Works by Le Corbusier*. Sotheby & Co., Tuesday 1st July, 1969.
*Lincoln, Louise (ed.) *Léger's Le Grand Déjeuner*. Minneapolis, MN 1980
Lynn, Greg.*Animate Form*. Princeton Architectural Press, NY, 1997. Also CD-ROM
*Mili, Gjon. *Picasso's Third Dimension*. Triton Press, NY, 1970.
Opheim, David C. *Point of View A Study in Perspective Drawing*. 1992.
Rubin, William. *Pablo Picasso: a Retrospective*. The Museum of Modern Art, NY, 1980.
Sadler, Arthur. *Paper Sculptur*e. Blandford Press, London, 1964.
Stearns, Marshall W. *The Story of Jazz*. Oxford University Press, NY, 1958.
Sutton, Keith. *Picasso*. Spring Books, Hamlyn House, London. 1962
Tsujimoto, Karen. *Wayne Theibaud*. San Francisco Museum of Modern Art, SF, 1985.
Tufte, Edward. *The Visual Display of Quantitative Information*. Graphics Press, Cheshire, CT. 1983.
van Doesburg, Theo. "Film as Pure Form." *Form*, Summer 1966.
Vignes, M. and Hofstein, F.*Oakland Blues*. Marchand Villa DÆlesia, Paris, 1989.
von Moos,Stanislaus.*LeCorbusierElements of a Synthesis*. MIT P, Cambridge, 1979.
Zorzi, Renzo.*Le Corbusier Pittore E Scultore*. Arnoldo Mondadori, Milano, 1986.

1.   MELODY

READINGS

Banham, Reyner. *Theory and Design in the First Machine Age.* MIT P, Cambridge, 1980.
Davies, Colin. *High Tech Architecture.* Rizzoli, NY, 1988.
Duddington, C.L. *Evolution and Design in the Plant Kingdom.* Crowell, NY 1974.
*Klee, Paul. *The Thinking Eye.* Jurg Spiller (ed.) Lund Humphries, London. 1964.
Klee, Paul. *The Nature of Nature.* Jurg Spiller (ed.) George Wittenborn, NY. 1973.
Prouvé, Jean. *Jean Prouvé, Constructeur.* Centre Georges Pompidou, Paris, 1990.
Tafuri, Manfredo. The *Sphere and the Labyrinth: Avante Gardes and Architecture from Piranesi to the 1970s.* MIT Press, Cambridge, 1980.

ADDITIONAL SOURCES

Acland, James H. *Medieval Structure: The Gothic Vault.* University of Toronto P. 1972.
Allen, Edward. *Stone Shelters.* MIT Press, Cambridge, MA. 1969
Arnheim, Rudolf. *The Dynamics of Architectural Form.* U. of California P. Berkeley, 1977.
Baer, Steve. *Zome Primer.* Zomeworks, Albuquerque, NM. 1970.
Baldwin, Jay. *Bucky Works: Buckminster Fuller's Ideas for Today.* John Wiley, NY, 1996.
Bernstein, Leonard. *What Is Jazz?* Lecture Album, RCA Victor, NY, 1959.
Berger, Horst. *Light Structures - Structures of Light: The Art and Engineering of Tensile Structures.* Birkhauser, Basel, 1996.
Bertomen, Michele. *Transmission Towers on the Long Island Expressway: A Study in the Language of Form.* Princeton Architectural Press, NY 1991
Calatrava, Santiago. *Dynamic Equilibrium.* Verlag fur Architektur, Zurich 1991
Calatrava, Santiago, *Il Folle Volo: The Daring Flight.* Electa Spa, Milano, Italy, 1987.
Chinese Calligraphy. The Philadelphia Museum of Art, 1971
Dyer, Geoff. *But beautiful: a book about jazz.* Farrar Strraus and Giroux, NY 1996.
Favier, Jean. *The World of Chartres.* Abrams NY 1990.
Fjeld, Per Olaf. *Sverre Fehn: The Thought of Construction.* Rizzoli, NY 1983.
Gans, Deborah. *Bridging the Gap: Rethinking the Relationship of Architect and Engineer.* Van Nostrand Reinhold, NY, 1991.
Glaeser, Ludwig. *Twentieth Century Engineering.* The Museum of Modern Art, NY. 1964
Goldscheider, L. *Michelangelo: Painting, Sculpture, Architecture* NYGS, Greenwich, 1964.
Halfman, Robert. *Dynamics. Volumes I and II.* Addison-Wesley, Reading, MA. 1962.
Hunter, S. and Hawthorne, D. *George Segal.* Ediciones Poligrafa, Barcelona, 1988.
Kagan, Andrew. *Paul Klee: Art and Music.* Cornell University Press, Ithaca, 1983.
Klee, Paul. *Pedagogical Sketchbook. Faber and Faber, London. 1968*
Lawrence, A.W. *Greek Architecture.* Penguin Books Baltimore. 1973
Leonidov, Ivan I. *Ivan Leonidov.* New York: Rizzoli, 1981.
Lodder, Christina. *Russian Constructivism.* New Haven: Yale U. Press, 1983.
Luce, H. Christopher. *Abstraction and Expression in Chinese Calligraphy.* China Institute, NY. 1995.
*Mainstone, Rowland J. *Developments in Structural Form.* MIT Press, Cambridge, 1975.
McCleary, P. (ed.) *Visions and Paradox: the Work of Robert Le Ricolais.* Catalog. University of Pennsylvania, Philadelphia, 1996.
Moore, Rowan ed. *Structure Space and Skin: The Early Work of Nicholas Grimshaw & Partners,* Phaidon, London, 1995.
Piano and Rogers. *Global Architecture.* A.D.A. Edita, Tokyo, Japan.
Pye, David. *The Nature of Design.* Van Nostrand Reinhold, NY. 1964.
Prouvé, Jean. *Jean Prouvé, Prefabrication: Structures and Elements.* Praeger, NY, 1971.
Read, Herbert. *The Art of Sculpture.* Princeton University Press, NJ, 1956.
Robbin, Tony. *Engineering a New Architecture.* Yale U. Press, New Haven, 1996.
Rose, Kenneth. The *Body in Time,* John Wiley and Sons, NY, 1988
Ross, Nancy Wilson. *The World of Zen.* Vintage Books, Alfred A. Knopf, NY 1960
Ross, Philip E. "Buckytubes". *Scientific American.* December, 1991.
Rudofsky, Bernard. *The Prodigious Builders.* Secker and Warburg. London. 1977.
Salvadori, M. and Heller, R. *Structure in Architecture.* Prentice-Hall, NJ. 1963.
Salvadori, Mario. *Why Buildings Stand Up.* WW Norton, NY, 1980.
Sankader, B. and Eggen, A. *The Structural Basis of Architecture.* Watson-Guptil, 1992.
Silver, Nathan. *Lost NY.* American Legacy Press, NY. 1967
*Snelson, Kenneth. *Kenneth Snelson.* Kunstverein, Hannover, 1971.
Stearns, Marshall. *The Story of Jazz.* Oxford University Press. NY 1958.
Sudworth, George, B. *Forest Trees of the Pacific Slope.* Dover, NY. 1967.
Thiis-Evensen, Thomas. *Archetypes in Architecture.* Norwegian U. Press, Oslo, 1987.

Vasari, Giorgio. *Lives of the Artists.* Penguin Books NY. 1965 [1568]
Vidler, Anthony. *Warped Space: Architectural Anxiety and Modern Culture.* forthcoming.
Weiger, S.L. *Chinese Characters.* Dover, NY, 1965.
Wilson, Forrest. *What It Feels Like to be a Building.* The Preservation Press, Washington, DC. 1988
Wittkower, Rudolf. *Sculpture: Process and Principles.* Harper & Row, NY. 1977
Villecco, Margot. "Rigged House". *Architecture Plus.* November/December 1974.
von Meiss, Pierre. *Elements of Architecture: From Form to Place.* Van VNR, NY. 1986.
*Yee, Chiang. *Chinese Calligraphy 3rd ed.* Methuen & Company, Ltd. 1973
Zion, Robert. *Trees for Architecture and the Landscape.* Van Nostrand Reinhold NY. 1968

2.   HARMONY: *SPINNING*

READINGS

Billington, David P. *The Tower and the Bridge.* Basic Books, NY. 1983.
Bruschi, Arnaldo. *Bramante.* Thames and Hudson, London. 1977
*Eames and Morrison. *Powers of Ten,* Scientific American Library NY 1982.
*Ghyka, Matilla. The *Geometry of Art and Life.* Dover, NY, 1978.
*Schwenk, Theodore. *Sensitive Chaos: The Creation of Flowing Forms in Water and Air.* Schocken, NY, 1976.
*Thompson, D'Arcy. *On Growth and Form.* Cambridge U Press. NY 1961. [1917]
*Wittokower, Rudolf. *Architectural Principles in the Age of Humanism.* Random House, NY. 1962

ADDITIONAL SOURCES

Ackerman, James. *The Architecture of Michelangelo.* University of Chicago Press, 1986
Boime, Albert. *Starry Night: A Matter of History; A History of Matter.* CD-ROM. Media for the Arts. Newport RI, 1996.
Ball, Philip. *Designing the Molecular World. Chemistry at the Frontier.* Princeton University Press. Princeton NJ, 1994.
Close, Frank. et.al. *The Particle Explosion.* Oxford University Press. NY 1986.
Denari, Neil. *Gyroscopic Horizons.* Princeton Architectural Press, NY, 1995.
*Doczi, Gyorgy. *The Power of Limits.* Shambhala Boulder CO. 1981.
*Frisch, Karl von. *Animal Architecture.* Van Nostrand Reinhold, NY 1983.
*Gabo, Naum. *Of Divers Arts.* Princeton University Press, Princeton NJ, 1962.
Glaeser, Ludwig. *The Work of Frei Otto.* The Museum of Modern Art. NY 1972
Huntley, H.E. *The Divine Proportion.* Dover, NY. 1970.
Marten, Michael *Under the Microscope: a Hidden World Revealed* Cambridge UP NY, 1990.
Pearce, Peter. *Structure in Nature is a Strategy for Design.* MIT Press, 1978.
Snyder, Gary. *Earth House Hold.* New Directions, NY. 1969.

2.   HARMONY: *GROOVING*

READINGS

*Arnheim, Rudolf. "Dynamics of Arches" in *Dynamics of Architectural Form.* University of California Press, Berkeley, 1977.
*Fuller, R. Buckminster. *Synergetics: Explorations in the Geometry of Thinking.* 2 vols. MacMillan, NY, 1979.
Kundera, Milan. *The Unbearable Lightness of Being.* Harper Collins, NY, 1988.
Mainstone, R. "Intuition and the Springs of Structural Invention" in *Via, Vol 2: Structures Implicit and Explicit.* Journal of the Graduate School of Fine Arts. [Bryan, James and Sauer, Rolf. eds.] University of Pennsylvania. Philadelphia, 1973.
*Marks, Robert. *The Dymaxion World of Buckminster Fuller.* Southern Illinois University Press, Carbondale, 1960.
Thorne, Kip. *Black Holes and Time Warps.* Norton, NY 1994
*Otto, Frei. *Tensile Structures.* MIT Press, Cambridge, 1969.
*Ozenfant, Amedée *Foundations of Modern Art. Dover, NY, 1952.*
Pauling, Linus, Hayward, Roger. *The Architecture of Molecules.* W.H. Freeman, SF 1964
Wachsmann, Konrad. *The Turning Point in Architecture.* Reinhold, NY 1961,
Wheeler, John Archibald. *A Journey into Gravity and Spacetime.* Scientific American Library NY 1990.

ADDITIONAL SOURCES

Adams, Henry. *Mont Saint Michel and Chartres* Viking Penguin, NY, 1986.
Alter, Dinsmore. *Pictorial Guide to the Moon.* 3rd ed. Thomas Y. Crowell, NY. 1973
Ames, Anthony. *Five Houses.* Princeton Architectural Press, NY, 1987
Baggott, Jim. *Perfect Symmetry: The Accidental Discovery of the Buckminster-fullerene.* Oxford University Press. NY, 1994.
*Bodanis, David. *The Secret House.* Simon and Schuster, NY, 1986.
Brandt, S. and Dahmen, H. *The Picture Book of Quantum Mechanics.* Springer-Verlag, Heidelberg, 1995.
Enaud, Francois. *Le Mont Saint Michel.* Caisse Nationale des Monuments Historiques, Paris. 1966.
Harries, Karsten. "*Building and the Terror of Time*" *Perspecta 19*, New Haven, 1982.
Misner, Thorne, Wheeler. *Gravitation.* W.H. Freeman and Company, 1973
Mitchell, William J. *The Logic of Architecture.* Halliday Lithograph. 1990
Nervi, Pier Luigi *Aesthetics and Technology in Building.* Harvard UP. Cambridge, 1990.
Nillson, Lennart. *Behold Man.* Little Brown and Company, Boston, 1978.
Plummer, Henry. "Vessels of Power" *A+U, Architecture and Urbanism*, February 1989.
*Roland, Conrad. *Frei Otto: Tension Structures.* Praeger, NY 1970
Sawkins, F. et.al. *The Evolving Earth: A Text in Physical Geology.* MacMillan, NY. 1974.
*Scharf, David. *Magnifications.* Schocken Books, NY, 1977.
Seike, Kiyosi. *The Art of Japanese Joinery.* Weatherhill/Tankosha, NY/Tokyo 1977
*Vitruvius. *Ten Books on Architecture.* Dover, NY, 1960.
Whitesides, G. "*Self Assembling Materials*", *Scientific American*, 9/95

Levenson, Thomas. *Ice Time.* Harper & Row, NY. 1989
Schey, H. *div grad curl and all that: an informal text on vector calculus.* Norton. NY. 1992
Singh, Simon. *Fermat's Enigma.* Walker and Company NY, 1997.
Summerson, John. *The Classical Language of Architecture.* MIT Press, MA, 1966
Treib, Marc. *Space Calculated in Seconds: The Philips Pavilion, Le Corbusier, Edgar Varese.* Princeton University Press. 1996.
Watson, James D. *Molecular Biology of the Gene. 2nd ed.* W.A. Benjamin, NY. 1970
Wittcower Rudolf *Allegory and the Migration of Symbols.* Westview Press, Boulder, 1977.
Yates, Robert C. *Curves and Their Properties.* The National Council of Teachers Mathematics. 1952

3.   CONCERTO: *WEAVING*

READINGS

Amatuzzo, Paul. *Niine selected Projects.* Sapienza Edizioni, Milan, 1994.
Feynman, Richard. *Lectures on Physics, Volume 2: Mainly Electromagnetism and Matter.* Callifornia Institute of Technology. 1964
Le Corbusier. *Oeuvres Complets. (8 volumes)* L'editions d'architecture. Artemis, Zurich. 1970. [1910-1965+]
Richter, Jean Paul. *The Notebooks of Leonardo Da Vinci.* Dover, NY. 1970.
Meier, Richard. *Richard Meier Architect.* Rizzoli NY 1984
Palladio, Andrea. *The Four Books of Architecture.* Dover, NY. 1965.

ADDITIONAL SOURCES

Adams, Colin. *The Knot Book.* W. H. Freeman, San Francisco, 1994.
Alvar Aalto: Architectural Monographs 4. St. Martin's Press, NY. 1978
Albertini, B. and Bagnoli, A. *Carlo Scarpa: Architecture in Details.* MIT Press, 1989.
Ambrose, James. *Design of Building Trusses.* John Wiley & Sons, NY. 1994.
Bach, Johann Sebastian. *The Well-Tempered Clavier.* Dover, NY. 1983. [1738-42]
Bar-Yam, Yaneer. *Dynamics of Complex Systems.* Addison-Wesley Longman, 1997.
Bovini. Giuseppi. *Ravenna: Art and History.* Longo Publisher. Ravenna. 1991.
Calvino, Italo. *Mr. Palomar.* Harcourt Brace Janovich, San Diego, 1983.
Carter, Robert. *Molecular Symmetry and Group Theory.* John Wiley & Sons, NY, 1997.
Carpenter, Edmund. *Eskimo Realities.* Holt Rinehart and Winston, NY, 1973.
Chihuly, Dale. *Seaforms.* Portland Press, Seattle. 1995.
Guerra, L. and Ojeda, O. *Henri Ciriani.* Rockport, 1997.
Elmore, William. Physics of Waves. Dover, NY, 1985.
Fuchigami, Masayuki (ed.) *Luis Barragan.* Yasusuke Hamada, Tokyo, 1992.
Gray's *Anatomy* World Publications, NY 1996. [1862]
Gray, Lee Edward and Walters, David. *Pattern and Context.* College of Architecture Monograph Series, Number One, University of North Carolina at Charlotte. 1992
Gutheim, Frederick. *Alvar Aalto.* George Brazillier, NY. 1960.
Hall, Stephen B. *Mapping the Next Millennium.* Random House, NY. 1992
Junger, Sebastian. *The Perfect Storm.* Norton, NY. 1997.
Kalil, Michael "A Melody and Three Harmonies" *UCLA Architecture Journal,* LA, 1989
Kalil, Michael "Leap of Faith" *Metropolis,* NY, May 1988.
Lessing, Gotthold Ephraim. *Laocöon: An Essay on the Limits of Painting and Poetry.* Bobbs-Merrill, NY. 1962. [1766]
Lobel, John. *Between Silence and Light,* Shambala, Boulder, 1979
Marein, Shirley. *Off the Loom.* The Viking Press. NY. 1972.
McCarter, Robert, Editor. *Frank Lloyd Wright A Primer on Architectural Principles.* Princeton Architecture Press, NY, 1991
Murray, Peter. *Renaissance Architecture.* Abrams, NY 197.
Nute, Kevin. *Frank Lloyd Wright and Japan.* Van Nostrand Reinhold, NY, 1993.
Panofsky, Erwin. *Renaissance and Renascences in Western Art.* Almqvist and Wiksell, Stockholm. 1960.
Panofsky, Erwin. *Studies in Iconology.* Harper and Row, NY 1967.
Parker, H. *Simplified Engineering for Architects and Builders.* John Wiley & Sons, NY. 1967.
Portoghesi, Paolo. *Roma Barocca.* MIT Press, Cambridge, 1970.
Rainey, Sarita. *Weaving Without a Loom.* Davis Publications, Worcester MA 1966.
Ruegg, Arthur ed. *Polychromie architecturale: Le Corbusier's 'Color Keyboards'.* Birkhauser, Basel, 1998.
Salvini, Roberto. *The Hidden Michelangelo.* Rand McNally Chicago IL 1978.

3.   CONCERTO: *BENDING*

READINGS

Benjamin, Walter. "The Work of Art in the Age of Mechanical Reproduction" in *Illuminations.* Schocken books, NY 1969.
Lipman, Jean. *Calder's Universe.* Viking Press, NY, 1976.
Deleuze, Gilles. *The Fold: Leibniz and the Baroque.* U. of Minnesota Press, 1993.
Hejduk, John. *Mask of Medusa.* Rizzoli, NY. 1985
Kopp, Anatole. *Town and Revolution.* Brazillier, NY, 1970.
Le Corbusier. *Creation is a Patient Search.* Frederick A. Praeger NY 1960.
Rowe, Colin. *Mathematics of the Ideal Villa and Other Essays.* MIT P. Cambridge, 1976.
Ryckwert, Joseph. *The Necessity of Artifice*
Kaufmann, Edgar (ed.) *Frank Lloyd Wright: Writings and Buildings.* Dutton, NY, 1974.
   Wright, Frank Lloyd. *Buildings, Plans, and Designs.* Horizon Press, NY, 1968.
   Wright, Frank Lloyd. *The Early Work.* Horizon Press, NY, 1968.
   Together these two reprint the 1910 "Wasmuth" *Edition.*
Wright, Frank Lloyd. *The Wendigen Edition.* Horizon Press, NY, 1965.
   This reprints the 1925 *Wendigen Edition.*

ADDITIONAL SOURCES

Ando, Tadao and Pare, Richard. *The Colours of Light.* Phaidon, London, 1996.
Bacon, Edmund N. *Design of Cities.* Penguin Books, NY. 1974
Brooke, Christopher. *The Monastic World.* Random House, NY. 1974
Bruschi, Arnaldo. *Bramante.* Thames & Hudson, Ltd., London, 1973.
Buonarrotti, Michelangelo. *Michelangelo Architetto.* Milano: ETAS. 1964.
Cook, Theodore A. *The Curves of Life.* Dover, NY, 1997. [1914].
Courant, Richard. *What is Mathematics? An elementary approach to Ideas and Methods.* Oxford University Press, NY, 1996.
Flatow, Ira. *Rainbows, Curve Balls, and Other Wonders of Natural Science Explained.* William Morrow, NY 1988
Giedion, Seigfried. *Mechanization Takes Command.* WW Norton, NY, 1969.
Grillo, Paul Jacques. *Form, Function, and Design.* Dover, NY, 1946
Hardison, O.B.Jr,. *Disappearing Through the Skylight: Culture and Technology in the Twentieth Century.* Penguin NY, 1989.
Heydenreich, Ludwig H. and Lotz, Wolfgang. *Architecture in Italy 1400-1600.* Penguin Books, Baltimore, MD. 1974
Huizinga, Johan. *Homo Ludens: a Study of the Play Element in Culture.* Beacon Press, Boston. 1950.

Slutzky, Robert. "Aqueous Humor" *Oppositions 19/20,* MIT Press, Cambridge 1980.
Snyder, Gary. *Regarding Wave.* New Directions, NY, 1970.
Tarrago, Salvador. *Gaudi.* Editorial Escudo do Oro, S.A., Barcelona, Spain. 1980.
van de Ven, Cornelis. *Space in Architecture.* Van Gorcum. Assen, Netherlands. 1977.
Vidler, Anthony. *The Writing of the Walls.* Princeton Architectural Press, NY, 1987.
von Miess, Pierre. *Elements of Architecture: From form to place.* Van Nostrand Reinhold, NY. 1986.
Walker, Lester. *The Tiny Book of Tiny Houses.* Overlook Press, Woodstock NY, 1993.

4.   SYMPHONY: *RESONATING*

READINGS

Ambasz, Emilio. *Italy the New Domestic Landscape,* Museum of Modern Art, NY 1972.
Ant Farm. *InflatoCookBook* Sausalito. undated, [1969].
Brand, Stewart, ed. *The Whole Earth Catalog.* Viking Penguin, NY, 1975.
Defoe, Daniel. *Robinson Crusoe.* Bantam Books, NY, 1981 [1719]
Isaac, Ken. *How to Build Your Own Living Structures* Harmony Books, NY, 1974.
Le Corbusier. *Le Modulor and Modulor 2.* Harvard University Press, MA, 1980.
Nilsson, Lennart. *Behold Man.* Little, Brown & Company, Canada. 1973
Ryckwert, Joseph. On *Adam s House in Paradise.* MIT Press, Cambridge MA 1981.
Wyss, Johann. *Swiss Family Robinson.* Putnam, NY, 1949.
Hutchins, Carleen (ed). *The Physics of Music.* W.H. Freeman, SF, 1978.
Turnbull, Colin. *The Forest People* Simon and Schuster, NY, 1987.

ADDITIONAL SOURCES

Ackerman, James. *The Architecture of Michelangelo.* U. of Chicago Press, IL, 1986.
Aladdin Company. *Aladdin "Built-in-a-Day" House Catalog, 1917.* Dover, NY, 1991.
Allen, Edward. *How Buildings Work.* Oxford University Press, NY, 1995.
Allen, Edward. *The Architect's Studio Companion.* John Wiley & Sons, NY, 1995.
Bishop, Jerry E. and Waldholz, Michael. *Genome.* Simon and Schuster, NY. 1990
Bonk, Ecke. *Marcel Duchamp The Box in a Valise.* Rizzoli, NY. 1989.
Brooke, C. Highfield, R. and Swaan, W. *Oxford and Cambridge.* Cambridge U. P. 1988.
Burns, Jim. *Arthropods: New Design Futures.* Praeger, NY. 1972.
Buttiker, Urs. *Louis I. Kahn Light and Space.* Whitney Library of Design, NY. 1994
Chiambretto, Bruno. *Le Corbusier A Cap-Martin.* Editions Parentheses, Marseilles, 1987.
Cook, Peter, et. al. *Archigram.* Birkhauser, Boston MA, 1996.
Cook, Peter. *Experimental Architecture* Universe Books, NY 1970.
Cooper, Geoffrey. *The Cell A Molecular Approach.* Sinauer, Boston, 1997. with CD-ROM.
Crosbie, Michael J. "Desert Shield." *Architecture,* May 1991.
Crosbie, Michael J. *Jersey Devil: Design/Build Book.* Gibbs M. Smith, Layton, UT. 1985.
Dadras, Aly S. *Mechanical Systems for Architects.* McGraw-Hill, NY. 1995.
De Tolnay, Charles. *The Medici Chapel.* Princeton University Pres, NJ. 1948.
Badanes, Steve. "Jersey Devil's Hill House: How a Design-Build Team Buried a House on a California Hilltop." *Fine Homebuilding,* Oct/Nov. 1985.
Davies, Colin. *High Tech Architecture.* Rizzoli NY, 1988.
Doubilet, S. and Fisher, T. "The Hong Kong Bank." *Progressive Architecture,* March, 1986.
Foster Norman. "Projets.Realisations.1980-1986." *l'architecture d'aujourd'hui.* 2/85. Paris.
Fuchs, Hans. *The Dynamics of Heat.* Springer-Verlag. Heidelberg, 1996.
Gebhard, David. *Schindler.* The Viking Press, NY. 1971
Goldstein, M. and Goldstein, I. *The Refrigerator and the Universe: Understanding the Laws of Energy.* Harvard University Press. Cambridge, 1993.
Goodsell, David. *The Machinery of Life.* Springer-Verlag. Heidelberg. 1993.
Gordon, Claude. *The Language of the Cell.* McGraw Hill, NY, 1993.
Halle, Francis. "A Raft Atop the Rain Forest." *National Geographic.* October 1990.
Hejduk, John. *Soundings.* Rizzoli, NY, 1993.
Helmholtz, Herman L.F. *On the Sensations of Tone.* Dover, NY. 1954.
Herzog, Thomas. *Pneumatic Structures: a Handbook of Inflatable Architecture.* Oxford University Press, NY. 1976
Hoberman, Chuck. *"Art and Science of Folding Structures."* Sites Architecture, 1992
Jellicoe, Geoffrey and Susan. *The Landscape of Man.* The Viking Press, NY. 1970
Jones, Wes. *Instrumental Form: Words, Buildings, Machines.* Princeton Architectural Press, NY, 1984.
Kahn, Louis. *Louis I. Kahn.* Williams College Museum of Art, Williamstown, MA. 1996

Kepes, Gyorgy. *The man-made object.* George Brazillier NY 1966.
Lawlor, Robert. *Sacred Geometry.* Thames and Hudson Ltd., London, 1982
Klepac, Lou et al. *Giorgio Morandi: The Dimension of Inner Space.* Bologna, 1997.
Levi Straus, Claude. *The Savage Mind.* University of Chicago Press, IL, 1968.
Logan, William. "Green Architecture" *House Beautiful,* June 1993.
March, Lionel and Sheine, Judith, (eds.) *RM Schindler.* Academy Editions, London, 1993
Masello, David. *Architecture Without Rules: The Houses of Marcel Breuer* and Herbert Beckhard. W. W. Norton, NY, 1993.
Novikoff and Holtzman. *Cells and Organelles.* Holt, Rinehart, NY. 1970.
Piedmont-Palladino, S. (ed.) *The Devil's Workshop: 25 Years of Jersey Devil Architecture.* Princeton Architectural Press, NY, 1997.
Rensenberger, B. *Life Itself: Exploring the Realm of the Living Cell.* Oxford U. P. NY, 1997.
Russell, Jeffrey. *A History of Heaven: The Singing Silence.* Princeton UP. NJ, 1997.
Sheldrake, Rupert. *Morphic Resonance: A New Science of Life.* Park St. Press, Rochester VT, 1995.
Sherwood, Roger. *Modern Housing Prototypes.* Harvard U.P. Cambridge, 1978.
Skurka, Norma and Naar, Jon. *Design for a Limited Planet.* Random House, NY, 1976.
Spence, William P. *Architectural Working Drawings.* John Wiley & Sons, NY. 1993.
Spitzer, Victor. *Atlas of the Visible Human.* Jones & Bartlett. 1997.
Villa-Real, Ricardo. *The Alhambra and the Generalife.* Grefol, Madrid, Spain. n.d.
Weber, Heidi. *Stahl und Form* Ausstellungsgebaude von le Corbusier. Verlag Stahleisen m.b.H., Dusseldorf, Germany. 1970.
Zuk, William, and Clark, Roger. *Kinetic Architecture.* Van Nostrand Reinhold, NY, 1970.

4.   SYMPHONY: *RADIATING*

READINGS

Benevolo, Leonardo. *The Origins of Modern Town Planning.* MIT P, Cambridge, 1967.
Gerster, Georg. *The Grand Design: The Earth From Above.* Knapp Press, LA, 1988.
Manuel, Frank *Paths in Utopia.* MacMillan, NY, 1988.
Michener, James. *The Source.* Random House, NY, 1965.
Morrish, William. *Civilizing Terrains: Mountains Mounds and Mesas.* Design Center for American Urban Landscape. Minneapolis, 1990.
Mumford, Lewis. *The City in History.* Harcourt Brace, NY, 1961.
Ryckwert, Joseph. *The Idea of a Town* Princeton University Press, NJ 1967.
Soleri, Paolo. *Arcology: The City in the Image of Man.* MIT Press, Cambridge, MA. 1969
Le Corbusier. *Radiant City.* Orion Press NY, 1967.
*Young, Louise B. *The Unfinished Universe,* Simon and Schuster 1986
Zajonc, Arthur. *Catching the Light: The Entwined History of Light and Mind.* Bantam Books, NY, 1993.

ADDITIONAL SOURCES

Anderton, F. "Learning from Jaipur." *Journal of Architectural Education,* Summer 1989
Andrews, George. *Maya Cities.* University of Oklahoma Press, Norman, 1977.
Baer, Steve *Sunspots: Collected Facts & Solar Fiction.* Zomeworks, Albuquerque, 1977.
Brand, Stewart. *How Buildings Learn.* Viking. NY, 1994.
Burckhardt, Jakob. *Civilization of the Renaissance in Italy. Random House NY 1995.*
Calvino *Invisible Cities.* Harcourt Brace, San Diego, 1978.
Calthorpe, Peter. *The Next American Metropolis.* Princeton Architectural P, NY, 1996.
de Coulanges, Fustel. *The Ancient City.* Doubleday, NY, 1956.
*Copper, Wayne. *The Figure/Grounds* "Cornell Journal of Architecture #2.* Rizzoli, NY, 1982.
Crocker, Andrew. *Mr. Sandman Bring Me A Dream.* Papunya Tula Artists Pty Ltd. Alice Springs and The Aboriginal Artists Agency Ltd., Sydney, Australia. 1981.
Couperie, Pierre. *Paris Through the Ages.* George Brazillier, NY. 1968.
Davies, Paul. *The Cosmic Blueprint.* Simon and Schuster, NY, 1988.
Eisenman, Peter. *Cities of Artificial Excavation.* Rizzoli, NY, 1994.
Foote, Timothy. *The World of Bruegel: c. 1525-1569.* Time-Life Books. NY. 1968
Friedman, Herbert. *Sun and Earth.* Scientific American Books, NY. 1986.
Friedman, Jonathan. "The Monuments of Chandigarth". *Central Papers on Architecture.* Spring 1990.
Friedman, Mildred, ed. "Suburbs." *Design Quarterly* 132. MIT Press, Cambridge, 1986
Geddes, Robert (ed.) *Cities in Our Future.* Island Press, Covelo, CA. 1996.
Garnier, Tony. *Une Cité Industrielle.* Auguste Vincent, Paris, 1918.

Gutkind, E.A. *International History of City Development.* Free Press, NY. 1973.
Ito, Teiji, Iwamiya, Takeji, and Kamekura, Yusaku. *The Japanese Garden: An Approach to Nature.* Yale University Press, New Haven, CT. 1972
Jacobs, Jane. *The Economy of Cities,* Random House, NY, 1969.
Jacobs, Jane. *Cities and the Wealth of Nations.* Random House, NY, 1992.
Kelbaugh, Doug et.al. *The Pedestrian Pocket Book.* Princeton Architectural P. NY, 1989.
Kelley, Kevin. *The Home Planet.* Addison-Wesley, Reading, PA. 1988.
Kostoff, Spiro. *The City Assembled.* Little, Brown, Boston, 1992.
de Landa, Manuel. "Theories of Self-Organization and the Dynamics of Cities." *Newsline,* Columbia University, NY, May, 1995.
Leoncini, Giovanni. *La Certosa Di Firenze Nei Suoi Rapporti con L'Architettura Certosina.* Analecta Cartusiana, Salzburg, Austria. 1979.
Ledoux, Claude-Nicholas. *L'Architetcure.* Princeton Architectural P, NY, 1993. [1847]
Lightman, Alan. *Einstein's Dreams: A Novel.* Warner Books, NY. 1994.
Mandelbrot, Benoit. *The Fractal Geometry of Nature.* W.H. Freeman, NY 1983.
Giorgio Morandi. Vancouver Art Gallery Catalog. Vancouver, Canada. 1977
Manuel, Frank (ed.) *Utopias and Utopian Thought.* Beacon Press Boston, 1966.
McHarg, Ian. *Design With Nature.* John Wiley and Sons. NY, 1995. [1969]
More, Thomas *Utopia.* Hendricks House, Putney VT. 1981 [1516]
Morris, A.E. J. *History of Urban Form Before the Industrial Revolution, 3rd Edition,* John Wiley and Sons. NY, 1994.
Pirenne, Henri *Medieval Cities: Their Origins and the Revival of Trade.* Princeton UP 1952.
Poryphyrios, Demetrios. *Heterotopia: A Study in the Ordering Sensibility of the Work of Alvar Aalto."* AD Academy Editions, London, 1978.
*Poundstone, William. *The Recursive Universe.* William Morrow, NY, 1985.
Reps, John. *Making of Urban America.* Princeton University Press, NJ, 1965.
Roberts, David. *In Search of the Old Ones: Exploring the Anasazi World of the Southwest.* Simon and Schuster, NY, 1996
Robinson, Kim Stanley *Red Mars, Green Mars, Blue Mars.* Bantam, NY, 1993, 1994, 1996.
Rowe, Colin and Koetter, Fred. *Collage City.* MIT Press, Cambridge, MA. 1978
Rykwert, Joseph. *On Adam's House in Paradise.* The Museum of Modern Art, NY. 1972.
Safdie, Moshe. *The City After the Automobile: an Architect's Vision.* Basic Books, NY, 1997
Saint Augustine *City of God.* Random House, NY. 1994. [c.400 ad]
Sauter Peter ed. *Finding Home Writings on Nature and Culture.* Orion Magazine, NY, 1996.
Schama, Simon. *The Embarrassment of Riches. Knopf, NY, 1987.*
Schwarz, Rudolf. *The Church Incarnate.* Henry Regnery Company, Chicago, 1968.
Simak, Clifford. *City.* Doubleday, NY 1992. [1952]
Stewart: T.C. *The City As an Image of Man.* Latimer Press, London, 1970.
Tafuri, Manfredo. *Architecture and Utopia.* MIT Press, Cambridge. 1976.
Trimble, Stephen. *The Sagebrush Ocean: A Natural History of the Great Basin.* University of Nevada Press, Reno and Las Vegas, 1989.
Updike, John. *Towards the End of Time.* A Novel. Alfred A Knopf, NY. 1997
Van der Ryn, Sim. *Ecological Design.* Island Press, Covelo, CA. 1996.
Weber, Max. *The City.* The Free Press. NY 1958.
Wilson, Johnny L. *The Sim City Planning Commission Handbook* McGraw Hill 1990 NY
Wright, Frank Lloyd. *Broadacre City* Taliesin Fellowship. Spring Green WI, 1940.
Wright, Frank Lloyd. *The Living City.* NAL/Dutton., NY. 1970.
Kalec, Donald G., Heinz, Thomas A. *Frank Lloyd Wright Home and Studios Oak Park Illinois.* Frank Lloyd Wright Home and Studios Foundation. Oak Park, IL . 1972

SELECTED AND RECOMMENDED SOFTWARE

ADAM INteractive Anatomy. Adam Software, Atlanta GA, 1997. CD-ROM.
Architectural Graphic Standards. John Wiley & Sons, NY. 1996. CD-ROM.
Architecture and Design Illustrated. Royal Institute of British Architects. CD-ROM.
AutoCAD. Autodesk. San Rafael, CA. 1998. CD-ROM.
Creatures. Mindscape Entertainment. Novato, CA, 1997. CD-ROM.
Dance of the Planets. ARC Science Simulations, CA, 1995. CD-ROM.
Dynamics: Engineering Mechanics. John Wiley & Sons. NY, 1993. CD-ROM.
Frank Lloyd Wright Presentation Concepts and Conceptual Drawings. Oxford University Press. NY, 1996. CD-ROM.
Form-Z. Ohio. CD-ROM.
Great Buildings Collection. Van Nostrand Reinhold, NY, 1994. CD-ROM.
HyperChem. Hypercube Inc. Ontario Canada, 1996. CD-ROM.
Lightscape. Discreet Logic, Montreal, 1998. CD-ROM.
Mechanical Desktop. Autodesk. CD-ROM.
Mountain High Maps. Digital Wisdom. CD-ROM.
MQPro, HumanCAD Systems. 1996. CD-ROM.
Populous. 1988. CD-ROM.
Poser 2. Fractal Design. 1995. CD-ROM.
Redshift 3. Piranha Interactive. NY. 1998. *CD-ROM.*
Sim City. Sim City 2000. Sim Earth. Sim Tower. Sim Isle. Sim Ant. Maxis. CD-ROM.
Softdesk Energy. Softdesk, Henniker, NH. 1995. CD-ROM.
Starry Night Deluxe. Sienna Software. CA, 1998. CD-ROM.
Woods of the World. Tree Talk, Inc. Burlington VT, 1995. CD-ROM.
Working Model; Working Model 3D. Knowledge Revolution. San Mateo, 1994. CD-ROM.
3D Home Architect. Broderbund. 1998. CD-ROM.
3D StudioMAX. Kinetix. 1997. CD-ROM.
Ultimate Frank Lloyd Wright. Microsoft Home Multimedia. CD-ROM. 1994.

SELECTED READINGS ON SPACE EXPLORATION

Apollo-Soyuz Summary Report. NASA Washington DC 1977.
Banks, Iain, *Feersum Endjinn.* Bantam Books, NY, 1994.
Crisswell, David (ed.) *Lunar Utilization* Lunar Science Institute NASA, Houston, TX. 1976
Heppenheimer, T.A. *Colonies in Space.* Stackpole Books, Harrisburg PA, 1977.
Johnson, Richard, and Holbrow, Charles. (ed.) *Space Settlements: A Design Study.* NASA Washington DC 1977.
O'Neill, Gerard K. *The High Frontier.* William Morrow and Co. NY, 1977.
Ruzic, Neil. *Where Winds Sleep*: Man's Future on the Moon. Doubleday, NY, 1970.
Sagan, Carl. *Pale Blue Dot: Vision of the Human Future in Space.* Random House, NY, 1994.
Zubrin, R. and Wagner, R. *The Case for Mars: The Plan to Settle the Red Planet and Why We Must.* Simon and Schuster, NY 1997.

5.   APPENDIX

5.1   A NEW MEDIUM

Downing, E. Hesselink, L., Rallston, J. and Macfarlane, R. "A Three-Color Solid State, Three Dimensional Display." *Science,* 30 August 1996.
"Inside Story" [On Voxels], *Scientific American* March 1994.
Kirkham, Pat. *Charles and Ray Eames: Designers of the Twentieth Century.* MIT Press, Cambridge, 1995.
Silver, Nathan. *The Making of Beaubourg.* MIT Press, Cambridge, 1994.

5.2   SPECTRUM

DESIGN & MODELING

Choisy, Auguste. *L'Art de Batir.* Arnaldo Forni, Bologna, 1986 [1883].
Ferguson, Eugene. *Engineering and the Mind's Eye.* MIT P. Cambridge, NY, 1992.
Giesecke, Mitchell, and Spencer. *Technical Drawings.* MacMillan, NY, 1958.
Le Corbusier. *The Journey to the East.* MIT Press, Cambridge, 1989.
Le Corbusier's Sketchbooks. 4 Volumes. MIT Press, Cambridge, 1982.
Linton, Harold. *Portfolio Design.* W. W. Norton, NY, 1996.
Richard Meier Collages. Academy Editions St. Martin's Press NY, 1990 .
Melville, Herman. *Bartleby the Scrivener.* Simon and Schuster, NY , 1997. [1853]
McGowan, Christopher. *Diatoms to Dinosaurs: The Size and Scale of Living Things.* Island Press. Covelo CA. 1994.
Weber, Bruce. "The Small Ships." *The NY Times Magazine,* November 4, 1990.
Yee, Rendow. *Architectural Design-Drawing Types and Methods.* RDW Publications, Daly City, CA. 1994

COLOR & COLLAGE

Albers, Josef. *Interaction of Color.* Yale University Press. New Haven. CT 1963.
Alvani, Getulio, ed. *Josef Albers,* L'Arcedizioni, Milan, 1988.
Itten, Johannes. *The Art of Color.* Van Nostrand Reinhold, NY. 1974.

Itten, J. and Birren, F. *The Elements of Color*. Van Nostrand Reinhold, NY. 1970.
Fuchigami, Masayuki (ed.) *Luis Barragan*. Yasusuke Hamada, Tokyo, 1992.
Jefferis, Alan, Jones, Michael. *AutoCAD for Architecture*. Delmar, Albany, NY. 1994.
Le Corbusier. *Oeuvre Lithographique*. Centre Le Corbusier. Heidi Weber. Zurich. n.d.
Lynch, David. and Livingston, William. *Color and Light in Nature*. Cambridge U. P. NY 1995
Lynch, David. *The New Munsell Student Color Set*. Fairchild Books, NY, 1995.
Pendleton-Jullian, Ann. "The Collage Poetics of Le Corbusier at La Sainte Baume."
a+u: Architecture and Urbanism, November 1987.
Rainwater, Clarence. *Light and Color*. Western Publishing Co, NY. 1971.
Swirnoff, Lois. *Dimensional Color*. Van Nostrand Reinhold. NY, 1992.

MUSIC MATHEMATICS & MIND

Blakeslee, Sandra. "The Mystery of Music: How It Works In The Brain", *NY Times*,
p. C1, May 16, 1995
Jourdain, Robert. *Music the Brain and Ecstasy: How Music Captures our
Imagination*. William Morrow, NY, 1997.
Greenfield, Susan. *The Human Mind Explained*. Henry Holt and Company, NY, 1996.
Gloor, O. Armhein, B. and Maeder, R. *Illustrated Mathematics*. Springer-Verlag,
Heidelberg, 1995. with CD-ROM.
Maor, Eli. *e: The Story of a Number*. Princeton University Press, Princeton, NJ. 1994.
"Exploring the Mandelbrot Set." *Scientific American*. August, 1985, Vol 253, No. 2. 1985.
Mitchell, W. Liggett, R. Kvan, T. *The Art of Computer Graphics Programming*. Van
Nostrand Reinhold, NY. 1987.
Partridge, Eric. *Origins: A Short Etymological Dictionary of Modern English*. Crown. NY 1983.
Pierce, John R. *The Science of Musical Sound*. Scientific American Books, NY, 1983
Peitgen, Heinz-Otto and Richter, Peter H. *The Beauty of Fractals: Images of
Complex Dynamical Systems*. Springer-Verlag Heidelberg, 1986.
Penrose, Roger. *The Emperor's New Mind*. Oxford University Press NY 1989.
Penrose, Roger. *Shadows of the Mind: A Search for the Missing Science of
Consciousness*. Oxford University Press NY, 1994.
Rothstein, Ed. *Emblems of the Mind: The Inner Life of Music and Mathematics* 1995
Schweber, Silvan. *QED and the Men Who Made It: Dyson, Feynman, Schwinger,
and Tomonaga*. Princeton University Press. Princeton NJ. 1994.

5.3   VISUAL GLOSSARY

Blake, Peter. *No Place Like Utopia*. Alfred A. Knopf. NY 1993.
Banham, Reyner. *Theory and Design in the First Machine Age*. The Architectural
Press. London, 1960.
Chaisson, Eric J. *The Hubble Wars*, Harper Collins, NY 1994
Curtis, William J.R. *Modern Architecture Since 1900*. Prentice-Hall. Englewood
Cliffs NJ. 1982.
Eliade, Mircea. *Cosmos and History: The Myth of the Eternal Return*. Garland, NY, 1985
Fletcher, Sir Bannister. *A History of Architecture on the Comparative Method*.
Charles Scribner's Sons. NY 1963.
Frampton, Kenneth. *Modern Architecture: A Critical History*. Thames & Hudson,
London. 1980.
Gardner, Helen. *Art Through the Ages*. revised ed. Harcourt, Brace & World, 1970.
Norberg-Schulz, Christian. *Meaning in Western Architecture*. Rizzoli, NY, 1974
Jencks, Charles. *Modern Movements in Architecture*. Penguin Books Baltimore. 1973
Kostof, Spiro. *A History of Architecture*. Oxford University Press, NY. 1985, 1995.
Lloyd, Seton et.al. *World Architecture: An Illustrated History*. McGraw-Hill NY 1963.
Pedoe, Dan. *Geometry and the Liberal Arts*. Penguin Books, Baltimore, MD. 1976
Robin, Harry. *The Scientific Image From Cave to Computer*. W.H. Freeman and
Company, NY. 1992.
Sofranko, Thomas A. *Teaching an Understanding of Three-Dimensional Space:
A Basic Architecture Course*. A thesis submitted to the Kent State University
Graduate College, December, 1991.
Watkin, David. *A History of Western Architecture*. Thames & Hudson, NY. 1986.

5.3.0   PRELUDE

Ball, Susan L. *Ozenfant and Purism*. Ann Arbor: UMI Research Press, 1981.
Ballinger, Raymond. Design *with Paper*. Van Nostrand Reinhold, NY 1982.
Besset, Maurice. *Who Was Le Corbusier?* The World Publishing Co., Cleveland, 1968.

Crary, Jonathan. *Terchniques of the Observer: On Vision and Modernity in the
Nineteenth Century* MIT Press. Cambridge MA 1994
Moholy-Nagy, Laszlo. *Vision in Motion*. Paul Theobald and Co. Chicago, 1969.
Muybridge, Eadweard. *The Male and Female Figure in Motion*. Dover, NY, 1984.

5.3.1   MELODY

Cheng, Fa-Hwa. *Statics and Strength of Materials*. Macmillan, NY, 1985.
Gresleri, G. et.al. *Le Corbusier: Il linguaggio delle pietre* Cataloghi Marsilio, Venice. 1988
Gewirtz, Herman *Essentials of Physics* Barron's Educational Series, Woodbury, NY. 1971.
Hudson, Ralph G., S.B. *The Engineers' Manual*. John Wiley & Sons, London, 1917.
Kernfeld, Barry. *What to Listen for in Jazz*. Yale University Press, New Haven, 1997
Riley, W. and Sturges, L. *Dynamics: Engineering Mechanics*. John Wiley & Sons. NY, 1993.
Thomas, George. *Calculus and Analytic Geometry*. 3rd Edition. Addison Wesley,
Palo Alto CA. 1960.
Starnet Structures, Inc. Catalog. West Babylon, NY. 1992.
Weaver, William and Johnson, Paul. *Structural Dynamics by Finite Elements*.
Prentice-Hall. Englewood Cliffs NJ. 1987.
Wilson, Forrest. *Architecture: Fundamental Issues*. Van Nostrand Reinhold. NY, 1990.

5.3.2   HARMONY

Delachet, Andre. *Contemporary Geometry*. Dover, NY. 1962.
Gabriel, Francois. *Beyond the Cube: The Architecture of Space Frames and
Polyhedra*. John Wiley & Sons, NY, 1997.
Gould, Stephen Jay. Wonderful *Life-- Burgess Shale and the Nature of History*.
WW Norton, NY, 1990.
Hyatt, Stephen L. (ed.). *The Greek Vase*. Latham, NY: Hudson-Mohawk Association
of Colleges and Universities, 1981.
Kappraff, Jay. *Connections: The Geometric Bridge Between Art and Science*.
McGraw-Hill, NY, 1991.
Lawrence, A.W. *Greek Architecture*. Penguin Books, NY. 1957, 1983.
Lotz, Wolfgang. *Studies in Renaissance Architecture*. MIT Press. Cambridge, 1977.
Richter, G. et al. *Shapes and Names of Athenian Vases*. Met. Museum of Art, NY, 1935.
Schenker, Heinrich. *Harmony*. MIT Press, Cambridge MA 1974. [1906]

5.3.3   CONCERTO

Allen, Woody. *Side Effects*. Random House, NY. 1980.
Borisenko, A. and Tarapov, I. *Vector and Tensor Analysis*. Dover NY 1979.
Ciufolini, Ignazio, and Wheeler, John Archbald. *Gravitation and Inertia*. Princeton
University Press. Princeton, NJ. 1995.
Hartt, Frederick. *History of Italian Renaissance Art*. Harry N. Abrams, NY. 1994.
Millon, Henry. *Baroque and Rococco Architecture*. Prentice-Hall, London. 1961
Murray, Peter. *Renaissance Architecture*. Harry N. Abrams, NY. 1971
Benevolo, Leonardo. *The Architecture of the Renaissance, Vol. II*. Westview
Press, Boulder, CO. 1968
Graves, William. ed. *Water: The Power, Promise, and Turmoil of North America's
Fresh Water*. National Geographic Special Edition. 1993.

5.3.4   SYMPHONY

Blaser, Werner. *Atrium: 5000 years of Open Courtyards*. Birkhauser, Basel, 1985.
Dagostino, Frank R. *Mechanical and Electrical Systems in Construction and
Architecture*. 2nd ed. Prentice-Hall, Englewood Cliffs, NJ. 1991.
Hale, Jonathan. *The Old Way of Seeing*. Houghton Mifflin, NY . 1994.
Katchor, Ben. *Julius Knipl, Real Estate Photographer*. Little Brown, Boston. 1996.
Olgyay, Victor. *Design With Climate*. Princeton University Press. Princeton NJ. 1963
Oakes, Baile. *Sculpting with the Environment-- a Natural Dialogue*. Van Nostrand
Reinhold. NY 1995.
Rapaport, Amos. *House Form and Culture*. Prentice Hall, Englewood Cliffs, 1969.
Rifkin, Jeremy. *Entropy into the Greenhouse World*. Bantam Books, NY. 1980.
Schama, Simon. *Landscape and Memory*. Knopf, NY, 1995.
Tobia, Michael. *Mountain People*. University of Oklahoma Press, Norman, OK. 1986.
Tulku, Tarthang. *Dynamics of Time and Space*. Dharma Publishing. Berkeley CA 1994.
Weinberg, Stephen et.al. *Life in the Universe*. Scientific American Special Issue. Oct. 1994.

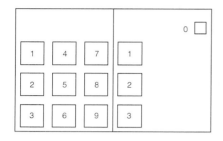

This book is primarily a visual meditation. Thus caption information often has been deliberately suppressed to permit the eye to read the image before reading the words about the image. Where appropriate, figure information is indicated vertically along edge of image on the page. Otherwise, the following identification information pertains.

Figures indicated by page and position. Thus, fig. 128-2, is figure number 2 on page 128. These charts show alternate positions. All student work is indicated near image. Fiigures are used by permission of copyright holder, unless otherwise noted. Unless indicated here, all other figures, including drawings and photographs, are by author.

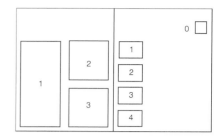

COVER

c Spiral galaxy M51   From *Galaxies* by Tim Ferris. © 1980. Reprinted by permission of Sierra Club Books.
c Modulor man   Le Corbusier © 1997 Artists Rights Society (ARS), New York/SPADEM, Paris
c spiral reverse   After Ferris, *op.cit.*
c animated galaxies   Galaxy NGC5195 passes M51 after Ferris, *ibidi*
i Beethoven's 5th   Author's drawing
iv daffodils   Photo by Charles Friedman, Author's father
v spring crystal   From *Physics for Students of Science and Engineering* by Halliday and Resnick. © 1960. Reprinted by permission of D. Halliday.
vi tensegrity model   Author's photo
vii dancing Shiva   From *Indian Sculpture* by M.M. Deneck. Photos by W. and B. Forman. Spring Books London by Artva, Czechoslovakia. 1962
xi drawing of bone   Le Corbusier, © 1997 ARS, New York/SPADEM, Paris.
xi ineffable space   From *New World of Space* by Le Corbusier. © 1948. Reprinted by permission of the Institute of Contemporary Art.
xiii Vertical Assembly Building   From *LIFE Magazine*, August 29, 1969. Time/Life Bldg. Rockefeller Center, NY 10020. Time/Life Inc.
xiii-0 hand+Algiers tower   Le Corbusier © 1997 ARS, New York/SPADEM, Paris.
xiii-1 brick and block   Author's drawings
xiii-2 medieval room   Pierre Desargues. *Perspectives*. © cliché Bibliotheque d'art et d'archeologie, Fondation Jacques Doucet, Paris
xiii-3 Vertical Assembly Building   Reprinted with permission of Simon & Schuster From *Experimental Architecture* by Peter Cook. © 1970 by Peter Cook.

SWING

1 swing icon   Author's drawing
2 children on swing   Author's drawing
3 tuning the universe   Author's drawings
4 windsurfers   Author's collage
5 forces   Kandinsky, Wassily. © 1970 by Editions Denoel. Reprinted by permission of Georges Borchardt, Inc.
6 Alaska Glacier   Photograph Courtesy of Art Wolfe.
7 *Fish*   Sculpture by Brancusi, Constantin. *Fish*. 1930. Gray marble, 21 x 71"; on three-part pedestal of one marble and two limestone cylinders, 29 1/8" high x approximately 65" diameter at widest point. Collection, The Museum of Modern Art, New York. Acquired through the Lillie P. Bliss Bequest.
8 Pisa, aerial view   Unidentified source
9-1 Pisa side view   Drawing, public domain
9-2,3 orbits   From *Mathematics and the Search for Knowledge* by Morris Kline. © 1985 by Oxford University Press. Used by permission of Oxford University Press, Inc.
10 blimp hangar   Goodyear Air-Dock postcard; Wilbur Evans Co.
11-1 Pantheon view   *The Interior of the Pantheon*, Samuel H. Kress Collection, © 1997 National Gallery of Art, Washington.
11-2 Pantheon   From Steirlin, Henri. *Encyclopedia of World Architecture. Van Nostrand Reinhold, 1983* © Georges Bertoud
12 castles+balloons   Photo © Michael St. Maour Sheil. Reprinted by permission of Susan Griggs Agency.
13-2 closepack circles   From *Mathematics and Optimal Form* by Hildebrandt and Tromba © 1985 by Scientific American Books, Inc. Reprinted with permis-

sion of W.H. Freeman and Company.
13-2 soap bubbles   From *Frei Otto: Tension Structures* by Conrad Roland. © 1970 by Frederick A. Praeger, Inc.
14 LEM/Moon/Earth   Photo Apollo 11 Mission. NASA
15 Voyager   Courtesy JPL The Jet Propulsion Laboratory
16 *Mr. Desmond Shute bends the shaft.*   Photo by Dr. Harold Edgerton, MIT, Cambridge, MA. Reprinted by permission of Palm Press, Inc.
16 Spiral Galaxy M51   After Ferris, Galaxies, op.cit.
17 Mickey Mouse   © Disney Enterprises, Inc.
18 wind combs   Sculpture by Eduardo Chillida, installation on the coast of San Sebastian, Spain, Courtesy of Galleria Maeght.
19-0 spoon on cup   Author's drawing
19-1 cosmic speedometer Author's drawing, after LC Epstein, *Relativity Visualized*.
19-2 strange attractor   From Scientific American, August '93, NY
19-3 bubble chamber   From *H. Robin, The Scientific Image* Harry Abrams, Inc.
20-21 Mickey Mouse   Animation sequence from "The Sorcerer's Apprentice" in *Fantasia*. © Disney Enterprises, Inc.
20-2 *Guernica*   Pablo Picasso. © 1997 Succession Picasso/Artists Rights Society (ARS), New York. Now in Museo Nacional del Prado, Calle de Felipe IV, Madrid Spain
20-3 "wooden" Mickey   © Disney Enterprises, Inc.
21 horse in motion   E. Muybridge. © Fotofolio. Reprinted by permission.
22-1 galaxy loops   Buckminster Fuller. *Synergetics.* © 1979 MacMillan NY
22-2 solar clock   Author's drawing
22-3 DNA model   Reprinted by permission of *Princeton Alumni Weekly*
22-4 space station   Michael Kalil. Reprinted by permission of Kalil Foundation.
23-1 sine and cycloid   Author's drawing
23-2 tuning fork wave   After Rogers, Eric. *Physics for the Inquiring Mind*. Princeton University Press. 1960
23-3 meter and rhythm   Author's drawing
24-1 color prism wave   Author's drawing
24-2,4 natural color system   NCS Natural Color System. With permission from the Scandinavian Colour Institute.
24-5 colorwave packet   Author's drawing, after *Scientific American*, 8/93
25-1 Goethe color scale   Author's drawing
25-2,3 color solids   After Ostwald and Munsell color diagrams
26-1 color wheel grid   Author's drawing
26-2 color scale   Author's drawing
26-3 *Still Life with Glass of Red Wine*. 1921. Oil. Ozenfant, Amedée. Oeffentliche Kunstsammlung Basel, Kunstmuseum. Donation Dr. H.C. Raoul La Roche 1963.
27-1 Slutzky cube   Paintings by and courtesy of Robert Slutzky. Photo NYIT
27-2 cube/chrome   From *CubeChrome*. Courtesy of Robert Slutzky.
27-1 Slutzky cube   Paintings by and courtesy of Robert Slutzky. Photo NYIT
28 Albers study   After Joseph Albers. *Study for Homage to the Square, 1976*
29-1 Unity Temple interior   Photo From *Frank Lloyd Wright, A Primer on Architectural Principles* by Robert McCarter. © 1991. Reprinted by permission of Princeton Architectural Press.
29-2 Heller house   Analytic drawings from McCarter, ibid.
30 Pazzi chapel   Filippo Brunelleschi, *Scala Insitituto* © Art Resource NY
31-2 medieval room   Pierre Desargues. *Perspectives. op. cit.*
32 *Rolling Stock series No. 9, for Reid.*   Painting 1989 © Bob Cottingham. Reprinted by permission.

PRELUDE

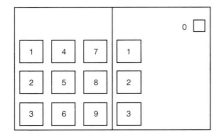

This book is primarily a visual meditation. Thus caption information often has been deliberately suppressed to permit the eye to read the image before reading the words about the image. Where appropriate, figure information is indicated vertically along edge of image on the page. Otherwise, the following identification information pertains.

Figures indicated by page and position. Thus, fig. 128-2, is figure number 2 on page 128. These charts show alternate positions. All student work is indicated near image. Fiigures are used by permission of copyright holder, unless otherwise noted. Unless indicated here, all other figures, including drawings and photographs, are by author.

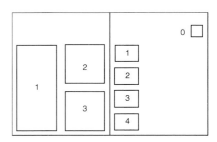

SECTION 1: MELODY

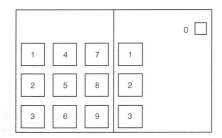

This book is primarily a visual meditation. Thus caption information often has been deliberately suppressed to permit the eye to read the image before reading the words about the image. Where appropriate, figure information is indicated vertically along edge of image on the page. Otherwise, the following identification information pertains.

Figures indicated by page and position. Thus, fig. 128-2, is figure number 2 on page 128. These charts show alternate positions. All student work is indicated near image. Fiigures are used by permission of copyright holder, unless otherwise noted. Unless indicated here, all other figures, including drawings and photographs, are by author.

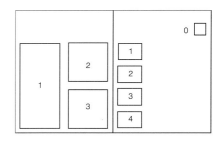

268 illustrations   Author's drawings
270-1 *Guitar Glasses and Bottle* Painting by Juan Gris. Public domain
270-2 *Violin and Newspaper* Painting by Juan Gris. Public domain
271 Carpenter plan   Author's drawings
273-1 guitar woman sculpture by Jaques Lifschitz, Hirshhorn Museum and Sculpture Garden, Smithsonian Institution, Gift of Joseph H. Hirshhorn, 1966. Photo by Lee Stalsworth.
273-2 *Guitar Glasses and Fruit Dish* Painting, 1919, by Juan Gris.

SECTION 3: CONCERTO   CHAPTER 3B: WEAVING

274 surf and headlands Photo courtesy of Cole Weston.
275-1 Wave (poem)   Gary Snyder: *Regarding Wave.* © 1970 by Gary Snyder. Reprinted by permission of New Directions Publishing Corporation.
275-2 curl wave photo Courtesy of Douglas Peebles.
276 Spiral stair at Sagrada Familia designed by Antonio Gaudi. Courtesy of Fisa-Escudo de Oro, S.A.
277-1 harmonic motion after Rogers, Eric. *op.cit*
277-2 Jupiter's moons Courtesy *Sky and Telescope* magazine.
278-1 green light   Illustration by Raymond Perlman From *Light and Color.* © 1971 Western Publishing Company, Inc. Used by permission.
278-2 light waves
278-3 light wave structure Illustration by Perlman, *op.cit*
278-4 ripples intersecting From Theodor Schwenk, *op.cit.*
279-1 solar fields   Author's drawing
279-2 monopole field Author's drawing
279-3 bipolar field   Author's drawing
280 Crescent, Bath   Aerial View of Landsdowne Crescent, Bath. Reprinted by permission of Aerofilms Ltd.
281-1 Baker dorm plan Reprinted by permission of Verlag fur Architektur.
281-1 Laocoön   Monumenti Musei E Gallerie Pontificie.
281-1 3D curve plates From *Developments in Structural Form* by Rowland J. Maidstone, reprinted by permission of the Author.
282-1 2 vanishing points Author's drawing
282-2 Candela shell   Reprinted by permission of Dr. Felix Candela.
282-3 candela plan/sect From *Santiago Calatrava* by W. Blaser (ed.). Reprinted by permission of Birkhauser, Basel, Switzerland.
282-4 St. Ivo interior The Conway Library, Courtauld Institute of Art
283-0 S.Carlo cloister plan Author's drawing
283-1 S.Carlo quattro fontana Fratelli Alinari I.D.E.A. S.p.A.
283-1 S.Carlo dome   Fratelli Alinari I.D.E.A. S.p.A.
283-3 S.Carlo plan   Author's drawing
284 roller coaster   Comstock Inc./Georg Gerster
285-0 shell drawing   Le Corbusier © 1997 ARS, New York/SPADEM.Paris
285-1 neck arteries   From Gray's *Anatomy*
285-2 enzyme map   From Hall, Stephen. *Mapping the Next Millennium*, Random House, NY 1992.
285-3 venous man   Courtesy of Francis Countway Library of Medicine.
286 Pallazzo Pellegrini plans From Letarouilly, *op. cit.*
287-1 St Stevens plan Seven Churches of St Stevens, Bologna, Italy. Unidentified source.
287-3 Pew House plan Frank Lloyd Wright drawings are © 1988 The Frank Lloyd Wright Foundation, Scottsdale AZ.
288 Perret concrete frame Maidstone, *op.cit.*
288 continuous beam From *Simplified Engineering for Architects and Builders*, 4th ed. by Harry S. Parker. Reprinted by permission of John Wiley & Sons, Inc.
289 reinforced concrete Author's drawing
289 concrete beams From Parker, *op.cit.*
290 Berlin Free University © 1997 ARS, New York/SPADEM, Paris
290 Wright tartan   From McCarter. *op.cit*
291 tartan stuidies   Author's drawings
293-1 Governor's Palace Author's drawing, after Le Corbusier
293-2 Savoye section Author's drawing
293-3 pas perdus   Author's drawing, after Le Corbusier
294 Strasbourg City Hall Le Corbusier © 1998 ARS, New York/SPADEM. Paris.
295-1 tartan overlays Author's drawing
295-2 Maison Domino Le Corbusier © 1997 ARS, New York/SPADEM, Paris.

295-3 Millowners plan Le Corbusier © 1997 ARS, New York/SPADEM, Paris.
297 doing diagrams Author's drawings
299 in concert   Author's drawings
300 4 homes/gardens Mike Falco. Reprinted with permission.
301 photos   Mike Falco. Reprinted with permission.
304 Eagle and Serpent Text From *Allegory and the Migration of Symbols* by Rudolf Wittkower. Reprinted by permission of Thames and Hudson International Ltd.
306 Magister Ludi   Text From *The Glass Bead Game (Magister Ludi)* by Hermann Hesse. © 1943 by Fretz & Wesmuth Verlag AG Zurich. Foreword by Theodore Ziokowski. © 1969 by Henry Holt and Company, Inc. Reprinted by permission.
306 Prelude and Fugue #11 in F J.S. Bach, From the *Well-Tempered Clavier* bwv 880, 1740.
308 "Reading the Wave" From *Mr. Palomar* by Italo Calvino, © 1983 by Giulio Einaudi editore s.p.a., Torino, English translation by William Weaver © 1985 by Harcourt Brace & Company, reprinted by permission of Harcourt Brace & Co.
308 *Great Wave Off Kanagawa* by Hokusai. Metropolitan Museum of Art. Arthur H. hearn Fund, 1950. Negative #MM7610. Reprinted by permission.
311 ocean wave   From *Luce Mare* by Giorgio Lotti, text by Vittorio G. Rossi, Rizzoli International Publishers, Inc., 1982.
313 Jupiter red spot NASA

SECTION 4: SYMPHONY   CHAPTER 4A: RESONATING

315 symphony icon   Author's drawing
316 xray crystal   Photo by Dr. Erwin Muller.
317-0 cubocta solid   Author's drawing
317-1 crystal pairs   Philip Ball. *Designing the Molecular World.* © 1994 by Princeton University Press. Reprinted by permission of Princeton University Press.
317-2 rebar grids   From *Developments in Structural Form* by Rowland J. Mainstone, reprinted by permission of the author.
317-3 Granada   The sacristy of the charterhouse, Granada. *The Architecture of the Renaissance,* by Leonardo Benevolo, Volume II, 1978 Routlegde & Kegan Paul, Ltd. and Westview Press, Boulder CO.
318 Angkor Tom plan After Stierlin *op. cit.* © Georges Bertoud
319-0 carving space   Author's drawing
319-1 Catherwood Maya U. of Illinois collection, reprint of 1844 London Edition
319-2 Angkor Wat plan Stierlin *op. cit.* © Georges Bertoud
319-3 Angkor view   Photo, Susan Jellicoe. From *The Landscape of Man* by Geoffrey and Susan Jellicoe, published by Thames and Hudson, London, 1975.
320 Hurva Synagogue Courtesy of George Pohl.
321-0 resonator sketch Author's drawing
321-1 Hurva simulation Reprinted by permission of Kent Larson.
321-2 Hurva plan,section Author's drawing, after Urs Buttiker
321-3 Hurva simulation Reprinted by permission of Kent Larson.
322 walk on watertube Designed Graham Stevens, image From *Pneumatic Structures* by Thomas Herzog, Verlag Gerd Hatje Stuttgart, 1976
323-0 walk on water tunnel Designed Graham Stevens, *Pneumatic Structures* op, cit.
323-1 freestone pillow Author's photo
323-2 frei otto inflato models From Thomas Herzog, *Pneumatic Structures* op, cit.
323-3 inflato community roof Author's photo
323-4 walk on water tetra Designed Graham Stevens, *Pneumatic Structures* op, cit.
324 South Pole dome Aerial photo, USA Public domain
325-1 dome home   Designed by R. Buckminster Fuller. From Marks, *op. cit.*
325-2 plan shapes   Author's drawing
325-3 cell and organelles From Novikoff and Holtzman, *Cells and Organelles* Holt Rinehart and Winston, NY 1970.
326 lunar man in space photo NASA, in the public domain
327-0 little waves   Author's drawing
327-1 Modulor man   Le Corbusier © 1997 ARS, New York/SPADEM.Paris
327-2 resonance   Author's drawing
327-3 Assembly Building Le Corbusier © 1997 ARS, New York/SPADEM.Paris
328-1 Medici Chapel dome From Norberg-Schulz, *op. cit.*
328-2 Medici chapel frontal From Charles de Tolnay, *op. cit.*
328-3 Medici drawings From Peter Murray, *Renaissance Architecture*, Abrams NY.
329-1 leonardo church sketch From *The Notebooks of Leonardo da Vinci.* Dover, NY
329-2,3 leonardo womb + birth From *The Notebooks of Leonardo da Vinci. op. cit.*
330 fan vaults   Photo of King's College Chapel.Reprinted by permission of Wim Swaan

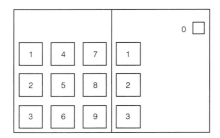

This book is primarily a visual meditation. Thus caption information often has been deliberately suppressed to permit the eye to read the image before reading the words about the image. Where appropriate, figure information is indicated vertically along edge of image on the page. Otherwise, the following identification information pertains.

Figures indicated by page and position. Thus, fig. 128-2, is figure number 2 on page 128. These charts show alternate positions. All student work is indicated near image. Fiigures are used by permission of copyright holder, unless otherwise noted. Unless indicated here, all other figures, including drawings and photographs, are by author.

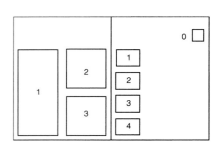

331-0 resonant load Salvadori/Heller, *op. cit.*
331-1 chladni patterns © by the Estate of Irving Geis. Reprinted by permission.
331-2 Friedman House Frank Lloyd Wright drawings are © 1988 The Frank Lloyd Wright Foundation, Scottsdale, AZ.
331-3 Portoghesi plan Presses Polytechniques et Universitaires Romandes, Switzerland.
331-4 harmonic mandala Doczi, *op. cit.*
332-1 Otaniemi inside From *Alvar Aalto Synopsis* by Alvar Aalto. Reprinted by permission of Birkhauser, Basel, Switzerland.
332-2 Otaniemi plan (2) Reprinted by permission of the Alvar Aalto Foundation.
332-3 Aalto sketch From *Alvar Aalto Synopsis op. cit.*
332-4 Aalto section From *Alvar Aalto Synopsis,* ibid.
332-5 Otaniemi section Reprinted by permission of the Alvar Aalto Foundation.
333-0 otaniem sketches Reprinted by permission of the Alvar Aalto Foundation.
333 piano From Steinway and Sons, NY.
333 resonant modes after Pierce, John R. The Science of Musical Sound. Scientific American Library NY. 1983
334-1 Oil platform Photo courtesy of the Royal Dutch Shell Group.
334-2 coop himmelblau From *Coop Himmelbrau.* © 1983 by Verlag Gerd Hatje.
334-3 envirobubble Design by Francois Dallegeret, Reprinted with permission of Simon & Schuster From *Experimental Architecture* © 1970 by Peter Cook.
334-4 MMU walker NASA
334-5 LEM on moon NASA
334-6 trumpet Photo From King Musical Instruments Inc. Eastlake OH
334-7 ADVmobile home Reprinted with permission of *Progressive Architecture*, Penton Publishing
335-0 clarinet Photo From King Musical Instruments Inc. Eastlake OH
335-1 Fully-Applianced House Designed by David Greene, Peter Cook, *op. cit.*
335-2 projects for houses By Jan Kaplicky. From Colin Davies, *op. cit.*
336-1 Carrier City Reprinted with kind permission of Hans Hollein. Collection Museum of Modern Art, New York
337 bricollage From Levi-Straus, Claude. *The Savage Mind.* University of Chicago Press. 1966.
338 Hill House Reprinted by permission of Steve Badanes
338 SnailHouse Reprinted by permission of Steve Badanes
339 *Ancient of days* William Blake
339 SnailHouse Reprinted by permission of Steve Badanes
340-1 expandable dome Courtesy of Chuck Hoberman.
340-2 Beam Builder Courtesy Grumman Corporation.
340-3 expandable dome Courtesy of Chuck Hoberman.
340-4 arch truck Peter Cook, *op. cit.*
341-1 greenhouse Designed and constructed by Author
341-2 structural sections Author's drawing
341-3 shelter arch From Design Magazine, #329. Reprinted by permission of the Design Council.
342-1 Hong Kong Bank Foster Associates
342-2 factory Foster Associates
342-3 Hong Kong Bank Window assembly. Reprinted with permission of Progressive Architecture, Penton Publishing.
342-4 factory assembly Foster Associates
343 table design Richard Rogers Partnership

344-1 zurich pavilion From *Stahl und Form, Ausstelungsgebaude von Le Corbusier.* © 1970. Reprinted by permission of Verlag Stahleisen, m.b.b.
344-2 carnot cycle Author's drawing
344-3 Dutch house assembled House near Amsterdam, by Benthem, Crouwel Architects. From Colin Davies, *op. cit.*
344-4 HFG structure Author's design, *Home for Generations*
344-5 Dutch house exploded From Colin Davies, *op. cit.*
345-1 greenhouse axonometric Author's drawing
345-2 tensegrity dodecahedron Author's drawing
345-3 little house axo Courtesy of Allan Wexler.
346 mobile environemnt by Marco Zanuso and Richard Sapper. From Ambasz, Emilio. *Italy: The New Domestic Landscape*, Museum of Modern Art, NY 1972
347 Hypercube Author's drawing
347 Trenton bathhouse Author's drawing after plan by Louis Kahn
348 Lovell house interior Reprinted by permission of David Gebhard.
349-1 Lovell house photo Reprinted by permission of David Gebhard.
349-2 planes intersect Author's drawing
349-3 schindler frame Author's drawing
350 shoji screens Two view of the interior of Kyusukien in Upper Tea House, Shugakuin Detached Pllace. From *The Japanese Garden: An Approavch to Nature* by Teiji Ito. Photos by Takeji Iwamaya. Yasle University Pres. Mew Haven CT. 1972.
351 tesseract shadow Author's drawing
352-1 umbrella table From *Sharper Image Catalog*, date unknown
352-2 suitcase Courtesy of Hartmann Luggage Company.
352-3 box in a valise Created by Marcel Duchamp. From *Marcel Duchamp, The Box in a Valise.* by Ecke Bonk. Rizzoli NY 1989.
352-4 Suitaloon Designed by Mike Webb. Peter Cook, *op. cit.*
353 doing drawings Author's drawings
355-1 world's largest suitcase Author's photo
355-2 stone into rock Author's drawing
357-0 tokonoma variations Author's drawings
357 renoant space Author's drawings
358 Lenin Institute By Ivan Leonidov. From *Town and Revolution* by Anatole Kopp, 1970, George Braziller, Inc.
359-1 sailboat Author's drawing
359-2 golf tee and bubble anchor Author's drawing
359-3 hose level Author's drawing
360 blimp over rainforest Photo by Raphael Gaillarde. Reprinted by permission of Liaison Agency, Inc.
361-1 "bottle rack" unité Le Corbusier © 1997 ARS, New York/SPADEM.Paris
361-2 bucky blimp Design by Buckminster Fuller. From Robert Marks,*op. cit.*
361-3 floating cities Design by Buckminster Fuller. From Robert Marks, *ibid.*
363 ThoreauTaf Author's drawing
364-1 Sistine ceiling Victor R. Boswell, Jr., © National Geographic Society.
364-2 Pollock wall *Number 3*. Painting by Jackson Pollock © 1998 Pollock-Krasner Foundation/ARS, New York.
365-1 Villa Caprarola Cutaway view, engraving. In the public domain
365-2 Arcology section From Paolo Soleri, *Arcology: City in the Image of Man,* MIT Press. Cambridge, MA. 1968
365-3 vortex ring rising upward through water From Theodor Schwenk, *op. cit.*
366ff *Walden* Text from *Walden*, by Henry David Thoreau. Public domain

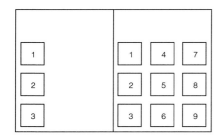

The graphic layout of this book is reversed in the **Appendix** and **Visual Glossary**. Thus the diagrams on this page indicate a reversal of layout, with text primarily on the *verso* page and images, including phtos, xerages, collages, and drawings, on the *recto* page. All images in e **Appendix** and **Visual Glossary**.are by author except as indicated below.

Figures indicated by page and position. Thus, fig. 443-2, is figure number 2 on page 443. These charts show alternate positions. All student work is indicated near image. Figures are used by permission of copyright holder, unless otherwise noted. Unless indicated here, all other figures, including drawings and photographs, are by author.

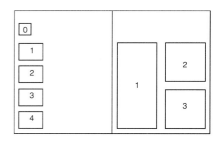

420-3 **Knossos plan**   From *Greek Architecture* by A.W. Lawrence. © by Yale University Press Pelican History of Art. Reprinted by permission.
420-4 **Venice Hospital**   Plan From *Le Corbusier Complete Works, Vol. 7, 1957-1965*, Verlag fur Architektur. © 1995 ARS, New York/SPADEM, Paris.
421-0 **Hadrian's Villa**   Plan From Lawrence. *op. cit.*
421-1 **doorway**   Edward Allen. *Stone Shelters. op. cit.*
421-2 **stairway**   Edward Allen. *Stone Shelters. ibid.*
422-1 **Certosa side view**   Photo by David Diamond.
422-2 **Certosa section**   After University of Kentucky poster
422-3 **Certosa air view**   Photo by David Diamond.
423-1 **Siena piazza**   Postcard, unidentified source
423-2 **heart interior**   From *Behold Man* by Lennard Nilson. © 1973. Reprinted by permission of Albert & Bonniers Forlag AB, Stockholm, Sweden.
423-3 **Certosa axo**   After Brian Johnston, University of Kentucky
424 **Taj Mahal**   Photo, Susan Jellicoe. *The Landscape of Man. op. cit.*
425-1 **taj mahal site plan**   Stierlin op. cit. © Georges Bertoud
425-2 **taj mahal plan**   Stierlin ibid. © Georges Bertoud
425-3 **radiance**   From *The Church Incarnate* by Rudolph Schwarz. © 1958 by Regnery Publishing, Inc. All rights reserved. Reprinted by special permission of Regnery Publishing, Inc., Washington, D.C.
426 **The Game of Life**   From William Poundstone, *The Recursive Universe.* © 1985 by William Poundstone. By permission of William Morrow & Company, Inc.
426 **glidergun**   Drawings From Poundstone, *ibid.*
427 **glider flotilla**   Drawings From Poundstone, ibid.
428 **collage cities**   Figure-grounds, p. 428-433. From Colin Rowe. *Collage City.* Reprinted by permission of MIT Press.
432 **"The Lives of a Cell"**   © 1971 by the Massachusetts Medical Society. From *The Lives of a Cell* by Lewis Thomas. Used by permission of Viking Penguin, a division of Penguin Books USA Inc.
434 **John Coltrane**   Reprinted by permission of Mosaic Records.
435 **Earth**   photo NASA, in the public domain

CHAPTER 5: APPENDIX

443-1 **XYZ joints**   Author's xerage
443-2,3,4 **joint drawings**   © Russell Jordan. Reprinted by permission.
443 **Belvedere stair**   From Letarouilly, *op. cit.*
447 **googolplex toy**   Reprinted by permission of Arlington-News, Inc.
451 **general to particular**   © Christopher Chimera. Reprinted by permission.
452 **complex surface**   3-D Visions Craftool
454-1 **mandelbrot set**   Mandelbrot, Benoit. *The Fractal Geometry of Nature* © 1983 by Benoit B. Mandelbrot. Reprinted with permission of W.H. Freeman and Company.
454-2 **Julia set details**   From H.O. Peitgen and P.H. Richter, *op.cit.*
455 **exploring Julia Set**   From H.O. Peitgen and P.H. Richter, *ibid.*
457-0 **KOP on CAD**   solid void B.. Amanzio, OP.CIT...
457-4 **KOP on CAD**   Victor Alvarez and Rick Kimball, students at University of California San Luis Obispo. courtesy Prof. Joseph Amanzio, University of California San Luis Obispo
457-3 **wireframe design**   Doug Doran, student at Univ. of Washington, Seattle
457-5 **Utrecht CAD study**   © Luis Diaz. Reprinted by permission.
459-1,2 **drawings**   Le Corbusier © 1997 ARS, New York/SPADEM.Paris

459-3,4 **collages**   By Richard Meier. Reprinted by permission of Richard Meier and Partners.
461 **Abers CD ROM**   © by Yale University Press Reprinted by permission.
466-2 **binary pulsar music**   From an illustration of gravitational waves on the Nobel Prize in Physics 1993. Produced by the Royal SwedishAcademy of Sciences.
466-3 **Arecibo Radio Observatory** David Parker, 1997/Science Photo Library.
467-2 **harmonic overtones**   From *The Power of Limits* by Gyorgy Doczi, © 1981. Reprinted by arrangement with Shambhala Publications, Inc., 300 Massachusetts Avenue, Boston, MA. 02115.
467-3 **Kepler solids**   Public domain
467-4 **Platonic polyhedra**   Public domain
465 **color piano**   Gyorgy Doczi, *op. cit.*
465 **e to the i pi**   Author's expression of Euler's equation.
465 **jazz grid Chandigarh** Le Corbusier © 1997 ARS, New York/SPADEM. Paris

CHAPTER 5B: VISUAL GLOSSARY

475 **Charlie with BOT**   Author's photo
476 **student project**   Photo © David Diamond
477-2 **spring cube**   Halliday and Resnick.*op. cit.*
477-4 **Nepal mountain**   From *Mountain People*, edited by Michael Tobias. © 1986 by the University of Oklahoma Press.
478,1 **perforatedTrombe wall**Author's drawing of Kelbaugh House, NJ.
478,3 **detail of Noisy 2**   © Henri Ciriani. Reprinted by permission.
479-1 **Weekend House**   Le Corbusier © 1997 ARS, New York/SPADEM.Paris
479-2 **exhibition BOT**   © Michael Manfredi. Reprinted by permission.
480 **Chandigarh plan**   Le Corbusier © 1997 ARS, New York/SPADEM.Paris
481 **manhattan air view**   Reprinted by permission of Aerographics.
486-1 **cubist diagrams**   © David Diamond
486-2 **student project**   Unidentified source
486-3 **cubist diagrams**   © David Diamond
488-1 **early structural science**   From Mainstone, *op. cit.*
488-2 **free body diagrams**   From Cheng. *op.cit.*
501-8 **curve plates**   Maidstone, *op.cit.*
501-9 **tensor fields...**   From *Gravitation* by Misner, Thorne, Wheeler *op.cit*
504-3 **before and after**   Courtesy Jonathan Reo. Reprinted with permission.
507-5 **Plastruct domes**   Illustration courtesy of Plastruct, Inc.
508-1 **skin and bones**   Illustration courtesy of Plastruct, Inc.
508-2 **lungs**   Le Corbusier © 1997 ARS, New York/SPADEM.Paris
509-3 **house and climate**   Drawn after Acland, *op. cit.*
510-3 **ripples**   From Theodor Schwenk, *op. cit.*
512-2-4 **plan types**   Frank Lloyd Wright drawings are © 1988 The Frank Lloyd Wright Foundation, Scottsdale, AZ.
513-3 **Piazzo San Marco**   From *An Atlas of Venice*, edited by Edoardo Salzano. © 1989 by Marsilio Editori. Reprinted by permission.
550 **the waves!**   Photo by Joe Snyder. Reprinted with permission.

BACK COVER
inside **space station**   NASA
outside **Eagle Nebula**   Gaseous pillars in M16 Eagle Nebula. J. Hester and P. Scowen. (Arizona State University). Hubble Space Telescope, NASA

A Note on Production

This book was begun before any GUI-WYSIWYG was available. The first volume was composed on a computer using Word software—the way that the text was written so as to match page for page the images on only the same double page spread required getting from the publisher a sample of text set in the Helvetica Light typeface at the required font size and leading (vertical spacing). Then the author composed on Word to match the page through tedious counting (each 47 line page of the book was a Word setup wider than the screen, scrolled through three times to get 3 x 19 lines to get 57 lines which had to be backed up two lines to avoid overlaps to get the correct 47 line count.) We have come a long way since then in the last 12 years. Computers, especially in the realm of graphics and interfacing, has been once again revolutionized, and this time it has revolutionized whole industries. This entire volume is set in PageMaker, a combined text and graphics format that permits the writer to flow text around images, alter type styles and sizes, and import graphics from other modes. We use PhotoStyler for modifying scanned images, CorelDraw to create original line art, and AutoCad to create 3D architectural drawings. Of course, the CAD drawings have to be translated into a DXB out format, then imported as DXB in, and again exported as DXF out before PageMaker can use them. The thousand plus images in this book were not originally scanned, because they would have taken up too much room for most of the time this book was written and composed. Now SyQuest, Zip Drive and other Gigabit portable memories make that possibility less daunting. Converting the layout into production-ready digital form with all artwork, captions, and text properly located and formatted has taken over 3 years– *after the manuscript was already completed!* This unfortunate development came about because of the overlap of the era of slow PC's with huge data demands for images. It would have been nice to be able to label each image with the requisite permission information, proper caption and caption location. Only when scripts were introduced to PageMaker was this possible.

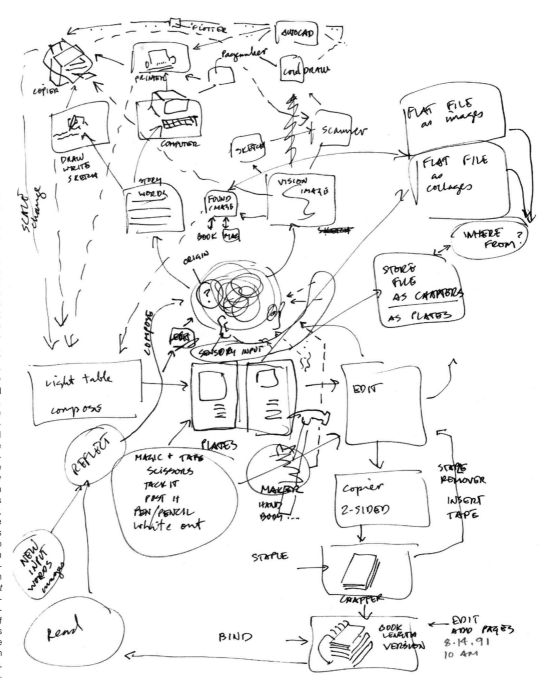

STUDENT ILLUSTRATIONS

Bob Albert, 127
Brad Anderson, 128
Chris Ballantine, 144
Scott Benson, 178, 298
Frank Bih, 306, 307
Shannon Bollinger, 264
Jeff Bottomley, 149
Joey Brusca, 356
Ed Butz, 264
John Cannataro, 302
M. Casdia, 131
Alan Chan, 43
Kunchul Chang, 406
Henry Chin-Hong, 356
Luigi Ciaccia, 131
John Conte, 85
John Cuhna, 296, 298, 337
Mike Cutita, 374
Maria Di Natale, 77
Jeff Dryer, 258
Alyssa Feldman, 128
George Figueroa, 144, 160
Sally Fried, 145
Kevin Fung, 476
Geoff Funston, 217, 362
Jerry Gallo, 354
Michael Giammarco, 296
Michael Gordon, 362
Ray Guitierrez, 89
Christina Halvorsen, 449
Jonathan Herdes, 434
Oscar Higuera, 144

Chris Hunt, 178
Benjamin Hurwitz, 131
Greg Isola, 267, 363
Ken Jerome, 79
John M. John, 75
Douk Hyum Kim, 264
Tracy Kosar, 362
Steve Kroner, 260
Sylvia Kumar, 258
Paul Kurklen, 362
Rick Lepic, 362
Art Lerian, 336
Michael Loo, 264, 312
Jackie Lopez, 178
Mark Lorentzen, 264
Jerry Maggio, 216
Bill Means, 351
Brian Medzinski, 261
Carlos Mitrione, 178
Kevin Molnar, 256
Vincent Muia, 336
Dafnia Myrick, 292
J. Nagle, 337
Kim Novick, 264
Todd O'Connell, 266
Lars Opedal, 258, 260
Joe Paone, 216
Nelson Parra, 292
John Pavlou, 69
Dayni Pelini, 302
Paul Pellicana, 266

Roberto Petrucelli, 70, 182, 211
Suzie Pezzello, 292, 336
Jorge Porta, 302
Richard Preston, 88
David Reinah, 351
Bil Reyman, 48, 182, 190
John Richards, 259
Dennis Rigosu, 228, 256, 257
Mike Rizzo, 130
Kim Robinson, 178, 179
Jeff Saldutti, 354
Phil Santantonio, 78
Ellen Santos, 356
Alan Sauberman, 78, 265
James Scala, 89
Scott Sepela, 406
Sagit Shayovich-Haklay, 264
Aleksandr Shkreli, 296
Madendratat Sitaram, 264
John Sodano, 216
Michael Sorano, 266, 267
Mark Sultana, 260
Emilio Susa, 84
Hiroyuki Tori, 254, 261, 406
Allen Tsang, 302
Neil Verwys, 256, 302
Charles Willis, 261, 272
John Wilson, Jr., 117
Marvene Worrell, 68, 100, 356
Todd Wright, 374
Yu Chi Yang, 88, 356

**Design Fundamentals 2 Faculty
(1983-1998)**

Don Alberto	Fred Gorree	Erin O'Keefe
Paul Amatuzzo	Michael Gorski	Theresa O'Leary
Angela Amoia	Virginia Greene	Terrance O'Neal
Amy Anderson	Carl Hauser	Sheri Olson
Steven Asaro	Laura Heim	Karen Payson
Todd Aufiero	Martin Hero	Ron Peterson
Maria Bentel	Linna Hunt	Vincent Polsinelli
Michael Berthold	Rudolfo Imas	Alex Pomarico
Michele Bertomen	Natalie Jabbour	Steven Potters
Phyllis Birkby	Scott Johnson	Frank Presta
Robert Braun	Russ Jordan	Pascal Quintard-Hofstein
David Busch	Beyhan Karahan	Irma Roby
Steven Buzbee	Carl Karas	John Reed
Marius Calin	Alyce Knight	Jonathan Reo
Frances Campani	Craig Konyk	Alan Sayles
Christopher Chimera	Kathy Krizek	Joe Scarpulla
Stephen Chung	Michael Kuenstle	Lindsay Shapiro
Marino Cimato	Stephen Leet	Judith Sheine
Victor Dadras	James Lesko	Joy Siegal
Felicia Davis	Steven Lesser	David Sirola
David Diamond	Mark Lorentzen	Edvin Stromsten
Luis Diaz	Wilbur Lupo	Gerard Sullivan
Liviu Dimitriu	Peter Lynch	Sumaida
Marie DiNatale	Michael Manfredi	Michael Szerbaty
Evan Douglis	Vera Marjanovic	Ian Taberner
George Downs	McAdams	Keat Tan
Kevin Fischer	David Mcalpin	Anne Tichich
Joseph Franchina	Merrell	Curtis Vasquez
Jonathan Friedman	Victoria Meyers	Maria Vera
William Gati	Vladimir Morosov	Robert Vuyosevich
Dennis George	Mark Motl	Warren Winter
Jason Gold	Dianne Neff	Ronald Zakrzewski

Honor Student Teaching Assistants
(1983-1998)

Vincent Affenita	George Chen	Betty Fouche
Ron Albinson	Henry Chin Hong	Joseph Franchina
Diana Allegretti	Nicole Chung	Carla Fritz
Wayne Alvar	Luigi Ciaccia	Geoffrey Funston
Angela Amoia	Patricia Cinque	Marie Furgiuele
Chris Anderson	John Clements, Jr.	Steven Gambino
Christopher Andron	Robert Cody	Michael Gargano
Kanayo Anekwe	Harold Conyers	Alexander Genna
John Angelos	Tommy Coronato	Vincent Gentile
Rhonda Angerio	Jason Coughlin	Dennis George
Vatche Aslanian	Suzanne Couture	Roman Georges
Dennis Austin	George Cumella	Peter Gerace
Joseph Bahan	John Cunniffe	Robert Gerardi
Thomas Baio	Daniel Cusick	Michael Giammarco
Brett Balzer	Michael Cuttita	Cesare Giaquinto
Iris Bar-Yehuda	Norman Davis	Stephen Giunta
Richard Bartlett	Peter Dawson	John Glavic
Sarah Bassin	Dominick Deangelis	Trevor Gordon
Ashraf Bekhet	Richard Decastro	Jonathan Grefaldon
Conrad Belluomo	Vincent Dellaquila	Hector Griffin
Barukh Ben-Haim	Ernest Demaio	Raul Gutierrez-Salgado
Paul Benoit	Daniel Dembling	Peter Hagemann
Thomas Berkoski	John Dias	Thomas Haggerty
Cesar Bettencourt	Luis Diaz	Cecilia Hagle
Paul Bisceglia	John Diehl	Doron Hakimian
Christine Bodouva	Erich Diller	Richard Hall
Gregory Bonsignore	Maria DiNatale	Wiliam Haskas
Frank Bonura	Johnny Donadic	Laura Haupt
Carey Boothroyd	Robert Drake	John Heidig
Jeffrey Bottomley	Ralf Dremel	Alex Helwig
Bruce Bowman	Michael Duignan	Keith Henshaw
Christopher Bradshaw	William Earls	Gregory Hermanowycz
Jose Branco	Michael Egan	Lourdes Hernandez
Robert Braun	Lucy Eichenwald	Danlys Hernandez
Nancy Bretzfield	Alexander Eng	Michael Himelstein
Paulette Buckheit	Eric Epstein	Andrew Holtzer
Gary Burke	Ronald Ervolino	James Hopeck
James Caleca	Zandra Fernandez	Barbara Hunt
Jack Caliendo	Jeanine Fetto	Eli-David Husravi
Mark Camera	Victor Filletti	Jason Hwang
Henry Cantwell	Robert Fitzgerald	John Iannacito
Annemarie Carragher	Thomas Fitzgerald	Michael Ingui
Edward Casper	William Fodor	Thomas Iovane
Mark Cassini	Regina Forteza	Hugh Isleib
Mark Chasmar	Eric Foss	Darryl Ivan

Michael Iwanyczko
Kenneth Jerome
Mark Kaminis
Joseph Karman
Nick Kazalas
Dawn Kelsey
Khalida Khan
Jennifer King
Charles King
Paul Klodowski
George Kloutis
Kenneth Koons
Paul Kurklen
Kurt Langjahr
Daniel Lasiewski
Rick Lavalley
Steven Lawler
Margaret Leporati
Adreas Letkovsky
Andrea Lightman
Ken Lin
Kenneth Lineman
Gino Longo
Michael Loo
Ryo Maekawa
Bryan Manning
Michael Mark
Robert Markovitz
Christopher Martin
Richard Massa
John Mastropietro
James McGorty
Christopher McGrath
John McGuire
Michael McNerney
Patrick Minze
Colin Montoute
Alessandro Moraca
Jose Mosquea
Joseph Mottola
William Mullan
Ross Muller
Marc Muller
Gen Mulone
Tiko Mulyawarko

Richard Napoli
Christopher Nardone
Orianna Nicoletti
John Nolis
Albert Notarnicola
Thomas O'Connor
Pearse O'Moore
Seak-Boo Ooi
Guy Page
Elizabeth Panzenhagen
Michael Paoli
Stephen Paolino
John Paone
Robert Papocchia
Steven Paquin
Kevin Paul
Michael Pena
Gustavo Penengo
William Pennock
Michael Peterman
David Phillips
Edward Pierson
Wayne Plourde
Kim Pomeranz
Hubert Poole
Jason Popkin
Joseph Porcelli
Audrey Porreca
Jorge Porta
Mark Powell
John Power
Carey Press
Mary Pyrovolakis
Frank Quatela
Peter Quinn
Maria Quintans
Christopher Raffaelli
Pamela Redmond
Erinn Reilly
Jonathan Reo
David Resnick
Joseph Rettig
Timothy Rice
Bryan Richter
William Ricket

Joyce Riggen
Diane Rinaldi
Michael Rizzo
Joseph Robinson
Michael Romani
Phil Rossillo
Paul Russo
Carla Saad
Juan Santos
Milan Savanovic
Thomas Scerbo
Gary Schiede
Bradford Schneider
George Schramm
Essam Sembawa
Joseph Sencen
Christopher Sepp
Ana Serra
Roma Shah
Janeen Shanahan
Russell Sherman
Kathleen Sherman
Judith Shirky
Robert Shoaff
Irwin Silverman
Betti Simpson
Michael Sleiman
Boris Slusarev
Christine Smirni
Jeffrey Smith
Clay Smook
John Soliman
Peter Somma
Michael Sorano
Suzanne Sowinski
Stephanie Stallone
Philip Stehling
Nancy Stoffel
Stacy Stoffel
Georgia Stokes
Gregory Straub
Keith Striga
Richard Sullivan
Imre Szabo
Mikolaj Szoska

Mikulaj Szoska
Christopher Taormina
Sergio Tedesco
John Tegeder
Lori Tepfenhardt
Ernesto Teran
Albert Thompson
Mark Thompson
Glen Tilkin
Alan Topel
Patricia Trifaro
Bart Trudeau
Robert Turner
Anastasios Tzakas
Joseph Uggino
Serda Urgancioglu
James Vandezander
Peter Van Geldern
Luis Vera
Maria Vera
Adam Volosik
Kevin Wallace
Mark Warren
Scott Waschitz
James Westcott
Jesse Whiteson
Katharine Whitley
Lois Wilhelmsen
Maria Wilthew
Mark Wittenberg
Margaret Woltzer
John Wong
Shai YSharabi
Michael Yacoub
Kok Yap
Yumi Yoshino
Jesse Zagarell
Linda Zahran
Samuel Zangi
Steven Zaweski
Vincent Zicchinolfi

INDEX

Symbols

A **COLOR POSTER** is provided with this text. These pages indicate the location of color images in the enclosed folded color poster. Printing economies normally require all color plates to be grouped together. Reviving the methods of early art books that included hand-tipped color plates, this poster allows for color images to be placed anywhere is this book. Reduced images (R) may be enlarged by rescanning and color printing, or via color xerography.

PAGE 3 · PAGE 26 · PAGE 24 · PAGE 26 · PAGE 90 · PAGE 24 · PAGE 24 · PAGE 24 · PAGE 26 · PAGE 72 · PAGE 66 · PAGE 68 · PAGE 93 · PAGE 99 · PAGE 374 · PAGE iv · PAGE 339 · PAGE 308 · PAGE 96 · R PAGE 64 · PAGE 364 · PAGE 155 · PAGE 232 · PAGE 447 · PAGE 381 · R PAGE 550 · PAGE 364

THE MODULOR SCALE IS SET AT 1/2" = 1' - 0" OR 1 : 24. IT SHOWS BOTH RED AND BLUE SERIES OF USEFUL DIMENSIONS. GIVEN IN BOTH METERS AND FEET AND INCHES. PROPORTIONS BASED ON THE GOLDEN SECTION PROGRESS UP AND DOWN INFINITELY. THIS SCALE WILL BE HANDY IN CONSTRUCTING HUMAN SCALED SPACES WITH THE BAG OF TRICKS.

We hope that future editions will provide die-stamping and sticky-back coating, so that these "stickers' can be just peeled and placed. But designers are resourceful.... The following method is suggested: (1) find the image on the poster (2) find its page number here (3) cut the image from the poster and cement into place (as in a stamp album) over the existing black and white version of the image. The location of the butterfly and the sun-earth gnomon are left for the reader to find.

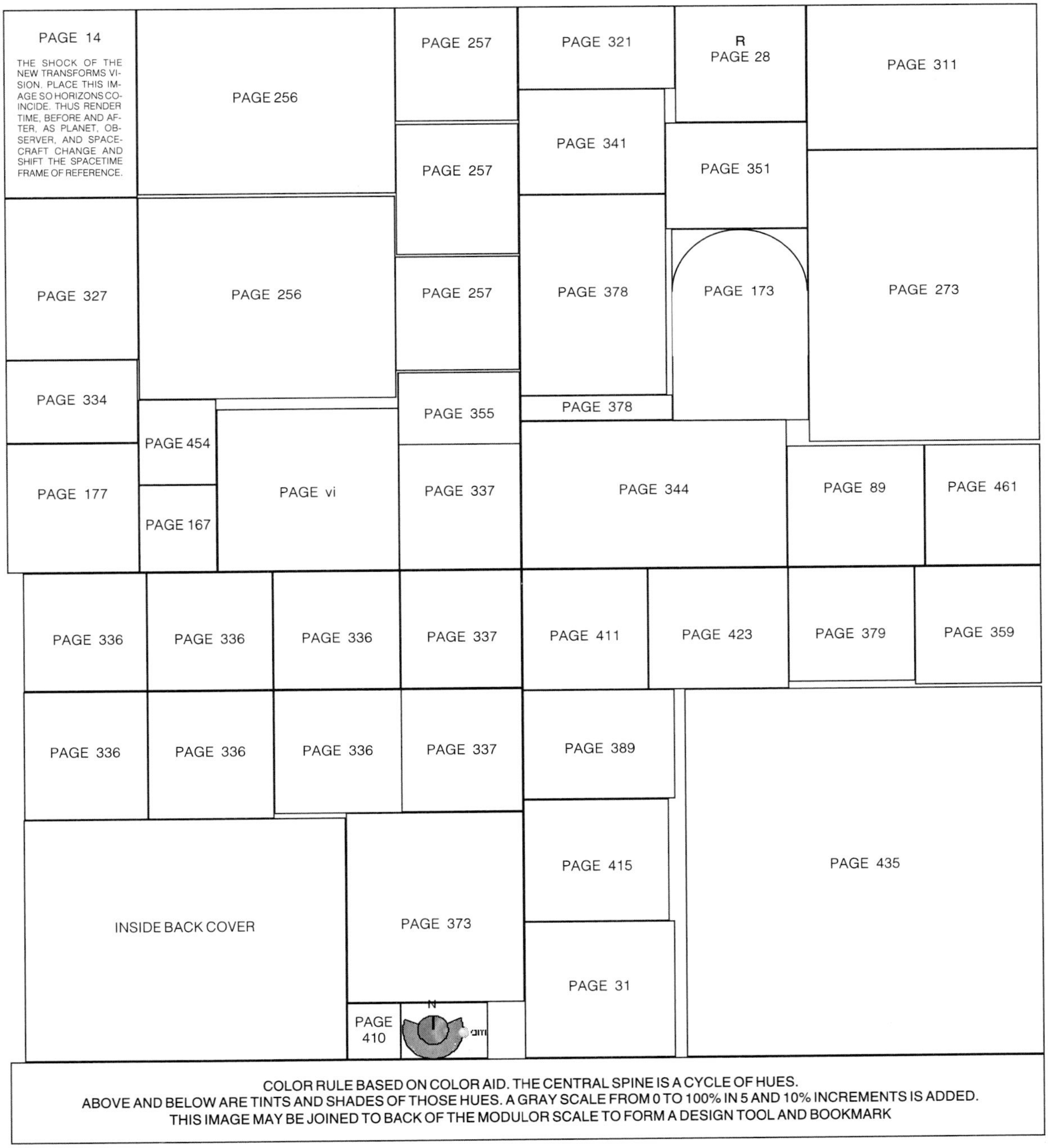

PAGE 14

THE SHOCK OF THE NEW TRANSFORMS VISION. PLACE THIS IMAGE SO HORIZONS COINCIDE. THUS RENDER TIME, BEFORE AND AFTER, AS PLANET, OBSERVER, AND SPACECRAFT CHANGE AND SHIFT THE SPACETIME FRAME OF REFERENCE.

PAGE 256

PAGE 257

PAGE 321

R
PAGE 28

PAGE 311

PAGE 257

PAGE 341

PAGE 351

PAGE 327

PAGE 256

PAGE 257

PAGE 378

PAGE 173

PAGE 273

PAGE 334

PAGE 454

PAGE 355

PAGE 378

PAGE 177

PAGE 167

PAGE vi

PAGE 337

PAGE 344

PAGE 89

PAGE 461

PAGE 336

PAGE 336

PAGE 336

PAGE 337

PAGE 411

PAGE 423

PAGE 379

PAGE 359

PAGE 336

PAGE 336

PAGE 336

PAGE 337

PAGE 389

PAGE 415

PAGE 435

INSIDE BACK COVER

PAGE 373

PAGE 31

PAGE 410

COLOR RULE BASED ON COLOR AID. THE CENTRAL SPINE IS A CYCLE OF HUES.
ABOVE AND BELOW ARE TINTS AND SHADES OF THOSE HUES. A GRAY SCALE FROM 0 TO 100% IN 5 AND 10% INCREMENTS IS ADDED.
THIS IMAGE MAY BE JOINED TO BACK OF THE MODULOR SCALE TO FORM A DESIGN TOOL AND BOOKMARK

CODA: *THE MOVES!!!*

A woman and child walk on the beach.
The child hurries to the waves.
And-- these solids are moving!
　　　　"the moves! the moves!"

Child now walks blocks
beyond tabletop and floor,
blocks bigger than pockets or hands.

Once each of us rode the full circuit for nine months in a relatively stress-free carriage, the womb, our own private nurturing ocean. But even there, the tug of gravity, the torsions shifts of mother's weight from leg to leg, the osmotic pressures on cells making protoplasm out of saline alien placental blood, were forces that made an endless dance of push and pull.

And then we each entered the room with the view-- our world of undreamed of, unexpected, unanticipated horizon. What amazement-- to discover that the one-way birth tug of gravity, the reference to the developing sense of balance through fetal otoliths, is exactly perpendicular to this planet's horizon! (There is no horizon inside the womb-- put your hands over your face and look towards the light, your may see light and dark areas-- but no horizon.) What such a moment must be for each of us, even if as we grow we become too busy with the action of the ocean, the magic carpet of grainy sand, the utter freedom of learning to walk beyond and faster than stately mother's (already again pregnant?) gait-- to find the intersection of our two most powerful means of position, orientation, and experience of space-- the "otolithic" with the visual!! Perhaps we drop a stone and see how it crosses the edge of ocean and sky exactly at the perpendicular. Is there any fundamental connection between these two? Can we pursue such wonders in a life of peace? On the edge of a next millennium, are we finally emerging from the 1000 year period of the Gothic wars, and the 2000 year period of the Roman-China wars? Will we begin another round of struggle for control over the illusion of limited resources, or shall we finally find the truth of the abundance all around us, and get on with the task of finding the right place and time for every thing under creation? Will we grow into peace, with time enough for joy--at last?

But not now does the child stop to ponder the infinite complex ramifications of such awesome simplicity . Now there is a spring in the dancing step! Now is the time to leap into the next moment, to keep up with the jubilation of the ever present now that comes tumbling out *from the Center of all Our Being* into the young drunken joyous mind-- *"the moves, the waves! the waves, the moves!"*